For the purpose of writing this book, **Ashok Mishra** spent over seven years studying more than 400 books, journals and monographs, to understand the roots of Hinduism. A double post-graduate in Electronic Engineering from Allahabad University, he was a resident of Muir Hostel from 1966-72. He then served as the CEO of an Indo-Japanese manufacturing venture and a Director in International Management Consultancy. Since 1981, he has been running a manufacturing business producing defence grade electronic components for US & other countries in Mumbai. His passions include Indology, Religion, History and listening to Classical music.

Author can be reached at **ashok@mishraashok.com**

Hinduism

Ritual, Reason and Beyond

Ashok Mishra

STORYMIRROR
Stories that reflect you

This is a work of research. Names, characters, businesses, places, events and incidents are result of author's extensive research on the hinduism subject. The book does not intend to hurt any religious sentiments in any manner.

First Edition and Print: July 2019
First Re-print: January 2020
Second Re-print: July 2020
Third Re-print: June 2021
Printed in India

Printed at Dhote Offset Printer, Mumbai
Typeset in Times New Roman

ISBN: 978-93-88698-10-8
Cover design: Prashant Gopal Gurav
Layout: Yogesh Desai

STORYMIRROR
Stories that reflect you

Publisher: StoryMirror Infotech Pvt. Ltd.
145, First Floor, Powai Plaza, Hiranandani Gardens,
Powai, Mumbai - 400076, India

Web: https://storymirror.com
Facebook: https://facebook.com/storymirror
Twitter: https://twitter.com/story_mirror
Instagram: https://instagram.com/storymirror
Email: marketing@storymirror.com

For the Ss and the As

Who gave me more than I could ever hope for in one life.

असतो मा सद्‌गमय, तमसो मा ज्योतिर्गमय, मृत्योर्मा अमृतं गमय ।

Lead me from 'Asat' to 'Sat', from darkness to light and from mortality to immortality.

(Pavamāna hymn - Brihadaranyaka 1.3.28)

Contents

PART II

PART III

PART IV

PART V

PART VI

Transliteration

Transliteration is the process of transferring a word from the alphabet of one language (in our case Sanskrit written in Devanagari script) to another (in our case English). It helps people pronounce words and names in foreign languages. For example Devanagari word सूत्र (usually spelt - sutra) is transliterated as sūtra; महाभारत (usually spelt - Mahabharata) as Mahābhārata; and कृष्ण् (usually spelt as Krishna) as Kṛṣṇa.

Devanagari Transliteration

Vowels

अ	a	A	आ	ā	Ā	इ	i	I	ई	ī	Ī
उ	u	U	ऊ	ū	Ū	ऋ	ṛ	Ṛ	ॠ	ṝ	Ṝ
ऌ	ḷ	Ḷ	ॡ	ḹ	Ḹ	ए	e	E	ऐ	ai	Ai
ओ	o	O	औ	au	Au	अं	ṃ	Ṃ	अः	ḥ	Ḥ

Consonants

क k K	च c C	ट ṭ Ṭ	त t T	प p P	tenuis stops
ख kh Kh	छ ch Ch	ठ ṭh Ṭh	थ th Th	फ ph Ph	aspirated stops
ग g G	ज j ś	ड ḍ Ḍ	द d D	ब b B	voiced stops
घ gh Gh	झ jh Jh	ढ ḍh Ḍh	ध dh Dh	भ bh Bh	breathy-voiced stops
ङ ṅ N	ञ ñ Ñ	ण ṇ Ṇ	न n N	म m M	nasal stops
ह h H	य y Y	र r R	ल l L	व v V	approximants
श ś Ś	ष ṣ Ṣ	स s S			

Illustrations

आसन	āsana	asana	ऋषि	ṛṣi	rishi
योग	Yoga	Yoga	शिव	Śiva	Shiva
महाभारत	Mahābhārata	Mahabharata	कृष्ण	Kṛṣṇa	Krishna
राम	Rāma	Rama	अन्तःकरण	antaḥkaraṇa	antahkarana
ज्ञान	jñāna	gyana	क्षोभ	kṣobha	kshobh
चक्र	cakra	chakra	सूत्र	sūtra	sutra
इच्छा	icchā	icchaa	प्रतिष्ठा	pratiṣṭhā	pratishtha
विक्लृप्	vikḷp	vikalpa	शास्त्र	śāstra	shastra
पतञ्जलि	Patañjali	Patanjali	अङ्ग	aṅga	anga

Abbreviations

AB	Aitareya Brāhmaṇa
AGS	Aśvalāyana Gṛhya Sūtra
ĀpDS	Āpstamba Dharma Sūtra
ĀpGS	Āpastamba Gṛhya Sūtra
ĀpSS	Āpastamba Śrauta Sūtra
ASS	Aśvalāyana Śrauta Sūtra
AV	Atharva Veda
AVPar	Atharva Veda PariSista
BD	Bṛhadadevatā
BDS	Baudhāyana Dharma Sūtra
BGS	Baudhāyana Gṛhya Sūtra
BSS	Baudhāyana Śrauta Sūtra
BU	Bṛhadāraṇyakopanisad
CU	Cāndogya Upanisad
DS	Dharma Sūtra, dharma sūtras
GB	Gopatha Brāhmaṇa
GDS	Gautama Dharma Sūtra
GGS	Gobhila Gṛhya Sūtra
GS	Gṛhya Sūtra,gṛhya sūtra
HAG	Hinduism, An Alphabetical Guide- Dalal
HD	History of Dharmshastra, Kane
HGS	Hiraṇyakeśin Gṛhya Sūtra
JB	Jaiminīya Brāhmaṇa
JGS	Jaiminīya Gṛhya Sūtra
JS	Jaimini Sūtra
KathGS	Kathaka Gṛhya Sūtra
KBU	Kauṣītaki Brāhmaṇa Upanisad
KhGS	Khādira Gṛhya Sūtra
KS	Kathaka Samhita
KSS, KSr	Kātyāyana Śrauta Sūtra
MBh	Mahābhārata
MGS	Mānava Gṛhya Sūtra

MP	Matsya Purāṇa
MS	Maitrayanisamhita
MS	Manu, Manu Smṛti
MSS	Mānava Śrauta Sūtra
MU	Muṇḍaka Upaniṣad
ParGS	Pāraskara Gṛhya Sūtra
PB	Pañcaviṃśa Brāhmaṇa
PGS	Pāraskara Gṛhya Sūtra
PMS	Pūrva Mīmāṁsā Sūtra
PP	Nitya Karma Pūja Prakāśa, RB Misra, LB Misra
RLTI	Religious Thought and Life in India, Monier
RV	Rg Veda
RVidh	Rg Vidhāna
S	Smṛtis
Sam K	Saṃskāra - kaustabha, Anantdeva
Sam P	Saṃskāra Prakāśa, Mitramisra
SB	Śatapatha Brāhmaṇa
SBE	Sacred Books of East
SC	Smriticandrika
SGS	Sañkhayana Gṛhya Sūtra
SRM	Saṃskāra Ratna Mala, Gopinātha
SSS	Śaṅkhāyana Śrauta Sūtra
SV	Sāma Veda
TA	Taittirīya Āraṇyaka
TB	Taittirīya Brāhmaṇa
TS	Taittirīya Saṃhitā
TU	Taittirīya Upanisad
VaiGS	Vaikhanasa Gṛhya Sūtra
VDS	Vasiṣṭha Dharma Sūtra
VGS	Vāraha Gṛhya Sūtra
Vi S	Viṣnu Smṛti
VMS	Vīramitrodaya Samskāra
VS	Vajasaneyi Saṃhitā
Yaj, Yaj S	Yājñavalkya Smṛti
YV	Yajur Veda

Preface

I recall clearly the late morning six-and-a-half years ago, when we had gathered for a small family function - the *munḍana* (tonsure) ceremony of my nephew's daughter - at my apartment. There must have been 15 to 20 of us; nephews and nieces, their spouses and children, and a barber to shave the head of the barely 1-year-old baby-girl. Those familiar with this ceremony, an important *saṃskāra* in every Hindu's life, know the head shaving is followed by a feast. The child, nestled in the lap of her mother, invariably resists the barber's attempts to hold its head still as he tries to remove all the hair. To prevent the baby from twisting and turning and getting injured by the razor, some member of family usually volunteers to hold the child firmly. Nobody enjoys this part of ceremony. Most certainly not the child who cries in protest right through the shaving which is repeated three times.

As the barber held the head of my nephew's daughter, she started to scream and hearing the child cry, her father (my nephew) intervened, instructing the barber not to shave, to use a pair of scissors instead to symbolically cut off a lock of hair. Many of nephews and nieces present murmured their approval, making me react more sharply than I had intended to. If I remember correctly, I said something along these lines: if you're not happy with the head being shaved, then better not have the ceremony at all! Let's not pretend that by clipping a lock of hair you would have performed *munḍana saṃskāra*. I remember adding - we can all have a nice party even without the *saṃskāra*, but if the idea is for the child to go through *munḍana*, then let's do it properly because it is an important milestone in the life of a Hindu child, and the family. There was a momentary silence - everyone gathered there thought I was upset because a tradition was not being followed. They were taken aback because they knew me as a non-traditionalist; not a 'conservative' Hindu, but as a great liberal. The child's father remarked that he did not know shaving of the head was a *saṃskāra*, an important milestone in the life of a child. I ended up explaining in detail what *saṃskāra*s are, what they mean for a Hindu, and how we've been performing *munḍana*, *upanayana* and *vivaha* as *saṃskāra* for well-nigh 4000 years. I must have spoken - uninterrupted - for about 20 minutes. Everyone, including my wife Shikha, who, despite her modern education, believes in following customs and traditions faithfully, heard me out in pin drop silence. Even the *paṇḍita* didn't intervene (I was speaking in Hindi, which the *paṇḍita* understood perfectly well). When I finished what I realised had embarrassingly become a lecture, several of the grown-ups spoke simultaneously, complaining - no one had ever told them anything about *munḍana* being a *saṃskāra*. They were also not sure what *saṃskāra* meant! At this point of time my wife, never short of words, remarked - 'He has time to read hours on end and write on other religions, but he has no time to write a book which can tell us about Hinduism, our ancient practices, our *pūjā*.' That stung me. Quite a bit. I temporarily shelved my writing project on Islam to write a book on Hinduism.

Hinduism is such a vast topic that it can hardly be covered meaningfully even in a dozen books. Fortunately for me, I was going to write in response to a very specific comment from my wife - she wanted a book that could explain to a lay reader like her about *Sanātana Dharma*, the Vedas, the importance of Purāṇas and other religious scriptures. More importantly, why we do what we do by way of worship.

This book is an endeavour to take the reader through some of these topics with the hope that the reader receives at least some satisfactory answers.

I was an engineering student, and in my university days always wanted to be a Lecturer. Coming from a family of civil servants, I was coerced, if not softly bulldozed, into abandoning my dream. I have been engaged in the manufacture of electronic components almost my entire working life, except for a short break of 14 months when I worked for the government. Having been born and brought up in, what is these days fashionably called a 'Secular' atmosphere, I had no special interest in learning about Hinduism. But after the very disturbing events of 9/11, when I decided to write on Islam, I learned Urdu from a Moulvi. I wanted to explore why Islam was at war with itself. In order to understand how Islam was different from other religions, I studied Christianity, Judaism, Zoroastrianism, Buddhism and Hinduism.

Later, having decided to write on Hinduism, I thought it necessary to learn Sanskrit. However, when I attempted to study the first volume of the Ṛgveda, I discovered that ordinary Sanskrit is of no use in understanding the Vedas. I struggled to find translations of the Vedas that weren't written by Western translators of the 17th and 18th centuries. It was then that I discovered that all Indian scholars of History and Indology - with very few exceptions - have written on Vedic literature reading from the secondary sources i.e. translations (more interpretations than translations, really). It was only towards the end of writing this book that I managed to procure a copy of Ṛgveda translations by Jamieson and Brearton. Reading Purāṇas, *Smṛtis*, *Gṛhya sūtras*, *Dharma sūtras*, and other literature opened a new world for me. I discovered that most modern Indians' Hinduism is a Hinduism of perception. None of the many educated old and young Hindus I interviewed possessed first-hand knowledge of any of the Hindu rituals/practices they come across in their homes from childhood. In an increasingly urbanised society, both parents are often employed and do not have the time to share mythological stories or explain why various festivals are celebrated or why holy places of pilgrimage are important. The *panḍita* rarely explains anything about the *pūjā* or any part of the ritual.

In fulfilment of Shikha's wish, I have attempted to present an account of Hinduism, which endeavours to explain how this religion started in ancient India, and its journey from a Ṛgvedic *yajña*-based society to a religion steeped in animal sacrifice, ritual, and even rank ostentation. I try to explore how sage gurus Aruni, Yajnavalakya, and many others, took it to new heights - the age of Reason - resulting in the creation of the Upniṣads, and how the attempts to resurrect *yajña*s by Jaimini (and his followers) was followed by the emergence of the *Vidhāna* practices. I also examine the fascinating strategy they employed to meet the challenges posed by Buddhism. The arrival of idol worship, and the easy to practice dharma of the Purāṇas which culminated in the religion that Hindus follow today, has also been discussed in some detail.

I have tried to explain and describe ritual practices of the Vedic period - an account of the '26 *karma yajñas*' and a detailed account of *Soma yajña*, the most important of all *yajñas*. This has been done so that the reader may see for himself how Hindu rituals transformed into present day *pūjā*. Descriptions of present day *pūjā*, and explanations - both the five and the sixteen offerings (*pancopchāra* and *śodaṣopcāra*) - are given in detail so that the reader can fully understand the intent of present day *pūjā*.

Saṃskāras and *tīrtha*, *dāna* and *vrata* raise many questions in our mind. I have tried to answer some of the common questions by describing and explaining these activities.

Two chapters have been included at the end on questions that set most Indians thinking: Do mantras have power? Do rituals have any meaning?

I hope the book provides Shikha satisfactory answers and explanations for the many things she does, and makes us do, as a religious Hindu housewife. And that it does the same for many like-minded Hindus, as well as fellow Indians, who may choose to read this book.

I have no words to express my gratitude to Vedika Jiandani. Forever patient and indulgent, she went through the manuscript several times. Even when her day of wedding was only a few weeks away, and she had resigned from her job in order to do the hundred things that an Indian 'would be bride' has to do, she found time to make one more revision of the transliterations. I am also grateful to Harish Puppala for going through a substantial part of the manuscript and his valuable contribution.

I interviewed a fair number of people who helped me understand better what Hindus think about their own religion: religious texts, gods and goddesses, customs and practices. I am thankful to all those who allowed me to interview them, and gave their valuable time, answering my several searching questions. I am especially grateful to Anjali Tandon, Anjana 'no argument' Bhargava, Nandini Baijal, Manjari Kakar, Manjushree Sahai, Meenakshi Kumar and Dipika Arora. Many of their replies were simply quote worthy.

The contribution of Madhav Pathak, an incisive and critical mind, and Arun Tandon, for ever helpful, encouraging, and patient has been immense. I simply cannot thank them enough.

Ashutosh Dixit has been my sounding board, every time I approached him he came up with a suggestion which resolved my dilemma. My sincere thanks to him for all his help.

And lastly I want to express my gratitude to the two gentlemen - Bibhu Datta Rout and Hitesh Jain, without whose help this book would not have been published and to the team at publishing house - StoryMirror - for all their time and help.

Ashok Mishra
Mumbai

Introduction

At no stage of my schooling, primary or secondary, was I taught anything about the pre-Indus Valley civilisation. Despite my habit of modest but regular reading, until about seven years back I believed - wrongly, as I now know - that Indian civilisation started with Indus Valley. During the course of my research for this book, I spoke to numerous school going children in Northern India, Maharashtra and Goa. Without exception, they shared the same mistaken notions about the beginnings of Indian civilisation. The name Mehrgarh doesn't ring any bells for them. I also interviewed a number of graduate and postgraduate housewives and working women - many of them teachers in the above regions. I found their responses no different from that of the students they taught!

For some strange reason we see our genesis only in Vedic Āryans! We seem to think that the India of pre-Vedic days (Indus Valley, Mehrgarh and earlier) belonged to some other peoples who were not our forefathers.

How strange, and yet not strange at all.

It is not strange because, as a student, I was never taught at any stage of my schooling that the history of my ancestors is at least as old as the skeletons, the mud bricks, and the broken pot shreds of Mehrgarh. Or that my ancestors baked the clay bricks and built those beautiful double storeyed houses which had bathrooms on the upper floor from where, through the vertical pipes, the water flowed down into the covered drainage system on the streets. For us, those people of the Indus Valley (and prior) were a different race that, for reasons we aren't very sure of, completely disappeared from the face of India.

And it is strange because we - the argumentative Indians, who like to question even that which is obvious - have believed for several generations, with nary a question, that an entire race disappeared with the Indus Valley civilisation. We do not enquire: How did a fairly developed civilisation, several centuries old, completely cease to exist, thereby leaving the slate of Indian civilisation clean for Vedic Āryans and their Hindu descendants to script their own story?

The 'Āryan Debate' is far from settled. But we do know that when the Āryans arrived, India was already populated with indigenous people. What cannot be said with certainty is whether the Āryans conquered and subjugated the original inhabitants as *dāsas* (serfs, slaves) or annihilated the Indus peoples and other inhabitants. Or was it a case of 'outsider' Āryans gradually settling down as agriculturists and assimilating with the natives? Linguists are still working on the interpretations of retroflexive words while Zoologists are trying to identify the origins of the Surkotada horse.

Were Āryans indigenous Indians who, over time, radiated out towards Central Asia and Europe? Or did the Āryans originate in Europe and Central Asia, and later migrate to India? This great debate, which has raged for several decades, seems to be taking a more definitive direction thanks to exponential advances in the field of DNA study.

The latest research paper (published on 31st March 2018) detailing the findings of a group of 92 scientists from around the globe has revealed that the very ancient inhabitants of India belonged to two groups - Ancient Ancestral South Indians (AASI) and Ancestral North Indians (ANI). The Indus Valley population was created by intermingling of Iranian agriculturists and South Asian hunter-gatherers. Around the second millennium BC, Steppe pastoralists (Aryans) from Central Asia moved toward the subcontinent and encountered the Indus Valley people. The exact nature of the encounter is not known. However, it resulted in the Indus Valley people moving deeper towards the South and mixing with South Asian hunter gatherers to create the ASI. The intermixing of Steppe pastoralists with the Indus Valley population led to the creation of the ANI grouping. Majority South Asian populations are a result of further mixing between ANI and ASI. An important outcome of these findings is that most extant Indian populations are connected through the bridge of Indus Valley civilisation to earlier populations. (bio Rxiv preprint first posted online Mar. 31, 2018; doi: http://dx.doi.org/10.1101/292581. Accessed on Dt 310718).

The religious inclinations and praxis of our ancestors prior to the Indus Valley period are not known to us. But we are in a much better position when it comes to the knowledge of the Indus Valley period. Any understanding of how Hinduism evolved to its present form has to start from the ruins of Mehrgarh (7000 BC) near the Bolan Pass in western Pakistan, where over 3200 figurines of clay and terracotta were discovered. The excavation by a French team, led by Jean-François Jarrige, between 1974 and 1986 yielded many more articles and objects that threw light on the civilisation which existed 4000 years, if not more, before Mohenjo-Daro and Harappa. Unfortunately, historians can only speculate that these figurines are related to the fertility practices of those people. Nothing much is known about the religious customs or practices of the people of Mehrgarh. However, we are better informed about the Indus Valley civilisation: the assembly halls, the public baths, the stone rings and *linga* shaped stones, a nude female figurine, the ithyphallic figure of a man sitting cross-legged in yogic posture etc., have given scholars more definitive clues about possible customs and religious inclinations of the Indus Valley people.

I interviewed a fair number of young and old educated Hindus to better understand what they thought was their religion. When asked - What are Vedas? What do they contain? Have they ever had an inclination to read these ancient books? - surprisingly, all of them, without exception, said the Vedas are the most important religious texts for Hindus, but they had never made any serious efforts to learn more about these texts. Following a standard format, I asked them to name some of the Vedic gods and goddesses. Not one of the many people I interviewed could name 'any three Vedic deities', though many did recall Indra! Unsurprisingly, for nearly all of them, there was hardly any difference between Vedic and Purānic Hinduism. All of them shook their heads in disbelief when told that almost none of the popular gods and goddesses of today existed during Rgvedic times.

This book begins with a brief discussion of the words Hindu and Hinduism, a 'gift' of the British in the 19th century. I have used the words Hindu and Hinduism anachronistically in this book. This is done because, in all my discussions about Hindu religion, I found people constantly referring to Vedic Āryans as Hindus. Not that they were not familiar with the term *Sanātana Dharma* - everyone I spoke to was acquainted with the phrase - but hardly anyone responded with *Sanātana Dharma* as an answer when asked "what is your religion?" Before embarking on a journey of Hinduism to try and understand - how a society that was entirely *yajña* centric and did not have any idols, transformed into an idol worshipping *pūjā* centric society? - understanding and familiarizing oneself with the terms Hindu and Hinduism, religion and dharma, and *Sanātana Dharma* was considered essential by this author. Accordingly, three chapters in the book deal with these topics.

Sanātana Dharma, the ancient religion that it is, has always been interpreted differently by different people at different times. I considered it prudent to lay before the reader how three prominent thinkers and scholars of the recent past interpreted it in their own ways. Nearly 125 years back, a British lady by the name Dr Annie Besant, internationally renowned for her spiritual discourses and writings (though a theosophist), was steeped in Indian culture and Hindu religion. She co-authored a book on *Sanātana Dharma* with Dr Bhagwan Das, an educationalist, freedom activist and a great scholar of Sanskrit. Shri Aurobindo, an Indian who received Western education in England from a young age, joined the Indian Civil Service (ICS) but resigned to pursue the path of spiritualism by becoming a saint. He wrote and spoke extensively on Hinduism and *Sanātana Dharma*. For that great mind, *Sanātana Dharma* was the same as nationalism - a radically divergent interpretation from the more conservative understanding of Annie Besant and Bhagwan Das. Dr RA Mall, a contemporary Indian scholar of religion and philosophy, has taught in Germany as well as in many other universities of Europe those very subjects. He considers *Sanātana Dharma* a secular concept. The reader will arrive at his/her own understanding of *Sanātana Dharma* having sampled these three points of view.

The traditional view traces the origin of Hindu religion to the Vedas. These sacred texts - the four Vedas - are believed to have been revealed directly to the ṛṣis orally, and are therefore called *Śruti* (heard). Each Veda comprises four different texts that were composed at different times; *Samhitās* (mantras), *Brāhmaṇas* (directions for conducting the rituals), *Āranyakas* (esoteric texts studied in the isolation of forests) and Upanisads (metaphysical discourses on *Ātmā* and Brahma); the four constituents together are called Veda. They are described in brief in a separate chapter, and four chapters follow that are devoted to each of the Vedas. An attempt has been made to give the description of the contents of each of the Vedas (*samhitā* part), the number of chapters, and the subject matter of each of the chapter, to help the reader understand what these different texts deal with.

I did face some trouble finding an authentic translation of the Vedas. After months of discussions with Sanskrit scholars as well as my own search of digital and physical libraries as well as book stores, I was surprised to discover that most, if not all, of what is written on the Vedas is based on nearly two-centuries old translations by German and English scholars' secondary sources. It was only when I was finishing this book that a properly detailed modern translation of the Rg Veda - by Jamieson and Brereton - came out in print. Most of what we rely on when we talk of Rgvedic *Samhitā* was translated from archaic Sanskrit into their language by English and German scholars of yore. This task was done in the absence of a standard Sanskrit-to-English dictionary. A serious debate raged at the time as to what constituted proper translation: Was it a precise word for word translation, or what the original author intended to convey, or what the original culture would mean in the culture of the translated texts? It was generally accepted that the translator had to have knowledge of the customs and culture of the people who composed the text in addition to the language of the original text. The ground reality was that there was hardly any interaction between Indians and these European translators.

Unless they were willing to undertake an arduous sea voyage - that lasted anywhere between four to six months - most of these translators were almost entirely cut off from the traditions, customs and culture of Hindus. The reader must, at all times, bear in mind the self-admitted prejudice of the sponsors of these translations - the East India Company - and that of the translators themselves who believed Christianity was the true religion, and that followers of false religions like Buddhism, Islam and Hinduism had to be converted to their faith. There is little doubt in my mind that in the absence of a standard Sanskrit-to-English dictionary as well as lack of exposure to, and an understanding of, Hindu culture and customs, taking into account their prejudices, such translations can, at best, be termed works of interpretation.

I had always taken it for granted that, right from the beginning, we had four Vedas. My study revealed that, for nearly a millennium and a half, Hindu texts spoke of only *Traividya* or three Vedas. It was only around Manu's time that the fourth Veda - Atharva - started appearing as the fourth Veda. I have tried to present as much evidence as a work of this nature permits to highlight this important point for the benefit of the reader. In many ways, admittance of the Atharva to the house of Vedas marked a major departure: On one hand it signalled the acceptance of non-Āryan practices of black magic as Āryan practice - a harbinger of the Hindu system of assimilating foreign or divergent ideas - and on the other, it opened doors to what was gross and 'unintellectual', and certainly uncharacteristic of Āryan religion. No doubt Rg too had 'magic' verses, but those did not relate to making one's neighbour impotent! Atharva had this and much more. It is truly intriguing how this Veda found a place for itself at the high table with Rg, Sāma and Yajur.

Since this book is written with the objective of placing before readers the evolution of Hindu practices, the change in the form of worship is an important topic that requires special attention. It has morphed from Vedic *yajña* to the present *pūjā*. Apart from descriptions of the various types of *yajña* practices prevailing in Vedic times, a fairly detailed description of a template of *Somayajña*, namely *agniṣṭoma*, has been provided in a separate chapter on *yajña* rituals. *Somayajña* was chosen because it is considered the most important among *śrauta* sacrifices.

A society that had moved away from the substance to the form (ritualism) underwent a remarkable change and shunned ritualism in favour of knowledge. This transformation of Hinduism, and its beautiful journey to what is more commonly known as Upnisadic period, eventually led to *Vedānta* or the end of Vedas. This journey has been divided into nine separate chapters. Towards the end of the Upnisadic period, the pendulum had swung to the other extreme. A society once completely immersed in ritualism experienced an age of reason and started speaking in terms of '*aham brahmāsmi*' (I am *Brahman*), and '*tat tvam asi*' (you are That). The unity of the Self and the Supreme became the ultimate goal of Hindu society. It was a concept so unique and so complex, it became almost impossible for a common Hindu to comprehend. He suddenly felt lost; if indeed there was only one ultimate reality which was nothing but unalloyed consciousness - the *Brahman* - having no attributes, then where, and to whom, could he turn to for help in overcoming the problems of this world?

Buddhism and Jainism had already started making deep inroads, hitting at the very core beliefs of Hinduism. Sages like Jaimini came forward to resurrect the crumbling *Vedism*. Employing the doctrine of *Mīmāmsā*, Jaimini argued that each and every word of Veda has meaning, and all rituals must strictly be adhered to. In *Mīmāmsā*, even the gods came to occupy a position that was secondary to the *yajña*; through *yajña*, the gods could be compelled to deliver *kāmya*. The rituals thus came to supersede everything else; *Karmakānda* and action were, in the *Mīmāmsā* scheme of things, supreme.

This undoubtedly was a 'revivalist' move by a staunch Vedic follower, an effort to stem the tide of Buddhism, Jainism and some of the other 'anti-Vedic' ideologies like *Ājīvikas* and *Śramanas*, which were threatening to destroy the very basis of *Vedism*. After all, the core teachings of these new 'religions' (Buddhism and Jainism) denied the existence of God, *ātmā*, *paramātmā*, and *svarga*, attacking the very foundation of Hindu religious thought, whether ritualistic or Upanisadic. Making ahimsa (non-violence) in thought and action the bedrock of their ideologies, and an integral part of daily practice, these religions had delivered a body blow to Hinduism which was, at the time, steeped in sacrificial (*yajña*) ceremonies that often extended over months and years (an *aśvamedha yajña* typically lasted more than an year). Many Hindus, disenchanted and disillusioned with opulent and often blood soaked ceremonies, did not need a great deal of persuasion to follow the path of Sangha (not to be confused with the modern day Sangh Parivar or RSS). They were desperately looking to tread a new path. Under such adverse conditions, Jaimini propagated an ideology which, even by the standards of those days, was 'conservative'.

Another section of sages devised a different plan. They came up with an abridged and modified version of *Vedism* and called it *Vidhāna*. *Vidhāna* practices provide a shortcut for achieving 'every day' desires - *kāmya* (desired object) - which were earlier achieved through cumbersome Vedic practices that, for an average Hindu without resources, were difficult to pursue. It was in that period of turbulence, when Hinduism was failing its followers who were drawn towards Buddhism and Jainism, that an easier form of worship, *mūrti pūjā*, tiptoed in as *Devāpūjā*, edging out *Devāyajña*, an important element of *panca mahā yajña*. *Mūrti pūjā* gained popularity among Hindus fairly quickly. And thus began the great journey of idol worship and Purānic Hinduism.

The Purānas became the new Vedas, and *mūrti pūjā* the new *yajña*. Where only four Vedas and 27 (some say 400) *yajñas* existed, 18 *Maha* Purānas and an equal number of Upa-Purānas were compiled over the next few centuries. The gods, who numbered less than a hundred in the Vedic period, grew exponentially and touched a staggering 33 crores (330 million)! Purānas introduced an easy to understand, and easier to practice, version of religion. A God in anthropomorphic form could be seen, spoken to, offered prayers and, more importantly, kept in the house and worshipped without requisitioning the services of a *purohita*. The wherewithal for *yajñas*, which had become a deterrent for most, was completely done away with in the Purānic scheme of bhakti. A Hindu could reap the benefits of even *aśvamedhá yajña* by *tīrth-yātrā*, *vrata* and *dāna*. Through simple and engrossing tales of the gods, their *avatāras* and demons, dharma was once again brought within reach of rich and poor alike. This was achieved with one very important distinction - women and *śūdra* were now allowed to practice this form of worship.

It is no easy task to describe what these Purānas are, or what constitutes their core contents; they go well beyond the topics spelt out as the *panca lakśanas* (five attributes), which they themselves have laid down. The Purānas cover nearly all aspects of Hinduism - custom, religion, *ācāra* and *vyavhāra* (rules and conduct); the dos and the dont's; atonement, crime and punishment; *samskāra*, cosmogony, philosophy etc. etc…the list is endless. In order to give the reader a flavour of this altogether different approach to Hindu dharma, topics like cosmogony and cosmography, time and *yuga*, gods and goddesses as well as tantrism are included in a chapter on Purāna. This will provide the reader an opportunity to see the wild swing from the age of reason and *Vedānta* to the seven oceans of honey, milk, curd, *ghī* etc., in Purānic cosmogony, and the replacement of the supreme realty, *Brahman*, with millions of anthropomorphic gods and goddesses.

This arrival - of many gods, and *mūrtipūjā* - heralded an entirely new form of worship, different from *yajña*. How '*devayajña*', a part of *panca mahā yajñas*, an exercise every *dvija* was enjoined to undertake daily, was replaced by *devapūjā* (idol worship), is not known with any degree of exactitude. But it is almost certain that *devapūjā* replaced *devayajña*. Given the important place various types of *pūjā* occupy in the average Hindu's life, and how little he tends to know when he, as a *yajmāna* (principal actor in the ceremony), is guided through the *pūjā* by a priest, I have provided very detailed accounts of short and long forms of *pūjā* (*pancopchāra* and *śodasopcāra*) in a chapter dedicated to *pūjā*. After reading these accounts, I hope that readers receive a deeper understanding of why we do what we do during a *pūjā*.

The Purānas undoubtedly were a significant factor in halting the march of Buddhism, and reigniting the flame of dharma in the residents of Bhāratavarsa. But the seeds of *Śaivism* and *Vaisnavism* had already sprouted in parts of India. The invasions by forces of Islam, a religion that thrived on forced conversion, coupled with the numerous social ills that afflicted Hindu society, which was itself becoming moribund due to the caste system and many other abhorrent practices, evoked a unique reformist movement from within - the Bhakti movement. Saints from high and low castes alike came forward to lead this movement by example. Tulsī, Sūr and Caitanya were *brāhmaṇas*, Mīrā was a *ksatriya*, while Nānaka came from the trading community. Kabīr, Dādu, Raidas were all from lower castes. Irrespective of their own caste, they brought a new wave of awareness to Hindu society. Both *saguna* and *nirguna* (with and without attributes) ideologies were presented in simplified forms that a common man could easily comprehend, and practice. Hinduism was revitalised by these saints, and the *Bhakti* movement was one important reason Hinduism survived a thousand years of Islamic rule.

In this author's view, every Hindu, whether practising or non-practising, does observe one or more *samskāra*. They could be classed as essential attributes of Hinduism. Three chapters have been devoted to this topic, and a detailed description of the two primary *samaskāras* i.e. *upanayana* and *vivāha* is given separately. While interviewing people, I had found that though they were familiar with the word *samskāra*, they did not quite understand what it entails. The first of the three chapters tries to explain the meaning of *samskāra*, and the context in which it is used in Hindu religion. The number of *samskāras*, and how they shrank from the original 40 to the present day 16, is also explored at length in this chapter. The next chapter contains descriptions of each *samskāra*, and explains how, and why, they are performed.

These days most Hindus do not perform most *samskāras*, and even the *samskāras* they do perform - like *nāma karna, annaprāsana, munḍana* or *cudākarma, vidyārambha* etc. - are not performed in the prescribed form But there are three *samskāras* which all Hindus continue to perform assiduously - *upanayana, vivāha* and *antyesti* (last rites). We do not take note of *upanayana* because, these days, in most cases it is not performed as a stand-alone *samskāra. Upanayana* is now performed a day before, or on the day of *vivāha*, and is mistaken as a prelude to *vivāha* ceremonies. In fact, in certain ways, it is a more important *samskāra* than the others - only after *upanayana* does a Hindu becomes a *dvija* or twice born. Without it, he is unsuitable to perform any religious rite! A detailed account of both, *upanayana* and *vivāha*, is provided in a separate chapter .

Vivāha is the single most important *samskāra* that a Hindu performs in his lifetime. It is also one of the most ancient, first finding mention in the Rgveda itself. The age, caste, *gotra*, *sapinda* et cetera continue to be important considerations at the time of marriage. This author took the opportunity of including a discussion on *jāti* and *varna* as part of the chapter on *vivāha* rather than giving them separate space in the book, which they ideally warrant.

Though very important, *antyesti samskāra* has not been selected for discussion in this book.

A question most Hindus often ask is, 'What is meaning of the various rituals we perform as part of every religious ceremony?' A modern day *pūjā* scene looks something like this: the *yajamāna* sitting in a *pūjā* is made to do a hundred things, big and small, at the behest of the *pandita*. He follows these instructions like a robot, almost never enquiring why he is to do those things, or what is their significance. None of those present dare question the *pandita* either; most sit reverentially with folded hands, while a few converse about inconsequential matters. Other than the *pandita's* instructions, which are usually spoken in the vernacular, the main proceedings are conducted in Sanskrit, a language that is now heard only in classrooms, or niche TV news bulletins. Those present at the *pūjā* understand almost nothing of what is being chanted, or done. It is not uncommon that the *pandita* himself understands little of what he is doing. It is not surprising then that rituals have become tedious, boring affairs that inevitably lead to the question: Why do we do this at all? What is the meaning of ritual?

No ritual is ever complete without the chanting of mantras. These mantras are in Sanskrit, and even more difficult to understand than the rituals. When questioned, those in the know tell us mantras have great power. So are the rituals meaningless? And are the mantras powerful and efficacious?

These questions can be looked at from two different perspectives: the traditional view, and the scholarly (Indian and Western) point of view. This is such a vast subject that a book of this size can hardly do justice to discussion of these two questions in the few pages that can be spared for this purpose. However, given the importance of these questions, one cannot ignore them altogether. The author has devoted one chapter each to these two questions.

Firstly, do mantras have power? Are they efficacious?

Mantras are collections of words in Sanskrit, and anybody familiar with the language will be able to comprehend their meaning. All mantras are laudatory in nature, addressed to various gods and goddesses, and at times to inanimate objects. They are recited during the course of *pūjā* for obtaining the desired results (*kāmya*). In another form of worship - *japa* - mantras are repeated over and over with some *kāmya* in mind. Their power and efficacy, at first level, can only be measured vis-a-vis the outcome of the *kāmya* through either of the above two forms of worship. But herein lies the catch: the texts prescribe that the *kāmya* is delivered provided the ritual is performed without a single error, with perfection, with complete dedication, and total focus on the deity (to the exclusion of all other thought). Since no ritual or *japa* can, in practice, ever be performed satisfying such stringent conditions, believers and traditionalists could exploit this 'trapdoor' when asked why the desired results are not delivered even after a ritual is performed. Any discussion on efficacy or the power of the mantra on these lines is therefore not likely to yield results.

The other route is non-traditional and/or scholarly. Applying this method, scholars have tried to question the efficaciousness of mantras by raising fundamental questions: for instance, do the mantra's qualify as proper language? If not, they are rendered meaningless and (hence) cannot possess any power. This is the route of Linguistic analysis; scholars like Frits Staal have followed this method to question the power and efficaciousness of mantras. There can be many other ways of examining/challenging the power of mantras. In this book I have restricted myself to the linguistic route, and tried to present a counter to Staal's assertions.

When we come to rituals, the issue becomes much more complex. Unlike mantras, there are innumerable kinds of rituals that pervade all aspects of an individual's life. Consequently, they have been studied, researched, and commented upon by many scholars in different parts of the world. In order to address the question 'Are rituals meaningless?' I have tried to discuss what rituals are, and whether they have any meaning i.e. do they serve any purpose? In the end, I have tried to explore how traditionalists approach this question.

Chart C-1

Chart Depicting Components of Vedic Literature

Vedic Literature — *Śruti*, *Smṛti*

Śruti

4 Vedas

- *Ṛg* — *Saṃhita*, *Brāhmaṇa*, *Āranyaka*, *Upaniṣad*
- *Sāma*
- *Yajur*
- *Atharva*

Each *Veda* has its separate *Saṃhita, Brāhmaṇas, Āranyakas & Upaniṣads*

Smṛti

6 Vedāngas

- *Kalpa* — *Śrauta Sūtras*, *Gṛyha Sūtras*, *Dharma Sūtras*
- *Śikṣā*
- *Chanda*
- *Nirukta*
- *Vyākaraṇa*
- *Jyotiṣa*

4 Upavedas

- *Āyurveda*
- *Arthaśāstra*
- *Dhanurveda*
- *Gandharvaveda*

6 Darśanas

- *Nyāya*
- *Vaiśeṣika*
- *Sāṅkhya*
- *Yoga*
- *Pūrva Mīmāṃsa*
- *Uttara Mīmāṃsa*

Purāṇas	*18 Purāṇa and 18 Upapurāṇa*
Itihāsa	*Ramāyṇa and Mahābhārata*
Dharmaśāstras	*Several texts*

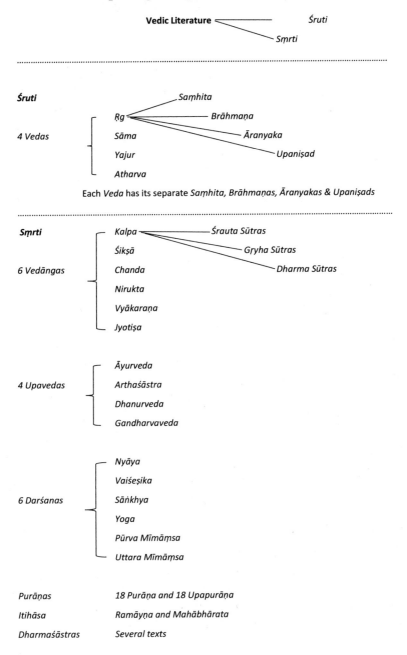

Chart C-2

Vedic Literature - A Brief Description

Vedic texts

Śruti - *Śruti* or 'what is heard', as opposed to what is composed, are revealed scriptures, self-authoritative, not composed by any human being. Vedas are *Śruti* texts. Each Veda had its own separate - *Samhita*, Brāhmaṇas, Āranyaka and Upanisads.

Post Vedic texts

Smrti - *Smrti* or 'what is memorised' are the traditional works of human origin solely based on the *Śrutis*. Called *Sūtra* texts, their most important part is vedāngas or 'limb of Veda'. Vedāngas are prescribed as essential reading for anyone wanting to learn the Vedas. They help students in reading and understanding Vedas and performing sacrificial rites.

i. *Kalpa* - ceremonial directory, including rules for Vedic rituals and sacrifices
ii. *Śiksā* - the science of pronunciation
iii. *Chandas* - metre
iv. *Nirukta* - etymology and meaning of words used in the Vedas
v. *Vyākarana* - grammar
vi. *Jyotiṣa* - astronomy, including the study of arithmetic and mathematics

Kalpa - These are texts concerned with ritual and have three categories-

- *Śrauta Sūtras* - Deal with Vedic sacrifices given in the Vedas and described in the Brāhmaṇas
- *Grhya Sūtras* - Deal with domestic ceremonies such as upanayana, marriage etc, and various daily and seasonal sacrificial rites, and mantras applied to these rites
- *Dharma Sūtras* - These address some of the topics dealt within the grhya sūtras and also deal with the provisions on matters concerning economics, politics, government, civil and criminal law

Later day Dharma Sūtra texts stopped having a clear link to a particular Veda school (*Śakhā*), and came to be called *Smrti* e.g. Devalā Smrti.

Other texts - Additional texts composed to clarify or explain certain aspects of the Vedas include: Padapāthas - samhita texts had words in the conjoined form (*sandhis*), the padapātha separates each word so in a sense it makes the text read as it was before the words were joined by *sandhi*; and *Anukramanikās* - the index of hymns, meters, deities and ṛṣis of each of the four Vedas.

The four Upa-Vedas (knowledge of Medical, Economic/Political, and Military Sciences and Music), the six *Darśanas* (branches of philosophy), the eighteen Puranas and Upa-Puranas each, *Itihāsa* (epics - Rāmāyana and Mahābhārata), later Upanisad and *Dharma Śastras* (Sanskrit texts that deal with the customs, practices, ethical conduct and laws of Hindus).

Chart C-3

	Veda	Ṛg	Sāma	Yajur Kṛṣṇā	Yajur Śukla	Atharva	Remarks
ŚRUTI TEXTS	**Brāhmaṇa**	*Aitareya Kauṣītaki*	*Pañcaviṃśa, Ṣaḍviṃśa, Jaiminīya-Upaniṣad-Brāhmaṇa, Chandogya-Upaniṣad-Brāhmaṇa*	*Taittirīya*	*Śatapatha*	*Gopatha*	*Pañcaviṃśa* is same as *Tāṇḍya Br.*
	Āraṇyaka	*Aitareya, Kauṣītaki*	- -	*Taittirīya*	*Śatapatha*	- -	*Kauṣītaki* is same as *Śaṅkhāyana Ār.*
	Upaniṣad	*Aitareya, Kauṣītaki*	*Chandogya, Kena*	*Taittirīya, Maitrayāni, Kaṭha, Śvetāśvatara*	*Bṛhadāraṇyaka, Iśa*	*Munḍaka, Praśna, Manḍūkya*	
	Śakha	*Śaklā, Bāṣkala*	*Jaiminīya, Rāṇāyanīya, Kauthuma*	*Taittirīya, Maitrayāni, Kaṭhaka, Kapiṣṭhala - Kaṭha*	*Vajasaneyi - Kāṇva, Mādyanandina*	*Śaunaka, Paippalāda*	Different recensions of *saṃhitas* or theological schools
SMṚTI TEXTS	**Śrauta Sūtras**	*Aśvalāyana, Śaṅkhāyana*	*Laṭyāyana Drāhyāyana Jaiminīya*	*Mānava, Vārāha, Baudhāyana, Bhāradvāja, Vādhūla, Hiraṇyakeśin, Āpastamba, Vaikhanasa*	*Kātyāyana*	*Āgastya, Vaitana*	*Sūtra* texts are concerned with rituals. *Śrauta* give details of solemn Vedic sacrifices in addition to *Brāhmaṇa*
	Gṛyha Sūtras	*Aśvalāyana, Kauṣītaki, Śāmbavya*	*Gobhila, Kauthuma, Drāhyāyana, Khādira, Jaiminīya*	*Mānava, Vārāha, Kaṭha, Laugākṣi, Baudhāyana, Vādhūla, Āpastamba, Bhāradvāja Hiraṇyakeśin, Vaikhānasa*	*Pāraskara*	*Kauśika, Paiṭhīnasi*	*Gṛyha* describe domestic ceremonies to be performed by Hindu every day and at important stages of life
	Dharma Sūtras	*Vasiṣṭha*	*Gautama*	*Mānava, Kaṭha, Baudhāyana, Āpastamba, Vaikhānasa*	- -	*Sumantu*	Earliest source of Hindu law, they deal with customs, rites, belief and ethics
	Smṛti			*Manu, Viṣnu, Vādhūla*	- -	*Yājñavalakya*	Later day *Dharma* texts

Indian Sages & Western Scholars

Some readers may want to know little more about the ancient ṛṣis, *Ācāryas* and gurus, and Indian and Western scholars who authored numerous texts on Hinduism, and whose names find frequent mention in this book. A brief introduction and timeline of some of these scholars is given below.

Indian Sages and *Ācāryas*

Oxford Dictionary tells us an *Ācārya*, a Sanskrit word, is 'a Hindu or Buddhist spiritual teacher or leader', and a Sage 'a profound wise man'. Authors of Vedic literature, other than the Vedic *Saṃhitas*, were Sages and *Ācāryas* in this sense. The extant *Śrauta* and *Gṛyha Sūtras* (texts which deal with Vedic, and domestic, sacrifices) as well as the *Dharma Sūtras* (texts which form the earliest source of Hindu law), the *Smṛti* (texts that generally include *Vedāngas* - the six limbs of Vedas, *Sūtras*, *Dharma* Śāstras, Purāṇas, Rāmāyana and Mahābhārata) composed by various Sages and *Ācāryas* are generally known by their author's name e.g. Gautama Dharma Sūtra was composed by Gautama. When we try to attach a timeline to these texts, we encounter several problems; the authors of these Vedic texts do not bother to give the year of composition, and since there were several *Ācāryas*/Sages by the same name in different periods - for example, Yājñavalkya, Manu - it is well neigh impossible to know which Yājñavalkya, or which Manu, is being referred to. The problem is compounded when we take in to account the fact that the members of the Sage's/*Ācārya*'s family often used the name of their forefathers while writing a given text: a descendent of Gautama did not hesitate using Gautama's name - while composing a text several generations down the line - himself! Given these limitations, the author of this book has compiled a list of important Sages and *Ācāryas* whose names the reader may come across frequently reading this book, along with their very brief background.

Names of important Western Scholars who made significant contribution to the Vedic study and study of Indology, with a very brief background, follows the list of Indian Sages and *Ācāryas*.

Briefly, according to PV Kane in his History of Hindu Dharmaśāstra, period of Vedic *Saṃhitas*, Brāhmaṇas and some of the Upaniṣads is 4000-1000 BC. Srauta Sūtras of Āpstamba, Aśvalāyana, Baudhāyana, Kātyāyana, Śaṅkhayayana, Laṭyāyana and some Gṛyha Sūtras like Āpstamba, Aśvalāyana etc belong to 800-400 BC. Dharma Sūtras of Gautama (600-400 BC), Āpstamba, Baudhāyana and Vasiṣṭha, and Gṛyha Sūtras of Pāraskara and some others belong to 500-300 BC.

Āpstamba - Founder of a *Śakha* (Vedic school) of Yajurveda, a teacher, and a mathematician. According to the Hindu tradition, he was the student of Baudhāyana, and had Hiraṇyakeśin as his student.

Aśvalāyana (400 BC?) - Author of the Aśvalāyana Śrauta Sūtra, a Vedic manual of sacrificial ceremonies, belonged to the 'forest tradition' of hermits and wandering holy men. In Vedic texts he is mentioned as a teacher as well as a sage. He is said to have been a student of the great grammarian Śaunaka.

Baudhāyana (~800 BC) - A teacher and a sage, was a formidable mathematician. He authored earliest *Śulba sūtras* which contains calculation of value of pi, Pythagoras theorem, square root of 2 and circling the square.

Manu - In the mythology of India, Manu was the first man and is the legendary author of an important Sanskrit law code, the Manu Smṛti (Laws of Manu).

Scholars believe Manu Smṛti or Manava Dharma Śastra was probably composed in the first few centuries of CE.

Yaska (800-500 BC) - Author of Nirukta - a Sanskrit text, is oldest known etymology or glossary of the Vedic *Saṃhitas*. He dates to before Paṇini.

Paṇini (~ 700-400 BC) - Sanskrit grammarian. Aṣṭādhyāyi, widely accepted as text on perfect grammar, is in *sūtras* (aphorism) which are explained by Patanjali and others.

Yājñavalkya - A sage and a teacher, he figures prominently in the earliest of the Hindu philosophical and metaphysical texts known as the Upaniṣads, the Brihadāranyaka Upaniṣad.

In Mahābhārata he attended *rajsūya yajña* of Yudhiṣṭhira, and in Rāmāyana he was in court of Janaka.

Yājñavalkya is also the name of the author of one of the principal texts of dharma or religious duty, the Yājñavalkya smṛti. This is an entirely different figure, however, since the Yājñavalkya Smṛti was written more than five centuries later than the Upaniṣad.

Jaimini (500-200 BC) - He was a commentator (*sūtrakara*) on *Mīmāṃsā* philosophy. His monumental work, Pūrvamīmāṃsā sūtra, giving fundamental theory of philosophy, contains 2644 *Mīmāṃsā Sūtras*, divided in to 16 sections.

Vātsyāyana (100-300 AD) - A philosopher, better known worldwide for his treatise on 'the art of love making' Kāmasūtra.

Śabara (~100 BC to 600 AD) - A philosopher of the *Mīmāṃsā* school of philosophy, composer of Śabara Bhaṣya (commentary).

Kumārila Bhatt (650-750 AD) - He was a philosopher and *Mīmāṃsā* scholar from medieval India. He is famous for many of his various theses on *Mīmāṃsā*, such as Mīmāṃsā Ślokavarttika, Tantra Vārtika.

Śankara (788-820 AD) - One of the greatest philosophers of India, an exponent of *Advaita* school of *Vedanta*. He set up 4 *maṭhas*, centres of religious authority and learning, Jyotir *maṭha* at Badrinath in north, Sharda *maṭha* at Shringeri in south, Kalika *maṭha* at Dvarka in west, and Jagannatha Govardhana *maṭha* at Puri in east. Died at the age of 32 at Kedarnath in Himalayas.

Medhatithi (820-900 AD) - Known for his extensive commentary on Manu.

Vijñāneśvara (1100-1120 AD) - Profound student of *Pūrvamīmāṃsā,* famous for his work Mitakshara.

Aparārkā (1125 AD) - A prince from North Konkan, authored voluminous commentary on Yājñavalkya Smṛti.

Swāmi Dayānand Sarasvati (1824-83) - Founder of Ārya Samāj and a great scholar of Vedas. He took *saṃnyasa* at 21. In 1875 inaugurated Ārya Samāj in Bombay to teach people to follow Vedas and lead a life of nobility (*ārya* = noble).

Western Scholars (In Chronicle Order)

Sir William Jones (1746-94 AD) - British scholar, a polyglot who knew 21 languages, Supreme Court Judge in British-India, founder of Asiatic Society - an institution involved in Indological studies, he propositioned Sanskrit is an Indo-European language, stressed its affinity to Greek and Latin. He translated the Śakuntalā in English, the Manu Smṛti in English and German, and edited the Ritusamhara.

Charles Wilkins (1750-1836) - A British scholar, his translation of the Bhagavadgītā (London 1785), was first Sanskrit book to be directly translated into a European language. His other works include - book on 'Sanskrit Grammar' (1808) and The Śakuntalā episode of the Mahābhārata (1793).

H.T. Colebrooke (1765-1837) - A British Scholar, described as "the first great Sanskrit scholar in Europe", he was first employed by East India Company at Calcutta in 1782. He edited and/or translated - The Śakuntalā (1830), the

Amaruśataka (1831), the Hitopadeṣa (1804), the Amarakoṣa (1808), the Śatakatraya of Bhartrihari (1804), Śāṃkhyakarika of Ishvarakrishna (1837). During his residence at Calcutta he wrote his 'Sanskrit Grammar' (1805), papers on the religious ceremonies of the Hindus, and 'Essay on the Vedas' (1805), for a long time considered the standard work in English on the subject, and two treatises on Hindu law of inheritance Mitākshara (1810) and the Dayābhāga, under the title Law of Inheritance. His work on algebra with arithmetic and mensuration based on Sanskrit works of Brahmagupta and Bhāskara preceded by a dissertation on the state of science as known to Hindus was published in 1917 in London.

A.W.V. Schlegel (1767-1845) - A German scholar who founded a periodical 'Indische Bibliothek' (1823). His works include the first critical edition of the Bhagavadgītā with Latin translations (1823), and the Rāmayaṇa and the Hitopadeṣa.

S.A. Longlois (1788-1854) - A French Sanskritist, he translated the whole text of the Ṛgveda into French, which was published in Paris, during 1848-51.

Horace Hayman Wilson (1786-1860) - An English orientalist, Dr. Wilson was the first occupant of the newly founded Boden chair of Sanskrit (1832) in Oxford University. He studied medicine at St Thomas's Hospital, and came to India in 1808 as assistant-surgeon on the Bengal establishment of the British East India Company and lived in India for a long time. Wilson prepared the first Sanskrit-English Dictionary (1819) from materials compiled by native scholars, supplemented by his own researches. He edited and translated the text of the Ṛgveda with the Sayana Bhashya into English and published the Sanskrit text with a free translation in English rhymed verse of Kālidāsa's poem, the Meghadūtam.

Hermann Grassman (1809-77) - He was a German Scholar, who made a poetic translation of the Ṛgveda and a Lexicon of the Ṛgveda in German titled, Worterbruchzum Rgveda.

Sir Monier Monier-Williams (1819-89) - British scholar, borne in Bombay, educated at Kings College, Oxford, was the second Boden Professor of Sanskrit at Oxford University. Wrote many books on Hinduism and translated and edited the Śakuntalā (1856), the Vikramorvaṣiyam, the Nalopakhyānam (1879). His biggest contribution is Sanskrit-English and English-Sanskrit Dictionaries.

William Dwight Whitney (1827-94) - An American scholar, known for his work on the Atharvaveda (1856). He wrote the Sanskrit Grammar (1879) and The Roots, Verb-forms and Primary Derivations of Sanskrit language (1885), edited the Atharvaveda Pratiśākhya (1862) and the Taittiriya Pratiśākhya, with commentary and translation, and the Sūrya Siddhānta, a treatise on Astronomy and Astrology.

Max Muller (1823-1900) - A German-born philologist and Orientalist, who lived and studied in Britain for most of his life, Müller became Oxford's first Professor of Comparative Philology. He was one of the founders of the western academic field of Indian studies and the discipline of comparative religion. Müller wrote both scholarly and popular works on the subject of Indology. He translated Upaniṣads and Āpastamba-Sūtras in English, edited the Ṛgveda with Commentary of Sayana (6 Vols.), and edited the Hitopadeṣa, the Meghadūta (1847), the Ṛgveda Pratiśākhya (1859-69) with German translations. He wrote many books on Philosophy, Grammar, and History related to Sanskrit. The Sacred Books of the East, a 50-volume set of English translations, was prepared under his direction and editorship.

A.Weber (1805-1901) - A French Missionery, he was very famous among those who contributed to Vedic literature. He translated the Śukla Yajurveda Saṃhita's ninth and tenth chapters into Latin and its 16th chapter into German. He also translated the Atharvaveda into German, published under the title Indische Studien.

R.T.H. Griffith (1828-1906) - He was the first and the last after H. H. Wilson, who translated the whole text of the Ṛgveda into English. He also published his poetic translation of the Yajurveda, the Sāmaveda, and the Atharvaveda. Elected Boden Professor of Sanskrit, he later held the position of Principal at the Benares College in India and later lived in Kotagiri, Nilgiri translating vedic works in English.

Alfred Ludwig (1832-1911) - A German, he was a Professor of Sanskrit in the University of Prague. He prepared the German translation of the Ṛgveda, titled Der Ṛgveda with 230 important Sūktas of the Atharvaveda translated into German.

AA Macdonnel (1854-1930) - A PhD from the University of Leipzig, Deputy Professor of Sanskrit at Oxford in 1888, and a Boden Professor of Sanskrit in 1899, Macdonnel was born in Muzaffarpur in India. He edited various Sanskrit texts, wrote a grammar, compiled a dictionary, and published a Vedic grammar, a Vedic Reader, and a work on Vedic mythology; he also wrote a history of Sanskrit.

A.B. Keith (1879-1944) - Prof Arthur Berriedale Keith was a Scottish constitutional lawyer, and a scholar of Sanskrit and Indology. He was student of Macdonell and translated Taittiriya Saṃhita into English, that was published under the Harvard Oriental Series in America, The Aitareya Āraṇyaka and Aitareya and Kauṣītaki Brāhmaṇas of the Ṛgveda.

Theodar Benfey (1909-81) - He translated 130 Suktas of Ist Mandala of the Ṛgveda into German and the whole text of the Kauthuma Śakha.

PART I

धर्मो रक्षति रक्षितः

Dharma protected, protects.

(Manu Smrity 8.15)

Prologue

Are we Āryans?
The beginning: From Mehrgarh to Surkotada Horse

If you ask Hindus about the origin of their religion, chances are nine out of ten times answer will be: from Vedas. They are left nonplussed at the suggestion that their religion could have originated many centuries earlier in the older Indus Valley period or deep in south, among South Asian hunter-gatherers, described as Ancient Ancestral South Indians or AASI, the oldest people of the subcontinent. Indians consider the Vedas' period as the beginning of Hinduism. Interestingly, even those familiar with the Indus Valley civilisation and its antiquity think of that civilisation only in terms of its advanced town planning, covered drainage system and the mysterious terracotta seals. They are likely to have no views or information about the religious practices and beliefs of their forebears. We have compartmentalised the Indus Valley civilisation and the subsequent Vedic civilization, as if there was a vacuum in the interregnum. In our minds, our civilizational and cultural inheritance begins with the Vedic period. Though there is no sensible possibility that every member of the Indus Valley civilization was annihilated, either by a natural disaster or meticulous military operations of the advancing Āryans - if indeed that was the case - yet, we like to believe that the slate of India's civilizational history was wiped clean before the history of Vedic civilisation was written on it!

Though people did reside in this part of the world - lands or the mountains and piedmonts bordering Iran - even before the Indus Valley civilization (Mature Harappan) flourished, very little is known about their religious thoughts and practices. It makes sense to start our journey of familiarisation with the origins of religious practices from the period of Indus Valley civilisation, because sufficient evidence exists to prove that more than 4500 years ago, an advanced urban civilisation flourished in India and parts of today's Pakistan.

Scholars believe that the Indus Valley civilization, which flourished between 2500-1900 BC, mysteriously disappeared when the Vedic civilization began to blossom. The Vedas, according to most scholars were composed between 1700-1400 BC. Thus, in addition to the religious thoughts and beliefs of the Indus people, we also need to look at the practices of people who lived in this region during those 800 years, i.e. between 2500 BC and 1700 BC. Using the latest scientific dating techniques, scholars at Indian Institute of Technology, IIT Kharagpur, are pushing back the origins of the Indus Valley civilisation to 5000 BC and beyond[1]. If that holds true, we are faced with a civilization of 3000 years or more, a long period that nearly or totally disappeared before Vedic civilisation began to take root in the Indian subcontinent.

∞

It may appear farfetched to many of us that 5000 years ago our ancestors built double storied houses, covered drainage system, and large public baths, using baked bricks of uniform shape and size - not unlike the bricks we use today. But it is true. In 1920, John Marshall discovered a Harrappan archaeological site buried under a seven-meter mound. The site was damaged by British engineers and contractors who used bricks from the ruins as a source for track ballast during construction of the Lahore-Multan railway line, as part of the Sindh and Punjab railway network in 1857. John Brunton, one of the two British engineers deputed on the job, when informed about the ruins of an ancient city called Brahmaṇabad, narrated: "I was much exercised in my mind how we were to get ballast for the line of the railway." To their delight, the ruins were full of hard and well-burnt bricks, and John was "convinced that there was a grand quarry for the ballast" he wanted. John's brother William Brunton's "section of the line ran near another ruined city further north, bricks from which had already been used by villagers in the nearby village of Harappa at the same site. These bricks now provided ballast along 93 miles of the railroad track running from Karachi to Lahore."[2]

The discovery of Harappan seals by J Fleet (1912) near the site prompted an excavation campaign under Sir John Hubert Marshall, who was Director-General of the Archaeological Survey of India at that time. As a result, the remnants of an unknown civilization - later called Indus Valley Civilisation - were discovered at Harappa by Marshall, Rai Bahadur Daya Ram Sahni and Madho Sarup Vats. Marshall, along with Rakhal Das Banerjee and E J H Mackay, also found remains at another ancient city, Mohenjo-daro, roughly 370 nautical miles to Harappa's west. Several important archaeological treasures were retrieved from both Mohenjo-daro and Harappa, but it is the objects that relate to religious practices of those people that are of special interest to us here.

A man sitting cross-legged, resembling a yogic position, with his hair in a topknot wearing a head gear displaying two horns and surrounded by deer, tiger, elephant and rhinoceros is an ithyphallic (representation of deity with an erect penis) figurine with possibly three faces. Many scholars, who believe in the antiquity of the Hindu religion beyond the Vedas period, see *Paśupati Śiva* in this figurine because of the three common features this ithyphallic man shares with *Śiva* -

(i) the yogic position, long unkempt hair resembling the *jaṭā* (matted hair)

(ii) presence of animals in the immediate vicinity

(iii) an erect penis, a feature associated with *Śiva*

To believers, these are clinching evidence, but much to their dismay, there is a section of scholars that does not buy this theory. This section points out that *Paśupati Śiva* is always surrounded by domesticated, not wild animals like tiger, rhinoceros, et cetera. Moreover, unlike *Śiva*, the figure appears - although it is unclear - to be of a man with horns, a common feature in various other old cultures and civilisations. These scholars also feel that too much is being read into the cross-legged sitting position of the man. This position has been a normal sitting position in the Indian subcontinent for ages, and hence, can hardly be termed 'yogic position'. Furthermore, the phallic emblem by itself is not sufficient evidence of being a representation of *Śiva*. In Hinduism, the presence of a humped bull, both standing and sitting, is associated with *Śiva's vāhana* (vehicle). Many representations of the humped bull depicted on terracotta seals and other engravings in both positions have been found in these sites. For scholars who believe that the Indus Valley inhabitants were worshippers of *Rudra* or *Paśupati*, all these are compelling evidence, but for those who do not subscribe to this interpretation, additional evidence is required before they accept this view.

Another important object in this context is a bronze statue, now commonly called the dancing girl. Here again, to scholars who are 'believers', it is a figure of the mother goddess. They associate findings of ring stones as emblems of *yoni*, especially when seen in conjunction with the abundance of phallic emblems found on the site. The worship of *Śiva* and *Śakti* has been popular in India in the embolic representation of *Śiva Liṅgaṃ* and *yoni*. It is believed the union of the two created the universe. However, scholars who do not consider these as representations of goddess *Śakti*, call these evidences just what they are - the dancing girl, and *yoni* or ring stones.

A figure of a bearded man with a shawl draped across his shoulders has attracted wide interest of scholars. The neatly trimmed beard and the delicate patterns on the shawl add an air of dignity to the figure shown wearing a head strap who could either be a priest or a priest king, or simply a headman.

Scenes depicting "figures in trees including a horned figure who may be a deity"[3] and *peepal* tree (Ficus religiosa) leaves indicate tree and/or 'tree god' worship. On terracotta seals, "in some scenes, a bull or a unicorn is shown in front of an altar or incense brazier. There are also birds and hybrid half human half animal figures which may have been deities."[4] Only one domestic animal, the bull, is depicted on the seals, the rest are all wild animals, such as tiger, rhinoceros, crocodile and a unicorn-like horned animal.

The presence of a series of fire altars at Kalibangān[5] points to worship involving sacrifice of animals. A part of Indus Valley Civilisation, Kalibangān in Hanumangarh district, Rajasthan was discovered by the Italian Indologist Tessitori (1887-1919) who reported it to John Marshall. Furthermore, the great baths at Mohenjo-daro ca 2600-1900 BC may have been sacred tanks used by people for washing or taking a dip before they offered prayers or conducted sacred sacrifices. Although no hard evidence has been found, the presence of fire altars, great baths, at least one structure in the citadel area of Mohenjo-daro - which looks like a temple - and a few other large covered areas probably used for religious functions, all indicate a society involved in collective and independent religious practices.

According to Dalal, "Because of wide variations in the analysis of the religion some see in it a proto-Hinduism; others identify the culture with that of the Ṛgveda or with an indigenous Dravidian culture later displaced by the Vedic culture. Still others see indications of shamanism, animism, or folk religions. No definite conclusions can be reached at present."[6]

The period from 2500-1900 BC is called Mature Harrapan by historians, and the periods from 7000-5500 BC and 5500-3300 BC named Mehrgarh I and II respectively. Phase II is also called the ceramic Neolithic phase, in which animals and agriculture were domesticated, and ceramic pots as well as other artefacts were made and traded.

The Mature Harappan phase is associated with urbanised centres and considerable knowledge of science. The excavations of this period have revealed "wide roads 'varying in width from 9 to 34 feet' intersecting at a right angle, aligned with accuracy, which can only come with the use of compass; perfectly laid out towns 'divided into square or rectangular blocks, each of which was divided lengthwise and crosswise by a number of lanes' with double-story living quarters with baths on upper floor, and vertical water pipes for drainage of water." These centres, interestingly, had large common facilities for its citizens - the Great Bath measures 180 feet by 108 feet and the largest assembly measures 80 feet square, i.e. 6400 square feet! "The vertical alignment in most of the buildings is marvellously accurate, showing that a plumb bob or a similar instrument was used."[7]

The Late Harappan period (1900-1300 BC), also called the Localisation Era, refers to fragmentation of the culture of the Integration Era (2600-1900 BC) when large urban centres were abandoned and smaller resettlements or new settlements emerged. Structures in the Late Harappan sites, generally dated after 1900 BC, are simple as compared to the Mature Harappan structures, with agriculture and domesticated animals. These sites are found extensively in western Uttar Pradesh along with OCP (Ochre Colour Pottery) sites, initially considered ill-fired, but later found to have acquired the colour due to peculiar weather conditions.

Apart from the OCP sites, Copper Hoard (CH) cultural remains have been discovered in the Late Harappan sites in western Uttar Pradesh. As the name suggests, many copper implements were found buried together in a hoard, mainly in the Ganga-Yamuna region extending to Orissa, Bihar and Bengal. There are also some finds in Haryana, Rajasthan and Madhya Pradesh. Since these three cultural sites dated between 1900-1200 BC, it is thought that communities that used copper hoards entered the Ganga-Yamuna region from the east and the Late Harappan region from the west. According to Dalal, "The OCP culture has some elements which are indigenous to the region, influenced by the Late Harappan culture. Both the OCP and the CH probably had an earlier level and could go back to 2500 BC."[8]

According to Dalal, "These three cultures are particularly significant for the Ṛgveda, as some theories equate the Ṛgvedic people with the late Harappans and some others with the CH culture." She adds, "Alternatively, CHs have been attributed to people represented in the Atharvaveda."

Dalal also mentions the Malwa (south-west region of state of Madhya Pradesh) culture (earliest dates between 2000-1750 BC), evidence of which was found at sites in Maheśwar, Nagda and Eran, where "a large pit in the floor of a house has been identified as the fire altar" and "another human figure with wild hair is thought by some to be a proto-*Rudra*." Interestingly, a shell amulet shaped like a tortoise found at Prakash, Maharashtra is considered a precursor to *Viṣṇu's Kūrma avatāra*.

∞

The Vedic period, as proposed by Max Müller and widely accepted by scholars, starts from 1500 BC. The period of Ṛgveda is generally believed to extend to 1200 BC. But what befell the Harappan civilisation? With all its knowledge of house building, bricks made of red sand and clay baked at high temperatures, covered drainage system and unmatched town planning, how did it suddenly disappear? Increasingly, the old theory of Āryan invasion or sudden floods resulting in complete destruction of the civilisation attracts fewer followers in the scholarly world.

Professor Shereen Ratnagar, an Indian archaeologist whose work has focused on the Indus Valley Civilization and author of several texts, questions the sudden disappearance, consequent to the invasion, in her article titled 'The End of Harappan Civilisation' and makes a keen observation that "the Samans, the rulers, craftsmen, shepherds, shipbuilders and pillars of the soil could not have disappeared or become extinct!" Ratnagar goes on to add that it is "the coherence of the civilisation as an overarching system with its regional crafts, modes of elite control, and systems of long-distance procurement that disappeared."[9]

To assume that an entire civilisation was suddenly and completely wiped off would be erroneous, particularly if it is based only on archaeological evidence of large-scale abandonment of cities, craft towns, garrisons and villages. Ratnagar notes that while Mohenjo-daro saw abandonment, Harappa saw squatters living in abandoned houses or crude shelters built using bricks from the structures.

So did these people give up urban life, revert to pastoralism, and chose to move, en masse, upstream along the Indus River and its tributaries because of a natural calamity or holocaust?

Ratnagar finds that the theory of large-scale desertion due to a natural calamity that many scholars subscribe to is simplistic, and gives the example of the Mesopotamian civilisation that survived the shift of channel by the river Euphrates, soil salinity and repeated invasions. The real cause, the actual reason, must be something else. She submits depletion of natural resources as an important reason for migration and relies on the findings of Walter Fairservis to bolster her argument. A prolific writer, Fairservis was a man of many talents. Apart from writing books on archaeology and anthropology, he also wrote many plays, and directed, produced, and acted in several films and served the US Army's Intelligence Branch in World War II before returning to work in a museum in New York as an archaeologist (New York Times Obituary, July 16, 1994). Fairservis prepared a model to calculate the food requirement of the estimated population along with the acreage under crops, number of cattle required for producing the crop, and grazing area required to support the cattle population, based on the natural resources of soil, forest, pasture around the city of Mohenjo-daro. The model concluded that there was a 'formidable assault' on the natural vegetation of the locality. Based on these findings, Ratnagar attributes mass migration to the depletion of natural resources which simply could not sustain the urban centre.

But the desertion of sites, Ratnagar points out, do not have a simple or straightforward explanation, and are not easy to 'read'. These are complex issues, and such movements have multiple triggers, such as inner conflicts, external enemies, et cetera. It is not certain whether this mass exodus arose because of the "hill people from the Kirthars, enemies in the plains, or local rebel factions, whom the rich feared." The desecration of the bust of the priest king and other sculptures suggests Mohenjo-daro had internal strife and domestic feuds. Archaeologists can often tell if people left in a hurry. Wooden doors, household valuables and caches of jewellery left behind in underground compartments are often tell-tale signs indicating that the owners feared a threat to their lives and departed suddenly. Even so, the real cause cannot be deduced accurately by reading these signs at abandoned sites. Ratnagar is right in pointing out that an archaeologist has an ability to tell "that there was no post Harappan culture at a particular site, but is rarely able to differentiate a quick total abandonment from gradual, house by house depopulation of a village over, say, a generation or two."

The abandonments can have many causes - an epidemic, famine or flood, or simply because better habitable sites were found. Ratnagar concludes that "the majority of towns and villages of Harappan culture failed to see sustained occupation after about 1800 BC and people seem to have emigrated."

However, this does not address the moot point - whether an urban centre with solid investment in its infrastructure was deserted solely due to a 'formidable assault' on vegetation, as Fairservis suggests. Even if we were to accept this contention, the abundance of virgin forests and water resources in that period makes it difficult to comprehend the sustained and concentrated assault resulting in complete denudation of land surrounding the urban centres, making it inhabitable for a relatively small population of approximately 23,500. After each rain cycle, the vegetation rejuvenated and the urban centres had an efficient agricultural system in place. The inhabitants were also aware of seasonal cycles and the basics of agriculture. They built granaries which indicate they produced more than they could consume in a season. With such depth of knowledge in agriculture and soil fertility, and the availability of ample water sources (the urban centres were located by the Sarasvatī river and its tributaries), it seems unlikely that a 'formidable assault' on natural resources was the only reason for migration, though it could have been one of the many reasons (even an important one). Even if one were to accept that this made the inhabitants give up their permanent settlements and emigrate voluntarily, it is difficult to understand why "there was a reversion to tribal cultures what we call Chalcolithic stage", as Ratnagar suggests.

[Ratnagar's arguments are from 'The End of the Harappan Civilisation', The Āryan Debate, Ed Thomas R Trautmann, Oxford University Press, 2008]

The Āryan Debate

Now, let us move to issues that are even more contentious. After the end of Harappan civilisation and before the beginning of Āryan Vedic civilisation, was there a cultural and civilizational vacuum? A vacuum, so total and complete, it blocked transmission of any knowledge or practice, from the older civilization to the new one? Or was it a continuum in which there was give and take of ideas, culture, and practices, between the two people?

A debate, called '*The Āryan Debate*', has been raging for more than three decades to settle this issue. It has divided scholars broadly into two groups. While one group believes that Indo Āryans belonged to an Āryan stock that originated in the Central Asian steppes, or at the very least were outsiders coming from the west of present day Pakistan, the other group holds that the Āryans were indigenous people.

Those who believe that Āryans migrated from Central Asia argue that the Āryans represented a more advanced civilisation than others, and shared common Indo-European languages with those who branched away and migrated westward towards Europe. They propose that the Vedic Āryans entered India through present day Afghanistan, and initially spread in the Sarasvatī river region and the cold climes of the Himalayas.

These migrants rode in on horses and chariots, and were physically and culturally different. They brought with them their Vedic gods, *Índra, Agni, Varuṇa,* et cetera, and decimated the native Dravidians, conquering their townships and either making them their *dāsas* (slaves) or driving them away deep down to the south of the Indian peninsula. The language of the 'superior' Āryans was Sanskrit, a branch of Indo-Iranian, which in turn is a branch of the mother group Indo-European. These people were militarily strong but pastoral nomads who practised the Vedic religion. It was due to these Āryans that the Vedic society emerged in India and imposed itself on the older Dravidian civilisation, culture and religion.

Other scholars hold a different view: they admit that the Āryans did indeed come from Central Asia, but not as marauder hordes invading Dravidian urban centres with their chariots and horses, conquering the supine inhabitants of the then India. According to this group of scholars, these Āryans came and settled as neighbours, interacted with locals and gradually spread from the Sarasvatī region to the Ganga-Yamuna plains (present day Haryana and western Uttar Pradesh), and finally to eastern Uttar Pradesh and Bihar, spreading in the piedmont of the Himalayas to the north of Ganga. It was through the interaction of these two - the immigrant Āryans, and local Dravidians and tribal folk - that Vedic civilisation emerged and blossomed in India, which in due course of time overshadowed the original Dravidian and other local cultures. The common core in both these theories is that the Āryans were outsiders to India; they were immigrants.

Another sizeable section of scholars holds an alternate view. They believe the Āryans, like Dravidians and tribal folk, were indigenous people and not immigrants.

∞

The crux of the 'Āryan debate' is the Sanskrit language, Vedas and interestingly, horses and chariots. Historians concur that Sanskrit is an Indo-Āryan language, which is a branch of Indo-Iranian language originating from the Indo-European language. This proposition, first put forward by Sir William Jones in 1786 in his lecture at the Asiatic Society in Calcutta, a society founded by Jones and presided by him at that time, remains a cornerstone of the origin of languages. More particularly, it suggests that Sanskrit is an Indo-Āryan language which has a close affinity with Indo-Iranian language.

It is also accepted by historians and linguists that Dravidian languages are indigenous to this country and do not belong to the Indo-European family, thus unconnected to Sanskrit. Spoken in the five southern states of modern India - Tamil Nadu, Karnataka, Telangana, Andhra Pradesh and Kerala - Tamil, Telugu, and Kannada languages share a common stock of roots and form of grammar which is different from Sanskrit. This subject was researched by Francis Whyte Ellis along with Indian scholars Pattabhiraman Shastri and Śaṅkara Shastri in 1816, while he was posted as the Collector of Madras. He published proof of his findings while working closely with his chief of staff Śaṅkara, and later extended his findings to Malayalam (spoken in Kerala), Tulu (spoken in and around Mangalore), Kodava (spoken in Kodagu or Coorg district of Karnataka), and surprisingly, Malto, a tribal language spoken, more than a thousand miles away, in the Gangetic plains of northern India.

It is only in Sanskrit that retroflex words are present. Words such as *ḍanḍa* (staff), *pinḍa* (lump), *mayūra* (peacock), et cetera are loanwords in Sanskrit from Dravidian. There are no retroflex consonants in either Indo-Iranian or Indo-European languages proving that Sanskrit acquired these words when it encountered the Dravidian language in India. Since Sanskrit was spoken by Āryans, it is clear that Āryans acquired retroflex consonants - which were not prevalent in Indo-European or Indo-Iranian languages - from the Dravidians. The alternate view that a proto Indo-European or Indo-Āryan language originated within India is difficult to sustain because it lacks a proper explanation on how this language radiated out of India towards Iran and Europe, since retroflex consonants are absent in the languages spoken in those two geographical locations.

Another argument forwarded in favour of Āryans being immigrants draws support from Vedic texts which are replete with references of fights between Vedic gods, led by the inimitable *Índra* and *Asuras*, who used fast-moving horses and chariots, and destroyed forts of wide-nosed, dark-skinned, phallic worshipping *dāsas*. They argue that it proves Āryans were pastoral, constantly moving with cattle, unlike local un-Āryas who lived in houses in their urban centres and were agriculturists.

This is a relatively easy problem to reconcile. Increasingly, historians are coming around to the view that not all Āryans were nomadic, many of them had settled down and engaged in agriculture. More importantly, these immigrants had settled down as neighbours of the local Dravidians. That is not to say that all was well between the Āryans and the locals. They had their own share of disagreements and wars, just as the Āryans had skirmishes amongst themselves. Moreover, there was give-and-take in not only language, but also religious practice and beliefs - children were born from marriages between Āryans and Dravidians.

The Horse puzzle

Perhaps the most insoluble problem after the indecipherable Indus seals is one related to horses, or rather, the absence of horses in the Indus civilisation period.

Vedic literature has multiple references to horses and chariots. In the Ṛgveda, parts of chariots are mentioned by name in great detail. But there is no evidence of horses, chariots and spoke wheels in the Indus Valley civilisation. If we are to assume that the Vedic Āryans were indigenous people, then why is there no evidence of horses, chariots or wheels with spokes in the Indus Valley civilisation? Staal, in his book 'Discovering the Vedas', has given fourteen pictures of wheels and its parts from Harappa (2600-1900 BC) - without exception all are solid wheels, i.e. wheels without spokes (figure 8). Likewise, all wheels attached to carts belonging to Harappa in figure 7 are also solid.[10] Absence of evidence is not conclusive proof that horses, chariots and spoke wheels did not exist in Harappan civilization. But as Trautmann observes in his Introduction to The Āryan Debate, "The burden of proof lies on those who wish to overturn the standard view (that there were no horses in Indus Civilization), and to meet it they need to come up with lots of evidence. So far, precious little evidence of Indus civilisation horses and chariots has been adduced by proponents of the alternative view, and the evidence adduced is doubtfull."[11]

However, Lal doesn't quite agree with Trautmann. In his article 'It is Time to Rethink' he says, "The horse has cleared the first hurdles, though no doubt one would like to have more and more examples."[12] He points to the terracotta figure found in Mohenjo-daro excavations by Mackay and, in more recent times, the molar of a horse along with a terracotta figure of the animal, the bones of a horse found at Surkotada and Kalibangān in India, and the discovery of terracotta figurines of horses by Jarrige and his colleagues at Naushahro in Pakistan, to emphasise why 'the horse has cleared the first hurdle'.

Surkotada in Kutch, Gujarat has become a familiar word among scholars of archaeology, particularly of the Indus civilisation period, for the remains of a horse found at a prehistoric Mature Harappan site of the late third millennium BC. These remains have generated extensive debate among scholars. J P Joshi found leg bones, hooves, phalanxes, molars, incisors and canine bones of what appeared to be the remains of a horse at an excavation site. However, many scholars viewed these excavations with great scepticism. Subsequently, in 1979, as mentioned earlier, a terracotta figurine of a horse, and bones of what were claimed to be horse's, were discovered at Lothal. Claims of Surkotada bones and Lothal remains of horses were largely ignored until Dr Sandro Bokonyi re-examined the bones in December 1991 and declared them to be those of a 'true domesticated horse'.[13a] This pronouncement would not have mattered much except that Dr Bokonyi was a name to reckon with. As Director of the Archaeological Institute of Hungarian Academy of Sciences, he was considered one of world's leading archaeo-zoologists. He made an observation that "the occurrence of true horse (*Equus caballus L.*) was evidenced by the enamel pattern of the upper and lower cheek and teeth and by the size and form of incisors and phalanges (toe bones)." He went on to add that "these horses were obviously imported from horse domestication centres recently discovered in Soviet Central Asia" and that the horse bones represented adult individuals, indicating that these horses were used for work.[13b] However, even this did not settle the debate.

Gupta holds the view that the horse has become a bone of contention between the so-called nationalists and the so-called Marxists. The former base their views on the archaeological findings, and maintain that the people of Indus Sarasvatī civilisation may have been Vedic Āryans known for their horse-driven chariots. The pro-Marxists find the evidence insufficient, and stick to the view that the Indus civilisation did not use horses and hence, were not Vedic Āryans. He finds this reasoning strange because "for the scientists, Indus Sarasvatī people were definitely horse users, whether they were Vedic Āryans or not, hardly concerns them."

Another interesting view indicates an early Āryan presence in India. Renowned Sanskritist and archaeologist Asko Parpola, bases his views on new archaeological evidence from Afghanistan and Pakistan. He believes that "the infiltration of a small number of Āryan speakers to the Indus Valley and beyond started as early as the last urban phase of the Indus civilisation from the twenty first century BC onwards." He theorises these immigrants came through Central Asia from "Eurasiatic steppes, the native habitat of the horse and the region where it appears to have first been domesticated."[14] Parapola is so convinced about the separate Vedic and Harappan cultures that, for him, any attempt "to conflate the identity of the Vedic and Harappan cultures and to deny the external origin of Sanskrit and other Indo-Āryan languages is as absurd as to claim, as Dayananda Sarasvatī did, that the railway trains and aeroplanes that were introduced in South Asia by the British in the 19th and 20th centuries had already been invented by the Vedic Āryans."[15]

In conclusion, what emerges after considering these different theories on the 'no horse, no Āryan' issue is that there is no clarity or unanimity among scholars. Not yet anyway. Perhaps Lal's approach is correct in this respect when he says it is time to rethink!

Conclusion

To sum up, starting from nearly 8000 BC down to the Late Harappan civilisation, evidence suggests, albeit tentatively, that people followed certain religious practices. Tentative evidence includes bathing pools - possibly used for dipping before a religious ceremony; figurines of women - possibly of a mother goddess or a fertility cult, the Indus Valley seals and figurines believed by many to be *Rudra* or proto-*Rudra*, phallic emblems and *yonic* links, the bust of the priest king, the Nandī bull and figures of humans in a tree. We will have to wait until the language of the Indus Valley is deciphered for a better understanding of their religious beliefs. It is possible that even that will not be sufficient.

Chapter 1

Arrival of Āryans and Vedas

There is evidence that all ancient religions started with nature worship - the rain gave them food to eat and water to drink without which life was impossible, but an excess resulted in floods that washed away their houses, their cattle and food, and often, their near and dear ones. The clouds that gave them life-supporting rainwater were also associated with life-taking thunderbolts. The life-giving air could show its fury when it blew strong, sucking away men, animals and dwellings in its whirlwind. Even fire that gave them warmth in cold weather, and helped them cook their food, could destroy everything they possessed and the forests on which they depended. Similarly, the sun was good only in the right measure; in excess, it resulted in loss of life and vegetation. It was natural for people to look at the elements and forces of nature as the handiwork of supernatural forces. In fact, this is true of all religions in all civilisations and cultures.

Empedocles, the fifth century BC Greek philosopher, scientist, and healer, in his work Tetrasomia, talks of the four elements not only as material substances but also as spiritual essence. He associates these elements with Greek gods and goddesses - air with *Zeus*, earth with *Hera*, fire with *Hades* and water with *Nestis*. This is not very different from the ancient Persians who had *Anahita* (the immaculate one), water goddess, fertility goddess, patroness of women as well as a goddess of war portrayed as a virgin dressed in a golden cloak wearing a diamond tiara (the dove and peacock as her sacred animals); *Asman*, the god of sky; and *Atar*, the Persian god of fires and purity, son of *Ahura Mazda*.

People venerated fire all over the world, particularly in the Celtic lands and other cold areas of Europe. They considered fire the terrestrial counterpart of the sun in the heavens and held fire festivals to acknowledge the power of the sun and replicate its heat and light on earth. *Agni* was the prime deity in Vedic rituals, and like the Iranian *Atar*, the object of a prominent fire cult. In Norse mythology, its destructive power manifests itself as the fire demon *Surt*: reducing the nine worlds to flame, then smoke, and then nothing but ashes.

Feng Po was the Chinese wind god, called the Wind Earl. He was perceived as the breath or soul of life, so they equipped *Feng Po* with tremendous powers.

The Greek mother earth, *Gaia*, the most ancient divinity born out of chaos, was the female creative principle and personification of the physical earth. As mother earth, *Gaia* is compared with similar personages in different cultures - *Pṛthvī* in India, *Papa* in Polynesia, and *Ki* in Mesopotamia.

Hephaestus forged the lightning boards in his smithy under Mount Aetna and was believed to return to his smithy each spring, when lightning storms were imminent, to craft a new supply. Then he gave the weapons to *Zeus*, who hurled them from the sky. *Aerun* hurled them in Russia, as *Adad* did in Mesopotamia and *Índra* used his thunder bolt *vajra* in India. These were storm gods, and the lightning bolts were their symbols.

AA Macdonell, an Indian born Sanskrit scholar and a Deputy Professor of Sanskrit at Oxford University in the late seventeenth century, observed, "Religion in its widest sense includes on the one hand the conception which men entertain of the divine or supernatural powers and, on the other, that sense of the dependence of human welfare on those powers which finds its expression in various forms of worship."[1]

∞

The Indian branch of Āryans who settled in the Sapta Sindhu region (*Hepta Hindu* in Avestan) or the land of seven rivers (present day Punjab in west India and eastern part of Pakistan) around 1500-1400 BC were no different. And because the worshippers did not understand how and why the forces of nature manifested in a way that affected their lives, many times benevolently and other times harshly, they began treating these forces with awe and respect. But the unpredictability of the behaviour of nature causing hardship and damage remained an issue, something beyond their understanding and control. Sometimes they faced excessive or untimely rainfall that caused floods and destruction, and at other times good weather made plentiful food available for men and animals. They had to find a way to influence these forces. It is not surprising therefore that these people, like their brethren across continents, accepted these natural forces to be caused and controlled by superior beings. Since these superior forces could not be tamed by any known means, they had to be cajoled, flattered and pleased, just as a king, or any other dispenser of favours. So people supplicated to be blessed with sufficient rainfall and sunshine, and to be spared the fury of thunder storms, floods and draughts, and forest fires. Even though these efforts were laced with adoration, it was 'physiolatory' ('physio' - what is from nature, ref Oxford dictionary, and 'latory' - worshiper, ref Webster New Colligiate Dictionary) developing itself more distinctly into forms of Theism, Polytheism, Anthropomorphism and Pantheism. The phenomena of nature were thought of as something more than powerful forces - to the worshippers they were like concrete personalities which had more personal attributes."[2]

Proto-Indo-Iranians worshiped many gods including 'nature gods', such as *Asman* - the lord of sky (*Aseman* in modern Persian), *Zam* - the earth goddess (*Zamin* in modern Persian and Hindustani) and *Hvar* and *Mah* (*Khorshid* and *Mah* in modern Persian) - the sun and the moon. There were two gods for wind, *Vāta* and *Vāyu*. *Vāta* was the one that brought rain clouds and *Vāyu* was responsible for blowing the wind.

To these people, the only known way to please supernatural powers controlling natural and cosmic phenomena was the way they supplicated their own superiors and fellow beings - through praises and offerings of gifts. The phenomenon of nature, treated as personalities with personal attributes, were invoked and praised in hymns and prayers just as the benefactors, kings, fathers, guardians, et cetera were in day to day life - "They were invoked in formal hymns and prayers (mantras), set in metres (*chhandas*)."[3]

Whether this was indeed the genesis of Ṛgveda or not is impossible to prove or disapprove. That this is a plausible explanation can hardly be disputed, especially because religions across the world, since the beginning, believed that supernatural personalities controlled the natural phenomena - these personalities were treated as gods of wind, water, fire and thunder bolt, and their worship and praises kept them in good humour.

Chapter 2

Hinduism - Dharma, not A Religion

The religion of these Indo-Āryan speaking immigrants was not Hindu religion - it was Vedism, variously called *Brahmannism* or *Vedic Brahmannism*; the three terms referring to the religious ideas and practices among Indo-Āryan speaking peoples of Ancient India. These religious ideas and practices of Āryans were based on the Vedas, and their gods were Vedic gods - very different, with a very few exceptions - from the Hindu gods as we know them now. The Vedism itself was not purely an Indo-Āryan affair, it had emerged 'as a syncretic mixture of old Central Asian and new Indo-European elements'[1] and one of the ingredients of this 'mixture' was ' Harappan heritage, incorporating some of its ritual customs (the construction of the fire altars, indoor rituals, the use of the stellar mantle [in the rajsua], ritual bathing, the fixing of festival days [of the goddess] on the equinoxes…) into their own religion.'[2]

The immigrant (Vedic) Āryans and the non-Āryans etc followed by their progeny and the non-Āryans, the older inhabitants of India (called *dāsas/dasu* by the Āryans), collectively came to be known as Hindus much later.

The word 'Hindu' was first used by Arabs after the eighth century AD for people living east of the river Sindhu (Persian - Hindu هندو, Enghlish - Indus), but it is the British writers of 1830 who first introduced and standardized the use of Hindu and Hinduism. The word 'Hinduism' refers specifically to the culture of thc Indian civilisation of the last 2000 years, which evolved from Vedism, the religion of Indo-European people who settled in India during the last centuries of the second millennium BC. As a religion, Hinduism is a composite of diverse doctrines and refers to the faith of the Hindus.[3]

But this Hinduism, the Hinduism we know today, has completely transformed itself from the Vedic religion of the immigrant Āryans, the 'syncretic mixture' or 'composite of the Indo-Āryan and Harappan cultures and civilization', prompting many scholars to call Vedic religion - 'ancient' Hinduism, and the Hinduism that we practice now, as 'recent' Hinduism. But it will be incorrect to think that these two are really different. The ideas and practices found in the Vedic texts had major influences that shaped contemporary Hinduism - indeed most of the important Hindu ceremonies have mantras from the Vedas. The Ārya Samāj movement, a reformist movement (1875) was founded with the express pupose of bringing Vedas centre stage to the Hindu way of life.

How the Vedic religion, passing through various stages, transformed itself into the Hinduism of today, is the subject matter of this book.

∞

From magic rites, animal and tree worship, worship of rivers and personal gods, to the belief in one supreme god, mysticism and intangibility, many divergent and different concepts co-exist in Hinduism. The contemplation of the abstract in *Advaita* and the worship of *kula-devatā, grām-devatā* (family and village deity) and one or more of the 33-crore *devī-devtā*, all find a place, often together under the same roof, in a Hindu home. It is not unusual, for what could appear to an outsider as great dichotomy, to find many of these beliefs and practices coexisting even in a single mind.

This has been made possible, among other reasons, due to Hinduism's belief that god transcends definition. It is repeatedly emphasised that god is beyond description, definition and comprehension. He is beyond all (sensory) perceptions and yet, present and manifests in all forms - animate and inanimate. He is omnipresent.

From this, it follows naturally to accept form, shape, and belief of countless 'products of imaginations' as manifestations of god.

Belief in one god does not clash with a simultaneous belief in other forms of gods. *Kuldev* and *grāmdev* (family and village deity) indeed share space with pan Indian gods and goddesses. Likewise, there is no clash in the mind of a Hindu if he or she also believes in non-Hindu god/s. In fact, the core idea of Hinduism does not lie in the belief that god exists!

Since there is no single founder of this religion, nor a central authority or a 'book' of teachings laying down a doctrine, when seen in conjunction with the flexibility it offers to believe or not to believe in the existence of god, it becomes evident why attempts to define Hinduism within the confines of a religion have been unsuccessful.

Any belief, once acquired in the realm of Hinduism, constantly undergoes moderation and revision, and keeps evolving; rarely is it ever completely rejected or jettisoned. For a Hindu, there are countless ways of looking at the truth - god may be present (and seen) in endless forms, in animate or inanimate objects, and even without form. So within Hinduism itself, such deviating, and at times opposing views coexist in such a way that a Hindu looks at divergence of views and beliefs not only as natural, but an essential element of the religion. This distinct aspect of Hinduism allows a Hindu to reconcile his beliefs with the followers of his own religion as well as followers of nearly all other religions, thereby imparting an almost unmatched tolerance. Accommodating, if not assimilating, vastly divergent and often opposing ideas and beliefs are an integral and indispensable part of the Hindu way of experiencing faith.

This practice is not new to Hinduism either. In the Ṛgveda, ṛṣi Viśvāmitra and ṛṣi Vasiṣṭha, despite their serious disagreements and unhesitant public name-calling, find a place side by side and receive equal respect. Similarly, later figures like Mahāvira Jain and Gautama Buddha, who did not hesitate in expressing what they thought of each other, at times in unrestrained fashion[4], are also treated with the same respect by non-Jain and non-Buddhist Hindus as *avatāras* (incarnations) of Hindu gods.

This contrasts starkly with religions founded on fixed basic tenets. A tight ring of religious beliefs within the ambit of which all adherents must think and act to qualify as followers, and stepping beyond which disqualifies them as practitioners, is the defining attribute of most other successful religions.

Chapter 3

Dharma - What is it if not 'religion'?

Manu, the famous law-maker, attributed a single factor behind every action of human beings - *kāma* (desire).

"Not a single act here (below) appears ever to be done by a man free from desire; for whatever (man) does, it is (the result of) the impulse of desire."[1]

The natural desires of all human beings are sexual and emotional pleasures, and *artha*. While we all are familiar with sensual and emotional pleasures, *artha* - according to the great sage Vātsyāyana, better known worldwide for his treatise on 'the art of love making' *Kāmasūtra* - is

"The acquisition of arts, land, gold, cattle, wealth, equipages and friends.

It is, further, the protection of what is acquired, and the increase of what is protected."[2]

According to this ancient text, all humans are driven by six basic impulses - desire (*kāma*), anger (*krodha*), passion (*moha*), greed (*lobha*), infatuation (*mada*) and enmity (*matsarya*). If not controlled, these natural impulses called the *arishadvarga* (the six enemies) lead to evil thoughts, evil actions and evil speech. They are believed to be the root cause of conflict between human beings.

Expounding, sage Manu says -

"Action which springs from the mind, from a speech, and from the body, produces either good or evil results;

Coveting the property of others, thinking in one's heart of what is undesirable, and adherence to false (doctrines) are the three kinds of (sinful) mental actions.

Abusing others, speaking untruths, detracting from the merits of all men, and talking idly, shall be the four kinds of (evil) verbal action.

Taking what has not been given, injuring (creatures) without the sanction of the law, and holding criminal intercourse with another man's wife are declared to be the three kinds of (wicked) bodily action.

That man is called a (true) *triḍanḍin* whose mind has controlled these three, the control over the speech (*vagḍanḍa*) the control over his thoughts (*manoḍanḍa*) and the control over his body (*kayaḍanḍa*) are firmly fixed.

That man who keeps this threefold control (over himself) with respect to all created beings and wholly subjugates desire and wrath thereby assuredly gains complete success." (MS 12.3 - 11)

But there were very few *triḍanḍin* who could voluntarily control 'these three'; most succumbed readily - and this led to inevitable clashes in the society.

The ṛṣis and wise men were quick to realize that for the society to function justly and in an orderly fashion, this matter of exercising control over the impulses and 'doing the right thing the right way' - which they called the way of Dharma - could not be left to individual's discretion. It required an external regulating mechanism which clearly lay down -

1. Righteous path, i.e. what are the right things and the right way of doing them; and

2. Consequences for the individuals who deviated from the Righteous path

These two aspects were codified as the *dharma sūtras*.

The enormous task of authoring the *dharma sūtras* was initially (600-400 BC) undertaken by sages like Āpastamba and Baudhāyana, detailing comprehensive rules that different members of society had to follow, and the expiation and punishment for their violation. A few centuries later, the *smṛtis* took this further. While Manu compiled the Manusmṛti, which later became a reference book for scholars and authors of Hindu texts in all ages, Yājñavalkya made his own very valuable contribution through Yājñavalkya Smṛti.

In this set up, every individual had the freedom to fulfil *kāma* and pursue his materialistic desires, i.e. acquire *artha*, so long as it was done adhering to the Righteous path in conformity with Dharma.

Sages warned that unacceptable or evil desire brought an individual in conflict with other individuals or the society. And the resulting disorder could disturb the peace, and cause unhappiness all around. Hence, such actions were proscribed by dharma. It was also understood that unhindered, unchecked and wholly selfish desires, if not regulated and controlled, could give the strong and the powerful a free hand to exploit the weaker members of society. Such conduct had to be controlled by a superior power, an authority that could enforce Dharma, and, if necessary, adequately punish those who transgressed.

The king was designated as the sovereign, enforcing the authority of Dharma.

The Oxford dictionary defines sovereign as 'possessing supreme or ultimate power', i.e. above the law, with the power to legislate, adjudicate and award punishment.

Giving unbridled power and making a king 'sovereign' - supreme, i.e. above the law, could have had serious repercussions, so the king himself was also brought under the rule of Dharma. The king had to follow *rājdharma*, and was thus bound by law. Detailed treatises prescribed *rājdharma*, the Righteous conduct of the king. He could judge and hand out punishment to those who deviated from Dharma, but only in accordance with the *dharmaśāstra*, and the punishment that he handed out, had to be in strict accordance with Dharma. A close look at *rājdharma* shows that the king in Hindu society did not have legislative powers. This difference between kingship in India and elsewhere in the world is truly remarkable.

Thus, Dharma became all pervasive. From the king to the *dāsa*, everyone was governed by it including the outcasts. Dharma was omnipresent because it covered every action of every member of society, from conception (*puṃsvana* and *garbhādhāna*) to death and becoming one with the elements (*antyeṣṭi*) and scattering of ashes in water. It governed every minute of an individual's life, from the moment s/he woke up in the morning to the time s/he went to sleep.

Since it was believed that every human action is triggered by the impulse of one of the six passions, *arishadvargya*, and their fulfilment had to be in conformity with dharma, the sages had to compile and prescribe the right course for every conceivable action and behaviour, for every member of society. These texts are called the *dharma śāstras*. Only when a man achieved *kāmya* by following the Righteous path could he experience the real satisfaction of savouring the results of his actions. But individuals often faced dilemmas when they encountered new situations - in business or with one's spouse, elders, youngsters, friends and even enemies - not already or fully covered in the existing *dharma śāstras*. As society evolved and became more complex, these situations arose more frequently. Additions and deletions were therefore made to suitably modify the existing *dharma śāstras*, and new texts composed to deal with the changing situation. Over a period of time, a comprehensive code of conduct emerged which formed the basis of Hindu law.

Adherence to the course of Dharma was not so much about creating a society which abided by the civil, criminal and constitution laws, i.e. a society free of crime, fair and just to all, as it was about prescribing a path, showing the right way following which everyone could achieve salvation (*mokṣa*). Of course, *vyavahāra* (conduct) and *prāyaścitta* (atonement/penance) were essential components of dharma, the Righteous course. Most modern societies have a charter of liberty and collection of laws enforcing proper conduct to preserve the concept of personal freedom and the right to justice, and any deviants are punished by the state. That is where the role of the modern state ends. The dharma prescription covered all this and went well beyond, to the spiritual territory. It prescribed right actions and conduct that led to the ultimate goal of every human's life - *mokṣa*.

This was achieved in a remarkably simple and effective manner. Members of society were told they were free to pursue objects of their worldly desires so long as the object of desire and the methods employed to achieve it, both were in accordance with the rules laid down in the *śāstras*, i.e. following only the Righteous path of dharma. By following the course of their dharma - from waking up to going to sleep, and from birth to death - not only they could obtain objects of desire and materials of pleasure they sought in this world, and avoid conflict with other members of society, but this adherence to the course of Dharma also eventually led them to eternal bliss or *mokṣa*.

Every individual, and society, striving for peace and happiness thus became a stakeholder in observing dharma. The twin goals of material and spiritual happiness could be achieved by following the course of dharma.

Hindu Dharma thus became a tempting proposition for all concerned; an offer too good to refuse.

Rather than being just a religion, it transformed into a way of life, touching and encompassing every action, thought and deed.

Acquiring *artha* and fulfilling *kāma* (desires) by consistently following the righteous path of Dharma leads to ultimate freedom, the final liberation! This is how the ultimate mission of life came to be defined.

The four *puruṣārthas*

Dharma, *artha*, *kāma* and *mokṣa* are called the four *puruṣārtha* - the goal of life for every Hindu.

Bhishma in Mahābhārata Sánti Parva 59-14 explains that an ideal state exists when people protect each other while acting in accordance with dharma. But they are also likely to stray from the path of Dharma when overpowered by sensual desires, passion and greed. Stronger people harassed the weak, and as a remedy to the situation, the threefold ideal called dharma, *artha and kāma* (*trivarga*) were laid down for the welfare and happiness of the people. The fourth ideal, *mokṣa* (the desire to eternal happiness) is attainable only if one adhered to the right course in attaining the first three. As stated earlier, the king was entrusted with the responsibility of enforcing dharma.

There was no dispute about the position of *mokṣa* as the ultimate objective of life. But situations arose where one had to decide which of the other three *puruṣārthas* was more important. *Dharma śāstras* unambiguously laid down that Dharma was supreme, followed by *artha*, while *kāma* was given the last position. Therefore, acquisition of wealth was acceptable and permitted, in this scheme of things, as long as it was attained using methods approved by dharma. Similarly, satisfying one's worldly desires was also legitimate so long as it was in conformity with what was prescribed as dharma.

In case of conflict between *artha* and *kāma*, *artha* took precedence.

It was believed, and rightly so, that acquisition of wealth and fulfilment of desires could give peace and happiness in the long run if, and only if, these were attained following the path of dharma. A fine balance was to be maintained where every action triggered by the impulse of desire was tempered with dharma. This led to a very detailed compilation of the Righteous course of action for members of the society, governing all aspects of their life. All actions, big and small, were covered by these compilations called *dharma śāstras*.

∞

From the early Ṛgveda to Yajurveda period, as the *varṇa* and *jāti* system evolved, numerous new classes started to emerge with their own local customs and traditions. This necessitated the formulation and prescription of a class-specific Righteous course. The *dharma śāstras* thus came to prescribe different Righteous courses under the same set of circumstances, for different classes of people. These texts stayed relevant by adapting to the prevailing socio-economic situation.

Depending on the social and political crisis afflicting the Hindu society at different times, these rules underwent amendments; some rules were overlooked or modified while others were jettisoned. At times, a new *Saṃhitā* was created. *Devala Saṃhitā* was composed in Gujarat/Sindh after the invasion (712 AD) and mass conversion of Hindus by Mohammad bin Qasim. According to Bhandarkar, "There were two *Devala Smṛtis*, one which was known, e.g. to Vijñāneśvara comprising all the essential constituents of a smṛti, and the other, the work which is engaging our attention here and which deals only with one subject, namely, that of the Hindus that had been defiled through contact with the *mlecchas*. The latter was composed to meet a special emergency created by the advent of the Muslim power whose ardent proselytising activity began to affect Hindu society seriously."[3]

This change in Dharma has been a continuous process since ancient times; nothing is inscribed on a tablet of stone.

This willingness to adapt, this readiness, at times the eagerness for embracing the new and good, and the alacrity with which many rules have been discarded and adapted also created peculiar problems. Many a times, such revisions led to unexpected situations where different *Saṃhitās* expressed differing views on the same subject, creating confusion in the minds of people about what is right and what is wrong, or rather, who is right and who is wrong. In fact, some *Saṃhitās* at times offer divergent views on the same subject in different places within the same book.

But before proceeding to explore the teachings of *dharma śāstras* any further, we should first understand: What does this word 'Dharma' really mean? What is the definition of dharma?

Chapter 4

Hindu Dharma and its sources

Dharma

It is almost impossible to put down a precise definition of Dharma, but what is certain is that it is not same as 'religion'. Various dictionaries define Dharma as ordinance, usage, duty, justice, morality, virtue, religion, et cetera. Interestingly, Dharma is also personified as a deity in the Mahābhārata.[1]

The meaning of the word Dharma, as it was understood, and the sense in which it was first used, in the Vedas, is quite different from its modern-day usage. Even within the Ṛgveda, the oldest of the four Vedas, Dharma conveys different meanings in different contexts. While in some verses (R.V. 1.22.18, V.2 6.6, V I I I.43.24, I X.6 4.1 et cetera) it refers to 'religious ordinances or rites', in some other (R.V. IV.53.34, V. 63) 'Dharma' is used for 'fixed principle or rules of conduct'. Elsewhere, in the Aitareya Brahmaṇa (a *Brahmaṇa* attached to the Ṛgveda) Dharma seems to have been used in an abstract sense - for the entire body of religious duties. Given its all-encompassing nature, it appears that tying the word 'Dharma' down to an exact definition was a challenge even in Vedas' times.

In the Upaniṣads, which were composed several centuries after the Ṛgveda, Dharma is widely used to imply duty. Living in the teacher's house as a *brahmacārin* (student) 'under the three branches of the law' is prescribed as the duty of the student.[2] In Taittirīya Upaniṣad, after teaching the Veda to students, the teacher instructs his pupil: "Say what is true! Do thy duty (Dharma!)." He instructs them to repeat the words: "Do not swerve from the truth! Do not swerve from duty (Dharma)!"[3] Clearly, here the word 'Dharma' has been used as a synonym of 'duty', which is how Max Müller translates it in his 'Sacred Books of the East' collection.

'Dharma' is used, more or less in the same sense (duty), by the sages when they request Manu (circa 200 BC), MS.1.2, the famous law maker of ancient India, to impart instructions on Dharma for all *varṇas*. Yājñavalkya Smṛti (100-300 AD) too uses it in the sense of duty. But the word 'law' can easily be substituted for 'duty' in many of these translations, and though the two words in the English language convey different meanings, both meanings make equal sense in these texts. In Yājñavalkya Smṛti (I.1), 'Dharma' appears to be the privileges, duties and obligations of a man; his standard of conduct as a member of one of the castes, and as a person at a particular stage of life, i.e. *varṇa* and *āśrama*. It is interesting to note that while Jaimini, in Pūrva Mīmāṁsā Sūtra (1.1.2), refers to Dharma as "a desirable goal or result that is indicated by injunctive (Vedas) passages", Manu in his *smṛti* (I.1) observes that "Dharma is that which is practiced by the learned that lead a moral life, that are free from hatred and partiality, and that is accepted by their hearts, i.e. conscience."

Thus, one may be right in drawing the conclusion that either 'Dharma' meant both duty and law, or the Sanskrit term had a more generic meaning and application such as 'Righteous conduct', which can be easily substituted for the previous meanings of duty and law.

Kumarila Bhat was a renowned philosopher and a *mīmāṁsākara* during ~700 AD. His Tantra Vārtika, a sub-commentary of Śabara's commentary on Jaimini's, often used as a reference by scholars, says all *dharma sūtras* are concerned with imparting instructions on Dharma of the *varṇas* and the *āśramas*, which appears to be a reference to the duties and obligations of individuals of different *varṇa*s and stages (*āśramas*) of life.

Perhaps McKenzie was close to the truth when he said, "In India, in those days, no clear distinction was drawn between moral and religious duty, usage, customary observance and law, and the term Dharma was applied to the whole complex of forms of conduct that were settled or established."[4] If we go by this observation, then religion, virtue, law and duty, these four concepts are subsumed in the usage of Dharma in Hindu texts.

Having said that, the most appropriate interpretation of Dharma does appear to be - the Righteous conduct.

Types of Dharma

Given the elasticity of the word, it is easy to understand that Dharma includes a wide range of activities spanning social, ethical and religious fields. These activities are usually different for the four different *varṇas* that constitute Hindu society. Thus, we have a variety of Dharmas - a social act could, and often did have a different Dharma for different *varṇas*. There were many ways in which Dharma could be classified, but the one provided by Manu is accepted by all. In his *smriti*, he describes Dharma as five-fold - *varṇa dharma, āśramas dharma, varṇaāśramas dharma, naimittika dharma* and *guṇa dharma*.

The distinctions between these five Dharmas can be better understood with the help of the following examples -

(i) *Varṇa-dharma*, or the law of castes, are the duties relating to classes, e.g. 'let a *Brahmaṇa* always abstain from wine' as enjoined in Gautama DS (I I.20)

(ii) *Āśrama-dharma* is the law of orders and relates to the duties of orders, e.g. begging of alms (for a student belonging to *brahmacārya āśrama*)

(iii) *Varṇāśrama-dharma* is the law of orders of specific castes (*varṇā*) and relates to their duties, e.g. a *brahmaṇa* student of Veda should carry a *palāsa* wood staff (Āp. GS. IV.11.15)

(iv) *Guṇa-dharma* is the law for people endowed with particular qualities, e.g. a king (endowed with the particular role of a ruler or kingship whose highest duty is to protect the subjects)

(v) *Nimitta-dharma* encompassed secondary duties, e.g. penances performed to atone for actions that are forbidden

Interestingly, Mitākṣarā texts (roughly meaning - in few words), a commentary on Yaj S (I.1) written by Vijñāneśvara, a scholar in the late eleventh and early twelfth century (considered to be a reference book of Hindu *dharma śāstras*) first discusses and illustrates the five-fold Dharmas and then prescribes a sixth category - *sādhāraṇa dharma* - duties common to men of all castes, including *candalas* (outcastes), e.g. *ahiṃsā* (non-violence). It goes on to quote a Veda passage in support: '*na hiṃsāyāt sarva bhūtāni.*' In summary, we can say that according to Medhātithi, Dharma is five-fold, but Mitākṣarā added *sādhāraṇ dharma* (duties common to all men) as the sixth Dharma. These guidelines are what Hindus all over the world continue to follow even today.

Sources of Dharma

Hindus consider Vedas supreme.

But the Vedas do not expound Dharma in a formatted manner. They mention the various aspects of Dharma in different contexts, but these observations are disjointed and scattered over several chapters. For the 'connect' and a formal treatment of the topics of the *dharma śāstra*, we have to look to the *smṛtis*. *Dharma sūtras* and *smṛtis* are the two important sources for the authentic study of the *dharma śāstras*. Both these texts are subsequent to Vedas and proclaim to have extracted the essence of Dharma from the Vedas.

According to Gautama Dharma Sūtra (I.1-2), the oldest of dharma sūtras: "The Veda is the source of Dharma वेदो धर्ममूलम । (१), and the tradition and practice of those that know it, i.e know Veda तद्विदां च स्मृतिशीले । (२)"

Similarly, Āpastamba observes that "the authority (for the Dharmas) is the consensus of those that know Dharma and the Vedas (I.1.1.2)." Vasiṣṭha in his

Dharma Sūtra I. 4-6 holds a similar opinion. The *smṛtis* have dealt with Dharma extensively and they too emphasise that the root of religion lies in the Vedas. Manu is more specific in explaining the sources of Dharma: "The root of religion is entire Veda, and (then) the tradition and custom of those who know (the Veda), and the conduct of virtuous people, and what is satisfactory to oneself (MS II. - Doniger)." Yaj S I.7 also declares the sources of Dharma as "the Veda, traditional law, the usages of good men, what is agreeable (to) oneself and (the) desire born of due deliberation - this is traditionally recognised as the source of Dharma."

From these quotes, one can infer that the principal sources of Dharma were conceived to be -

1. The Vedas
2. The *smṛtis*, and
3. The customs

The inclusion of customs as a source of Dharma is an interesting aspect that needs to be understood better. As mentioned earlier, the Vedas, which are the *mūla* (the source) of Dharma, are not treatise on Dharma; they do not profess to be so. However, references to numerous topics in the Vedas, which form part of Dharma, were culled by *smṛtikāras* and *sūtrakāras* (authors of *smṛtis* and *sūtras*) in formulating their works. Apart from these, there are several stories and narrations in the Vedas, such as the *vivāha* of *Sūrya's* daughter *Sūryā*, or the practice of gifting cows, horses, gold and clothes that came to be used as model standard practices and were incorporated into Dharma. In the first instance, what *Sūrya*, a god, did in his daughter's wedding was emulated by the mortals as an ideal form of the ceremony, and in the second instance, the eulogy of Veda (Ṛ.V. X.107.2) signalled this custom as appropriate to be considered a part of Dharma. However, there is yet another meaning to 'using customs as sources of Dharma'. The prevalent socio-economic and geographical conditions of different sections of the society moulded their customs, which in turn caused changes in the way people came to practice Dharma. For example, the less affluent could hardly afford gifting a bull or a cow to a guest, as recommended in the Aitareya Brahmaṇa (1.15): "People offer a bull or a cow when a king or a worthy guest comes, making it the Dharma of the householder towards the distinguished *atithi*." These communities modified the practice, gifting less expensive items such as fruits or other edibles. These revised customs were permitted within the fold of Dharma. Likewise, some local twists to rites in *vivāha* ceremonies came to be practiced as Dharma.

Dharma Śāstras

These are "Sanskrit texts which deal with the customs, practices, ethical conduct, and laws of the Hindus." (HAG-Dalal)

In a broad sense, *dharma śāstra* comprises *gṛhya* and *dharma sūtras*, metrical *smṛtis*, like those of Manu, Yājñavalkya, Bṛhaspati, Parāśara, and commentaries on them as well as the digests (*nibandhas*). However, the term sometimes includes all texts dealing with Hindu laws. Manu (Manusmṛti I I.10) states that *smṛti* is *dharma śāstra* or 'remembered literature' rather than *śruti* or 'revealed literature' that includes the four *Saṃhitās*, i.e. Ṛg, Sāma, Yajur and Atharva, and the associated Brahmaṇas and Upaniṣads.

Manusmṛti, also known as Mānava Dharmaśāstra, which belongs to the pre-Christian era, is considered the oldest of the *smṛtis*. Yājñavalkya's smṛti from a later date, third century AD or thereabouts, is considered only next in authority to Manu's work. There are several other *dharma śāstras*, such as Āpastamba, Bādarāyaṇa, Angiras, Bṛhaspati, Gautama, Kātyāyana, Kaśyapa, Parāśara, et cetera. These were composed in the subsequent period extending to mediaeval times by sages, or their descendants, with the same name as that of the texts. These *śāstras* are often cryptic and difficult to understand, but fortunately, several commentaries on these works are available for interpretation. Mitākṣarā and Dāyabhāga are two such invaluable works. Mitākṣarā - literally meaning 'in a few words' - was composed by Vijnāneśvara at the court of *cālukya* emperor Vikramāditya VI around 1075-1127AD on customary Hindu laws such as the laws of inheritance. Dāyabhāga, compiled by Jīmūtavāhana around the twelfth century AD, is a detailed treatise on Hindu laws of inheritance. Dāyabhāga has influenced the formulation of contemporary inheritance laws in India.

When were *Dharma Śāstras* composed?

It is not possible to accurately determine the period the first formal composition of texts on Dharma was undertaken. But there is a reference in Nirukta (III.4-5) to a controversy of property inheritance involving the rite of *putrikā* (when a man without a son declared his daughter to be *putrikā*, the daughter's son after her marriage belonged to the father of the daughter, and not her husband's family). The right of inheritance, without a doubt, is a matter falling in the domain of law. Similar other controversies on the correct way of doing things, more particularly issues of inheritance, must have led to acrimony and heated discussions, and the conclusions of these discussions may have found their way from the meetings of wise men into formal works. A dispute on inheritance that found its way into the text of Yaska's Nirukta suggests that matters of law had gone beyond informal arrangements and practices and were already codified.

Yaska's Nirukta belongs to 800-500 BC and so, one would not be in error when assigning the earliest of formal laws an antiquity of at least Nirukta's period. These dates seem to make sense when we examine the oldest of the *dharma sūtras* written by Gautama (widely accepted as belonging to 600-400 BC) which speaks of *dharma śāstras*, a word that also appears in Baudhāyana *DS* (IV.5.9). There are numerous other references to *dharma śāstra* in subsequent literature.

Such evidence places the works of *dharma śāstra* prior to Yaska, or at least prior to 600-300 BC.

Kalpasūtra and *Kalpa*

There are six limbs of Veda, called *vedāngas*, which are prescribed as essential reading for anyone wanting to learn the Vedas. In the words of Monier: "The very essence of *smṛti* may be said to include six principal subjects or departments, viz six *vedāngas*, 'limbs for supporting the Veda', or in other words, help to aid the student in reading, understanding and applying it to sacrificial rites."[5] The six limbs are -

i. *Kalpa* - ceremonial directory, including rules for Vedic rituals and sacrifices
ii. *Śikṣā* - the science of pronunciation
iii. *Chandas* - metre
iv. Nirukta - etymology and meaning of words used in the Vedas
v. *Vyākaraṇa* - grammar
vi. *Jyotiṣa* - astronomy, including the study of arithmetic and mathematics

Kalpasūtra is a term used for Sanskrit texts of Hinduism which deal with *kalpa* or rituals. According to Kane[6], *kalpa* is used in two senses -

1. Comprehensive: By including the aphoristic works on (i) Vedic rituals; (ii) domestic ceremonies; (iii) law, government and administration of justice
2. The second sense covers only those aphoristic works that deal with Vedic sacrifices and related matters

The 'comprehensive sense' refers to *Kalpa Sūtras* as a trilogy of -

- *Śrauta sūtras* - These deal with sacrifices given in the Vedas and described in the Brahmaṇas
- *Gṛhya sūtras* - These deal with domestic ceremonies such as *upanayanaaa* (thread ceremony), marriage, and various daily and seasonal sacrificial rites, and mantras applied to these rites
- *Dharma sūtras* - These address some of the topics dealt within the *gṛhya sūtras* and also deal with the provisions on matters concerning economics, politics, government, civil and criminal law

Many scholars believe that each of the four Vedas (and its *śākhā*) initially had their own *kalpa* i.e set of *śrauta, gṛhya* and *dharma sūtras*. Unfortunately, only for three *kalpas* - Āpastamba, Hiraṇyakeśin and Baudhāyana Sūtracarana - we have all three components, i.e. *śrauta, gṛhya* and *dharma sūtras* available to us. It is a matter of conjecture whether other extant stand-alone *dharma, śrauta* and *gṛhya sūtra* texts actually had accompanying texts of trilogy (which constitutes a set of *kalpa*).

The *dharma sūtras*, or guidebooks of Dharma, were composed by sages in typical *sūtra* style between 600 BC and the medieval period. The *sūtra* style is so terse that it is nearly impossible for a lay reader to comprehend its meaning. The *sūtras* discuss the duties and rights of people in the four *āśramas*, i.e. *brahmacārya, gṛhyastha, vānaprasthas* and *saṃnyāsa,* personal and criminal law, the duties and rights of a king, et cetera. They do not cover, save for a few exceptions, topics of rites and rituals covered in the *śrauta* and *gṛhya sūtra* texts of *kalpa*.

Some of the more important and popular *dharma sūtras* with their approximate date of composition are listed below. The following content list of Gautama's Dharmasūtra will help understand the topics covered in similar other texts.

Gautama DS - Oldest among the *dharma sūtras* (600-400 BC), it is entirely in prose and divided into three *praśna* (questions). The first and second *praśna* have nine *adhyāyas* (sections) each, and the third *praśna* has ten *adhyāyas*.

The first *adhyāya* deals with Dharma, *upanayana*, purificatory rites and rules for students. The second *adhyāya* covers rules for a *brahmacāri*, observance and prohibitions. *Gṛhyastha, vānaprasthas* and *saṃnyāsa āśramas*' rules are listed in the third *adhyāya* and Dharma of *gṛhyastha*, marriage, and types of son adopted, et cetera are given in the fourth *adhyāya*. The fifth *adhyāya* covers *punca mahāyājña* and *madhuparka* (a ceremony for greeting guests); the sixth covers rules of greeting and conduct towards important and respected people; and the seventh deals with the topic of serving a guru (teacher) and the duties of a *brahmaṇa*. The eighth *adhyāya* covers the king and the *brahmaṇa's* position in society, *bahuśruta* person's special rights (one who has learned the four Vedas and *vedāngas*), enumeration of forty *saṃskras* and eight *ātmanguṇas*. The ninth and final *adhyāya* in the first *praśna* deals with *vrata* (fast) and rules of every day conduct.

The second *praśna* covers duties of the four *varṇas* in its first *adhyāya*, and the qualifications and duties of the king and administration of justice by the king are in the second *adhyāya*. Crime and punishment, interest and loans are addressed in the third *adhyāya*; the fourth *adhyāya* speaks of dispute resolution, law of evidence and conduct, speaking the truth and the man delivering justice, i.e. judge. The fifth *adhyāya* deals with death and impurities related to birth, the sixth covers *śrāddha* rites and rituals, the seventh talks of the study of Veda and *anadhyāya* (study breaks), the eighth details the rules governing edibles and drinks, and the ninth *adhyāya* of the second *praśna* deals with the Dharma of women.

The third *praśna*, in its first section, deals with penance, in the second with people to be shunned, in the third with *pātaka* and *mahā pātaka* (sinner and great sinner). *Adhyāyas* four to seven talk about penance, while the eighth and ninth deal with penance fasts. The tenth *adhyāya* explains property and its division.

Baudhāyana DS (200-500 BC) - It is split in four *praśnas*, the last being *pariśiṣṭa* (appendix) and a later day addition. It refers to Gautama's name twice and once to his *dharmasūtra*, and is older than Āp DS.

Āpastamba DS (600-300 BC) - It has two *praśnas*, each with eleven *patalas* (literally screen, sections), and is the briefest of all *sūtras*. It appears to be connected to *Pūrva Mīmāṁsā* and is one of the most quoted since it is considered authentic.

Hiraṇyakeśin DS - This is not considered an independent *dharma sūtra* since it has borrowed from hundreds of Āp Dharma Sūtras.

Vasiṣṭha DS (300-200 BC) - This *sūtra* has many versions. The *Jeevanand* version has twenty *adhyāya* and part of the thirty-first *adhyāya*. A few other versions also have thirty, six and twenty-one *adhyāyas*, suggesting that these are later additions.

Viṣṇu DS - The earlier parts are believed to have been composed between 300BC and 100 BC. It belongs to *Kathā śākhā* of Yajurveda and has 100 *adhyāyas*, with the first and the last two in verses and the rest in prose. It includes many references of Manu and Yājñavalkya Smṛti as well as the Bhagavada Gītā.

Śaṅkhā DS (300-200 BC) - It belongs to *vājasaneyī śākhā* of White Yajurveda. It has been quoted in the Tantra Vārtika, and finds mentions in Yājñavalkya and Parāśara. The Jeevanand Smṛtisangraha contains eighteen of its *adhyāyas*, and three hundred thirty and ninety-three *ślokas* from Śaṅkhā and Likhita Smṛtis respectively.[7]

Some important characteristics of the *sūtras*

While the authors of *dharma sūtras* do not claim to be inspired ṛṣis or superhuman beings, the *smṛtis*, such as Manu and Yājñavalkya, are ascribed to gods like *Brahman*.

While the *dharma sūtras* are in prose, mixed prose or verse, the *smṛtis* are in verse.

The language of the *dharma sūtras* is generally more archaic than that of the other *smṛtis*.

While the *dharma sūtras* do not proceed upon any orderly arrangement of topics, the *smṛtis* arrange their contents and treatment of the subjects under three principal heads, namely acara (established practices- covering caste, rules concerning diet, domestic ceremonies etc), *vyavahāra* (practices of law and kingly government) and *prāyaścitta* (rules of penance and expiation).

Most *dharma sūtras* are older than most of the other *smṛtis*.

Chapter 5

Santāna Dharma

'*Sanātana*' means eternal or immemorial. Depending on the context in which the elusive word 'Dharma' is used, the meaning of *Sanātana Dharma* also changes - from eternal religion, eternal laws, eternal practices, eternal Righteous conduct to any other contextual use demanded by the word 'Dharma'.

Britannica[1] defines it as 'a term used to denote the eternal or absolute set of duties, or religiously ordained practices incumbent upon all Hindus, regardless of class, caste, or sect'. However, it also cautions that 'different texts give different lists of the duties', and proceeds to add - 'but in general *Sanātana Dharma* consists of virtues such as honesty, refraining from injuring living beings, purity, goodwill, mercy, patience, forbearance, self-restraint, generosity, and asceticism'.

As discussed, it is difficult to locate an 'absolute set of duties or religiously ordained practices' anywhere in the Vedic texts that are 'incumbent upon all Hindus', since these texts do not directly define religion. Naturally, this has resulted in diverse interpretations of *Sanātana Dharma*, at times, an understanding lacking any logical or factual basis. Given the elasticity of the word 'Dharma', various interpretations by scholars, commentators, and religious leaders, over the last century and a quarter can be sampled in the following three examples -

1. A British lady by birth, Dr Annie Besant (1847-1933) was a leading reformer and secularist who knew India and Indian culture well. She participated in India's freedom struggle and was elected President of the Indian National Congress in 1917. At the time, Theosophy (defined by Oxford dictionary as 'any of a number of philosophies maintaining that the knowledge of god may be achieved through spiritual ecstasy, direct intuition or special individual relations') was a big international movement attracting some of the better-known names in the western world as well as India. As President of the Theosophical Society, she toured around the world extensively, holding

meetings and delivering lectures. Dr Bhagwan Das (1869-1958), a collaborator of Dr Besant in the Theosophical Society, was a freedom activist and one of the founder of Kashi Vidyā Peeth University at Benaras, and other educational institutions. He was also a reputed Sanskrit and Hindi scholar who authored thirty books (mostly in Sanskrit). Dr Das was the fourth recipient of the Bharat Ratna - the highest civilian award bestowed by the Indian government. Both, Dr Das and Dr Besant, wrote extensively on Indian religion and culture, and their writings are a window into the thinking current of the late nineteenth and early twentieth century. They co-authored a book titled *Sanātana Dharma* which is described as based on the Vedas. According to them, "The *Sanātana Dharma*, is also called Āryan Religion, a religion followed or practiced by Āryans." Importantly, the authors use the word 'Āryan' more as a descriptor of noble conduct than an ethnonym.

According to Besant and Das, these Āryans were "a great race, much finer in character and appearance than the races which went before it in the world history."[2]

The foundation of *Sanātana Dharma*, according to the two authors, is based on '*śruti*', a Sanskrit word meaning 'that which has been heard' and refers to the Vedas which are believed to have been heard. The Vedas were teachings and wisdom received by wise men (the ṛṣis) directly from *devas*. They were learnt by heart, not written down. The *śrutis* consist of *catur* (four) Vedas, i.e., Ṛg, Yajur, Sāma and Atharvaveda, while *smṛti*, Sanskrit for 'that which has been memorized or remembered', is founded on *śruti*, and is second to *śruti* in importance and authority. It consists of *dharma śāstra* - laws and regulations, duties and responsibilities, and the correct way of doing things in life as an individual, family and society.

The four *smṛtis* that lay down these laws and regulations include:

i. Manu Smṛti or Mānava Dharma Shāstram
ii. Yājñavalkya Smṛti
iii. Shankya Likhit Smṛti
iv. Parāśara Smṛti

2. Shri Aurobindo (1872 - 1950), born Aurobindo Ghose, was sent to England to study when he was barely seven years old. He completed his college education at King's College, Cambridge and joined the elite Indian Civil Service, a career he did not pursue for long. He returned from England and joined the Indian independence movement (1906-1910), but eventually found peace in *yoga sādhanā* and became a spiritual reformer. He introduced his vision on human progress and spiritual evolution, and was recognised as a *yogi*, guru and philosopher. Aurobindo wrote extensively on the Vedas, *yoga*, Hinduism and spiritualism, and had a large following, especially among the educated and elite of the world.

For Aurobindo, the cosmic spirit was moving towards the realization of an all-embracing world religion based on a wider Hinduism. He believed that *Sanātana Dharma* signified the eternal truths and principles of human life, and the cosmos, as well as this body of knowledge that India has always been the guardian, exemplar and missionary of. He emphasized that *Sanātana Dharma* itself is nationalism. In support of this conclusion, he said, "I say no longer that nationalism is creed, a religion, a faith; I say that it is the *Sanātana Dharma* which for us is nationalism. This Hindu nation was born with the *Sanātana Dharma*, with it, it moves and with it, it grows. When the *Sanātana Dharma* declines then the nation declines and if the *Sanātana Dharma* were capable of perishing, with the *Sanātana Dharma* it would perish. The *Sanātana Dharma* is nationalism." Aurobindo's deep involvement in the independence struggle before he turned to spiritualism is worth remembering. He practiced *yoga sādhanā* for nearly four years and was charged with sedition on multiple occasions by the British government for his writings and activities. Fortunately, he narrowly escaped jail term or worse punishment. His interpretation and understanding of *Sanātana Dharma* was greatly influenced by nationalism. Many of us may not agree with Aurbindo's logic of equating nationalism with *Sanātana Dharma*, but it does illustrate the elasticity of the words '*sanātana*' and 'Dharma', and how some of the great minds of the nineteenth and twentieth centuries viewed the term '*Sanātana Dharma*'.[3]

3. Ram Adhar Mall is a Senior Professor and Chair of Religious Science at the University of Jena in Germany since 2016. He has spent his entire life teaching philosophy and religious sciences in universities across India, Austria and Germany. He is the Founding President of the Society for Intercultural Philosophy (SIP) and his important works include publications in the fields of empiricism and phenomenology, comparative and intercultural philosophy, religious philosophy and comparative religion. Mall's interpretation of the term '*Sanātana Dharma*', unlike Besant, Das and Shri Aurbindo, is quite contemporary. For Prof Mall, "*Sanātana* or *shāshvata* (eternal) Dharma is not itself a Dharma, in the sense of being a positive religion with its own cult and other religious practices." What he is trying to imply here is that Hinduism is almost universally understood to be *Sanātana Dharma*, which is not a religion in the conventional sense.

Mall then makes an important observation that *Sanātana Dharma* is like the transcendental ego, which is not over and above the empirical, and yet, given to us at a higher level of consciousness. He adds, "One who ascribes to such a reading of *Sanātana Dharma* is committed to know one particular religion as the only true religion. Its neutrality is its strength, which must not be confused with disinterestedness."

According to Mall, it is not necessary to identify the *tadekam* (meaning 'that one alone') with the positive religion of Hinduism to be true to the spirit of the Veda's dictum. To do so would mean committing the mistake of *pars pro toto* (defined by Oxford dictionary as 'a part or aspect of something taken as representative of the whole'). Mall insists that the richness and tolerance of Hinduism lie in its conviction that different religions, including Hinduism, are different expressions of one eternal Dharma. He arrives at the conclusion that "*Sanātana Dharma* can, thus, be interpreted in the real spirit of the Vedas dictum as a regulative, basic religiosity, which is the very cornerstone of inter-religiosity. It may also function as a guiding principle on the methodological level."[4]

Besant and Das's laws and regulations, duties and responsibilities, and the correct way of doing things; Aurobindo's eternal truth and principles of human life and the cosmos, and identification of nationalism with *Sanātana Dharma*; and Mall's 'interpretation of real spirit of the Vedas dictum', all go beyond the narrow definition of religion. Together, they embody *Sanātana Dharma*, which has guided generations of Hindus, as a broad and flexible concept beyond the fixity of any definition tied to religion.

Before concluding this discussion, we must have a quick look at a strange interpretation of *Sanātana Dharma* by a section of Hindus who have foisted a very different construct on this term. They insist that one can be a Hindu only by birth and Hinduism does not permit 'converts' into its fold. This characteristic, according to this section of people, has remained unchanged from the very beginning - it is eternal or *sanātana*. And that is why, they say, Hinduism itself is *Sanātana Dharma*.

Smṛtis, which are repositories of Dharma, provide ample evidence to dispel this misconception.

As we already know, the *smṛtis* detail laws and regulations, duties and responsibilities, and the correct way of doing things in life as an individual, family and society.

But with changing times and socio-political situations, the laws needed modification or change.

Acknowledging this, Parāśara in his smṛti emphasizes that the laws are different for different *yuga's* periods -

"In conformity to the character of the age, the rules of law (suitable) for men differ from age to age. The rules for the *krita* differ from the *tretā* rules; the *dvapara* laws are not identical with the *kali* rules." (Parāśara Smṛti 22)

He then goes on to name his own *smṛti* as suitable for our time, i.e. *kaliyuga* - "For the *krita*, the laws of Manu are suited; for the *tretā*, those by Gautama (are) prescribed; for the *dvapara*, those by Shankha and Likhita; for the *kali*, those by Parāśara are prescribed." (Parāśara Smṛti 24)

With the passage of time, change in place, and evolution of society, new *smṛtis* were composed incorporating these factors in their prescriptions and recommendations at different times in different parts of the country. Their main, if not the sole, purpose was to provide guidelines for people to follow in their time and place, and carry out their duties and responsibilities righteously, i.e. according to their Dharma. It can be reasoned that the *smṛtis* were composed to fulfil a popular want and reflected the prevailing state of the society.

Thus, the *smṛtis* were brought into existence as and when the circumstances demanded. Initially, practitioners of Hinduism, particularly women, often faced expulsion from the Hindu *varṇa vyavastha* (*varṇa* system) when they voluntarily or involuntarily committed sins. Hindu women, who were raped (and at times conceived) by *cāndālas* or *mlecchas* (a non-Indian barbarian - Śaka, Yavana etc; outcastes), were often excommunicated. The *smṛtis* came up with a practical solution for this problem. They prescribed a process of *śuddhi* (purification), which would enable these women to reconvert to Hinduism. Similar *śuddhi* procedures were laid down for re-admitting Hindu males who were coerced into converting to Islam. In his book 'Some Aspects of Ancient Indian Culture', Dr Bhandarkar has cited examples of Devala Smṛti, which "was composed to meet a special emergency created by the advent of the Muslim power whose ardent proselytizing activity began to affect Hindu society seriously".[5a]

According to Bhandarkar, "Devala Smṛti expressly lays down that everybody, male or female, healthy or diseased, shall perform purificatory rites, if he or she is between 11 to 80 years old. That this picture of mass *śuddhi* depicted in our *smṛti* is real and not imaginary may be seen from what the Muhammadan historians themselves have written about this matter." The Devala Smṛti is widely accepted to have originated in the tenth century AD and composed consequent to Muhammad bin Qasim's Sindh adventure. According to the author, Devala Smṛti also considers "the case of women who have been ravished by the *mleccha* and have even conceived. Devala adopts a very liberal point of view. But he is not alone. The same view is expressed by Vijñāneśvara (the commentator) on this subject in the same restraint in his gloss in chapter III, v.265 of the Yājñavalkya Smṛti. He quotes verses from many *smṛtis* to show that a woman can be taken back into the caste even if she is raped by a *cāndāla, pukkasa* or *mleccha.*[5b]"

In his work 'Social and Cultural History of India', explaining who constituted *cāndāla* and *pukkasa*, and their social status, Bose says, "Below the *śūdras* or untouchables existed groups of people who were looked upon as quite outside the pale of āryandom. They served society in very menial and dirty tasks. They were the untouchables who were called fifth class or *pancamas*; but the term *puncama* was not usually accepted as if to insist that they were to be excluded from Āryan society altogether. These were *cāndāla, nishada, kaivarta, vena, karvara, pukkas, rathakara,* et cetera. Some of these were probably of non-Āryan origin."[6]

This demonstrates that both men and women could be re-converted to Hinduism following the correct procedure laid down in the *smṛtis*. Furthermore, until the times of Devala Smṛti, and subsequently when Vijñāneśvara wrote his commentary in the twelfth century AD, these practices were in vogue. Interestingly, as known from multiple sources, much before these texts were written, many foreign tribes had intermingled with the locals and settled in India. In due course, they not only adopted local customs and practices, but also converted to Hinduism or Buddhism. In the words of Bhandarkar (in the above cited book, pp. 67-68), "There was a time when any foreigner could become a Hindu. Whatever foreign tribes entered India, they became Hinduized and gradually got lost into the Hindu masses. Even the self-complacent Greeks who were proud of their Hellenism and branded all foreigners as barbarians, were glad to become either Buddhists or *vaiśnavas*."

This practice continues unabated even today. The ISKCON or Krișṇa Consciousness movement, started by Bhaktivedanta Prabhu Pada in 1966, attracted hordes of foreigners from all continents, and is evidence of the presence of this practice. In another example, the Ārya Samāj *śuddhi* movement resulted in the reconversion of thousands of tribal folk, who had previously converted to Christianity. In the last few years, many *dalits* have willingly reconverted to Hinduism (from Buddhism and at times Islam, which they had adopted as a protest against the inhuman treatment meted out to them by fellow Hindus).

PART II

एकं सद्विप्रा बहुधा वदन्ति

Truth is one, but the wise men know it as many.

(Rg Veda 1.164.46)

Chapter 6

Earliest Body of Indian Scripture : Vedas

Sacred Knowledge

Composed between fifteenth and tenth century BC 'by men of light and leading (ṛṣis) among the Indo Āryans immigrants, who were afterwards held in the highest veneration as patriarchal saints', Vedas are compositions in archaic Sanskrit - a language very difficult to understand even by scholars of modern Sanskrit. "Eventually these hymns were believed to have been directly readily revealed to rather than composed by the ṛṣis and were called divine knowledge (Veda), or the eternal word heard (*śruti*) and transmitted by them."[1]

Derived from root word '*vid*', 'to know', Veda in Sanskrit means knowledge.

All Vedas are in Sanskrit, but their archaic Sanskrit, used before Pāṇini standardised Sanskrit grammar, is very challenging. They have come to us as a work of translation done mostly by German, English and some French scholars of the eighteenth and nineteenth century AD who accomplished this job without the help of a standard dictionary. The first volume of Ṛgveda (Max Müller's, engaged by East India Company) appeared in 1849; many years before the first Sanskrit-English dictionary (Wilson's in 1872 - considered incomprehensive by scholars) and Sanskrit-German dictionary, Grosses Petersberger Worterbuch, (Bohtlingk and Roth's in 1855) were published. Readers can well imagine how well these works of translation represent what was intended to be conveyed by the ṛṣi poets through these Vedas.

It is this work of translation (of Vedas) by German and British scholars that is used as a source material by nearly all scholars, and general readers get to know this interpretation of Vedas.

∞

When the British came to India, India was seeing the tail-end of several centuries of Muslim rule. With a few exceptions, the worst of the Muslim rulers often destroyed (Somnath, Vishvanath and other temples) or suppressed (*jezia*) Hindu religion and its associated heritage, and the benevolent best simply ignored it. Apart from Dara Shikoh and Akbar, in nearly 900 years of Muslim rule, it was only during the British rule that any serious attempt was made to understand the roots of Indian religion and culture in a systematic manner. More precisely, it was Warren Hastings, Governor of Calcutta Presidency, who first saw immense political opportunity in serious study of Hindu religion. In 1785, he was presented with the excerpts of the first-ever English translation of Gītā by Charles Wilkins. Wilkins, a British subject, was a familiar name in the East India Company circles. Studying Wilkins' grammar had become a regular feature for all civil servants coming to India. Hastings was very impressed after reading the excerpt of the translation titled The Bhagavata Gītā, not by its philosophical content or teachings of *Niśkām Karma Yoga*, but by the opportunity he saw in it - as an ideal means of propaganda to make a case for an Indianised administration. Addressing a letter to the Chairman of East India company, Nathaniel Smith, Hastings wrote, "Every accumulation of the knowledge and especially such as is obtained by social communication with the people over whom we exercise a dominion founded on the right of conquest, is useful to the state", because, Hastings clarified, "It lessens the weight of the chain by which the natives are headed in subjection and it imprints on the hearts of our own countrymen the sense and obligation of the benevolence."[2] He appealed the East India Company to undertake publishing of the translation.

It was in this context that the eighteenth century saw a politically sponsored thrust on translation of oriental literature. William Jones' arrival on the scene provided Hastings with just the right man for the job. A hyper-polyglot, Jones was a man of exceptional talent with languages. He had mastered thirteen languages, including Latin, Greek, Persian, French, Hebrew, Arabic and Chinese, and had a reasonably good working knowledge of twenty-eight other languages. While on an assignment as a Supreme Court Judge in India, Jones felt naturally inclined, as a jurist, to read ancient Hindu texts on which the Hindu law was based. But all these texts, including the laws of Manu (Manusmṛti), were originally written in Sanskrit. Being a language expert, Jones was sceptical about the fidelity of translation by native interpreters and thought even less of these interpretations through Persian. With great difficulty, he managed to hire the services of a Sanskrit scholar who taught him the language. Over the years, Jones made immense contribution through his lectures, translations and discourses on Indian history and civilisation. But, it is his work on the relationship among European and Indian languages (which later came to be known as Indo-European languages) that made him immortal. His biggest contribution to India was the establishment of Asiatic Society which attracted a vast number of scholars. The Society became a repository of valuable work on Indian culture and civilisation. He also started The Asiatick Researches, first ever journal to be published in India.

Jones' passion for translation of Sanskrit texts, in part, was further fuelled by his own first-hand experience of the difficulty he faced in finding a Brahmin tutor prepared to teach the language of the gods - the *deva bhāshā* - to an untouchable foreigner. The knowledge of Sanskrit gave the key to read the Vedas to anyone who wanted, which was prohibited. As per directives of Manu, only certain class of people among Hindus were entitled to recite Vedas; people belonging to the *śūdra* (lower) *varṇa* attracted severe punishment if they as much as heard the Vedas, let alone recite them. The *brahmaṇas* had created a monopoly on the knowledge of Vedas. Jones hoped that 'the apparent monopoly of a form of indigenous knowledge by certain classes could only be broken through translation.'[3] But his passion was not solely driven by this noble cause, Jones also hoped that the translations would serve 'to domesticate the orient and thereby turn it into a province of European learning'[4] a view which attracted considerable adverse comments.

Whatever be Jones' reason or intention, the work of serious study of Hindu/Indian religion and civilisation was started by a foreign power, the East India Company, as they considered translation of native texts of great significance for political reasons. The Asiatic Society of Bengal, founded in 1784 by William Jones with Thomas Colebrooke and Nathaneil Halhed, started the journal Asiatick Researches which became the springboard of study of Indian history and civilisation. When this new trend of studying the native culture and civilisation emerged in the Indian subcontinent, the great Western thinker and philosopher, Schopenhauer, was still nearly two decades away (1802-04) from laying his hands on the Latin translation of the Persian manuscript of Oupnekhat (Persian translation of Upaniṣads for Dara Shikoh by *brahmaṇas* from Benaras/Kāśī) and making his famous pronouncements -

"In the whole world there is no study, except that of the originals, so beneficial and so elevating as that of the Oupnekhat. It has been the solace of my life, it will be the solace of my death!"[5]

His observations did more than a little to arouse the interest of western public and scholars in Indian Vedic texts and Indian civilization. Mohenjo-daro was still nearly a century and quarter away from being discovered and the Europeans still considered the Indian continent an area of darkness, an area which had very little to offer, either by way of culture, or civilisation.

It was Max Müller, a German Scholar, who, while studying with eminent philologist Eugene Burnouf in Paris, heard his lectures on Ṛgveda and felt that it had "opened a new world" to him. He decided to collate and copy manuscripts of this ancient text and prepare an edition. The library of East India House in London was known to keep masses of manuscripts that became Max Müller's destination. With the help of well-wishers in London, he convinced the board of directors of the East India Company to finance his project by paying him 'pound 4 per sheet on the basis of 50 sheets a year.'[6] The first volume of Ṛgveda appeared in 1849 and the last (sixth) volume was presented in 1874 to Queen Victoria.[7]

As a continuation of Hasting's policy of using the translations of native religious work to extend the British colonial interest, the sacred text of Hinduism, Ṛgveda (mostly produced in Oxford), was brought to India: 'The volumes presented by the Prince of Wales on tour in India to his colonial subjects, and were studied by Brahmin pundits near Poona.'[8a]

But to Max Müller, who had become a naturalised British citizen in 1855 and did not understand the cunning complexities of colonial politics, the study of Sanskrit established a deep connection between India and Europe - not the kind that exists between a ruler and its subjects, but a connection of an entirely different kind. He observed, '(It) owes its permanent interests chiefly to the fact that the ancient language of India has proved to be most intimately connected with the classical language of Europe'[8b]. For him, unlike Hastings, the edition was meant to shed light on the cultural, religious and linguistic affinities between the East and the West.

Perhaps, it was mainly the theory of Āryan race and Jones' proposition of Sanskrit being part of the Indo-European language that invoked curiosity and interest among scholars and the public, particularly in Germany and across Europe.

Britain continued to look at these developments through the prism of politics of colonisation and religious conversion. The superiority of Christian religion and 'conversion' of natives had so thoroughly permeated the great seats of learning in Britain that the Oxford chair of Sanskrit was established with money bequeathed to the university by Joseph Boden 'as a means of enabling Englishmen to proceed in the conversion of the natives of India to the Christian religion.'[9]

In the words of Hastings, 'Every accumulation of the knowledge about the people, over whom we exercise a dominion founded on the right of conquest, is useful to the state.'[10]

The Empire concurred and promptly put the Hastings plan of translating Indian scriptures in to action.

It is important to remember that no standard dictionary of Sanskrit to English and Sanskrit to German existed at this time.

Translation of Vedas: Or is it Interpretation?

One of the biggest controversies, still unresolved, concerns translation of the Vedas. The moot point is - What we get to read as a work of translation, is it really translation? Or is it interpretation of Vedas?

Sanskrit language is generally divided in to Vedic and Classical form. The ancient Vedic texts are in Vedic Sanskrit - an archaic form which differs significantly from the classical Sanskrit. The Vedas' Sanskrit itself is not uniformly the same across the Vedic literature; with time it evolved in clearly distinguishable stages till it got modernised and merged in classical Sanskrit.

The difference between the two becomes at once remarkable when we compare the verses of the two period, they differ not only in grammar, vocabulary and metre but also, what Gaurinath Sastri, a Professor of Sanskrit, calls, 'in respect of matter and spirit'[11]

The difference which has greater bearing on our discussion i.e. translation and interpretation of Vedas, is the 'form' of language. The single most important difference between the Vedic and Classical Sanskrit is use of accents. There are mainly two accents *uddāta* (acute) and *anuddāta* (grave). *Uddāta* - the raised note is indicated in the text by a vertical stroke over the letter, *anuddāta* - the lowered note by a line under the letter. 'The list of books which use the accent-system consists of all Vedas, *Taittiriya Brahmaṇa* and *Āraṇyaka* and *Shatpatha*'.[12]

Depending on the accent the meaning can change completely, thus for instance, the word *Índraśatru* with one kind of accent will mean '*Índra* as an enemy', and the same word with a different kind of accent will imply 'enemy of *Índra*'.[13] But the classical Sanskrit literature has no role for these accents.

An important fact to remember is - the Vedic Sanskrit is a language to be recited and heard - a sonic language. Vedas were essentially 'audio' material, which were later reduced to 'visual' texts.

So herein lies the real issue - How do we translate and interpret what are essentially 'Sonic' texts, where meaning of word changes according to the accent?

∞

Let's look briefely at how and why Vedas were first translated.

Warren Hastings, during his tenure (1773-1785) as first de facto Governor General of India, conceived the policy of using translations of native religious work to extend the British colonial interest in India. Soon a Company sponsored programme to collect religious texts was put in place and set in motion. Normally public libraries and libraries of universities and colleges are repository of books. India of eighteenth century had neither any public library, nor any university or a college. For Muslims, the institutions of learning were traditional *maktabs* (elementary scools) and *madarsās* (instituitions of higer education) - run, primarily, with help and support of the Mughal rulers. Nearly every *madarsā* had its own library - but as a rule, they did not keep religious texts of any religion other than Islam. Sanskrit was taught in traditional *pāthshālās* (Sanskrit schools), and unlike *madarsās*, these *pāthshālās* rarely had a library of their own. During centuries of Muslim rule, these *pāthshālās* did not receive the patronage of rulers they deserved, and were treated, at best, indifferently. *Madarsās* and *pāthshālās* both lacked a formal system of education; they did not have any standard curriculum, and each establishment followed its own course.

The first college - Hindu College at Calcutta - was established by David Hare, with the help of Raja Rammohun Roy subsequent to the Charter Act of 1813; and the first public library was established in1835 in Calcutta. But Asiatic Society Library (est. 1784) with a strong collection of Indological and oriental literature by now was already in existence.

An important reason why not many libraries could be setup in India was also due to non-availability of the published material; until 1817 there were very few printing presses in India. There is no record of any Veda text that was printed before this time.

The Hindu religious literature, up until this time, was available only in the form of manuscripts - scattered all over the country/side. These manuscripts, often found in very bad condition, were procured - for a small price - from sources in far flung villages, and brought to Presidencies, where they were restored, as best as they could be, catalogued, and packed in boxes for onwards sea transportation to England.

There were no dedicated passenger ships between India and England at this time. Suez Canal was not opened till 1869; Sea voyage between Indian ports and Southampton normally took four to six months in fair season, and in monsoons it took much longer. The manuscripts, mostly on palm leaves, and in a fragile condition to begin with, were exposed to corrosive sea air and humidity for extended period of up to six months. Naturally, by the time they arrived in England, MS suffered further damage, making the task of deciphering what was written on the leaves even more difficult. These MSs were then distributed for translation among the few English and German Sanskrit scholars. This is how Max Müller, who was assigned the task to translate Ṛgveda and other texts, received Vedic texts from India and produced the first ever complete English translation of Ṛg in 1849.

Consider this.

(i) Since the entire Vedic literature is in Sanskrit, the German and the English scholars engaged to translate these manuscripts must necessarily have used Sanskrit to English language dictionary for consistant and uniform translation of Sanskrit words. At this time, the theory of literary translation was centred around the concept of fidelity as defined in the beginning of nineteenth century. Later, in the beginning of twentieth century, it was modified to Franz Rosenzweg's concept of 'double fiedely'; according to this concept, 'to translate means to serve two masters' (1926:23).

But the first Sanskrit to English standard dictionary was not compiled till much later (1899). This monumental work by Sir M. Monier-Williams - even though he could not see the first print of the dictionary, he had the satisfaction of seeing the final proof before it went for print - was completed by Monier-Williams only days before he died on April 11, 1899.[14]

Considering Monier's was the first Sanskrit to English dictionary, it is difficult to understand how any work of translation predating this dictionary was accomplished with any degree of uniformity, leave alone accuracy or fidelity. In absence of a standard dictionary, different 'translator' scholars, using different source for finding meaning of a given Sanskrit word, must have translated it differently in English.

Śruti (*Saṃhitā*), Brahmaṇa, Upaniṣad texts were composed prior to Pāṇini (500-300 BC); Sanskrit before him was archaic, did not have codified grammar, and was open to different interpretations, often causing confusion even among indigenous Sanskrit scholars of that time (ref. accents, *uddāta* and *anuddātta* in preceding paragraph). This was why a need was felt to standardise it, prompting Pāṇini to give a detailed system of grammar. Translation of the *śruti*, which are in accented form, must have complicated the task of translation and search of appropriate word manifold.

(ii) As we know, a translation can never be one hundred per cent reflection of what the author originally intended to convey. It becomes even more difficult when the original text is in verse form rather than prose. If the translator is alien to the culture, customs, and thinking of the society, to which the author/poet of the original text belonged, even the best translations may end up quite off the mark (ref. above - *Índrasatru* with one kind of accent will mean '*Índra* as an enemy', and with a different kind of accent will imply 'enemy of *Índra*').

(iii) Language in all Vedic literature is invariably Sanskrit. However, in the early Ṛgvedic period, an archaic form of Sanskrit, different from modern Sanskrit, was used, which by the time of Pāṇini was transformed into a perfect grammatical language. One of the most important aspects of the Sanskrit language is root (origin) of the words, and their *sandhi* (joining the words together). The language gradually evolved from the early Ṛgvedic period to the *vedānga* and *vedānta* period, adopting a strict grammatical discipline over time. Add to this constant change the variable of imperfections inherent to any translation and we end up having a very foggy picture.

(iv) Furthermore, the Sanskrit language is unique in the sense that the same word can have vastly different and often completely unconnected meanings. Prof Monier points this out in his famous lectures compiled in a book titled 'Wisdom of India'; Quoting Yaska's Nirukta he gives example[15] of *gamati* (he goes), or *gati* (going), whose synonyms include *vartate* (he turns), *lotate* (he rolls), *sarpati* (he creep), *sravati* (he flows), *sransate* (he drops), *plavate* (he swims), *diyate* (he flies), *patati* (he falls), and 122 other words!

Yaska was a linguist and an etymologist belonging to ~400 BC, who in his Nirukta (meaning 'exposition') text undertook compilations of words from the Vedas with the same meaning. These words alluded to different interpretations by various schools of Vedas which existed before him - more than seventeen such interpreters are mentioned by name preceded by Yaska. It is thus evident that even in Yaska's time a great difference of opinion existed among scholars of Veda as to the correct meaning of the words in *ṛcas*.

A reader of 'translation' of the Vedic literature, particularly the Vedas, is well advised to keep in mind above factors. To this author's mind - any translation of the Vedas should be more accurately referred to as an interpretation, not translation.

∞

The works of translations of Vedic texts, normally used as reference by western and Indian scholars, can broadly be put under two categories -

(a) Translators of non-indigenous variety: The leading names in this catogory are HH Wilson (1786-1860), J Stevenson (1798-1858), H Grassman (1809-1877), Monier Williams (1819-1899), Rudolf Roth (1821-1895), Max Müller (1823-1900), RTH Griffith (1826-1901), A Ludwig (1832-1912), G Buhler (1837-1898) and A.B. Keith (1879-1944) who all belonged to early period.

(b) Indigenous translators: Swami Dayanand (1824-83) and Shri Aurobindo (1872-1950) are two leading authorities who have given most comprehensive interpretation and translation of Vedas. In more recent times, PV Kane (1880-1972) interpreted Hindu scriptures in English and produced an unparalleled compendium of Hindu Dharmaśāstra. He was honoured with the highest national award of Bharat Ratna by the government of India for this super human work running in to over 6600 printed pages.

One should always remember that different translations could be vastly divergent in the interpretation of the same verse/prose depending on the translator (or interpreter). Sometimes, these interpretations can be so different that they may lead to opposite conclusions!

There is one factor that makes these matters even more complex, it is something intrinsic to India and the Indian way of thinking (or the Hindu way of thinking). From time immemorial, it was recognised that knowledge is to be imparted at two levels -

(i) gross, superficial or exoteric; and

(ii) subtle, deep or esoteric

In India, even in primary classes in schools, a clear-cut distinction is made between *śabdārtha* (word meaning) and *bhāvartha* (intended or deeper meaning). Perhaps this is in recognition of the fact that in society, the common man is not always blessed or equipped with the ablity and the desire to understand the deeper meaning of things. However, a small section - the elite - is forever in pursuit of the deeper knowledge.

Composed nearly 500 years back, Tulsi Dasā's Rāmāyaṇa, in *Awadhi* (a dialect of Hindi), is a good example. This great epic was composed with the purpose of making available the story of lord *Rāma* to the largely semi-literate and illiterate masses in the age of revival of religion, i.e. *bhakti* period. And yet, as any reader would notice, lord *Rāma's* story is interwoven with complex metaphysical discourses, difficult even for a highly learned reader to fully comprehend!

Chapter 7

Constituents of Vedas

It will be rare to find a Hindu, indeed an Indian, who has not heard of the Vedas. And, it will be equally difficult to find a Hindu who has read all four, i.e. Ṛg, Yajur, Sāma and Atharva Veda, or who knows the different constituents and subject matter of these ancient books of knowledge. In fact, for most Indians, the Vedas are simply the oldest books of Hindu religion; they hardly know anything about its contents. In short, the Vedas, the ancient '*vid*' or knowledge, are a closed book for most Hindus.

Along with The Book of the Dead, Enuma Elish, I Ching and Avesta, the Ṛgveda is among the most ancient religious texts still in existence. The Vedas are also the most ancient extensive texts written in an Indo-European language. Before proceeding with Vedas, let's have a brief look at these religious texts of other religion.

The Book of the Dead is a collection of ancient Egyptian funerary texts that describe the Egyptian concept of an 'afterlife'. It consists of hymns, spells and instructions that help the deceased pass through various obstacles in the afterlife. These texts were developed from a tradition of funerary manuscripts dating back to the Egyptian Old Kingdom - the first funerary texts were the Pyramid Texts, originally used in the Pyramid of King Unas of the fifth dynasty around 2400 BC. They remained in use for nearly 1500 years.[1]

Enuma Elish, also written as Enûma Eliš, the Babylonian creation myth~1400 BC, was recovered in fragments in 1849 by Austen Henry Layard in a ruined Library of Ashurbanipal at Nineveh (Mosul, Iraq), and published by George Smith in 1876. The Enûma Eliš has nearly a thousand lines recorded on seven clay tablets, each holding 115 to 170 lines of Sumero-Akkadian cuneiform script. The text is almost complete.

This epic is one of the most important sources for understanding the Babylonian worldview, centred on the supremacy of *Marduk* and the creation of humankind for service of the gods. Its primary purpose, however, is not an exposition of theology or theogony, but the elevation of *Marduk*, the chief god of Babylon, above other Mesopotamian gods.

The copy found at Ashur has the god *Ashur* in the main role, as was the custom of the cities of Mesopotamia. Each city considered its own god the best and most powerful. *Marduk*, the god of Babylon, figures as prominently as he does in the story because most of the copies found are from Babylonian scribes.[2]

Avesta texts, also called Zend-avesta, is the sacred book of Zoroastrianism (Parsees). It contains its cosmogony, law and liturgy, the teachings of the prophet Zoroaster (Zarathushtra) in Avestan language. They were collated over several hundred years. The extant Avesta is all that remains of a much larger body of scripture, apparently Zoroaster's transformation of a very ancient tradition. The original voluminous manuscripts are said to have been destroyed when Alexander the Great conquered Persia. The oldest Gatha is believed to have been composed by Zoraster himself around 1000 BC.

The Avesta is in five parts. Its religious core is a collection of songs or hymns, the *gāthās*, thought to be, in the main, the very words of Zoroaster. They form a middle section of the chief liturgical part of the canon, the Yasna, which contains the rite of the preparation and sacrifice of *haoma*. The Visp-rat is a lesser liturgical scripture, containing homages to many Zoroastrian spiritual leaders. The Vendidad, or Vidēvdāt, is the main source for Zoroastrian law, both ritual and civil. It also gives an account of creation and the first man, *Yima*. The Yashts are twenty one hymns, rich in myth, to various *yazatas* (angels) and ancient heroes. The Khūrda Avesta (or Little Avesta) is a group of minor texts, hymns, and prayers for specific occasions.

I Ching is one of the oldest classical Chinese texts describing an ancient system of cosmology and philosophy intrinsic to Chinese cultural beliefs. In modern times, it is sometimes regarded as a system of divination. Yijing, Chinese for 'Classic of Changes' or 'Book of Changes', Wade-Giles Romanization I-Ching or Yi-Ching, also called Zhou Yi, an ancient Chinese text, is one of the Five Classics (Wujing) of Confucianism. The main body of the work, traditionally attributed to Wenwang, who flourished in the twelfth century BC, contains a discussion of the divinatory system used by the Zhou dynasty wizards. Many believe it originated with mythical Fu Xi around 2800 BC.

A supplementary section of 'commentaries' is believed to be the work of authors of the Warring States period 475–221 BC and, as a philosophical exposition, represents an attempt to explain the world and its ethical principles, applying a largely dialectic method. For this, the work came to have great importance in the history of Chinese philosophy.[3]

Given the briefest of introduction of four of the oldest texts belonging to four different civilizations and the subject matter they deal with, we now turn to the Vedas, which in the words of Drs Besant and Das, deal with the 'religion of the Āryans'. Perhaps not in terms of timeline, but the Vedas do seem to be very close to the Avesta in terms of its geographical proximity and affiliation with the language of the region. According to Dalal, "There are certainly close similarities between Ṛgvedic Sanskrit and Gathic Avestan. There is also similarity between the deities of the younger Avestan texts and the Ṛgveda though, at the same time, there are many differences." She points out that the homeland for Gathic and younger Avestan speaking people - between Central Asia and eastern Iran - is very close to the homeland of the Vedic people. In the Ṛgveda, this region is indicated as between Afghanistan and the river Yamuna. Both group of texts 'provide little idea of the date,'and, 'in fact, the Gathas are dated on grounds that they must be approximately of the same date as the Ṛgveda.'[4]

∞

The word 'Veda' is derived from the Sanskrit word '*vid*', meaning 'to know'. There are four Vedas - Ṛg, Sāma, Yajur and Atharva.

The oldest parts of the Ṛgveda, the *Saṃhitā*, which are in verse form, are thought to be 3000 to 4500 years old and widely accepted to have been codified around 600 BC. Even though it is unclear, it is generally accepted that the Ṛgveda was committed to writing around 300 BC. The Vedas are a compilation of ancient knowledge and wisdom, and form the basis of Hindu Dharma. This is the fountainhead of Hinduism from which sprang countless ideas, beliefs and practices followed by Hindus even today. The Vedas are not the result of an individual or a group of people working collectively to produce a 'book', but a collection of the efforts of sages, ṛṣis or ṛṣi *kulas* (families) over time that were eventually compiled in book form.

Each Veda has its *Saṃhitā*, Brahmaṇa, Āraṇyaka and Upaniṣad (Charts C -1 and C-3).

Ṛg is, mostly, a collection of laudatory hymns - called mantras - praising Vedic gods and goddesses. *Saṃhitā*, which means 'collection' in Sanskrit, has many *manḍalas* (literally circle) - just like a book divided in chapters. Each *manḍala* has *sūktas* (literally 'well told' or 'well said'), which are hymns devoted to one or more *devī* or *devatā*. Each *sūkta* is the work of one or more ṛṣi whose name is mentioned at the beginning of the *sūkta*. Further, each *sūkta* has several *ṛcas* - couplets or *ślokas*. In summary, each *Saṃhitā* has several *manḍalas*, each *manḍala* has several *sūktas*, and each *sūkta* may have several *ṛcas*. In another system *Saṃhitā* is divided amongst eight *khandas* (portions), or *aṣtakâs* (eighths), each of which is again subdivided into eight *adhyâyas*, or lectures.

***Aṣtakâ* System**

Aṣtakâ	*Adhyāya*	*Varga*	Mantra
1	8	265	1370
2	8	221	1147
3	8	225	1209
4	8	250	1289
5	8	238	1263
6	8	331	1730
7	8	248	1263
8	8	246	1281
Total	**64**	**2024**	**10,552**

***Maṇdala* System**

Maṇdala	*Anuvāka*	*Sūktas*	Mantra
1	24	191	2006
2	4	43	429
3	5	62	617
4	5	58	589
5	6	87	727
6	6	75	765
7	6	104	841
8	10	103	1716
9	7	114	1108
10	12	191	1754
Total	**85**	**1028**	**10,552**

The Yajurveda is a ritual-oriented collection of liturgical formulae mostly in prose form. The invocations or prayers are borrowed from the Ṛgveda and are applied for the consecration of utensils and other materials used in the ceremonial worship and praise of Vedic gods. The Sāmaveda is concerned with chanting of hymns on different ceremonial occasions and is compiled wholly, with a few exceptions, by rearranging the Ṛgveda *ṛcas* to fit in forms suitable for musical chanting. Often, additional words called *stobhas*, which have no meaning, are inserted to make the hymns suitable for chanting. Atharvaveda considered a much later Veda - with a language and style different from the other three - also includes many hymns fom the Ṛgveda, but deals with entirely different subjects - like sorcery, charms and such.

Apart from the *Saṃhitās*, the other important components that constitute the Vedas are the Brahmaṇas. These are a collection of rules for applying the mantras, providing directions for performing rites and citing hymns, and offer explanations of rites, often through illustrative stories. Āraṇyaka - not meant for an ordinary reader of Vedas - are believed to contain esoteric knowledge so special that only those who are in the third phase of life, the *vānaprastha*, are recommended to read them in *āraṇya* (forests) away from habitation, hence the name Āraṇyaka. The latest addition to the Vedas, are the Upaniṣads. These books contain abstract and complex metaphysical thoughts of various sages, and represent Hinduism's major departure from rituals to a knowledge-based society.

According to Wilson, the original denominations of the divisions of the Veda, *Saṃhitā, manḍala, aṣṭaka, adhyāya, anuvākyā, sūkta* and *varga* are the English substitutes for collection, circle, book, lecture, chapter, hymn and section, but they convey erroneous impression.[5] In this book we have retained the original Sanskrit words like Veda, *Saṃhitā*, et cetara.

The importance of Ṛgveda lies in the fact that it is the oldest, as is evident by the extensive inclusion of Ṛgveda *ṛcas* in the other three Vedas. 'In truth, it is to the Ṛgveda that we must have recourse, principally, if not exclusively, for correct notions of the oldest and most genuine forms of the institutions, religious or civil, of the Hindus'.[6]

∞

The first *sūkta* of the first *manḍala* of Ṛgveda in which ṛṣi Madhuchandas, the son of famous Viśvāmitra praises *Agni* in nine *ṛca*, is given below. The meter is *gāyatri* and the translation is Wilson's. This will give readers an idea of the nature of Ṛg *ṛcas*-

1. I glorify *Agni*, the high priest of the sacrifice, the divine, the ministrant, who presents the oblation (to the gods), and is the possessor of great wealth.
2. May that *Agni*, who is to be celebrated by both ancient and modern sages, conduct the gods hither.
3. Through *Agni* the worshipper obtains that affluence which increases day by day, which is the source of fame, and the multiplier of mankind.
4. *Agni*, the unobstructed sacrifice of which thou art, on every side, the protector, assuredly reaches the gods.
5. May *Agni*, the presenter of oblations, the attainer of knowledge, he who is true, renowned, and divine, come hither, with the gods.
6. Whatever good thou mayest, *Agni*, bestow upon the giver (of the oblation), that, verily, Angiras, shall revert to thee.
7. We approach thee, *Agni*, with reverential homage in our thoughts, daily, both morning and evening
8. Thee, the radiant, the protector of sacrifices, the constant illuminator of truth, increasing in thine own dwelling.
9. *Agni*, be unto us ease of access; as is a father to his son: be ever present with us, for our good[7].

Reading of the first translation of Ṛg (Wilson ~1860) left me cold.

There are 110 similar *sūktas* in praise of *Agni*, or *Agni* and another deity, in the Ṛgveda alone. If we assume ten *ṛcas* per *sūkta* on an average, nearly 1100 *ṛcas* take a reader through a long, monotonous journey in praise of *Agni*. Until nearly 1000 AD every *brahmaṇa* was expected to learn at least one Veda by heart. It made me think that the religious life of *vedins* (one who learnt or knew Veda) in those days must have been tedium of insipid repetitions. Reading Griffith's translation of Ṛgveda in verse form (sample given below), in the hope that some of the spark of the original poetry might come through in this monumental work, did not help. Sample Griffith's translation of the foregoing hymn in verse form -

1. I Laud *Agni*, the chosen Priest, God, Minister of sacrifice,
   The Hotṛr, lavishest of wealth.
2. Worthy is *Agni* to be praised by living as by ancient seers.
   He shall bring hitherwards the Gods.
3. Through *Agni* man obtaineth wealth, yea, plenty of waxing day by day,
   Most rich in heroes, glorious.
4. *Agni*, the perfect sacrifice which thou encompass about
   Verily goeth to the Gods.
5. May *Agni*, sapient minded priest, truthful, most gloriously great,
   the God, come hither with the gods.
6. Whatever blessing, *Agni*, thou wilt grant unto thy worshipper, that, Angiras, is indeed thy truth.
7. To thee, dispeller of the night, O *Agni*, day by day with prayer bringing thee reverence, we come.
8. Ruler of sacrifices, guard of law eternal, and radiant One, increasing in thine own abode.
9. Be to us easy of approach, even as a father to his son: *Agni*, with us for our weal.

I then tried reading Avesta - the holy texts of Parsees - since this ancient text is known to have commonality of language style and deities with the Vedas. But this attempt too proved unhelpful and futile. I kept wondering: Why do these ancient texts remain popular, and have such a powerful effect on the followers of the religion despite followers' lack of familiarity with the language?

The mystery began to unfold when I stumbled upon Catherine Armstrong's work on Islam: she has recorded reactions of Muslims to *Azan*, call for *Namāz*, and Qurān recitations. The sound of words of Qurān, not necessarily their meaning, have a very special effect on the 'believers'.

I found the answer to this puzzle a decade back, at a religious function in northern India, when I heard a dozen *vedins* chanting Veda hymns in unison. The effect was simply electric; not only this author, but nearly a hundred men and women gathered for the occasion stood still for several minutes listening to modulating chants in a language they did not understand. Every one present listened in complete silenc, and many confirmed later, they were deeply affected. A prayer, a hymn of praise, is an expression of faith in the powers of the supernatural. Unless the person who is offering, or listening to the prayer believes in the existence of this supernatural entity, the prayers may appear puerile. However, to truly understand and comment on any religious text, or faithfully translate it, the commentator/

translator need not necessarily be a faithful follower of the religion. He should, in addition to be knowledgeable in the language and the subject matter, also know the culture and customs of the concerned people intimately. And more importantly, he should be above religious and cultural prejudices and bigotry.

So, when several western Vedic scholars and translators, like Monier Williams, found the Vedas containing many 'puerilities'[8], was it because they lacked this prerequisite faith to enjoy (the power of) these religious texts? Or was it due to the strong prejudice and belief, the self confessed belief, in superiority of their own faith, Christianity? On this aspect, Monier Williams observes, "It appears to me high time that all thoughtful Christians should reconsider their position, and - to use the phraseology of our modern physicists - readjust themselves to their altered environments." But this observation came much after he was exposed to Vedic texts initially. Admitting that western scholars were susceptible to bias, the Oxford Professor of Sanskrit goes on to add that 'the ground is now being rapidly cleared for a fair and impartial study of the writings of eastern nations. The sacred books of the three great systems opposed to Christianity - *Brahmanṇism*, Buddhism, and Islam - are now at length becoming accessible to all; and Christians can no longer neglect the duty of studying their contents."[9] One cannot help but wonder, how Monier arrived at the conclusion that the sacred books of *Brahmanṇism*, written at least a millennium and a half before Christ, could have been written in opposition to Christianity! It appears, even later in life, the good professor did not entirely succeed in shedding his own religious prejudices altogether.

∞

The Ṛgveda is not an epic like Rāmāyaṇa, Mahābhārata, or the Iliad, which owe their popularity to interesting tales of a bygone period, nor is it a compendium on how to perform rituals. It is simply a collection - *Saṃhitā* - of hymns by different sages, created at different times, in praise of one or more deities unknown outside the Indian subcontinent. It belongs to a period associated with the dawn of the Āryan civilization more than three millennia ago. In words of Horace Wilson, the man who first translated the Ṛgveda, 'These hymns are put together with little attempt at methodical arrangement, although such as are dedicated to the same deity sometimes follow in a consecutive series. There is not much connexion in the stanzas of which they are composed; and the same hymn is, sometimes, addressed to different divinities.'[10]

He adds, 'There are, in the Veda (Ṛgveda) itself, no directions for the use and application of the *sūktas*, no notices of the occasions on which they are to be employed, or of the ceremonies at which they are to be recited. These are pointed out, by subsequent writers, in *sūtras*, or precepts relating to the ritual.'[11]

For those who believe in the Vedas (close to a billion or more across the world), this is no ordinary collection of hymns. These mantras were not created by ṛṣi or any mortal, but are *apaūruśey*, i.e. self-existent. They were revealed only to worthy recipients, the ṛṣis, who could comprehend their special meaning and power. The truth or fallacy of this belief is beyond the scope of this work. However, whether the mantras have meaning and efficacy has been a topic of great interest to believers and scholars alike, and is separately dealt with in a subsequent chapter.

∞

The first *manḍala* of the Ṛgveda has 191 *sūktas* and 2006 *ṛcas*. It is easy to refer to a specific *ṛca* by denoting the *manḍala* number, followed by the *sūkta* number and the *ṛca* number. For example, Ṛgveda 3.62.10 refers to the tenth *ṛca* of the sixty-second *sūkta* in the third *manḍala*. This happens to be one of the most beautiful prayers popularly known as the *gāyatri mantra*. The *ṛca* itself is minus '*Om Bhurbhuvasvah*'. *Sūkta* sixty-two was composed by ṛṣi Viśvamitra and Jamadgāni who together contributed eighteen *ṛcas* devoted to *Índra, Varuṇa, Brihaspati, Pūṣan, Savitar, Soma, Mitra* and *Varuṇa Dev*. *Chhandas* are *Gāyatri* and *Triśtubh*.

The Ṛgveda is divided into ten *manḍalas* with 1017 *sūktas* and 10472 *ṛcas*. While ṛṣi Bhārgava, Viśvamitra, Atri, Vaiśiṣṭha, Vāmdeva and Kaṇva Kula have contributed to nine *manḍalas*, the tenth *manḍala* is thought to have been added at a later period and written by another ṛṣi.

The Ṛgveda *sūktas*, with few exceptions, are praises. For a lay person, reading most of the Ṛgveda *sūktas* would be a tedious task as they seem repetitive.

The ancient wisdom of the sages does not stand out in most of the *sūktas*; there is hardly any scope for that. These *ṛcas* were created with the purpose of praising gods in a thousand different ways! But wherever there is scope for creativity, the sheer beauty of the poetry is compelling. First, in praise of dawn -

> The radiant dawns have risen up for glory, in their white
> splendour like the waves of waters.
> She makes paths all easy, fair to travel, and, rich, has shown
> herself benign and friendly.

And in praise of *rātri* (night) RigVeda (X.127) -

> The darkness she produces; soon advancing
> She calls her sister morning to return,
> And then each darksome shadow melts away.
> Kind goddess, be propitious to thy servants
> who at thy coming straightway seek repose,
> Like bird's who nightly nestle in the trees.[12]

∞

As the author discovered, reading 10,000 invocatory or laudatory *ṛcas* is a challenging task, made even more monotonous by repetitions.

Therefore, the question arises - Why does the Ṛgveda occupy a special place in the hearts of Hindus even though only a minuscule number of Hindus have read it, and especially since it is far from gripping, unlike epics such as Rāmāyaṇa and Mahābhārata?

There are obviously many reasons for this, but the main reason appears to be that a Hindu child grows up learning that the Vedas are the fountainhead of Hinduism, and that all the knowledge of the world is available in the Vedas. However, matters don't quite end there - we are also told that the Ṛgvedic ṛṣis not only had knowledge of metaphysics and religion, this life and the afterlife, but also of aircraft building, modern weaponry, missile technology, grafting surgery and stem cells, all of which modern scientists are beginning to discover only now. We (Hindus) are told that our foreign rulers in the past - the English, the Portuguese and the Dutch - took away, euphemism for 'stole', our Vedas. On the one hand, this reduced the once spiritually and materially most advanced nation (Bhāratvarṣa) to the status of a poor and helpless country that India is in the comity of nations. On the other hand, it catapulted cunning western countries, particularly the Germans and the English, to the top! This conspiracy of the west, this grand theft of knowledge of all Vedas, makes Hindus look at the Vedas, not just as a repository of ideas and beliefs of our forefathers at the dawn of the Vedic civilization that laid the foundation of Hinduism, but also as mystical texts which contain all knowledge of physics, chemistry, aerodynamics and other modern sciences. In short, for us, the Vedas contain the knowledge of all developed and developing modern sciences and technologies associated with it.

Although several Hindus, including a fair section of the educated, believe in the above theory to a varying degree, they do not bother to procure a copy of this ancient text and find out the truth for themselves. They do not bother to read the Vedas, if not in the original Sanskrit version then atleast its translation, which is now readily available across India in any decent bookshop in many local languages. One of the many reasons they don't do so is because, they believe - all the real knowledge of science and technology originally contained in the Vedas, the knowledge that really mattered, was siphoned off by the Westerners. What the Westerners gave back to us was 'left overs' of the Vedas. It is this concept of the 'lost knowledge of Vedas' that makes the Vedas so great in our eyes. Aggrieved Hindus believe that all physical laws, mathematics, modern inventions, and other aspects of material universe, were, as quoted by sage Dayanand, in essence, contained in the Vedas. However, these believers completely overlook the possibility that Swami Dayanand's observations can be interpreted in a metaphysical sense - that all aspects of creation had an eternal existence in the un-manifested supreme principle, and this was reflected in the eternal words of the Vedas.[13]

Another likely reason is that the Ṛgveda is written in archaic Sanskrit, the *deva bhāshā*, or the language of gods, and less than 0.005% of Indians understand this beautiful language. A mere 14,035 Indians reported Sanskrit as their mother tongue in 2011 government of India census.[14] There is hardly any occasion in a Hindu household, social or religious, when a *pūjā* is not performed, and *pūjā* is always performed only by a *paṇḍita*, a *brahmaṇa*. Much of what the priest recites and performs - the mantras and the rituals - are, most of the times, not understood by the priest himself, let alone the audience. But what is conveyed to the audience, in what has now become an alien language to all but a select few, is the power of mantras and the rituals that are performed. We do not understand what the priest is saying or doing, yet we are told it has great hidden power - power to benefit us beyond our expectations, and harm us beyond imagination. Though no one tells us why and how these mantras and rituals came to possess such power, it is this belief that makes us look at these texts with awe and respect, never mind that the original Vedic gods - *Mitrá*, *Varuṇa*, *Aditi*, et cetera - who bestowed these favors, have disappeared from the Hindu pantheon a long time ago. They have been replaced with *Rāma*, *Kṛṣṇa*, *Hanumān* and *Gaṇeśa*, who are not even mentioned in the oldest of our Vedic texts - the Ṛgveda.

More on this later. For now, let us examine what the Vedas contain.

Chapter 8

Ṛg - The collection of mantras

Yāska, a great linguist and Veda scholar during 800-500 BC, is best known for authoring Nirukta (Niruktam). Nirukta in Sanskrit means 'explained/interpreted'. Yāska's Nirukta is a study concerned with the correct interpretation of Sanskrit words in the Vedas. However, it differs from *vyākaraṇa* (grammar); while *vyākaraṇa* deals with linguistic analysis to establish the exact form of words to properly express ideas, Nirukta is a glossary that helps understand archaic and uncommon words, given their context and etymology.

Although the study of Nirukta has been closely related to the ancillary Vedic science of *vyākaraṇa*, it has a different focus and form. The two are part of the six limbs of *vedāṅga* - a compulsory study for all students of the Vedas. Yāska's remarkable work has helped us immensely in understanding Vedic texts. In the Sanskrit language, the same word can have multiple meanings, which, among other reasons, has led to varying interpretations of the Vedic texts by different scholars, causing considerable confusion. In his Nirukta, Yāska interpreted the correct meaning of these words in the given context with appropriate explanations. His work holds unique value because all other such *Niruktas* of the time (authored by other scholars) are unfortunately lost.

Explaining the word '*rik*'(*ṛca*), Yāska says, "It is so called because 'Ṛg *archani bhavati*' ('by Ṛg is offered homage or worship')." The Ṛgvedic compositions are essentially praises and homages to *Agni, Índra, Sūrya* and other deities but they have different subject matters too. Yāska classifies these hymns into three categories - *pratyakṣa krut* (where the subject matter and meaning are evident), *parokṣa krut* (where the meaning is hidden/implied), and *ādhyātmika* (where the subject matter is spiritual in nature).

All *manḍalas*, except the eighth which begins with exhortations to praise 'only mighty *Índra*', open with a hymn to *Agni*. Apart from *Índra*, perhaps the maximum number of hymns is dedicated to *Agni*.

Not all hymns in the Ṛgveda are homage and worship hymns- many are invitations for blessings or seeking benefits and favours. When we closely examine the subject matter of these hymns, we find that they cover a wide spectrum: religious, cosmological, social, philosophical and literary, to light-hearted, secular and even the magical. The range is truly impressive! Perhaps this is why eminent Vedic scholar Prof V S Ghate classified Ṛgvedic *sūktas* under four heads - religious, secular, philosophical and worldly (pertaining to the material world).

With the view to give readers a whiff of a few hymns from the Ṛgveda on a wider range of topics, the author has chosen to follow the classification of the Sanskrit scholar and Indologist Dr Moriz Winternitz, an associate scholar who worked with Max Müller and (according to Dr Pravesh Saxena[1]) categorized the *sūktas* under eight heads -

1. Songs/poetry
2. Sacrificial *stotra*
3. Philosophical
4. Narrative/Legends
5. Magical
6. Secular
7. Praise of gift *(Dānastutis)*
8. Riddle *(Brahmodya)*

Representative examples of English translation of hymns from different categories will help reader understand the nature of contents of Ṛg better. Translations of the verses (not literal in some cases) are by Griffith (1825-1906), Macdonell (1854-1930) and Monier Williams (1819-1899) - three eminent Indologists of nineteenth century, who, coincidentally, at different times were Boden Professor of Sanskrit at Oxford University. We will begin with the 'sacrificial *stotra*', as sacrifice is what the Vedas are all about.

There are fewer than ten *āprī* ('the one that pleases') hymns in the Ṛgveda which were specifically used during a sacrificial ritual. Three *ṛcas* or mantras of *āprī* hymn in the third *sūkta* of the second *manḍala* are given below -

> *Agni* is set up on the Earth well kindled; he stands in the presence of all beings.
> Wise, ancient, God, the priest and purifier, let *Agni* serve the gods for he is worthy. 1

The hymn ends requesting *Agni* to carry away consecrated oblations.

> *Vanaspati* shall stand near and start us, and *Agni* with his arts prepare oblation.
> Let the skilled heavenly Immolator sent to the Gods the offering thrice anointed. 10

Oil has been mixed; oil is his habitation. In oil he rests; oil is his proper province. 11

Come as you wish: O you steer (*Agni*), rejoice; carry away the oblation duly consecrated.

Dāna stutis - hymns in praise of donors - are even fewer, only half of the *āprī* hymns. The following two mantras give a flavour of these *stutis* -

He, whose two red steers, seeking goodly pasture, plying their tongues move on 'twixt earth and heaven,

Gave Turvasa to Sranjaya, and, to aid him, gave the Vrcivans up to Daivavata. 7

Two wagon teams, with damsels, twenty oxen, *O Agni, Abhydvartin Vayamdna,*

The liberal *Sovran*, giveth me. This guerdon of Prthu's seed is hard to win from others.[2] 8

Under the Narratives/Legends category, three examples of important narratives, also known as dialogue *sūktas*, including *Pururva-Urvaṣi* (10.95), *Yama-Yami* (10.10) and *Sarma-Pani* (10.130) are noteworthy. All three belong to the tenth *manḍala*. On the very first read, one gets the impression these dialogues must have formed a part of plays/dramas, or as Dr Winternitz has suggested these are examples of ancient traditional ballads.

In the *Pururva-Urvaṣi* narrative[3], *Urvaṣi* (an *apsarā* or celestial nymph), while returning to heaven along with other *apsarās* just before dawn, after completing her task of breaking the penance of ṛṣi Vibhandaka, was abducted by a demon. *Pururava*, a brave king and regular guest at *Índra's* court, chased the demon in his chariot and freed *Urvaṣi* from his clutches. The brief period their bodies touched changed their lives forever. She united with the human king. But after living with him for four autumns, she left him when he inadvertently violated one of the conditions. The love poem describes *Pururva's* heartbreak due to the separation.

Śatapatha Brahmaṇa (11.5.1) has also dealt with the love story of *Pururva* and *Urvaṣi* in detail, which, many centuries later, the great poet and playwright Kālidāsa recreated in his play Vikramōrvaśīyam.

The *Yama-Yami* dialogue[4] (X.10) is about incestuous love. According to the Ṛgveda, *Yami* is the twin sister of *Yama* and they have a divine lineage. Their mother *Saraṇyū* is the daughter of *Tvaṣṭr*, the artisan god, and their father *Vivasvanta* is associated with the sun.

Yami is in love with her brother *Yama*. Expressing her love for him, she invites him to her bed, but he rejects her advances saying, 'The gods are always watching us, and shall punish the sinful.' She is heart-broken.

In another story, *Yama* finds the way to the land of his fathers. He voluntarily chooses death and becomes the first man to die. So great was *Yami's* grief that she would not stop crying. When the gods tried to console her, she replied, 'How can I not mourn, for today is the day of my brother's death.' To cure her, the gods created night. From then on, night follows day and the cycle of time began. This story is cited as an example of the power of time as a healer of grief.

[According to some of the later Purāṇas, *Yami* is actually the wife of *Yama*, not his sister.]

In the legend of *Sarama* and *Panis*[5], a group of demons named *Panis* steal the cattle (cows) tended by *Angirasa*, son of sage Angiras. The *Panis* hide the cows in a cave, until *Sarama*, at the bidding of *Índra* and Angiras or Bṛhaspati (two variants of the legend), follows the tracks of the thieves and helps *Índra* recover the cows. *Sarama* is described as having found the cows 'by the path of truth'.

This myth of *Sarama* and *Panis* is found in Ṛgveda (X.108).

Interestingly, there are two different translations of the colloquy. In Griffith's version, the *Panis* carry off the cows (or rays of light) and hide them in caves, which *Índra* then wishes to recover. And in Macdonell's version, *Índra* wants to capture the cows belonging to the *Panis*. The cows are tracked by *Sarama*, who then asks the *Panis* to hand over the cows to the mighty *Índra*, whose bravery he describes in detail to the *Panis*.

There are certainly some messages conveyed through the *Sarama-Panis* story of *Sarama* finding the cows 'by the path of truth', and the *Yama-Yami* story where *Yama* warns his sister about punishment from the gods for committing a grave sin. Was conveying these morals the chief reason why the *sūkta* dialogues were included in the Ṛgveda? Or they find a place in the Ṛg because they were a crucial element of popular folklore, handed down through generations as ballads, an important part of the society's cultural inheritance? These are not easy questions to answer. What cannot be denied however is that the inclusion of these legends made these ancient texts, one of the oldest known to humankind, rich and fascinating.

Some *sūktas* are brilliant showcase of poetic creativity, and one such *sūkta* is the hymn of the dawn offered to *Uṣa* -

> The radiant dawns have risen up for glory, in their white splendour like the waves of waters.
> She makes paths all easy, fair to travel, and, rich, has shown herself benign and friendly. 1
> We see that you are good: far shines your lustre; your beams, your splendours have flown up to heaven.
> Decking yourself, you make yourself seen, shining in majesty, you Goddess Morning. 2
> Your way are easy on the hills: you pass Invincible!
> Self luminous, through waters.
> So lofty Goddess with your ample pathway, daughter of heaven, bring wealth to give us comfort. 3

Dawn, bring to me wealth: untroubled, with your oxen you bear riches at your will and pleasure;
you who, a goddess, a child of heaven, has shown yourself lovely through bounty when we called you early. 4
As the birds fly forth from their resting places, so man with a store of food rise at your dawning.
Yes, to the Liberal mortal who remains at home, oh Goddess dawn, much good you bring. 5

Yet another example of excellent poetry is the following hymn dedicated to *rātri*[6] (night), a part of which we examined earlier -

The goddess of night arrives in all her glory,
Looking about her with her countless eyes.
She, the immortal goddess, throws her veil
Over low valley, rising ground, and hill,
But soon with a bright effulgence dissipates
The darkness she produces; soon advancing
She calls her sister Morning to return,
And then each darksome shadow melts away.
Kind goddess, be propitious to thy servants
who at thy coming straightway seek repose,
Like bird's who nightly nestle in the trees.

Receive, O night, dark daughter of the day,
My hymns of praise, which I present to thee,
Like some rich offering to a conqueror.

Why the riddle *sūtras* were included in the Ṛgveda is perplexing, to say the least. Leaving aside the difficult ones, most other *sūtras* are simple and might have been used for light-hearted exchanges. In one such hymn[7] (8.29.1-4), the main characteristics and features of deities are described, but the names are for the hearer to infer -

1. One is a youth brown, active, manifold he decks the golden one with ornament
2. Another, luminous, occupies the place of sacrifice, sage, among the gods
3. Of one brandishes in his hand and eye and knife, firm, in his seat amid the deities
4. Another holds the thunderbolt, where with he slays the *Vrtras*, resting in his hand

The secular *sūktas*, as the name suggests, do not - directly or indirectly - concern religion. A hymn in which a gambler describes his suffering as a consequence of the game of dice makes an interesting read. Yet, it is difficult to understand why it finds a place in this ancient book.

1. Sprung from tall trees on windy heights, these rollers transport me as they turn up on the table.
   Dearer to me the dice that never slumbers than the deep draught of *Mujavan's* own *Soma*.
2. She never vexed me nor was angry with me, but to my friends and me was ever gracious.
   For the dice's sake, whose single point is final, mine own devoted wife I alienated.
3. My wife holds me aloof, her mother hates me; the wretched man finds none to give them comfort.
   As of a costly horse grown old and feeble, I find not any profit of the gamester.

We are now left with two interesting categories of hymns - philosophical and magical. The philosophical *sūktas* deal with issues of cosmology, nature and god. These *sūktas* are, as is typical of the Ṛgveda, not collated, serialised or gathered in a *maṇḍala*, but randomly distributed. The famous *Puruṣa* (10.90), *Hiraṇyagarbha* (10.121) and *Vāksūkta* (10.145), along with the great hymn of creation, *Nasadiyasūkta* (10.129), all find a place in the tenth *maṇḍala*, whereas the ponderings of ṛṣi Dīrghatamas on 'one reality' described by learned men in different ways are placed in the first *maṇḍala* (1.164).

It is in the *Puruṣasūkta* that we come across the earliest ideas of a supreme being as the chief creator, and more importantly, the first-ever reference to caste[8] (towards the end) -

> The embodied spirit has 1000 heads,
> 1000 eyes, 1000 feet, around
> On every side enveloping the Earth,
> Yet filling a space no longer than a span.
> He is himself this very universe,
> He is whatever is, has been, and shall be.
> He is the Lord of immortality.
> How did they cut him up? What was his mouth?
> What were his arms? And what his thighs and feet?
> The *Brahmaṇa* was his mouth, the kingly soldier
> Was made his arms, the husbandman his thighs,
> The servile *Śūdra* issued from his feet.

The hymns of creation - *Nasadiyasūkta*[9] - are remarkable contemplations over creation and its creator -

> In the beginning there was neither not nor aught,
> then there was neither sky nor atmosphere above.
> What then enshrouded all this teeming universe?
> In the receptacle of water was it contained?

Was it enveloped in the Gulf profound of water?
Then was there neither death nor immortality, then was there neither day, nor night, nor light, nor darkness,
only the existent one breathed calmly self-contained.
Not else than him there was - not else above, beyond.
Then first came darkness hid in darkness, gloom in gloom.
Next all was water, all a chaos indiscreet.
In which the one lay void, shrouded in nothingness.
Then turning towards he by self developed force
of inner fervour and intense abstraction, grew.
And now in him desire, the Primal germ of mind,
arose, which learned men, profoundly searching, say
is the first subtle bound, connecting entity
with nullity. This ray that kindled dormant life,
where was it then? Before? Or was it found above?
Were there parturient powers and latent qualities,
and ficund principles beneath, and active forces
that energised aloft? Who knows? Who can declare
how and from what has sprung this universe? The gods
themselves are subsequent to its development.
Who, then, can penetrate the secret of its rise?
Whether it was framed or not, made or not made; he only
who in the highest heaven sits, the Omniscient lord,
assuredly knows all or haply knows he not.

Our ancestors, while deliberating over abstract metaphysical ideas of truth, the self, creator and creation, appear to have concluded in the early Ṛgvedic times that there is a single ultimate reality. Ṛṣi Dīrghatamas's 3500-year-old mantra '*Ekam sad vipra bahudha vadanyagnim yamum matarishvanmahu*' continues to define the core of Hindu belief even today.

They call him *Índra, Mitrá, Varuṇa, Agni*, and he is heavenly nobly winged *Garutman*.

To what is One, sages give many a title they call it *Agni*, *Yama and Mātariśvan*. (1.164.46)

These are but a few examples of philosophical ideas and thoughts that emerged in Vedic society more than three millennia ago, and which the compilers of the Ṛgveda thought fit for inclusion in this ancient book of Hindus. It seems nigh impossible to understand why those wise compilers thought it appropriate to include magical mantras in the same text. Here are four of the ten mantras recommended for keeping the husband away from the affections of a rival wife -

1. From out the Earth I dig this plant, a herb of most effectual power,

where with one quells the rival wife and gains the husband for oneself.

2. Auspicious, with expanded leaves, sent by the gods, Victorious plant, blow thou the rival wife away, and make my husband only mine.
3. Stronger am I, O stronger One, yea, mightier than the mightier; and she who is my rival wife is lower than the lowest dames.
4. Her very name I utter not: she takes no pleasure in this man. Far into distance most remote drive we the rival wife away.

Apart from the eight categories classified by Dr Winternitz, there is, unsurprisingly, a hymn for cows - unsurprising because this animal, besides playing an important economic role in the daily lives of Vedic Āryans, also had great importance in various religious ceremonies. Cows were important economically, and central to an emerging agricultural society. They were counted as wealth -

6. May we be friends of one like thee, O *Índra*, with the wealth of kine,
   Comrades for lively energy.
7. For thou, O *Índra*, Art alone the Lord of strength that comes from kine
   So grant thou us abundant food.
   (4.32.6-7)

These bovines were also important because their milk, butter, *ghī* and even urine and dung were used in religious ceremonies.

5. To me the cows seem *Bhaga*, they seem *Índra*, they seem a portion of the first poured *Soma*.
   These present cows, they, O ye *Índra*. I long for *Índra* with my heart and spirit.
6. O Cows, ye fatten e'en the worn and wasted, and make the unlovely beautiful to look on.
   Prosper my house, ye with auspicious voices. Your power is glorified in our assemblies.
   (6.28.5-6)
   [See RV (10.169) - for more on cows.]

Finally, we come to assorted hymns, numbering under a dozen - in praise of mountains (4.53), rivers (3.33), dice (10.34), weapons of war (6.75), *yūpa* (the post a sacrificial animal is tied to) (1.136), *sita* (furrow implements) (4.57), *kṣatrapati* (owner of land or landlord) (4.57), *manḍuka* (frogs) (7.103), herbs (10.97), and *rājā* (king) (10.174). The most likely explanation for these hymns of praise is that the Āryans considered any useful object or product praiseworthy, much like the forces of nature such as rivers and mountains. Why a *rājā* is considered worthy of praise needs no explanation!

The tenth *manḍala*

It is widely believed that the tenth *manḍala* is an extrapolation of the Ṛgveda - and was added later. The contents of this *manḍala* are, without a doubt, out of sync with the earlier nine *manḍalas*. Consisting of 191 *sūktas* (same as the first *manḍala*), it deals with strange subjects, such as hymns against a demon who injured children, rival wives and enemies - topics more consistent with the contents of the Atharvaveda. However, one should also remember that the famous *sūkta* of creation, *Nasadiyasūkta*, also belongs to this very *manḍala*, as does the *Puruṣasūkta*. Hymns of creation and cosmological speculation, the unforgettable dialogue between *Yama* and *Yami* as well as *Pururva* and *Urvaṣi*, all find place along with hymns for begetting children. Diverse is the range of topics covered in this unique *manḍala*.

It is in this *manḍala* that we come across wedding hymns as well as hymns for funeral for the first time, which nearly 4000 years later are still an integral part of *saṃskāra* in every Hindu's life. Scholars believe that not all tenth *manḍala* compositions are later-day additions to the Ṛgveda. It is most likely that the tenth *manḍala* is a mixed bag, not only in terms of its contents, but also in terms of timeline.

Chapter 9

Yajur - The Veda of rituals

The Yajurveda is considered the Veda of *karma* or action.

Underlining its importance, Manu observes, "Anyone who, with a concentrated mind, recites three times the collection of the Ṛgveda, or of the Yajurveda or the Sāmaveda, together with the secret texts, is freed from all evils." (MS11.263)

Yajurveda literally means Veda of '*yajus*', a Sanskrit word with the following meanings -

(i) Mantras employed in *yajña*

(ii) A sentence ending in irregular letters

(iii) '*Śaiśe yajuh*' or mantras (in prose), other than Ṛgveda and Sāmaveda mantras in verses

Nirukta, a glossary of Vedas, defines '*yajus*' as *pūjā* and *yajña.*

From these definitions, it is clear that Yajurveda is so titled because of its collection of mantras in prose (and verse) form, and differs from the mantras in the Ṛgveda and the Sāmaveda, which are only in verses.

Traditional Veda scholars who believe in the primacy of *yajña* and *karmakāṇḍa* consider Yajurveda to be a collection of mantras and directions for application in various *yajñas* as per Brahmaṇa and *śrauta sūtras*. They also subscribe to Manu's views that "from fire, wind and the sun he milked out the triple eternal Veda, consisting of the Ṛg, Yajur and Sāma, so that the sacrifice could be accomplished." (MS1.23)

In the modern (scholarly) view, Yajurveda is a primary text for (whole sacrificial rituals which consist of a number of hymns taken from the Ṛgveda. Apart from the hymns, it also has directions for the use of mantras in various sacrificial rituals. It is these directions in prose form that distinguish Yajurveda from the Ṛgveda and Sāmaveda, which consist of verses (Ṛg) and chants (Sāman).

Although some Purāṇas (such as *Matsya*) consider Yajur as the oldest Veda, there is little doubt that Ṛgveda is the older. This is evident from the description of the socio-economic order in the two Vedas: While Ṛgveda contains the first mention of *brahmaṇa, kṣatriyas, vaiśya* and *śūdra* (order of *varṇa*) in the tenth *manḍala*, the *varṇa vyavasthā* (order) takes a clear shape in the Yajurveda; there is proliferation of occupations in Yajur, which are lacking in the Ṛgveda. But this should not lead us to the conclusion that the entire Ṛg *Saṃhitā* is older than the Yajurveda. As discussed elsewhere, the Vedas were not composed in one go - different parts of the Vedas are anthologies of various ṛṣis, collated over a period of time; some parts of the Yajurveda could have been composed earlier than some later parts of the Ṛgveda.

Yajurveda has two versions: *śhukla* (white) and *kṛṣṇa* (black). The *śhukla* version comprises, exclusively, mantras in verse form unlike the *kṛṣṇa* version, which has a mix of both verse and prose. Many believe that it is this purity of collection of mantras - exclusively in verse form - that makes *śhukla* superior and pure (or white) as compared to the other version whose purity was diluted because of the induction of prose in the collection of mantras, and thus becoming black. While *śhukla*, also called Vājasaneyi Saṃhitā, became popular in the north, *kṛṣṇa* or Taittirīya spread widely in southern India, where it continues to be practised even today.

While some texts refer to 101 different *śākhās* (branches/schools) of Yajurveda, unfortunately, only seven are extant of which two, kānva and madhynādina, belong to the *śhukla*, and the other five, Taittirīya (Āpastamba), kapiṣṭhala (*Hiraṇya keśi*), kaṭha, kāṭhaka and maitrāyaṇīya (*kalpa*) belong to the kṛṣṇa Yajurveda.[1]

Whether *kṛṣṇa* or *śhukla*, the Yajurveda is essentially a book of rituals and deals with the subject of *yajña*, i.e. *karmakāṇḍa*, which is central to all important activities of a Hindu's life from conception (*garbhādhāna*) to cremation (*dāh karma saṃskāra*).

Yajñas are sacrifices 'that can be undertaken for any purpose including conferring blessings, purifying the house, workplace, curing illnesses, bringing rain, at various rituals performed in temples or sacred places, or at the *saṃskāras* or rituals of daily life including those connected with birth, marriage, and death'[2] and are 'usually performed according to the methods prescribed in Vedic texts.' The Yajurveda describes various Vedic sacrifices - new and full moon sacrifices (*darśapūrṇamāsa*), sacrifices offered every four months (*cāturmāsa*), sacrifice for the *pitṛ́* (*piṇḍapitri-yajña*), *agnihotṛ* and animal sacrifices - along with prayers offered with the sacrifices. Most of the names of these *yajñas* may appear unfamiliar to the reader, having gone out of practice for many, many years, with the exception of a few like *aśvamedha* and *rajsūya*. These two names sound familiar because of their frequent reference in popular mythologies - Mahābhārata and Rāmāyaṇa.

Yajurveda also describes the preparations for conduct of the *yajña*, for example seating arrangements of priests and *yajamāna*, direction in which the participating priests and *yajamāna* must face, location of *yūpa* (a post to tie the sacrificial animal) shape and size of the fire altar, consecration of the implements and bricks, et cetera. In doing this, it relies heavily on its own Brahmaṇas.

Śhukla Saṃhitā

The Śhukla Saṃhitā has forty *adhyāyas* (chapters) divided into sections or segments called *kandika*, each consisting of a prayer or mantra. *Adhvaryu*, the priest of Yajurveda, and his three assistants, not only recite mantras and Brahmaṇas of their Yajurveda school, they also mutter *yajus*, which are brief formulas in prose form.

The first three *adhyāyas* contain 2086 mantras for *darśa* (first night of the new moon), *pūrṇamāsa* (full moon), *agnihotṛ* (morning and evening *homa*) and *cāturmāsa* (rituals performed at the beginning of every four-monthly season).

The next seven *adhyāyas* have mantras for three important *yajñas* - *soma*, *vājapeya* and *rajasūya*. The construction of fire altar for *homāgni*, called *agnicayana*, was considered a matter of great importance - the subsequent eight *adhyāyas* (from 11 to 18) deal with this matter in detail. The fire altar was built using bricks in special shapes and sizes, and arranged in the form of a large bird, a trough, a chariot wheel, and few other designated shapes. The process of building the fire altar was time consuming and extremely complex requiring knowledge of geometry. As described in Vajaysaneyi Saṃhitā, it took one year to complete using 10800 kiln fired bricks of various shapes including triangles, squares and rectangles, piled in five layers of 200 bricks each. There are very detailed instructions in the texts which had to be followed diligently. Some of the mantras with which the bricks were consecrated occur in Maitrāyaṇīya in the earliest Yajurveda Saṃhitā (nearly 1000 BC). The bricks may be deposited in any order, but the order in which they were consecrated with mantras was fixed. For example, in case the shape of the altar was large bird, the first consecrated brick used at the bottom line of the tail was a square; the second brick placed at the bottom of the tip of the wing stretched in south was a triangle, and so on. Undoubtedly, this required advanced knowledge of geometry. [Stall - Discovering the Vedas, page 267-268, four figure of the bird ref figure 22; Kane - History of Hindu Dharmashastra, Vol II, part II etc for Citi types, construction method etc.] No wonder the study of Vedic geometry was considered essential, and formed a part of *śulbasūtras* of Baudhāyana, Āpastamba and Mānava which are attached to *śrautasūtras* of the black Yajurveda, and Kātyāyana, which is attached to the white Yajurveda.

The Brahmaṇa mantras explain the spiritual interpretation of the different shapes and sizes of the fire altar and bricks.

The sixteenth *adhyāya* is famous for prayers to god *Rudra Śatarudriya*. The next *adhyāya* describes various kinds of bricks used in fire altars along with prayers for taking possession of the altar. The eighteenth *adhyāya* has mantras related to *vasordhārā*, meaning 'flow of wealth'. *Agnicayana* is an important aspect of *somayāga* involving quite a few rites, *vasordhārā* being one of them. It is the name of the entire rite in which several hundred offerings of *ājya* (*ghī*) are made with a *sruc* (ladle made of *uḍumbara* wood), which is also cast into the consecrated fire at the end. The purpose is to secure all the powers of the deity *Agni* for the sacrifice. The mantras used are mostly from the Taittirīya and Vājasaneyī Samhitās. The next two *adhyāyas* deal with the *sautrāmaṇi* sacrifice in which *sura* (a type of wine) is used instead of *soma*. The sacrifice is dedicated to *Índra*, the *Aśvins*, and *Saraswatī*. It is performed by a *brahmaṇa* for success, by a king for a lost throne, and by a *vaiśya* for riches.

The next four *adhyāyas* deal with mantras employed in the famous *aśvamedha* sacrifice performed by kings to demonstrate their universal sovereignty. Detailed description of the *aśvamedha* is given in the thirteenth *kāṇḍa* of Śatapatha Brahmaṇa and the twentieth *adhyāya* of Kātyāyana śrauta sūtra. While *adhyāyas* twenty-six to twenty-nine have supplementary mantras for various sacrifices, the thirtieth and thirty-first *adhyāyas* have mantras for *puruṣamedha*, which are only symbolic sacrifices. These *adhyāyas* contain descriptions of arts and crafts, professions and occupations, useful in extending our understanding of the society in that period. The *sūkta* in the thirty-first *adhyāya*, like *puruṣasūkta* of the tenth *manḍala* of Ṛgveda, is a fine example of spiritualism.

As the name suggests, *sarvamedha* is the sacrifice of everything. The *sarvamedha yajña* is dealt with in the thirty-second, thirty-third and thirty-fourth *adhyāyas*. Some of the *Hiraṇyagarbha sūtras* of the Ṛgveda and the famous *Śivasaṃkalpa sūktas*, concerning matters of human psychology, can be found here. The *pitṛmedha* and funeral verses are explained in the thirty-fifth *adhyāya*.

In *pravargya*, a flat vessel of clay is heated red-hot and hot milk is poured on its surface to produce a column of flame considered to represent the sun. After worshipping the sun, the hot milk is offered to *Aśvin*. This ritual is described in *adhyāyas* thirty-six to thirty-nine. The final *adhyāya*, the fortieth, of Vājasaneyi Saṃhitā contains *Iśavasyopaniṣad*, the only Upaniṣad to be included in any Veda. It has no connection with the *Saṃhitā*.

Kṛṣṇa Saṃhitā

There is an interesting story on how Taittirīya got its name from *tītar*, a variety of partridge. Texts of four *śākhās* of Kṛṣṇa Yajurveda - Kāṭhaka, Kapishthala, Maitrāyaṇi and Taittirīya - are extant. The *Saṃhitā* devoted to *karmakāṇḍa* is divided into seven *kāṇḍas*, each of which is subdivided into forty-four *prapathakas* which are further divided into 631 *anuvākas*.

The first *kāṇḍa* describes how to conduct the *darśapūrṇamāsa*, *vajāpeya* and *rajasūya yajñas*, and the mantras to be used in the rituals. Here, *agniṣṭoma*, an important Vedic fire sacrifice which consists of offering *soma* to *Índra* and other deities, is also described in detail. The sacrifice is performed for the religious merit of a *brahmaṇa* householder and can also be performed for fame, health, good rainfall, et cetera. It usually takes five days and sixteen priests to perform this *yajña*[3]. The second *kāṇḍa* describes the process for animal sacrifices and related rituals, detailing which animal is to be sacrificed to fulfil a given desire. For example, anyone who desires prosperity should sacrifice a white animal to god *Vāyu*, and those who wish to have children should sacrifice a horn-less goat to *Prajāpati*. In this *kāṇḍa*, *daivas* too are described as making sacrifices for fulfilling wishes and desires.

Not all *kāmyas* required animal sacrifices. *Prapathakas* 2-4 describe how offerings of *puroḍāśa* (cakes of grain) on potsherds to various deities using appropriate mantras can help achieve victory over the enemy, birth of an offspring, attainment of *svarga*, et cetera.

The third *kāṇḍa* provides additional instructions for conducting *soma* sacrifices, describing the role of the *adhvaryu* priest, and how the Sāmans and *stotras* are to be used. *Atirātra*, as evident from its mention in the Ṛgveda, is a very old *soma* sacrifice among the *vikrti*-type (variant). While *ekāha* sacrifices can be completed in one day, the *atirātra* takes the whole day and night - hence the name. Among the four *ekāha* type of *soma* sacrifices, *ukthya* is the second, while the others are *agniṣṭoma*, *ṣoḍaśin*, and *atirātra*. The *ekāha soma* sacrifices have one pressing (*sutyā*) day, one or many *dīkṣa* days and three or twelve *upasada* days[4].

It also indicates when offerings should be made to minor deities such as *Dhatr*, *Aurthnumati*, *Raka*, et cetera. The fourth *kāṇḍa* deals with mantras used in building the fire altar and *agnicayana*, and prayers and offerings to *Rudra* - *Śatarudriya* (which also find place in the sixteenth *adhyāya* of Vājasaneyi). Prayers of *aśvamedha yajña* are also included here. The fifth *kāṇḍa* describes how to make *ukha*, lay bricks, build the fire altar, and elucidates offerings and rituals of *aśvamedha*. The sixth *kāṇḍa* gives the description of the *soma* sacrifice, *dakṣiṇā* offerings and *ṣoḍaśin* sacrifice. The *ṣoḍaśin* sacrifice forms a part of the *atyagniṣṭoma* which is the formal order of the ritual texts that succeeds the *agniṣṭoma* and precedes the *ukthya* sacrifice. According to the Maitrāyaṇīya Saṃhitā and Yajñatatva Prakaśa, the *ṣoḍaśin* is not a separate (independent) sacrifice, but a name of *agniṣṭoma vikrti*, which ends with the *ṣoḍaśin-stotra*.

This *kāṇḍa* also includes instructions for the selection of an appropriate piece of land and various implements for the *yajña*, educating the *yajāmana*, et cetera. The seventh *kāṇḍa* deals with the *soma*, *panchrtāra*, *aśvamedha* and other sacrifices. There are narrations on how *Índra*, who was initially afraid of *asuras*, used the power of *agnistuti* to destroy evil. Detailed explanations of the *soma* sacrifices and rites that extended as long as a year (including nights) are given below.

Interestingly, the hymn 5.25 explains the symbolic meaning of *aśvamedha* as similar to the Upaniṣads.

The Taittirīya Saṃhitā (3-4 and 6-7) exemplifies how the mantras were mixed with explanations in prose. The mantras and their commentary are thus mixed in the Kṛṣṇa Yajurveda, thereby taking away the purity associated with Śhukla Yajurveda, which has only the mantras and no prose or explanations.

Importance of Yajurveda

Yajurveda 's importance lies in it being a directory of rituals with commentaries. According to Dr Pravesh Saksena[5], the prose form was first used in sentences like *Índraya svāhā* and *Agnaye svāhā* in the Kṛṣṇa Yajurveda. The single letter '*bīja*' (literally seed) form of prayers, such as *ong, shreen, bhū, bhuvaḥ, svaḥ,* et cetera are also found here. The Ṛgvedic tradition of addressing the same god by multiple names was taken to a new level in the Yajurveda. There are a hundred different names of *Rudra*[6] in *Śatrudriya*, which evolved into *Śivasahastranāma* and *Viṣṇusahastranāma* in the later *purāṇic* tradition. On the other hand, as mentioned earlier, some of the simpler prayer mantras that evolved in the Yajurveda are examples of extreme simplicity, for example, '*Sūryo jyotih, jyotih Sūryo*'. In Yajur, *Sūrya Pūjā*, symbolic in the Ṛgveda, was firmly established as a part of Hindu Dharma. *Yajña*, rituals and more importantly, the role of *purohita* became central to Hindu religion, relegating even the role of gods to a secondary position. A *purohita* could help fulfil even the most difficult wishes of the *yajamāna* through rituals.

It marked the beginning of a new chapter in the long history of Hindu Dharma.

Chapter 10

Sāma - The Veda of songs

In Sanskrit, Sāman means 'song', therefore, Sāmaveda means Veda of melodies and chants. It is collection of hymns to be chanted at sacrifices. Even though its main purpose appears to be teaching how to chant the Vedic verses during sacrifices, Sāmaveda's objective was more than simply converting Veda verses to 'pleasant-to-hear' tunes. This is evident in the observations of Bṛhad devatā that go to the extent of saying that only he who knows Sāma truly understands the real meaning of Vedas - "*Sāmani yo vetti sa veda tattvam*" (Bṛhad Devatā 8.130). The Yājñavalkya Smṛti (3.4.11 - 2) also holds a similar view: the one who sings and carefully practices the Sāmagāna attains *Brahman*. The Cāndogyopaniṣad (1.1, 2) considers it the essence of the Ṛgveda, the very foundation of Vedic religion! Although falling third in the list of Vedas (after Ṛg and Yajur), Sāmaveda is considered next only to the Ṛgveda in importance. In fact, in the Gītā, *Kṛṣṇa* says, "among the Vedas, I am the Sāma" (10.22).

In Sāmaveda, all but 75 of the 1800 odd *ṛcas* are from Ṛgveda, which have been modified and rearranged for chanting, thereby attracting comments that Sāmaveda is "the Ṛgveda set to music."[1] In archaic Sanskrit, just as in modern Sanskrit, phonetics was very important and accents were used to indicate change of emphasis. While the Ṛgveda has vertical and horizontal accents, the Sāmaveda uses numbers 1, 2 and 3 (either in the numerical or syllabic manner) to mark the accents, indicating importance of phonetics in both. Typically, first, a mantra from the Ṛgveda is chosen, and then its words are marked according to their *ādhār* (base/foundation) and *yoni* (source). The Sāmaveda consists of such *yonis* that are modified by changing, transforming or embellishing the words and inserting - wherever necessary - sounds called *stobha*, which, though meaningless, are crucial in converting an existing string of words into a melody. *Stobha* consist of words like *huva*, *hova* and *bhū*. Thus, a mantra from the Ṛgveda is first modified into a basic verse (*yoni*) and then into chants, as indicated in songbooks or *gānas*. For some reason, "They have almost universally been neglected by scholars."[2]

The Sāmaveda comprises two major parts: the first part includes four melody collections or *gāna*, and the second consists of three-verse 'books' or *ārchika*. The song book indicates how the verses are to be sung and used in rituals. A melody in the *gāna* book corresponds to a verse in the *ārchika* book.

Melody Books (*gāna*)	**Verse Collections (*ārchika*)**
Grāmegeya gāna	*Pūrvārcika*
Aranyayegeya gāna	*Āranyaka Sāmahitā*
Ūha gāna	*Uttarārcika*
Ūhya gāna	*Collection of stobhas*

[*Āraṇyaka Saṃhitā* is attached to *pūrvārchika*.]

In its first part, the Sāmaveda *Saṃhitā* closely follows the arrangement of the Ṛgveda. In the *pūrvārchika*, the verses addressed to *Agni* and *Índra* come before those addressed to *soma*. Just as in the ninth Ṛgveda *manḍala*, the *Soma* book comes only after the family books, which typically begin with hymns for *Agni* and *Índra*. Furthermore, the verses are arranged in descending order according to their metres. Although the Sāmaveda mostly contains hymns from the Ṛgveda, it is believed, they have not been accurately transmitted among the *Sāma vedins*.

In the *pūrvārcika*, the first verse of the common unit, the *triśtica*, is used to indicate the melody of the whole *tristica* (*tṛca*). In the *uttarārcika*, however, groups of verses (mostly *triśtica*) and *pragāthās* (strophes - a group of lines forming a section of a two-verse lyric poem) or strophes of four, six, seven, nine or ten verses, have been collected. This collection contains verses used for melodies sung at various *śrauta* rituals. In the *uha* and *uhagāna*, melodies of the *soma* ritual are found which rest on the verses of the *uttarārchica*. While melodies of *uhagāna* correspond to the verses of author's *ārcika* and *grāmegeya-gāna*, the melodies of *uhya* (*rahasya*) *gāna* correspond to those of the *Āraṇyaka Saṃhitā* and *Aranyageya-gāna*.

The *gāṇa* collection is divided into *grāmegeya* or melodies for *grāma* (village or public recitations), and *āranyageya* (melodies of the forest) for use by anyone meditating in solitude. *Ārchika* or verse collection on the other hand has *pūrva* (earlier or first) *ārchika*, which has 585 single stanza verses organised in the order of deities, and *uttara* (later or second) *ārcika*, which has verses grouped in triads or *tricas*. Each triad is sung together in one melody and the verses are arranged in order of the rituals. In the *uttaragāna*, chants are serialised according to the order in which they are used in the *soma* rituals. The *uha* and *uhyagāna* are divided into seven sections each, of which the first five (*daśaratra*, *sāmavatsāra*, *ekaha*, *ahina* and *sattra*) are arranged according to the length (in days) of the rituals. The remaining two sections are *prāyaścitta* (expiation) *gāna*, sung for expiation, and *kśūdra*, sung for fulfilling wishes.

Ahina is the name of a class of *soma* rite in which the pressing days last two to twelve days and always within *atirātra*.

Ekaha is a day-long *soma* sacrifice; reckoned as a class of *soma* different from *ahina* and *sattra*. *Agniṣṭoma* is an *ekaha* sacrifice, since the main rite relating to the *soma* is performed in a single day. There are several *ekaha* sacrifices prescribed for fulfilling various desires.

Sāmavatsāra, or *Sāmavatsāra Sattra*, is a year-long sacrifice in the shape of *gavam āyana, ādityanam āyana*, *Angirasāma āyana*, et cetera. It occupied a very important place in the life of an ancient Indian.

Daśarātra comprises ten principal days of a twelve-day *Sattra*; *Sarvamedha* is a *Daśarātra*.

[*Sattras* are those which last thirteen to a hundred nights or more.]

Even though the *gānas* are not a part of the Sāmaveda, they play an important role. The first two, *grāmegeya* and *āranyageya*, together are called *pūrvāgāna* (earlier or first song book) and *prakṛtigāna* (principal song book). *Uha* and *uheyāgāna* are called the *uttaragāna* or subsequent song book. Since they are derived from the principal *prakṛtigāna*, they are known as *vikṛtigāna*. Each *ārcika* verse forms the base of chants in the village songs. The chants of the forest song are based on verses of *Āraṇyaka Saṃhitā* (with a few based on *pūrvārcika*).

Since the contents of the Sāmaveda are almost entirely drawn from the Ṛgveda, it is considered to be the later Veda. However, many scholars believe the melodies of SāmaVeda must have been of the Ṛgvedic period or even earlier, sung as folk songs or semi-religious songs by ordinary people, magicians or priests. According to Staal, "The melodies were held in extraordinary awe and it looks as if they might not have been created for the sake of the verse, but were in existence already." He goes on to add that, "sometimes we have a series of chants in which the words fit the music in the first instance but less closely, or hardly at all, in those that follow. It shows that the words for the first had been carefully selected to fit the melody; after which others, different in length and number, were forced into the Sāmaveda format as if confined in a straitjacket."[3]

It is also possible that Sāmaveda may be older than even *Kṛṣṇa* and Śhukla Yajurveda texts; both have chants from the Sāmaveda. Moreover, Sāmaveda is used in Yajurveda *śrauta* ceremonies, and according to Staal, "The organisation and fixation of its chants in one large collection during the Kuru period must have been undertaken in close cooperation with the *Yajur vedins*, many of them indigenous inhabitants of the subcontinent like the *Sāma vedins* themselves."[4]

According to another theory, verses of the Sāmaveda were initially taken from the Ṛgveda, modified, set to tune and composed as *uttarārcika*. Typically, the *śrauta* rituals have *stotra* or *stutis*, and each stuti consists of five portions - prelude (*prastāva*), chanted by *prastotṛ* priest; chant (*udgitha*), chanted by *udgātr* priest; response (*pratihāra*), chanted by *pratihāra*; accessory (*upadrava*), chanted by *udgātr*; and finale (*nidhāna*), chanted by all three. Each of the *stuti* sections must be sung in one breath, which is not an easy task because chants are long and the sound of 'O' is stretched for an extended period. During these long stretches, the *prastotṛ* (priest) signals the halfway mark to other participating priests who have their own roles to play. Since this process was quite complex, the *pūrvārcika* lists of *yonis* were composed along with the *Āraṇyaka Saṃhitā* to make memorisation of the melodies and chants easier. According to Dalal, even though the melodies could have been pre-Ṛgvedic, the majority, including all the village songs had Sanskrit names, such as *Rathantara*. However, the names of certain forest songs may have been non-Sanskrit in origin, indicating the existence and intermixture of different groups of people.[5]

Śākhās (schools/branches)

The *Patañjalimahābhāshya* and Purāṇa mention a thousand paths, but only thirteen *śākhā* are found listed in texts, of which only three, *Kauthuma*, *Ranayaniya* and *Jaiminiya*, are known today. The first two have the same order of mantras and differ only in division. Whereas *Kauthuma* is divided into *prapāṭhaka*, *ardhpāṭhaka* and *daśati*, *Ranayniya* is divided into *adhyāya*, *kāṇḍa* and mantras.

While *Kauthuma* is popular north of Vindhyas, *Rananiya* is better known in the south. All parts of *Jaiminya* or *Talavkar* recension - *Saṃhitā*, *Brahmaṇa*, *Śrautāsūtra* and *Gṛhyāsūtra* - are extant. Primarily, it is the difference in pronunciation that led to the emergence of different *śākhā* (recensions/schools)[6]

There are 1810 *ṛcas* in the *ārchika*, of which some have recurred, leaving 1549 *ṛcas*. Keeping aside 75 of these 1549 *ṛcas*, the rest are from the eighth and ninth *manḍalas* of the Ṛgveda. The *ṛcas* of the first *prapāṭhaka* of *pūrvārchika* are related to *Agni* and appropriately called *Agneyākāṇḍa*. The second to fourth prapāṭhaka contain *stutis* of *Índra* and are collectively called a *Índraparva*. The fifth *prapāṭhaka* is called *pavamānaparva*, as this contains *stutis* of *Soma*. The sixth *prapāṭhaka*, known as *Āraṇyaka parva*, has a variety of *candas* and different deities. The *mahānammnyārcika* contains ten *ṛcas* and is like an appendix at the end of *pūrvārcika*. The *pūrvārcika* has 650 *ṛcas*.

The *uttarārchika* has nine *prapāṭhaka* and 1225 mantras of which 267 are repeats. A *gīta* or chart is made using three *ṛcas* and the *sāmāgīta* have been used to compose *srotras* sung in *yajñas*. Only ninety-nine SāmaVeda mantras are original to the Sāmaveda, i.e. not common to the Ṛgveda. The mantras common to SāmaVeda and Ṛgveda (in *ārchika* section) - number 15041.

Scheme of singing: from three notes to seven notes

Any verse can be read or sung - it is the composer who creates melodies, turning groups of words into songs. Tulsi's Rāmāyaṇa, depending on the creativity of the melody composer, is sung in a hundred different ways. As mentioned earlier, the Ṛgveda *ṛcas* use three notations for accent, showing the importance attached to the pronunciation of words. Sound was central to oration of the Vedas, and it is no surprise that all Ṛgveda *ṛcas* were composed in meters (*candas*) with accent notations. Therefore, the method of chanting of the *ṛcas* naturally became a sufficiently important matter to be included in a separate Veda - the Sāmaveda. It is the Sāmaveda that gives melody to the verses of the Ṛgveda.

Initially the Sāma Vedas hymns were typically sung in three notes. The upper note was called the '*uddāta*' and its sound was produced from above the palate. This was denoted with a small vertical line over the syllable. The lower note in which sound was produced from below the palate was called the '*anuddāta*' and denoted with a horizontal line underneath the syllable. *Svarita*, a central note, and combination of *uddāta* and *anuddāta* didn't have notation. In an alternative method, instead of vertical or horizontal lines, numerals 1, 2 and 3 were added above the letters indicating *uddāta*, *svarita* and *anuddāta* notes.

Example: Sâma Veda (1), first 2 pādās.

२ ३ १ २ ३ १ २ ३ २ ३ १ २
अग्र आ याहि वीतये गृणानो हव्य दातये

Udātta (१): आ, त, व्य
Svarita (२): अ, या, ये, नो, दा
Anudātta (३): ग्र, वी, णा, ह
Prachaya: हि, गृ, त, ये

With the development of Sāmagāna, these three notes evolved into four, five and eventually seven notes. The Sāmavidhāna Brahmaṇa, while associating these seven notes or *svaras* with Sāmagāna, asserts that each note was favoured by human, *deva*, *gandharva*, animal, birds, vegetation and *rākṣasa*, as listed below -

1. *Prathama-ma*: Humans
2. *Dvitya-ga*: *Gandharva* and *apsarā*
3. *Tritīya-re*: Bull and other animals
4. *Caturtha-sā*: Birds
5. *Pancama* or *mandra* (low)-*ni*: *Rākṣasas*
6. *Ṣasta* or *krusts* (high)-*dha*: Herbs, vegetation, et cetera
7. *Antya* or *atiswara* (very high)-*pa*: gods

In a different explanation, the *Nardiya Śikṣā* (1.5.3-4) says that each Sāma *svara* was derived from the sounds of animals and birds in the appropriate seasons. Thus, the *krauncka's* (heron) cry was *madhyama*, an elephant's trumpet was *niṣādha*, a bull's roar was *riṣabha*, a *koel's* (cukoo) whistle was *pancama*, et cetera.

Readers familiar with Indian music would notice the diminishing nature or *avaroha krama* (descending order) of the *Soma* notes. This order of *svaras* in *soma* music - *ma*, *ga*, *ri*, *sa*, *ni*, *dha* and *pa* - was revised subsequently to *sa*, *re*, *ga*, *ma*, *pa*, *dha* and *ni*, which are used even now. The Yājñavalkya Śikṣā text talks of the present order of the notes and insists that the seven *svaras* belonged to *Āraṇya Gāna*.

For purists of the Vedic period, correct recitation of the mantras and performance of rituals was important, not for the sake of perfection alone. It is believed that the benefits of chanting Veda mantras accrues only if there is -

- correct pronunciation of words, i.e., *akṣara śuddhi*
- correct duration for utterance of words, i.e. *mātrā śuddhi*
- correct intonation of words, i.e. *svara śuddhi*

The scriptures warn of severe blowback in case mistakes are made in the pronunciation of mantras or conduct of rituals. Volumes were written covering every minute act of a ritual and study of *vedānga*. The study of *vedānga* was made essential for every student of Veda to ensure correct recitation of mantras. Of the six limbs of the Vedas, *śikṣā* - the 'phonetics directory'- is very important. This "science of proper pronunciation, especially as teaching the laws of euphony peculiar to the Veda " comprises knowledge of "letters, accents, quantity, the right use of the organs of articulation, and phonetics generally."[7]

The study of *śikṣā* includes correct pronunciation of syllables and compound letters - *varṇa*; correct pronouncement with proper accent - *uddāta*, *anuddāta* and *svarita* (*svara*); and the duration required for pronouncing a syllable - *mātrā*. The time spent on consonants and vowels, long and short duration vowels, and consonants (not accompanied by vowels), et cetera has been critically examined here, besides stress (*balam*), continuity (*sanātana*) and tone (*sāma*). Together, these seven elements make for a complete study and recitation of mantras.

The issue of appropriately fitting the Ṛgvedic *ṛcas* in melody form must have been critical for those sound-sensitive people, who lay great emphasis on purity of sound; *vac* was a *devī* for them! The Sāmavidhāna Brahmaṇa, Nāradiya Śikṣā, Arśeya Brahmaṇa and other texts deal with this issue in great detail. The Sāmavidhāna Brahmaṇa lists six modifications or deviations to fit the Ṛgveda mantras or *ṛcas* into Sāmagāna. These are[8] -

1. *Vikār* - Modifying a word according to the need. For example, '*agneya*' is replaced by '*o gna yi*'
2. *Viśleśhan* - Breaking a word
3. *Vikarśan* - Stretching a *svara* or note. For example, '*yay*' as '*yaaa ye*'
4. *Abhyās* - Repeating a word or *padā* several times
5. *Virām* - Stopping midway for the convenience of the song and beginning again, as if the remaining word is a new one
6. *Stobha* - Adding meaningless words like *ho*, *hu*, et cetera

The ṛṣis composed many Sāmagānas using these seven notes and the six *Sāmavikāras*.

The melodies and notes of *gāna* formed the basis and source of music in India. The *Dhrupad* traces its origin to Sāmaveda and practitioners of *Dhrupad*, the famous Dagar family, even today whisper the Sāmaveda mantras in the ears of a new born child.

Chapter 11

Atharva - A Veda?

Time and again, the scriptures have spoken of *traividyā* (triple learning) or three Vedas.

In the very first chapter of Manusmṛti, the author refers to the *traividyā* ('*trai*' means 'three' and '*vidyā*' means 'knowledge') in reference to the three Vedas, "From fire, wind, and the sun he milked out the triple eternal Veda, consisting of the Ṛg, Yajur and Sāma, so that the sacrifice could be accomplished." (MS 1.23) In the second chapter, clarifying what it means to be a good priest, Manu again refers to only three Vedas; he explains that a priest who has curbed himself and only knows the verse dedicated to the Sun god is better than a man "who is not curbed, who eats everything and sells everything, even if he knows the three Vedas." (2.118) There are several other references to three Vedas in Manusmṛti: "The vow for studying the three Vedas with the guru is for 36 years, or half of that, or a quarter of that, or whenever the undertaking comes to an end" (3.1).; kings were exhorted to rise early in the morning and respectfully attend to learned priests "who have grown old in the study of the triple learning, and abide by their advice" (MS 7.37); "From those who have the triple learning he should acquire the triple learning, the eternal science of politics and punishment, philosophy, and the knowledge of the soul" (MS 7.43). The famous lawgiver speaks of the three Vedas several times, but does not mention the fourth Veda anywhere.

Early Buddhist texts, for example *Nikāya*, also refer to the three Vedas; they too do not recognize Atharvaveda as the fourth Veda.

The Manusmṛti is universally acknowledged to have been composed somewhere between 200 BC-100 AD. For Manu to not acknowledged the Atharvaveda in his *magnum opus* can be attributed either to a lack of recognition of the Atharva as a Veda during his era (even though it existed), or for reasons unknown to us, it's delisting from the list of Vedas. The Atharvaveda, in the first seven of the total twenty books, extensively deals with sorcery (black and white magic) as well as medicine, healing and funerals. It is possible that because of this association with *jādu-toṇa* practices of magic, and medicine - references that were considered impure - the whole composition was considered unworthy of occupying the same shelf as the other three Vedas. After all, the Vedas were the purest of the pure - the very fountainhead of Hindu Dharma.

Although it has proven nearly impossible to attach a fixed date of compilation to any of the Vedas, their relative antiquity can be deduced based on multiple factors, such as their language and grammar, description and evolution of the Vedic gods and their function, description of society, et cetera. The language of the Ṛgveda, the earliest of the Vedas, is different from the later texts, characterised by different word roots and compound words. The Ṛgvedic gods differ in their personal attributes and functions from gods described in the later Vedic texts. The *varṇa* system, which finds only a passing reference, and is in its infancy in *Puruṣasūkta* of the Ṛgveda, matures in the Atharvaveda (by this time, the *brahmaṇa* had become a powerful and respected *varṇa*) and there are parts that refer to the Kuru kings, who came much after the early Ṛgvedic *manḍalas*. Based on these studies, scholars believe that Atharva is the latest (and the last) addition to the Vedas. But again, like other Vedas, some or many parts of Atharva may be as old, or perhaps older, than some parts of the Ṛgveda.

Interestingly, the literal meaning of Atharvaveda is 'the knowledge of magic formulas' - the first seven books of the total twenty deal with magical poems. But many of the 6000 verses deal with serious topics like cosmology, philosophy, the concept of time and *yajña*. The word '*ātharvaṇa*' occurs in the Vedic texts in various contexts. Ṛṣis Bhisaj Atharvaṇa, known for his knowledge of the healing practices, and Ghora Angirasa, known for his magic spells, both are associated with this Veda. The Ṛgveda too mentions an Atharvaṇa, a priest who produced *Agni* and was responsible for bringing order through sacrifices[1]. *Angirasa* is one of the six 'mind-born sons' or 'spiritual sons' (*manas putras*) of *Brahman*; the others being *Māric*, *Atri, Pulatsya, Pulaha* and *Kratu*, all of whom became great ṛṣis (Mahābhārata Ādiparva chapter 65, Stanza 10). Ātharvaṇā is also a generic term in Sanskrit language for priests, similar to Atharvaṇa (note the difference in spelling) who is a fire priest in the Avesta, indicating its Indo-Iranian origin.

Atharvaveda is known by many names - *BrahmaVeda* (after ṛṣi Brahman?), *Bhṛgvangiroveda* (after ṛṣis Bhṛgu and Angiras) and *AngiroVeda* (after ṛṣi Angiras). Bloomfield thinks that the name *BrahmaVeda* was acquired because these texts dwell on *Brahman* and related matters. But in reality, these texts devote more space to non-spiritual and non-philosophical topics, such as magic, charms, sorcery and healing, rather than *Brahman*. It is also possible that the name *BrahmaVeda* was given since 967 *sūktas* out of the nearly 6000 mantras were composed by ṛṣi

Brahman. Probably, prefixing the word '*Brahman*' to the title, was an attempt to give the text a status higher than other texts of the same class.

In Bloomfield's view, "The term 'Atharvaṇa' refers to the auspicious practices of the Veda, the *bheṣajani* (*bheṣaj* - drug, medicine) (AV. X I.6.14), those parts of the Veda which are recognised by the *ātharvaṇa* ritual and orthodox Brahmanical writings, as *santa*, 'holy', and *pauṣtika*, 'conferring prosperity'." He further adds, "The term Angiras refers to the hostile sorcery practices of the Veda, the *yatu* (S.B. X. 5.2.20), or *abhicāra*, which is terrible (*Ghora*)."[2] This means that the Atharvaveda consists of Atharvaṇa and *angiras* matters, and it appears that the Veda was given its name based on considerable logic.

With so many possibilities, it is anybody's guess how this fourth Veda acquired the name Atharva.

Śākhā

Śaunaka's Caraṇa-vyūha lists nine *śākhās* (branches/schools), namely Paippalāda, Mauda, Stauda, Jajala, Jalda, Brahmavada, Śaunakiya, Kuntapa and Devadarsh. In Patañjali's list of schools, which otherwise appears partly unrealistic, there are a surprising twenty one schools of the Ṛgveda, 101 schools of the Yajurveda, and 1000 of the Sāmaveda ! This concurs with Caraṇa-vyūha's nine *śākhās* of Atharvaveda. However, Paippalāda and Śaunakīya are the only two recensions that have survived through time.

Maurice Bloomfield's translation and commentary of the Atharvaveda is a thorough work, one that most scholars and readers rely upon. In the Introduction to Hymns of Atharvaveda [3], Bloomfield observes that "the most difficult problem, hardly as yet ripe for final solution, is the original function of many mantras, after they had been stripped of certain adaptive modifications, imparted to them to meet the immediate purpose of the Atharva *vedin*." He goes on to add, "New meaning is read into the mantras, and any little stubbornness on their part is met with modifications of their wording." This leads critic to a very difficult situation of "searching investigation of the remaining Vediv collections" before a connection can be made "from the more original meaning to the meaning implied and required by the situation in a given Atharvan hymn." While Rudolph Roth and William Dwight Whitney were among the first western scholars to publish the *Śaunakīya* text in 1856, Shankar Pandurang Pandit was the first Indian scholar to produce a comprehensive scholarly treatise on the Atharvaveda in the 1890s.

The study of the Atharvaveda again came alive in the 1950s, when Durga Mohan Bhattacharya announced the discovery of several palm-leaf manuscripts of the Paippalāda Saṃhitā in Odisha. These manuscripts helped scholars clarify the numerous corrupt passages in the Kashmir manuscript of Paippalāda Saṃhitā. In the 1990s and early 2000s, several *kāṇḍas* of the Paippalāda Saṃhitā were edited and translated, and a few collections of papers on the Atharvaveda appeared, especially Ghosh (in 2002), and Griffiths and Schmiedchen (in 2007), which rekindled interest in the study of the Atharvaveda.

Date

The subject matter of the two, i.e. Paippalāda and Śaunaka, can be broadly divided into four heads - sorcery hymns, speculative hymns, special topics of *gṛhya* rituals, and a few royal rituals and appendices. Iron is introduced in texts of 1200 BC (the mantra period), and speculative hymns of both Paippalāda and Śaunaka Saṃhitās mention *shyam aysa* or iron (AVS 130307=PS 16.63.12 and AVS 9.5.4=PS 16.97.3). According to Witzel, "AVŚ 1-5, 8-12 = PS 1-15, 16-17 are the two older sections. They form the core of the Atharvaveda texts dealing with sorcery and speculation, and can be dated *ad quem* with the introduction of iron (1200 BC)." and Atharvaveda 13-18 = PS 18 "at least in part, of a slightly later age, that of the later *Saṃhitā* period (Taitteria Saṃhitā), or even that of some early Brahmaṇas, such as the older parts of Atharvaveda."[4]

∞

Society tends to consider all ancient knowledge, and practices, superior. We accept the old sayings as gospel, even though modern scientific findings may not support, or may even contradict, many of these ideas and beliefs. For an Indian, *neem* (Indian lilac or *Azadirachta indica*) tree products remain a more effective disinfectant and germicidal than any that modern science has produced. In India, we tend to accept ancient knowledge and wisdom without much questioning even though, as a country and culture, we are more critical and argumentative than most others; modern knowledge attracts the full glare of our critical faculties before passing muster. For many Indians, everything written in the Ṛgveda is not only good, but also correct. After all, how could the ṛṣis say anything incorrect? Their pronouncements are admitted as the ultimate truth, leaving no scope for any modification of ideas or beliefs expressed therein. These purists, including not only the uninitiated but also the well-read, educated and well-informed, believe that in the times of the Ṛgveda, only rational and philosophical thoughts and ideas could emanate from the great sages we call ṛṣis. They trust that the entire discourse in the Ṛgveda is only about 'serious' matters. The non-serious matters, in their opinion, simply do not belong to the pure '*satayuga*' period in which the Ṛgveda was revealed to the ṛṣis. Applying this elliptical logic, they defend magic and charm mantras of the Ṛg, as serious matter. Some even argue that the powerful mantras could help achieve impossible feats, such as curing diseases like leprosy or destroying the enemy! This proclivity has led to several debates that continuc unabated, at times dragging in venerable saints and scholars of the Vedas like Dayanand Saraswati.

The Atharvaveda extensively deals with magic, charm and sorcery. But it also deals with theosophy, philosophy, cosmology and some important rites of passage of life as well as matters pertaining to royal rites. According to Carr and Mahalingam, "The Atharvaveda, despite its more popular character (seen in the lack of connection with the ritual on the whole and in the proliferation of spells instead), does in fact contain a greater number of speculative hymns than the Ṛgveda," unlike what many believe[5].

While both Ṛgveda and Yajurveda concern themselves with mantras and *yajña*, the Sāmaveda is more about the chanting of mantras while performing *yajñas*. However, the contents of all three Vedas, such as cosmology, worship of forces of nature and Vedas deities, method of worship and philosophy, are 'serious' and *yajña* centric. This certainly does not mean that 'non-serious' matters like magic or charm are completely excluded from the *tri-vidyā*. Though present, these matters are addressed peripherally, and don't form the core subject matter of the other three Vedas. No one can dispute that the objective of creating the three Vedas was not to teach magic, charm or sorcery. The problem arises when purists, who insist that everything Ṛgvedic is rational, philosophical and spiritual, and that Vedic sages and their Āryan followers entertained only 'serious thoughts', surmise that the pure, clear and pristine flow of the Ṛgvedic stream was contaminated by 'non-serious' impure matters (like *jādu-toṇa* and witchcraft) in the Atharvaveda, much after the Vedic Āryans had learned and practiced the first three Vedas for generations. This position needs to be disputed by presenting facts which demonstrate that while the great thinkers of the Ṛgvedic period were pondering in their mantras abstract matters, such as the 'One Creator' and 'Ultimate reality', they were also composing mantras for destroying the enemy and his children -

> May he be swept away, himself and children: May all the three earths press down beneath them.
>
> May his fair glory, O ye gods, the blighted, who in the day or night fain destroy us. 11
>
> So may I die this day if I have harassed any man's life or if I be a demon.
>
> Yea, may he lose his 10 sons together who with false tongue hath called me *Yātudhāna*. 15

And praying and exhorting *Índra* to destroy fiends shaped like birds and animals -

> Destroy the fiend shaped like an owl or owlet, destroy him in the form of dog or cuckoo.
>
> Destroy him shaped as evil or as vulture as with a stone, oh *Índra*, crush the demon. 22
>
> (RV. VII.104)

In reverse, the Atharvaveda which has more space devoted to black and white magic, also has nuggets- such as about *kāla* (time) -

By him this (universe) was urged forth, by him it was begotten, and upon him this (universe) was founded. Tying, truly, having become the *Brahman* (spiritual exaltation), supports *Parameśtin* (the highest lord). 9
(AV. XIX.53.9)

So, how does one deal with a text like the Atharvaveda?

Many portions of the Atharvaveda belong to the Ṛgvedic period, possibly even earlier. There is ample evidence to show that the magical practices, which occupy a significant part of Atharvaveda, were prevalent in the Ṛgvedic times and known to the authors of Ṛgveda. There are several hymns in Ṛg, Yajur and the Sāma Vedas which relate to the pursuit of 'non-serious' practices. Even in the golden age of *satayuga*, these practices were so common among Vedic people that they were included in the main body of the Ṛgveda. Had these activities been confined only to a limited, or so-called uninitiated and uninformed section of society, the concerned mantras would not have been known by the names of great ṛṣis. It is possible that these practices were prevalent among the non-Āryan inhabitants of Kuru-Panchala area (and to the east of this region) even before the arrival of Vedic culture and civilisation. It is possible, that due to cultural osmosis, these practices found their way among the Āryans too. Such exchanges are common enough when two different cultures interact. It is fairly obvious that even as these alien practices were accepted by Ṛgvedic people, they remained on the fringe and did not become mainstream until much later, i.e. the Atharvavedic period.

Let us now refine our search for possible evidence in the Vedic literature in support of this proposition. The following questions will help us find answers -

- Do the Ṛg, Yajur and Sāma Vedas (*Brahmaṇa* and Upaniṣad) refer to Atharva as the fourth Veda?
- What are the essential ingredients/characteristics for a text to qualify as a Veda?

  Since the Vedas are self-existent or '*apauruṣeya*' (not created by humans), they do not have qualifying characteristics/attributes like the Purāṇas. This presents a fundamental problem - what kind of attributes a text should have in order to be recognised as a Veda? And did Atharva have those attributes?
- Is it only the inclusion of 'magic and healing' which made Atharva impure? Are these topics missing in other Vedas?
- At what point in Vedic literature was Atharva accepted as a Veda?

As discussed earlier, the Manusmṛti (200 BC to 100 or 180 AD) has repeated references to only three Vedas and *tri-vidyā*, making no mention of a fourth. It can well be argued that Manu did not accept the Atharva as the fourth Veda, but there were other thinkers and sages during his time who held a contrary view. This argument appears untenable and should be rejected since Manu chose to refer to only three Vedas in his seminal work Manusmṛti, which was not compilation of only his opinion, but "the culmination of the work of several authors". "By the early centuries of the common era, Manu had become, and remained, the standard source of authority in the Orthodox tradition for that centrepiece of Hinduism, *Varṇāśrama-Dharma*."[6] Furthermore, early Buddhist literature (~400 BC) mentions only three Vedas. This supports the contention that up to the time of the Manusmṛti (200 BC to 100 AD), Atharva had not earned a place for itself among the Vedas. It is challenging to say with any degree of certainty when this position changed.

Atharva Veda : Reference in other Vedas

If it is assumed that different parts of the Atharvaveda came into existence at different times - some pre-dating or coeval with the Ṛgveda, and others much later in time - only then is there a possibility of Atharvaveda finding a mention in the Ṛgveda. On the other hand, if the Atharvaveda came into existence (or came to be recognised) as a Veda, in part or as a whole, later than the other three Vedas, then such a reference would obviously not be available in the Ṛgveda. There is also a third possibility: that different books or parts of Atharvaveda existed in the Ṛgvedic times but had not been compiled into a single text, hence, there is no reference of the fourth Veda in the Ṛgvedic texts.

Whatever be the reason, it is certain that there is no mention of Atharva as a Veda anywhere in the Ṛgveda. In fact, there is no mention of the existence of the fourth Veda anywhere, even though in the Ṛg, Yajur and Sāma Vedas find frequent mention.

From that great general sacrifice *ṛcas* and Sāma hymns were born:
Therefrom were spells and charms produced; the *Yajus* had its birth from it.
Puruṣa (RV X.90.9)

One plies his constant task reciting verses. One sings the holy psalm in *Sakvari* measures.

One more, the *Brahmaṇa*, tells the lore of being, and one lays down the rules of sacrificing.

Jnanam (RV X.71.11)

It is important to note that the above quoted mantras belong to the tenth *manḍala* - the youngest of the Ṛgveda *manḍalas* - and along with the first *manḍala*, widely believed to be a much later addition. This means that when the tenth *manḍala* was added to the main body of the Ṛgveda, Atharva had either not been compiled as a Veda, or if already compiled, was not recognised as one. Otherwise, *Puruṣasūkta* had no reason to ignore it. Furthermore, names of ṛṣis Atharvans, Angiras and Bhṛgu frequently occur in the Ṛgveda, but nowhere are they mentioned as having made any literary contributions towards 'a fourth' Veda. The centrality of magic and sorcery to Atharva, despite many of these practices being well known and in vogue even in early Ṛgvedic times, could have been a strong reason for its exclusion from the house of Vedas.

Maurice Bloomfield, an associate of Whitney, who contributed hugely to the translation and commentary of the Atharvaveda, gives strong counter arguments: "There is no positive evidence - barring the *argumentum ex silentio* - that the names current in other texts as designations of Atharvan hymns (*bheśajani*, *Atharvanah*, *Angirasah*, et cetera) were unknown at the earliest period of literary activity." Bloomfield further argues that "the sorcery and house practices there were in India at all times", and, "the failure of the Ṛgveda to mention any systematic redaction of charms by a collective name like *Atharvāṅgirasa* must be gauged by the slenderness of its opportunities to mention the Veda as a generic name or Vedic collections or redactions in particular."[7]

There is one direct reference to the fourth Veda '*Atharvāṅgirasa*', in the Atharva Veda (translation- Griffith) -

> Who out of many, tell me, is that *Skambha*
> From whom they hewed the *ṛcas* off, from whom they
> chipped the *Yajus*, he
> Whose hairs are Sāma-verses and his mouth the *Atharvāngi*-verses?
> (AV. X.7.20)
> To sacrifice, to worshipper, hymns, songs, and healing charms, we speak,
> To priestly acts and *Yajus* texts: may they deliver us from woe.
> (AV. XI.6.14)

We come across Atharvana and *Angirasa* again in the nineteenth *kānda*, the hymn in the praise of *kāla*; albeit a connection has to be drawn from *ṛca* and *Yajus* made earlier in the third mantra.

> In *Kāla* erst the text produced what is and what is yet to be.
> From *Kāla* sprang the *ṛcas*, and from *Kāla* was the *Yajus* born.
> They formed in *Kāla* sacrifice, eternal portion for the Gods.
> In *Kāla* the *Gandharvas* and *Apsarās* and worlds abide.
> Atharvan and this *Angiras* in *Kāla* are supreme o'er heaven.
> Both this world and the world that is most lofty, the pure worlds and pure
> intermediate spaces
> (AV. XIX.54.3- 5.)

The first prose hymn of homage (to ṛṣis and *Brahman*) to various portions of the Atharvaveda again makes a direct reference in the first five chapters of '*Angirasanamadyāiyah*' texts -

> With the first five chapters of the Angirases, Hail!
> To the sixth, Hail!
> (AV. XIX.22.1-2)

A more direct reference perhaps comes in the prose hymn of homage to various portions of the Atharvaveda classed according to the number of verses contained in their hymns -

Hail to the four-verse strophes of the Atharvanas. (AV. XIX.23.1)

Together, these references in the Atharvaveda strangely indicate reluctance, if not aversion, to using the term 'Veda' for this fourth composition. Bloomfield again, generously, feels that it is not a case of conscious neglect or contempt "but rather of esoteric restriction to the sphere of the great Vedic ritual (*śrauta*)."[8]

He goes on to add that additional Atharvana passages (I X.6.1, 2; X I.7.5, 24; 8.23; X I I.1.38; XV.3.6 - 8; 6.3), wherein Atharvana is not mentioned alongside other Vedic compositions, indicate that the Atharvaveda, "unlike ritualistic adjuncts, is in no wise engaging either in the self-glorification, or in polemics against the other Vedas."[9]

The position is similar in the other two Vedas. The first three Vedas, by their very nature, relate to *śrauta* performances, and contain numerous mantras that qualify as magical or relating to Atharvan charms. Whether it is Ṛg, Sāma or Yajur Veda, Atharvans form an integral part of Vedic sacrifice. But there is a fundamental difference between these applications and what we find in the Atharvaveda. Bloomfield was unambiguous about the distinction between Atharvan practices in the three Vedas, and Atharvan practices of black magic and sorcery in the Atharvaveda: "In the *sruti* literature, the sphere of the Atharvan is restricted to matters that are incidental and subsidiary, intended merely to pave the way for the main issue, the successful despatching of the sacrifice to the gods, and the undisturbed gratification of the priests (the *iṣtam* and the *pūrtam*)."[10] These claims are substantially different in the case of Atharvan applications meant for private purposes and selfish gains. While the charm to arouse the passionate love of a woman is understandable, the charm to make the rival sterile is definitely a very private use of Atharvan.

All our thoughts do ye, *O Mitra* and *Varuṇa*, drive out of! Then having deprived her of her will put her into my power alone! (AV. I I I.2 5.6)

Turn him into a eunuch that wears his hair dressed, and into one that wears a hood! Then *Índra* with a pair of stones shall break his testicles both! (AV. VI.138.2)

Whether it is *bheṣajani* or *abhicārini*, the objective of these charms makes them qualify as '*jādu-toṇa*' or black magic.

Bloomfield (1855-1922) - a Sanskritist, scholar of Vedas, and Professor of Sanskrit and Philology at Hopkins University - explains that the *śrauta* texts devote themselves to the mention and laudation of *traividyā* either without recounting its literary varieties or by full citation of the terms Ṛg, Sāma and Yajur. On the other hand, whenever the *śrauta* texts mention or draw upon other literary forms like *itihāsa*, Purāṇa, *gātha*, *sūtra*, Upaniṣads and others, the Atharvan literature is almost unfailingly included. Usually, they follow the order of first *traividyā*, then Atharvana, *itihāsa*, et cetera.[11]

Surprisingly, the *gṛhya sūtras*, where one expects frequent references to the Atharva Veda because of its very nature (i.e. its dependence on *Atharvanic* practices and the *vidhāna* literature) seem to rely more on Ṛg, Sāma and Yajur Vedas. According to Bloomfield, the *gṛhya sūtras* of Gobhila and Khādira, and Āpstamba "do not seem to mention the Atharva at all; *Asvalāyana* (i.e. I I.3.1 - 3) on the occasion of the *Swādhyāya* recommends Atharvan."[12] However, we can find the reference of Brahma Veda in *gṛhya sūtras* of *ankh* (I.16.3), of Atharvāṅgirasa in Hiraṇyakeśin (I I.3.9) and of Atharvaveda in (I I.1 8.3; 20.9). In *Pārakara Gṛhya Sūtras* I I.1 0.7, the fourth Veda is directly mentioned as Atharvaveda.[13]

Thus, it is safe to conclude that the completed *Atharvāṅgirasa* texts are slightly younger than Yajurveda and Sāmaveda, but they did not attain 'Veda ' status until the *sūtra* period (or later epic period). *Śāṅkhayana śrautasūtra* is perhaps the first text to call the collection 'Atharvaveda', even though Manu's code only talks about three Vedas. However, the Mahābhārata fully considers and advertises Atharva as the fourth Veda.

Magic - black and white

As observed above, the predominant characteristic of Atharvaveda is neither it's philosophical *sūktas* in fair number, nor the *sūktas* related to a king and his rule; it is magic and charm, sorcery and witchcraft (Oxford dictionary: The practice of magic, especially black magic, use of spells and invocation of spirits) which sets it apart from the other three Vedas. The debate on the status of Atharva as a Veda remained unsettled for centuries, until the times of Mahābhārata and *Sāṃkhya Sūtras*. These texts clearly referred to Atharva as the fourth Veda. It is almost certain that the occultly content was the biggest obstacle to the inclusion of these texts alongside the three preeminent Vedas. However, this line of thinking poses yet another argument - magic and charm are not peculiar to the Atharvaveda alone, all the three Vedas have hymns unambiguously of 'non-serious' nature, and these occurrences are not exceptional. They can neither be ignored using the 'exception proves the rule' logic, nor be treated as an 'odd example of a later date inclusion or interpolation'. These mantras are there because the sages wanted them to be there, to be read and applied on appropriate occasions. What distinguishes the Atharvaveda from the other three is the quantity and quality of magic and charm hymns.

Since the beginning of civilized societies, every culture has believed in magic and charms (Oxford dictionary: an object or saying believed to have magic power) and practiced them. Despite the dawn of the age of logical reasoning and advances in the field of science and technology, this belief has not disappeared. The only change is perhaps the scale at which such magic and charms are now practised. Interestingly, although the number of practitioners has dwindled, the belief in magic and charm has not significantly reduced. Human belief and faith in the possibility of achieving desired results through irrational, inexplicable and unrelated acts appear to be unshakeable. Whether it is writing an exam using a lucky pen for better results, or belief that a black cat crossing the traveller's path brings bad luck, both are manifestations of faith in (and practice of) the same magic and charm, though admittedly by different names. In another instance, the Azande tribe in Central Africa are known to rub a curved crocodile tooth on a banana leaf in the hope that the tree would regenerate bananas, just like the crocodile does its fallen tooth. This tribe is guided by the same belief that makes a famous cricketer in England put his right foot first in his slippers while getting out of bed in the morning, in the hope of scoring a test century that day. But when it comes to these beliefs and practices, unfortunately, matters quite don't stop there. Soon, believers of magic start looking towards appropriating the neighbour's plot of land, or the love of his beautiful wife, or even wishing death for the enemy. It is the latter variety of such practices (meant to inflict harm) that distinguish the magical practices of Atharvaveda from the other three Vedas. These occult-like practices of the Atharvaveda are called *abhicārni*. They are qualitatively different from magical practices aimed at acquiring a beautiful girl for a bride, a good harvest, good health, riddance from fever or leprosy, et cetera. The Atharvaveda is a potent armoury of abundant *abhicārni* hymns/practices for different situations.

The use of *gandā-taveej* (charm amulet) is not peculiar to Indian civilisation alone. Many other societies across the world have believed in the effectiveness of charms since ancient times. The Atharvaveda recommends a variety of herbal charms for preventing diseases, akin to modern-day inoculation against smallpox and diphtheria. It has a fair number of mantras for maintaining good health as well as ridding the body of several diseases, along with hymns of praises for herbal medicines. But why should these mantras for prevention and cure of diseases be the reason for ostracization of the Atharva from the house of Vedas? It may sound strange to us, but the Ṛgvedic Āryans treated practitioners of medicine as impure, a class of people in whose presence the Sāmaveda chanting was halted! The reason for such a practice is obscure, but it appears that the practitioners of medicine had to physically make contact with and/or be in constant close proximity of their patients, rendering them 'untouchable'. But that still doesn't explain why this physical impurity or lack of '*śauca*', apart from making them unsuitable and unsafe for physical contact, rendered them unfit to even hear, from a distance, chanting of the Vedas?

For many centuries, these two peculiarities (black magic and practice of medicine) appear to have prevented Atharva from attaining the status of 'the fourth' Veda.

So how did *Atharvanists* manage to break down this wall of segregation and make a place for themselves at the high table of the Vedas?

The *brahmaṇas* and the *kṣatriyas* joined hands to make this shared objective possible. They came up with a potent combination: the might of the *kṣatriyas* as rulers came to be aligned with the power of knowledge, and interpretation of religion, exercised by the *brahmaṇas*. While the *brahmaṇas* were constantly looking for economic and political supremacy, the kings continually strived to expand their kingdoms and secure them from enemies. For this, they sought the extra help of the power of magic and sorcery which only the *brahmaṇas* could provide.

A king was dependent on the *brahmaṇas* for all rituals relating to his consecration as the ruler and, subsequently, for conducting *yajñas* without which no ruler could continue his reign. He had an army to protect the boundaries of his kingdom, to attack, conquer, and subjugate other kingdoms. But all this was not possible with the might of the army alone - the magical support of powerful rituals was considered an absolute must. Not only that, it was impossible for any ruler to survive without conducting various *śrauta* ceremonies, especially *aśvamedha* and *rajasūya*, which could only be accomplished with the help of *brahmaṇas*. In fact, with the arrival of more Āryans and formations of new urban centres and kingdoms in the Kuru-Panchala range, Videha region became increasingly populated. People of these newly emerging Videha kingdoms had migrated from the core of *Āryavratta* lands, a distinguishing feature of their identity. Despite the geographical relocation, the identity of their native land had to be visibly kept alive. Kings like Janaka and Ajātaśatru achieved this by encouraging immigration of heavy weights, such as Yājñavalkya, into their kingdoms. In front of the public, they took the likes of Uddālaka head-on (at times nine or eleven of them combined) and decimated them in the *śāstrārtha* (debate on Dharma). This helped the *kṣatriya* rulers establish credibility as belonging to the original Āryan stock despite their geographical relocation.

An interesting development was thus underway. The *kṣatriya* and *brahmaṇa*'s mutual dependence grew exponentially - their common interests conveniently converging like never before. The *brahmaṇas* seized this opportunity and carved out a permanent new position for themselves in the courts of these kings - office of *purohita* or private chaplain.

The *brahmaṇas* eventually accomplished three goals -

(i) They managed to get the *Atharvanic* texts, 'a compilation' of - what were so far - peripheral practices of magic and charm, the status of the fourth Veda, the *BrahmaVeda* or Atharvaveda.

(ii) A *brahmaṇa* earlier oversaw the *hotṛ*, *udgātṛ* and *adhvaryu* priests, during a *śrauta yajña* ceremony, and intervened if he noticed any errors in proceedings; now he was required to be an *Atharvanic* practitioner as well. This made the

Atharvaveda priests supervisor of the Ṛg, Sāma and Yajur Veda priests.

(iii) They institutionalised the position of *purohita* in court of every king. Without a *purohita*, not only were some of the most important rituals impossible to conduct, but because the Atharvaveda enjoined "the gods, the fathers, and the twice born (priests) do not receive the oblation of the king in whose house there is no guru that is skilled in the Atharavana" (2.3) it became mandatory for every king to have a *purohita* who was an *Atharvavedin*.

Each of these achievements is an outstanding example of 'environment management' which would make any modern-day management guru proud. Social and political opinions were moulded and managed in a remarkable manner to achieve the desired objectives. Let's take the case of *Atharvanic* texts attaining the status of a Veda. As we have seen, the Vedas are *apauruṣeya* (self-existent). They were revealed through the ṛṣis, but not created by them. They simply re-emerge after every *mānvantara* (when all creation is annihilated and recreated); the Vedas are perpetual. Mythologically speaking, the Vedas were produced from the exhalation of god *Brahman*. Thus, whatever the Vedas revealed was the ultimate truth, the ultimate source of knowledge and the fountainhead of Dharma.

Now, as discussed before, the three *Saṃhitās* do not mention the existence of Atharvaveda anywhere, nor do the second or third layers of the Vedas, i.e. *Brahmaṇa* and Āraṇyaka/Upaniṣad. Time and again only *traividyā* and the corresponding three Vedas (Ṛg, Sāma and Yajur Vedas) find mention in the Vedic texts. A millennium down the line, Buddhism emerged in the neighbourhood of the Videha region. Fortunately, Buddhist literature is available to us from Indian sources as well as foreign travellers who have commented, at length, on the Vedic religion practiced in India. All authentic early Buddhist writings of this period (~400-100 BC) only speak of three Vedas. And later, Manu, the great lawgiver of his time, also only spoke of three Vedas and the *traividyā*. All the *śrauta* rituals up to this period talk of Ṛg, Sāma and Yajur Vedas, and the three classes of priests (*hotṛ*, *udgātṛ* and *adhvaryu*) associated with each of these Vedas. The ritual texts are categorical when they talk of the role of the fourth priest, the *brahmaṇa*, who, so to speak, was the stage manager of the whole show. He ensured that the three priests carried out their duties properly, and pointed out if any errors were made.

In this watertight compartment of self-existent *triveda* (three Vedas) and *traividyā* (triple learning), how did a fourth Veda find acceptance from people and sages alike? It must be recognised as the biggest and most successful exercise in the history of moulding public opinion - a *coup de maître*, a master stroke. Undoubtedly, the *brahmaṇas* and the *kṣatriya* kings were interested parties and played a key role in this endeavour. But any such endeavour could hardly have succeeded unless the society itself didn't, in large measure, believe in, or was susceptible to, concepts like magic.

Brahman and *Brahmaveda* - A deliberate misinterpretation by *Athrvavedins*?

Let's see how and why.

Magic existed much before religion emerged. But even today, we find it difficult to clearly grasp what magic is, and have far greater clarity with respect to religion. It will be instructive to study how these two practices - magic and religion - evolved in tribal societies in the recent past (and continue to do so in the present), and the influence of scientific developments on this evolution, especially the medical sciences. Among tribal communities, the role of a medical practitioner was often rolled into one with that of the magician, or perhaps the other way around - magic playing a more dominant role in every-day life. What could not be achieved by human endeavour and available knowledge was achieved through intercession of (external) agencies like spirits and witches. It was the shaman, or the Druid who made intercession of these spirits possible (or enabled the powers) either through coercion or supplication. As these societies evolved, clearer and firmer outlines of what came to be 'religion' emerged. The duties of the man who could call upon these spirits were redefined and came to be labelled 'priestly'. The magico-medical practitioner now became the priest. Thus, as societies evolved, the magical and medical practices were closely intertwined, the jobs eventually rolling into one - the shaman's. And later, when religion arrived, yet another, the third strand was added to the existing two. This pattern of evolution is evident in all ancient religions - Egyptian, Greek, and Chinese - and Vedic religion was no exception.

There is sufficient evidence that supports the presence of human habitation in this part of the world even when the Āryans arrived. There is also enough evidence to prove there was give-and-take between the Āryans and non-Āryans over the centuries, not only in terms of commerce, but also socially and culturally. The older inhabitants, regardless of their religion (since their religious practices are unclear) and the new arrivals, the Āryans, influenced each other mutually; the interactions even led to alliances in marriages.

The first literary text of the Āryans, the Ṛgveda, has more than a few mantras classified as magic mantras. This could be attributed to the existence of such practices among Vedic Āryans before their arrival in India, or the interaction and intermingling of the Āryans with the indigenous population consequent to their settlement in the foothills of Himalayas, Sapta-Sindhu and the Doab. It is more than likely that the Vedic Āryans arrived in India carrying with them a fair share of magico-medical practices (and beliefs) of their own, which both influenced, and were influenced by, the practices of the non-Āryans. A small number of magic mantras in Ṛgveda indicate these were not considered very important. At the same time, the very presence of magic mantras in these holiest of the holy texts of Āryans, tells us, these were considered important enough to find a place in these texts.

Without going into details, it is important to appreciate that magic, in this context, was not merely about winning the love of a neighbour's wife or destroying the virility of the man next door. It was about a king winning a war, a businessman completing a trip successfully, a profitable commercial transaction or safeguarding the wealth and happiness of a household from evil eyes or spirits. It was equally about protection from diseases, recovery from various illnesses and ailments, and good health.

Although there is little evidence of black magic in the Ṛgveda, we almost certainly know that a wide range of magic or medical practices did exist at that time the world over. Herein lies the important point - given that good and bad magical practices existed in Ṛgvedic times, why did the *abhicāra* - practices which cause harm to others - find no mention in the Ṛgveda? The exclusion of black magic or *abhicāra* meant excluding not only those practices, but also the practitioners or followers of these 'inferior' customs from mainstream Vedic Hinduism. In other words, the *shamans* or priests were shut out from Ṛgvedic (good) practices probably because they did not have the required skills, knowledge, inclination or abilities to join mainstream religion. These were the *Atharvanic* practitioners. Not only did they stand to lose economically from this exclusion, they were about to lose their superior position in society as agents of spirits, witches and demons. Their black magic had put them on a high pedestal, and exclusion from the Ṛgveda meant coming down to the level of mere pedestrians!

At the cost of repetition, it is important to note that the Ṛgveda did incorporate magic practices organic to Āryans and even non-Āryans local inhabitants, thereby sanctifying the magico-medical practices. Since black magic mantras and practices are totally absent in the Ṛgveda, it can be inferred that they were considered unfit for a place in the Ṛgveda 's main body. It is safe to say that the Ṛgveda had no issues with magic or magico-medical practices per se, and in fact, shared a common belief in efficacy of these practices with the non-Āryans, leaving the door open for proponents of Atharavana magico-medical followers to eventually find a place for themselves in the house of Vedas. This was made possible because of vested interests - powerful *kṣatriyas* who believed in magical rituals for extra protection, in addition to their army; and the common man who was not satisfied simply by winning the love of the damsel next-door, but wanted to destroy the wealth of his enemy. These baser instincts could only be satisfied through black magic. The recipe for good health, wealth and happiness (as prescribed in the Ṛgveda) was not enough for these ends. The Atharavana practices were their answer to these unchaste goals. Hence, the two interests - of the *Atharvanic* practitioners/priests, and those who stood to gain from these baser practices coalesced. When the time was ripe, these forces came together to elevate the *Atharvanic* texts to the status of the fourth Veda.

However, this did not come to pass until the *Atharvanists* incorporated major changes in their texts. Discussions on *Brahman* and matters of creation as well as speculative texts, outnumbering even those in the Ṛgveda, were incorporated into *Atharvanic* texts. Whether this was purely a strategical move, or the thinkers genuinely adapted and accepted Ṛgvedic concepts may perhaps never be known with certainty.

It would be wrong to conclude that the *Atharvanists* were solely responsible for creating the post of *purohita* in the courts of kings. The credit, or blame, cannot be laid at the feet of the *Atharvanists* alone. *Atreya Brahmaṇa*, a *Brahmaṇa* attached to Ṛgveda *Saṃhitā*, describes the functions of a *purohita* and his relationship with the king, which confirms that this office did exist in Ṛgvedic times. In the Atharvaveda, the *purohita* safeguards the king's royalty, strength, empire and people (VI I I.2 4.7). His people do not die young, his own life's breath does not leave him before he has reached the full limits of his life and he lives to a ripe old age. A *brahmaṇa* imbued with this knowledge and holding the position of a *purohita* becomes the shepherd of the kingdom. The subjects of such a king are loyal and obedient (VI I I.2 5.2 - 3). Even Manu, who refused to accept Atharavana as a Veda, recommended that a priest should not hesitate to deploy the revealed canonical texts of the Atharavana and Angiras, and since speech is the weapon of the priest, a twice born man can slay the enemies with it (MS X I.33). These *purohitas* were undoubtedly familiar with the magic rites which formed a part of the Ṛgveda *Saṃhitās* and the *Saṃhitās* of the Sāmaveda and Yajurveda.

Priest - As *guru*, magician, healer, and *purohita* rolled into one

In the early Vedic period, the main function of the priests was to conduct *śrauta* rituals. All *kāmya* was achieved through the power of *yajña* conducted by purohits. Additionally, as a guru, the priest advised the king in matters relating to Dharma - the Righteous path - and guided him to the path leading to *brahmajñān* (knowledge of *Brahman*) through philosophical speculation. *Yajña*, the Righteous path, and the *brahmajñān*, could all do with a bit of help from another source - magic. In the words of Bloomfield, given the situation that "the interests of the King and the Sovereignty (*kṣatriya* and *kṣatram*) are too obviously dependent upon magic rites", it was natural to assume that "at all periods the safety of the King, the prosperity of his people, his ascendancy over hostile neighbours, must have depended upon the skill of his *purohita* in magic."[14] Under the circumstances, it made eminent sense for the king to look for Atharvana priest who could perform this role and provide extra protection. This called for two *purohitas* with different expertise and trainings - an expert in *rājakarmaṇi*, and another who specialised in Atharvana practices that provided security to the kingdom and the king through magic and charm. Hence, the king readily supported the *Atharvanic* proposition that a *purohita* must be from the *Atharvanic* stock. Not all practitioners of Veda were prepared to acquire 'the baser' knowledge associated with *Atharvanic* practices, and chose to stay out of the race. But *Atharvanic* practitioners did not have any qualms about learning the *traividyā*, which was not forbidden to them in any case.

And finally, let us also discuss briefly, whether the *Atharvavedins* really possessed knowledge of *śrauta* ceremonies and practiced it in real life, or did they simply put forth these arguments to usurp positions of *purohita* and supervisor priest in *śrauta* ceremonies. To better understand this matter, we can examine the evidence available to us from the Atharvaveda itself. Apart from devoting more space than the Ṛgveda to speculative and theosophical matters, the Atharvaveda deals with *Brahman vidyā* extensively, and includes "mantras which could have had no sense and purpose except in connection with *śrauta* performances - series of formulae like AV. (VI.47 and 48) have no meaning except in connection with the three daily presses of *Soma* (*savana*), and the *Vait. Sūtra* (21.7) exhibits them, properly no doubt, as part of an ordinary *śrauta* rite, the *Agniṣṭoma*."[15] Apart from six chapters of *Prāyaścitta* in *Vaitana Sūtra*, evidence that the *Atharvavedins* practiced *śrauta* rites is presented by the hymns which are expiatory formulas for faults committed at the sacrifice in Atharva Veda (VI.114). No text would go to the extent of cooking up records to show how to correct the faults committed at the sacrifice by way of inclusion of expiatory formulas. Bloomfield sums it up thus - "It would seem then that *Atharvavedins* possessed the knowledge of, and practised, *śrauta* rites prior to the conclusion of the present redactions of the hymns and thus perhaps, after all, the *purohita* in case of his being an upper one was not altogether unequipped for taking a hand in the broader Vedic rites with the three fires and the usual assortment of priests."[16]

Contents of the Atharvaveda

Let's take a brief look at the contents of the Atharvaveda. It contains twenty books which are a mix of verse and prose. There are prayers for the destruction of the enemies as well as prayers to various deities for protection, prosperity, health and happiness. There are hymns meant to secure the supremacy of the king's throne and his consecration benediction; spells for childbirth, for curing a woman's infertility or conceiving a baby boy; a charm to gain a young man's love, et cetera. The second *kāṇḍa* looks at the causality of everything apart from prayers for protection against the enemy and charms to cure diseases. It also instructs the use of amulets and prayers to get a wonderful husband for a girl. Apart from the usual charms for curing ailments, the third *kāṇḍa* also includes blessings for a newly built house, prayers for triumph in battle and increasing a king's strength. The fourth *kāṇḍa* has charms and prayers for protection, health, rain, ridding the body of poison and healing broken bones, besides charms for acquiring superhuman powers of sight and success in gambling.

The fifth *kāṇḍa* has charms against fever, witchcraft, worms and other sicknesses, and conceiving a child. This *kāṇḍa* includes hymns that condemn harassing *brahmaṇas*. The sixth *kāṇḍa*, apart from prayers and charms against diseases, contains love charms, mantras to ensure the birth of a son and to strengthen his growth. It also contains prayers for peace, security, prosperity, power, health and longevity. The seventh *kāṇḍa* also has charms that are said to help achieve success in battle and prayers for the prosperity of a king and his kingdom, apart from charms to win a wife's favour, banish problems, enemies and demons. There are prayers in praise of sacrifices to attain fruits of secret knowledge and to obtain knowledge of the Vedas. This *kāṇḍa* also contains funeral hymns, a charm for a king to make his subjects obedient and a few verses for sacrifices.

The eighth *kāṇḍa* hints at the possibility of recovering a dying man, charms for removing evil spirits and demons, and invocations against a hostile army. There are two hymns of great interest here - the first deals with cosmological and ritual doctrines, and the second concerns the mystical concept of *Viraj*. As per the Ṛgveda, this secondary creator was born from *Puruṣa*. The ninth *kāṇḍa* has hymns in praise of *karma* and a few that elaborate on cosmological doctrines. The tenth *kāṇḍa* has a non-*Puruṣa* and *skambha* (the basis or support for all existence), and begins with a charm against witchcraft! There are speculative hymns on a supreme being and a hundredfold oblation. The eleventh *kāṇḍa* contains verses for a boiled rice mixture used in sacrifices such as the *brahmaudāna*; prayers to *Bhava*, *Sarva* and *Rudra*; spells to destroy a hostile army and speculations on the origins of gods and creation. The *kāṇḍa* is known for funeral hymns and *Ahina* to *Pṛthvī*. The thirteenth *kāṇḍa* contains hymns praising *Rohita* (a form of fire and sun) as the highest being. The fourteenth *kāṇḍa* has hymns dealing with marriage ceremonies and the marriage of *Suryā*, the sun god *Sūrya's* daughter.

The fifteenth and sixteenth *kāṇḍas* are a mix of prose and verses difficult to interpret. These hymns deal with *Vrātya* - a group of people who did not follow the Vedas or the brahmanical guidelines, and were often ascetic wonderers. The sixteenth *kāṇḍa* also includes charms and blessings.

The seventeenth *kāṇḍa* is unique and contains only one hymn - a prayer to *Índra*, where *Índra* is identified with *Viṣṇu* and the sun.

The eighteenth *kāṇḍa* has funeral ceremonies partly taken from the Ṛgveda. The nineteenth has hymns which are philosophical, offered to various deities including *kāma* and *kāla*, and for victory in battle. There are charms for the destruction of enemies, against disease, for good health, long life and in favour of a newly elected king. It contains hymns praising amulets and curative herbs, the *Puruṣasūkta* and a prayer to twenty-eight *nakṣatras*. Importantly, it has mantras and prayers to be used with sacrifice.

The twentieth *kāṇḍa* has 143 hymns, most of them from the Ṛgveda. The new additions to the Ṛgveda hymns are part of a sacrificial ritual called *kuntapa* hymns.

Importance of the Atharvaveda

The importance of the Atharva Veda lies in its addition to the list of the Vedas after a delay of nearly a millennium. This indicates an obvious resistance by the purists among Vedic Āryans, who were not prepared to accept texts containing magic or medical practices as part of Vedas. The first three Vedas were only about power of *yajña*, the belief that it could coerce even the gods into submission. The *yajña* was supreme and could help mortals achieve just about anything - it could elevate them to the status of gods and above. With the induction of Atharva as the fourth Veda, the pure stream of *yajñik Vedism* became a stream of mixed ideologies. One may call Atharavana practices contained in Atharvaveda by any name, the fact remains that these went against the original teachings of the Ṛgveda, which were about the good of all. Admittedly, the Ṛgveda had its own share of magical mantras, but those mantras were for the greater good - *abhisjaya*. The Atharvaveda, despite containing matters concerning *Brahman*, is predominantly a Veda of non-serious matters and, unfortunately, many mantras are meant to adversely affect the lives of fellow members of society. The Atharvaveda also diverted the flow of the mainstream Vedic ideology from *śrauta* (public ceremonies) to Atharavana ceremonies, which were essentially private in nature. This gave rise to a major shift in Vedic religion.

Chapter 12

The ritual sacrifice - *Yajña*

It is likely that the simple act of expressing gratitude towards the gods for their blessings soon changed, in the words of Monier, to "seek(ing) the favour of celestial beings capable of conferring good or inflicting harm on crops, flocks, and herds," and "was conciliated by offerings and oblations of all kinds, and especially of the products of the soil."[1] Men assumed what pleased them must also please the gods. So they offered food and gifts to the gods in a manner that they would like to receive such tributes themselves. However, the gods were invisible and the only sensible way of ensuring that the nourishments reached them was vaporising the solid and liquid offerings by putting them in fire. Since drinking *soma* juice was so exhilarating for humans, it was poured into the fire so the gods too could have that most extraordinary experience. It is easy to imagine the genesis of *homa* in these actions before the Vedic Āryans formalised them as *yajña*.

The *Puruṣasūkta* of the Ṛgveda narrates that this creation emerged as a result of the great primordial sacrifice of the parts of the body of *Puruṣa*, the primeval man. This famous hymn, in which *Puruṣa* is the sacrificial offering, spring the clarified butter, summer the fuel, and autumn the oblation, belongs to the tenth *maṇḍala*, universally acknowledged as the last of the additions to the Ṛgveda. But *yajñas* were central to the Ṛgveda long before the *Puruṣasūkta*; they predate the tenth *maṇḍala*, the imitation of the act of *Prajāpati* (creator of heaven and earth, the chief god), and the Śatapatha Brahmaṇa by centuries. It is well established that in the pre-*Prajāpati* period there existed a rich tradition of *yajñas* in the Ṛgveda (e.g. *agnicayana*) which had its genesis elsewhere i.e. other than the myth of the primordial man. But after the advent of the *Puruṣasūkta*, the purpose of all *yajñas* came to be defined as, "This (ritual act) done now is that which the gods did then (in the beginning)." (SB. 7.2.1.4; 9.2.3.4) All older Ṛgvedic *yajñas* also came to be performed with this new objective.

As more Brahmaṇa texts were composed, the *śrauta* rituals began to occupy centre stage; ritualism proliferated and became extremely complex resulting in an exponential growth of sacerdotalism.

The meaning and purpose of *yajña* underwent further change in the *sūtra* period (800-400 BC). Āpastamba, in his Yajña Paribhāshā Sūtra (literally - *yajña* definition rules/aphorism), observes: "*Yajña*, sacrifice, is an act by which we surrender something for the sake of the gods. Such an act must rest on a sacred authority (*āgama*), and serve for man's salvation (*sreyo*rtha*)."[1a] According to Āpastamba, *yajñas* were prescribed by the three Vedas (*sūtra* III) for the three *varṇa*s - *brahmaṇa*, *kṣatriya*, and *vaiśya* (*sūtra* II), and should be considered synonymous with *yaga* and *iṣṭi*.

The system of sacrifice (*yajña*), which started as an expression of gratitude for blessings received from the Vedic gods and 'for man's salvation', soon transformed into propitiation. Sacrificial offerings began to be made to the gods not just as gratitude for blessings received or man's salvation but also for attaining worldly pleasures and gains.

The great sage Manu (200 BC-200 AD) observes, "Not a single act here (below i.e. in this world) appears ever to be done by a man free from desire; for whatever (man) does, it is (the result of) the impulse of desire."[2]

Manu attributes a single factor behind every action of human beings - *kāma* (desire). What are these human desires?

The natural desire of human beings is to have sexual and emotional enjoyment, and material pleasure (*artha*). Sage Vātsyāyana, better known worldwide for his treatise on 'the art of love making' Kāmasūtras, defines *artha*[3] as -

The acquisition of arts, land, gold, cattle, wealth, equipages and friends. It is, further, the protection of what is acquired, and the increase of what is protected.[3]

It is this 'desire' that makes us do what we do in this world. It is all about the fulfilment of *kāmya*.

The Vedic religion believes that through *yajña*/sacrifice, a man can achieve the desired objectives in this life - from wealth (*prasava*), food (*vaja*), health (*anāmaya*), mental acuity (*dhīti*), vigour (*ojas*), friendship (*anamitram*), fearlessness (*abhaya*), tranquality (*sarma*), to enlightenment (*jyoti*) and more (XVIII.1-10). The Yajurveda Saṃhitā declares that it is indeed possible to attain *svarga* through *yajña*. Thus, a Hindu has assurance from the highest religious authority - the Vedas - that no matter what his desire, material or spiritual, it is attainable through a properly performed sacrifice (*yajña*).

Types of *yajña*

The Vedas speak of 400 *yajñas*, which can be broadly segregated into four categories:

i) *Swadhyāya yajña*

ii) *Japa yajña*
iii) *Karma yajña*
iv) *Mānasa yajña*

Swadhyāya is self-study, a *yajña* that is carried out sitting at the feet of the guru in the *gurukula. Japa yajña* is constant repetition of mantras and focusing the mind. *Karma yajña* is performed through sacrificial rites; and in the *manas yajña*, also known as *Ātma yajña*, the entire sacrifice is internalised. This last is considered the most powerful and also the most difficult *yajña* to perform. Each of these *yajñas* is believed to be ten times more efficacious than the previous one.

All ritualistic rites involving *karma*, performed in accordance with procedures detailed in the concerned Vedic literature fall under the category of *karma yajñas*. Though the names of some of the *karma yajñas*, such as *aśvamedha* and *rajasūya yajña*, are familiar to us through mythological stories and their picturization in television shows, in real life these have nearly disappeared. They are hardly ever performed anywhere, except in certain parts of states of Maharashtra, Andhra, Karnataka, Tamil Nadu and Kerala, where many of these practices are kept alive - more particularly among the *Nambūdiri brahmaṇas* of Kerala. *Yajña*, *yāga*, *yagana*, and *iṣṭi* are considered synonymous.[4]

There are twenty-six main *karma yajñas*, classified under four heads -

i *Panca mahā yajña* (numbering 5) - Every man is indebted to five (Sanskrit: *panca*) debts (*riṇas*). *Brahman, pitŕ, deva, bhūtāni* and *manuṣya yajñas* are the means by which he makes offerings to discharge each of his debt.

ii. *Sapta pāka yajñas* (numbering 7) - In this *yajña*, cooked (*pāka*) offerings, such as boiled grains mixed with butter, are offered in the *aupāsnāgni* or *gṛha agni*. These sacred fires are consecrated at the time of marriage and are kept alive by a householder until his death. *Aṣṭaka, sthalipāka, parvana, śravani, agrahayani, caitri* and *aśvāyuji* are the seven *pāka yajñas*; they help attain material gains and prosperity.

iii. *Sapta havir yajñas* (numbering 7) - *Havis* is, generally, an uncooked oblation which contains offerings of barley, rice, milk and clarified butter, poured into a consecrated Vedic fire. The seven *havir yajñas* are *agnadheya*, *agnihotṛ*, *darśa-pūrṇasmāsa*, *cāturmāsya*, *āgrayaṇa*, *nirudhapasubandha* and *sautrāmaṇī*. These *yajñas* are performed in the three *śrauta agnis*, namely *gārhapatya*, *dakṣiṇā* and *āhavanīya*.

iv. *Sapta soma yajñas* (numbering 7) - *Soma yajña* is a major sacrifice performed in an elaborate ceremony involving multiple priests and participants. In *soma yajña*, the juice of *soma* plant is the main ingredient in the offering to the gods. *Agniṣṭoma*, *atyagniṣṭoma*, *ukhtya*, *shodasi*, *vājapeya*, *atirātra* and *apotrayama* are the seven *soma yajñas*.

Kalpa

Many ṛṣis, including Āpastambaa, Aśvalāyana, Baudhāyana, Bharadvāja, Kātyāyana Satyashada, and their family names (ṛṣi *kula*) are associated with the authorship of *dharmaśāstras* called *Kalpa. Kalpa* has *śrauta*, *gṛha* and *dharma sūtras* as well as *śulba sūtras*. There are different *yajña* procedures authored by these ṛṣis, which are faithfully followed by the respective sects. Depending on whether the *yajña* was a public or a private affair, it fell under the category of *śrauta* or *gṛha* rituals. *Śrauta* rituals deal with solemn rituals, whereas *gṛha sūtras*, the householder's rituals or domestic rites.

A very important distinction between the *śrauta* and the *smṛti* (*gṛha*) rituals is the role of the priest. The *śrauta* rituals are necessarily performed by priests - their numbers vary and extend to sixteen or seventeen in certain cases, depending on the ritual. On the other hand the *gṛha* rituals (many of which are required to be performed daily) are performed by the householders themselves.

Another important distinction is the fire in which the *yajña* is conducted.

The *aupāsna agni* lit at the time of the grooms wedding is divided into two in a sacrifice called *agnyadhana*. One part becomes the *gṛhyagni* the other becomes the *śrautagni*.

Fire is taken from the *gṛhapatya* (*gṛhyagni*) and kindled in the remaining two fires.

Whereas in *śrauta* rituals, three *agnis* including *gṛhapatyāgni* had to be used, the *smṛta* ceremonies were performed in *gṛhyagni* by the householder or by those required to carry out the ceremony in his absence, at home.

The *śulba sūtras* contain principles of geometry essential to Vedic rituals, particularly in the construction of the *yajñashālā* (the place of *yajña*) and *vedi* (the fire altar).

The *Kalpa Sūtras* give detailed instructions and guidelines not only for public rites (*śrauta sūtras*) and private householder's rites (*gṛha sūtras*), but also rules of moral conduct for individuals and rulers, and laws for society, in texts called *dharma sūtras*.

With the compilation of *gṛha sūtras*, the passage ceremonies of life, such as *upnayana* and marriage - which indicate a crossover from childhood to studentship, and then to householder's life - were formalised as *saṃskāras* and became an integral part of Hindu life.

Śrauta rituals

"When taken seriously sacrifices, quite bluntly, are an act of significantly controlled death and destruction. This act purports to force access to the other world… or in simple terms one must sacrifice a cow in order to obtain cows." - (attributed to) JC Heesterman

The Vedas emphasise that every man is born with a debt - a debt to death. And this debt can only be redeemed through sacrifice. *Yajña*-centric society believed, attainment of *kāmya* (what is desired), material or otherwise, is through *yajña*; at some level it boils down to sacrificing 'a cow' to get 'many cows'. This is an important pillar on which the ideology of sacrifice rested in later Vedic times.

In accordance with the principle of 'a cow for cows', if a debt of life must be redeemed, it could only be done by giving away life. This created a huge problem in the sacrifice system. While it was (practically) possible to give away 'a' cow for 'many' cows, it was practically impossible to give away one's own life for immortality in the next life, simply because for the concerned person, it meant the end of the show.

As mentioned earlier, the scriptures exhorted men to imitate gods in the act of redemption through sacrifice. In *Brahmaṇas*, it was depicted as the sacrifice of the primordial deity, *Prajāpati* (Lord of Creatures), who was perpetually regenerated by the sacrifice: "This (ritual act) done now is that which the Gods did then (in the beginning)." (SB. 7.2.1.4; 9.2.3.4) But emulating *Prajāpati's* sacrifice, i.e. sacrificing one's own life in imitation, would have been self defeating - the *kāmya* (desired objective) of the sacrifice being immoratlity!

Therefore, when it came to redemption of *riṇas* of death, basic principle of sacrifice for redemption, was impractical, if not impossible to practice. There was an additional problem: even if one was prepared to sacrifice one's life, suicide was forbidden in all Vedic practices. So the *brahmaṇa* thinkers had to find a way to circumvent this tricky issue of debt redemption of death, without anyone having to end his life. The sages came up with a complex system of rituals to work around this dilemma. They prescribed -

i. substituting an animal's life for the life of the sacrificer, i.e. *yajamāna*
ii. sacrificer the passive role of a *yajamāna*, though he remained the main beneficiary of the *yajña*
iii. instead of the *yajamāna*, priest perform the actual sacrificial rite, thus insulating the real sacrificer (and the beneficiary of *yajña* i.e. *yajamāna*) from causing the animal's death

The word '*bandhu*' literally means one who is bound or tied - physically, notionally or metaphysically. As a concept, it is extensively used in Vedic and post-Vedic Hindu texts and practices, and differs in many ways from 'symbolic' attachment. *Bandhu* concept was extensively used in resolving the apparently insoluble problem of a sacrificer having to sacrifice his own life. Following paragraphs try to explain how the concept was put into practice -

i. The sacrificer was symbolically substituted by an animal (later even with vegetables) and/or a gold replica in the rituals. To make this symbolism as true to life as possible, a physical contact, albeit indirect (for reasons explained later), as well as an emotional and metaphysical bond had to be created between the victim (animal) and the sacrificer.

Accordingly, the sacrificer (*yajamāna*) first purchased the victim animal and became its owner. He then went through several steps designed to make this representation as total as possible, such as tying the animal overnight to a post located in his (sacrificer's) home prior to the actual killing, making indirect contact with the animal via the priest who in turn was in physical touch with the animal either directly or through a cord, et cetera. To impart an air of volunteer to the victim, the sacrifice owner, i.e. the *yajamāna*, followed an elaborate procedure of seeking permission from the victim animal's parents to proceed with the act. To further strengthen the *bandhu* bond between the *yajamāna* and the victim, the animal was tied to the *yūpa* (a post to which sacrificial animals were tied in a *yajña*) located at a prescribed distance from the scene of action and seat of the sacrificer. The *yūpa* itself was designed with specifications matching the physical attributes of the sacrificer (*yajamāna*).

ii. The sacrificer was assigned the passive role of a *yajamāna*; the priest, as an intercede, assumed the central role in this scheme of circumvention. The complexity of the *śrauta* ritual required expertise that could only be acquired through lifelong training. To that extent, even the regular 'cow for cows' rituals could not be performed by an ordinary sacrificer without the active participation of a full quorum of *hotṛ*, *udgātṛ* and other priests. The presence of these priests was critical for the success of the sacrifice as the sacrificer had to pay back his debts by giving a life in the ceremony. In this scheme of things, the priest actually performed all functions and the role of the sacrificer (*yajamāna*), and the sacrifice for actual slaughter was represented by the victim animal. In the world of *yajña*, though the *yajamāna* was the institutor, sponsor of a sacrifice, he engaged a priest to perform the ritual on his behalf. No benefit of the *yajña* accrued to the priest, he was receipient of only *dakshina* given him by the *yajamāna*. All benefit of the *yajña* went to the *yajamāna*. Thus, the priest played the role of a cut-out and a *bandhu*. The *yajamāna*, who had to be in physical contact with the victim, instead made physical contact with the priest (his representative) who in turn contacted the victim.

For victim animal to represent the sacrificer, it was important that the sacrificer remained in physical contact with the victim, but any physical contact with a victim which was about to die caused impurity (*aśaucha*) in the sacrificer, and hence had to be strictly avoided. This dichotomy - of touching the victim to symbolically identify himself with it, and yet not touching it - was resolved by bringing the victim in contact with the sacrificer in an imperceptible (*paroksha*) manner (SB.3.8.1.10) through the cut-out (the priest).

The term '*paroksha*' is employed here to indicate the animal victim was held metaphysically by the sacrificer.

While amplifying and emphasising this point, Śatapatha Brahmaṇa (3.8.1.10) prescribes that "the victim must not be held on to by the sacrificer, for they lead it unto death". But at the same time, it prescribes to "let him nevertheless hold onto it; for that (victim) which they lead to the sacrifice they lead not to death; therefore, let him hold onto it" - two opposite actions explaining the necessity for each. The sacrificer performing the *yajña* was required to stay clean and '*śauca*', away from the negative and '*aśauca*' acts leading to imminent death of the victim. This death was no ordinary death, but an event eventually leading to regeneration of life and immortality through the successful completion of the rite in which the gods themselves were the invitees! By not holding onto the animal, the sacrificer would have 'cut himself off from the sacrifice', an unthinkable situation. The *Śatapatha* therefore recommends that the animal be held on to "in a mysterious way; by means of the spits *pratiprasrhatri* (holds onto it); to the *pratiprasthṛtṛi* the *adhvaryu*, to the *adhvaryu* the sacrificer; thus then it is held on in a mysterious way." This way, the *bandhu* conceptually helped the sacrificer hold the animal without actually making physical contact.

Dakṣiṇā

At the conclusion of the *yajña* ritual, the *yajamāna* gave *dakṣiṇā* (gift) to the priest. An important ritual, *dakṣiṇā* was a defining act which very clearly differentiated the officiant, who actually performed *yajña* and recieved the gift, and the actual beneficiary of the *yajña*, the *yajamāna* (or the sacrificer) who made this gift. Act of accepting *dakṣiṇā* prevented the priest from accruing any benefit of the *yajña* and *kāmya* for himself.

To ensure that the efforts of the priest were not equated to the give-and-take of a commercial transaction, any prior agreement of the nature and quantum of *dakṣiṇā* was prohibited. It was also emphasised that the "sacrifice of his then goes forth towards the world of the gods: after it follows the fees which he gives (to the priest), and holding onto the priest's fee (follows) the sacrificer."[5] Without giving the sacrificial gift, the sacrifice would not have been complete ("for no offering, they say, should be without a *dakṣiṇā*") (SB. 4.5.1.16.).

Dakṣiṇā was not an inducement to the priest to carry out the rituals; it was an integral part of the ritual. This idea is further reinforced in *Brahmaṇas*, they specify gifts to be given for expected benefits from the sacrifice - "He (the sacrificer) gives to them four thousand (cows) in order to his gaining and securing everything, for 1000 means everything, and the *Aśvamedha* is everything. And (he gives them) four gold plates weighing hundred grains." (SB. 13.4.1.6) For the *iṣṭi* of *sāvitrī* in *aśvamedha*, "The priest's fee is gold weighing 100 grains" (SB. 13.4.2.13); and for the *punarādheya* or re-establishment of the sacred fires, a *dakṣiṇā* of gold is prescribed because "the sacrifice belongs to *Agni*, and gold is *Agni's* seed: this is why the priests fee consists of gold." (SB. 2.2.3.28). Likewise, for a sacrifice belonging to *Agni*, *dakṣiṇā* of an ox is also recommended because "*Agni* is oblation bearer to the Gods, and that (ox) bears (or draws, loads) for men: this is why an ox may be given as the priest's fee."[6]

While it was easy to determine the *dakṣiṇā* in an ordinary 'cow for cows' situation, matters became quite complex when it came to 'an immortal life for life' ritual. The Śatapatha recommended the sacrificer give his voice to the *hotṛ*, his mind to the *brahmaṇa*, and his breath to *vāyu* as *dakṣiṇā*. Fortunately, the *Śatapatha* allows the *yajamāna* to substitute a suitable gift in lieu of his various body parts.

∞

The *śrauta* oblations, also called *vaitanika*, are public sacrifices (*aśvamedha, agniṣṭoma,* et cetera) performed in three fires, collectively called *tretā agni*. These fires are *gārhapatya, dakṣiṇā* and *āhavanīya;* the latter two are lit from the *gārhapatya* fire.

i. *Gārhapatya* - kept in a round fire place
ii. *Dakṣiṇāgni* - kept in a fire place shaped like the half orb of the moon
iii. *Āhavanīya* - kept in a square fireplace

The *smṛta* oblations, as observed earlier, are to be performed only in the domestic fire (*gārhapatya*) brought from the bride's home at the time of marriage and kept alive until the householder dies.

The *Smṛta Sūtra* is a comprehensive term for rules unrelated to the usually grand and publicly conducted *śrauta* ceremonies. It concerns private and personal religious ceremonies that have two divisions -

i. Family or domestic rites (*gṛha*) - These are performed at specified periods (*gṛha sūtra*)
ii. *Samayāchāra*, conventional usages and everyday practices (*samayāchārika sūtra*)

Apart from the *panca mahā yajña*, which a householder is to perform daily, *agnihotṛ* and *aupāsna yajñas*, performed morning and evening every day, are also obligatory for every *brahmaṇa*. The new and full moon sacrifices as well as a few other animal sacrifices are also part of *gṛha* sacrifices.

Smṛta or *Gṛha* rituals

The great five *yajñas* (or *panca mahā yajña*) are enjoined to be performed by all householders in nuptial fire every day, starting from the day he holds the hand of his spouse in marriage until the day of his death (Āp DS. I.4.13, 22, 14.1; Yaj. S. I.99; MS IV.25). This *gṛha* fire is kindled on the day of the couple's wedding, and brought from the bride's house in a vessel called *ukha*. The *gṛha sūtra* emphasises daily worship of the domestic fire. In case the householder is unable to perform this duty, the wife, son, daughter or pupil (in that order) must perform it in his stead.[7]

The five *mahā yajña* are *deva*, *pitŕ*, *bhūtāni*, *manuṣya* and *Brahman yajñas*. When one makes an offering in the fire, it becomes *deva yajña*; when one offers *shrāddha* repast, it becomes *pitri yajña*; an offering of *bali* (a ball of food) to the beings becomes *bhūtāni yajña*; food given to *brahmaṇa* becomes *manuṣya yajña*; and when one studies the Vedas, it becomes *Brahman yajña*. An offering of even two fuel sticks in fire, a few drops of water, or muttering a single *ṛca* of the Vedas also fulfils the criteria of *deva*, *pitŕ* or *Brahman yajñas* respectively.

These *panca mahā yajñas* prescribed in the early Vedic texts, are described as *mahā yajñas* or the great sacrificial sessions. In reality, all five do not even fully qualify as *yajñas*. Their names are figurative and they are termed great by way of laudation.[8] By the time of Manu (post the advent of Buddhism and Jainism in India), a wave of *ahiṃsā* was sweeping through India and these *mahā yajñas*, though still a part of daily religious routines, were now being performed by way of expiations of the five 'slaughterhouses' in every household - "A householder has five slaughterhouses, whose use fetters him: the fireplace, the grindstone, the broom, the mortar and pestle, and the water jar."[9] Professor Wendy Doniger, an eminent Indologist, explains that these are called slaughterhouses because small creatures are often inadvertently killed through their use. This inadvertent killing termed 'slaughter' appears to be a consequence of the growing influence of the non-violence doctrines of Buddhism and Jainism on the Hindu society. It is also likely that Mahavir Jain's followers made this insertion in the Manusmṛti later. But the ideology of *ahiṃsā* did not give birth to these mahā *yajñas*; as explained below, they existed since the Vedic times when *paśu bali* or animal sacrifice was a part of *yajñas*.

[*Aupāsna* and *agnihotṛ yajñas* are part of daily religious routines. Although *aupāsna* is a *pāka yajña*, it is not included in the group of seven *pāka yajñas* mentioned above.]

The *agnihotṛ yajña* is one of the seven *havir yajñas*. While the *darśa-pūrṇasmāsa yajña* is to be performed once in fifteen days, the other *havir yajñas* and *soma yajñas* are to be performed once a year or at least once-in-a-lifetime.

The *pravani yajña* (*shrāddha*) is to be performed once a month, the *sthālipāka yajña* every *prathama*, and the other five *pāka yajñas* once a year. In summary, the five *mahā yajñas*, together with *agnihotṛ* and *aupāsna*, are to be performed every day; the *darśa-pūrṇasmāsa* and the *sthālipāka* once a fortnight; and the *parvani shrāddha* once a month. The other *yajñas* were to be performed once a year (if possible) or at least once-in-a-lifetime.

Origin and institutionalization of *Gṛha Sūtras*

The *śrauta* ceremonies were in accordance with prescriptions of the *Saṃhitās* and *Brahmaṇas*. But how and when, and more importantly, why were the *smṛta* composed and compiled, needs examination before we proceed to the various *smṛta* rituals. These rituals are performed in accordance with *Gṛha Sūtras*, which form part of *Kalpa*, compiled much later than the *Brahmaṇa* (600-400 BC) and authored by many ṛṣis and their families.

There are enough indications in the Brahmaṇa texts that the *gṛha* fire and many associated acts were not unknown at the time. The Aitareya Brahmaṇa quotes *gṛha agni* and describes the ceremony to be performed over this fire. In SB.I.8.1.7, the *pāka* sacrifice is performed under its *gṛha sūtra* name when Manu (not to be confused with Manu of Manusmṛti fame) desirous of an offspring, "engaged in worshipping and austerities. He also performed a *Pāka* sacrifice: he offered up in the waters clarified butter, sour milk, whey and curds." In the subsequent book of the same *Brahmaṇa*, the great disputant sage Yājñavalkya adjudicates *agnihotṛ* as *pāka yajña* and not *havis*: "On this point Yājñavalkya said, 'It (the *agnihotṛ*) must not be looked upon as a (*havis*) sacrifice, but as a domestic sacrifice (*pāka yajña*); for while in any other (*havis*) sacrifice he pours into the fire all that he cuts off (from the sacrificial dish and puts) into the offering a spoon, here, after offering and stepping outside, he sips water and licks out (milk); and this indeed (is a characteristic) of the domestic offering'." (I I.3.1.21)

Yet, despite the *Brahmaṇa's* familiarity with the *gṛha* fire and associated *pāka* ceremonies, there is no mention of separate *gṛha* ritual texts. This leads us to conclude that the recognition of *smṛta* rites, as a separate system analogous to *śrauta* rites, came many centuries after the *Brahmaṇa* period.

According to Hermann Oldenberg - a prominent eighteenth century German scholar of Indology, Pali and Sanskrit, and Professor at Kiel (1898) and Göttingen (1908), who made the translation of the *gṛha sūtras* - the domestic sacrifice fire and ritual peculiarities of *pāka yajña* were given in the *Brahmaṇa* in prose and there were *ślokas*, which explained, in metrical form, certain points of the *gṛha* rituals similar to *śrauta* rituals. Though there were no definite *gṛha* texts, many elements that we find later in the text were either already formed or were in the process of formation. Most verses used for *gṛha* acts bear the formal imprint of the *Brahmaṇa* period. In Oldenberg's view, many ceremonies and verses were first developed (in *Brahmaṇa*) not as universal rites or duties but as special possessions of individuals who desired to attain special goods and advantages by performing certain ceremonies in a specific manner. It was only later that these became universal and were incorporated into the *gṛha sūtras*.[10] This was the period of literary development of *Kalpa* and it was natural that "the domain of *gṛha* sacrifices was recognised and expounded as the second great principal part of the ritual of sacrifices alongside the *śrauta* domain which was alone attended to in the earlier period."[11] There is striking similarity between the *gṛha sūtra* and the *śrauta sūtra* on treatment of their subjects. In addition to this, the assumption made by the authors of the *Gṛha sūtras* on its familiarity with *śrauta sūtras* leaves little doubt that either the same authors were responsible for *Gṛha sūtras* as had originally written the *śrauta* or it was the work of the family of ṛṣis who followed the same Veda schools.

These 'human authored' *gṛha* acts came to be accepted as duties by Hindus, at par with the *śrauta* acts based on self-existent texts, because *gṛha* acts were also "based on *śākhā* of the Veda, but that this *śākhā* is hidden, so that its existence can only be demonstrated by reasoning."[12]

Apart from daily rites, the *gṛha sūtras* contain the rites to be performed at fixed times such as *śrāvani* (a rite performed during *śrāvana* - fifth month in Hindu calander beginning on first day of full moon in late July and ending in late August). Some rites were copied from *śrauta* rituals like *darśa-pūrṇasmāsa*; rites for a particular occasion, such as building a new house or undertaking a long journey; rites of passage from one stage to other in life; and funeral rites, apart from *pāka yajñas* or *sthālipākas*. Finally, the *gṛha sūtras* also deal with *kāmya* rites associated with attaining worldly desires.

Saṃskāra as *Gṛha* ceremonies

From the time of conception (*garbhadāna*), and once the child is born, from showing him the sun for the first time, to making him lick the first mess of food, his sacred thread ceremony, marriage and up to his last rites, are series of sixteen rites of passage - ceremonies called *saṃskāras* - which gave him an identity as a Hindu. As these ceremonies are private and performed at home, the *saṃskāras* form a part of the *Gṛha Sūtras*.

The life of a Hindu is a cycle with no fixed beginning or end. The most important event in the life cycle is not necessarily birth or death. Accordingly, the rites of passage from one stage to other are not treated in the *gṛha sūtras* in any fixed manner. Most ṛṣis chose *upanayana* as a starting point as this was a very important stage in life, when a child was handed over to the guru for learning the Vedas, or at least one of the Vedas, away from home for a period extending from eight to forty-eight years or even lifelong! On completion of his studentship, in another milestone called *vivāha* (marriage), the individual was ready to marry and enter the life of a householder. It was at this point that he brought the nuptial fire from the bride's house which he was supposed to keep alive lifelong and in which he was to perform daily *yajñas* and other *gṛha* sacrifices. Since he was enjoined to produce a son, the ceremony of *garbhādhāna* soon followed.

Not all *saṃskāras* were associated with sacrificial ceremonies. Many were simply important milestones in the life of the pregnant mother, e.g. *seemantonayan*, or of the newly born child, e.g. *annaprāśana* - occasions for the immediate family to rejoice and celebrate at home. To that extent, though the *saṃskāras* were *gṛha* ceremonies performed at home, in many ceremonies, the fire and *yajña* were crucial components, such as in *vivāha*, *upanayana*, et cetera and in many others, fire and *yajña* were both absent and the only thing which made these social occasions like *annaprāśana* a religious function was the use of mantras.

As these ceremonies were private and performed at home, the *saṃskāras* formed a part of *gṛha* ceremonies.

∞

Apart from *agnihotṛ*, which had to be performed thrice (some say twice) every day, the householder was also required to perform the *panca mahā yajña* daily. What came to be known as the 'seven *pāka yajñas*' were, in the beginning of the *gṛha uūtra* period, simply *pāka yajñas*, divided in different ways.

Laugakshi and Sankhayana divide the various *pāka yajñas* into four classes[13] - the *huta*, where offerings are poured into the domestic fire; the *āhuta*, where offerings are made to the fire, presents are given to the *brahmaṇa* and received from others; the *prahuta*, where rice balls or *piṇḍas* are offered to ancestors and presents are given to the *brahmaṇa* and others; and the *praśita*, where offerings are made to the *brahmaṇa* as food - "A distribution which may coincide with that of the four *mahā yajñas*."[14]

The division into seven classes, it appears, was influenced by the division of *havir* and *soma yajñas*, each of which include seven further classes:

"The seven kinds of *pāka yajñas* viz the *aṣṭaka*, the *parvana* (*sthālipāka*, offered on new and full moon days), the funeral oblations, the *śravani*, the *agrahāyaṇi*, the *caitrī*, and the *aśvāyugi*."

Or,

"*Hutas*; *āhutas*; *prahutas*; and *prasitas*, the spit ox sacrifice, the *bali* offering, the redescent (on the *agrahāyaṇa* day), the *aṣṭaka* sacrifice."[15]

Description of *Yajñas*

Śrauta sacrifices

These community rituals can be categorised into *havir*, and *soma yajñas* - each contains seven different types of sacrifices. The distinguishing feature of *soma yajña* is that *soma* juice is used in all its seven sacrifices, which the performing priests and *yajamāna* also drink. On the other hand, the *havir yajñas* have offerings of clarified butter, boiled preparations of rice, barley or wheat, fuel sticks of selected trees and such. The *pitṛ yajña* (funeral sacrifices) and *Bṛhaspati sava* (the consecration of a *purohita*) are also included in *śrauta* sacrifices.

Havir yajñas - These seven sacrifices are performed by the householder. The fact that he is apprised of this obligation during the wedding rites at the time of his marriage indicates the importance of these *yajñas* in a householder's life. The seven sacrifices include -

i. *Agni-ādhana* or *agnyādheya* - This is spread over two days, allowing the householder to prepare for the sacrificial ceremony for the first time after his wedding. The preliminaries are performed on the first day, and the main rituals, in which offerings of *ghī* and *caru* (unpounded rice or balrley cooked in water with butter or milk) are made in the fire, are organised on the second day. The *yajña* is conducted in three fires assisted by four priests and involves making fire through *agni-manthan*, i.e rubbing wood sticks together.

ii. *Agnihotṛ* - This rite is to be performed every day in the mornings (offerings to *Sūrya* and *Prajāpati*) and evenings (offerings to *Agni* and *Prajāpati*). The precise time that this offering is to be made is debated even today. The offerings are made from the fresh milk of an *agnihotṛ* cow. The milk is then heated over embers drawn from *gārhapatya*, and allowed to cool. While the Āpstamba *śrauta* allow a *śūdra* to milk the cow (VI.3.11-14), he is categorically barred from milking by Kātyāyana (K.Sr IV.14.1). The evening prayers include a prayer for the cow that supplied the milk, *āhavanīya*, home, night, and thereafter for *gārhapatya*. The Mahābhārata calls it the best of Vedic sacrifices. *Agnihotṛ* brings great merit and life in *pitṛiyāṇa* - the *loka* (after-world) of the ancestors.

iii. *Darśa-pūrṇasmāsa* - These are new and full moon rites performed over two days with assistance from four priests. The preliminaries are performed on full and new moon days, and the main rite is conducted on *pratipad* day (*pratipad* - an introductory verse). Offerings to *pitri* are made on *amāvāsyā* (new moon day), after which *pūrṇimā* (full moon day) offerings are made to *Agni* and *Índra*, and *Agni* again. Following *amāvāsyā*, offerings are made to *Agni*, *Prajāpati*, *Soma*, and *Índra*. The term '*darśa*' literally means the time when the moon is seen only by the sun, i.e. *amāvāsyā*. *Pūrāṇasmāsa* (or *pūrṇimā*) is when the moon is full. It is an *iṣṭi* type rite performed with four principal priests on *amāvāsyā* and *Pūrāṇasmāsa* and the principal offerings made on the next day, the conjunction between the *parvan* (four periods/parts of *caturmasya* rite) and *pratipad*. It is an archetype (*prakṛti*) of all other *iṣṭis*.

On the first day, *upávastha* (fasting day before the main rite), the sacrificer performs preliminaries such as bathing and shaving. The *anvadhana* (offering fuel sticks into sacrificial fire) rite is performed by feeding logs of wood to the fire and arranging *vedi* with *prastara* (place on the *vedi* for keeping ladles filled with butter, made using fistful of *durba* grass cut with sickle tied in bundle). In the afternoon of the new moon day, *piṇḍa pitri yajña* is conducted where *piṇḍas* (balls) of cooked rice are offered to the father, grandfather and great-grandfather. After the *agnihotṛ*, the cows are milked the same evening and their milk is purified, heated, curdled and preserved for later use.

The havir *yajña* performed on every *prathama* (first day) is called '*darśa-pūrṇa-iṣṭi*.' As mentioned earlier, the '*iṣṭi*' or sacrifices conducted on the day following the new and full moon (the two *prathamas*) are together given the name of *darśa-pūrṇa-iṣṭi*. The two rituals are also referred merely as '*iṣṭi*'. This is the *prakṛti* (model or standard form) for *havir yajñas*.

On the second day, grains are pounded and winnowed, flour is mixed in *madanti* water (boiling water used for mixing flour) and stirred by *mekshana* (a mixing rod of *aśvāttha* wood having a square board at one end for stirring hot mix) to prepare a dough. Thereafter, the altar is prepared and utensils are placed on it.

Fuel sticks are then fed into the fire while the *samidheni* verses (eleven verses recited by *hotṛ* when *Agni* is being kindled) are being recited. The *pravaras* (ancestor ṛṣis) of the sacrificer are announced by the *hotṛ* followed by an *aghara* libation (libations of butter) of the *adhvaryu*. The next step is the *prayajas* (five preliminary *ājya* i.e. *ghī* oblations before principal offerings) and *ājya bhāgas*. Then, the principal offerings are made along with *puronvākyas* (invitatory verse recited by *hotṛ*) and *yājyas* (mantras composed of verses) for *darśa*; a cake to *Agni*; *upāṃśu* oblation (oblations of butter offered silently or with muttered prayers) to *Prajāpati*; a cake each to *Agni*, *Soma* and *Vaimridha Índra*; one cake each to *Agni* and *Índra-Agni* for *purṇasmāsa*. These are further followed by an offering called *pārvana homa* and the *sviṣtakrit* offerings (a secondary tribute offered to *Agni* after the principal one). *Ida* (portions of oblatory material divided and sprinkled with *ājya*) is offered and consumed by the priests. The *adhvaryu* offers three *anuyaja* oblations (made after principal offerings) into *āraṇya* and five or eight *patnī samyaja* oblations (*ājya* offerings made to the wives of four gods) into the *gārhapatya*. Then, the *yoktra* (cord of munja grass) is removed from the waist of the sacrificer's wife and the rite is concluded with the three *visnukramas* ('*Viṣṇu* steps' taken with appropriate mantras) of the sacrificer.[16]

This is both a *śrauta* as well as *gṛha* rite.

iv. *Āgrayaṇa* - This is a celebration of the season's first harvest wherein, twice a year, the householder offers the first grains of the harvest to the sacred fire. During spring, offerings of barley cake are made and a rice cake is offered to *Índra* and *Agni* in autumn, besides *Viśvedevās*, *Dyaus* and *Pṛthvī*. The first calf born in the year is given as *dakṣiṇā* to the priest.

v. *Cāturmāsya* - These are four-monthly sacrifices, marking the advent of a new season and performed on full moon days. *Vaiśvedevā* is performed in the spring, *varuṇa-praghasha* during the monsoon, and the *sakamedha* in autumn. In *Vaiśvedevā*, *Agni, Soma, Savitṛ, Saraswatī* and *Pūṣan* are worshipped first. A cake is offered to the *Maruts* followed by a dish of milk to the *Vaiśvedevā* and a cake to *Dyaus-Pṛthvīi*. *Varuṇa Praghasha* also prescribes the worship of these five deities in the beginning. Representations of a ram and ewe made in barley flour are offered to *Varuṇa* and *Maruts* respectively. *Karira* fruits are offered in the hope of increasing flock, inviting rains and yielding a good harvest.

In the sacrifice, the wife of the sacrificer worships *Varuṇa*, confesses the names and number of her lovers and offers plates of gruel to the southern fire.

The *pitri yajña* forms an important part of *sakamedha* in which the *dakṣiṇā* fire is prominent. Here, an offering is made to *Rudra Trayambak* for ensuring the safety of the flock.

vi. *Nirūḍh paśu bandha* - These, too, are four-monthly sacrifices, each marking the beginning of a new season and performed on full moon days like *cāturmāsya*. It involves the sacrifice of a disembowelled animal, reconstructed by *sūtrakāras* as an independent rite from animal sacrifice, as prescribed in the *Brahmaṇa*, like *agnishomiya*. It is considered a model for all optional animal sacrifices to be performed every six months or more. The rite takes one to two days wherein six priests are engaged for the *iṣṭi*, besides an additional two priests. The altar is prepared as in *varunpraghasha* rite; *āhavanīya* is installed on the *nābhi*, i.e. navel (see diagram D-1) of the *uttara vedi*. The principal part of the rite begins with putting logs into fire while reciting *sāmídheni* (verse recited while kindling *Agni*). The sacrificial animal (a goat) is bathed, anointed with *ājya*, and touched with a twig and *darbha* blades. The animal is led to *śāmitra* shed (see diagram D-1- place where limbs of animal are roasted)) by the *āgnīdhra* (the priest who kindles fire), while the *hotṛ* recites the *āvāhana* (an invocation), and immolated. The priests then return to the sacrificial shed. After the immolation, the sacrificer's wife is led to the *śāmitra* shed to pour water on the animal's limbs.

The animal's belly is cut open by the *adhvaryu* to draw out the omentum, which is roasted on the *āhavanīya* by the *pratiprasthṛtṛ* (priest), sprinkled and offered as an oblation to *Índra* and *Agni*. The animal is dissected and its limbs are cooked over the *śāmitra* fire followed by an invocation to and partaking of the *ida*.

When the slaughterer (of animal) replies in the affirmative to the question, "have the limbs been properly cooked?" (asked thrice), *prasādājya* (curdled milk mixed with *ghī*) is poured over its heart and *ājya* (*ghī*) over its limbs. The parts are taken to the altar where the *avadānas* (portions of the heart, lungs and the tongue) are cut into the *juhu*, *upabhrit* and *idapatri* spoons, and offered with the utterance of *vaṣat* (mystical exclaimtion uttered loudly by the *hotṛ* priest). The invocation to, and partaking of, the *ida* (holy milk) are then repeated, preceded by the *sviṣṭakṛt* (secondary oblation offered to *Agni* after the principal one). The *patnī samyaja* (four offerings of *ājya* made to wives of gods) are made with the flesh of the offering's tail, which is also offered to the *hotṛ* and the *āgnīdhra* (priest who kindles the fire).

The sacrificer, his wife, and all the priests go to the *utkara* (a little mound of earth) from the *cātvāla* (a pit dug near the *vedi*). They respectfully place the animal's heart outside the *vedi*, insert it into the pit, sprinkle themselves with water, return to the sacrificial shed without looking back and, finally, pray to the *āhavanīya*.

vii. *Sautrāmaṇī* - Described in the Yajurveda, this sacrifice is in honour of *Índra* and distinguished by use of *sura* (wine) instead of *soma*. The wine is consumed as part of the sacrifice, not by the officiating priest, but a *brahmaṇa* especially hired for the purpose. The sacrifice, dedicated to *Índra*, *Aśvins* and *Saraswatī*, is offered by a *brahmaṇa* for a king to regain a lost throne or a *vaiśya* seeking riches. It lasts four days, of which three days are allotted to the preparation of *sura* which is re-designated as the *pariśrut* after purification. (Āp. SS. X I X.1.8, 18) A goat for the *Aśvins*, an ewe for *Saraswatī* and a bull for *Índra Sūtraman* are slaughtered. (K. Sr. X I X.1 - 7, Āp. SS. X I X. 1 - 10)

Soma yajña - Of all the sacrifices, these are considered most important and usually performed by kings or very rich individuals. The *brahmaṇas* spent large portions of their wealth in performing *soma yajña*, and poor *brahmaṇas* often begged to perform this *yajña*.

Oblations of *soma* juice and singing *stotras* of Sāmaveda is the principle aspect of *soma yajña*. *Soma yajñas* are also known as *somasaṃsthās*. According to the Dictionary of Vedic Rituals, *saṃsthā*[17] is the 'termination or conclusion of a rite' or a 'basic form of sacrifice'.The conclusion of the Sāmavedic hymns chanted by the *udgātṛ* is also called *saṃsthā*. Compositions recited in praise of deities are known as *stotras*. In the Vedic tradition, hymns which suggest seven notes of the *saptasvara* are called '*sastras*' in the Ṛgveda and '*stotras*' in the Sāmaveda.

Singing the Sāman creates a mood of ecstasy. When a musician elaborates a *rāga* and touches the fifth *svara* of the higher octave, the *puncamasvara*, the listener is transported to another world. When *stotras* of the Sāmaveda are recited during the *saṃsthā*, all those assembled for the sacrifice have an experience bordering on ecstacy. This is one reason why *soma yajña* is also known as '*somasaṃsthā*'.

The *somasaṃsthā* are also of seven type. In each there is a sacrificial post (*yūpa*) for animal sacrifice, chanting of Sāmans, and *soma* pressing and offering. Each sacrifice requires four days of initial preparations -

- *Ekaha* are performed in one day during which pressing of the *soma* stalks (*sutyā*) is concluded - this is principal part of *soma* sacrifice
- *Ahina* requires two to twelve *sutyā* days
- *Sattra's* duration varies from twelve days to a year or more, even up to a hundred years (theoretically). The *prakṛti* of *sattra* is *dvādaśāha* (twelve) and the essential feature is *shadaha* - six *soma* days - especially from the second to the seventh day of the *dvādaśāha*[18]

The seven *somas*

i. *Agniṣṭoma* - This name is derived from a *stotra* called *agniṣṭoma* chanted during the rite. The word '*ṣṭoma*' means sacrifice and this is classified as *ekaha*, the *prakṛti* (model or archetype) for all *soma yajñas*. It is performed every year in spring and lasts five days - four preparatory days and one *sutyā* day (day of *soma* pressing). On the final day, *soma* is offered thrice - morning, midday and evening. *Agniṣṭoma* includes twelve *śāstras* and twelve *stotras*.

The rite is performed for religious merit, fame, health, good harvests and abundant rainfall. It requires participation of sixteen priests, who along with the venue are selected on the first day and then the householder and his wife are consecrated. On the second day *soma* stalks are purchased and cermoniously brought to the the cite in a procession. *Upasada* ('homage or investment') and *pravargya* ceremony is performed twice - morning and evening - daily. *Pravargya* is an independent elaborate rite, incorporated as an essential part of *agniṣṭoma*. The altar is prepared on the third day, and a goat is offered to the gods *Agni* and *Soma*. The sons, grandsons and relatives of the sacrificer also participate in this ritual. On fourth day the infrastructure is prepared and various sheds erected. The fifth day is *sutyā* day, when *soma* is offered to *Agni*, *Uṣa* and *Aśvins* followed by another animal sacrifice in honor of *Índra* and *Agni*. Finally, the *śāstra* is recited followed by the *avabhritha* ceremony where all implements are cast into the river.

ii. *Atyaganaṣṭoma* - This includes thirteen *śāstras*, thirteen *stotras* and thirteen libations of *soma* as well as a live offering to *Índra*.

iii. *Uktyā* - This has fifteen *śāstras* and fifteen *stotras*, and similar to *agniṣṭoma* two animals (one each for *Índra* and *Agni*) are offered in sacrifice on the pressing day.

iv. *Ṣoḍaśin* - A variant of *uktyā* in which libation of *soma* is offered to *Índra*, and one *śāstra* and one *stotra* are added in the evening. A ram is also offered to *Índra*. As the name suggests, *ṣoḍaśin* has sixteen *śāstras*, sixteen *stotras* and sixteen offering cups. *Ṣoḍaśin* cups receive special care and are placed in vessels made of *khadira* (*Acacia catechu*) wood.

v. *Vājapeya* - This important *soma yajña* lasts seventeen days during which seventeen animals are sacrificed, and seventeen *stotra* and *śāstras* are recited for libations of seventeen cups of *soma*. Seventeen bags of salt are tied to a *yūpa*. Interestingly, this *yajña* also involves a chariot race where the distance is fixed by seventeen arrow shots - each successive arrow is shot from the landing spot of the previous arrow.

vi. *Atirātra* - This is an optional form of *jyotiṣṭoma*, performed on the third day of the *soma* pressing in *aśvamedha yajña* and lasts an entire day and a night. In twenty-four hours, twenty-nine *stotras* and *śāstras* are recited, and the last verse (*prātaranuvāky*) is recited after sunrise. *Prātaranuvākya* is a morning litany recited by the *hotṛ* in the last part of the night following the *sutyā* day. The *hotṛ* sits between the yokes of two carts (*havirdhāna*) placed side-by-side in the *mahā vedi* and voices hundreds of verses, gradually modulating his voice upwards through seven tones (*yama*) of the deep scale (*mandasvara*).[19] A cup of *soma* is offered to the *Aśvins* followed by a cake. A major part of the ritual is offering a male goat to *Saraswatī*.

This is an *ahina* sacrifice as it lasts more than a day.

vii. *Aptoryama* - A modification of *atirātra*, this ritual requires recitation of thirty-three *śāstras* and *stotras*.

The *atyagniṣṭoma, vājapeya* and *aptoryama* are not part of *jyotiṣṭoma* (name of an *ekaha*) - *agniṣṭoma* is an extended form. *Jyotiṣṭoma* is often a synonym of *agniṣṭoma*[20] in older texts, believed to have been added later to reach the mystical number seven.

Gṛha sacrifices

These are simple domestic ceremonies characterised by offerings of cooked food into *gṛhāgni* - the household fire. These sacrifices called *pāka yajñas* are performed by the householder without the assistance of a priest. The word '*pāka*' means cooked as well as small, both fitting the description of this *yajña*. As discussed in the preceding paragraphs, the *gṛha yajñas* are categorised under seven varieties most likely to bring them in line with the seven varieties of *havir* and *soma yajñas*. These include -

i. *Aupāsna homa* - Three daily offerings in the domestic fire

ii. *Vaiśvedevā* - Daily offerings of cooked rice to various deities

iii. *Parvana* - Monthly offerings

iv. *Aṣṭaka* - Performed in honor of ancestors in the month of *maghá* in the *kṛṣṇa pakṣa* (dark lunar fortnight) on the eighth and ninth days

v. *Masi-śrāddha* - An important *yajña* which is the *prakṛti* (model) for all other *śrāddhas*. This is performed on the new moon night or *amāvāsyā* of every month for the *manes*

vi. *Sarpabali* or *śrāvaṇi* - A *sthālipāka* (a sacrifice in which barley or rice grains are cooked and offered as oblations) ceremony, conducted in the month of *śrāvaṇa* after sunset, and continued every night until the *agrahāyaṇa*, four months, to overcome any curses of infertility. On the full moon night of the month of *śrāvaṇa*, *caru* rice and *ghī* are placed in the fire and forest flowers are also offered. Designs are drawn with rice flour over an ant-hill or another such place. Offerings are also made to snakes while chanting mantras. This ceremony must be held every full moon night up to *margazhi* (mid-December to mid-January).

A rite that forms the basis of many other rites is called '*prakṛti*' (archetype or model). Rites performed after the *prakṛti*, but with some alterations, are known as '*vikṛti*'. *Sthālipāka* is the *prakṛti* for the *sarpabali* called *śrāvaṇi*, and the *pāka yajña* called *agrahāyaṇi*.

vii. *Ishāna bali* or *caitrī* - Performed for *Rudra* on the full moon night of the *caitra* month at a crossroad.

Pāka yajñas are minor sacrifices performed at home. Even *śrauta* rites like the first four *havir yajñas* - *adhāna, agnihotṛ, darśa-pūrṇasmāsa* and *āgrayaṇa*

- are performed at home. The last three *havir yajñas* - *cāturmāsa, nirūḍh paśu baṃdha* and *sautrāmaṇī* - are always performed in a *yāgśāla*.

Rashtriya yajñas

This class of sacrifices were performed only by *rājanyas* or *kṣatriyas*. Many people call it *rashtriya* sacrifices or national rituals, though the *sūtras* do not contain this separate classification.

i. *Aśvamedha* - Performed by emperors to establish sovereignty and for the absolution of sins
ii. *Rajasūya* - Performed by the ruler to assert his superiority
iii. *Sarva medha* - Performed by a sole monarch in which all his accumulated wealth is gifted away
iv. *Puruṣa medha* - Involved symbolic human sacrifice. It should be emphasised that there is no evidence that an actual human sacrifice was ever performed
v. *Aindra mahābhiśeka* - Performed for obtaining extraordinary qualities and special energy
vi. *Vājapeya* - Performed to confer superior restraint and divinity on the ruler. This sacrifice was also permitted for a *brahmaṇa*

Aśvamedha

Best known of all ancient sacrifices today is *aśvamedha*, which as the name suggests, involves *aśva* (horse) sacrifice. A *soma* sacrifice, it is one of the most ancient of Vedic sacrifices and finds mention in the Ṛgveda (I.162; I. 163). It was performed by kings to increase their power, and demonstrate and establish sovereignty. Not only was this *yajña* the most prestigious, it was considered important for all kings; many kings performed several *aśvamedha yajñas* during their reign.

A horse possessing certain qualities was selected and after purificatory ceremonies, it was branded with the name of the king and allowed to gallop freely across the land for one year, protected by a hundred princes and four-hundred armed guards. During the year, the horse was not allowed to mate. Territories where the horse wandered during this period were considered to have accepted the sovereignty of the king. Anyone challenging this sovereignty was welcome to stop the horse and settle matters on the battlefield. Theoretically, even if the horse covered a measly 25km a day, the steed would have travelled nearly 9000km in an year - across several princely states, and covering large mass of land.

While the horse was away, the king was kept busy with several *iṣṭis* he had to perform, entertained by laudatory hymns and popular legends (*pāriplava*) recitals composed of the *Sunehshepa* legend wherein several hundred *riks* and *gāthās* were collected. These were recited by the *hotṛ* and renewed every ten days throughout the year (K. SS. XX.3.1; Āp. SS. X V I I I.1 9.10) to keep the king connected with the year-long sacrifice on an everyday basis, while the actual scene of action lay with the galloping steed far from the capital of the kingdom.

With the return of the horse, the principal rites began - starting with an animal sacrifice, consecration (*dīkṣā*) lasting twelve days, measurement and preparation of the altars, and twelve *upasada* days followed by three *sutyā* days. *Upasada* is an *iṣṭi* comprising a group of rites performed between the conclusion of the *dīkṣā* and *sutyā*, but always after the *pravargya* of the *soma*. Performed twice a day for at least three days, in this *iṣṭi* the oblations of clarified butter are offered to *Agni*, *Soma* and *Viṣṇu*, into the *āhavanīya* fire with an offering spoon having cup-shaped bowl (*juhu* ladle). *Sutyā* is the day of pressing *soma* stalks, constituting the principal part of a *soma* sacrifice in contradistinction to preliminaries, like *dīkṣā* and *upasada*. The first day of pressing is the ordinary *agniṣṭoma*. On the second day, the horse is led to a pond, anointed by the queens and adorned with 101 golden beads. The horse is then strangled to death and the queens walk around the carcass, fanning it with their garments. Then, they untie their hair and beat their left thigh with the left hand in mourning. Other animals are also sacrificed. While Yajurveda provides a list of animals to be sacrificed, Ṛgveda talks of offering a goat to *Pūṣan*. Then comes what has become a very controversial set of actions over the last two centuries. The chief queen spent a night near the horse. In the rituals that follow, she lies down besides the dead horse, covering herself and the horse, and stimulates sexual copulation while abusing the dead horse. (Āp SS XX.1 8.3 - 4, K.SS. XX.6.15 - 17). Simultaneously, the priests and women exchange obscene and crude dialogues followed by *brahmodaya* (riddles between priests and the sacrificer). Thereafter, the horse is cut up along with the other sacrificial animals and offerings are made. The flesh of the horse is consecrated to the gods, and eaten by the participants of the sacrifice. On the third day, *atiratra* and *avabhṛtha* (the final purificatory bath marking the end of a sacrifice) are conducted, which is an *iṣṭi* involving the sacrificer, his wife and priests who bathe in the river/reservoir, then dispose utensils smeared with *soma* in water[21], thereby marking the end.

A hefty fee of 48,000 cows for each of the four principal priests is the prescribed *dakṣiṇā*.

Aśvamedha was regularly performed, and records prove that many kings of the Gupta, Chalukya and the Chola dynasties practiced it. However, by the time of the Cholas, the practice had become rare and gradually died out.

Rajasūya

'*Su*' in Sanskrit is 'to press out or generate' and '*rajasūya*' literally means 'birth of king'. It is the rite of royal consecration performed by a *rājan* (*kṣatriya*).

There are four main consecration rituals for kings - *rajasūya*, *vājapeya*, *punarābhiṣeka* and *Aindra mahābhiṣheka*. The *rajasūya* follows *soma* sacrifice pattern and lasts more than two years. It begins with *dīkṣā* ceremony on the first day of the bright half of *phālguna* (Feburary/March) month, followed by five days of *pavitra* of *agniṣṭoma-soma* rite, and a series of *iṣṭis*': *anumati catur* (lasting a year), *índraturiya*, *pancavatiya*, *iṣṭi's* for *Mitra*, *Bṛhaspati*, etc. The main ritual commences only in the thirteenth month with gifts to the chief queen and court officials, followed by *abhiṣecaniya* (anointing) and *abhiṣeka* (sprinkling of water) with a mixture of seventeen types of water brought from different sources, including dew, a pond, a well, a whirlpool, the river *Sarasvatī* and the sea. Once the gods were invoked and *abhiṣeka* was performed, the king made many symbolic gestures, such as walking in different directions indicative of his rule extending in all directions, and wearing tiger skin to gain the strength of a tiger.

These were followed by a chariot race, a mock battle or enactment of a cattle raid. The king then alighted from his chariot to be enthroned. Thereafter, he won a game of dice, and recited the story of dog's tail in *Sunahshepa* after listening to a *hotṛ*. For the next ten days, ten *iṣṭis* were performed to make him a *dīkṣitā* ready for the next *soma* rite, *daśapeya*. The king was to observe *devavratas* (vows) for one year, at the end of which *keśhavapaniya* was performed at dawn. *Keśhavapaniya* was an *atirātra* type haircutting ceremony of the king in which the number of verse of the *stotra* decrease at each *savana* - twenty-one in the morning, seventeen at mid-day, fifteen at third and nine at dawn. (Āp SS. X V I I I.2 2.9 - 11)

A steep fee was paid to the priests - 32,000 cows for each of the four principal priests, 16,000 each to the *dvitiyins*, 8000 each to the *trityins* and 4000 to each of the *padins* in *abhiṣechaniya* (unction).

Vājapeya

Vājapeya, meaning 'drink of strength', is one of the four consecration rites for kings; it confers superior status on the king. Although it follows the patterns of *ukhtya*, it has several features different from all other rites of the class. *Ukhtya* is a *soma* sacrifice (one of the *saṃsthās*) which contains fifteen *stotras* and *śāstras* each, besides *Agniṣṭoma* (sacrifice of a goat for *Índra* and *Agni*) and an additional animal sacrifice.

Vājapeya incorporates many popular rites. There are seventeen *stotra* in the *śāstras*, seventeen animal sacrifices over seventeen days (thirteen *dīkṣit*, three *upasada* days and one pressing day) and preparation of seventeen cups of wine and *soma* (ready-made wine is purchased). The special feature begins with the mid-day pressing. Seventeen chariots are prepared; each yokes four horses except that of the sacrificer's chariot, which has three horses. An archer shoots arrows in succession, starting from where the prvious one fell, and wherever the seventeenth arrow hits the ground, it is marked as the finish line for the chariot race. The *brahmaṇa* fixes a wheel on a pole and sits on it. When the sacrificer and competitors start the race, seventeen drummers beat seventeen drums placed on the northern *śroṇi* ('hip') of the *vedi*. After *soma* cups have been offered, sixteen wine cups are given to sixteen competitors. The sacrificer and his wife reach up the ladder onto the top of *yūpa* and seventeen bags of salt (tied to a long pole) are raised to them to the top of the *yūpa*. (Āp SS. X V I I I.1 - 7, K. SS. X IV)

After participating in the race between seventeen chariots, the sacrificer and his chief queen ascend a pole signifying a seat high up in the air (above others) - "He then descends (and treads) upon a piece of gold; gold is immortal life" and then they "bring a throne seat for him; for truly he who gains a seat in the air, gains a seat above (others), thus these subjects of his sit below him who is seated above." (SB.V.2.1 - 14, 20 - 22). Once the ruler sits down on the throne covered with goatskin, the *adhvaryu*, endowing the ruler with royal power, explains the king's duty and responsibility towards his people: "This is thy kinship", "Thou art firm and steadfast!", "Thee for tilling!", "Thee for peaceful dwelling!", "Thee for wealth!",and "Thee for thrift!" (SB. V.2.1.25)

Puruṣamedha

As the name suggests, *puruṣamedha* refers to human sacrifice. A type of *soma* sacrifice lasting five days, it finds mention in the Yajurveda, Taittirīya, *śrauta sūtra*, et cetera. And according to Śatapatha Brahmaṇa, it is the highest sacrifice. The Kātyāyana Śrauta Sūtras explain that one who performs the *puruṣamedha* excels over everyone else in the world. One of the most controversial topics of the *yajña* in the recent past, starting from the time of Weber (Indische Streifen), is the big debate whether *puruṣamedha* involved human sacrifice or it was a symbolic act: "As many as 180 forms of human beings were to be offered to various deities including a *brahmaṇa*, a *kṣatriya*, a *vaiśya*, a *śūdra*, a murderer, a eunuch, a blind man, a deaf man, a washer man, a barren woman, a vina player, a flute player, cripple, a bald man, and many more." According to Dalal[22] (The Vedas, page 264), it is unlikely that all these victims were located and sacrificed. She cites inclusion of the *Puruṣa sūkta* hymn of Ṛgveda, in which *Puruṣa* performs the highest sacrifice from which creation emerges. He is also identified with *Prajāpati* and *Brahmanṇ* in the same section in which Yajurveda deals with *puruṣamedha*. Dalal concludes this as a reason for *Puruṣamedha* to be a symbolic act.

Dalal also cites GR Sharma's (Professor at Allahabad Unversity and the excavator of Kaushambi fame) claim of discovering the site of an ancient *puruṣamedha* - "*Śyenachiti Agnicayana* with the remains of human and animal bones and human skulls, as well as with the different types of bricks described in texts." Dr. Vishambhar Tripathi, in his exceptional work '*Agnicayana*' in Hindi language has successfully demonstrated that the bricks and earthenware unearthed by Sharma do not hold true to the specifications of bricks used in *agnicayana*. Tripathi goes a step further and demonstrates that the site had nothing to do with *agnicayana*.

Julius Eggeling (1842–1918) - a Professor of Sanskrit at the University of Edinburgh, and translator of Śatapatha Brahmaṇa too, in his introduction to Śatapatha Brahmaṇa (SBE volume 44), has discussed the issue of human sacrifice at length. In his view, such sacrifices were a universal custom in ancient times, and Indians too practised these as is "clearly shown by unmistakable traces of them in the ritualistic works". He rightly frames the next question - Was this practice maintained at the time with which we are concerned? In his view, the Yajurveda, the main textbook of sacrificial practices, no longer recognised human sacrifice. In his opinion, the story of *Sunahshepa* does not support the presence of human sacrifice because it doesn't answer the question - why would a childless king pray for the birth of a son only to sacrifice him? If it is on the say-so of Nārada, and the story is given merely to try the king's faith in truthfulness, then this case is similar to Abraham's sacrifice in the land of Moriah. The coarseness of the synonymous names - dog's tail - of the three sons of *brahmaṇa* further indicates that it is symbolic.

The clearest, most unambiguous reference to the old practice of human sacrifice is found in building of the fire altar[25] where heads of a goat, sheep, ox, horse and a man are planted in the bottom layer to provide stability to the altar. According to Eggeling, some subsequent remarks by the authors of *Brahmaṇa* (VI.2.1.37 seqq.) "go far to show that his previous statements are referred only to the traditional practice which, however, was no longer in use in his own day, and had probably not been so for generations past". The *Brahmaṇa* author summarily rejects substitutes of victim's head made of gold or clay confirming that "*Prajāpati* was the first to slaughter, and *Śyaparna Sayakayana* the last; and in the interval also people used to slaughter them." But importantly, the *Brahmaṇa* goes on to say, "but nowadays only these two are slaughtered, the one for *Prajāpati*, and the one for *Vāyu*." (SB. VI 2.1.39). Explaining why he slaughters this animal (a bearded, hornless white goat), the author quotes: "In this animal doubtless the form of all (the five kinds of) animal is (contained): in as much as it is hornless and bearded, to the form of a man, for man is hornless and bearded; inasmuch as it is hornless and furnished with the mane, that is the form of the horse, for the horse is hornless and furnished with the mane; inasmuch as it has hoofs, that is the bulls form, for the bull is eight-hoofed; inasmuch as its hoofs are like those of the sheep, that the form of the sheep; and in as much as it is a he goat, that is that of the goat. Thus, when he slaughters this one, thereby indeed all those (five) animals are slaughtered for him." (SB. VI 2.2.15). For *Prajāpati*, the animal is dark grey: "For the grey has two kinds of hair, the white and black; and two make a productive player: that is *Prajāpati*-characteristic. It is a hornless one, for *Prajāpati* is hornless." (SB. VI.2.2)

Finally, while discussing the relative value of non-animal offerings and five sacrificial animals, it is stated that because the gods used these five animals, the sacrificial essence was passed from one to the other, rendering the previous one useless for sacrifice until it finally entered the earth. From there it entered the rice and the barley, used afterwards for sacrificial dishes. This passage clearly indicates a gradual tendency towards substituting lower animals for higher ones and ultimately vegetables for animal offerings. (SB. I.2.3.6)

Vedic deities

There are many Vedic deities. In the Ṛgveda's first *manḍala* we come across *Agni*, *Vāyu*, the Aśvins, *Índra*, *Mitra*, *Savitṛ*, *Pūṣans*, *Rudra* and *Brahmaṇapati/ Bṛhaspati* - names which reappear, besides many other deities, all the way to the tenth *manḍala*. Of these, *Agni* and *Índra* undoubtedly appear to be more important and influential than the rest. *Uṣa*, *Maruts*, *Rudra*, *Mitra-Varuṇa* and *Viṣṇu*, apart from *Soma*, *Ribhus*, and *Ka*, have also been praised with hymns in the first *manḍala*. *Dadhikara* and *Bributaksha* find a place in the fourth and sixth *manḍala*, whereas *Saraswatī* appears only in the seventh *manḍala*. The eighth *manḍala* has some interesting names, such as *Asanga*, *Vibhindu*, *Trindara Parshvya*, *Anila*, *Trasadayu Paurukutsa*, *Chitra Raja*, *Prithushrava Kanita* and *Shrutva Arkshya*. And finally, we have *Apah*, *Yama*, *Yami*, *Asamati*, *Hasta* and *Bhavavrita* in the last *manḍala*. These deities rarely appear more than once in the entire Ṛgveda after the eighth *manḍala* - it appears they were of lesser importantance at the time.

The most important deity in the Ṛgveda without any doubt is *Índra*. Nearly 250 hymns are devoted to him alone, and nearly fifty hymns are jointly addressed to *Índra* and other deities. He is depicted as the leader who constantly leads battles. Apart from using the now famous thunder bolt (*vajra*) and other weapons in his armoury, he displays a penchant for living large and often manipulates situations to the advantage of the gods. Described as having tawny hair and beard, and a big belly (the result of imbibing *soma* liberally, no doubt), he rides a golden chariot drawn by two, and at times a thousand, horses. (ref RV 10.119) *Agni* and *Pūṣan* are considered his siblings.

However, *Índra* gradually ceded his position in the scriptures. In the Mahābhārata and Purāṇas, he is secondary to *Brahman*, *Viṣṇu* and *Śiva*.

After *Índra*, *Agni* is the second most important Vedic deity. A personification of the sacrificial fire, *Agni* is central to all sacrifices. There are more than 200 hymns dedicated to this deity in the Ṛgveda. Interestingly, the Vedas contain several adjoined names of deities, such as *Mitra Varuṇa*, making it difficult to understand if *Mitra-Varuṇa* is a separate deity, different from *Mitra* and *Varuṇa*, or not. Similarly, gods who are jointly praised and worshipped like *Agni-Índra, Índra-Agni, Agni-Soma, Agni-Sūrya,* et cetera occur several times in the Vedic texts. Like other gods, *Agni* has a fondness for *soma*; he removes darkness and brings light everywhere. He bestows all kinds of boons like granting children and prosperity. *Agni* takes many forms, such as *Jātaveda* and *Vaiśvanara* to name two, and was constantly reborn - *Agni* is both, the old and the new.

An important deity, *Varuṇa* normally finds a place in the Ṛgveda alongside *Mitra* as *Mitra-Varuṇa*. In the only hymn where he is without *Varuṇa*, he is said to 'bring men together uttering his voice'. While *Mitra* relates to the morning and sunrise, *Varuṇa* symbolises evening darkness in the Vedas. This could be because *Mitra* is similar to the *Zoroastrian Mitra*, the god of light and sun. In the Mahābhārata and Purāṇas, we come across *Mitra*, but as one of the *Ādityas*. *Mitra*, like *Varuṇa*, has only a single hymn in his name, the rest are in praise of *Mitra-Varuṇa* together. Although he is associated with mornings in earlier Veda texts, by the time of the *Brahmaṇa*, he had become a day time god. Interestingly, *Mitra* is one of *Śiva*'s names in the Mahābhārata.

Savitṛ has dozens of references and eleven hymns of the Ṛgveda dedicated to him. Another important deity, he grants immortality and protects his worshippers. The *gāyatri mantra* is addressed to *Savitṛ*. Riding a golden car drawn by radiant brown horses, he is said to light up the air, heaven and earth. *Savitṛ* follows the laws of the universe; even the wind and water move according to his orders. *Índra* too abides by his will. Many times, he appears to be identical to *Sūrya*. In the Mahābhārata, he is one of the twelve *Ādityas*. Later, *Savitṛ* is the name of *Śiva* and *Viṣṇu*.

Pūṣan, which means to prosper and grow, has eight hymns dedicated to him in the Ṛgveda besides finding dozens of mentions jointly with *Índra* and *Soma*. Described as the lord of all things, he too carries a golden spear and goad, has braided hair, sports a beard and rides a chariot drawn by goats. He is the protector of cattle and horses, and safegaurds travellers from dangers. In the Atharvaveda, he is described as leading the dead to the world of gods. Although he is mentioned in the Mahābhārata and the Purāṇas, he had become lesser known by that time.

Maruts are a group of deities, the sons of *Rudra*, responsible primarily for thunder, lightning and rain. Their number varies from twenty-one to 180. Invoked for providing rain and bringing healing remedies from mountains, seas and rivers, they were helpers of *Índra*, at times in conflict with them, self-luminous, of the same age and born at the same place. In the Vedic texts, they are storm as well as wind gods. They are often depicted carrying spears and golden helmets, riding golden chariots with golden wheels swiftly drawn by horses. In the time of the Rāmāyaṇa and the Purāṇas, they do find mention, but had dimished in importance.

Viṣṇu has less than half a dozen hymns dedicated to him in the Ṛgveda. However, he is mentioned several times in context of the three steps he took to cover both the earth and heaven. In Taittirīya Saṃhitā, *Viṣṇu* assumes the form of a dwarf and decimates *asuras* to free the earth from evil. In the Ṛgveda, there are stories of *Viṣṇu* and *Índra* conquering ninety-nine forts of *Shambara* and killing *Emusham*, the boar, which finds a place in the *Brahmaṇa* and, subsequently, in the Purāṇas. But he remains a second-rung deity all through the Vedic texts, nowhere close to *Índra* and *Agni*. He achieved prominence several centuries down the history of Hinduism.

Vāyu, the god of wind, is also known as *Vāta* in Ṛgveda. He finds mention in the very first *manḍala* of Ṛgveda ; an entire hymn is dedicated to him, and there are several references to *Vāyu* jointly with other gods. As a god who bestows wealth and fame, he also protects the weak and disperses their enemies. Riding a chariot drawn by red horses, he is believed to prolong life and heal. Never a first-rung deity, *Vāyu* continued to be important in the Mahābhārata as the father of *Bhīma*, and in the Rāmāyaṇa as *Hanumān's* father. Gradually, he descended the ladder and in the Purāṇas was named one of the guardians, *dikpāla* of the north-west.

Yama and *Yami* are siblings. *Yami* fell in incestuous love with her brother, the god of death. He is one of the most feared deities and not a popular god for the obvious reason. By the time of the Mahābhārata, he had become the son of *Sūrya*. *Yama* imparts to *Yami* a lesson in Dharma and correct actions, which forms an important part of Vedic literature. *Yami* is also the personification of river *Yamunā*.

Sūrya is the sun as well as a deity; there are ten hymns dedicated to him in the Ṛgveda. *Sūrya* keeps away bad dreams, sickness and disease, and provides a long life to the entire world. He rides a chariot drawn by seven white horses which represent rays of the sun. He is also known as *Āditya*, son of *Dayus*. Although in the Vedas, they also appear as individual deities *Savitṛ*, *Āryaman*, *Pūṣan*, *Mitra* and *Bhaga* are considered synonyms of *Sūrya*. Later, *Sūrya's* importance dimished, but he continued to be worshipped and finds several mentions in the Mahābhārata, the Rāmāyaṇa, et cetera.

Soma is god of the moon in the Ṛgveda, a plant, and the divine drink made from the mysterious *Soma* plant. The entire ninth *manḍala*, with all its 114 hymns, is dedicated to *soma* as a deity and a plant. The Ṛgveda provides a detailed method for the extraction of juice from the *soma* plant, also called *soma*, which is an elixir of immortality called *amṛta*. *Soma* is not merely a drink, but a ṛṣi, the soul of *Índra*, and his friend. There are several joint references to *Soma* in the Ṛgveda with *Índra*, *Agni* and *Pūṣan*. As a deity, *Soma's* abode is in the heavens. After the Vedic period, *soma* continued to remain important in many *yajñas* which were performed right through to the time of the Mahābhārata. Gradually, *soma* came to be identified more as the name of the moon.

Rudra has three hymns dedicated to him in the Ṛgveda, where he is the storm god in an earlier form of *Śiva*. He is described as copper coloured with a blue neck and blue tuft in Yajurveda. He is addressed as *Mahādeva* and *Shri Rudram* (*Śatarudriya*), one of the most powerful chants in Taittirīya Saṃhitā 4.5, 4.7 which describes him as a dweller of mountains, clothed in skin, young, fierce, strong and wise, one whose wrath is to be feared by all. He is also the most benevolent.

Aśvins are twins described as young, honey coloured and riding a three-wheeled golden chariot drawn by a deer, horse, buffalo or an ass. Among Vedic deities, *Aśvins* are fourth in the heirarchy after *Índra*, *Agni* and *Soma*. The Ṛgveda contains fifty hymns and more than 400 references to the *Aśvins*. Radiating golden brilliance, they were considered owners of horses (*aśva*) and often described rescuing people from water. They are helpers not only to distressed humans, but also to animals. Numerous tales describe them as healers of earthly beings and physicians of gods. According to Yaska in his Nirukta, some considered them to be heaven and earth, others day and night. They continued to be mentioned frequently until the times of the Mahābhārata and the Purāṇas.

Aditi is a goddess in the Ṛgveda, mother of a group of gods, the *Ādityas*. Bright and luminous, she supports all creatures and is invoked in the morning, at noon and sunset. She provides freedom from bonds of suffering (meaning of *aditi* is 'unbound'), she is sky and space, the mother, father, son, all there was, all that has been and will be. Though there is no hymn dedicated to her, there are close to a hundred references to her name in the Ṛgveda. Her sons, the *Ādityas*, who have half a dozen hymns dedicated to them in the Ṛgveda, are *Mitra*, *Varuṇa*, *Bhaga*, *Daksha*, *Amsha* and possibly two or three more, including *Mārtanda* and *Āryaman*. By the time of Mahābhārata, four more *Ādityas* were added to the list of eight who later came to be worshipped along with the nine planets (*navagraha*).

Ambikā, later known as *Durgā*, was not known in Ṛgvedic times. In later texts - Taittirīya Āraṇyaka - we come across *Ambikā* who is also called *Durgā*, *Vairocani* and *Katyayani*. It is later in the Upaniṣads that we come across *Umā*, *Haimāvati* and *Kāli*, who become full-fledged *Durgā* in the Mahābhārata and the Purāṇas.

Brahman is the creator god, also known as *Viśva Karman*, *Hiraṇyagarbha* and *Prajāpati*. Śatapatha Brahmaṇa describes him as the creator of gods and the source of all. *Brahman* continued to hold the same importance in the Mahābhārata and subsequent texts.

Bṛhaspati has eleven hymns dedicated to him in the Ṛgveda and has more than a hundred mentions. Born of the light in the heaven, he is also known as *Brahmanṇāpati* who drives away the darkness with thunder that has seven mouths, seven rays and a hundred wings. He is right and pure with a chariot drawn by red horses. Described as a friend of *Índra*, he is also identified with *Agni* and in subsequent Vedic texts is invoked as a priest. Later, he came to be identified with the planet of his name and is worshipped as one of the *navagrahas*.

Dyaus is both the sky and god of heaven or sky. In the Ṛgveda, he is associated with the earth (*Pṛthvī*) and the dawn, *Uṣa*, his daughter. *Dyaus* and *Pṛthvī* have half a dozen hymns dedicated to them, and are called father and mother who sustained the world and all its creatures. In the later Veda period, *Dyaus* became a lesser-known god.

Chapter 13

Soma Yajña

Participants

Yajamāna - The *yajamāna* or sacrificer is the cause of the *yajña*; he initiates the whole process for his *kāmya*. The etymological meaning of *yajamāna* is 'one who is the performer of a sacrifice'. In Vedic thinking, the *ṛtvij* (priests), who are seen performing all the actions, are believed to only assist the *yajamāna*. They do not get any benefit of the sacrifice; it is the *yajamāna* who accrues fruits of the sacrifices. What *ṛtvij* receive for their effort is *dakṣiṇā* - a gift given by the *yajamāna* to the priests at the conclusion of the ceremony.

A *gṛhastha* (married man) belonging to the *brahmaṇa*, *kṣatriya* or *vaiśya varṇa* is entitled to maintain the Vedic fire and perform *yajñas*. Once established, it was mandatory to maintain the fire for rest of one's life. If the fire died, it had to be rekindled following an elaborate procedure. Though the householder was entitled to maintain the Vedic fire immediately after marriage, in real practice people avoided keeping the fire immediately post-marriage as it constrained their travel from one place to another creating an additional burden.

Patnī - Wife of the *yajamāna* who played an important role in *yajñas*.

***Ṛtvij* or priests** had crucial roles to play in *yajñas*, from planning to execution of the whole exercise. The *yajamāna* selected them to take over procurement of all utensils, implements and materials needed for the sacrifice, and requisition materials for building infrastructure for the *yajña* (in larger *yajñas*, it was a huge task for *ṛtvij* - requiring great skill, experience and knowledge). However, their main role lay in conducting the *yajña* as per *Brahmaṇa* and other *sūtras* which went in incredible detail and required a high degree of perfection in executing numerous steps spread over several days, months or even years.

Priests who came from the line of traditional priests and belonged to a good stable were favoured. The *gurukula* from which they graduated weighed heavily in their selection as priests, just as an IIT or IIM does in our time.

The discussion or demand for a fee was a big no-no and completely forbidden. A *dakṣiṇā* was purely a gift which the *yajamāna* unilaterally decided. Usually, the *yajamānas* were extremely generous in their *dakṣiṇās* because it also brought them additional credit, besides the benefits they accrued from the *yajña*. There are records showing that tens of thousands of cows, in addition to land, were given to individual priests for performing *yajñas* like *aśvamedha* or *vājapeya*.

A priest was disqualified and barred if he had any physical disability or deformity.

The priests were classified in four categories according to the Vedas -

- The *hotṛ* with the Ṛgveda;
- The *adhvaru* with the Yajurveda;
- The *udgātṛ* with the Sāmaveda; and
- The *brahmaṇa* with the Atharvaveda

Each of these four main priests had three assistants - *dvitīye*, *tritiye* and *padi* - as per the table given below:

Veda	**Main Priest**	***Dvitīya***	***Tritīya***	***Padi***
Ṛgveda	*Hotṛ*	*Sautravarun*	*Accāvāka*	*Avastut*
Yajurveda	*Adhvaryu*	*Pratiprasthatṛ*	*Neṣtṛ*	*Unnetṛ*
Sāmaveda	*Udgātṛ*	*Prastotṛ*	*Pratihartṛ*	*Subhramanya*
Atharvaveda	*Brahmaṇa*	*Brahmanṇācchamśin*	*Āgnīdhra*	*Potṛ*

The number of priests required for a sacrifice depended on the type of *yajña*. Not all *yajñas* required presence of sixteen priests, however, all *soma yajñas* did.

The duties assigned to the priests were in accordance with the hierarchy, clearly defined for each of the assistant. The same was reflected in the *dakṣiṇā* - the *dvitīye* received half, *tritīyi* one third, and *padi* one fourth of the main priest's amount.

Since *soma* is a Yajurveda *yajña*, *adhvaryu* played the key role in the ceremony. The *brahmaṇa* on the other hand was a silent observer who sat aloof and keept a hawk-eye to ensure that the ceremony was conducted exactly as per the prescribed texts. He intervened whenever a slip occurred and gave directions for immediate correction. The *brahmaṇa* had to be the most knowledgeable of all and fully conversant with all aspects of the ceremony to function as a supervisor and stage manager of the whole show.

Adhvaru's main tasks involved selection of a suitable ground for the sacrifice, preparation of the ground and marking it with the exact measurements to build various facilities as prescribed in the texts, including construction of the *mandapa*, plinths, *mahávedi*, and enclosures, besides procurement of all implements, vessels and other materials to be used in the sacrifice.

The *mahávedi*, *vedi* and *yajñashālā* simply cannot be prepared without knowledge of *Śulba Śāstra* (part of *Vedanga*, involving study of geometry). The success of any *yajña* is contingent on the right setup of *yajñaśhālā*, and so the role of *adhvaryu* and his knowledge of geometry (*Śulba Śāstra*) was critical.

Agni

Agni as "the chosen priest, God, minister of sacrifice, the *hotṛ*" (RV.1.1.1), is the most important constituent of any Vedic *yajña* who not only brings "hitherwards the Gods" (RV.1.1.2) to the *yajña*, but also carries the sacrifice to the gods - "*Agni*, the perfect sacrifice in which thou encompasses about; Verily goeth to the Gods" (RV. 1.1.5). For spiritualists, sacrificial fires are the threefold knowledge leading to good-hood and the supreme means of liberation.[1]

The three *agnis* (*tretāgnis*) are *gārhapatya*, *dakṣiṇā* and *āhavanīya*. The latter two are sourced from *gārhapatya* and classified as -

i. *Vihāraniya* - fire which can be moved from one place to another; and

ii. *Upastheya* - fire which is fixed and cannot be moved

There are eight types of *vihāraniya* (mobile fires) kept next to eight priests: *āgnīdhra*, *hotṛ*, *maitra varuṇa* (the first assistant of the *hotṛ*), *brahmaṇa chamśi*, *potṛ*, *neśtṛ*, *acchāvāka* and *mārjala* (the one who does *marjana* - purification).

Upastheya are also of eight kinds, located at - *dhruva sthali* (the fixed place of *dhruva*, an offering spoon of *sruc* class on *vedi*), *cātvāla sthāna* (a pit admeasuring appox 2.25 feet square, dug outside the *vedi* from where loose earth is drawn for various *yajña* purposes), *śamitra* (the place of *paśu*), an *uḍumbara* (a post of *uḍumbara* wood located at a central point of *sadas*), *brahmaṇa* - the chief *ṛtvij*, *sukhashālā* and the *yajamāna*.

Oblations

The offerings made in the consecrated fire to please gods, such as *ghī*, rice, corn, blades of grass, milk, curd, barley, fruits, vegetables, *soma* juice, other cereals, and parts of a victim.

Vedi

In Vedic language, the sacrificial altar is termed *vedi*. It is either a dug, or elevated, plot of ground where different sacrificial materials, implements and utensils used in the sacrifice are placed on the *durbha* grass. Located between the *āhavanīya* and *gārhapatya*, the rectangular *vedi* is supposed to be in the shape of a young woman with broad hips, shoulders and a slender waist. The north and the south sides are made concave to make the resemblance complete. (ref diagram D-1)

The measurements and shape of a *vedi* vary according to the type of *yajña* and are elaborated in the Śatapatha Brahmaṇa and concerned *Kalpa* texts. Interestingly, the unit of measurement is not absolute and depends on physical attributes of the *yajamāna* - such as his height from toe to the tip of the raised right hand's middle finger, elbow to tip of the middle finger (*hasta*), or length of his normal step (*pada*), thereby emphasising the link between the *yajamāna* and creation of *yajñashālā*, and as a reflection of *Prajāpati's* sacrifice.

Mahāvedi is the great altar, also called *saumika*. It is a trapezium facing *śālā* two parallel arms running north to south measuring 56 feet and 45 feet, separated by 67 feet. An oblong shaped shed, called *sadas*, a shed where two bullock-carts are parked (*havirdhanā mandapa*) and a high altar (called *uttaravedi*) is constructed within the *mahāvedi*.

Agnicayana

Also called *cayana*, it is the rite of piling the fire altar in which five layers of fired clay bricks numbering thousands are used on the *uttaravedi* for setting up the *āhavanīya* for *soma* sacrifices.

Yajña implements

The ten principle *yajña* utensils or *pātras*, also called *yajña āyudha* (TS-I.6.8.2 - 3), include -

i. *Sphya* - a sword-shaped *khadira* wood implement, one *pradeśa* (9 inches) in length, used for various sacrificial acts, symbolically ensuring the safety and unhindered performance of a sacrifice. It is used to perform various acts related to the *vedi*, such as drawing the *vedi* outline and other lines (*lekha*), removing the upper layer (*tvac*) of the *vedi*, etc.

ii. *Kapālas* - square-shaped small troughs made of burnt clay and used for cooking *puroḍāśa* cakes

iii. *Agnihotṛ ahavani* - a large ladle made of *vaikankata* wood used for pouring oblations of milk into the *gārhapatya* fire

iv. *Śurpa* - a winnowing basket made of bamboo or reed, used for winnowing grains

v. *Krisṇajina* - deerskin on which *dṛṣad* and *upala* are kept before pounding rice grains

vi. *Śamya* - a wooden yoke made of *khadira* wood used for measuring the *uttaravedi*, either 32 *angulas* (two feet) long or the same length as *juhu*. Its thicker portion is called *kumba*.

vii. *Ulukhala* - mortar made of *palāsa* or *uḍumbara* wood used for pounding corns;

viii. *Mūsala* - pestle made of *khadira* wood used for pounding

ix & x. *Dṛṣad* and *upalā* - grinding stones used to pound grains for making rice cakes (*puroḍāśa*). *Drishad* is the flat lower stone and *upala* is the upper grinding cylindrical stone.

Some more utensils include -

- *Madanti* - vessel for heating water to cook the *puroḍāśa* cakes;
- *Praṇanita pranayana* - a long rectangular vessel made of *aśvāttha* wood used by the *adhvaru* priest to carry holy water;
- *Idā* and *dāru pātra* - oblong-shaped look alike vessels made of *aśvāttha* wood used to retain the remnants of *havis* after offering, and store the *puodasha* and *caru*;
- *Dohana* - vessel used to collect milk during milking;
- *Sannaya tappani* - two bronze vessels in which milk is collected in the morning and evening, and heated together;
- *Sruc* and *ṣruva* - small wooden spoons for offering clarified butter (*ājya*);
- *Juhū* and *upabhṛt* - wooden spoons like *agnihotṛahavani*, but smaller in size;
- *Yoktra* - a rope made of *munja* grass straw used as a belt;
- *Chamṣa* - deep wooden bowls with short handles to keep *soma* juice;
- *Daśapavitra* - a small cloth sieve used to strain *soma* juice;
- *Droṇakalaśa* - a wooden vessel for collecting the strained *soma* juice;
- *Anvāhāryasthali* - a big metal vassel in which food is cooked for distribution amongst priests after completion of the main sacrifice;
- *Araṇīs* - two pieces of wood used to generate a fire by vigorously rubbing one against the other. The upper piece, called *uttaraṇī*, is shaped like a round pestle, and the lower piece has a slot to insert the upper piece;
- *Ājyasthali* - a bronze vessel for storing *ājya* or *ghī*;
- *Yūpa* - an octagonal wooden post to tie the animal to be immolated

Yajña - dravyas and the *pātras*

Homa, in the '*laukika*' (worldly) fire, is core of a *yajña* and the purification rites are integral to this exercise. *Dravyas*, ingredients used in a *yajña*, and the implements required for performing *agni kārya* (exercise connected with the fire) are listed below -

- *Sruc* and *śuva* - wooden ladles used for making offerings in the fire
- *Idhma* - wooden sticks or samidhas used as fuel in the sacrifice
- *Pātras* - bowls or plates containing different ingredients

Pātras can be categorised under three heads based on their use. The *prokshini* is used for sprinkling (to purify); *ājya* is used to hold *ghī*; and *pūrna pātra*, as the name suggests, is used for keeping all other ingredients needed for a *yajña*.

Chapter 14

Soma yajña ritual

What is *soma* - plant, drink or the god *Soma*?

Soma the elixir, the drink discovered by gods themselves, was considered so important it was personified as a deity, *Soma Deva*, and all 114 hymns of the ninth *maṇḍala* of the Ṛgveda dedicated to it. Immitating their gods when mortal humans drank *soma*, they had a sense of finding god and immortality -

> "We have drunk the *soma*; we have become immortal; we have gone to the light; we have found gods.
> What can hostility do to us now, and what the malice of mortal, O! immortal one?" (RV. V I I I.48.3, J & B)

In Ṛgveda, hymns are dedicated to all three i.e. *soma* the plant, its juice, and *Soma* the deity, and even the method of juice extraction and identification of the plant is described in detail. The exhilarating drink can be compared to Avestan *haoma* which was extracted from the *haoma* plant, and considered a divine drink by followers of that religion in olden times, in present-day Iran.

Though *soma* plant has now been extinct for a long time, we know from Vedic texts that it was found in the hills. Suśruta Saṃhitā says that apart from mountains of (ancient) India - the Himalayas, Mahendra, Devagiri, Vindhya, et cetera - a few *soma* varieties also grew in the aquatic habitats around Devasunda Lake, Sindhu River and Manas Lake in Kashmir. According to the famous Ayurvedic scholar Suśruta, the best *soma* is found in the upper Indus and Kashmir region[1]. The Ṛg describes *soma* as a 'stalk' of green colour whose juice is extracted by pressing and pounding (9.74.2 - 5) which makes it fibrous, like twigs or roots. It is then strained using fleece (RV. 9.13.1) or a woollen cloth (RV. 9.13.6) to contain the sediments and other impurities (9.16.2-4). The juice is described brown or tawny (9.11.4,7; 31.5; 5.4), but also a bright red (9.8.6) in other texts, indicating that plants from different geographical locations had different botanical characteristics.

Extraction of juice from the stalks required a high degree of skill. The plant stalks were pressed (*savana*) between stones (9.3 4.3) which resulted in copious quantities of juice flowing out like 'a flood' (9.1 6.1).

Apart from exhilaration - it 'inflamed' one 'like a churned fire', made one feel 'conspicuous' and 'better off' apart from making think of oneself as ' rich'and all set to 'prosperity'.[2]

Considered a divine drink, it had deep affect -

> "I of good wisdom have partaken of the vitality of the sweet drink, which is rich in purpose and excellent at finding wide space,
> which all the gods and mortals, calling it honey, converge upon.
> When you have gone within, you will become *Aditi* [/boundless ness], appeaser of divine wrath.
> Drop, enjoined the comradeship of *Índra*, like an obedient mare following the chariot - pole, you should follow riches to fulfilment."
> (RV. VI I I. 48.1 - 2, J&B)

No wonder it was variously called *Amrit*, nectar which conferred immortality.

Why is *soma yajña* performed? What does it deliver?

All *yajñas* bestow the desired '*kāmya*' upon the *yajamāna*. *Soma yajña* is considered particularly efficacious in conferring prosperity (RV, 9.90.3; 40.5-6), strength and power, the ability to bring down an enemy's might whether enemy is near or far (2. 19), drive away the enemy, and give victory in battles (8.8). It can ennoble a man by conferring general prosperity, wealth of cattle and horses, and strength to uphold the law (8.7-9). The Ṛgveda describes *soma* as the destroyer of fiends (1.2). Apart from these worldly gains *soma* had spiritual power to confer bliss and give the kinship with the gods (10.8).

With so much to give, *soma*, naturally, was considered the most important of all *yajñas*.

The sages called upon the gods to drink *soma* juice in *yajñas*, not only because it was considered fit for the gods (1.4), but also because it was food that the gods relished. Its offering thus ensured their presence in the *yajña*, and thereby its success.

***Agniṣṭoma* : *Soma Yajña* Ritual**

A description of *Agniṣṭoma* is given below. Those readers who will like to go through the detailed *vidhi* of this *Soma yajña* may refer to the Appendix - 1 where a step by step account is given.

Agniṣṭoma or 'praise of *Agni*' is a *Soma* sacrifice. There are seven basic or fundamental forms of *Soma* sacrifice, and *Agniṣṭoma* - considered a model of *Soma* sacrifice (Āp Sr. X.2.3) - closely related to *Jyotiṣṭoma*, is one of them and. Its name is derived from the last *stotra* chanted in the rite.

It takes only one day to perform the core of the rite (*sutya* - the day of pressing and libations), and it therefore falls in the category of *ekāha* (one day *Soma* ceremony). But the full rite lasts for 5 days - first four days devoted to preparatory rites and rituals, and the fifth day - the day of extraction and libations of *Soma*. *Agniṣṭoma* is performed annually in spring.

First day - The day starts with the householder (sacrificer) formally resolving to perform the sacrifice.

The priests are selected by the householder (sacrificer) who then requests the king to allot a suitable piece of land for erecting infrastructure of the *Soma* ceremony. A hut is built on the land in which the sacrificer lives during the entire period of sacrifice. In preparatory ceremony, he is consecrated: his hair and nails cut, he is given bath, and he observes restraint - practices celibacy and eats and draiks restricted diet. He wears black antelope skin, carries a staff, and keeps his hands clasped in imitation of an embryo. No one pronounces his name or touches him and he is forbidden to talk to *śudras*. His wife lives in another hut nearby under similar conditions.

A shed measuring appox. 30 feet in length and 22 in width is erected inside which are located - the three fires, woman shaped rectangular altar (*vedi*), place to tie the victim lambs etc.

Second day - *Soma* stalks are symbolically purchased by a *brahmaṇa* in exchange for a cow, which are then brought by priests in a cart and received ceremoniously as an honoured guest, and a 'hospitality-sacrifice' held in its (*Soma's*) honour. The priests then make a compact of mutual loyalty - not to spoil proceedings arising out of mutual disagreements. In another rite of intermediate consecration, a priest brings boiling water in a vessel which is touched by all, the sacrificer tightens his girdle, clasps hands tighter and cuts down his food intake to warm milk, indicating intensified austerities. The cart carrying *Soma* stalks, accompanied with the litany, is brought under a shed admeasuring 22 X 22 feet, specially ercted for parking carts, and the King *Soma* (stalks) is transferred on the throne (chair).

Pravargya, an independent complex rite, in which a specially handmade, baked earthen pot is heated red hot, and boiling *ghī* and milk poured over it producing a column of fire, is performed two times every day - mornings and evenings - except on the day of actual pressing. It is performed either before or after a rite (*upasadas* - 'sessions'/'homage') in which a series of oblations and recitation of sayings referring to *Agni* and other myths are performed.

Third day - After *pravargya* and *upasada* have been performed twice, the large and high altar are constructed. The large altar is a trapezium shaped arena; two parallel arms of the trapezium measuring 56 feet and 45 feet, separated 67 feet apart. The high altar is also shaped like a trapezium - the two parallel arms 6 and

4 feet long respectively, separated by a distance of 10 feet - in which the navel, a square hole of the size of a cow's hoof is located. The parking shed for the two carts, which is constructed next day, is also located within the large altar.

Fourth day - *Pravargya* and *upasada* - both are performed twice.

Parking shed for two carts - measuring 22 X 22 feet - is constructed where the carts carrying the *Soma* stalks are parked. In this shed near the carts four 'resonance' holes are dug which are roughly a foot and quarter deep and about a foot in diameter. Each hole is separated over the ground by a distance of about a foot, and inter- connected under the ground. Another large shed - 40 X 19 feet - is constructed towards the westernmost side of the large altar, for the priests, six fire hearths, seating for the householder and the supervisor priest. A wooden post of *Udumbara* (Ficus glomerata tree) is located in this shed and the spectators who are allowed to witness the rites sit here.

Huts for cleaning sacrificial utensils, and for keeping fire, are also constructed on this day and are located inside the large trapezium.

After dedicatory and other rites the priests and the family come in a procession carrying the *Soma* stalks and the *āhavanīya* fire to offer a goat to *Agni-Soma*. The procession is led by the priest, the sacrificer holds the priest who in turn is held by his wife, who agin in turn is held by the sons, the sons are held by the grandsons so on. The consecration ends following some more rites.

An animal sacrifice of a goat is performed. The householder keeps awake the whole night, watching over the *Soma* stalks.

Fifth day - The final day, the day of action called *sutyā*, has three pressings of *Soma* stalks (*savana*) - in the morning, midday and afternoon. Preparations begin very early- soon after midnight and long before the dawn. All utensils are arranged and kept at their proper place.

Sitting between the yoke, the priest offers oblations of *ghī* and starts the morning recitations of (Rigveda) mantra. Nearly a fifth of Rig verses are sung, passing through the seven tones of the deep scale. Then begins the first pressing of the stalks. The four 'resonance holes' are covered by two wooden boards and red hide of a bull, cut to fit the boards, spread over them. The stalks, soaked in water, are crushed between two stones on this board; the sound of crushing and flow of juices gets amplified and resonates due to hollow under the boards, giving the name *uparava* (resonance) to the holes.

The juice fall in a jar containing water from where it is transferred by the designated priest to another vat belonging to the priest responsible for reciting mantras to invoke gods. The householder pours this mixture of juice and dregs through a filter of wool to obtain 'pure' *Soma*, and this 'pure' *Soma* juice is filled in various cups for libation and drinking. During this process of filtration, the priests chant hymns and offer oblations. This is preceded by a ritual procession in which the priests and the sacrificer hold on to each other's garments, and proceeded stealthily - in a creeping movement, bending their heads and licking lips, manoeuvring like a hunter in pursuit of a deer. They move to the adjacent shed (containing the six hearths) and return to the hut by the same route.

Cups of libations - *graha* - of *Soma*, cakes, hot mixture of milk and sour milk etc., are offered, followed by special libations of *Soma* brought from various vats of different priests. After a recitation of 'inviter'(a subordinate priest), more cups of *Soma* are offered followed by an oblation to *Agni*.

Drinking of *Soma*, followed by another sacrifice of goat brings to end the morning proceedings.

The midday proceedings mark the climax. These follow the same pattern as the morning proceedings except for an extra offering of hot sour milk. With distribution of *dakṣiṇā* the midday services conclude.

Immediately after the midday services are over the third service starts which follows the pattern of midday service. Animal sacrifice which began in the morning service is concluded, and offering made to the deceased ancestors followed by chanting by the assistant priest responsible for chanting.

[Note - Beside the sacrifice of single victims, sacrifice of eleven animals is sometimes performed; rites varied. Ref. Barnett Lionel D (1999). Antiquities of India. New Delhi. Atlantic Publishers and Distributers. fn page 161]

Householder and his wife thereafter bathe, wash each other's back, and wear new clothes.

The proceedings conclude with oblations and a barren cow is offered to *Mitra* and *Varuna* etc.

PART III

तत्वमसि

Thou art That

(Chandogya Upanishad 6.8.7)

Chapter 15

From Action to Knowledge - Veda to Vedānta

Before we begin to understand how Jaimini (400-200 BC), his students and subsequent commentators - down the centuries to Mandāna Mishra - looked at the Vedas, vedānta, sacrifices and related rituals, it will be useful to first look at how things changed in Bhāratvarṣa from what started (around 1700-1500 BC) as a *yajña*-based Vedic society of Āryans.

Ṛgvedic society was centered around *yajña*. The Āryans believed *yajñas* yielded all that a man desired - sons, cattle,protection from natural calamities and diseases. If properly performed, *yajñas* also ensured heaven in the afterlife. In the early Vedic days, *yajñas* were simple affairs requiring little more than a place for *vedi* (sacrificial altar), fuel sticks, oblation materials and one or more priests. The society itself was pastoral wanderer, and this 'portable religion' fit well with its nomadic impulsion.

When the society started settling down to agriculture, these Āryans started building homes for themselves. *Śrauta* were the only ceremonies performed at this time, so called because these *yajñas* were performed in the three *śrauta agnis*, namely *gārhapatya*, *āhavanīya* and *dakṣiṇāgni*. Most such ceremonies were performed by the householder himself. *Śrauta yajñas* were of two types - *havir* and *soma*; each in turn was further classified into seven different *yajñas*. The oblations in *havir* were grains, butter, curd, *ghī*, et cetera. With the exception of three *havir yajñas*, which were performed outside in a *yajñashāla*, the rest were performed in the *yajamāna's* house. Two of the *havirs* involved animal sacrifices. *Havirs* were largely private affairs in which members of the household or friends and relatives participated. On the other hand, *soma yajñas* were essentially public affairs performed only by kings or the very affluent in a *yajñashāla* (a temporary structure requiring a large piece of land specially created for a *yajña*) outside homes. *Soma yajñas* derived their name from the oblation of *soma* (juice of *soma* plant) used in these *yajñas*.

In addition to the usual gains that he accrued, the *yajamāna's* social status was also enhanced by performing the *yajña*. The priest also benefitted - apart from earning name and fame, he received land, large number of cattle and significant sums of money as *dakṣiṇā*. We should not overlook this important and complex sociological and economic function served by the ritual even in its earliest stages.

Our knowledge of *śrauta* - the oldest rituals - does not come from the Ṛg *Saṃhitā* which contains only occasional and oblique references to the *yajñas*. It is the Brahmaṇas that provide details of the rituals. However, the real repository of these *yajña* rituals are the *śrauta sūtras* which were created solely for this purpose, they contain all details of *śrauta* ceremonies,. We know that *śrauta* literature was created centuries after the *Saṃhitā* and later than the Brahmaṇas - between 800 to 400 BC - but, as is the case with most pre-Buddhist Vedic texts, a fixed date cannot be assigned to any of the *śrauta sūtras*, even the ones ascribed to sages Āpastamba, Baudhāyana, Aśvāyana, Latāyana, et cetera. It was during this time that Āryan society transformed from pastoral to agrarian, with far reaching and, in many cases, radical, social, religious and political changes. These changes had a deep and lasting effect on the evolution of Indian civilization.

Karl Jaspers, the Axial Age, and the *Śhrauta*

Between 900-200 BC, across most of the inhabited world, great intellectual, philosophical and religious systems emerged almost simultaneously, shaping human society and culture. During this period, thinkers in India explored the doctrine of *karma* and how *mokṣa* (liberation) could be attained; Socrates in ancient Greece emphasised the use of reason in the relentless investigation of truth; Plato laid the foundation of Western Philosophy by theorising how the world of everyday existence and the eternal world of ideas interrelate. Nearer home, the Chinese thinkers (disciples of Confucius) argued that the '*dao*' (way) for human society lay in promoting human civilisation, while some others (Zhuanji) came to look at the cosmic '*dao*' as a guide for life. The Hebrew prophets came to view the god of nation of Israel as the one who created heaven and earth and shaped the destiny of all people. In Persia, Zoroastrianism claimed that human history was conceived as a microcosm of the cosmic struggle between good and evil, and humans were living the struggle of choosing good over evil.

Karl Jaspers, a German psychiatrist and philosopher called this period the 'Axial age'. Jaspers found this nomenclature appropriate since he observed a shift during this period, a turning away (as if on an axis), from predominantly localised concerns towards transcendence. A defining feature of the Axial age is that these significant developments in the history of human civilisation took place quite independently, often thousands of miles apart in different geographical and cultural locations. These thinkers though dispersed in different part of the world, had one thing in common - finding solutions to life's questions, not only for their own selves, but for the society. The question related to existence or experience beyond the normal physical plane i.e. transcendence. Charles Taylor is a Canadian sociologist and philosopher. In his book The Secular Age, he has put his views contradicting seculerization thesis, which holds that as modernity (a bundle of phenomena including science, technology, and rational forms of authority) progresses, religion gradually diminishes in influence. Taylor argues that the modern world has not seen the disappearance of religion but rather its diversification and in many places its growth.

Taylor saw a qualitative change in thinking in the 'transcendence' - stepping away from a passive acceptance of the existence of the cosmos and the way it functions as *fait accompli*, these philosophies questioned the how and why of it. They pondered and speculated about human beings' relationship with the cosmos and importantly, about 'the good' and how human beings can be good.

During the Axial age, accelerated by technological advances like use of the iron plough, major socio-economic-political changes were afoot in Vedic India as well. Though there are references to other metals in the Ṛgveda, it does not mention iron. However, this evidence is used for determining the antiquity of the Ṛg as pre-Iron age. [According to latest path breaking studies by Tewari R., Man and Environment XXXV(2): 81-97 [2010], iron was known in this part in early second century BC. The technology of using iron in the ploughs probably came much later.] The hymn in praise of agricultural divinities in the fourth *maṇḍala* of the Ṛgveda praises the plough in several verses -

> 'O Prosperity and Plow, take pleasure in this speech here.'
>
> 'Let *Índra* lay down the follow; let *Pūṣan* extend her straight.'
>
> 'For prosperity let our plowshares till through the Earth; for prosperity let our plowmen advance with the draft - animals.'[1]

Such praise points to the use of the plough in agriculture - a technological advancement which must have resulted not only in ease of land tilling, but also a high yield resulting in surplus food production. In the words of Eraly[2]: "This constituted a momentous change, which provided relative security of livelihood to the people, steady revenue to the state, and laid the economic basis for the advancement of civilisation." Eraly makes an important observation that "all the cultural activities of the society depended on his (farmer) productivity." How true! The ploughs become more significant in later texts. *Índra*, the most powerful Vedic god and leader of the *devatās*, is praised as 'Lord of the plough', and the *Maruts* as ploughmen, in subsequent Vedic texts (Atharva) belonging to the middle Vedic period.

Migratory pastoral Āryans who had started taking to agriculture in early Vedic period in the Indus valley region had now upscaled it, thereby adding pressure on availability of arable land. This resulted in a search for virgin lands as well as pastures. People moved eastward from the Indus Valley (present day Punjab and beyond, towards the west) through the Himalayan regions (north of the Ganges), and into the Gangetic plains towards the end of second millennium BC. Over time, these Āryans settled in the Gangetic plains and coalesced into more rooted agricultural societies. This resulted in surplus food production and the formation of increasingly larger and more complex settled communities and the emergence of new occupations.

Mark Taylor talks extensively of the axial age and the radical changes it wrought in the conception of the 'world' and 'self'. Early Vedic religion which was restricted to *yajñas* for propitiating gods and beseeching them for sons, cattle, et cetera also adapted to the socio-politico-geographical changes associated with the emergence of large agrarian communities. The Brahmaṇas and *srauta sūtras* - which give details of the *yajña* rituals - were composed during this period.

Yajña began assuming importance not due to religion alone, but because it elevated the social status of the *yajamāna* in society and showered the priest with financial rewards. This was probably an important reason the *brahmaṇas* turned the previously simple *śrauta* rituals into increasingly complex and lengthy affairs.

∞

These rituals became further complex and grew in size from the early Vedic to the Brahmaṇa period and, finally, to the late Vedic *sūtra* times. Urbanization of society had resulted in many new occupations, and with the emergence of new *jātis* (example: *rathakāra* - chariot maker), more frequent interaction and social intermingling among different *varṇa*s gave birth to new castes. In this fast-emerging urban economy, new laws and codes of conduct had to be formulated for new *jātis* and castes - a job strictly in the domain of *brahmaṇas*, which made their role as vital as the king's, for the smooth functioning of society. They (*brahmaṇas*) were not only the sole conductors of rituals, but were also tasked with slotting these new *jātis* and castes under appropriate *varṇa* groups and prescribing religious duties. While *kṣatriyas* became *rājans*, *rajās* and *mahārājās* - wielders of state power - the *brahmaṇas* became indispensable to royalty - no *yajña* could be performed without them, nor any victory expeditions launched. A *ksatriya* could not even be anointed a king and ascend the throne without the appropriate *yajña* and associated rituals!

Śrauta Yajña : Big is Beautiful?

Large scale urbanization leading to formation of *janapadas*, and kingdoms extending from Gandhara to Kuru, Panchala, Kosala and Videha regions, brought with them many new economic challenges. While food and housing security gave stability to the population in fixed dwellings, as well as new occupations in cities and towns, new lifestyle presented new complications. Questions of morality, inequality, social justice and the like arose, for which this newly agrarian society was not fully equipped. By this period, the caste system had fully embedded itself in society and caused its own disparities.

In the late Vedic period, *yajñas* began spanning several weeks, months, and even years, requiring huge financial and logistical resources which went beyond the reach of even wealthy members of the society. In a following chapter on *soma yajña* ritual, reader will get a fair idea of the resources required for conducting a *soma* ceremony like *vājapeya*, if one chose to perform it in present times. An ordinary citizen desiring to perform these *yajñas* was forced to abstain from his occupation for long periods which directly affected his earnings in a fast urbanizing economy. In some cases, people had to spend a lifetime's savings on performing just one *yajña*, such as *vājapeya*.

Brahmaṇas desirous of performing these *yajñas* for themselves often had to beg for prolonged periods to collect enough capital for conducting a *soma yajña*. These *yajñas* gradually came to be performed only by the rich and powerful - to demonstrate their status, to show that they had arrived. That is not to say that the sole purpose of *soma yajñas* was reduced to demonstrating or asserting the power of the sacrificer (usually a king or a nobleman). From the beginning, it was, and it remained, essentially a religious ceremony, but the occasion was eventually used more for demonstrating one's position and standing in the society, and consequently, *soma* sacrifices grew bigger and grander. The very nature of these ceremonies provided scope for upscaling - the number of animals to be sacrificed, the number of guests to be fed and, indeed, the duration of the ceremony itself, not to talk of the quantum of *dakṣiṇā*. These were all quite flexible. And the sacrificers kept pushing for ever bigger ceremonies extending over longer periods. For example: *aśvamedha*, which anyway required a minimum of one year to complete, was often extended to two years. While the stallion roamed from kingdom to kingdom and the army of soldiers, princes and servants followed it, a series of grand functions centered around the king were held every day back in the capital where thousands participated. Sacrifices associated with the function ran into the hundreds if not thousands. The minimum prescribed *dakṣiṇā* of 48,000 cows to each of the four principal priests is simply mind-boggling! The religious core was completely overshadowed by the pomp and show, just as the religious core of *vivāhaā saṃskāra* (marriage) - *pāṇigrahaṇa* and *saptapadī* - are completely pushed off the center stage in present-day marriage celebrations; cocktails, *mehndi*, et cetera have overshadowed the essence.

Very large religious functions like *rājasūya* and *aśvamedha* performed by the rich and powerful increasingly became more common, and the *śrauta* rituals performed by the householders receded in to the background. They simply drowned in the pomp of Vedic mantras chanted by scores of priests, and the sacrifice of hundreds of animals daily, performed on behalf of a *rājana* desiring to conquer the world and dislodge *Índra* from his celestial throne; by performing a hundred unblemished *aśvamedha yajñas*, all this, and more, was acheivable. *Śrauta* rituals were thus appropriated by the upper crust, reducing the commoner to the role of bystander. And *brahmaṇas*, despite knowing that their actions encouraged these *yajña* practices, continued to perform them for self-serving reasons, though it often meant selling all their possessions, leading them to begging, when they chose to perform it for themseves!

∞

Confronted with complex new scenarios born of socio economic changes and faced with new dilemmas of morality, inequality and social justice, the perplexed and confused populace turned to their religion for answers - a religion which had immersed itself in gaudy displays and interminable, tedious rituals. Their religion at the time was concerned more with form than substance and could not furnish any satisfactory answers. It was so consumed with ritual, it had little intellectual resources left to deal with the urgent issues that society faced. The *brahmaṇas*, who were traditionally tasked with providing answers and solutions to such spiritual quandaries kept busy with ritual and *yajña*, small and big, and had no answers outside of what they had practiced all their lives - conduct *yajñas* and rituals. They could recommend little more besides performing more *yajñas* as solutions to these problems. Confused and restless, people soon became disillusioned with their religion.

The dismay and despondency was not confined to ordinary people. Records show the disenchantment of even rich and ruling classes with blood soaked religious ceremonies and rituals. Disillusioned, several members of the society, affluent or otherwise, started deserting the comfort of their homes in search of a new meaning to life and existence - they became mendicants or *śramaṇas*. This created 'a movement' similar to the hippie movement of the 1960s in the west. But was this situation created solely due to grandiose ritualistic displays? No. There were many factors which combined and formed a 'critical mass' triggering this chain reaction. Apart from the socio-economic- religious factors and political changes, the (Indian) 'Axial age' had certain aspects which are not fully understood yet.

The jury is still out on the contentious issue of what really caused this movement where people took to the life of *śramaṇas* and mendicants, and started leaving the comfort of an agrarian and urban society.

There is a view that the seeds of asceticism, renunciation and supremacy of reason over rituals were embedded in Vedic literature itself.

Aruni's teachings to Śvetketu is one of the most famous Upaniṣadic narrations - The '*Brahman*', all pervasive, permeating the cosmos and yet unseen and invisible, is explained by way of analogies : salt dissolved in water, a river flowing into the sea, seed of a tree cut open (which, though it does not contain anything resembling the tree, does have the essence of the tree). Aruni explains to his son that *Brahman*, although invisible to the eye, can be understood in different ways such as in the above examples. After each example, Śvetketu is told '*tat tvam asi*', which has been widely translated in 'King James' English as 'that art thou' or 'you are that' or 'that is what you are' (essence). Each example shows that there is an ineffable essence which is the inner reality of all things, including 'the self'. [Brereton however argues that the proper translation of '*tat tvam asi*' is not 'that is what you are', but 'that is how you are'.]

Many centuries later, Śaṅkara saw '*tat tvam asi*' as 'each one of us in our deepest essence is God'. This - in the earliest Upaniṣads - Bṛhad Āraṇyaka and Chāndogya - was a move away from the rituals; although the efficacy of rituals was not in dispute, a new element- the factor of knowledge was introduced. The best way to obtain this knowledge, the texts recommended, was through the chaste and contemplative life of the ascetic. The Bṛhad Āraṇyaka Upaniṣad also identifies the *Brahman* as the essence of all these phenomena and more. (BU. 4.1.1-7)

As we move to the later Vedic period, and deeper into Jaspers' Axial age, the later Upaniṣads display clear emergence, indeed dominance, of the age of reason, and a frontal attack on rituals. The Upaniṣads increasingly advocate right knowledge, contemplation and the discipline of renunciation to apprehend this deeper reality -

'By truthfulness, indeed, by penance, right knowledge, and abstinence must that Self be gained; the Self owned spotless anchorites gain is pure, and like the light within the body.'[3]

But even before Muṇḍaka Upaniṣad, a late Vedic period or later composition, there was a significant shift in reward theory of rituals i.e. *yajñas*, leading to an afterlife in heaven, propounded in the Brahmaṇas. As we move away from the Brahmaṇas into middle and late Veda period, i.e. towards the middle of the Axial-age band, the concept of rebirth (*Ātman* reborn in a new life-form) determined by the *karma* (actions) in this life emerges in early Upaniṣads. Birth in the next life 'as a worm, or as an insect, or as a fish, or as a lion...' determined by *karma* (actions) 'according to his deeds and according to his knowledge' is clearly spelt out in Kauṣitaki Upaniṣad.[4]

First mentioned in Kaṭha Upaniṣad (1.2), this on-going cycle of birth, death and rebirth - *saṃsāra* - could only be broken by attaining *mokṣa*, a final liberation which was attainable through renunciation and constant pursuit of knowledge of the ultimate reality, *Brahman*. Was this the trigger which turned several Āryans towards the life of mendicants or *śamanas* is difficult to deduce, but constant hammering of ideas of Muṇḍaka and Bṛhad-Āraṇyaka that the karmic chain can only be broken by banishing all desires and through renunciation (BU.4.4.6

and MU. 1.2.10-11) definitely helped in pushing many on the ascetic path. The renunciatory ideal is based on the assertion that by severing desire-driven ties with family, worldly things, the body and even sacrificial merit, one can eventually break the karmic chain and realise oneness of *Ātman* and *Brahman*, i.e. *mokṣa*, as taught by Yajñavalakya in Bṛhad-Āraṇyaka 4.4.6. A deep scepticism of ideology of the Vedic rituals and culture, which had resulted in a near iron grip of *brahmaṇa* priests on religion and the power they had attained, likely played a major part in this key shift.

Ford's view that the debate among scholars about the origins of this ascetic ideal - whether "it emerged out of the Vedic tradition, specifically out of the privatisation of ritual', or others who "trace the renunciatory ideal to the indigenous non-Āryans populations", "better be left behind" - seems to be the best way to deal with this issue.[5]

Cometh the hour, cometh the man (John 4:23)

The imagination of these disillusioned, wandering *śramaṇas* and mendicants was caught by Gautam Buddha and Vardhamāna Mahāvīra Jain.

Siddhartha (Gautama Buddha), a prince, had abjured the kingdom of Lichchhivi (present-day northern Bihar and terai region of Nepal) and, in the middle of night, left his sleeping wife and son, in search of life's real meaning. This he found, after nearly starving himself to death while meditating under the '*bodhi*' tree near the present-day city of Gaya in Bihar. He had an epiphany - the *Bodha*, an experience which he then shared with anyone who cared. Very few did in the beginning. What started with a handful of followers at Saranatha near Kaśi (Varanasi), where Buddha first spun the wheel of Dharma negating the existence of any god or *Brahman*, heaven or hell. Buddhism eventually spread as a religion of peace in most of Asia and later across the world. But at that time, Buddha had raised quite a storm in Vedic India by denying the existence of god, heaven and hell - a raging controversy. His views struck at the very root of Hindu religion as it was practiced at the time. Naturally, there was stiff opposition to his ideas and his preaching.

Perseverance pays. Buddha soon started attracting hordes of inhabitants of the *Āryavratta* who were weary from the endless rituals, violent sacrifices, ostentatious display of wealth and power, through huge quantities of food and drinks served at religious rituals (*śautrāmaṇi* and other *soma yajñas*). Not surprisingly, Buddha made *ahiṃsā* (non-violence) and renunciation of material comforts the core of Buddhism. Violence of any kind against any living creature was completely forbidden in thought, word and deed. There was no place for *yajña* or any ceremony involving money and priests. Religion was restored as a private affair with no place for an intermediary. Acquisition of worldly wealth was a big no. Renunciation was the key to happiness and *mokṣa* in this new order.

What a turnaround!

There is little doubt in the author's mind that great emphasis on renunciation of worldly possessions - a common denominator of Buddhist teachings and the ascetic life of Hindu sages, and the course prescribed for all householders in the third stage of life of *vānaprasthas āśrama* - made Buddha appear more like a Hindu reformist than an adversary of Hinduism. The image of Buddha in a saffron robe, shaved head, moving from place to place in wooden sandals, with no possessions save for a begging bowl for *bhikṣā*, must have looked remarkably similar to the image of Hindu *sādhus*, who lived in great numbers in and around the holiest of Hindu city, Kaśi (Varanasi), and were widely respected for their austere choices. Whether the saffron garments and wooden footwear were deliberately chosen to give the impression of a *sādhu* so that people would gather to listen to the preaching of a Buddhist monk, is difficult to prove, but it was definitely effective in gathering a crowd of Hindu believers!

Mahāvīra Jain was another prince (599-527 BC) from Vaishali (in present-day Bihar), also known as Vardhamāna, who was a contemporary of Buddha (563-483 BC). He gave up the life of a prince, renounced material comforts and experienced 'self-realization' like Siddhartha, though at a different place and time. Remarkably, Mahāvīra Jain was also a married man, with a wife (Yashoda) and a son. He left them both and walked away from the lap of a luxurious, palatial life. The single most important teaching, the very foundation of Jain religion, is the tenet of *ahiṃsā* (non-violence).

Soon, these twin ideas and teachings caught the imagination of commoners, rich, and powerful alike. Gautama Buddha and his followers, dressed in saffron, moved in groups from village to village, city to city and kingdom to kingdom. They not only covered plains and mountains within Bhāratvarṣa, but even neighbouring countries, and soon travelled across seas and the imposing Himalayas - to China, Thailand, Vietnam, Sri Lanka, *et al.*

In India, Buddhism probably reached its zenith during Ashoka's reign (304-232 BC). In the name of Emperor Ashoka the Great, edicts were issued to show compassion and love to all living creatures, and to stop animal killings - the first animal hospitals in the world were built during his reign. From deep in Afghanistan to the east of India, we still find evidence of how Ashoka propagated the teachings of Buddha and gave up the violence of war. After the bloody Kalinga victory, Ashoka turned a devout Buddhist.

Buddha and Mahāvīra were just two of the many thinkers who took a radically different approach to the 'why' and 'how' of life; Gosala of the *Ājīvikas* was another rationalist with a large following. It appears that in the sixth century BC, the conundrums of the purpose of life and the world around us, and the relation of an individual with the world, agitated people extensively (you may recall the earlier discussion on the Axial age); especially those who were not prepared to accept the answers provided by Vedic rituals and *brahmaṇa* priests. Similarly, in more recent times, an entire generation of Americans had turned away from material comforts and their homes. They became hippies to get away from the confusing ideology of fighting someone else's war - thousands of miles away in Vietnam, far from their home and country. Thousands of Americans and other western youth simply gave up the normal life of comfort and became wanderers (hippie) seeking answers, just like the *parivrājaka* of 600 BC. Both men and women *parivrājakas* wandered around the country seeking answers and engaging in philosophical debates, often surrounded by onlookers who were equally curious to hear their entirely unconventional views.

Non-conformism (as Jataka confirms) became an 'in thing' among people disenchanted and disillusioned with life. Many turned into wanderers or *śramaṇas* and mendicants in 600-400 BC India.

Renunciation of worldly things has been considered a noble ideal in a Hindu's life from the beginning - asceticism was respected even in the Ṛgvedic period. *Rṣis*, *munis* and *yatis* occupied the highest place in society and commanded the respect of people from all occupations and *varṇa*s because they renounced the world and worldly possessions. Of the four stages in life - *brahmācārya*, *gṛhastha*, *vānaprasthas* and *saṃnyāsa* - the fourth involves giving up all worldly things and attachment with people. Ideally, a Hindu should give up everything in the final stage of life and retire to the forest to meditate and contemplate the divine.

Divorcing oneself from society and practicing celibacy are not unique to Hindu religion, the practice existed among a Jewish sect in times of Jesus - "A handful of sects, such as the aforementioned essence and another called Therapeutae, practiced celibacy, but these were quasi-monastic orders; they not only refused to marry, they completely divorced themselves from society."[6]

But the ascetics of 600- 400 BC India were very different from the 'normal' Hindu ascetic. They had not reached the third or fourth stage (*āśrama*) of life. In fact, they were all in the first or second '*āśrama*'. They renounced material pleasures not to comply with *āśrama dharma* of Hinduism, but in opposition to the dogma of Hinduism, and openly rebelled against the teachings of Dharma.

They were nonconformists and wanted to show that they were so.

Chapter 16

Questioning Minds and Unanswered Questions

Thousands of ideologies bloomed during this period. Most, if not all, questioned the efficacy of *yajñas*, rituals, and their purpose. Philosophical debates and arguments about the abstract and the divine, about the world being eternal or finite, real or illusory, became the most popular occupation. So much so that auditoria called *kautuhala-shāla* were designated for conducting these debates and arguments in public.

Here, we must pause and consider some important aspects of this 'movement'.

Was this a revolt against the Vedic religion/society which had increasingly come under the iron grip of priests and had become something of a religious oligarchy?

Or, were those people questioning the relevance and prescriptions of the *śrutis* and *smṛtis*?

When the freedom to ask questions, express diverse opinions, or attempts to bring about change is taken away, history is proof that such suppression invariably gives bith to a 'movement' or a revolt. Did this movement in Vedic India start because individuals in Vedic society were denied the freedom and platform to question rituals, religious practices, and priests?

Had Hindu society reached this *nadir*?

No, says Thomas William Rhys Davids (1843 –1922), a British scholar, and an officer in the British civil services, who spent a long time in this part of the world. According to Rhys Davids, the ancient people of India enjoyed "the most perfect freedom probably unequalled in the history of the world"[1] at that time.

It is well-known that debates and arguments on religious ideas, thoughts, and abstract matters were not only freely allowed, but quite popular in those times. In fact, this trend is clearly reflected in most scriptures of that time - which are written in question - answer format; the enquirer constantly questions the one who is depicted imparting knowledge.

One thing that consistently stands out during this period is the freedom of expression in all aspects of life, including rituals. Yet the fact is that several members of that society were not engaging with the proponents of the 'non-ritual, non-*yajña* based' school existing within Hinduism. Much before Buddha sat under the banyan tree meditating, seeking answers to his questions about suffering and pain, life and death, at least five Upaniṣads had already become part of the Vedic literature. These Upaniṣads were openly critical of rituals and priests, and declared the pursuit of knowledge as the supreme goal of life![2]

Not only the traditionalists, but the scholars also acknowledge that the focus had already started shifting from ritualism to the individual-self.

All dialogues in the Upaniṣads have one common feature - the teachers are shown presenting knowledge about the self as a fundamental part of their teachings and discourse.

Śandilya identifies *Ātma* with *Brahman*, Uddalka Aruni describes *Ātma* as the fundamental essence of life, Naciketā learns from *Yama* that he can find the secret meaning of sacrifice within himself, and *Prajāpati* presents *Ātma* as the agent for sensing and cognizing.

Though these teachers (and many others) had different, and sometimes contradictory, understanding of *Ātma*, they all present knowledge about the self as a new way of thinking, opposing Vedic ritualism. This ideology formed a fundamental part of an Upaniṣadic student's education.

And yet, large scale migration to Buddhism, Jainism, Shramanism, mendicant and the ascetic way of life continued, threatening to drain life out of the Hindu society. Why?

The unanswered questions

1. Buddhism and Jainism were both devoid of rituals - at least in their initial stages. Both taught that there is no god, hence idol worship or rituals had no place in these religions. The five *śīlas* of Buddhism were a simple affair and included prohibition of injury and destruction of life, prohibition of sexual impurity, lying and intoxicating liquors. Did Buddhism, with its simple, uncomplicated teachings, strike a chord among commoners, rich, and powerful alike? Since *gṛhya* and other Hindu rituals were excessively time consuming, was the absence of these rituals in Buddhism the main attraction in an increasingly commercial, materialistic society?
2. Hinduism also offered a 'non-ritual' path since the period of the Ṛgveda, Upaniṣads taught that knowledge was more valuable than ritual. So why did these ideas not become popular? Was it because Hindu religion always had two levels of teachings - abstract and metaphysical for its intellectuals, and

mythological for the commoners? Is it that commoners, who were in much larger numbers, simply could not grasp the abstract path of knowledge?

3. Was the Sanskrit, language of Upaniṣads/*gṛhya sūtra*, a barrier even for educated *shreshthis* and upper-class people? It is known that during this time, the lower class were increasingly using Pali - a corrupted version of Sanskrit. It is noteworthy that Buddha rejected Sanskrit and chose Pali for his teachings.[3]
4. Had the Brahmaṇas and *purohitas* acquired such dominance that very little space was left in society for the rich business class and other non-*kṣatriyas*?
5. And finally, why did Buddha attack the knowledge-based stream in Vedic Hinduism that was emerging and asserting itself? Was he as opposed to this knowledge-based alternative in Hinduism as the ritualistic *yajña*-based Hinduism?
6. Or was Buddha by now committed to opposing Hinduism per se, as he had 'concluded' that Hinduism could not be reformed?

[For further reading on this subject - ref. History of Dharmashastra, Kane.]

Buddhism and Jainism - A brief look

Granted the situation was ripe for a drastic shift in religious practice, but what was so unique and attractive in Gautama Buddha's teachings that people were drawn to them rather than to other alternatives available within the Hindu fold? Whatever the answer, some important questions arise which need investigation, even if the answers that are uncovered are not wholly satisfactory.

First, let's look briefly at the core values and tenets of Buddhism. In Buddhism (as well as in Jainism), the basic precepts are -

There is no god, no *Ātma*, no heaven or hell, and that in this *saṃsāra*, there shall always be sorrow with joy, pain with pleasure, hate with love, and such like, eventually leading to suffering. The only way to liberate oneself from this cycle is to distance oneself from both, become equidistant from happiness and sorrow alike, by following a sensible path of renunciation - the middle path. This 'middle path' can help attain a state of perpetual bliss, something akin to *nirvāṇa* - an enlightenment or wisdom which will end all suffering in this world.

For proceeding on this middle path, these religions recommended, one must follow certain basic rules while exercising self-discipline.

There are five rules called *śīlas* that are binding on all Buddhists - prohibition of injury and destruction of life, prohibition of sexual impurity, prohibition of lying, and prohibition of intoxicating liquors.

Buddhist priests must follow an additional five provisions - prohibition of eating at forbidden hours, training worldly amusements such as dancing, song, music, et cetera, using unguents (greasy, perfumed rub-ins) and jewelry, or the use of a large ornamented couch and receiving gold and silver.

The striking thing about this code is the simplicity of Buddha's message. In his first discourse in Saranath, near Varanasi, he expounded the four noble truths -

Suffering (*duhkha*), the cause of suffering (*duhkha samudaya*), the suppression of suffering (*duhkha nirodha*) and the way leading to suppression of suffering (*duhkha nirodhagamini pratipada*).

This last is the noble eight-fold path -

Those who practice the Right views, Right thoughts or aspirations, Right speech, Right actions, Right living, Right exertion, Right in the collection or mindfulness, Right meditation, i.e. speaking briefly, lead a virtuous life.

Sabbasavasutta (9 - 13) says that a wise man walking the noble eight-fold path understands what things ought to be considered and what things ought not to be considered[4]. (SBE volume 11 page 298 - 300)

Buddha's teachings were very basic, uncomplicated,easy to understand and practice, free of ritual and priestly intervention. He, in his original teachings, regarded it a waste of time to ponder questions like - Did I exist during the past ages or not? Do I after all exist or not?

According to PV Kane[5], "Buddhism brought half of Asia under its influence not only by its promise of salvation to all by self-help, but more so by its teachings of profound tenderness, active charity, goodness and gentleness."

Buddha's original doctrines aimed at individual effort and salvation of the self by one's own effort and self-culture. Early Buddhist texts deny the existence of anything like a soul and find no place for the idea of god. And interestingly, though Buddha spoke of *nirvāṇa*, he did not clearly define it nor did he specify the condition of an individual upon reaching *nirvāṇa.*

Aśvaghoṣa compares *nirvāṇa* to the extinction of a flame[6]. Because the doctrine of *karma* was deeply rooted in the popular mind, Buddhism took over that doctrine. To non-Buddhists, this appears to be contradictory to denial of the existence of a soul. But this was undoubtedly conceived by an expert tactician!

The word '*dhamma*' has three meanings in the Pali '*dhamma pada*' - mentioned in Milinda's questions, and predating the second century BC -

1. the truth or law preached by Buddha
2. thing or form
3. way or mode of life

As stated above, the original Buddhism preached by Buddha and his followers in the first hundred years or so, after his *parinirvāṇa*, was a strict ethical code for individuals who sought salvation from the misery of the world. The three central conceptions of early Buddhism were the following three refuges (or *ratnas*) -

(i) Buddha

(ii) Dharma and *sangha*

(iii) The four noble truths and the eightfold path

From this strict ethical code, gradually a new doctrine evolved based on the thought that it was rather selfish to care for one's own deliverance, and spend all time and effort thereon. As Buddha himself served the suffering humanity for forty-five years and led men to salvation by his exhortations and sermons, so also a Buddhist must put off his own deliverance and work for the deliverance of fellow men out of compassion (*karuṇā*) for their misery. In doing so, he should be ready to incarnate again and again, unoccupied with own salvation and unafraid of the *saṃsāra*.

Those holding the latter views deified Buddha, taught that Siddhartha attained Buddhahood after undergoing numerous births, rendering help to others in every birth. To these followers, this was a superior code of conduct - the great vehicle *Mahāyāna*. In comparison, the more self-serving code for the salvation of the individual came to be called the lesser vehicle *Hīnayāna*.

The gospel of *Mahāyāna* was attractive and won great support in most Asian countries as it taught profound tenderness, charity, goodness and gentleness more than the promise of salvation by self-help. *Mahāyāna* laid great stress on *bhakti* and doing good unto all.

∞

Now let's examine whether it was *ahiṃsā*, the core value of Buddhism, or the *Panch Śīla*, a wider ethical code, which led 'Vedic Hindus' to embrace Buddhism.

It is unlikely that *ahiṃsā* or the five *śīlas*, the core of Buddha's teachings, were the only (or even the main) attraction towards Buddhism.

Consider the following passages, authored by two of Hinduism's real heavy weights of all time: Yājñavalkya and Gautama -

The author (now) describes the general duties - *Sādhāraṇa Dharma* - harmlessness, veracity, non-stealing, purity, controlling of the organs, liberality, self-control, mercy, and forgiveness, are the means of religion for all (Yājñavalkya S. 122).

Mitākṣarā's commentary irradiates Yājñavalkya's sūtra -

Harmlessness - non-doing of or injuring living beings. Veracity - truthful speech, not causing pain to anybody. Non-stealing - not taking of things not given. Purity - external and internal. Control of organs - employment of the intellect and the organs of action in lawful objects. Liberality - removal of the pain of living creatures by giving food and water. Self-control - repression of the internal organ (mind). Mercy - protecting the afflicted. Forgiveness - non-emotion of the mind under injury.

These are the means of acquisition of Dharma for all men, beginning with the Brahmaṇa and ending with the *Cāndāla*.[7]

Chāndogyopaniṣad too emphasizes *ahiṃsā* in several passages. In (I I I.1 7.4), it says -

"Tapas, charity, straightforwardness, *ahiṃsā*, speaking the truth - these are the fees of this (sacrifice without ceremonies)"

While describing how a person who attained true knowledge of the self does not return to the *saṃsāra*, the Chāndogyopaniṣad says,-

"He causes no pain to any creature except at Tīrthas."[8]

Gautama DS (24 - 25) specifies two virtues of the soul, of which the first is compassion for all beings and the second states that he who has the forty *saṃskāras* performed on him, but does not possess the eight virtues, does not secure absorption into *Brahman*.

There are several other examples of '*ahiṃsā* being preached as a great Dharma', and at times 'the highest Dharma', in post Buddhist literature. But these are perhaps consequent reactions (and influences) of the teachings of Buddha.

It is clear in the foregoing Chāndogyopaniṣad passage that much before Buddha encapsulated his teachings in the *Panch Śīla*, nearly identical teachings had already gained importance in the *yajña*-based Vedic ritualistic society. More importantly, an authority like Yājñavalkya had incorporated these very practices for every member of society in his *smṛtis*, covering all four *varṇa*s from *brahmaṇa* to *cāndāla* as part of *Sādhāraṇa Dharma*.

∞

It is not as if Yājñavalkya alone realized that 'form' (ritual) was squeezing 'substance' out of the Vedic religion and that a deep cleansing was the need of the hour. Other thinking men - Śandilya, Uddalka and others - were also preoccupied with serious anomalies and aberrations threatening to affect, if not permanently damage, the core of the Vedic religion and culture. Fortunately, this 'self-correcting and self-healing' internal mechanism which has always kept Hinduism 'alive and going' was in place even at that time. The 'movement' (if it can be called that) changed the original course of mainstream Hinduism forever by firmly planting the concept of knowledge-based religion in its path. The 'knowledge-less' ritualistic stream of religion, which had become turbid and shallow, and was nearly running dry of new ideas, received fresh impetus : a gush of debates and discussions of the 'supremacy of knowledge'.

An important point to note is that Yājñavalkya's concerns were not because of the lurking threat of Buddhism - Buddha was still 200 years away from being born!

This author is of the view that the awareness of the need for reform in Vedic practices, and discussions among various intellectuals had put the pot of Hinduism on 'simmer' and a constant stream of bubbles was emerging on the hitherto 'still' and 'unstirring' surface of Hinduism. Over time, various new thinkers emerged with their own ideologies and thoughts.

These thinkers who were aware of the need for reform were large in number, as indicated by the near simultaneous rise of the *Ājīvikas*, Jains and Buddhists, among others. After all, the proponents of these divergent faiths were all part of the same 'imperfect ritualistic Vedic society' until well into their adulthood. All three, Gosala, Vardhamāna and Siddhārtha, very likely started off as Hindu reformers before they realized that the changes they wanted to implement were so radical and/or called for such complex mechanisms (requiring enormous amount of time and energy) that it was easier to step away and create a new channel of their own belief, rather than attempt to alter the course of the mighty mainstream of Vedic Hinduism. There is enough evidence to infer that Buddhism, at least initially, was only a reformist movement and a subset (or a sect) of Hinduism. Though some of these thinking men - like Buddha, Mahāvīra and Gosala - eventually left the 'house' of Vedic Hinduism permanently to build a house of their own, several other thinkers stayed back. They continued to make it a religion of a more meaningful way of life.

Be that as it may, there is no denying that an intense reformist movement was afoot within the ritualistic Vedic society because of the emergence of new faiths and ideologies (Buddhism, Jainism, *Ājīvika*). These new ideologies were attracting an increasingly large number of followers from the ancient faith, and therefore, there was more pressure from within Hinduism for quicker and greater reforms. It appears that the Hindu reformists finally worked out a successful strategy. They understood full well that for the change to happen -

(i) Institution of *purohitas* and *brahmaṇas* (as birth right) had to be first reformed; and

(ii) Elaborate ritualism had to be diluted.

It is inconceivable that the *brahmaṇas* adopted a passive attitude towards these changes. The growing voices of disaffection were directly, and indirectly, questioning the *brahmaṇas* and the role they played in peoples' lives (according to *Āhnika* accounts, nearly two thirds of an individual's daytime was devoted to rituals, leaving little time for any commercial pursuit in the ever-growing urban society). The *brahmaṇas* must have been deeply concerned because this was the first time that their position as the sole agent qualified (by birth) to understand, interpret and conduct affairs of *karmakāṇḍa*, was being directly challenged.

Here, it is important to understand the stakes. The dissatisfaction and disenchantment in the society was no doubt due to changes in rituals over time - both qualitatively and quantitatively - which had been appropriated by the rich and powerful of the society. But, it was equally a vote of no-confidence in the *brahmaṇas*, who, as the final arbiters of Dharma had allowed - even connived with the rich and powerful - to take these rituals (*yajñas*) to a point where ordinary people felt alienated and were reduced to a role of mere spectators. When things go wrong, leaders do not always succeed in deflecting blame. During this period, things were going horribly wrong in the society and *brahmaṇas* were in the direct line of fire!

The exalted position that the *brahmaṇas* occupied in society was due to the role they played as interpreters and conductors of what was prescribed in the Brahmaṇas (the text). Undeniably, they occupied this position after many years of study and training. But they had what many call today an 'unfair advantage' of being born to a *brahmaṇa* family. Only a *brahmaṇa* by birth was qualified to go through studentship and training to become a performing *brahmaṇa*.

Coming to the second point - for the supremacy of 'practice' (sacrifice and ritual) to make way for supremacy of 'knowledge' was no easy task either. This required that several Vedic religious practices be diluted, if not entirely discarded.

The two issues were closely linked and the *brahmaṇas* had a strong vested interest in preserving and continuing old complex ritualistic practices in Sanskrit language, which the increasingly Pali-speaking population was (perhaps) unable to understand properly.

Next, we shall see how, and how far, this reformist movement succeeded.

Chapter 17

The Reforms: Upaniṣads

It will be useful to learn more about the Upaniṣads before discussing the reforms, since these reforms were led by the Upaniṣads.

In fact, these reforms may well be called 'Upaniṣadic reforms'.

What are Upaniṣads?

The Oxford dictionary defines philosophy as the study of the fundamental nature of knowledge, reality, and existence, especially when considered as an academic discipline.

If we go by this definition, then the Upaniṣads mark the beginning of philosophy in India. According to Black[1], "Upaniṣads occupy a similar place within the Indian tradition as the writings of the pre-Socratic philosophers do in the history of Western philosophy, as they mark the beginning of a reasoned enquiry into philosophical questions like how one should live one's life, what happens to the self at the time of death, the nature of the self and the being, et cetera..."

Meaning of Upaniṣad

Though widely accepted by scholars to mean 'a session consisting of pupils assembled at a respectful distance around the teacher', Max Müller is emphatic that no precedent has been met with in which 'upaniṣad' is used in the sense of pupils approaching and listening to their teacher. He goes on to add that besides being the recognized title of certain philosophical treatises, Upaniṣad also occur in the sense of doctrine and secret doctrine, and that it seems to have assumed this meaning from having been used originally in the sense of session or assembly in which one or more pupils receive instruction from a teacher.

Max Müller goes on to identify the following four different meanings of the word Upaniṣad [2], as found in Upaniṣads themselves -

1. Secret or esoteric explanation, whether true or false
2. Knowledge derived from such explanation
3. Special rules or observances incumbent on those who have received such knowledge
4. Title of books containing such knowledge

Who wrote the Upaniṣads and when?

These texts formed a part of the oral tradition of *śruti* and were handed from one generation to the next, possibly in the latter part of the Brahmaṇas period. However, the first germs of the Upaniṣad's doctrines go back as far as the mantra period (1000-800 BC).

Although the Upaniṣads formed a part of the Āranyaka, they were subsequently detached, edited and compiled separately.

It is safe to say that the modern generations owe it to Prince Dara Shikoh, the eldest son of the Mughal emperor Shāh Jahān, for being able to read the various Upaniṣads. The prince, a learned, lettered man, was deeply interested in Hindu religion. He engaged the services of Brahmaṇas from Kāśī (Benaras) to get fifty of the then extant Upaniṣads translated from Sanskrit to Persian language. Persian was the language of Mughal courts and cultured folk in the east. The Kāśī *brahmaṇas* were natural masters of Sanskrit, and being learned and living in the cultural hub of Hindu society, knew Persian well. They were hand-picked for the translation task which was accomplished in 1657 AD in the form of fifty 'Oupnekhats'.

Alas, the liberal prince's skills with the sword were not in the same class as his skills with the pen. Dara Shikoh was killed by his younger brother Aurangzeb, a devout Muslim better known for his lack of tolerance towards other religions particularly Hinduism, in a battle for succession to the throne of India. Aurangzeb called his elder brother Dara Shikoh, the rightful inheritor of the throne, 'an infidel' because of Dara's liberal leanings towards Hinduism. Among other things, Dara's love for the 'Oupnekhat' must have been a contributing factor in building such an image.

Thus, for the next half a century (Aurangzeb ruled for nearly forty-nine years and died in harness in 1707 AD), the 'Oupnekhat' stood little chance of receiving any royal indulgence, let alone patronage. It is a miracle that these manuscripts were not destroyed on royal orders, and survived Aurangzeb's rule!

Nearly 125 years later, M Gentil, a French resident at the court of the Nawab of Awadh, Shuja ud Daula, sent one of the manuscripts of the Persian translation of 'Oupnekhats' (Upaniṣads) to the well-known traveler and discoverer of Zend Avesta, Anquetil Duperron. After receiving the second Persian manuscript of the 'Oupnekhat', Duperron collated the two and translated them into French and Latin. Of the two, the Latin translation was published in 1801 and 1802 under a very long title 'Oupnek' Hat (id Est, Secretum Tegendum): Opus Ipsa In India Rarissimum,

Continens Antiquam Et Arcanam... Studio Et Opera Anquetil Duperron' in Europe. This is how it reached the great German thinker and philosopher Schopenhauer. Schopenhauer was deeply affected by Oupnekhat, and observed[3] -

"How is everyone who by their diligent study of its Persian Latin has become familiar with that incomparable book, stirred by that spirit to the very depth of his soul! How does every line display its firm, definite, and throughout harmonious meaning! From every sentence deep, original and sublime thoughts arise, and the whole is pervaded by a high and holy and earnest spirit. Indian air surrounds us, and original thoughts of kindred spirits."

And, finally -

"In the whole world there is no study, except that of the originals, so beneficial and so elevating as that of the Oupnekhat. It has been the solace of my life, it will be the solace of my death!"

Numbers and classes of Upaniṣads

Traditional vedānta divides the Vedas into -

Karmakāṇḍa - consisting of *Saṃhitās* and Brahmaṇas that deal with rituals, and

Jñānkāṇḍa - consisting of Upaniṣads and Āraṇyaka that deal with more philosophical subjects

The early Veda literature primarily focuses on the description and meaning of the ritual actions, i.e. *karmakāṇḍa*, whereas the Upaniṣads are focused on the self. The early Upaniṣads are usually lodged in Āranyaka, considered esoteric and recommended to be studied in the privacy of *āraṇya* (forests), and fall under *jñānkāṇḍa*.

According to philosophers of vedānta and Brahman Sūtra, equivalence of *Ātma* and *Brahman* is the fundamental message of all Upaniṣads.

The five 'early Upaniṣads' - Bṛhad-Āraṇyaka, Chāndogya, Kauṣītaki, Taittirīya and Ātreya - were composed in prose form, sometime before the advent of Buddha and Mahāvīra (800-600 BC). They consist of a diverse set of material, much of which either existed independently or formed part of other texts before being collected in one of the Upaniṣads.

The later Vedic Upaniṣads are post-Buddhist and in verse form. These include Kena, Katha, Īśa, Svetasvatra, et cetera. Important ideas, such as *saṃsāra* (cycle of life, death and rebirth), *mokṣa* (final liberation) and *yoga*, were developed only in these later texts.

Number of Upaniṣads

There are many claims to the correct number of Upaniṣads. This author has chosen to go by Max Müller's account[4] -

There are fifty Upaniṣads translated by Dārā Shikoh.

The number given in Mahavākyamuktavali and Muktikā Upaniṣad is 108.

(Prof Webber thinks that the number, as we know at present, may be reckoned at 235).

However, to arrive at so high a number, every title of an Upaniṣad would have to be counted separately. In several cases, the same Upaniṣad has been quoted under different names.

I had published an alphabetical list in 1865 wherein the number of Upaniṣads reached 149.

New names are constantly being added in the catalogues of MS published by Buhler, Burnell, Rajendralal Mitra, et cetera, and I shall therefore reserve a more complete list of Upaniṣads for a later volume.

Another view: When were the Upaniṣads composed?

Many Indologists hold onto the vague notion that the principal Upaniṣads were composed before Buddhism arrived. Paul Deussen, however, succeeded in making a general classification. He determined the date order for the principal Upaniṣads by closely examining the style, language, content and parallel passages in fourteen old Upaniṣads. He divided them into three groups -

1. Upaniṣads of the early period (chiefly prose) - Bṛhad Āraṇyaka (particularly I - IV), Taittirīya, Kauṣītaki, Chāndogya Aitareya and Kena.
2. Upaniṣads of the middle period (poetry) - Kāṭhaka, Svetasvatara, Mahānārāyaṇa, Īśa, Muṇḍaka
3. Upaniṣads of the late period (poetry) - Praśna, Māṇḍūkya and Maitri

The listed order of these fourteen Upaniṣads represents the order of their composition as well.

This order has been accepted by many scholars. Keith however opposed this chronological order. He is of the view that the Aiterya is the oldest Upaniṣad and must have been composed around 600 or 550 BC.

Chapter 18

The Upaniṣadic reforms

Given the backdrop of turmoil, Hinduism urgently needed reformation to survive the tsunami of Buddhism and the backwash of Jainism. On the one hand, it was important for this old religion to stop new conversions to Buddhism/Jainism, and on the other, to bring back to its fold those who had already converted to these new religions. What emerged can be seen as the twin strategies of Upaniṣadic reforms -

A. Reform of institution of *purohitas* and Brahmaṇas
B. Dilution, if not not complete eradication, of 'supremacy of sacrificial, ritualistic' practice of Vedic religion.

Reform of institution of *Purohitas* and *brahmaṇas*

Even though knowledge (particularly of *Ātman* and *Brahman*), instead of rituals and sacrifice, was increasingly beginning to be considered worthy of pursuit, texts permitted access to knowledge based only on birth (for *brahmaṇas*). Were these restrictions getting relaxed? Was society now becoming more inclusive?

The answer to both these questions must be yes. The rigid practice of allowing 'only *brahmaṇas*' to have access to knowledge was gradually giving way to participation and admission of *kṣatriyas* (Prāvāhana, Janaka), women (Gārgi, Maitrāyaṇīya) and even *śūdras* (Satyakāma) in this club.

To see how this change happened, let us look at this transformation more closely -

A commoner desiring a son, good crop or wealth, and a king with huge resources desiring to perform *aśvamedha* or *rajasūya yajña* - both were equally dependent on the *brahmaṇa*, who alone was qualified to chant appropriate mantras of the *Saṃhitās*, conduct *yajña* and other rituals. The 'key-stone' which held the arch of religious acts in place was the *purohita* - a *brahmaṇa* by birth - who had acquired this specialized knowledge of rituals and mantras after spending many years (sometimes even a lifetime) mastering these arts. A non-*brahmaṇa*, even if he memorized these mantras and the directories of rituals, could not become a priest. There was an all-important condition to being a *brahmaṇa* - a *purohita* had to be a *brahmaṇa* by birth! This criterion effectively disqualified all but a miniscule population from becoming a *purohita* - a high position in the society before which even the kings bowed.

This period is marked by rapid social, economic and political changes and proliferation of new urban centeres, particularly to the east of Kuru and Panchal region, i.e. in Kosal and Videha. On one hand urbanized people tended to be less enthusiastic participants and sponsors of long drawn ritual practices, on the other, the urbanization nudged them to a more materialistic life. People now needed better and bigger houses, better clothing and wider range of worldly possesions. The society faced a dillemma; people were pulled in two opposite directions -

1. A quest for knowledge and desire to move away from rituals led to introspection and public debates about *Ātma* and *Brahman*;
2. A strong desire to have worldly possessions - a son, a good crop or wealth - kept driving them to *yajñas* and rituals

Alternative ways for obtaining *kāmya*, other than through the traditional ways of mantra and sacrifice-based rituals, were yet to be discovered and institutionalized. In this new search for knowledge of the self and *Brahman*, one could not lose sight of the more pressing realities of fulfilling desires of having a son, wealth or a fuller harvest! Torn between these opposing ideas, society chose not to sever its umbilical cord with traditional rituals.

But this churn brought a marked shift - from *yajña*-centric religious beliefs rooted in Vedic mantras and Brahmaṇa rituals, to a 'reason and analysis' based system. In due course, it received support and 'recognition' from sages, found a permanent place in the Upaniṣads, and became a part of organized religion.

The old ritual (*yajña*) practices and systems capable of delivering material pleasures survived alongside the new 'reason and analysis' based system. As a result, the *purohitas* and *brahmaṇas* too lived on, because without them these rituals could not be performed.

Thus, the priests appear to have won the day yet again! And the two systems, despite the obvious dichotomy, continued to exist in tandem.

Though the *brahmaṇas* and *purohitas* managed to weather the storm, there was no going back on the pursuit of knowledge, and the *Ātma* debates could not be ignored or wished away. This was an irreversible change. The Upaniṣadic literature openly started running down those who wanted to stay on the top of the heap solely by virtue of birth. Uddālka told his son Svetaketu to go to school "for there is none belonging to our race, darling, who not having studied (the Veda), is, as it were, a Brahmaṇa by birth only"[1]. (CU VI.1.1)

The 'necessary condition' of being a *brahmaṇa* to access the vault of knowledge was about to be abolished. In Cāndogyopaniṣad, when Satyakam Jabala approached Gautama to accept him as his student -

He (Gautama Haridrumta) said to him, "Of what Family are you, my friend?" He replied, 'I do not know, Sir, what family I am. I asked my mother, and she said, 'In my youth when I had to move about much as a servant, I conceived thee. I do not know of what family thou art. I am Jabala by name, thou art Satyakāma.' I am therefore Satyakāma Jabala, Sir."

Gautama's response is remarkable -

He said to him, "No one, but a true Brahmaṇa would thus speak out. Go and fetch fuel, friend I shall initiate you. You have not swerved from the truth."[2] (CU. IV.1.3-5)

Gautama equated 'speaking the truth' to the status of a '*brahmaṇa* by birth', attacking the root of the *brahmaṇa*-by-birth doctrine. And Satyakāma, born of a servant mother and an unknown father, was found fit to become a *brahmachārin* (student) of sage Gautama.

∞

The tradition of public debates, which were attended by wandering sages, ascetics, women and men from all walks of life, is a unique feature of the early Upaniṣads. Many of these debates took place in the courts of kings. There is evidence of even women (Gārgi Vachaknavi) participating in these debates occasionaly. Upaniṣadic narrations are usually in the form of questions and answers, and involve the *brahmaṇas* as well as *kṣatriya* rulers. For this reason, many scholars call it a political alliance between power and knowledge.

It was not only the intellectual inquiries of the Upaniṣads that triggered and contributed to the reforms - moving away from pompous rituals of *Brahmannic* society - but, the socio-economic changes that were taking shape in society were equally important; reforms are signified by -

i. Large scale participation in the public debates by people from all walks of life
ii. The public participation by women in debates - many times as active participants: Gārgi Vachaknavi (BU. 3.6.8) and Maitreyi, the wife of Yājñavalkya (BU. 2.4; 4.5)
iii. In a major departure from the old order signalling a complete role reversal - the *brahmaṇas* going to *kṣatriyas* for knowledge (King Jaival in CU. I.3.7)

Based on the Upaniṣadic narratives and other Vedic literature, it can be safely assumed that the Kuru-Panchala society, centered around northwest of India (in and around present-day Haryana), was increasingly losing out to the new centers of urbanization emerging in Kosala-Kāśī-Videha regions (present day eastern Uttar Pradesh and north-eastern Bihar). The Bṛhad-Āraṇyaka Upaniṣad champions the eastern city of the Videha presenting it as superior to the more orthodox western Kuru-Punchala area.[1] This increasing urbanization was a direct consequence of growing commercial activity. With the shift of socio-economic-political activity to the east, it was natural for artisans and scholars to migrate and seek the patronage of rulers in these new kingdoms. Since many of them belonged to the eastern tribes, the eastern rulers were equally keen to be recognized by scholars and teachers of the older western kingdoms. The emergence of the east as an important center of Vedic culture is clearly indicated in the often-cited passage of[3] Śhatapatha (SB.1.4.1.14 - 17).

When Janaka of Videha in the east organized *Brahmodaya* (a public debate) between Yājñavalkya, a known ritualist and scholar of repute in his kingdom, and more than half a dozen scholars from the Vedic heartland of Kuru-Panchala, he was trying to make more than a point of being a scholar-king and a patron of scholars. In the public debate held in his court, Yājñavalkya demolished all challengers from 'the west' Kuru-Panchala region, and emerged the undisputed winner. This demonstrated to the world that Yājñavalkya, a truly formidable *brahmaṇa* teacher and ritualist, who, by the time of Bṛhad-Āraṇyaka Upaniṣad (6.5.3), had become known as the founder of Yajurvedic school and author of parts of Śatapatha Brahmaṇa as well as Bṛhad-Āraṇyaka Upaniṣad, chose 'patronage' of the eastern kingdom of Videha over Kuru-Punchala!

One can only imagine how desperate and keen the new rulers of the emerging kingdoms of Kosala-Videha must have been nearly three millennium ago to establish themselves as true Āryan kings, and to be accepted as equals of the well-established Kuru-Panchala branch of the original heartland of the Āryans! They must have bent backwards to woo *brahmaṇas* who had the power (through rituals) to confer on these aspiring kings' divine authority to rule.

There can be little doubt that the *brahmaṇas* of the Vedic period were equally interested in migrating to the new states in Videha and other eastern regions since these were lands of emerging opportunities. The migrant *brahmaṇas* carried with them repackaged old ritual practices to attract and impress new clients, expecting to be suitably rewarded by the patron kings of the east. These migrant *brahmaṇas*, according to Olivelle and other scholars, helped create narratives of the *brahmaṇas* going to *kṣatriyas* for knowledge, as a calculated move aimed at securing royal patronage: "Some segments of *Brahmannical* community - which was not a monolithic entity - must have perceived it as advantageous to present doctrines they favored as coming from the Royal elite."[4] Their motive could also have been to quickly cement a new alliance with royalty in a new and changed situation. In addition, a suitable reward must also have been a potent motivation. Bodewitz, for example, points out that much of the material spoken by kings or members of the *kṣatriya* class (rulers and warriors) in general, which was presented as new to the

Brahmaṇical tradition, appears in older sections of the Jaiminīya Brahmaṇa and SB.

Nearly 2500 years later, when the great *marātha* warrior Śivaji desired to be anointed as *catrapati*, the conservative and staunch *mahārāshtrian brahmaṇas* refused to perform the religious ceremony leading to his *rājtilak* and ascent to the throne on the ground that Śivaji was not a *kṣatriya*. Eventually, Śivaji enticed the *brahmaṇas* of Kāśī (1500 km to the north-east of Raigad and Satara) with bags full of gold as *dakṣiṇā* to perform the rituals leading to his ascent to the throne as *maharaja*!

Whatever be the truth, for the Vedic *brahmaṇas*, finding their place in the new kingdoms of the east came after a major trade-off. These *brahmaṇas*, who had hitherto enjoyed unequalled respect in society by virtue of knowledge acquired over a lifetime and were treated as next only to the gods and above kings, now had to cede power to the *kṣatriya* rulers as scholars. Janaka and Prāvāhana are but two such examples.

Whatever the (true) reason of these rulers gaining prominence, the emergence of *kṣatriya* rulers as intellectual leaders was an important development. The *brahmaṇas* came away bruised from this churning.

Dilution, if not not complete eradication, of 'supremacy of sacrificial, ritualistic' practice of Vedic religion

Socio-political and economic changes

The early Upaniṣads consist of texts which either formed parts of other texts (Āraṇyaka, Upaniṣad et cetera) or existed independently, and Āranyaka were considered their natural depository. As the name suggests, Āranyaka contained esoteric knowledge so arcane that they were to be studied away from human habitation, in the solitude of *āraṇya* (forest). Many of these secret discourses were considered equivalent to ritual performances. Keith however thinks that "the Āraṇyaka seems originally to have existed to give secret explanations of the ritual, and to have presupposed that the ritual was still in use and well known."[5]

In the early Upaniṣads, knowledge has been lauded time and again (but) without directly criticizing or running down the rituals. In fact, it is clearly stated that the one who performs rituals with knowledge is superior to the one who does so without knowledge.

"The sacrifice which a man performs with knowledge, faith, and the Upaniṣad is more powerful."[6]

Aśvapati Kaikeya, a *kṣatriya* king, while imparting knowledge of the self to his *brahmaṇa* 'students' said[7] -

1. "If, without knowing this, one offers an *agnihotṛ*, it would be as if a man were to remove the live coals and pour his libation on dead ashes."

2. "But he who offers this *agnihotṛ* with the full knowledge of its full purport, he offers it (i.e. He eats food) in all worlds, and all beings, in all Selfs."
3. "As the soft fibers of the *ishika* reed, when thrown into the fire, are burnt, thus all his sins are burnt whoever offers this *agnihotṛ* with the full knowledge of its true purport."

Here, the king is seen acknowledging the centrality of rituals while underlining the importance of knowledge of the self.

Thus, knowledge - till this stage - was considered more of a 'force multiplier' than an alternative to rituals. It was nowhere near an 'either-or' situation; not yet, anyway. And in any case, this trend of according importance to knowledge and bringing it center-stage next to rituals was not new. It had emerged in the late Brahmaṇa and Āraṇyaka period itself: "*paro kshama hi devah*" which translates to "the gods love what is mysterious (secret)." (SB. 6.1.1.1 - 15; BU. 4.2.2 AU. 1.3.14) In its earliest textual contexts, the Upaniṣads described a connection between things, often presented in a hierarchical relationship. According to Harry Falk (1986), in the Brahmaṇas, Upaniṣad refers to the final teaching that is the foundation for everything else.

By associating Upaniṣads with esoteric knowledge, the knowledge of connectedness between things and adding emphasis on knowledge as a force multiplier, the Vedic texts were revealing the growing tendency of accepting knowledge as an important factor into what until then was a system entirely based on practices (rituals).

The Upaniṣadic knowledge is based on reason of the self and *Brahman*, death and rebirth, and its fundamental message is about equivalence of the *Ātma* and *Brahman*. Documentary and archaeological evidence shows that this Upaniṣadic period coincided with radical developments in northern India. Expansion in agriculture, rapid growth in trade and commerce, and the emergence of craft specialists was accompanied with urbanization and emergence of new political centers in the east. All these factors - economic, social and political - contributed to the changes (decline in Vedic ritual practices) as reflected in the Upaniṣads, and also contributed to the shift from ritual to a knowledge-based system. Thapar singles out economic strain as the main reason for decline in Vedic sacrifice practices. She argues that the consequent "discontinuance of the Vedic sacrificial ritual would break the nexus between the *brahmaṇa* and the *kṣatriya* and would provide a new role for the *kṣatriya* more in consonance with the broader changes of the time." (1994.318)

While there is little doubt that conducting rituals like *pravargya* and *agnicayana* required enormous human and financial resources, and rituals were becoming impossible for any ordinary man to organize, it would be an exaggeration to say that this caused the demise of ritual practices. For example, it becomes difficult to explain why early Buddhist texts continue to criticize the Vedic rituals, if they had already died. Laurie Patton has suggested that the *gṛhya sūtra* rituals (actually) continued to be composed during this period and "the *brahmaṇa* composers of *gṛhya sūtras* continued to perform Vedic rituals, i.e. the rituals were not dead and that we should acknowledge all the while that the sacrifices were still happening." (2005, 185)

Declining rituals or ritualizing differently

Increased commercial activities and urbanized living have had an adverse impact on the number of participants in rituals in western societies. As societies industrialized and became more modernized, fewer people visited churches to attend Sunday mass and other Christian rituals. In modern day India too, people living in metropolitan and urban areas demonstrate similar tendencies. Due to time constraints, the available time gets divided between family, friends and entertainment, leaving very little 'disposable time' for individuals to participate in religious rituals. A similar situation must have existed in societies in the Upaniṣadic times as well. It is difficult to imagine an artisan or a craftsman with limited financial resources, abandoning his work for several days consecutively to participate in a *cāturmāsya* ceremony or *pravargya* ritual. Additionally, as discussed elsewhere in this book, people in general were growing averse to the pomp and violence involved in the animal sacrifice associated with these rituals. They were increasingly orienting towards understanding the self, the world around them, death, and the afterlife. Answers to these questions could not be found in the protracted ritualistic practices of *yajña* conducted under the supervision of the *brahmaṇas*.

Masters as they were of the ritualistic ceremonies, these *brahmaṇas* did not possess the answers to questions about the self and *Brahman*, death and afterlife, et cetera. Consequently, people started looking out for others who could answer their queries.

The ritual priests thus began losing their following, and respect, from the members of society. The dwindling following must have acted as a wake-up call for the *brahmaṇa* community, especially for its economic implication - fewer rituals meant fewer cows, fewer gifts of land as *dakṣiṇā*, and a decline in their financial fortunes. The author is of the view that this might have been only a small consideration for them. The *brahmaṇas*, as keepers of faith and Dharma, were undoubtedly equally, if not more, concerned with the dwindling influence of Hindu religion among rural and urban population alike. Someone had to stand up and provide satisfactory answers to the disillusioned and confused people who were turning away from the helpless ritualist *brahmaṇas*.

Chapter 19

Age of Reason: Ritual gurus as teachers of knowledge

Many heavyweights - Śandilya, Yājñavalkya and Uddālka - came forward not as ritual leaders, which they already were, but in new role as teachers who could answer puzzling questions about *Ātma* and *Parmātma*, life and death, and the purpose of life. These *brahmaṇa* sages were helped by intellectual *kṣatriya* rulers, like Aśvapati, Ajatshatru and Prāvāhana, as well as women and *śūdra* members of the society, such as Gārgi and Satyakāma. This was the beginning of the golden age of reason - the Upaniṣadic renaissance - which took Hinduism to new heights in a new direction. This journey culminated in the vedānta - the ultimate knowledge.

The Upaniṣads essentially deal with knowledge of the self, *Brahman* and equivalence of the self with the *Brahman*. They also deal with life, death, and life after death.

Many centuries before the Upaniṣads came into existence, the Ṛgvedic poets had already explored these metaphysical questions. The 'hymn of creation' is an outstanding example of not only the creative talent, but also representation of complex thoughts of the poet. It also clearly shows that at the dawn of civilization, those ṛṣi poets were not composing prayers praising forces of nature just as observers, but going beyond mere appearances and reflecting on the existence (or not) of a Creator. Even in its English translation (by A L Basham), the hymn is stunning -

> नासदासीन्नो सदासीत्तदानीं नासीद्रजो नो व्योमा परो यत् ।
> किमावरीवः कुह कस्य शर्मन्नम्भः किमासीद्गहनं गभीरम् ॥ १॥
> Then even nothingness was not, nor existence,
> There was no air then, nor the heavens beyond it.
> What covered it? Where was it? In whose keeping?
> Was there then cosmic water, in depths unfathomed?

न मृत्युरासीदमृतं न तर्हि न रात्र्या अह्न आसीत्प्रकेतः ।
आनीदवातं स्वधया तदेकं तस्माद्धान्यन्न परः किञ्चनास ॥२॥
Then there was neither death nor immortality
nor was there then the torch of night and day.
The One breathed windlessly and self-sustaining.
There was that One then, and there was no other.

को अद्धा वेद क इह प्र वोचत्कुत आजाता कुत इयं विसृष्टिः ।
अर्वाग्देवा अस्य विसर्जनेनाथा को वेद यत आबभूव ॥६॥
But, after all, who knows, and who can say
Whence it all came, and how creation happened?
the gods themselves are later than creation,
so who knows truly whence it has arisen?

इयं विसृष्टिर्यत आबभूव यदि वा दधे यदि वा न ।
यो अस्याध्यक्षः परमे व्योमन्त्सो अङ्ग वेद यदि वा न वेद ॥७॥
Whence all creation had its origin,
he, whether he fashioned it or whether he did not,
he, who surveys it all from highest heaven,
he knows - or maybe even he does not know.

This author has wondered many a time, 4000 years ago, why these men spent long hours contemplating the birth of the universe, the beginning of it all, and other abstract matters like - when 'even nothingness was not, nor existence', and 'there was that One then', and wondering whether 'he, who surveys it all from highest heaven, he knows - or maybe even he does not know'? Surely they had many other pressing matters related to their daily existence staring them in the face. They could certainly have used their time more productively in, say, reinforcing the leaking thatch roofs of their dwellings, tending cows or barricading their houses and fields from wild beasts.

One likely explanation that comes to the author's mind is that humans tend to divide their time according to priorities. People of the Ṛgvedic period, struggling to work out a design of a more efficient wheel for their *ratha* (chariot), basic implements for agriculture, or better ways to save their crop from floods, had clearly defined priorities. They preferred spending their time contemplating over philosophical matters rather than devoting it entirely, to hunting animals, tilling fields, and producing and storing food for the family, which back then was undoubtedly a cause of major insecurity and should have been a bigger priority compared to beholding the cosmos. Perhaps this was made possible because that society was already divided into different classes, each fulfilling different needs of the society. Still, question remains - what drove them to search for this sort of (abstract) knowledge?

The author believes that the habitants of India were not unique in this respect. The quest for such knowledge, as a trait, can be spotted in other old Asian civilizations of the same period. It was a remarkable trait in civilizations still in their infancy. In the Indian context, its significance lies in the speed with which this trait evolved from the later Brahmaṇas to the Āraṇyaka period, and soon matured into a formidable ideology in the form of Upaniṣads and Vedānta, nearly squeezing the *yajña*-based ritual practices out of the Hindu way of life. By the time of Śaṅkara (early eighth century), *śrauta* rituals were on their way out, and *vedānta*, *gṛhya* rituals, idol worship and *bhakti* were in vogue.

Gods: From Many to One - *Puruṣa* to '*tad-ekam*' and finally '*tat tvam asi*'

Immortality and the desire for heaven after death occupied the minds of our ancestors every bit as much as it does our's now. Veda's idea - good deeds in this life fetch rewards and bad deeds attract pain and suffering in the afterlife - too remains popular in our present Hindu society. This carrot and stick policy is as popular in modern management as in the sphere of religion. Not much seems to have changed in this respect in the last 4000 years! In the very first *sūkta* of the Ṛgveda, the 'liberal giver' and 'him who hath worshipped, him who now will worship' indicates a journey to the gods and heaven: "on the high ridge of heaven he stands exalted, yea, to the Gods he goes" (RV.I.125.4-7 Griffith). The heaven is described as "that deathless, undecaying world" where "the light of heaven is set, and everlasting luster shines." The desire for immortality "in that realm where they move even as they list, in the third sphere of inmost heaven where lucid worlds are full of light" is unambiguous. However, immortality is described to be not so different from life in this world in terms of pleasures: "the region of the radiant Moon, where food and full delights are found", and, "where joys and felicities combined, and longing wishes are fulfilled." (RV IX.113.7-13 Griffith)

For the evil doers, the Śatapatha Brahmaṇa[1] warns, "whatever food a man eats in this world, by the very same is he eaten again in the other world" - a simple and straightforward principle of retribution and recompense.

∞

According to the 'early Ṛgveda ', the life of a Hindu appears to have been simple and uncomplicated - do good deeds, stay away from evil in this life, and chances are you'll end up in heaven getting good food, uninterrupted happiness and joy, and an afterlife in another world. Interestingly, immortality was a persistent desire, but only in the afterlife. It is difficult to say whether this was an early, indirect expression of wanting to be free of the cycle of *saṃsāra* full of *dukkha*, or simply a desire to have a good time in heaven forever. Nevertheless, what it does tell us without any ambiguity is that our ancestors believed in god, afterlife, heaven, and good deeds. They trusted they would find an entry to heaven if they were liberal givers and worshippers: "flow to profit him who hath worshipped, him who now will worship" and "to him who freely gives" of the 'liberal giver'. (RV. I.125. 4-7)

Though there are many *sūktas* in the early, mid and later parts of the Ṛgveda which talk of various gods and the Creator(s), some also hint that 'all plurality is one'(RV I.164.46 J&B) - "They call him *Índra*, *Mitra*, *Varuṇa*, *Agni*, and also it is the winged, well- feathered (bird) of heaven (=the sun). Though it is One, inspired poets speak of it in many ways. They say it is *Agni*, *Yama*, *Matravisan*." The earliest signs of such Upaniṣadic ideas are found in the late Ṛgvedic period. With "a 1000 heads, 1000 eyes, and a 1000 feet" pervading earth on every side, *Puruṣa* - a supreme creator - appears only in the tenth chapter around 1100 BC in the famous sixteen hymns of *Puruṣa-sūkta*. He is credited with all that is and that is to be: "The Man alone is this whole (the world): what has come into being and what is to be." (RV. X.90.1-2 J&B)

And the same tenth chapter of the Ṛgveda also contains a philosophical contemplation in the hymn of creation (X.129), where for the first time, the poet reflects on creation and the imponderable in a very direct manner -

> "There was then neither '*asata*' (what is not, non-being) nor '*sata*' (what is); there was no sky nor the heaven which is beyond; what was it that covered all? Where was it and under whose shelter? Was there abyss unfathomable of waters?" 1
>
> "There was no death, hence nothing immortal; there was no consciousness (distinction) of night and day; that one breathed by its own nature (power) without there being any air, really nothing other than that existed." 2
>
> "He from whom arose this creation, whether he made it or did not make it, the highest seer in the highest heaven, he indeed knows or even he does not know?"......7

This breathtaking poetry, with its creativity and stunning content, speaks with a degree of uncertainty about how all this came about, and whether 'He' made it, or if 'He' even knows who made it?

Deussen (1845 - 1919), a German Indologist and professor of Philosophy at University of Kiel had observed (Vide Bloomfield's) that "no translation can ever do justice to the beauty of the original." Completely taken in by the sheer beauty of this Ṛgvedic hymn in Sanskrit, he lamented what we all lament when we (having read it earlier in the original language) read translations of poetry.

Until this point in time, the scriptures reflect a mind dissatisfied (but not agitated) with any of the prevailing beliefs in power of *yajña*, Vedic gods or *Puruṣa* as Creator. This period heavily identifies itself as *yajña* or sacrifice centric, and only when we move to the late Brahmaṇa period does the emergence of knowledge distinguish itself as an important element in narratives - a counterpoint, a rival to ritual, so to speak.

Ritual knowledge vs knowledge

For a modern reader, 'knowledge' is like any other word of the English language. To know its exact meaning, he will simply pick up a standard English language dictionary and look for its meaning under the appropriate section. However, the way the word 'knowledge' is used in the Vedic texts can be very confusing, even misleading. The importance of knowledge is emphasised in Vedic texts frequently, it is evident that it has been used in a different sense in different contexts. In the early Ṛgvedic period, knowledge implied 'mantra', making it a ritual-specific knowledge. As we move towards the Upaniṣadic period, i.e. late Brahmaṇas early Upaniṣads, knowledge is initially used more in the sense of knowledge of the self (*Ātma*), and subsequently *Ātma*, *Brahman* and other metaphysical matters.

Traditionalists consider memorizing the Vedic texts synonymous with knowledge of Vedas. Those who mock the tradition of 'memorization' of the Vedic scriptures argue that this 'knowledge', i.e. 'memorizing', doesn't involve acquisition of knowledge of what is said in the Vedas as we understand it. [Interestingly, Jamison and Brearton have translated 'Wisdom' as the title of the seventy-first hymn of the tenth chapter of Ṛgveda : "According to Anukramani, X.71 is dedicated to *jñāna* 'wisdom' or 'knowledge'," observe the two, and add, "but it is knowledge in the form of sacred speech (Vac)." They clarify that "the word *jñāna* does not occur in the hymn, or indeed in the Ṛgveda." (2014: 1496)]

It is important to bear in mind that in addition to 'memorizing' one or more Vedas by heart, Veda student had to master the six vedāṅgas (six limbs of Vedas which included grammar and etymology without which the learning of Vedas was considered incomplete). Radha Kumud Mookerji in his scholarly work 'Ancient Indian Education: Brahmanṇical and Buddhist'[2] observes -

"The contemplation and comprehension of their meaning was considered as more important and vital to education than a mere mechanical recitation and correct pronunciation. The Ṛgveda has several significant passages condemning and holding up to ridicule those whose knowledge is confined only to the repetition of its words without insight into their inner meaning, and emphasizing the supreme need of realizing that meaning by constant and concentrated contemplation."

RV. VI I. 103. 1 also refers to a period of contemplation in silence, during which the Brahmaṇas achieved enlightenment and burst out into speech like frogs quickened into activity by the clouds after a year's slumber. It is this enlightenment which fits the pupils (called *brahmaṇa vratacharinah* explained by Yaska in his Nirukta IX.6 as *abruvanah*, i.e. maintaining the vow of silence) for expounding the sacred texts.

"He who does not realize the ultimate Truth behind the Rik and *akshara* (word and letter) in which rest all gods - what we do by merely reciting and repeating the Riks? The Ṛgveda is *apara* (inferior) *vidyā* to one who does not go behind its words to their inner meaning (Sayana) (i.164.35.3/38)."

Yaska (Nirukta I.18) further condemns the mere reciter of the Veda, who does not attend to its meaning, by quoting the following two passages as translated from Saṃhitopanishad Brahmaṇa :

"He is only the bearer of a burden, the blockhead, who having studied the Veda does not understand its meaning (like an ass, carrying a load of sandalwood whose weight it feels without enjoying its fragrance). Learning without understanding is called cramming; like dry wood on ashes, which can never blaze."

Sayana (1300-1386 BC), the author of *Bhāshyas* (commentary) of Vedas *Saṃhitās* and Brahmaṇas, explains this passage as: "The words of the Veda which are received from the teacher without their meaning, and are repeatedly recited as texts, do not kindle, and reveal their inner essence."

Sayana's opinion is that the mere reciter of Vedic texts does not lose his caste or count as a *Vrātya*, but he is incapable of performing any sacrifice or winning its fruit, such as attainment of heaven.

For aims and methods of education - ref RV(X.71).

Knowledge vs Knowledge

However, Sayana's opinion has not settled the issue. The fundamental question 'cynics' continue to pose is - Can the mere understanding of the words in the Vedic texts be termed as (acquisition of) knowledge?

For this class of people, the contents of most of the *Saṃhitās* and Brahmaṇas are not of any intrinsic worth and do not qualify as knowledge. Therefore, even the most thorough knowledge of mantra recitation and ritual execution, carried out with objective of, say, warding off the influence of a co-wife in conformance of Atharvaveda's directions, hardly qualifies as knowledge, notwithstanding the complete understanding of grammar, etymology, and meaning of words by the performing *brahmaṇa.* For these skeptics, the mastery of associated procedures (rituals) that kept away the evil influence of the co-wife on one's husband (in this example), certainly does not count as knowledge.

These skeptics are of the view that the content of the Vedas and early Brahmaṇas contain very little (if any) 'real' knowledge (of use) - real knowledge as defined in dictionary (ref. Oxford Dictionary) i.e. 'facts, information, and skills'. Because, in their opinion, most of the literature of this period has only unscientific and non-rational content, they reject all early Vedic literature as devoid of meaning and 'unhelpful' in acquiring any knowledge. They quote the Vedic ritual literature, referring to 'mantra and ritual specific' knowledge as devoid of any real substance, a knowledge which is very different from the real knowledge as we understand it today (ref. Staal, The Vedas, for meaningless rituals and mantras). According to this line of argument - when authors of the Vedic texts speak of the importance of knowledge (as in the examples above), they are referring to the ability to memorize and recite mantras accurately and correctly in an error free manner, rather than its implied or explicit significance - what is intended to communicate its real purpose. And therefore, these authors should not be credited as having a high regard for knowledge (as we understand this word today). Simply put, they point out absence of 'advocacy of scientific temper and questioning mind (which are necessarily associated with knowledge as we understand it today) in early Vedic literature' and consider it a farce.

But even such cynics can not deny that things were changing in the late Ṛgvedic and early Brahmaṇa period. The poet of the hymn of creation ~ 1100 BC was pondering not on how to steal affections of a woman next door (as in the Atharvaveda mantra), but about more philosophical questions of who created this universe and whether He himself has all the answers or not: "He indeed knows or even He does not know?"

∞

In the early periods, the Upaniṣads formed part of the Brahmaṇa Āranyaka and were composed at different locations in different *pariṣads* (a group of followers or retinue). Consequently, the develapment of the Upaniṣadic thought was not a uniform or sequential process across the country - in fact it was quite random. The two surviving manuscripts of Chāndogya, the oldest (~800-600 BC) Upaniṣad, and Bṛhad Āraṇyaka (composed nearly at the same time as Chāndogya), were composed in two different geographical locations. The Chāndogyopaniṣad is associated with the Kuru-Panchal region of the northern Himalayan region and Haryana, while Bṛhad Āraṇyaka far to the east of the Videha region. Whereas Chāndogyopaniṣad is attached to the Sāmaveda, the Bṛhad Āraṇyaka is part of the Yajurveda. The difference in narrative of the same story in the two Upaniṣads, such as Svetaketu's interaction with Uddālka, mirrors the differences in societal thinking separated by what must have been considered a good physical distance in those days.

The shift in the thought process from the occasional metaphysical pondering in the hymn of creation, when nearly everything was ritual centric, to the CU and BU times ~600 BC is quite apparent, when 'full knowledge' became important in successfully conducting rituals, *agnihotṛ* -

1. "If, without knowing this, one offers an *agnihotṛ*, it would be as if a man were to remove the live coals and pour his Libation on dead ashes."
2. "But he who offers this *agnihotṛ* with the full knowledge of its full purport, he offers it (i.e. He eats food) in all worlds, and all beings, in all selfs."[3] CU V.24.1-2

But so far, this shift was bereft of any criticism, direct or indirect, of the prevailing ritual practices.

Even in CU, when Nārada approaches Sanata Kumāra to teach him about the Self to overcome his grief, Nārada is not critical of his own 'traditional' knowledge of mantra and the sacred books. Explaining what he had already learnt, Nārada enumerates,

"ṚgVedas, ... the *vakovākya* (logic); the *ekayana* (ethics); the *daiva vidyā*; the *Brahman vidyā*; the *bhūtāni vidyā*; the *kshatra vidyā*, the *nakṣatras vidyā*"[4] CU.VI I.1.3

He asks to be taught the knowledge of the self "which will help me overcome grief", implying that this knowledge (*vidyā*) of the self which he had not attained thus far, was like other *vidyās* (*kṣatriya vidyā*, *Brahman vidyā*, et cetera). It also indicates that Nārada, at least until then, did not consider this other *vidyā* about the Self as supreme knowledge. It was merely another type of knowledge or discipline that one acquired to destroy grief (like *kṣatriyas vidyā* - knowledge of weapons was acquired to destroy one's enemy). Nārada's behaviour was in many ways akin to a patient seeking a specialist in a suitable branch of medicine (*vidyā*) to cure a specific ailment (overcome grief).

Why is this debate important?

Does knowledge, here, mean correct understanding of the meaning of the words in the Vedic texts, or knowledge of subjects beyond memorization, recitation and ritual practices? This debate is important for our purpose because the entire argument of disenchantment with meaningless mantras and rituals, that drove people away from Hinduism, stands on the assumption that the pre-Buddhist Upaniṣadic movement was a move away from traditional dogmatic Vedic teachings towards knowledge centric teachings concerned with the self or metaphysical exploration.

But this confusion about the real knowledge was soon laid to rest.

Chapter 20

Cosmos, the Creator and the Self

Matters of life, death, and eternal bliss

In the Ṛgveda, *Puruṣa* with his 1000 heads, feet and eyes, is termed the supreme creator of "all that has come into being and is yet to come" (X. 90), which is not very different from Taittirīya Upaniṣad's creator *Brahman*. This is evident from what *Varuṇa* teaches his inquisitive son *Bhṛgu* about *Brahman*: "That from whence these beings are born, that by which, when born, they live, that into which they enter at their death, try to know that. This is *Brahman*." (III.1). Both, Ṛgveda and Upaniṣad, subscribe to the doctrine of 'a supreme creator'. This doctrine contradicts that of an immanent (existing or inherent) universe, but is widely accepted in the Vedas and other subsequent literature much like the existence of god. Interestingly, in Hinduism, god was accepted without a debate (unlike other theologies where arguments are given in favor of the existence of god).

The early Upaniṣads (~800-600 BC) extensively talk of *Brahman* as the Creator of the universe -

"In the beginning, my dear, there was that only which is one only, without a second. Others say, in the beginning there was that only which is not, one only, without a second; and from that which is not, that which is was born." (CU. VI.2.1)

And, verily in the beginning this was *Brahman*, that *Brahman* knew (it's) Self only, saying, 'I am *Brahman*'. From it all this sprang." (BU. I.4.10)

Having created it all -

"that being (i.e. that which had produced fire, water, and earth) thought, let me now enter those three beings (fire, water, earth) with this living Self, and let me then reveal (develop) names and forms." (CU.3.2)

In some Upaniṣads, *Brahman*, the creator, preserver and destroyer, assumes the additional role of 'the ruler god' - "That puller (ruler) within (*antáryamin*), who within pulls (rules) this world and the other world and all beings?" (BU I I I.7.1 - Uddālka Aruni debate)

Although both terms, *Brahman* and *Ātma*, are frequently used as concepts in the Ṛgveda (II.2; VI.21; X.72), Brahmaṇa, and Upaniṣads, they are widely discussed, employed and commented upon only in the early Upaniṣads. Since no special effort is made in these texts to distinguish between the two concepts i.e. *Brahman* and *Ātma*, and at times they are freely interchanged, it becomes confusing for the reader to understand whether they are different or the same, and what these two distinct words imply.

Brahman

Brahman, a Vedic Sanskrit word, is a key concept that first occurs in the Ṛgveda, and is extensively discussed, debated and expounded in the Upaniṣads. The Vedas conceptualise *Brahman* as the cosmic principle. In some of the oldest Ṛgvedic verses, it is identified as a power immanent in sounds, words, verses and rituals, and evolves as the "essence of the universe", the "deeper foundation of all phenomena", the "essence of the Self (*Ātma*)," and the "deeper truth of a person beyond apparent difference". Thus, *Brahman* didn't mean the same thing even during the Vedic period. Its ancient meaning (according to Gonda) was never the only meaning, the concept evolved and expanded throughout ancient India, conveying "different senses or different shades of meaning." Gonda goes on to add that there is no one single word in modern western language that can render the various meanings of the word *Brahman* in the Vedic literature. In fact, *Brahman* has such flexible meanings throughout the Upaniṣads that it may mean 'formulation of truth', the Veda, or the ultimate and basic essence of the cosmos.[1]

But there is no dispute about *Brahman* meaning the supreme, the ultimate truth or the ultimate reality.

In the early days of the Upaniṣads, sages were expounding their concept of *Brahman* using different words and examples. As noted earlier, the action did not take place in a single *janapada* or kingdom. These debates and discussions took place at different locations. The main actors came from differing backgrounds and interacted with participants who, in turn, belonged to diverse cultural, and (possibly) racial, backgrounds. Though these sages used different words to describe their concepts, the thought flow progressed in nearly the same direction - Uddālka's 'essence of life' was similar if not the same as *Prajāpati's* 'agent for sensing and cognizing'. Naturally, in this stage of Upaniṣadic evolution, as Brereton suggests, "Brahmaṇa (i.e. *Brahman*) remains an open concept." Furthermore, *Brahman* is "the designation given to whatever principle or power a sage believes to be behind the world and to make the world explicable." (1990, 118)

Ātma

The word *Ātma*, also a Sanskrit word, appears in the first *manḍala* (I.115.1) and nearly half a dozen more times in the subsequent manḍalas - VII.87.2, VII.101.6, VIII.3.24, IX.2.10 and IX.6.8 of the Ṛgveda. But Yaska (~800-500 BC), the ancient Indian linguist and grammarian, explains its meaning based on its use in the last chapter (ninety-seventh hymn of the tenth chapter) - "The pervading principle, the organism in which other elements are united and the ultimate sentient principle." The concept of *Ātma* is a key concept of Hindu metaphysics referring to the soul or the self, and was widely used in the early Upaniṣads by different sages. The fact that they defined it differently shows that the idea of *Ātma* was still evolving. But as a concept, it had taken firm root among intellectuals and public alike. This is evident from most narratives that depict teachers imparting knowledge of *Ātma* to their students, indicating a definitive move away from the teaching of rituals and *karmakāṇḍa*. Yājñavalkya, Śandilya, Uddālka (and others) are all shown either teaching or discussing the Self time and again, confirming that this new thought revolved around seeking knowledge of the Self rather than mastering the art of sacrifice.

According to the early Upaniṣads, *Ātma* is the core of every person's self - also referred as the Self - which is not the body, mind or ego. *Ātma* is the essence in all creatures, their innermost being which is eternal and ageless. BU describes *Ātma* as that in which everything exists, which permeates all, which is the essence of all, which is bliss and, most importantly, beyond description. It goes on to liken *Ātma* to *Brahman* (ref Yājñavalkya identifies *Ātma* with *Brahman*).

The socio-political-economic situation in that society was ripe for, and triggered this process of, transformation of the staid traditional ritualistic Vedic society into an intellectually vigorous *vedāntic* society in pursuit of knowledge of the *Ātma*, *Brahman*, and the meaning and purpose of this life, through deeply engaging metaphysical debates and discussions.

∞

This evolution of the idea of *Ātma* and *Brahman* also primarily took place in and around the Kuru Panchala-Kosala and Videha belt in 800-600 BC. A common denominator that soon emerged from these diffused and often divergent ideas of the Ultimate Reality was the Supreme, which had no *guṇas* (attributes), and hence could only be conceptualized or described as - '*neti, neti*' - 'not this, not this', negating the Supreme's identification with any known attribute of worldly objects. This *neti* became the foundation of Upaniṣadic thinking which finally developed into the *Vedantic* philosophy. So many different ideas, concepts, explanations and interpretations emerged and were subsumed under the head of Upaniṣads over a period of 600 years that the total number of Upaniṣads soon crossed two hundred.

(Prof Webber thinks that the number, "so far as we know at present", may be reckoned at 235, Ref - Max Müller, above, in this chapter on Upaniṣad.)

Naturally, many of these creations did not merit a place on the same shelf as the older Upaniṣads initially compiled as part of different Vedas. Even among the Upaniṣads containing serious matter, views and ideas expressed often needed to be restated to be correctly understood, and conflicting concepts rationalized and unified. Badrāyana (~200 BC-200 AD) accomplished this monumental task in his masterpiece *Brahman Sūtra*, systematically summarizing (authentic) spiritual and philosophical ideas contained in the Upaniṣads. The 555 sūtras of the Brahman Sūtra became the founding text of the Vedānta school of Hindu philosophy and remain so even today.

However, understanding any composition in *sūtra* form is about as easy as deciphering clues in the Times of India cross word puzzle. As a perplexed George Thibaut once lamented[1] -

"In these *sūtras* the most essential words are habitually dispensed with; nothing is, for instance, more common than the simple omission of the subject or predicate of a sentence. And when here and there a *sūtra* occurs whose words construe without anything having to be supplied, the phraseology is so eminently vague and obscure that without the help derived from a commentary we should be unable to make out to what subject the *sūtra* refers."

The Brahman Sūtras belong to the category of an even more cryptic variety of *sūtras*, thus they remained beyond the understanding of the public then, just as they remain now. Those interested in understanding it relied heavily on various available commentaries. But even this was no easy task, as Thibaut realized: "When undertaking to translate either of the *Mîmâmsâ-Sūtras* we therefore depend altogether on commentaries; and hence the question arises, which of the numerous commentaries extant is to be accepted as a guide to their right understanding."

Several interpretations emerged in the form of commentaries further adding to the difficulty of students and followers. Fortunately, the great *Vedāntin*, Sri Adi Shankarāchārya ~ 900 AD, explained Badrayana's complex *sūtras* in his exhaustive commentary Brahmāsūtra Bhāshya. This, along with his commentaries on four pre-Budha-Mahāvīra age Upaniṣads (Chāndogya Bṛhad Āraṇyaka, Aitareya, Taittirīya) and six other key Upaniṣads - Īśa, Ken, Katha, Praśna, Muṇḍaka and Māṇḍūkya - is the most authoritative work for understanding the Upaniṣads. Nearly 1100 years later, Shankarā's commentaries remain some of the most authoritative works on philosophy and religion for all Hindus.

∞

It is evident that with the evolution of the Upaniṣads, Hinduism moved to a different intellectual plane. As discussed in the foregoing paragraphs, this renaissance was a result of several things happening simultaneously which moved Hinduism from an archaic ritualism of the Vedas to a knowledge seeking *vedāntic* society. This transforming society saw the emergence of concepts "that include the doctrine of re-birth, the law of *karma* that regulates the rebirth process, and the techniques of liberation from the cycle of rebirth, such as mental training associated with *yoga*, ascetic self-denial and mortification, and the renunciation of sex, wealth, and family life."[2]

Following paragraphs will throw light on three important aspects -

- How rituals, initially allowed to retain their central role with knowledge playing a supporting role, were eventually severely criticised in the Upaniṣads
- How the *Ātma* and *Brahman* debate progressed from the early Upaniṣads, leading to *Parabrahmā* and *Aparabrahman*
- How *vedāntins* accommodated ritualism with the concept of an indestructible, perpetual, and attribute-less *Brahman*, into Hindu tradition

All three strands are so closely intertwined that it is impossible to consider any of them in isolation without encroaching onto the other two.

Knowledge - from a mere 'force multiplier' to 'all that matters': The importance of knowledge in context of ritual sacrifices starts emerging strongly in the early Upaniṣads (~800-600 BC). In the first *kāṇḍa* of the first *prapāṭhaka* of CU, it is clarified that knowledge and ignorance are different - "Now therefore it would seem to follow, that both he who knows this (the true meaning of the syllable *Aum*), and he who does not, perform the same sacrifice. But that is not so, for knowledge and ignorance are different" and that "the sacrifices which a man performs with knowledge, faith, and the Upaniṣad is more powerful."[2] In his commentary[3], Max Müller explains the difference between knowledge and ignorance as: "In case of a jeweler and a mere clod selling a precious stone the knowledge of the former bears better fruit than the ignorance of the latter."

The story of Ushasti Chakrayāna and his virgin wife amply demonstrates that society had accepted, and indeed was practicing, the teachings of gurus that - action performed with knowledge is superior to action performed in blind faith. Living in abject poverty, Chakrayāna goes to the king who was preparing to offer a major sacrifice, with the purpose of being chosen for all the priestly offices to gain wealth for himself. Before the *udgātṛis* (priests) began singing hymns of praise, Chakrayāna warned the *prastotṛa* (the leader) saying, "*Prastotṛa*, if you, without knowing the deity which belongs to the *prastāva* (hymns et cetera of *prastotṛa*) are going to sing it your head will fall off." (CU 1.10.8-9)

The reason Chakrayāna warned the *udgātṛa* (priests) is - (in those times) if an uninitiated priest (who didn't know the secret meaning) chose to conduct the *yajña* while an initiated priest was present, he ran the risk of being punished and losing his head[4]. An uninitiated priest was, however, permitted to conduct sacrifice without running the risk of any punishment provided an initiated priest was not available! The underlining principle is not difficult to grasp - sacrifice, even by an uninitiated priest, was preferable to no sacrifice. At the same time, recognizing that the right knowledge was crucial, an uninitiated priest ran risk of his life, if he chose to conduct a sacrifice while an initiated priest was available to conduct the *yajña.*

While the anecdote shows that society had accepted the supremacy of knowledge decisively, the transition ultimately succeeded because of the inbuilt incentives that this arrangement offered -

i. Priests with 'knowledge' were treated as better qualified, and so they were 'more sought after'. They commanded more respect and enjoyed greater fame, were more in demand to perform the rituals (in comparison to uninitiated priests), and consequently, earned more money.
ii. Uninitiated priests were prevented from performing rituals by deterrent punishment (death by shattering of the head) if an initiated priest was present among the attendees. Their prospects of better clientele and earnings reduced if they chose to remain uninitiated.

By the seventh and eighth *prapāṭhakas* of CU, we see proponents of supremacy of knowledge becoming less diffident; a hesitancy in putting rituals (sacrifice) before knowledge becomes evident, and even the Vedas are called inadequate - 'mere names'. A melancholy possessed and the despondent Nārada is depicted confessing that he learnt the Vedas and the six *vedāngas* as well as several other *vidyās*, and yet this learning is not helpful in shedding his grief. He beseeches Sanata Kumara, "Teach me, Sir!" and Sanata Kumara responds, "Whatever you have read is only a name" (CU VII.1.3). He pointedly adds, "A name is the Ṛgveda, Yajurveda, Sāmaveda and as the fourth the Atharvana as the fifth the *Itihāsa*-Purāṇa."

Imparting *Bhuma vidyā* to Nārada, he concludes, "He who sees, perceives, and understands this, loves the Self, delights in the Self, revels in the Self, rejoices in the Self - he becomes *svaraj*, (an autocrat or Self ruler); he is Lord and master in all the worlds." (VII.25.2) The last two lines of the seventh *prapāṭhaka*, often overlooked, contain telling evidence of the changing mindset - "The venerable Sanata Kumara showed the other side of darkness to Nārada after his faults had been rubbed out. They call Sanata Kumara *Skāṇḍa*, yea, *Skāṇḍa* they call him." Chāndogyopaniṣad underlines that it is the knowledge of the Self that (finally) made Nārada see the light by rubbing out his faults, which his learning of the four Vedas, *itihāsa* and Purāṇa had failed to do!

Knowledge of the self thus lifted the darkness that persisted in Nārada's mind despite learning all the Vedas.

Staying with Chāndogyopaniṣad a bit longer, in the eighth *prapāṭhaka* (last chapter), Nārada makes an important observation that the gains of sacrifices are temporary and perish: "Whatever has been acquired by exertion, perishes, so perishes whatever is required for the next world by sacrifices and other good actions performed on earth." Since knowledge is superior for "those who depart from hence after having discovered the Self" they receive a greater reward "for them there is freedom in all the worlds." (V I I I.1.6)

It is not Chāndogyopaniṣad alone which propagates the superiority of knowledge over rituals. Aiteraya-Āraṇyaka Upaniṣads classify people in three categories according to their quest for knowledge, or the lack of it. They place those who have turned away from the world and are single-mindedly fixed 'to be free at once' in the highest class to be taught knowledge of *Brahman* (Aitareya Ar I I.4 - 60), and those who do not care either for immediate or gradual freedom and desire nothing but offspring, cattle, et cetera in the lowest class. They cling strongly to the letter of the sacred text to gain knowledge of either *prāṇa* or *Brahman*. *Yama* also teaches the same to Naciketā in Kaṭha: "Wide apart and leading to different points are these two, ignorance, and what is known as wisdom. I believe Naciketā to be one who desires knowledge, for even many pleasures did not tear thee away." (Katha U 1.2.4)

It is the Muṇḍaka that categorically asserts knowledge of the Self as over and above even the Vedas: "That Self cannot be gained by the Veda, nor by understanding, nor by much learning" (III.2.3) Muṇḍaka's radical stand of running down Vedas reflects how the idea/concept of *Brahman* had evolved and found acceptability and following in society.

The term *vedānta*, which also means end of the Vedas, is first[5] used in Muṇḍaka. Is that a mere coincidence?

Returning to the discussion of knowledge in Upaniṣadic society - even though there are odd instances of the Vedas being run down (as in Muṇḍaka), the early, and even later, Upaniṣads did not take a confrontationist stance favoring knowledge in opposition to the traditional ritual practices. As is typical of Hinduism, the Upaniṣads - including Muṇḍaka - accommodated rituals, and without wasting energy in removing the rituals from the life of Hindus, they accorded recognition to ritualism, and termed rituals a stepping stone for climbing to the highest level, i.e. *Brahman*. To understand how and why this happened, we need to dwell a bit more on the evolution of the concept of the Self from '***tat tvam asi***' and '***aham brahmāsmi***', to an 'attribute-less' *Brahman* alongside the concept of Īśvara, a personal god.

Chapter 21

Meeting of *Saguṇa Brahman* and *Vedānta*

We have seen how Jaimini and Bādarāyaṇa produced, perhaps simultaneously, what later became foundational texts for the two most important, divergent and often competing ideologies that are a part of every Hindu's life even today. The concise compilation of ideas in the form of *sūtras* is a fascinating feature of Hinduism since ancient times. The *sūtras* were so terse that it was nearly impossible for a normal mortal to fully comprehend its meaning. The explanation was done through *bhāshyas*, i.e. commentary, either in verse or prose form, composed by scholars who invariably interpreted it differently, leading to sub-commentaries. This led to the creation of camps, each with its own strong following. These camps constantly engaged in animated debates and discussions, presenting their own different view points on the same subject which helped create an open minded society - a society which tolerated dissent and criticism. But there was a flip side to this accommodating sprit. The same Vedānta Sūtra has been interpreted so differently by various sages that if one read only the conclusions of Śaṅkara and Mādhava, it would seem as if the two *vedāntins* arrived at their conclusions by reading two different *sūtras*!

The concept of the *Nirguṇa Brahman* - *Brahman* without any qualities or attributes, the only and absolute reality - is the core of Śaṅkara's philosophy of *Śuddha Advaita* or non-dualism. *Saguṇa Brahman* of Mādhava, in complete contrast, has the fullness of qualities and is producer of the world due to its intrinsic nature. Mādhava identifies and includes five types of differences in support of his philosophy of dualism. Yet, both these systems form a part of the same *vedānta darśan*. It is remarkable that such opposing ideas became part of the same philosophical system. The contradiction is absolutely glaring, and not just in the scriptures, but also in the minds of most Hindus. Yet, this is nothing new or unusual - such contradictions have coexisted in Hinduism for millennia. Scholar after scholar has noted that Hindus of the twentieth and twenty-first centuries quote and follow teachings of Śaṅkara in everyday life. But it is not the *Brahman* - the unalloyed consciousness, it is the *Īśvara*, the personal god, who is remembered by all practicing and non-practicing Hindus. It is the personal god that they visit in temples and in *pūjā* rooms located in a nook or kitchen of their dwelling, demarcated often by nothing more than an imaginary line, which no person is allowed to cross wearing footwear.

Śaṅkara's brilliant mind which conceived an attribute-less and non-dual reality also saw clearly the improbability of such an abstract metaphysical concept being understood and accepted by the majority of people (even) in 900 AD - a period called the 'logical period'[1] by Dasgupta, an Indian philosopher noted for his authoritative A History of Indian Philosophy in 5 volumes. Śaṅkara was quick to accommodate *Aparabrahman* or *Saguṇa Brahman* as an important stopover in the ultimate journey of self-realization and the *Brahman*. But there was another reason why Śaṅkara accommodated and compromised his idea of *Śuddha Advaita*. He followed the principles that he had laid down himself - reasoning should be allowed freedom only as long as it does not conflict with the scriptures. In matters regarding super-sensible reality, reasoning itself cannot deliver certainty, for according to Śaṅkara, every thesis established by reasoning may be countered by an opposite thesis supported by an equally strong, if not stronger, reasoning. The sacred scriptures, which embody the results of the intuitive experience of seers should therefore be accepted as authoritative, and reasoning should be made subordinate to them[2]. Consider this masterpiece from the greatest champion and advocate of *Śuddha Advaita*, Śaṅkara -

"Our first duty consists in performing sacrifices, such as are described in the first portion of the Veda, the *Saṃhitās*, Brahmaṇas, and, to a certain extent in the Āranyaka also. Afterwards arises a desire for knowledge, which cannot be satisfied except a man has first attained complete concentration of thought (*ekāgrata*). To acquire that concentration, the performance of certain *upāsanas* or meditations is enjoined, such as we find described in our Upaniṣads viz in Ar.II.1-3."

Nearly 1000 years before him, Bādarāyaṇa too had arrived at the same conclusion. Instead of completely rejecting or contradicting Jaimini and his *karmakāṇḍa*, he accommodated the *Vaisvānara* of Jaimini as the *Brahman*: "There is no contradiction in taking *vaishvānara* as the supreme *Brahmaṇa* (i.e. *Brahman*) (VS 1.2.28). In 1.2.31, Jaimini is again quoted by Bādarāyana as saying that the *nirguṇa* (attribute-less) *Brahmaṇa* can manifest itself in a form. In 4.3.12, Bādarāyana again cites Jaimini saying that the *mukta* (liberated) *Puruṣa* attains *Brahman*.

Several other instances of Jaimini referring to the supreme god are present in his *sūtras* - from Jaimini 6, 3.3 to the "Omnipotent Main Being" (*api vāpy ekadeśe syāt pradhāne hy arthanirvṛttir guṇamātram itarat tadarthatvāt*; Jaimini 6, 3.2). *Karma-Mīmāṃsā* supports the Vedas, and the Ṛgveda says that the one truth is variously named by the sages. It is irrelevant whether we call Him *Pradhāna, Brahman, Vaishvānara, Śiva* or god.

It would be apt to conclude this section by giving the example of Mandāna Miśra, a staunch follower of Jaimini's *karmakāṇḍa.* After losing *shāstrārtha* (debate) to the great advocate of *Śuddha Advaita*, Śaṅkara, he became his follower and went on to write some of the finest commentaries on *Advaita Vāda.*

Conclusion: The doctrine of the non-difference of the individual self or inanimate world from First Principle or Essence is one of the most characteristic features of Hinduism[3], and India's greatest contribution to the spiritual development of the man.

All plurality is one - this was hinted at in RV (I.164.46) [They call him *Índra, Mitra, Varuṇa, Agni,* and he is heavenly nobly-winged *garutman.* To what is One, sages give many a title they call it *Agni*, *Yama*, *Matravisan*] and VIII.58.2 - showing germs of Upaniṣad 's ideas; RV X.90.2 finally says very clearly 'all this universe is one *Puruṣa* only'.

Chapter 22

Īśvara, the personal god : *Para* and *Aparabrahman*

In the ancient Vedic times, an ordinary man's concept of god was an almighty who created everything animate and inanimate, and ruled over the world. This concept was in line with the cosmological argument of philosophy in support of the existence of god, which claims that all things in nature depend on something else for their existence (i.e. they are contingent), and that the whole cosmos must therefore depend on a being which exists independently or necessarily. In this world order of the ordinary Vedic man, good deeds were rewarded after death by a sojourn in heaven, and bad acts attracted punishment! If pleased, god blessed individuals with immortality and a good life. These ideas connecting good deeds with heaven - "To him who freely gives" and "the liberal giver", and rewards - "on the highly range of heaven he stands exalted, yea, to the gods he goes, the liberal giver" appear in the early Vedas[1]. According to the Brahmaṇas, evil or harmful acts attracted retribution - "For whatever food a man eats in this world, by the very same is he eaten again in the other world"[2]. Apart from life in heaven, good deeds also brought the reward of immortality and good health - "For those who give rich meeds are made immortal; the givers of rich feasts prolong their lifetime"[3]. The "deathless, un-decaying world" "wherein the light of heaven is set, and everlasting lustre shines"[4] was the ultimate goal achieved through good deeds of sacrifice, the Vedic rituals. Interestingly, in the early stages, Vedic gods that were identified with forces of nature - the all-purifying *Agni*, *Varuṇa* and the thunder bolt god, *Índra* - did not deliver heavenly rewards. It was the *yajña* (the sacrifice ritual) that had this capability. This is why the early texts define sacrifice as 'good deeds' leading to haven. The 'liberal giver' of RV (I.125.4-7) is also a suitable candidate to go 'to the gods' and stand exalted 'on the highly ranges of heaven'. The word 'giving' here is associated with *dāna*, which to this day is recognised as *puṇya karma* (sacred/

meritorious acts), and puts the 'liberal giver' at the same pedestal as the *yajamāna* performing a *yajña*.

During the early Upaniṣads, the idea of *Ātma* and *Brahman* had rapidly started taking definite shape through vigorous public discussions, debates, and also contemplation and meditation - the opening *shloka* of Chāndogya implores meditating on *Om*. What was emerging was an abstract concept, an attribute-less, indestructible, all pervasive, timeless *Brahman*, the essence of it all, *tad ekam* (That One), very different from the *Puruṣa* of Ṛgveda. But, the change was restricted only to the idea of god; the concept of heaven, and consequences to good and bad deeds remained intact at least in the early Upaniṣads. When Arthabhaga asked Yājñavalkya, "What happens to the person himself when he dies?" he responded saying, "A man turns into something good by good action (*puṇya karma*) and into something bad by bad action (*pāpa karma*)" (BU).

This burst of metaphysical activity associated with the Upaniṣadic era soon took the level of debates to another intellectual plane involving complex abstractions beyond the understanding of most men. The concept of the Self evolved from the often confusing *Ātma*, described by different sages at times in contradictory terms, to '*neti, neti*' (not this, not this) *Brahman*, and finally *Brahman* as the only reality. Equivalence of *Ātma* and *Brahman* is the ultimate message of the Upaniṣads.

Interestingly, while this evolution in the concept of god occurred in isolation, other important pre-Upaniṣadic concepts like inevitability of consequences of good and bad deeds, heaven and afterlife remained unchanged. But the new concept of *Brahman* as the only reality came in direct conflict with the belief of the common man who simply could not grasp the idea that the world which he saw, experienced and lived in was not real. For him, this world was as real as himself and both were creations of the god, the ultimate ruler. But, even this belief in the reality of his own existence was denied in the new concept - that the 'absolute *Brahman* is the only reality, everything else is unreal'. The concept of the creator god as described in Taittirīya Upaniṣad (III.1) -"Desire to know that from which all *bhūtānis* (being or nonbeing) spring, by which, after being created they live (are sustained) and to which they return and are absorbed therein; that is *Brahman*" - was a common man's idea of an orderly world administered by an *antāryamin* god ruling the universe - "Dost thou know Kapya, that puller (ruler) within (*antaryāmin*), who within pulls (rules) this world and the other world and all beings"[5], and "he is the guardian of the world, the king of the world, he is the lord of the universe"[6]. The reader would immediately spot the different strands and ideas propagated in the Upaniṣads - Bṛhad-Āraṇyaka and Kauṣitaki both belong to the early Upaniṣad era, Bṛhad-Āraṇyaka in its very first chapter gave that *mahā vākya* (great saying) which is perhaps the most quoted of any Upaniṣads *mahā vākya* - '*aham brahmāsmi* - 'I am *Brahman*'[7].

[Note - The *mahā vākya* are 'The Great Sayings' or the words of wisdom of the Upaniṣads, the foundational texts of Vedanta. There are many *mahā vākya*, but the four - one from each of the four Vedas - that are mentioned as *mahā vākyas* are-

1. *prajñānam brahma* - "Consciousness is *Brahman*" (Aitareya Upanishad 3.3)
2. *ayam ātmā brahma* - "This Self (Ātman) is *Brahman*" (Mandukya Upaniṣad 1.2)
3. *tat tvam asi* - "Thou art That" (Chāndogya Upaniṣad 6.8.7)
4. *aham brahmāsmi* - "I am *Brahman*" (Bṛhad-Āraṇyaka Upaniṣad 1.4.10)]

They talk of a *Brahman*, who apart from being creator of all *bhūtānis*, is described as the guardian and king of the world, and lord of the universe, which clearly clashes with the concept of an absolute *Brahman* as the only reality.

This is a typical example of a society where different ideas and concepts were allowed to be freely put forward in public domain, and old ideas and beliefs criticised unhesitatingly. If found unsuitable, old ideas were sidelined or rejected, and new ones adopted through discussions and debates. Because this process was not a 'managed process' - by authorities (temporal or spiritual) - many old ideas and concepts like supremacy of rituals, *Puruṣa* and *Prajāpati* continued to exist and practised by sections of people. Simultaneously, new ideas and beliefs, often contradicting and severely criticising the old ideas and belief, also thrived, without its proponent getting ostracised or labelled heretic.

The sages, *brahmaṇa* teachers, *kṣatriya* rulers, and many others who commanded authority in such matters, must have played a crucial role together in devising a course of action acceptable to all, a masterpiece example of managing contradictions. So, here was a society where the majority believed in a creator god (creator, sustainer and destroyer), a god who created the self (individual beings) and this world. The thinking man - the sages and intellectuals - however, had started seeing things differently. In the early Upaniṣads, they conceptualised god as the *Ātma* and *Brahman* which evolved into the Supreme, the ultimate reality and finally as '*Brahman*, the only reality', negating existence of everything else as unreal, including the self and the world.

This abstract concept of an attribute-less (*nirguṇa*) *Brahman* must have been extremely difficult, if not impossible, for an average member of the society to grasp then, as it is now (despite a high rate of literacy). For an average man, the concept of an almighty god, as the Creator of the self and the whole universe, was difficult to grasp, but something that also made eminent sense. What did not make sense was that this world in which he lived, grew up and died, the world he experienced in every living moment with all his senses, was unreal. And worse, that he himself was unreal! The higher philosophic minds resolved this problem by simply accommodating the common man's view and conceding that the universe exists. In truth, however, they said, it is nothing but the *Ātma* entered into the universe. They said that the world was phenomenal (perceptible by the senses or through immediate experience), not false or nothing, but *Ātma* was behind the world, and they called *Brahman* a creator, and *Īśvara* a personal god. This is theism [belief in existence of a god(s), specifically of a creator who intervenes in the universe - Oxford Dictionary], which acknowledges three entities viz a real world, the *Paramātma* (creative *Ātma*) and the individual (self) dependent on the *Paramātma*. But while accommodating this viewpoint, it was emphatically pointed out that the final goal for all human beings was beyond this personal god, *Īśvara*. The ultimate objective was to strive for the attribute-less (*nirguṇa*) *Brahman*, the only reality.

For common people, the path of *Saguṇa Brahman* - also identified as *Aparabrahman* - was prayer and worship (*upāsana*), distinguished from *Parabrahma*, the attribute-less *nirguṇa Brahman*. But, it was made quite clear that although it was acceptable for people to pursue *Īśvara* (*Aparabrahman*) and go down the route of *upāsana*, it was really a path of *avidyā* (ignorance) - a stopover on the way to the final goal, the *nirguṇa Brahman*, the only reality.

Thus, the *saguṇa Brahman* concept, instead of being rejected and ending up taking a competitive or alternative role, came to coexist with the *nirguṇa Brahman* concept in a complimentary way.

It'll be wrong to conclude that because majority of the population believed in, and practised *upāsana*, they were not in tune with the current Upaniṣadic thoughts of the *Ātma* and *Brahman*. The early Upaniṣads are full of concepts of a creator God, indicating a transition from Vedic cosmological ideas of the golden egg (*Hiraṇyagarbha*) and *Puruṣa* to the *Ātma* and *Brahman* assuming the role of a creator. But more importantly, it shows that the masses were in sync with this transition and easily adapted these changes. However, when it came to the next transition- to *nirguṇa Brahman*, people could not make the leap and continued their old practices, showing their inability or reluctance to change. This indicates that for the common man, this change was either too radical to adopt or too difficult to understand, or probably both. Its difficulty lay in its abstractness and radical viewpoint; it meant giving up the concept of a personal saviour god. It is simple to conclude that the idea of 'the *Brahman* being the only reality' was too complex and difficult to comprehend. Hence, it was never readily adopted by the masses. One of the main reasons why *nirguṇa Brahman* was not completely accepted by the society (in large numbers) was, and continues to be, for a very practical reason. It is same as why Hindus never gave up *yajñas* even though they were disillusioned and disenchanted with the associated pomp and violence and moved to a knowledge-based society away from - *kāmya*. *Upāsana* and worship of a personal god, i.e. *Īśvara*, is believed to be capable of delivering a son, a good harvest or other worldly possessions that *nirguṇa Brahman*, by its very definition having no desire - being attribute-less, and untouched by any prayer, is not expected to deliver.

Thus, *nirguṇa Brahman* remained lonely; its popularity restricted only among intellectuals, *vānaprasthas*, and *saṃnyāsīs*, a small fraction of the total population, and could never become a common man's god.

Chapter 23

Pūrva and *Uttara Mīmāṁsā*

Pūrva Mīmāṁsā and *Devatās*

Why is it that, despite the strong sense of disenchantment with *yajña* and related practices, people were not entirely driven away by ritual practices, even though a logical viable alternative had clearly emerged? The alternative 'path of knowledge' was made available by none other than 'the *brahmaṇa* teachers and *kṣatriya* rulers combine' and ably aided by other thinking members of society.

This was due to two interrelated reasons -

i. *Yajña* and rituals were considered more important than even the *devatās*
ii. Only *yajñas* - not even the *devatās* - could fulfil human desires

The first point is explained by Jaimini in V I I I.1.32 - 34 that - in a sacrifice, *havis* (offering) is the principal matter while the *devatā* is the subordinate (*gauṇa*), and in case of conflict between the two, the conclusion is to be arrived at by relying on *havis*. Explaining why it is so, the texts say although the Vedas connect the *devatā* with the sacrificial act (as in Taittirīya S. I I.2.1.1), the *phala* or reward is achieved by the sacrifice (not the deity), and the words '*Índra* and *Agni* confer progeny on the sacrificer' are purely laudatory.[1] The Vedas clearly say, "One desirous of heaven to perform sacrifice", it is *Veda-vākya* (literally - said in Veda), *shruti*. It comes from 'the' final authority. It was natural for people to follow *Veda-vākya*; thus they had greater faith in *yajñas* than in the deities, and relied on the efficacy of *yajña* rituals for fulfilling their worldly desires.[2]

As pointed out earlier, it was also due to the failure of the new system in providing a credible, authoritative alternative to *kāmya* practices (which helped solve practical every day issues of life, including but not restricted to neutralising enemy's nefarious designs, winning the heart of the maiden next-door or getting an ailing child good health) that the people persisted with old ritualistic practices. Upaniṣadic debates of *Ātma Paramātma* quenched the thirst of the mind, but the hunger of worldly acquisitions could not be satisfied with metaphysical discourses. The Upaniṣads had nothing to offer by way of alternative to *kāmya* practices, therefore *kāmya* rituals continued unabated. This was not without more than a little help from all those who genuinely believed in the efficacy of the ancient ritualistic Vedic system - the true and committed believers from the members of the public. The priestly class, which stood to lose position and wealth in case the old system was dismantled, was determined to resist any change. Despite such direct conflict of interest and even though it was in a state of turmoil, the society was nowhere close to revolting against the *brahmaṇas*. In fact, nothing in available records even obliquely suggests that any section of society had even contemplated any violent action against the *brahmaṇas* and *purohitas* - the very cause of this very unsatisfactory state of affairs in the society.

In any case, the early Upaniṣadic discourses progressed, hand-in-hand with *kāmya* rituals, smoothly and peacefully. But the major upheaval caused by the Upaniṣadic movements was staring squarely in the face of the *brahmaṇas* who were a divided house. The priests were no more a monolith bound by the same set of common beliefs, practices and rituals. One should bear in mind that by this time, so many *śākhās* and *caranas* of the Veda school had mushroomed across society (each with its own peculiar prescription and practices) that Brahmaṇa directories no more enjoyed the position they initially did as a single reference book for all *purohitas* and *paṇḍitas*. There was a great proliferation of recensions of the Vedas, making it very difficult to ascertain what was right and authentic, and what was not. Five *śākhās* of the Ṛgveda, eighty-six of the Yajurveda, one of Atharvaveda and a staggering 1000 of SāmaVeda are indicated in the *Śaunaka Pariśiṣṭa*.

Jaimini (400-200 BC), chose to correct this situation. A purist, he formulated rules (*nyāya*) prescribing the performance of rituals and sacrifices in his monumental work Mīmāṁsā Sūtra, the largest of all philosophical *sūtras*. Divided into twelve chapters, it is a collection of nearly 2500 aphorisms.

Whether purist Jaimini was driven more by a desire to provide a consolidated authentic text to all ritualistic Hindus, or it was an attempt by a conservative ritualist to push back the onslaught of Upaniṣadic thinking by uniting ritualistic Hindus through a common directory of rituals, cannot be said with certainty. Perhaps it was a bit of both. Jaimini's monumental work claims that each and every word of the Veda is injunctive and related to the Dharma; that it is only *havis* that lead to *svarga* or *kāmya*; and that the *devatās* have no existence or power beyond mere words. A man of Jaimini's intellect would have known that his work was not only a persuasive way to re-establish the supremacy of traditional Vedic ritualism, but also a reminder to those who had strayed from the flock that *kāmya prāpti* (achievement of desired object) could only happen through the ritualistic practice of *havis*. In a way, Jaimini was offering the word of the Veda as the only reality, countering the Upaniṣads' idea of the *Brahman* being the only reality. Jaimini had an edge over Upaniṣadic thinkers because he offered the traditional tool of *havis* for *kāmya prāpti* which, by definition, the Upaniṣadic thought/ideology was incapable of providing.

As is the case with all *sūtras*, Jaimini's *sūtras* too could not be fully understood without the help of commentaries. Śabarasvamin's ~ 100 BC-300 AD Sabra Bhāshya is not the first but the earliest available commentary on Mīmāṁsā Sūtras - Pūrva Mīmāṁsā or Karmakāṇḍa. Nearly 400 years later, Kumārila Bhatt and Prabhākara wrote separate commentaries on various aspects of Śabara's Bhāshya - though Prabhākara is believed to be a student of Kumārila, the two have some important differences.

Kumārila Bhatt (seventh century AD), founder of the first school of *Mīmāmsā*, commented on both the *sūtra* and its Śabara Bhāshya. His treatise consists of three parts - the Ślokavārttika, the Tantravārttika and the Ṭupṭīkā. Mandāna Miśra (eight century AD) was a follower of Kumārila, who wrote Vidhiviveka and Mīmāmsānukramanī.

Prabhākara (eight century AD), the originator of the second school of the *Mīmāmsā*, wrote his commentary on the Śabara Bhāshya called Bṛhatī. Śālikanātha's Ṛjuvimalā (ninth century AD) is a commentary on the Brhatī. His Prakaranapañcikā is an independent work of this school and the *Pariśishta* is a brief explanation of the Śabara Bhāshya.

The founder of the third school of the *Mīmāmsā* was Murāri, whose works have not reached us.

Jaimini's *Pūrva Mīmāmsā*: Core teachings

Mīmāṁsākas hold that the Vedas are - 'eternal, authorless, infallible' injunctions (Veda *vidhi*) and mantras in rituals prescriptive actions (*kārya*), and rituals are of primary importance in merit. The *Mīmāṁsā* school has little interest in examining the existence of god - it holds that the soul is an eternal, omnipresent, inherently activist ritual essence. Just as there was no need for an author to compose the Vedas, there was no need to postulate a maker for the world. The gods named in the Vedas have no existence outside the mantras that mention their names and, to that extent, it is the power of mantra that the *Mīmāṁsākas* see as the power of gods.

The *Mīmāṁsā* school believes in the theory of intrinsic validity of all cognition. It holds that all knowledge is *ipso facto* true (Sanskrit - *svataḥprāmāṇyavāda*). Thus, what is to be proven is not the truth of cognition, but its falsity. *Mimāṃsākas* advocate self-validity of knowledge both in respect of its origin (*utpatti*) and ascertainment (*jñapti*) which is used to establish the unchallengeable validity of the Vedas. The core tenets of *Pūrva Mīmāṁsā* are orthopraxy-ritualism, anti-asceticism and anti-mysticism. The central aim of the school is elucidation of the nature of Dharma - understood as a set of ritual obligations and prerogatives to be performed properly. Dharma is held equivalent to following the prescriptions of the *Saṃhitās* and their Brahmaṇa commentaries relating to the correct performance of Vedic rituals. The source of the knowledge of Dharma is neither through sense, experience nor inference, but through the knowledge of words and (their) meanings according to the Vedas.

Therefore, *Pūrva Mīmāṁsā* is essentially ritualist, placing great weight on performance of *karma* or action as enjoined by the Vedas.[3]

Pūrva Mīmāṁsā does not expressly talk of the existence of a soul in any of the *sūtras*, although it does talk of *svarga* (PMS IV.3.15) - it provides that *svarga* is the reward of all religious acts (such as *visvajit*) for which no express reward is provided by the texts. Śabara in I.1.5 deals with the topic of the existence of the soul as different from the body, senses, et cetera. The Shloka Vārtika devotes 148 verses to this subject and the Tantravārtika also briefly deals with it in PMS I I.1.5.

Śabara states that "happiness is *svarga* and all seek that."[4] The idea of heaven entertained by Jaimini, Śabara and Kumārila is different from the description of heaven in the Vedas and Purāṇas (ref RG. I X.11 3.7 - 11) - that immortal world where there is continuous light, where all desires are fulfilled, where there are joys of various kinds (RV. VI.4 6.12). In Atharva Veda IV.3 4.2 and 5 - 6, *svarga* has many women, great edible plants and flowers of various kinds, streams of *ghī*, honey and wine, milk, curds and lotus ponds all round. Śhatpatha (XIV.7.1.32 - 33) promises that the joys of heaven are a hundred times greater than those on earth. Kauṣītaki Upaniṣad (1.3 and 4) becomes more specific, assuring '500 *apsarās*' (nymphs) will meet those who reach heaven: "100 with garlands in their hands, 100 with ointments, 100 with perfumes, 100 with garments and 100 with fruit." However, fruits of sacrifices are not always *svarga* - Taittirīya S. I I.4.6.1 provides 'one desirous of (plenty of) cattle should offer the *citra* sacrifice', or 'one desirous of (leadership or control over a) village should offer an *iṣṭi* called *sangra-hani*' (Taittirīya S. I I.3.9.20). According to Śabara, the Veda does not say that the result of sacrifices cannot be attained in this life.

Another important doctrine, the doctrine of *Apūrva*, is about 'invisibility' or 'potency'. The Vedas laid down that one desirous of heaven should perform sacrifice. But the reward of heaven doesn't follow immediately in the wake of the sacrifice; there is no direct immediate connection between the cause (sacrifice) and the reward (heaven). Before the act of sacrifice is performed, men have no capacity for *svarga* and likewise, sacrifices are also incapable of delivering *svarga* by themselves. The acts in a sacrifice when carried out properly remove this incapacity and produce a certain capacity or potency - *svarga*. This capacity or potency, which either resides in the man as an agent or arises from the sacrifice performed, is called *apūrva*. *Mīmāṁsākas* do not admit that the result of the religious acts is given by god. According to Prakaranapañcikā page 186, the invisible force or potency is not in the agent but arises as a subtle form from the action itself.

There are many deities, eternal Vedic nature gods. However, these deities do not exist in space and time - they are not anthropomorphic beings. They do not even grant boons or benefits for the sacrificial offerings given to them. The deities cannot be at par with or superior to the Vedas.

As a whole, the universe has no beginning or end and 'the description of creation and dissolution in the Vedas are only meant to illustrate the power of *daiva* (fate or destiny) and the vanity of human effort and urge men to perform duties enjoined by the Veda'.[5]

Neither the PMS nor Śabara or Prabhākara deal with the topic of *mokṣa*. Kumārila in Śloka Vārtika and Śalikanatha ~700 AD in Prakaranapañcikā (one of the very few texts available to us for studying the Prabhākara school of *Pūrva Mīmāṁsā*) deal with liberation consisting of not having to assume human form again. Śhloka Vārtika states that one desiring *mokṣa* should not do any act that is forbidden or is *kāmya* (prescribed for those who desire an object like riches, a son, et cetera); he should perform the rites such as *agnihotṛ* and *naimittika* (like a bath, *japa*, gifts on an eclipse, et cetera) to avoid the sin that would accrue owing to non-performance of those two. If he does not desire the rewards of doing it and the *naimittika* acts, they will not come to him - because a reward comes to one who seeks it. The results of acts in a former life would be eliminated by undergoing them in the life in which he seeks liberation.

This differs from Śaṅkarachārya's position, who holds that there is no other way to *mokṣa* except knowledge and the realisation of the *Ātma*, as declared in Svet Upaniṣad III.8. According to Kumārila, Upaniṣad passages about the knowledge of *Ātma* are only *artha-vada* as they convey to the performer that he has a soul and that the soul has certain characteristics, while Śaṅkara maintains that the *phala*, the subject of investigation, and the Vedas exhortation (*codāna*) are different in *Pūrva Mīmāṁsā* and in Brahman Mīmāṁsā.[6]

Mīmāṃsā doctrine claims that Veda is eternal, of absolute and unquestioned authority. This school devised a logic of their own that governed the interpretation of Vedic passages. Although this provided *Mīmāṁsā* with a psychological and semantic technique for interpreting the sentences of the scriptures that are clearly in the injunctive form, there are also other kinds of sentences - prayers, glorifications, those referring to a thing by a name and prohibitions. Attempts, sometimes comical, were therefore made to show, how each one of these types of words and sentences, directly or indirectly, could be interpreted to fit as injunctive texts.

Summary: Unlike other *darśanas*, *Pūrva Mīmāṁsā* appears to be much more about faith than inquiry. An abiding faith in the Vedas and an equally strong commitment to discharging the duties commanded by the Vedas is the core of *Pūrva Mīmāṁsā*. Heaven was the goal, although the later *Mīmāṁsākas* seem to have nodded in favour of liberation from the cycle of birth and death. The *Jinas* and *Bauddhas* (*Jina* - a title given to great Jain teachers, followers of Jain religion; *Bauddha* - follower of Buddha) seem to have rebelled against the extreme ritualism of *Pūrva Mīmāṁsākas*. *Uttara Mīmāṁsā* or *vedānta* seems to be a response to the reaction of the *Jinas* and *Bauddhas*.[7]

***Uttara Mīmāṁsā* or *Vedānta*:**

While the serious effort of resurrecting ritualistic aspects and belief in the meaning of every word of Veda was underway through the *Pūrva Mīmāṁsā* route of Jaimini's work, the followers of *Jñāna Kāṇḍa*, following later Upaniṣads and the concept of *prajñānam Brahman* (*Brahman* is the supreme knowledge - *Aitareya* Upaniṣad's 3.3 (and *brahman satyam jagan mithya*) *Brahman* is real; the world is unreal - (Vivekachudamani), were constantly moving away from archaic ritualism. Bādrāyaṇa, a contemporary of Jaimini, was the other major interpreter of Vedic thought. His monumental work Vedānta Sūtra laid the basis for the development of *Uttara Mīmāṁsā* - *vedānta* philosophy - by doing something similar to what Jaimini had done by producing a consolidated work of *Karmakāṇḍa*, i.e. Mīmāṁsā Sūtra.

Your author thinks that it is more than a mere coincidence that the two contemporaries - Bādrāyaṇa and Jaimini - two heavy weights belonging to two fundamentally differing ideologies, decided to consolidate, nearly at the same time, their divergent views, ideas and practices in their respective fields of interest - pursuit of perfect ritualism and pursuit of pure knowledge. It was undoubtedly a consolidation of forces by the two ideologies, engaged in a battle of supremacy being fought in the Bhāratvarṣa of that time.

Chapter 24

Vedānta

The later Upaniṣads increasingly occupied themselves with discourses and discussions on *Ātma* and *Brahman*, devoting hardly any space to the orthopraxy of Vedic ritualism. Since the Upaniṣads formed the last part of Vedas, and the study of *Ātma* and *Brahman* was central to the later Upaniṣads, these texts came to be called *vedānta* or *Uttara Mīmāṃsā*. Collectively known as *prasthāna-traya* (triple foundation), the Upaniṣads, along with the Bhagavad Gītā and the Brahman Sūtras, are the primary sources for all schools of *vedānta*, and are the critical objects of commentaries.

Bādrāyaṇa's Brahman Sūtra is a four-chapter long work comprising 564/555 *sūtras* (pithy aphorisms) considered a foundational work on *Uttara Mīmāṃsā* or *vedānta*. But it was not the first to systematize the teachings of the Upaniṣads; Bādarāyaṇa himself refers to seven other *vedāntic* teachers before him. The time gap between later Upaniṣads and Śaṅkara is approximately 1000 years. What happened during the thousand years between the Upaniṣads and Śaṅkara, considering that "originally these scriptures were not put down in writing, but were orally transmitted - with oral tradition there must not be even a single break in the teacher pupil line. Since both, the teacher and the student understood Sanskrit they could master the doctrines completely and immerse themselves in philosophic reflection and thought. ....There is a definite history of more than 1000 years before Śaṅkara in the evolution of this school, but the actual position of that period remains unclarified."[1]? We know commentaries were written since both Rāmanuja and Śaṅkara refer to *vrittis* (a learned work or commentary) of Baudhāyana and Upavarsha in their work. Unfortunately, no commentary on the *vedānta sūtras* written between Śaṅkara and Badarāyaṇa is available to us today. Hence, we are not in a position to say with certainty how vedāntic thoughts evolved in this period.

Although *vedānta* is one of the six *darśanas* (*ṣadaḍarśanas*) or systems of orthodox hindu philosophy bound together by adherence to the *traiy prasthanas* (the Upaniṣads, the *Vedānta Sūtra,* also known as Brahman Sūtra, and the Bhagavada Gītā) - various schools flourished within the *vedānta* system, each with a different viewpoint born out of their varying interpretations of the three *prasthanas*. Sometimes, these interpretations are so radically different that they appear to draw their ideology from an altogether different source. These differences arise out of their diverse ways of looking at the nature of *Brahman*, the status of the phenomenal world, the relation of finite individuals to the *Brahman*, and the nature and means to *mokṣa*, or liberation.

The three main schools - Śaṅkara's (eighth century AD) *Śuddha Advaita* or unqualified non-dualism; Rāmanuja's (eleventh-twelfth century AD) *Vishishtadvaita* or qualified non-dualism; and Mādhava's (thirteenth century AD) *Dvaita* or dualism, tell it all. While Śaṅkara believed in the thesis that the one, universal, eternal, and self-illuminating self whose essence is pure consciousness without a subject (*āśraya*) and without an object (*viṣaya*) from a transcendental point of view alone is real, Rāmanuja rejected Śaṅkara's conception of *Brahman* as an indeterminate, quality-less, and difference-less reality on the ground that such a reality cannot be perceived, known, thought of, or even spoken about, in which case it is nothing short of fiction. Rāmanuja defended his thesis saying *Brahman* is a being with infinitely perfect virtues, a being whose perfection cannot be exceeded. Both the world and finite individuals are real, and together they constitute the body of *Brahman*. The subject of body and soul is central to his way of thinking - the body is that which can be controlled and moved for the purpose of the spirit. Rejecting Śaṅkara's conception of reality, the material world and the conscious spirits, Rāmanuja argues that although substantive realities, they are inseparable from the *Brahman*, thus qualifying him in the same sense in which the body qualifies the soul - *Brahman* is spiritual-material qualified, and liberation is a state of blessedness in the company of god. Rāmanuja emphasizes on a path which requires complete self-surrender (*prapatti*) to god's will and making oneself worthy of his grace.

Mādhava (born 1199?) belonged to the *vaiṣnava* tradition and showed great polemical spirit in refuting Śaṅkara's philosophy, and converting people to his own fold. An uncompromising dualist, he traced back dualistic thought even to some of the Upaniṣads.

He also glorified the differences. There are five types of differences central to Mādhava's system - difference between soul and god, soul and soul, soul and matter, god and matter, and matter and matter. *Brahman* is the fullness of qualities, and by its own intrinsic nature, *Brahman* produces the world. The individual, otherwise free, is dependent only upon god. The *Advaita* concepts of falsity and indescribability of the world were severely criticized and rejected.

PART IV

पुराणमित्येव न साधु सर्वं न चापि काव्यं नवमित्यवद्यम्।
सन्तः परीक्ष्यान्यतरद्भजन्ते मूढः परप्रत्ययनेयबुद्धिः॥

Not all that is old, is good;
Not all that is new, is bad;
After examining wise men know the difference;
Dull-witted are led by somebody else's intelligence.

Chapter 25

Ancient sacred mythology and legends - Purāṇas

The response to *Vedic Brahmaṇism* manifested in different ways. Finding no space for their belief system within the fold of *Vedic Brahmannism*, Buddhism and Jainism branched out into new religions. Within the Vedic school of thought, Upaniṣadic ideas started to gain prominence as the dominant philosophy, initially tolerating but later openly criticising, and finally, frontally attacking, the ritual practices of *Vedic Brahmannism*. The last 500 years of the first millennium before the advent of the Christian Era (500 BC to the beginning of Christian Era) witnessed some of the most far reaching changes in the history of Hinduism and Bhāratvarśa. The *śramanicas*, *ājīvikas*, and many other schools of thought and practices blossomed in this period.

The author must emphasise that the use of the word Hindu in this context is anachronistic. First used by Arabs after the eighth century AD for people living east of the Indus, its use was standardized by British writers in 1830. The word 'Hinduism' now denotes the Indian civilisation of approximately the last 2000 years, which evolved from *Vedism*.

This period - 500 BC to the beginning of the Christian era - witnessed the emergence of knowledge (Upaniṣadic philosophy) as superior, indeed as a substitute for action (ritualism). The *brahmaṇas* - attempting to assert their eminence - responded. For instance, Mīmāṁsāka Jaimini and his followers reasserted the importance of Vedic sacrifices, insisting that every single word in the Veda is meaningful. The emergence of *Vidhāna* practices as a substitute of large-scale, expensive, blood soaked and time-consuming *śrauta* rituals and, crucially, the evolution of *Bhāgvata* and *Śaiva* sects and the beginning of *mūrti pūjā* (idol worship) marked this era. But it was idol worship that captured the imagination of a large section of the Hindu population.

Cutting across social, economic and caste boundaries, it found favor in all sections of society, eventually expanding to encompass the whole of India and Hinduism itself. *Mūrti pūjā* then took firm root in post-Vedic India. Today, all over the world, idol worship has become the most distinguishable characteristic of a Hindu, and of Hinduism.

∞

Purāṇic Hinduism, as it came to be later called, was a response to the urgent need to counter internal as well as external (international) threats that the Hindu religion faced at this juncture. The Greek and Saka invasions brought social and religious practices which challenged *brahmanṇical* values. A greater challenge came as a consequence of the ascension of non-*kṣatriyas* to kingship. The Nandas and the Mauryas, both *śūdra* clans, established powerful kingdoms across the northern plains. Purāṇic Hinduism offered a simpler, less orthodox religion which promised *svarga* and *mokṣa* through simple acts such as *bhakti*, *dāna*, *vrata* and *tīrtha* etc.. All members of society - including women and *śūdras* - could freely practice this form of religion, without having to depend on the services of a *brahmaṇa* priest. A new class of texts, Purāṇas, were compiled as the new 'Vedas' of ordinary and excluded people.

Wendy Doniger, writing on Purāṇa in Britannica, says - 'With the epics, with which they are closely linked in origin, the Purāṇas became the scriptures of the common people. Unlike the Vedas, which were restricted to initiated men of the three higher orders, the Purāṇas were available to everybody, including women and members of the lowest order of society (*śūdras*).'

The Purāṇas propagated:

- An all-inclusive form of Hinduism
- Simple *bhakti*, *dāna*, *tīrtha* and *vrata* practices, leading to *svarga* and *mokṣa*
- A choice of worshipping god in an iconic form (*mūrti*) that the devotee could relate to
- Through mythological stories, simplified, more accessible teachings of Dharma

∞

As Hinduism recast itself from *yajña* centric *Vedic Brahmanṇism* to an idol worshipping purāṇic faith, the *vidhāna* practices played a key role - Bhatt has acknowledged this role of Ṛg and Yajur *vidhānas* as the connecting link between *brahmaṇism* and the purāṇic Hindu religion[1a]. *Vidhāna* texts had, in the words of Bhatt, marked 'a new period of literature and a new outlook in the religious life of India, since they were written with a practical object in view, to wit: the simplification of the complicated and burdensome ceremonies treated in the *śrauta* and *gṛhya sūtras*, and this was achieved by adjusting the matters, with the help of magic, in such a way that observances became easier in practice'.[1b] It is easy to see why, compared to Vedic ritual, these simple, result oriented magico-religious *vidhāna* practices became popular with the common man. They offered an economical and quick solution to problems like finding a stolen cow, winning back the love of a straying husband, or getting rid of a quarrelsome neighbour. Religion became a useful implement in solving problems, big or small, spiritual, material or mundane, and even means of realising such baser goals as making one's enemy impotent! Thanks to the simple and economical nature of *vidhāna* rituals, religion was now within the reach of everyone and had become a useful 'tool' of everyday use. Though many complex, archaic Vedic rituals were done away within the emergent *vidhāna* practices, they did retain more than a few ritual features from the past - mantras and priests continued to play a significant part in this highly compressed and modified form of Vedic ritualism.

From this 'stop over' of *vidhāna* practices, the ancient religion next moved to its simplest and easiest form of ritual practice - *pūjā*.

Described by Dalal as 'the act of worship in Hinduism, which may take place in a temple or at home'[2], *pūjā* has two equally important parts - prayer and offerings. Both are manifestations of *bhakti* (devotion) which aims for union with god in any form through total surrender and personal love. In Hindu belief, god manifests in countless forms - animate and inanimate. The object of worship could be anything - a river, a tree, an animal, a mountain, a rock, an image or an idol. Likewise, the offerings could be almost anything - flowers, leaves, fruits, milk, curd, honey, food or water. Or just a simple act of obeisance - folding hands and bowing down. Two important features differentiate *pūjā* from earlier forms of ritualism. First, *pūjā* can be performed in a temple, at home or any place where the object of worship is situated; second, it can be performed with or without an officiating priest.

Such worship includes rituals (*pūjā*) that should be performed on festivals; places to go on pilgrimage; prayers to recite; and stories to narrate and listen to.

All *pūjā*, as the object of devotion, usually have an icon or *mūrti.*

What began as an exercise in focusing one's mind (meditation or the act of *dhārṇa*) on abstract *Om* (ref Chāndogya Upaniṣad) eventually assumed the physical form of a *mūrti*. The practice of idol worship, with some variations, was common to both *vaiṣnavas* (*Bhāgvatas*), i.e. followers of *Viṣṇu*, and *śaivas*, the followers of *Śiva*. How and why *Brahman* - the Creator, and the third deity in the Trinity - fell out of favor has many reasons, apart from the most popular mythological one - his incestuous attraction towards his daughter. The two sects, *Bhāgvatas* and *Śaivas*, came to be identified as followers of purāṇic Hinduism, a term that differentiates them from the followers of *Vedic Brahmaṇism*.

∞

The centrality of *yajña* is the defining characteristic of Vedic practices. Over time, the royalty, the rich and powerful, and the *brahmaṇas* appropriated Vedic practices, completely excluding women, *śūdras*, and even the ordinary *dvija*. Purāṇic Hinduism was a major course correction; it created 'user friendly' practices and texts, available to every member of Hindu society. Cutting across *varṇa*, *jāti* and gender barriers, in purāṇic practices, women and *śūdras* could read the Purāṇas, recite mantras, and perform *pūjās*, with or without a priest. Drawing from the mythology, religious customs and practices (for example, fertility rites) of non-Āryan and Āryan clans and cults, pre-Vedic texts (like the *āgama* from Southern India) and Vedic texts, and the epics (Ramāyāna and Mahābhārata), purāṇic Hinduism evolved into a new form of Hinduism centred around *bhakti* and *mūrti pūjā* instead of *yajña*.

Non-Āryans, women, *śūdras*, et cetera, who had been kept away in *Vedic Brahmannism*, were brought into the fold of purāṇic Hinduism. Priests, as intermediary between men and gods, saw their clout decline. True to Hindu tradition, purāṇic Hinduism did not outright reject Veda mantras or sacrificial practices - both were retained, but in a highly modified and diluted form.

∞

Literally meaning old or ancient in Sanskrit, the Purāṇas, according to Dalal, are 'Sacred Hindu texts…which include myths, legends, methods of worship, geography, historical details and a lot more'.[3]

Purāṇas are to purāṇic Hinduism what the Vedas are to *Vedic Brahmannism*.

Because purāṇic Hinduism was conceived as a simplified version of complex *Vedic Brahmaṇism*, its authors and compilers ensured its contents were easy to understand, and its practices easy to perform. Dealing with their primary concerns, like how to live a pious life or how to worship the gods, all the Purāṇas narrate countless tales of gods and goddesses, ṛṣis and sages, kings and subjects, especially their ideals and good deeds that the believer is encouraged to emulate in real life. They also have a number of stories portraying evildoers who reaped the fruits of the evil they had sown. All the Purāṇas use the medium of *kathā* (story) to make a moral, worldly or spiritual point. Since the purāṇic texts were compiled over 1000 years, what they prescribe as the Righteous path differs from one Purāṇa to another, as do the practices, form of worship, as well as the names and importance of the gods.

As mentioned earlier, the Purāṇas retained many Veda mantras but added several of their own. These purāṇic mantras could be recited even by the non-*dvijas*. According to the Purāṇas, *bhakti* (devotion), *dāna* (gift), *vrata* (fast) and *tīrtha* (pilgrimage) lead to union with the gods. There are many other practices, but these four practices are central to purāṇic Hinduism, and all the Purāṇas narrate tales underlining their importance.

∞

The Śatapatha Brahmaṇa mentions Purāṇa, and so does Gopatha, but 'The term Purāṇa, indicating the type of text, is first used in the Atharva Veda'.[4]

Composed in narrative couplets, all the Purāṇas are in Sanskrit and follow the free-flowing form of the two great epics - the Mahābhārata and the (Valamiki) Ramāyāna. Occasionally they lapse into prose form. There are eighteen major *mahā* Purāṇas, and an equal number of minor or Upa-Purāṇas, besides a large number of *sthala*-Purāṇas (local Purāṇas) or *mahātmyas* (magnifications), which glorify temples or sacred places and are recited in services at those places.

All eighteen *mahā* Purāṇas - Brahman, Padma, Viṣṇu, Vāyu or Śiva, Bhāgvata, Brihannārdiya or Nārdiya, Mārkaṃḍe, Agni, Bhaviṣya, Brahmāvaivarta, Liṅgaṃ, Varāha, Skāṇḍa, Vamana, Kūrma, Matsya, Garuda and Brahmaṇda Purāṇa are extant.

The Padma Purāṇa classifies Purāṇas into three categories according to *guṇas* of *Sāmkhya* philosophy. Sattva with Viṣṇu, Nāradiya, Bhāgvata, Garuda, Padma and Varāha; *Rājas* with Brahman, Brahmaṇda, Brahmāvaivarta, Bhaviṣya, Mārkaṃḍe and Vāmana; and *Tamas* with - Matsya, Kūrma, Liṅgaṃ, Vāyu or Śiva, Skāṇḍa and Agni.

Matsya, on the other hand, links these with the three deities. Thus, Sattva Purāṇas are associated with *Viṣṇu*, *Rājas* with *Brahman* as the creator, and *Tamas* with *Śiva* as the destroyer. Skāṇḍa has yet a different classification - it assigns the Purāṇas to five deities - *Brahman, Sūrya, Agni, Śiva* and *Viṣṇu.*

It is not accurate to classify the Purāṇas in this manner because several of them have mixed themes and cannot be assigned to any one *guṇa* or a deity.

Though the list of *Upapurāṇa* varies, the commonly accepted eighteen texts are -

Sanatakumāra, Nāradiya, Narasiṃha, Śiva, Kapila, Mānava, Uṣanas, Varuṇa, Kalika, Saura, Āditya, Maheṣvara, Devi Bhāgavata, Durvāsa, Viṣṇudharmottara and Nilamata Purāṇa.

Besides these, there are a few other texts that call themselves Purāṇa, including a number of texts composed by Jains which are also known as Purāṇas. For example Padma Aparahna, a version of the Ramāyāna, the Jain Harivamsha Purāṇa, et cetera.

Newer Purāṇas continued to be composed down the centuries in response to the need of the times - there is even a Krista Purāṇa on Jesus![5]

Date

While the exact time of their composition is still uncertain, it is widely accepted that -

(i) the earliest nine Purāṇas - Brahmaṇda, Devi, Kūrma, Mārkaṃḍe, Matsya, Vāmana, Varāha, Vāyu, and Viṣṇu - were composed in the Gupta period, between 350 AD and 750 AD;

(ii) Agni, Bhāgavata, Bhaviṣya, Brahman, Brahmāvaivarta, Devibhāgavata, Garuda, Liṅgaṃ, Padma, Śiva, and Skāṇḍa - were compiled between 750 and 1000 AD; and

(iii) the most recent, the Kalika, Kalki, Mahābhāgavata, Nāradiya, and Saura, were composed between 1000 and 1500 AD.

Lakṣaṇas

Amarakosha (original name Namaliṅgaṃnushashanam, or 'Instructions concerning nouns and gender') the oldest known thesaurus of Sanskrit was compiled by Amar Siṃha, believed to be one of the nine jewels (*navaratnas*) at the court of Chandragupta (480 AD). Hazra, quoting Amarkosha, cites an ancient definition of Purāṇa 'a Purāṇa is to have five characteristics or *lakṣaṇas*: creation (*sarga*), re-creation (*pratisarga*), genealogy (*vaṃsa*, of gods and sages), cosmic cycles (*mānavāntara*), and accounts of royal dynasties (*vaṃshanucharita*)'.[6]

Virtually all the Purāṇas cite the same five *lakṣaṇas* as a defining characteristic of Purāṇa. But in praxis, only the earlier Purāṇas conform to these *lakṣaṇas*. The later Purāṇas contain material on topics like the social customs and glories of god, and their contents do not always satisfy the criteria of the five *lakṣaṇas*. As a matter of fact, in many Purāṇas, these *lakṣaṇa* have been neglected, their place taken by detailed accounts of rites and duties, not unlike the *smṛtis*. According to Kane, who disagrees with Amarsiṃha (Amarakoṣa) and Hazra, the Purāṇas are not characterised by these five traditional topics - *panca-lakṣaṇa*. He claims they actually form less than 3% of the total contents of *Mahā* Purāṇas.[7]

∞

In his seminal work, 'Purāṇic Records on Hindu rites and Customs', his thesis for a PhD in the 1940s, still widely cited by scholars, RC Hazra drew a table showing how the Purāṇas began to incorporate *smṛti* philosophy. During the first stage of the development -

(i) From the beginning of third to the end of the fifth century AD - the Purāṇas dealt only with *varṇāśramadharma*, *ācara*, *āhinika*, *bhakśyaabhakśya*, *vivāha*, *aśauca*, *śrāddha*, *dravyaśuddhi*, *pātaka*, *prayścita*, *narka*, *karma vipāka* and *yuga dharma*.[8] These topics are covered in the early *Smṛti Saṃhitā*, for example, by Yajñavalakya and Manu.

(ii) From the sixth century AD, new *smṛti* topics were added to the Purāṇas. These included various kinds of gifts, initiation, sacrifices to planets and their pacification, *homa*, consecration (*pratishtha*) of images, *saṃdhya*, glorification of *brahmaṇas* and their worship, glorification of holy places, *tīrtha*, *utsarga*, *vrata* and the *pūjā*.

'These topics are found neither in the works of Manu and Yaj, nor in the Purāṇas or portions thereof, which were written earlier than about the beginning of the sixth century AD.'[9]

Hazra then goes on to investigate the reasons this significant change in the characteristic of the Purāṇas took place. He divides followers of religion in four categories.

Vedas - those that believed in *śrauta, smṛta* and *yajña* centric Veda practices

Anti-Vedas - those opposed to *Vedic Brahmannism*, such as Buddhists, Jains, Ājīvikas

Semi-Vedas - those that followed *Vaiṣnavism* and *Śaivism*

Non-Vedas - followers of *Śaktism*

He then adds an important fifth category - those that followed *vaiṣnava* or *śaiva* practices but also had faith in Vedic practices. People in this category believed they could attain *mokṣa* through worship of their chosen gods, but they also demonstrated great respect for the Vedas as the highest authority of Dharma. They followed Vedic practices like *varṇāśrama-dharma* and *smṛti* rules.[10] According to Hazra, "Purāṇic Dharma originated with this last-mentioned class of people."[11]

Contents of Purāṇa : Cosmogony and cosmography

Cosmogony deals with the origin of the universe. All purāṇic texts delve into this subject, but they present differing versions of how it all came to be. Many Purāṇa stories were developed on themes contained in the Brahmaṇas, the Upaniṣads, and the epics. The most common, and popular, version has *Brahman*, born in a lotus growing out of the navel of *Nārāyaṇa* (*Viṣṇu*) who is reclined on a bed formed by the coiled *ananta nāga* (endless snake), floating in the primeval waters, reciting Vedas from his four heads. *Nārāyaṇa* (Sanskrit - nara=water, ayana=home) had remained for a year inside a golden egg which came into being by itself. And creation - the earth, the heavens and also the sky, directions, time, and senses - was thus manifested (ref. Brahman Purāṇa). Unlike the Vedas, which do not deal with end of the world, purāṇic cosmogony accounts for the periodic destruction of the world at the close of an aeon. *Śiva*, the lord of destruction, dances his famous *tāṇḍava* heralding the destruction of the world (*pralaya*), after which the cycle of creation begins anew.

The three-tier concept of the universe described in the Vedic literature has been expanded upon, and expounded, in almost all the Purāṇas.

Bhū-manḍala, literally circle of earth, has been dealt with extensively in the Bhagavata Purāṇa. It calls the earth a disc that bisects the *Brahmaṇda*, the spherical purāṇic universe. Seven annular rings - alternate islands and oceans - divide the central region of *bhū-manḍala*. Islands are *dvipa* in Sanskrit - we live on *jambudvipa* which is located in the innermost ring.

In the Purāṇas, *jambudvipa* is a disk 100,000 *yojanas* (one *yojana* = eight miles) in diameter, situated in the centre of *bhū manḍala*. At the centre of *jambudvipa* is Mount Meru (or Sumeru) which, in one interpretation, corresponds astronomically to the polar axis of the earth. The cardinal directions east, west, north and south are defined from this point.

The disk is separated into nine *varshas*, or continents, by a series of mountain ranges. It is first divided into seven horizontal strips by six ranges that run east to west. Each strip is 10,000 *yojanas* high and 2,000 *yojanas* wide. The three strips to the north, and the three to the south, are single *varshas* extending 9,000 *yojanas* in a north-south direction.[12]

Dvipas* and oceans of *bhū-manḍala

***Dvipa* (Islands)**	**Surrounding Ocean**	**Named After**
Jambu	*Lavnoda* (salt water)	Rose Apple Tree
Plaksha	*Iskura* (sugarcane juice)	Indian fig tree
Salmali	*Suroda* (liquor)	Silk-cotton tree
Kusha	*Ghratoda* (*ghī*)	*Kusha* grass
Krauncha	*Kshiroda* (milk)	Mt Krauncha
Saka	*Dhyoda* (curd)	Teak tree
Pushkara	*Svadudaka* (fresh water)	Lotus flower

Each of the *dvipas* divided into seven regions are called *varshas*, with seven mountains and seven rivers. *Varshas* are ruled by the grandson of Mahārāja Priyāvrata, who created the second sun.

These accounts of cosmogony run against the well-established scientific facts of modern times. They attracted ridicule in the west, as they do amongst educated Indians at home. Any person with the most basic schooling understands that oceans contain only salt water. Milk, curd and *ghī* are commodities sold over the counter in markets precisely because they are not available free of cost in the oceans.

For the Purāṇas' cosmogony to remain relevant, a deeper and different meaning has to be assigned to their theories. One example of such an attempt is by Thompson. "Certainly, this is not geography in the familiar European sense of the term. However, as we will see later on, the geography of *Bhū-manḍala* encodes a combination of astronomical and geographical maps which is both rational and scientific. It appears that the elements of *Bhū-maṇḍala* geography have either been introduced or adapted to convey a number of meaningful messages, some of which still remain obscure."[13]

Richard L. Thompson received his Ph.D. in mathematics from Cornell University, specialising in probability theory and statistical mechanics and has done research in quantum physics, mathematical biology, and remote sensing. He has extensively investigated ancient Indian cosmology and authored nine books on subjects ranging from archaeology to ancient astronomy. Delivering a lecture - "An Accurate Map of the Solar System in an Ancient Sanskrit Text"[14] - in the Patanjali series at The Center for Indic Studies at the University of Massachusetts Dartmouth, Dr. Thompson observed:

"This system looks like an elaborate account of a flat earth, with precise dimensions of geographical features given in terms of a unit of distance called the *yojana*. However, when these dimensions are carefully examined, they reveal a map of the solar system out to Uranus, with accurate values for the closest and greatest distance of each planet from the earth."

Time and *Yuga* - essentially from Śiva Purāṇa

Time (in Purāṇas) is under the control of lord *Śiva*. Since time contains the element of *Śiva* (*Śivattatva*), its momentum will not be checked by any power, except that of *Śiva*. One who understands the meaning of *kāla*, has a *darśana* (audience/sight) of lord *Śiva*.

The smallest unit for measuring time is called '*nimesh*'. The time taken to drop one's eyelid is one *nimesh*. A *kala* consists of fifteen *nimeshas*; thirty *kalas* make a '*muhūrta*'. Thirty such '*muhūrtas*' make a day and a night. A month consists of thirty days, divided into two fortnights. One fortnight is known as *kṛṣṇa pakṣa* (dark lunar phase) and the other is known as *śukla pakṣa* (bright lunar phase).

In *pitṛloka*, the day consists of one fortnight and night of the same number of days. *Śukla pakṣa* is the day of the *pitṛloka* and *kṛṣṇa pakṣa* the night.

One '*ayana*' consists of six months. Two '*ayanas*' form one year. A year on earth is equivalent to a day and a night in the heavens. The six months when the sun is in the southern hemisphere (*dakṣiṇāyana*) is the time the deities experience night. Conversely, the six months when sun is in the northern hemisphere (*uttarāyana*) is the day time of the deities. One year in the life of the deities is equivalent to three hundred and sixty years in our world.

Yugas are calculated on the basis of the years of the deities. According to scholars, there are four *yugas* - *Satya* or *Kretā Yuga*, *Tretā Yuga*, *Dvāpar Yuga* and *Kali Yuga*.

Time itself deteriorates, for the ages are successively shorter. Each *yuga* is preceded by an intermediate 'dawn' and 'dusk'. The *Kretā Yuga* lasted 4,800 years, with a dawn and dusk of 400 years each; *Tretā yuga* spanned 3,600 years; *Dvapara* was 2,400 years long; and *Kali* (the current one), is 1,200 years long. A *mahāyuga* thus lasts 12,000 years and observes the usual coefficient of twelve, derived from the twelve-month year, the unit of creation.

One thousand *mahāyugas* form one *kalpa* (aeon), which is one day in the life of *Brahman*. *Brahman's* life lasts 100 years. Each *kalpa* is followed by an equally long period - *pralaya*, of abeyance in which the universe is asleep. *Brahmans* are innumerable, and a new universe is reborn with each new *Brahman*.

According to Purāṇas, the present period is the midpoint of *Brahman's* life.

Gods and Goddesses

Saṃhitās and the Brahmaṇas categorically speak of thirty-three gods - the eight *Vāsus*, the eleven *Rudras*, and the twelve *Ādityas* - these are thirty-one. *Índra* and *Prajāpati* make up the thirty-three.[15]

'This division into the three classes of the terrestrial *Vāsus*, the aerial *Rudras*, and the celestials *Ādityas* distinguished by the poets of the *Saṃhitā* as well as the compilers of the Brahmaṇa and surviving as the constituent groups of the thirty-three gods in epic times, may probably be considered to have eventually paved the way for the constitution of the classical triad of high gods'.[16] Usually, the gods are referred to as 'the Thirty-Three'.

According to the Mahābhārata (1.1.39), there are 33,333 Hindu deities. In other sources that number is multiplied a thousand-fold. In modern times, Hindu gods are believed to number a staggering thirty-three crores, i.e. 330 million!

The tendency towards the worship of many gods (pantheism) rapidly escalated in purāṇic Hinduism and led to a kind of theism - belief in the existence of a creator who intervenes in the universe. Several supreme gods, none prominent in the Vedic texts, were exalted. At the same time, many of the Vedic gods simply faded and eventually disappeared. Vedic notion of *ṛta*, the basis of the conception of cosmic order, began emerging as Dharma, or the religious-social tasks and obligations of humans in society that maintain order in the universe. There was also a broader vision of the universe and the place of divinity.

All Purāṇas are strongly sectarian—some devoted to *Śiva*, some to *Viṣṇu*, some to other gods (*Gaṇeśa*, *Garuda*, *Vāyu*, et cetera), and goddesses (*Devi*, *Kalika*, et cetera). Yet, even the ones devoted to a particular god often dwell on other gods. The most popular Purāṇa is the Bhāgavata-Purāṇa. The treatment of the childhood and early life of *Kṛṣṇa* makes it particularly popular among rural and urban folks alike.

Tantrism

An important feature of the Purāṇas is the inclusion of tantrism. The customs we associate with Tantrism are 'purely of non-Vedic origin.'[17] It is widely accepted that these practices pre-existed many of the Vedas and its followers did not accept the superiority of the Vedas. These practices gained such popularity that it was considered prudent to accommodate tantrism, albeit in a watered-down form, in Hinduism. The five M's - *matsya* or fish, *maṃsa* or meat, *mada* or liquor, *mudrā* or hand gestures, and *maithuna* or copulation - which found a place in purāṇic Hinduism continue to be practiced even in our time. While incorporating these popular tantric customs in Purāṇa, the authors tried to add Vedic elements to these practices in an attempt to purge them of features associated with pure tantrism.

However, some Purāṇas categorically state that scriptures influenced by what we brand tantric characteristics are *shruti-smṛti-viruddha*, or incompatible with *śruti* and *smṛti*, and that they can lead people astray. Those that revere such texts, we are informed, must be expelled from the kingdom by the righteous ruler.

Summing up, it will not be wrong to say - '…the battle against the influence of Tantrism was a losing one, and Tantric elements are very noticeable in those parts of the Purāṇic corpus that date from the ninth century. New material continued to be added to the Purāṇas, and while things Vedic became increasingly rare over time, Tantric features became more pronounced.'

Description of Customs, Saṃskāra, *Pūjā*

The Purāṇas touch upon various topics concerning religious developments that occurred between ~400 and 1500 AD. Those additional topics include customs, ceremonies, sacrifices, festivals, caste duties, donations, construction of temples and images, places of pilgrimage, and many others.

Topics like *varnāśrama*-dharma, *ācāra*, *āhnika*, *bhakṣyābhakṣhya*, *vivāha*, *aśaucha*, *shrāddha*, *dravya-śuddhi*, *pātaka*, *prāyaścitta*, *naraka*, *karmavipāka* and *yuga*-dharma, are discussed in Purāṇas from beginning of the third to the fifth century AD.[18]

The appended table T-1- gives a rough account of contents and the period in which these topics came to be included in the Purāṇas (Hazra, Studies in Puranic Records on Hindu Rites and Customs, 1940).

Chapter 26

Devotion - *Bhakti*

Devotion, faith, and union with god through love is described as *bhakti*.

Bhakti implies worship, total surrender and personal love of god in any form. Forgetting everything and everyone else, the devotee yearns for a glimpse of god, and finally for total union[1].

In Monier's Sanskrit-English dictionary, *bhakti* is defined as attachment, devotion, fondness for, devotion to, trust, homage, worship, piety, faith or love or devotion (as a religious principle or means of salvation, together with *karmaṇa*, 'works,' and *jñāna*, 'spiritual knowledge'). Apart from these, the dictionary also provides several other meanings of the word. What we know from texts available to us is that word *bhakti* was first used in the Gītā, 'as a technical term to designate a religious path'; love, affection, attachment, et cetera - its earliest usages, had a narrow and more specific meaning. The Gītā distinguished *bhakti* to denote 'a method of religious experience that leads to liberation.'[2]

Bhakti transformed the way Hindus worshipped gods. It was fundamentally different from Vedic practices which required a suitable place and preparation of altar, fuel, items of sacrifice, and, most important, a *barahmaṇa* priest who conducted the *yajña* and a *yajamāna*. In *bhakti*, so long as an individual's mind was focused on god, no matter the social strata he originated from, he was engaging in the act of worship and this could eventually lead him to *mokṣa*. When lord *Kṛṣṇa* proclaimed '*sarva-dharman parity ājya mam ekam sharanam vraja, aham tvam sarva-papebhyo mokṣayishyami ma shuchah*' (Abandon all varieties of religion and just surrender unto me alone. I shall deliver you from all sinful reaction. Do not fear) in Gītā (18.66), He placed *bhakti* above all other forms of worship. This came after he had explained the knowledge of the supreme *Brahman*, the various kinds of knowledge on religious processes, the different types of orders and statuses of social life, the renounced order of life, sense and mind control, meditation etc.

It is this technical meaning of *bhakti* that almost edged out Vedic ritualism from the everyday life of a Hindu, and due to its sheer simplicity, replaced structured Vedic practices. It also prevailed over all other forms of worship in the domain of Hindu religion. All the old rules, that lay down where, how and by whom the religious worship was to be carried out, were made redundant by this new *bhakti* practice. It gave a believer the liberty to revel in his *bhakti* almost anywhere, at any time, and while the person was engaged in whatever he was doing. The god of gods, lord *Kṛṣṇa*, himself promised salvation to his *bhaktas* (followers/worshippers) overriding their gender, caste or past sins provided they surrendered to him completely.

According to Prentiss, a Professor at University of Drew, 'This technical meaning of *bhakti* became a qualitative, and the Gītā was considered one of the three foundational texts (*prasthānatraya*) for a Hindu religious commentary by the great philosophers Śaṅkara and Ramanuja, as well as later Sanskrit philosophical tradition.'

Bhandarkar, says Parentiss, endows *bhakti* with the revival of devotion that had once, but no longer, inspired *Brahmannical* sacrifice: "Cold and dead formalities took the place of warm and living devotion, and the very verses and hymns which contained the fervent prayers of the old ṛṣis, were repeated mechanically in the course of the formal worship, without even an attempt to apprehend the sense." This image of the history of *bhakti* would influence subsequent scholarship up to the present day.[3]

Much before *Kṛṣṇa* showed the Right path to his friend Arjuna in the Bhagavad Gītā, the germs of devotion had already started growing in the Vedas. The prayers and praises offered to Vedic gods were the beginning of *bhakti* tradition. Prentiss, quoting Professor Biardeau (a French Indologist, an expert in Indian philosophy and religion, teaching Indian religion at the École Pratique des Hautes Études (EPHE)) says, the Yajur Veda provides a model for the importance of action for salvation, which is a major thread in *bhakti*. The Taittirīya school of the black Yajur Veda (TS 4.5,4.7) may be most directly influential; for example it's this version of the *Śatrudrīyastotra - stotra* paying homage to lord *Rudra* or *Śiva* - that appears to have been quoted in Tamil *Śiva bhakti* poetry.[4] As we know, the Yajurveda is manual of praxis in a ritual context, and the *Śatrudrīya*, a liturgical prayer.

The Purāṇas are replete with tales glorifying gods and goddesses. They are valuable material that throw light on how *bhakti*-centric traditions took firm root in a society which, for nearly 2000 years, had followed *yajña* centric religion. Though all the Purāṇas include devotional prayers and praises, the Bhāgavata Purāṇa is invariably singled out for its detailed treatment of *bhakti*. Not just prayers, praises or glorification of an intensely personal and passionate nature, it also includes the philosophy of *bhakti*, and -

(i) A doctrine of the *avatāras* of *Viṣṇu*; and

(ii) Teachings of *vaiṣnava* theology

Avatāra, Sanskrit for 'descent', is the incarnation of a deity in human, animal, or hybrid form to counteract particular evils in the world. *Viṣṇu* is said to descend as *avatāra* to restore cosmic order. His *Dashavatāra*, or the ten incarnations, are - *Matsya*, the fish; *Kūrma*, the giant tortoise; *Varāha*, the boar; *Narasiṃha*, the half-man, half-lion; *Vamana*, the dwarf; *Parashurāma*, the warrior with the axe; Rāma, the prince and king of Ayodhya; *Balarāma*, *Kṛṣṇa's* older brother; *Kṛṣṇa*; Buddha and Kalki.

Kalki ('Eternity', 'White Horse', or 'Destroyer of Filth'), will be the final incarnation of *Viṣṇu*, foretold to appear at the end of *kali yuga*, our present epoch. He will be atop a white horse and his sword will be drawn, blazing like a comet. He is the harbinger of end times in Hindu eschatology, and will destroy unrighteousness and evil at the end of *kali yuga*.

∞

In *vaiṣnava* theology, god is transcendent and beyond human understanding. He creates the world merely because he wills to do so, and this creation and destruction is his *līlā* (sport or playfulness); he expands himself into the universe and pervades it through *māyā*, but through *bhakti* a man can unite with him. It lists nine characteristics of *bhakti* - praising god's name, listening to the sacred histories, remembering and meditating on his nature leading to union of the devotee with god, serving his image, adoring him, respectful salutation, servitude, friendship, and self-surrender. Meritorious deeds are also an element of *bhakti*.

Accordingly, it recommends that a true *vaiṣnava* must worship *Viṣṇu* or one of the *avatāras*, construct temples, bathe in holy rivers, study religious texts, serve superiors, and honor cows.

Bhāgavata-purāṇa, by far the most popular Purāṇa and a veritable handbook of *vaiṣnavism*, teaches that *bhakti* delivers *mokṣa* to one and all irrespective of caste, but retains caste division. Sin is antithetical to *bhakti* irrespective of status and cannot be expiated if one is not free from falsehood, hypocrisy, envy, aggression and pride. According to Bhāgavata, someone belonging to a low caste, but who is devoid of these, i.e. falsehood, hypocrisy, et cetera, may be treated higher than *Brahman*, yet it does not speak up against caste division!

Bhakti was a way of life which involved a ceaseless longing for god, constantly thinking of god following non-violence (*ahiṃsā*), truth (*satya*), kindness, charity, wishing good for all, helping others and maintaining cheerfulness and hope. Such ideas popularized the *bhakti* movement between the seventh and tenth centuries in the south of India (present day Tamil Nadu and Kerala), where Nayanars emerged as worshippers of *Śiva*, and Alvars of *Viṣṇu*. *Bhakts* or disciples hailed from diverse social backgrounds, ranging from *brahmaṇas* to artisans, cultivators and even from castes considered 'untouchable'. They were itinerants, moving from place to place singing hymns in Tamil praising their gods.

The Nalayira Divyaprabandham ('Four Thousand Sacred Compositions') - one of the major anthologies of compositions of the twelve Alvars - was compiled by the tenth century. This was frequently described as Tamil Veda.

Bhakti gained popularity in the region of Maharashtra around the twelfth century, and later in Gujarat, Bengal and other areas. It soon became widespread across the length and breadth of the land. Devotional poems and songs dedicated to god were composed in several languages, many of which are available today.[5] It swept over east and north India from the fifteenth century onwards, reaching its peak between the fifteenth and seventeenth century AD.

The period from the Gītā up until the thirteenth century, before Islam penetrated into the interior of the country, saw the growth of *Saguṇa* (god with attributes) *bhakti* movement through the southern saints Rāmanuja (1017-1103), Nimbārka (~1162), and Mādhva (1238-1317). All three produced valuable works of philosophy and *vaiṣnavism*. The *bhakti* movement from the thirteenth century to the seventeenth century was, quantitatively and qualitatively, quite distinct. Sūr, Tulasī , Mīrā, Caitanya, and Vallabhācarya became symbols of spiritual yearning of Hinduism which was under attack from Islam, they took the *Saguṇa* movement forward; Kabīr, Nānak, Raidas, Dādu, and others became champions of the *nirguṇa* (attribute-less god) movement.

All over India, a large number of mystics and poet-saints took to writing and social reform. Almost all of them were *sādhakas* (meditators) and wanderers in the name of god. Remarkably, most of the *nirguṇa* poet saints belonged to the lower strata, and it was among these classes they preached their form of *bhakti*. It would not be wrong to say that between Kabīr, a weaver from Benaras, Ravidās (also known as Raidās), a contemporary of Kabīr's from the same city and a cobbler by profession, and Nānak, a grain merchant from Punjāb, a trinity of the leadership of the monotheistic movement was formed. While Dhannā was a Jāt peasant from Deoli in Rajasthan, Dādu was the cotton weaver from Gujarat, Nāmdeva, a calico painter from Maharashtra, they all had one thing in common - they preached social equality and *nirguṇa bhakti*. For them god was one and was *nirākāra* or formless, with no human attributes.[6] These saints and reformers tried to purge Hinduism's evil practices, particularly those relating to rigours of caste and image worship. They started a movement which is popularly known as the *bhakti* movement.

They had, indeed, the conscious feeling that they had opened the path to god for the poor.[7]

Mīra, Tulsī, Sūr and Caitanya, on the other hand, belonged to the *saguṇa* school of *bhakti*. For them, god had human attributes and responded to love, adoration, and affection and, of course, devotion. According to them, god is like a man with supernatural qualities. The *saguṇa* school believed in the authority of the Vedas and did not abandon the traditions of the past. Caitanya was perhaps a (rare) exception; he was the only *saguṇa* saint who actively led an anti-caste movement despite his spiritual connect with *vaiṣnavism.*

The *bhakti* trend placed *mūrti* and *pūjā* at its center. Purāṇic traditions were constantly rewritten to suit the need of changing times. Today the path of *bhakti* is very popular because it has no restrictions (unlike in Vedic sacrifices) and is open to all. It generally involves singing devotional hymns, chanting the name of the god and worshipping an image or visualising a form of the deity.

Chapter 27

The gift - *Dāna*

The simplest interpretation of word '*dāna*'is gift. But Mauss' (well known French sociologist and anthropologist, d. 1950) view of gift - a total social fact which means reciprocation in material terms - is not what *dāna* is all about. Not only does *dāna* have a soteriological (doctrine of salvation) goal, it also contradicts universal norms of reciprocity: *dāna*-dharma does not require repayment in any material form. Or at least, it didn't in the early periods.

Dāna involves a donor and a recipient - an essential condition of any gift - but in its religious form the act of gifting by itself doesn't constitute *dāna* unless it satisfies certain other criteria. When, where, what is to be given, and how it is to be given, are governed by certain rules; the act itself is to be accompnied with the chanting of mantras for it to qualify as *dāna*. Minus the mantras, a gift, even without any expectation of material reciprocity, is alms or *bhikṣā*. Another important condition that a gift has to fulfill in order to be recognized as *dāna* is categorical acceptance of the gift by the receiver.

In all three - *homa*, *yaga* and *dāna* - something is given. Commentator Śabara in Jaiminīya (IV.2.28) clarifies the difference in three: 'giving up what belongs to one is common to all the three, but *yaga* means simply giving up something intending it for a deity and accompanying it with the mantra; and in *homa* there is in addition the throwing of a thing in fire; *dāna* consists in abandoning the thing that belongs to one and creating the ownership of another in that thing.'[1]

The word *dāna* first occurs in early Ṛgvedic texts. There are numerous *dānastutis* (eulogies of gifts) where the gifts made by kings are praised.[2] Cows are the most favoured gifts. Horses, camels, young damsels[3], garments, gold, chariots are other standard gifts that find mention in Vedic texts. What was usually expected in return was life in heaven, victory in battle, et cetera. At this time, land does not find a mention as an item of gift, indicating it was not considered wealth.

By the time of Brahmaṇa texts, the *brahmaṇas* had become very powerful and were often equated to gods on earth - 'Verily, there are two kinds of gods; for indeed the gods are gods; and the *Brahmanṇs* who have studied and teach sacred lore are the human gods,' and, Śatapatha continues, 'With oblations one gratifies the gods, and with gifts to the priests the human gods, the Brahmaṇas who have studied and teach sacred lore.'[4]

The magico-religious Vedic rituals which accrued supernatural benefits to the *yajamāna* also conferred social status on *rājanya*, *kṣatriyas* as well as the *brahmaṇas*. *Dāna* and *dakṣiṇā* thus became very common in this period; there was an important difference between the two - *dāna* was gift while *dakṣiṇā* was the sacrificial fee. The *brahmaṇa* gods, as they were often referred to and continue to be referred to sometimes even in present day, gradually started to receive (and accept) land in addition to cows, horses, gold, et cetera.

The notion of giving gifts was legalised with the rules and regulations in the Christian Era. Jaiminīya (500 - 200 BC) mentions *dāna* was transference of ownership - proof that *dāna* was already institutionalised in late Vedic India.

∞

Any discussion of *dāna* would be incomplete without *iṣṭapurta*, a word first used in the Ṛgveda to imply 'the humility of a spiritual result or merit due to a man's performance of sacrifice and charitable acts'.[5] Subsequently, Taittirīya (V.7.7.1–3), Atharva (II.12.4) and the Upaniṣads, all used it. *Iṣṭa* dharma is the acquisition of spiritual merits by giving gifts at the time of sacrificial rituals (*gṛhya* and *śrauta*), and what is given outside of the sacrificial altar is *purta*, e.g. dedication of wells, tanks, temples, groves, food and also gifts on occasion of eclipse, on the twelfth day of the month, et cetera.

The Vedic rites were performed for *iṣṭapurta*. The meaning of *iṣṭapurta*, in accordance with the religio-philosophic essence of Vedic thoughts, is the merit of sacred rites performed in the previous life and stored up in heaven in the world of *Yama* after death. According to Kane (ref HD, Vol II part II, p 843-44), it (*iṣṭapurta*) is an important word from the Ṛgvedic period where it appears to have been used in the sense of 'the cumulative spiritual result or merit due to a man's sacrificial rites and charitable acts'. Aprārka (1100 AD), on page 290, quotes Mahābhārata to define *iṣṭa* and *purta* as - "Whatever is offered in the single fire (i.e. *gṛhya* fires) and what is offered in the three *śrauta* fires and the gifts made inside the *vedi* (in *śrauta* sacrifices) are called *iṣṭa*; while dedication of deep wells, oblong large wells and tanks, temples, distribution of food, and maintaining public gardens - these are called *purta*." Elaborate rituals were developed in the Vedic literature for *ishtapurta*, which were centred around sacrificial rites performed to propitiate the gods in order to obtain desired goals. These sacrifices were made in *Agni* (the fire-god) regarded as the messenger of gods on earth and the carrier of oblations to them. Dedicating wells, large water tanks, temples, et cetera were considered good for the society. Both actions earned merit.

The *dāna* could be *iṣṭa* or *purta*, depending on one's means, and had to be given to a worthy person (*pātra*) willingly and happily. *Śraddhā* - not to be confused with a similar Sanskrit word '*śrāddha*', rituals for deceased relatives - means 'respectful or reverential offering'. A *dāna* without *śraddhā* led both the donor and the donee to hell - 'Both he who receives with honour and he who gives with honour go to heaven; in the opposite case to hell'.[7]

By the time of the Mahābhārata, *dāna* had become an important and integral part of religion. A major portion of *Anuśasana parva* in the Mahābhārata is devoted to *dāna*. Matsya (chapters 82–91 and 274–289), Agni (208–215 and 217) and Varāha (99–111) Purāṇas contain detailed accounts of *dāna*. The Arthaśāstra attributed to Kautilya, and other similar early texts, have also dealt with *dāna*. It became a subject of *nibandha* by the tenth century BC, and commentators like Hemādri, Govindānanda, Nīlkantha, and Bhallasena all wrote extensively on this topic indicating the significant role it came to play in purāṇic India.

It is interesting to see how purāṇic ideas and practices replaced Vedic rituals and beliefs. They offered simpler alternatives like *bhakti*, *dāna*, *tīrtha*, *vrata* to cumbersome Vedic rituals. The Vedas concept of the three *rinas* - debt to forefathers, gods and sages - which could only be repaid through *yajñas* could now, in the purāṇic scheme of things, be repaid through *dāna*, and one could now earn the same merit by *dāna* that he earned by reciting Vedas. Unlike Vedic rituals, women and *śūdras* could also participate in this act, purify themselves and earn merit (*śūdras* could only perform *purta* dharma). All sins, big and small, heinous or ordinary, could be expiated, and the sinner purged, simply by making appropriate gift to a *brahmaṇa*.

According to Matsya Purāṇa, *purta* yielded the same results which large scale Veda *yajñas* promised -donor would benefit of *agniṣṭoma yajña* by consecrating a tank during the *vṛṣhti* (rain), *śarada* (autumn); benefit of *vājapeya* and *atirātra* by consecrating a tank during *hemnta* (fall) and *śiśira* (winter); and the benefit of *aśvamedha* by constructing it in *vasanta* (spring) season; and if constructed during *grīṣma* (summer), one would get the benefit of *rājasūya*.

Besides these benefits one was promised region of *Viṣṇu* or *Śiva* in afterlife, as a bonus.

∞

The Purāṇas list six constituent elements of *dāna* - *dātā* or donor, *pratigrahita* or recipient, *śraddhā* or respectful attitude, *deya* or appropriateness of the gift, *tithi* or appropriate time, and *desha* or proper place.

Some important characteristics of *dāna* were as follows. The donee had to be a *snātaka* and a *storotiya*, i.e. one who knew the Vedas and was not a hypocrite or self-centered; *dāna* was to be given with a liberal spirit because only then did the donor receive *puṇya* (merit); acceptance of a gift in the proper place and at a proper time (with proper mantras) alone made it a religious offering; since there was the danger of loss of *tejas* (energy) associated with *dāna*, which only a worthy recipient could withstand, it was important that the chosen recipient be suitable for the gift; the benefit of *dāna* was purely religious, without any material reciprocation; and, finally, the donor was higher in the status than the recipient.

Exception: During an emergency (*āpadā*), a *brahmaṇa* could accept anything from anybody.

A word about *pratigraha* i.e. acceptance of gifts. *Dāna* was not considered complete unless the donee mentally, vocally or physically, specifically accepted what was given to him. *Dharmaśāstrās* prescribe one should accept a deer skin by touching it on the hairy side, the cow by its tail, an elephant by the trunk and the horse by its mane, a female by touching her head, and land by enjoying its produce. *Pratigraha* was not only acceptance but also involved reciprocation with *puṇya.*

The qualities of the recipient were also important. Hypocrite *brahmaṇas* and those who did not know the Vedas, those who recited over sacrifice for *śūdras*, suffered from disease, seller of Vedas, wicked, et cetera, were considered unfit to receive *dāna*.

Things which were considered *deya*, i.e. fit to be given, were divided into three categories: The first, considered superior, included food, curd, honey, protection, cow, land, gold, horse, and elephant. The next category consisted of learning, house for shelter, domestic supplies, and medicines. And the inferior category consisted of shoes, swings, carts, umbrellas, vessels, seats, lamps, wood, fruits, and other objects. However, there was no unanimity among the authors of *dharmaśāstra* as to what constituted the best gift or *atidāna*.

Law books are categorical that one should give only what he owned and that, too, within his means. What was borrowed, property jointly owned, children, son and wife, entire property et cetera, were declared unfit for *dāna*.

Dāna was often divided into *nitya*, daily; *naimittika*, given during special occasions such as an eclipse or penance; and *kāmya*, with a desire for things or persons such as crop, progeny, victory or wife. Similarly, gifts were also of three kinds. *Nitya* - given every day such as food for *vaiśvadeva*; *naimittika* - given at a specified time, for example, on eclipses or on account of certain acts like penances; and *kāmya* - given with the desire of attaining prosperity, wife, progeny and the like.

Types of *dāna*: The Bhagavad Gītā (17.20-22) divides *dāna* into *sātvika*, *rājasa* and *tamasa*. When a donor feels it his duty to gift and does so, to a proper person at a proper time and place, that is *sātvika dāna*; when it is made reluctantly, with the expectation of something in return or with an eye on reward, that is *rājasa dāna*; when the gift is given to an unworthy person, without *śraddhā* and with contempt, at an improper time or place, that is *tamasa dāna*. The proper time for gifts is laid down in the *dharmaśāstras*. Special emphasis is placed on the gift given on the first day of the *ayana*, i.e. the passage of the sun to the north or south, eclipses of the sun or moon, new moon day, twelfth day, *saṁkrānti* and other such *tithis*.

Night time was not considered appropriate for *dāna*, except during eclipses, marriage, birth of a child and *saṁkrānti*. With reference to a proper place for *dāna*, there was a mention of increase in denomination of benefit depending on the place where the gift was made.

Place: An appropriate place for *dāna* was considered, in a way, a force multiplier. Gifts, given at home, would yield ten times as much merit, in the cow-pen hundred times, at *tīrthas* a thousand times, and infinite times if made near a *Śiva-liṅgaṃ*. Holy places like Prayāg, Kuruksetra, Puskara, Banaras, and banks of rivers such as the Ganga, Yamuna, Narmada, et cetera, and forests were considered ideal. The benefit from making gifts in such places was proclaimed as infinite.

The Matsya Purāṇa discusses extensively *dāna* related rules, regulations and procedures, as do the Agni and Vāraha Purāṇas.

Dāna: Best object and best type

What constituted the best gift? The Matsya speaks of sixteen *mahādāna* (*mahā* - best, great) while the Agni Purāṇa mentions ten *mahādāna*, including gold, horses, sesame elephants, chariots, land, house, a bride, and dark brown cow; *sumeruparvatadāna* of ten hills; and cow *dāna*.

A cow was considered the best *dāna*, as it erased all sins. As *Rudrani*, a favorite of *Śiva*, and believed to be a form of goddess *Lakṣmī*, the cow was revered by *vaiṣnavas* and *śaivas* alike. Matsya describes ten forms in which *dhenu* (cow) was gifted - *guda dhenu* or made of raw sugar; *ghrita dhenu* or of clarified butter; *tila dhenu* - of sesame; *jala dhenu* - of water; *kshira dhenu* - of milk; *madhu dhenu* - of honey; *sharkarā dhenu* - of sugar; *dadhi dhenu* - of curd; *rasa dhenu* - of syrup or juice; and a living cow (MP 82.18-19).

Sumerparvatadāna (*sumer parvata* - a mythical mountain of gold), considered incomparable *dāna* by the Purāṇas, consisted of *dāna* of ten hills of grain, salt, raw sugar, gold, sesame, cotton, clarified butter, jewels, silver and sugar. According to Matsya, 'the blessings conferred by this form of charity cannot be attained otherwise, not even by reading of, or listening to, the Purāṇas, Vedas, performing sacrifices, and worshipping or erecting temples for the *devas*'.[8]

Another *dāna* which vied for the top position was *mahādāna* or great gift. Any one performing these sixteen *mahādānas* was, as reward, said to be liberated from the cycle of birth and death, purged of all sins and promised *Viṣṇu's* realm for one *kalpa* with his wife and sons (MP 289.17).

Apart from the main items of *dāna* - listed below - from which it derives its name, other paraphernalia were included as well.

(i) *Tulā-puruṣa* - weighing the person against gold or silver

(ii) *Hiraṇyagarbha* - items to be given included a cow decorated with ornaments

(iii) *Brāhmāṇda* (*Brahman's* egg) - gifts included ten cows, gold

(iv) *Kalpapadapa* - golden tree or *kalpa vraksha dāna*

(v) *Gosahsra* - included gifting ten cows decked up in ornaments, along with a bull

(vi) *Kāmadhenu* - a cow and calf made of gold

(vii) *Hiraṇyaśvā* - golden horse

(viii) *Aśvaratha* - golden chariot

(ix) *Hemahasti ratha* - a golden chariot of the shape of *puṣpaka* (mythical aircraft mentioned in Ramāyāna) studded with precious stones

(x) *Pancalangalaka* - land measuring five ploughs (MP283); the text states any marketplace, town or village should be given with ornaments

(xi) *Dharādāna* - a golden replica of the earth, i.e. *jambudvipa* along with hills, rivers, et cetera

(xii) *Viśvācakra* - golden wheel

(xiii) *Mahākalapalatā* - golden creeper

(xiv) *Saptasāgara* - seven oceans crafted in gold

(xv) *Ratnadhenu* - a cow studded with precious stones

(xvi) *Mahābhūtānighata* - golden vase/pot

Each of these *dānas* led to atonement of sins, afterlife in *Viṣṇu*, *Śiva*, *Brahman*, *Go* (cow), *Índra* or *Sūrya loka* (realm), often along with one's family and forefathers.

Stories abound in various Purāṇas how, through *dāna*, a better life was attained in the next birth. Benefits increasingly became more than just atonement for sins. What began as spiritual benefit gradually turned into unmitigated materialism.

Women and *Dāna* - For women, the *dānadharma* specifies items of gold, land, cow or other material objects are not to be gifted, instead, trees such as *āmra*, *kadamba*, *campā*, *aśoka*, *aśvattha*, et cetera are recommended as *dāna* items. The benefits she accrued are neither spiritual nor material, but physical - the breast of women were supposed to take the form of wood-apple, her thighs that of the plantain tree; she would become adorable like the *aśvattha* tree and sweet smelling like the *nīm*. She would become illustrious like the *campaka* and free from sorrow like the *aśoka* tree. She would turn sweet like the *mahua* and soft like the leaves of the banyan tree (MP 187.31-32). Women making gift (*dāna*) became *saubhagyavati* (blessed with good fortune and prosperity).

Compare this, in following passages, to what men got in return of *dāna* - *apsarās* who like "black bees drink with the aroma of his lotus face" and lady "whose face is like a moon and whose colour is like burnished gold, her breasts are bloated, waist slender, and eyes are like lotuses." (MP 283)

Women were required to observe a proper fast before they gave *dāna*.

Type of gift

The type of gift given also had a bearing on the benefits that would accrue - deer skin decorated with gold, silver, pearls, and other jewels when given to an *agnihotṛ brahmaṇa* expatiated the sin of speaking falsely about a cow and a virgin (Matsya 206.1–31). Benefits bestowed included the ability to fly like a bird, father and son not perishing, never being separated from one's wife, never losing wealth and having all wishes fulfilled.

Benefits

Apart from an afterlife in different *lokas* and expiation of all sins, benefits typically included adoration by *apsarās* for many *kalpas*, rebirth as an emperor and conquest of 1000 things (MP 274.19); liberation of self and of the paternal relations from hell (275); *brahmaṇa dāna* resulted in liberation of maternal and paternal family (a few instances of maternal family liberation); *kalpapadamahādāna* liberated the donor's present family and future generations, and he accrued the benefit of *aśvamedha yajña* (MP 277); a sojourn in *Śiva Loka*, where the donor performed 100 *aśvamedha*, and liberation from bondage (MP 278) by the *gośaharsa mahādāna*; in *aśvaratha* (MP 281) the donor was not only liberated from all sins, he attained the realm of *Śiva*, where nymphs like "black bees drink with eyes the aroma of his Lotus face"; not just father and grandfather, even friends are promised the realm of *Śiva* in *panca langlaka* (MP 283); liberation of self and family for twenty-one generations as a benefit of *dharadāna* (MP 284); an assurance of attaining eternal form with four hands, among *apsarās*, for 300 *kalpas* in the realm of *Viṣṇu* in *viṣvacakra*, (MP 285) apart from prosperity, wealth and long life, destruction of enemies and freedom from the cycle of rebirth; liberation of 400 generations, and adoration by *apsarās* (MP 286) from the *mahākalpalatā*.

Thus, the benefits of *mahādāna* are cosmic as well as material, accruing wealth, longevity, beauty, et cetera.

The calving cow, when gifted, was to be decorated with gold, silver and pearls to bring the donor the same benefit as gifting land along with four oceans. It liberated his father, grandfather and great-grandfather from hell, from where they would proceed to *goloka* and *brahmāloka*. The surprising bonus included a lady "whose face is like a moon and whose color is like burnished gold, her breasts are bloated, waist slender, and eyes are like lotuses".[9]

Chapter 28

Pilgrimage - *Tīrtha*

Tīrtha is a Sanskrit term denoting a sacred place visited for religious reasons.

Both *tīrtha* and *tīrthayātra* (journey to *tīrtha* or pilgrimage) are described extensively in ancient Hindu texts. These are sites along rivers, lakes and pools, hills, mountains and shrines, and most importantly, temples across India which are considered holy. They derive their importance from legends - ṛṣis and other saints who visited these holy places, or mythological stories glorifying the benefits of pilgrimage. Subsequent purāṇic scriptures sanctified these locations as *tīrtha*.

The Skāṇḍa Purāṇa describes *tīrtha* in I.2.13.10 succinctly - 'a spot of the earth resorted to by ancient good men for the collection of merit is called *tīrtha*, and that the main thing is to go to (i.e. associate with holy) men, and pilgrimage is only a secondary object'.[1]

Though the Ṛgveda does not speak of *tīrtha* specifically in the sense that we understand it now, it does describe the great rivers Saraswatī, Saryū and Sindhu as divine and as mothers (I.3 2.12, 34.8, 35.8, I I.1 2.12, VI I I.2 4.27). The river Sarasvatī was particularly important to Āryans - they called it the best of rivers and goddesses (I I.4 1.16) - the Ṛg has three hymns devoted to it as a deity (VI.61, VI I.95 and 96). Such veneration for rivers, undoubtedly, was the reason river banks, their confluences, and their origins later became *tīrthas*.

Ṛg uses *tīrtha* to mostly mean a road or a way (I.16 9.6, 173.11 IV.2 9.3, et cetera), or a ford or a river (V I I.4 7.11, I.4 6.8). And up to Yaska's Nirukta, i.e. 500-250 BC, this position remains constant. There is no etymological explanation listing pilgrimage as synonym of travel (*yātra*), indicating *tīrtha* and *tīrthayātra* were not part of social or religious praxis till at least Yaska's time.

There is mention of *tīrtha* in *śrauta* and *dharmasūtra* literature. Gautama 19.14, Baudhāyana 3.1 0.12 and Vaṣiṣṭa Dharma Sūtra 22.12, all have references to bathing places (*tīrthas*) as places for expiation of sin. Though *tīrtha* here does not seem to refer to some particular pilgrimage spot, it eventually took on that meaning.[2] The ancient *smṛtis* do not confer any such importance on *tīrthas*. As we know them today, *tīrtha* and *tīrthayātra* were first used in Mahābhārata's later chapters - *Tīrthayātraparavan* of *Āraṇyakaparvan*[3], chapters in *Shalyaparvan*[4] and *Anushashanaparvan*[5]. But it is the Purāṇas that serve as our basic source of *tīrtha* material; they describe innumerable places of pilgrimage, their geographical location and legends (*mahātmya*) associated with the particular center. Apart from the Upapurāṇas (minor Purāṇas) which are eighteen in number, there are *Sthala* (literally 'place') Purāṇas that are attached to a particular temple or a place and narrate tales of the significance of that particular *tīrtha*. The central premise of *tīrtha* discussion in Purāṇa is making available to everyone a practicable solution to wash off all their sins.

Hindu Dharma is not alone in extolling the benefits of pilgrimage. The Quran enjoins every able-bodied Muslim to perform the Haj - a journey to the holy Kaaba in Mecca - at least once in a lifetime. Christians consider visits to Jerusalem as having great religious significance. Buddhists, from all over, visit Gaya in Bihar for a glimpse of the Bodhi tree under which Gautama attained enlightenment- as sacred, and Sārnatha, where Buddha first spun the wheel of Dharma. Jews consider their individual religious evolution incomplete without a visit to the Wailing Wall and Sikhs from all over the world come to take a holy dip in the *sarovar* (pond) and seek blessings in the Golden Temple in Amritsar. Every religion propagates that a visit to the holy place purifies its adherents, absolves them of sin and accrues benefits which otherwise come only with great effort.

In the twelfth century AD, Lakṣmīdhara Bhatta, a political essayist and a minister in the court of the king of Kanyakubja, compiled a systematic description of *tīrthas* and essentials of the *naksatra* in his monumental work Krityakalpataru. Often quoting the Brahmāpurāṇa, Lakṣmīdhara classifies *tīrthas* into four types: *Daiva* - of the gods; *Asura* - founded by *asuras*; *Arśa* - of the ṛṣis; and *Manuṣya* - founded by great beings or other people. Krityakalpataru lists Badrikāśrama, Dvarka, Kedara, Kubjamraka (Haridwar), Kuru kshatra, Madhura (Mathura), Narmada, Prayag, Pushkara, Sukura (Soron on Ganga) and Kashi (Varanasi) as important *tīrthas*. As is the wont of Hindu Dharma, *tīrthas*, like mountains and rivers, were personified - the Padamāpurāṇa contains an instance of *Índra* summoning them to his court.

The long list of *tīrtha* from early Purāṇa days, systematised by Lakṣmīdhara, grew over time. New saints and new sects brought with them new locations that were sacralised as *tīrthas*. *Śaktism* added the *śakti pīṭhas* (literally seat). According to mythology, *śakti pīṭhas* are locations where 108 different parts of *Sati* fell on earth after *Viṣṇu* used the *sudarśana cakra* (disc weapon) on her corpse.

Later, during medieval times, even Sufi shrines were included in the list of *tīrtha*. Visits to *tīrthas* initially included *vratas* and *pūjā* rituals, but with the passage of time, these have come to be replaced by reverence and devotion.

∞

As discussed earlier, *tīrtha* became an essential feature of Purāṇic Hinduism which had evolved as an alternative to the ancient sacrifice-based Vedic system. It is therefore not surprising that in the Mahābhārata and the Purāṇas, *tīrtha* is considered more valuable than sacrifice. Vanaparva (82.13-17) pointedly observes that sacrifices (Vedic rituals) required numerous implements, collection of materials, co-operation of priests, presence of a wife and, hence, could be performed only by rich people with the requisite financial resources. A man without wealth, without a wife or other resources simply could not perform those sacrifices. But by visiting holy places (*tīrtha*), a man can seek and receive rewards that cannot otherwise be secured even by performing *agniṣṭoma yajña*. Of course, the full reward of pilgrimage was contingent on, the Purāṇas add, the individual cultivating high moral and spiritual qualities.

Control of the mind and limbs, possession of knowledge, austerities and good reputation were extolled; one was asked to be free of hypocrisy or deceit, to not eat heavily, to control rage, and to always speak the truth in order to derive the full benefit of pilgrimage[6]. In a similar vein, the Skāṇḍa Purāṇa clarifies that *snāna* (bath) does not mean simply washing the body with water, one who has controlled his senses and is pure and relieved of all taint is the true *snata* (as having had a bath). The Vāyu Purāṇa (77.125) clearly states that a wise and steadfast man with faith, in control of his senses, would be purified of sin by visiting *tīrthas*. Brahman Purāṇa (25.4-6) concurs - a wicked heart is not purified by baths at holy places.

Many Purāṇas give detailed procedures of a *tīrthayātra*. *Pūjā* is an integral part of any pilgrimage, be it a temple in Mathura or Kashi or one of the four *dhamas* in the four corners of the country; to the rivers Ganga, Yamuna, Narmada or Godavari, or the lakes Pushkara and Mansarovar. When a Hindu pilgrim visits any of the holy places, he always offers *pūjā*, with or without the help of a priest. In modern times, this is done independent of what is laid out in the Purāṇas and other relevant texts. These visits, which are to be accompanied by vows (*vrata*) and rituals, are gradually ceding space to devotion and reverence accompanied by a holy dip in the river or the lake.

Not Geography, history or nationalism, nor even the Bollywood - the *tīrtha* is the biggest unifying factor in India. Rameswaram and Kanyakumari at the southern end, Badrinath and Kedarnath nestled in the Himalayas up north, the Kāmakhya śakti pīṭha at the eastern tip in Assam, Pushkara and Dwarka in the extreme west - all these are considered holy by Hindus. This results in a massive cross-country pilgrimage by members of all sections of Hindu society.

The idea of *chāra dhāma* (four abodes) has become synonymous with the idea of pilgrimage in Hinduism. Hindus believe that pilgrimage to these four holiest of holy places purges them of all sins and ensures *mokṣa*. Interestingly, either by design or by chance, these temples are located in the Eastern (Puri), Western (Dwarka), Northern (Badrinath), and Southern (Rameswaram) corners of India. Hindus from different parts of the country travelling across various states discover a common thread of Hinduism running through diverse peoples across vast distances, speaking different languages, dressing differently. They discover the common religious belief that they share, the common gods that they worship, and common methods of worship they employ when seeking the divine. This engenders a kinship, a sense of belonging, and, perhaps stronger than any other, a sense that they are all united as a nation.

The great *Advaita* philosopher Śhankarāchārya, travelling literally the length and the breadth of India in 788-820 AD, established four *mathas* (religious orders) -

- The *Dakshiānmnāya Śri Śarada Pīṭham* (main *matha*) at Ṣringeri Śaradā Pīṭham in Ṣringeri, Karnataka in the south
- The *Uttarāmnāya matha* (northern *matha*) at Jyotir *matha* in the city of Jyotirmath or Joshimath, Uttarakhand, in the north
- The *Pūrvāmnāya matha* (eastern *matha*), or the Govardhana *matha* at Puri, Odisha in the east, and
- The *Paśchimāmnāya matha* (western *matha*), or the Dwaraka Pītha at Dwarka, Gujarat, to the west

A great scholar philosopher, who lived just thirty two years, covered a distance of 7125 kilometre (based on google road map) on foot to establish these *mathas* with the idea of propagating *Advaita* philosophy, and to promulgate *Sanātana Dharma* in India. Whether he believed in concept of the *chāra dhāma* or not, cannot be ascertained, but what can be said with confidence is that Shankarāchārya was driven by the idea of integrating the vast and diverse Hindu population using the adhesive of *tīrthas*.

Kumbha melā

Kumbha melā ('*kumbha*' means pot and '*melā*' is fair) too merits a brief mention here.

This religious festival is celebrated four times over every twelve years on the bank of the rivers - Ganges at Haridwar, Shipra at Ujjain, Godavari at Nashik as well as the confluence of Ganga, Yamuna and the mythical Saraswatī at Prayag or Allahabad. Celebration is based on the conjunction of the sun, the moon and the planet Jupiter.

But it is the *kumbha melā* that occurs once every twelve years, that is considered most sacred by all Hindus. Several million devotees take a holy dip in the freezing waters of river, starting before sunrise until late in the day. An even greater occasion, the *mahā kumbha*, arises once every 144 years following a rare conjunction of heavenly bodies. The last *mahā kumbha*, which was in 2001, saw sixty million devotees bathe in the river at Prayag!

The veteran journalist Mark Tully, whose name is synonymous with the BBC in India, wrote of his experience thus - "I had never been in such a peaceful crowd. There was no frenzy, just the calm certainty of faith; the knowledge that what had to be done had been done."

Faith is the key to the *kumbha melā*. It is a spectacle, a great demonstration of the variety and vigour of Hinduism, an occasion to preach politics and conduct business, but there would be no *kumbha melā* were it not for the faith that draws millions of pilgrims to the Sangam in Allahabad.[7]

Chapter 29

Pious observances - *Vrata*

Vratas are vows, regimens and austerities of many kinds. The present discussion is about religious vows. Non-religious or secular vows, though a part of Vedas and purāṇic lore, were more in the nature of *pratijñā* (vow), either to carry out an act (in the Mahābhārata, Arjun's resolve to kill Jayadratha before sundown) or not to carry out an act (Bhīṣma's *pratijñā* to remain a celibate for life).

In today's Hindu society, *vratas* have come to mean innumerable religious vows and austerities, especially by women. Since *vratas* invariably involve *upavāsa* (fasting) on religiously important *tithis* (dates in Hindu calendar), the two words are used interchangeably and have come to mean the same thing.

But the line was not always as blurred. In early Vedic literature, *vrata* had many meanings. It was only during the days of the Brahmaṇas that *vrata*, "had come to have two secondary meanings of 'religious observance or obligation'; viz. 'a proper course or pattern of conduct for a person' and 'an *upavāsa*' i.e. the sacrificer's stay at night near *gṛhyapatya* fire or fasting."[1]

The term *upavāsa* had a very different connotation in those days - it was not fasting as we understand it now. Manu has used *vrata* at many places in his *smṛti* to mean *prāyaścitta* as they (*prāyaścittas*) involved observance of several strict rules (X I.117, 170, 176, et cetera.); Yajñavalakya Smṛti (I I I.251, 252, et cetera) and many other *smṛtis* also use *vrata* in much the same sense, signifying that the meaning of *vrata* in *smṛti* period was not fasting.

Subsequently, in the Mahābhārata, it came to mean a primarily religious undertaking, or vow, in which one has to observe certain restrictions regarding food, or general behavior, vide *Vanaparva* (296.3) and *Anusāshanaparva* (103.34). The great epic also contains instances of *vrata's* nonreligious or secular use as discussed in the foregoing paragraphs.

Vrata can also be understood as mental activity. For instance - a resolve by Bhīṣma (in Mahābhārata), to remain a bachelor right through his life. Or more recently, in our times, *vratas* have come to mean restrictive rules, a resolve by people to abstain from an activity, e.g. to not eat a particular food item for rest of their lives, or a student's resolve not to watch a movie till he qualifies in a competitive examination et cetera. Acknowledging this restraint as *tapās* (power generated by ascetic practice), Agnipurāṇa observes, 'restraint of senses and other rules are but special incidents of *vrata*; *vrata* is called *tapās* because it causes hardship to the performer and it is also called *niyama* since therein one has to restrain the several organs of sense', and remarks, 'a restrictive rule declared by the *Śāstra* is called *Vrata*' (175.2.3).

According to Kane - 'It's (*vrata's*) principal meaning from at least the first centuries of the Christian Era onwards has been that of a religious undertaking or vow, observed on a certain tithi, week day, month or other period, for securing some desired object by the worship of a deity, usually accompanied by restrictions as to food and behavior'.[2] This is what *vrata* means for Hindus all over the world today. One should remember that Hindus are not alone when it comes to religious fasts - the Passover in Judaism, Lent in Christianity, Ramzan or Ramadan in Islam, and Paryushan in Jainism form the core of religious practices in these leading religions of the world.

We cannot determine with any certainty if popular customs - with necessary modifications - were adopted and came to be known as *vratas*, or these *vratas* emerged from Purāṇic traditions. But it is clear that *vratas* are creature of the Purāṇas. The Brahmaṇa authors assiduously promoted vows, visits to holy places, gifts and the *bhakti* form of worship as a substitute for Vedic practices. 'Feasting and fasting: the *vrata* tradition and its significance for Hindu women' was Mary McGee's Ph. D. dissertation submitted to Harvard University in 1987. In her remarkable work she describes[3] the difference between Vedas and purāṇic *vrata* as a shift from impersonal to personal acts, and from mandatory to optional observances (1987:33). The idea of vows made voluntarily to a deity leading to spiritual and material rewards gained popular acceptance - an ordinary man found it an easy alternative to the assiduousness of Vedic rituals. *Vratas*, along with *dāna*, *tīrtha*, *pūjā*, et cetera, offered a 'package deal' to all members of society, including women and *śūdras*, which was difficult to reject. Even foreigners - Yavanas, Shakas, Turks, Andhras, et cetera - were promised the same reward as a Hindu, if they observed *vrata*[4], indicating that even these non-Hindu foreigners were susceptible to the lure of this easy route to expiation of sins and obtaining objects of desire. The Purāṇas made it look as if *vratas* had been a part of Hindu Dharma forever. In the words of Davis, "The Dharma tradition just took everything from the Purāṇas and presented their long praises and descriptions of *vratas* as though they had been Dharma all along."[5]

According to Davis, "Beginning with Lakṣmīdhara in the twelfth century, the *dharmaśāstra* authors simply decided that the Purāṇas are authoritative sources for rules regarding vows, pilgrimage, the consecration of image, and the *pūjā* (footnote 2)." In other words, the Dharma authors accepted temple Hinduism in a way that they had not done previously.[6]

Women and *vrata*

Though the commentator Hemādri (late thirteenth century) describes only thirty-five vows for women and 175 for men and women[7], these days it is Hindu women who drive *vrata* practices. The domestic *pūjā* is another area where they are more active than the men folk. This is a significant departure from earlier times. In Viṣṇu Dharma Sūtra (25. 15 -16), it is said that *yajña* or *homa* when performed by a woman by herself (alone) does not lead her to *svarga*, i.e does not beget her any benefit, and warns 'if a wife performs a vow of fasting while her husband is alive, she robs her husband of his life and also goes to hell.' Mediaeval authors agree that this passage and other similar passages mean that women must ask for permission from their fathers, husbands or sons before undertaking a vow.[8]

Vratas in our time have become key practices, and in today's Hindu household it is women who dominate the world of *vrata*.

Dos, Don'ts, and Food

On the morning of the commencement of *vrata*, one should use *pancāgavya* in place of tooth stick (for brushing teeth) and avoid use of collyrium. *Pancāgavya* is a concoction of five products from a cow-three direct constituents are cow dung, urine, and milk; the two derived products are curd and *ghī*.

One who is fasting should reject bell-metal, flesh, *masura* (lentil), chickpea, *koraduśaka* (a species of grain), vegetable, wine, food from others, (association with) a woman, flowers, ornaments and dress, incense, perfume and unguent.[9]

Anyone who wants to undertake *vrata* should bathe daily, eat moderately, and worship preceptors, gods and *brahmaṇas*. There are ten general virtues that are prescribed to be followed during *vratas*: forebearance, truth, compassion, charity, cleanliness, control of the senses, worship of gods, making oblations to fire, happiness and not stealing.[10] Many believe that daily *snāna*, moderate eating and worshipping preceptors are preconditions that should be met by the person proposing to undertake the *vrata*.[11]

During all *vratas*, persons undertaking it should sleep on the floor, perform *homa, japa* and *pūjā* of the image of the deity from whom one is seeking favour.[12] And at the conclusion, *brahmaṇas* should be worshiped, *dāna* given, and the preceptors fed.[13]

Nāradiya Purāṇa (Pūrvārdha 110.48) discussing food and sexual relations during *vrata* remarks, "*Bramhachārya* is prescribed for being observed in all *vratas* and it is declared that generally sacrificial food is eaten."[14] The sacrificial food or *havishyāna*, according to Manu, is 'food eaten by hermits, milk, *soma*, and dressed meat, and natural salt' (MS 3.257). According to Kane, "Though flesh was offered in *śrāddhas* in the times of the several early *smṛtis* such as that of *Yaj*, flesh must be excluded from the list of proper foods in the case of *vratas* owing to the express provisions contained in Devala Smṛti and others."[15]

Samāyapradipa by Harihara (~1510 AD) is an important Sanskrit text of the early sixteenth century, it deals with appropriate astral conjunctions and times for performance of rites and ceremonies. The Kṛtyaratnākara, **(कृत्यरत्नाकर)**, a Sanskrit text by commentator Caṇḍeśvara, quoting Samāyāpradipa text prescribes what food should be partaken in *vratas* - "First come *yavas* (barley), on failure of them *vrihi* (rice), on failure of this, other food except *masa* (black beans), *kodrava*, gram, *masura* (a kind of pulse), *china* and *kapittha*."

On items that should not be eaten, unsurprisingly, there is no unanimity. Agni Purāṇa says *kṣarā* (alkali), *lavana* (salt), honey and flesh should be eschewed in *vrata* (175.12), then includes among *kṣarā* all cereals in pods excepts sesame and *mudga*, later saying *kusumanda* (pumpkin), *alabu* (bottle gourd), and *vartaka* (eggplant) should be avoided. In different texts bell metal vessels, flesh, *masura*, gram, *kodarva*, vegetables, honey and the food cooked in another's house (Bhujabala and Garuda); conversation with women, *śūdras* and *patitas* (sinful, fallen) (*Śhāntiparva*); conversing with one guilty of heavy sins, heterodox sectarians, atheists and speaking what is untrue and obscene (*Harita*) are forbidden during *vrata*.[16]

A *vrata* undertaken must be completed. Dire consequences are laid down for him who gives it up through tediousness. During *aśauca*, i.e. impurity on birth and death, *vrata* is not to be undertaken.

Drinking water, partaking of roots, fruits and milk and sacrificial offering, the desire or command of a *brahmaṇa*, the order of one's guru and medicine do not affect a *vrata*.[17]

Hemādri permits drinking of milk - and the rest that follows - if the performer is a woman, a child or one who is in extreme pain.

A person undertaking *vrata* should refrain from anointing the body or head with oil, chewing *tāmbūla*, applying sandal paste or anything else that increases physical strength or passion.[18]

∞

In Śhāntiparva (65.13–25), *Índra* is made to say to king Mandhata that even Yavanas, Kirata, Gandharas, Chinas, Sakas, Andhras were permitted to give gifts to *brahmaṇas*. Bhaviṣya in Brahman Parva (16.61–62) states that Haiyayas, Turks, Yavanas and Sakas desiring to reach the status of *brahmaṇas* observed fasts on the first *tithi* (*pratipad*).[19]

Brahmaṇa and *kṣatriyas*, according to Mahābhārata Puruṣa Sambhava (106.12), should not engage in a continuous fast exceeding three days, and *vaiśyas* and *śūdras* can observe a continuous fast no more than two days.[20]

The bulk of *vratas* practiced in medieval and modern times are *kāmya*, performed to secure some object in this world, sometimes in the next world, or both.

There are many ways to classify *vratas*. Eating just once in a day is *ekāsani* (literally taking seat once); eating once a day after sunset is *nakta*; fasting the whole day, fasting without eating and drinking - not even water is *nirjala*; subsisting on food one gets without asking for it is physical *vrata*. *Vratas* of speech include speaking truth, not speaking ill of anyone, recitation of gods names, stories etc. Another type of *vratas* are those that are observed on particular days (*tithis*), occasions (like solar and lunar eclipse), et cetera.

Some *vratas*, like *Haritalika* and *Vata-Savitṛi*, are meant for women alone. Some are to be performed by men alone, and some other *vratas* can be performed only by kings or *kṣatriyas* or by *vaiśyas*.

According to Kane's calculation, the Purāṇas contain, at the minimum, around 25,000 verses on this topic alone.[21]

Number of *vratas*

It appears that the number of *vratas* in the first centuries of the Christian era was not very large. One of the earliest digests on *tithis* and astrological matters in relation to *dharmaśāstra* is the Rajamartanda of *Raja Bhoja* (first half of eleventh century AD) which mentions only about twenty-four *vratas*. The next important extant work where the number of *vratas* is specified is Lakṣmī Dhara's Kratyakalpataru (first half of twelfth century AD), where he mentions 175 *vratas*; Sulapāni (1375–1430 AD) in his Vratakālaviveka mentions only eleven *vratas* and Hemādri gives 700 *vratas*. This was the time foreign invaders were ruthlessly razing temples and converting the local population.

The number increased by leaps and bounds thereafter, reaching around 1000. [The Vratakosha edited by MM Gopinath Kaviraja (in the Sarasvatibhavana Series in 1922) lists 1622 *vratas*.[22]]

Chapter 30

Arrival of *mūrti*, and many gods

The Ṛgveda does not specifically describe Vedic gods as having human form, nor does it mention image or idol worship. However, the early Ṛgveda does contain instances where ṛṣi poets allude to human attributes in the gods. RV (X.96.8) says *Índra* has dark green hair (*hari*) and a beard; RV X. 96.8 suggests that the hair on his chin is dark green; X. 105.7 claims *Índra's* chin is never injured; and RV VIII.17.8 suggests he has a powerful neck ('*tuvigrīva*') and belly ('*vapodara*'). Similarly, RV II.33.5 portrays *Rudra* with a soft abdomen that is brown (*babhru*) and a fine chin or nose (*suśipra*). Vaj S 16.7 speaks of *Rudra* having a dark blue throat and a red complexion. It also ascribes another human attribute - *kṛtti* or skin.

Further, the gods had homes or abodes during the times of the Ṛgveda (RV. III.53.6). In one instance, *Índra* is asked to return to his charming wife and delightful house after he has consumed *soma*. It is possible the ṛṣi poets used human attributes to depict *devās* in the hymns because the *devās* were once normal human beings themselves, with beautiful features, spouses and homes. It was only after a series of successful *yajñas* that they attained immortality and the status of *devās*.

One probable instance of worship of *Índra's* idol occurs in Ṛgveda (II.1.50) which says - "Oh *Índra*! I shall not give thee for even a great price, not even for 100, 1000 or an *ayuta* (ten thousand)." We could surmise here that the poet is referring to a *mūrti*, or an idol, of *Índra*. In Taittirīya too, the *hotṛ* priests are exhorted to worship the three devis - *Bhārti*, *Ida*, and *Sarasvatī*..."that are golden, that are endowed with beauty that are great ones" (Tai B. II.6.17), giving an impression that the golden images depict goddesses[1]. That said, we find almost no overt references to *mūrtis*.

Índra, *Varuṇa*, *Mitra* and other Vedic gods, were originally human beings, who achieved the status of *devtā*, and the right to live in *svarga loka*, by way of successful *yajñas*. These *devtās* were wary of mortals challenging their divinity through successful completion of the very same *yajñas*. For instance, any mortal could challenge *Índra's* right to his throne if he completed 100 successful *aśvamedha yajñas*. Not surprising then that *Índra* kept a close watch on mortals who harboured such ambitions, and wasted little time disrupting any imminent threats. Many stories in the Purāṇas (composed much later than the Vedas) tell us how the king of all *devtās* was not averse to employing chicanery towards this end.

Devtās were accorded lesser importance in *yajña*-centric early Ṛgvedic society; *kāmya phala* was believed to be delivered not by *devtās* but by the sacrifice. *Devtās* played only a more benign, secondary role in this scheme of things.

Jaimini (V I I I.1.32 - 34), as discussed earlier, observes that in a sacrifice, *havis* (offering) is the principal matter while the *devatā* is the subordinate (*guṇa*). In case of conflict between the two, the conclusion is to be arrived at by relying on *havis*. It is the Vedas that connect the deity with the sacrificial act.

Until this period, the Ṛgveda makes no clear mention of any supreme being: *Yajña* was all-powerful, and the *devatās* decidedly played a secondary role.

Then, in the *Nasadiya sūkta* and elsewhere (*Puruṣa sūkta*), we begin to see the outlines of what would eventually become *Brahman*.

It is therefore safe to conclude that in Ṛgvedic times, gods were worshipped in abstract (as described in the Brahmaṇas) - as the divine forces behind natural phenomena or cosmic processes. These gods received offerings like butter, boiled rice, grains, animals or *soma* sacrifices in the holy fire. Sages had little to do with idol worship, save for occasionally ascribing human traits to such deities.

Many scholars are of the view that *Śiva* predates the Vedas in the form of *Rudra* and that his idol was worshipped in the Indus Valley civilization. Most Hindus, who have received formal education, too argue along similar lines. Their assertions draw, in the main, from the discovery of an ithyphallic figurine in Mohenjo-daro. This steatite seal (~ 2000 BC) depicts a seated human form with an erect phallus and a mass of knotted hair on his head. He is surrounded by a variety of animals and bears a striking resemblance to *Śiva* - the *Paśupati*, protector of animals. This figurine is undoubtedly useful material evidence that supports the pre-Vedic antiquity of *Rudra* (in *mūrti* form), an argument that cannot be ignored despite declarations by some scholars that the seal is merely a human figure with the head of a bull.

Noting that "phallic emblems (representing *Śiva*) were found in ruins of Mohenjo-daro," Kane observes that "apart from these, (the) earliest known *Lingas* discovered at the time of writing the book (1936) did not go beyond the first century BC." He adds, "But the worship of images had become widespread in India many centuries before Christ."[2]

[A large *Śiva linga* found in Gudimallam in south-eastern India, dated to the second or first century BC, indicates *linga* worship (atleast) from this period.[3]]

If we go with Kane's assertions that image worship in Hinduism had begun much before the Christian Era, we must bear in mind that no idols or phallic emblems representing *Śiva* have been found between the period of Mohenjo-daro *Paśupati* and the second or first century BC. This discontinuity needs to be convincingly explained by scholars who assert that idol worship of *Śiva* was prevalent since the Mohenjo-daro period.

Kane makes another interesting point[4]. Even in Ṛgvedic times, not everyone followed Vedic practices, possibly due to different genetic stock (in this author's opinion, there could have been other reasons at play, some purely social). He cites RV (VII.21.5) where sage Vasiṣṭha prays to *Índra*: "May *Śiśna devās* not overwhelm our *rta*", and "May he striking the *Śiśna devās* overcome them by his form or power." (X.99.3) While some scholars believe phallus worshippers were non-Āryans who followed non-Vedic practices, others contend that the term 'phallic worshipper' is used metaphorically for those immersed in sexual gratification. Yaska, in Nirukta (IV.19),quoting RV (VI I.21.5) explains that the word means "those who do not serve rules of *brahmacāri* or celibacy."

There is evidence within the Ṛgveda that people who followed non-Vedic practices were not uncommon. RV. VII.104.24 says *Índra* was called upon to kill male and female *Yātudhāna*s (evil spirits or sorcerers), and adds, "May the *muradevā* perish bereft of their necks and may they not see the sun rising up from the horizon." Yaska explains *mura* as *mūdha* or stupid[5]. If Ṛgvedic poets knew of people who indulged in witchcraft and considered them *muradevās*, or stupid people who were enemies of the Āryans, then these people could also have been following non-Vedic practices of worshipping *Śiśna devās*. Such a possibility cannot be ruled out.

But when we come to the late and post Vedic period, we can say with some certainty that idol worship had become an accepted practice in the Āryan society; we find many *sūtras* that deal with idol worship. Mānava gṛhya sūtra (circa 300 BC) clearly prescribes that if an image of wood, stone or metal burns down, is reduced to powder, falls or breaks into pieces, laughs or moves to another place, the householder must offer ten oblations to the fire with certain Vedic verses (Mānava GS. I I. 15. 6). Āpastamba (7 patala, 20 section, 1-3), in his *gṛhyasūtras*, recommends offerings to the images of three gods - the *Īśana*, *Midhushi*, and *Jayanta*[6]. Āpastamba makes it abundantly clear that stretching feet out "towards a fire, water, a *brahmaṇa*, a cow, the gods, a door, or against the wind" is a big 'No'.[7]

This appears to substantiate Kane's contention regarding image worship in ancient India. Image worship was, evidently, quite prevalent in the *gṛhya sūtra* period between 800-500 BC.

It is also certain that in the time of Gautama, temples referred to as *daivakula* by Sankhāyana (Gṛhya Sūtra. IV.12.15 and II.6.6) were common, for he forbids answering calls of nature in front of these images, or stretching feet in their direction (I X. 66). Pāṇini, universally accepted as belonging to a period no later than 300 BC, teaches that-

An image which is not for sale (like a *mūrti* in a temple), and is being worshipped by a devotee (*pūjārī*) who earns his livelihood attending on the image as (if it were) *Śiva* or *Skāṇḍa* (himself), has the same name as the god whose image it is. Meaning, if a *pūjārī* worships an idol as *Śiva*, the *mūrti* becomes an idol of god *Śiva* (and should not be treated as 'a figure' made of stone, clay or metal).

This indicates popular acceptance of both *mūrti* and *pūjārī* in that society, and the construction of temples for public worship, as common practice.

He goes on to add that a *vāsudevaka* is one who is a votary of *vāsudeva*; that *vāsudeva* was not a mere *kṣatriya*, but that the word was the name of god.

Commenting on the practice of Mauryas, who crafted images of gods, Patañjali (~100 BC-300 AD) says such a rule would not apply to these images, but only to the images of gods used for *pūjā* (worship).

By this time, *mūrti pūjā* was no longer confined to 'a (select) few' who practiced this form of worship in their homes, akin to the *gṛhya* ceremonies. It had gained a significant following in society - temples had become public places of worship and collective *pūjā* ceremonies, much like the public *śrauta* ceremonies. Interestingly, this period coincides with the emergence of the Mauryan Empire (~300 BC), the golden period of Hindu civilisation. Kautilya's recommendation in the Arthaśāstra for the construction of temples dedicated to *Śiva*, the *Aśvins*, *Vaiśravaṇa*, *Lakṣmī* and *Mādirā*, in the centre of the capital is indicative of how *mūrti pūjā* and temples had firmly become a part of Hindu society.

By Manu's time (~200 BC-200 AD), *mūrti pūjā* was fully institutionalized. The *brahmacāriṇs* were being regularly directed to worship images of deities. (MS I I. 176) They were to "circumambulate to the right, clockwise" the holy images they met on their journey. (IV. 39) They could not step intentionally "on the shadow of the (images of) deities, nor of a guru, king, Veda graduate, teacher, tawny (creature), or anyone consecrated for *Soma* sacrifice." (IV. 130) This placed the images on par with the guru and the king. Soon, *mūrti pūjā* found official recognition among the bureaucracy - the swearing-in of witnesses was done in the presence of images of gods and *brahmaṇas*. (MS.VI I I. 87)

This was the period when idol worship was subsumed into Hinduism and temples achieved formal status as places of public worship that were to be shown due respect and deference uniformly by all members of society.

Manu's code, which many refer to as the bible of Hindu practices, includes directives relating to temples and idol; it accorded a permanent place for idol worship in Hindu religion.

An interesting point about the pujāris in the temples needs readers' attention: *Devalaka brahmaṇas* were the individuals who sustained themselves by attending on images or *mūrtis*; either for a salary or by appropriating part of what was offered to the images. These *brahmaṇas* were, significantly, degraded in Manu's code (III.152), put at par with "doctors, people who sell meat, and people who support themselves by trade," and accorded inferior status in society. They were not to be invited for śrāddha or offerings to gods, implying that *mūrti pūjā* had perhaps found only grudging acceptance and was considered an inferior act (as compared to Vedic rites) not fully embraced by *Brahmannical* society.

When, how and why did *mūrti pūjā* begin?

It is not known precisely how idol worship began - first in the individuals' homes, for private, and subsequently the temples, for public worship. But there are substantive reasons to believe that the *devā yajña* (part of the five *mahā yajña*) assumed the form of *devapūjā*.

In order to examine how this transformation took place, it will be helpful to refresh our understanding of *pūjā* and *yajña* briefely.

Pūjā, according to Dr Roshen Dalal, a scholar of history, religion, and philosophy and author of several books, is - The act of worship in Hinduism, whether in a temple or a home. Prayers, along with offerings such as fruit, flowers or incense, are made to the image of a deity, or to a symbol of the divine. *Pūjā* may be done according to prescribed rituals, or in any other spontaneous way.[8]

Explaining *yajña*, Āpastamba, a formidable *sūtrakara* (800-400 BC), in his Yajña Paribhāshā Sūtra (literally - *yajña* definition rules/aphorism), observes: "*Yajña*, sacrifice, is an act by which we surrender something for the sake of the gods. Such an act must rest on a sacred authority (*āgama*), and serve for ma1's salvation (*sreyo*rtha*)."[9]

Yajñas - which, according to Āpastamba, should be considered synonymous with *yaga* and *iṣṭi* - were prescribed by the three Vedas (sūtra III) for the three *varṇa*s - *brahmaṇa*, *kṣatriya*, and *vaiśya* (sūtra II).

Monier has a pragmatic take on the genesis of sacrifice: "Every worshipper praised the gods because he liked to be praised himself. He honoured them with offerings because he liked to receive presents himself. He pretended to feed them because he required food himself."

He concludes,"...in its purest and simplest form it (sacrifice) denoted a dedication of some simple gift as an expression of gratitude for blessings received." This was a simple yet logical explanation of why sacrifice gained currency. The forces of nature - viewed as manifestations of divine powers - were believed to have the power and will to wreak havoc when the heavens were displeased and dispense favours when pleased, like granting a son or a good crop. Sacrifices were used to attract "the favour of celestial beings who were capable of conferring good or inflicting harm on crops, flocks and herds." Sacrifice gradually transformed from an expression of gratitude to "an act of propitiation for purely selfish ends." It was now used for obtaining *kāmya* on one hand, and for propitiating against the wrath of divine power on the other. Monier suggests that people invoked the gods at every meal and offered a share of the food hoping for such benefits. The gods, given their ethereal bodies, could consume such offerings only in the form of essence and aroma - the fumes from libations of grains, the *ghī*, and the exhilarating *soma rasa* offered in *homa*. According to Monier, "Of course all offerings and libations were accompanied with the hymns of praise. A certain amount of ceremonial was gradually added. The whole sacrificial service was called *yajña*."[10]

Devā yajña is one of the five '*mahā*' *yajñas* that every householder was required to perform daily, the other four being *Brahman*, *pitŕ*, *bhūta* and *manuṣya yajña*. *Devayajña* is enjoined to be performed in the nuptial fire by a householder every day of his life, starting from the day he first holds the hand of his spouse in marriage until the time of his death. (Āp D.S I.4.13, 22, 14.1, YAJ I.99, Manu IV.25, et cetera). This fire, called *gṛhyāgni* (*gṛhya* fire), is kindled on the day of the wedding and carried from the bride's house to her husband's in *ukhā* vessel. The *gṛhya sūtras* place special emphasis on the daily worship of this domestic fire. In case the householder is unable to carry out this duty, his wife, son, daughter or pupil, in that order, are enjoined to perform the worship in his stead. (Āp. GS. 2.5.12-16 and Aśhv.GS. I.9.1 - 2)

Why were the five *yajñas* lauded as '*mahā*' *yajñas*?

It has been repeatedly explained that all *yajñas* (other than *nitya karma*) were performed to attain *kāmya* (that which is desired) - be it expansion of the boundaries of a kingdom (*aśvamedha*), begetting a son (*putraiṣṭikarma* as mentioned in Rāmāyaṇa), prosperity, or the destruction of one's enemies. Hindu scriptures of the Veda period were unabashed in admitting that *yajña* was an effective instrument for worldly gains. All *yajñas* required the *purohita*, a *brahmaṇa*, as an agent. The actual beneficiary, the *yajamāna*, played a passive role and merely followed instructions from the priests. It was believed that all of the benefits from the sacrifice accrued to the *yajamāna*, and the performing priests only received *dakṣiṇā* (fee) as reward. The ancients had a rather practical approach to *yajña* in their time!

Nevertheless, none of this was applicable to the *panca mahā yajña*, which was performed without any stated *kāmya* objective or priests. The householder performed the *yajñas* himself, and the five *yajñas* were carried out with no expectation of material or worldly gain. It was a truly selfless exercise in pursuit of higher ideals. By offering oblations, the householder demonstrated his humility and devotion to the gods. By reading the Vedas, he expressed his gratitude to the great sages for wisdom imparted through sacred literature, and reverence toward his forebears for granting him the most precious of inheritances - his life and his ability to think. By offering *tarpaṇa* (water), he conveyed kindliness and tolerance to all beings, and conveyed the goodness of sharing by scattering food for all *bhūtas* before feeding himself.

Little wonder then that Manu calls this an ennobling act that frees the soul from rank selfishness and elevates the body to a vehicle worthy of higher things. "By the study of the Veda, by vows, by offerings into the fire, by acquiring the triple learning, by offering sacrifices, by sons, and by the great sacrifices and the (other) sacrifices, this body is made fit for ultimate reality."[11] Both Manu and Gautama looked upon these *yajñas* as *saṃskāras*.

[These *panca mahā yajñas* were considered great sacrificial sessions in early Vedic times. In reality though, none of the five fully qualify as *yajñas*, and are referred to as such only figuratively. They are termed 'great' by way of praise. (Tattiriya Āraṇyaka I I.10; Āp. Dharma Sūtra 1.4.12.14)]

The earliest observations about these five *yajñas* are seen in the Vedic texts of Śatapatha Brahmaṇa, where the adjective '*mahā*' (meaning 'great) is first used - "There are five great sacrifices, and they, indeed, are great sacrifice of sessions - to wit, the sacrifice to beings, the sacrifice to men, the sacrifice to fathers, the sacrifice to the gods, and the sacrifice to the *Brahman*." (X I.5.6.1) The Brahmaṇa text goes on to enjoin that "day by day one should offer an oblation to beings: thus he performs that sacrifice to beings. Day by day one should offer (presents to guests) up to the cupful of water: thus he performs that sacrifice to men. Day by day one should offer with *svadha* up to the cupful of water: thus he performs that sacrifice to the fathers. Day by day one should perform with *svāhā* up to the log of fire wood: thus he performs that sacrifice to the gods."(X I.5.6.2) This centrality of *mahāyajñas* in an Āryan's daily life remained unchanged for several centuries, as is evident from their presence in the *dharma sūtra* (500-300 BC) rules of Baudhāyana (I I.6.11.1 - 2) and Āpastamba (.I.4.12.13 - 14) concerning observance of the five daily sacrifices.

However, over time, only *devā yajña* retained its significance. Further inquiry by scholars is necessary if we are to understand fully the reasons the other four *yajñas* diminished in importance. [The *Brahman-Yajña* is still performed by most Brahmaṇas of the deccan- recited only once a year in the *śrāvaṇa* month[12].]

Devā yajña was performed by offering fuel sticks and food to the holy fire, as oblations, to Vedic deities (the deities differ in different texts) with the chanting of their names or distinguishing attributes, followed by the lexical word *svāhā*. (Āp.DS. I.4.13.1, Baud DS. I I.6.4, Gaut DS.V.8 - 9). The offerings of food or fuel sticks in fire were also called *homa*, a generic name for any oblations made in the fire. But, the *panca mahāyajña* and *homa* were two separate items in the *āhnika* list of daily duties of every *dvija*, indicating that in addition to *devāyajña*, another *homa* activity was prescribed.

Manu (I I.176) and Yaj. (I.99, 100, 102), both show that *devapūjā* is different from *homa* and was performed after the latter according to Marīci and Harita quoted in the Smriticandrika, Smritimuktaphala and other digests.[13]

Āhnika

Let us have a quick look at *āhnika* before proceeding with the discussion of *mahāyajña*. In numerous *smṛtis*, Purāṇas and digests, the duties of householders have been described in detail. Some works contain moral exhortations to the householder, but fall under the category of *Sādhāraṇa Dharma*. The *dharmaśāstras* also prescribe the most important daily duties, a strictly regulated daily routine for all *dvijas*. Such duties which were performed during the day or '*ahan*' were called *āhnika*. Every activity - even those pertaining to the physical needs of the body, like bathing or brushing teeth - was performed as religious duty. Such an attitude was considered conducive to the spiritual welfare. Day-time (before sunrise up to after sunset) was divided into eight equal parts for practical purposes and different activities of the daily routine were assigned to different periods of the day.

Study of activities listed in different *smṛtis* is important as it can throw light on the *smṛti* period when the worship of gods or *devapūjā* was introduced, and to understand whether or how it (*devapūjā*) replaced *devāyajña*.

While Parāśara Smṛti (600-900 AD) (I.39) lists bathing, performing *saṃdhyā* prayers, *japa*, *homa*, worshipping gods, honouring guests and *vaiśvedevā* as the six compulsory duties, Manu's morning duty list (IV.152) includes answering calls of nature, bathing, brushing teeth, applying collyrium to eyes and worshipping gods.

संध्या स्नानं जपो होमो देवतातिथिपूजनम्
आतिथ्यं वैश्वदेवं च षट्कर्माणि दिने दिने ३९

Mitākṣarā, commenting on Yājñavalkya Smṛti (I.98), states that after answering nature's calls, brushing teeth and completing the morning prayers, sacrifice should be offered according to the prescribed rules to the fires named *āhavanīya* and *aupasna* i.e. *homa*. Thereafter, the sun deity hymns should be repeated with concentration (I.99), followed by study of the Vedas, and visiting the ruler for the sake of attaining *yogakhema*, i.e. 'acquisition and preservation'. Later at noon, after bathing in the river, libations of water are offered to the gods, the *pitris* and ṛṣis. Mitākṣarā prescribes that "he should worship according to the prescribed rules with sandal paste, flowers and rice the gods *Hari*, *Hara*, *Hiraṇyagarbha*, &c., or others as he may prefer with the hymns of the Ṛg, Yajur or the Sāmaveda specifically addressed to those deities or by joining the word *namaḥ* (salutation) to the fourth declension (dative case) of the name of the God (as *Namaḥ Haraya Namaḥ Haraye* &c, salutation to *Hara*, salutations to *Hari*,

&c.)" (I.101). Thereafter, Mitākṣarā prescribes *japa* in (I.101), and goes on to say in (I.102) that the "five great *yajñas* should be daily performed, because they are permanent duties."

This clearly demonstrates that -

i. Idol worship or *devapūjā* with sandal paste, flowers and rice had become a part of daily routine or *āhnika* at the time of compilation of the Yājñavalkya Smṛti
ii. Idol worship was performed (after *snāna*) during the mid-day, before *japa* and *panca mahāyajña* (including *devāyajña*)
iii. *Mahāyajña* continued to be performed (as before) in its totality i.e. without dropping *devāyajña*.

Interestingly, Manu, in his *smṛti* (in 2.176), which was composed a few centuries before the Yājñavalkya Smṛti, also prescribes the same sequence of daily duties - *snāna*, followed by *tarpaṇa* (water oblations) to *devatās*, manes and *pitris* followed by *devapūjāṇa* and *homa*, quite distinct from the *mahāyajñas* -

नित्यं स्नात्वा शुचिः कुर्याद देव -ऋषि -पितृतर्पणम I देवताभ्यर्चनं च -एव समिधादानम
एव -च II २-१७६

"Every day, having bathed, and being purified, he must offer libations of water to the gods, sages and manes, worship (the images of) the gods, and place fuel on (the sacred fire)."

This translation, from an unknown source, has translated '*devātbhyarchanam*' to mean 'worship (the images of) the gods', whereas Doniger, in translating the same *sūtra*, has simply used the phrase 'worship the deities' without referring to their 'images'. The former translation appears to capture the sense of the *sūtra* better. The important point here is that Manu also speaks of *devatāpūjān* as a constituent of the daily duties.

With time, the ancient idea of *homa* receded into the background and an elaborate procedure of *devapūjā* (worship of images kept in the house) took its place in the medieval through modern times[14]. Interestingly, though the *devā yajña* morphed into *devā pūjā*, the use of Veda mantras continued almost seamlessly, recommending application of three Ṛgvedic mantras.

Why did *mūrti pūjā* begin?

There are numerous theories on why a society that practiced portable religious practices (*yajña*) and rituals for over 1500 years, took to *mūrti pūja* - requiring fixity of place of worship and erection of temples. Portable here applies to *yajña*, which could be performed almost anywhere by preparing a small *vedi*; the implements needed for such rituals could be ported easily from one location to another. This portability had definite roots in the pastoral lifestyle of the Āryans, who moved constantly in search of new lands fit for rearing animals. Vedic Āryans practised this religion for more than a millennium, with the core revolving around *yajña*. As society evolved and urban centres emerged, *śrauta* ceremonies, which required temporary but large infrastructure, gained popularity; the large infrastructure which was erected for these *yajñas* was dismanteled and set afire after the conclusion of the ceremony. But the change from the *śrauta* to the *mūrti pūjā* was radical - it led to creating permanent places of worship (temples), partly, no doubt, a result of a pastoral society taking to urbanisation.

∞

It seems inconceivable that *mūrti pūjā* was a sudden development. It was, in all probability, triggered by one or more of the following factors, or combinations, thereof:

1. We observed that even in the earlier parts of the Ṛgveda, *Índra* was portrayed with a green chin and a big tummy. It is likely this was little more than the poet's own imagination - he perhaps could not restrain himself from picturing *Índra* (and the other gods) as possessing human form, along with other human attributes. The genesis of idolising *devatās* could also lie in the belief that *devatās* were originally ordinary humans who attained divinity through a series of successful *yajñas*.
2. The Vedas prescribed the concept of '*dharnā*' while engaging in *yajña*. The *yajña* performer must focus his mind on the *devatā* being invoked and, deep in such contemplation, establish him in his '*hṛdaya*' (heart). The idea was to focus one's mind on the deity. This was essential to all *yajñas*. Max Müller found this to be a 'Hindu specific' attribute alien to the western mind. Describing '*ekāgratā*' or single-mindedness, he observes that the western mind works like a kaleidoscope when concentrating or focusing on an object.[15] The idea behind *ekāgratā* was to consciously focus on only one object and shut out all other thoughts from the mind. This made the *yajña* all the more arduous due to the absence of a form or shape of object to focus on. It became necessary to have some form or shape to establish it in the *hṛdaya*. Chāndogyopaniṣad opens with the edict - meditate on the *akshar* '*Om*' (letter '*Om*'). This again calls upon the performer to concentrate and focus not just on the sound but also on the imagery of *Om*. This was a move towards associating the word and its sound with a mental image, of associating names of *devatās* with images. There were many *devatās*, like *Sūrya* or *Agni*, whose forms were easily discernible. It must have proved difficult for worshippers to not attribute shape and form to other *devatās*, especially during a *yajña* where they could clearly visualise *Sūrya* and *Agni* while invoking them.

Kane makes a compelling point: even in the times of the Brahmaṇas simple *gṛhya* sacrifices were raised to the level of *śrauta* rites, which gradually became less frequent. When a man invoked a deity through an offering, he was asked to contemplate upon that deity before saying '*vasata*'.[16] Patton too, while discussing *viniyoga*, asks us to 'consider the usage of the important verbal phrase, *manasi samnyasya* "having brought the deities to mind," found in the Vajasaneyi Anukramani, and the Brhaddevata 8.132." She concludes, 'This and other related phrases suggest that the deities are to be thought of, and thought about, as the recitation is happening. The phrase implies that the deities are to be imagined, and imagined properly, in order for the ritual to be efficacious.'[17]

Naturally, this led, if not coaxed, the worshipper to assign anthropomorphic attributes to the deity.

By the time of Nirukta (800-500 BC), deities with anthropomorphic forms came to coexist with formless Vedic gods. While dealing with Vedic mantras concerning deities, Yaska propounds three views - they have anthropomorphic form, they do not have anthropomorphic form, and they may assume both characters, i.e. though non-anthropomorphic, the deities may assume various forms for carrying out specific activities.

3. Finally, there was the concept of 'internal *yajña*'. Its symbolism equating the various elements of *yajña* (fuel sticks, *ghī*, mantra) with human attributes like eyes, ears, tongue and speech, led to the devout imagining the *devatās*, and the supreme being *Brahman* himself, as having a form.
   (a) Interestingly, personification is a favoured device among poets and authors alike because humans look for parallels between themselves and other objects. Human-like shapes among clouds, vegetation, rocks and mountains attract both - children and adults. The poets of the Ṛg and other Vedas were no different; the Vedas are replete with such devices. In fact, esoteric knowledge is the core of Vedic studies where symbolism plays a significant role. It appears that Vedas' studies constantly nudge, even coax, the reader's imagination towards association of that which is written with that which is implied. Given these circumstances, it was only a matter of time before *Índra's* green chin and *Rudra's* sharp nose found expression in images carved from wood, stone or metal.

Prāṇāgnihotṛ was an important development in the Vedic period when scholars composed Upaniṣads shifting focus from external rituals to the knowledge of the self. The literal meaning of the word *prāṇa-agni-hotṛ* is sacrifice (*hotṛ*) of breath or life force (*prāṇa*) to the fire (*agni*). What it meant was that the external *śrauta* rituals and other *yajñas* were being given up and replaced by *prāṇāgnihotṛ* or internal rituals. Henk Bodewitz states that the *prāṇāgnihotṛ* is an internalized direct, private ritual that substituted the external, public *agnihotṛ* (a *śrauta* rite). According to Bodewitz[18], when external gods are replaced by internal gods, this sacrifice is no longer a *devāyajin*. The self of the sacrificer becomes the object of the rite.

(b) In words of Śhatapatha Brahmaṇa - "As to this they ask, 'Who is the better one, the self offerer (*Ātmāyajin*), or the god offerer (*Devāyajin*)?' Let him say, 'the self offerer; 'for a self-offerer, doubtless, is he who knows, 'this my (new) body is formed by that (body of the *yajña*, the sacrifice), and this my (new) body is procured thereby'. And even as a snake frees itself from its skin, so does he free himself from his mortal body, from sin; and made of the *Rik*, the *Yajus*, the *Samana*, and of offerings, does he pass on to the heavenly world."[19]

The *śrauta agnihotr* sacrifice thus evolved into a *prāṇāgnihotṛ* sacrifice. Heesterman describes the *prāṇāgnihotṛ* sacrifice as one where the practitioner performs the sacrifice with food, and his own body as the temple, without any outside help or reciprocity. This ritual allows a Hindu to "stay in the society while maintaining his independence from it"; its simplicity marks the "end station of Vedic ritualism."

This evolution of the Vedic idea of *devas* (gods) having human-like sensory organs, and the human body being the temple of the *Brahman*, the metaphysical unchanging reality, is found in the Bṛhad-Āraṇyaka Upanishad section 2.2, Kena Upaniṣad sections 1.4 and 2.1–2.5, Praśna Upanishad chapter 2, and other Upaniṣads. In fact, even in our day-to-day conversations, we refer to the body as a *devālaya* - an abode of the gods.

Śatpatha has several examples where worldly objects are likened to the components of a *yajña*[20]. For example, the *praṇīta* water is equated with the head of the sacrifice, the fuel is equated to the breath, and the kindling verses are the spine. The two libations of *ghī* are its mind, and speech *Sarasvata* and *Sarasvatī* (XI.2.1-3). In context of the *aśvamedha yajña*, Max Müller explains: "*Yajña*, the sacrifice, is here, as so often, to be understood as the abstract representation of the victim (here the horse), as well as of the *Puruṣa*, i.e. *Prajāpati*, and the Sacrificer."[21] The *Brahmaṇa*, in the next *kāṇḍa*, using symbolism observes - the year is sacrifice, the officiating priests the seasons, the oblations are the months[22]. Such symbolism, which equated sacrifice and its elements with various objects, and its vivid imagery moved people towards embracing anthropomorphic personas for the *devatās*. When one worships the sun, moon, fire and water, one can see and feel them. It would not be unnatural if someone were to create images of the *devatās*, especially because the gods were humans to begin with.

Over time, another factor - icon worship - must have compelled the devouts to create images of gods and goddesses as well. Here, the word 'icon' indicates an object or thing regarded as a representative symbol worthy of veneration. In all the religions of the world, icon worship is either an integral part of the faith or practiced despite censure, as in the case of Islām.

In Christianity, the first of the Ten Commandments states -

"You shall have no other gods before me. You shall not make for yourself a graven image, or any likeness of anything that is in heaven above, or that is in the earth beneath, or that is in the water under the earth; you shall not bow down to them or serve them." (Exodus 20:2–5)

And,

"Ye shall make you no idols nor graven image, neither rear you up a standing image, neither shall ye set up any image of stone in your land, to bow down unto it: for I am the Lord your God." (Leviticus 26:1)

Yet, Catholic and Orthodox Christians use religious objects such as statues, crosses, icons, incense, the Gospel, the Bible, candles and religious vestments. In dogmatic theory, these are venerated as objects suffused with God's grace and power, and Eastern Orthodoxy even declares that they are not 'hollow forms' or cult images.

The offering of veneration in the form of *latria* (the veneration due god) is doctrinally forbidden by the Orthodox Church. However, revering religious pictures or icons in the form of *dulia* (reverence accorded to saints and angels) is not only allowed but also obligatory. Some outside observers find it difficult to distinguish these two levels of veneration in practice. Nonetheless, the distinction is maintained and even taught by the faithful in many hymns and prayers that are sung throughout the liturgical year.

Buddhism and Jainism are other two faiths where icon worship is extremely popular. In Islām, despite stringent opposition from the Wahabi sect, the respect accorded to photographs of the great Mosque of Mecca, to the hair of Prophet Muhammad and to the Holy Qurān is not vastly different from icon worship. Likewise, in Sikhism, worship of icons is quite common.

Even though gods had no shape or form in Vedic Hinduism, icon worship was commonplace. Not just the implements but also the place of *yajña* (including the pillars of the structure where *śrauta* was conducted) had to be purified through mantras and other prescribed procedures. In a religion where both, the animate, and inanimate, were believed to be permeated by the *Brahman*, it was only a matter of time before *mūrti pūjā* of the *devatās* began.

4. We finally come to the theory that *mūrti pūjā* predated the Vedic period amongst non-Āryan inhabitants of the land. This is evidenced by the discovery of an ithyphallic figurine in Mohenjo-daro and various stones representing phallic emblems. The reference to *Śiśna Devās* in the Ṛgveda lends credence to the theory that there were people of non-Āryan stock who worshipped *mūrtis* including phallic symbols. With the passage of time, as non-Āryans were absorbed into society as *śūdras* and intermarried, the practice of *mūrti pūjā* entered Āryan households.

5. The contention that Buddhists introduced Hindus to *mūrti pūjā* does not hold water because there is ample evidence, by way of prescriptions and directions in various *smṛtis* and *sūtras*, of *devālayas*, i.e. public places of idol worship, which predate the birth of Gautama Buddha.

Arrival of many *mūrtis* and *āgama*

The concept of a personal god (ref. chapter on 'Īśvara, the personal god: Para and Aparabrahman') was meant to help the common person prepare himself for the arduous journey towards the ultimate realization and merge his self with the *Brahman*, the Supreme Being. It was not a licence to portray the gods in anthropomorphic forms or to worship images. As explained earlier, a personal god was a 'convenience' for ordinary people. It helped them believe that the world around, including themselves, was real, even though the true *Vedantin* knew that the world (including himself) was unreal and that reality, the *Brahman*, was but one. Belief in a personal god was important because this god, by virtue of possessing *guṇas* (human-like attributes), was amenable to blessing worshippers with health, wealth, progeny, et cetera when pleased by *pūjā* or fasting, whereas the inactive *Brahman*, devoid of all guṇas, could not do any of this. This belief in a personal god was conceptualised to serve as a stopover in a long and difficult journey to the final destination, the *Brahman*, the supreme reality.

Once the idea of a personal god obtained official sanction, different people - depending on their imaginations and preferences - began praying to different gods in different physical forms. A multitude of gods proliferated, and continue to do so. One modern instance is Santoshī Mā, considered an avatar that gained popularity in the 1970s. *Jai Santoshi Maa*, a low-budget Hindi film, was released in 1975 and went on to become one of the biggest hits of all time in India. Thanks to the immensely successful film, *Devi's* popularity peaked, particularly in the northern states. There is no mention of the *Devi* in any of the major Hindu religious texts of the eighteenth century or earlier!

As a concept, this (*mūrti pūjā*) was nothing new. From the early Vedic period, fire, whether in hearth, forest or a *yajña vedi*, was a physical manifestation of *Agni devatā*; just as *Sūrya*, *Candra* and *Vāyu devtā* had a physical presence. In some ways, the religion had grown quite comfortable with visible and invisible gods since the early Veda times. Thus, a personal god conceptualised in different physical manifestations was not a radical departure for the Vedic Āryans or for those who created images of their personal gods for worship around 800-300 BC.

It is surprising that a considerable section of society vehemently defends the view that there was no image worship in the Vedic period. The (paraphrased) arguments put forth are -

Even in instances where *Índra* and *Rudra* are said to possess human attributes, like a green chin or a big belly, these are nothing but metaphors used by the Vedic poets. The Vedic gods were abstract.

This view is patently incorrect. The worship of *Sūrya*, *Candra* and *Agni* refutes any such argument. Even the claim that *Agni* and *Sūrya* deities represent merely the attributes of fire, and heat or energy, respectively, is countered by the fact that in *yajña* rituals, after invocation, oblations were offered to the very 'visible' fire, and water was offered facing the direction of the 'visible' sun! 'Finally let us consider usage of the important verbal phrase *manasi samnyasya* or "having brought the deities to mind," found in the Vajasaneyin Anukramani and the Brahad Devta 8.132. This clearly suggests that the deities are to be thought of, and thought about, as the recitation is happening.'[23]

The author is of the opinion that the anti-idolatry teachings of Christianity (and Judaism) are responsible for this defensive attitude in Hindus. It appears that right from inception, Vedic society believed - not only in strong associations - as evident in *viniyoga*,[24] but also in worshipping gods, both - 'formless' as well as with 'definite form'. Importantly, that society felt neither shy nor apologetic about it. Not in the earlier days anyway. Apologists, and their diffidence, came much later. That is not to say that there was no criticism of worship of symbols or images within Hinduism. But Hinduism has always been the sum of divergent ideas, beliefs and practices. This divergence is represented in various *śākhās* of the Vedas, and their followers, since inception. The black and the white YajurVedas are a shining example of this seamless coexistence since ancient times.

The emergence of the concept of a personal god was something very fundamental - *devāpūjā* started replacing *yajña*, which was relegated to secondary status in Āryan homes. It is no surprise that *pūjā* soon became the recognized way of worshipping gods in physical forms.

This trend was probably also encouraged by Hindu religious leaders to counter Buddhism which had emerged as a potent threat to *Brahmanism*. The new religion gained widespread acceptance because of its simplicity - in practice and in teachings - as opposed to the complexities of the Upaniṣads, the *Nirguṇa Brahman*, and *yajña* rituals.

The Upaniṣads were a product of the age of reason and the core teaching was equality of *Ātmā* and *Brahman*, i.e. *Brahman* permeating everything animate and inanimate. As discussed earlier, this concept of a transcendental god was too abstruse even for the educated elite. The less enlightened members of society simply failed to comprehend such an entity. There was another issue - the Upaniṣadic system did not have a place for worldly pursuits (*kāmya*) through *yajña*. If a common person chose to truly follow the Upaniṣadic path, he was required to renounce material desires. This was unrealistic, a utopian dream. Most people desired worldly comforts and had many unfulfilled wishes; they believed these 'out of reach' objects of worldly comfort and desire could be attained by performing the appropriate *yajñas*. Therefore, an 'inactive and indifferent' *Brahman*, that pure, unadulterated consciousness, had to make room for new personal gods who 'delivered' people's wishes.

But even such materialistic individuals, who cared little for any higher path of renunciation and struggled to grasp the abstract concept of a supreme being, unquestioningly believed in the Upaniṣadic teachings. However, realising their own limitations, they chose to tread the easier path of worshipping a personal god, *Īśvara*. The great teacher Śaṅkara himself endorsed *Īśvara* and called it the stepping stone to *moksha*, realisation and salvation of a human being!

Trimūrti

The personal god, unlike a supreme being, is a 'doing god'. The world is created by *Brahman* (a four-faced god not to be confused with the Supreme Being, *Brahman*-neu.). If there is a creator, then there must be a preserver, and someone responsible for the dissolution. These three specific duties were assigned to the gods *Brahman*, *Viṣṇu* and *Rudra* (or *Śiva*). It is interesting to note that in the Vedas, *Rudra* is associated with storms, which are forces of destruction, leaving the preserver's job to *Viṣṇu*. Both *Viṣṇu* and *Rudra* find mention in the Ṛgveda, though not specifically as gods of preservation and destruction; that happened much later.

The emergence of these three gods could have clashed with the concept of the 'one' ultimate reality - the supreme being, *Brahman*. The *Trimūrti*, a three-faced unit or trinity of *Brahman*, *Viṣṇu* and *Maheśa*, resolved this conflict as well as other possible issues regarding superiority among the three. The concept of the Trinity is not alien to other religions - in Christians there is the holy Trinity of God the Father, God the son, and God the Holy Spirit. However, to assume that the Hindu trinity was borrowed from any foreign religion would be erroneous for the simple reason that this concept is fundamentally different from the holy Trinity of Christianity.

While a *vedantin* believes in one supreme spirit as the only reality (the universe being unreal), he/she also admits to a personal god who engages in creation, preservation and dissolution, and thus intervenes in the world. However, in Śaṅkara's *Vedantic* scheme of things, the personal god is a step below the ultimate reality. This personal god, like all humans and unlike the supreme reality, has *guṇas* (qualities or attributes) identified as *sattva* (serenity and purity), *rajasa* (energetic activity) and *tamas* (dullness). Most humans have all three *guṇas*, with one dominant *guṇa* in every individual. According to the Purāṇas, *guṇas* reflect the principal attributes of the three deities - *Brahman* (the god) the *rajasa*, *Viṣṇu* the *sattva*, and *Śiva* the *tamas* (vide definition of *guṇas* in Dalal's Hinduism). Monier admits to a great difference between the understanding of the pantheisms of India and Europe. He observes that these three *guṇas*, which are the same as those in the *Sankhyayan* system, are the constituents of *prakṛti* - activity, goodness, and indifference (*rajasa*, *sattva*, *tamas*). They are sometimes regarded as equivalent to passion or pain, purity or happiness, and apathy or ignorance. According to Monier, "Dominated by activity (*rajasa*), the supreme being is *Brahman* the creator; by goodness (*sattva*), he is *Viṣṇu*, the preserver; by indifference (*tamasa*), he is *Rudra*, the dissolver."[25]

He, interestingly, observes, "Nothing was easier for them than to maintain that the one sole, self-existing Supreme self, the only real existing Essence, exercises itself as if sportively (*lilaya*), in Infinite expansion, in Infinite manifestations of itself, in Infinite creation, dissolution, and re-creation, through Infinite varieties and diversities of operation."

He reminds that the name *Brahman* derives from the Sanskrit root '*brih*' meaning 'to increase', which was expressive of this growth. Thus, all things animate and inanimate are believed to emanate from the supreme self. And above man, a series of higher forms of existence such as demigods, supernatural beings, lesser gods, superior gods, et cetera eventually lead to the primeval male god *Brahman*. Monier describes this first personal product of the purely spiritual *Brahman* as "the first evolution and hence the apparent evolver of all the inferior forms. To draw any line of separation between the stalks, stones, plants, animals, men, demigods and gods is, according to the theory of *Brahmanism*, impossible. They are all liable to run into each other, and the number of gods alone amounts to 330 million."[26]

It appears the holy Trinity concept was introduced to accommodate the concept of a creator, preserver and destroyer, as well as to address disputes regarding the supremacy of *Brahman*, *Viṣṇu* or *Maheśa* by uniting all three gods as one and accommodating them as equals in the classic Hindu way. However, this idea of the *Trimūrti* never gained much traction. Like all such ideas in this ancient religion, it was never completely abandoned either. For inexplicable reasons, *Brahman* (as creator) did not become a popular deity. He has just the one popular temple at Pushkar in Ajmer (Rajasthan). It is believed he was shunned because of his incestuous inclinations towards his daughter *Sarasvatī*. On the other hand, *Rudra* or *Śiva* (though destroyer), is one of the most popular deities even today, as is *Viṣṇu* (the preserver), the serene one. Followers of *Śiva* and *Viṣṇu* came to be known as *shaivas* and *vaiśnavas*, two of the largest sects of Hinduism, and the two schools of faith as *shaivism* and *vaiṣnava* respectively.

Interestingly, *Śaivas*, *Vaiśnavas* and followers of all other 330 and 2 gods continue to believe in the supremacy of the Ṛgveda which asserts that all gods are one being under different names (I.I16. 4.46)

Śaivism and *Vaiśnavism*

Buddhism had become a religious movement to reckon with in Buddha's lifetime itself. A large number of Hindus converted to the faith of the *Śakyamuṇi*. This compelled Hindu religious leaders to counter the growing popularity of Buddhism in the Hindu heartland. After the demise of Buddha, his body parts and personal belongings became objects of reverence (as expected), and were sacralised by his followers who enshrined these remnants in stupas near and far. It seems natural for followers to worship the remains of the great man though it went against the core of his teachings. This may have given *Brahmanical* leaders the idea to encourage image worship within the Hindu fold.

It is important to appreciate here that the distinguishing feature of Buddhism, as preached by Buddha, was its simplicity. This uncomplicated, easy-to-grasp idea was in stark contrast to Upaniṣadic *Brahmanism*, which was so complex and abstract that even among the educated only a few could fathom it. One such simple notion in Buddhism was the absence of a designated place of worship and refrain from worship of any object or symbol. More importantly, the lack of possession of any material objects that led to attachment and eventually *dukkha*. Even food was not allowed to be possessed (stored) - a *bhikṣu* was beholden to seek alms daily for food to satisfy his hunger. This humility and austerity associated with the life of a *bhikkhū* was helped along considerably by the construction of large *vihāras* (monasteries). These monasteries provided a permanent and secure dwelling to several Buddhist monks with a minimum assured safety from hunger and elements of nature. The monks increasingly began to prefer various *stupas* (to worship relics of Buddha) to 'any place' suitable for meditation, and 'any home', suitable for *bhikṣa*. The itinerant nature of Buddhism, where a monk went from door to door seeking daily *bhikṣa* (food) and did not have a fixed place for meditation (worship), quickly transformed to a 'rooted' or fixed life. As an alternative to *caityas* (halls for meditation with a *stupa* at one end), *Brahmanical* religious leaders cleverly offered *devālayas* as fixed places of worship.

In the earliest phase of Buddhism, using his own example, Buddha recommended a life of renunciation. A *bhikṣu* had to forsake all worldly possessions and comforts, beg for sustenance by going door-to-door and survive on such *bhikṣa* alone. Buddhism taught that *dukkha* emanated from worldly possessions that must therefore be abjured. *Śiva* (the god) exemplified the same principle, and, just like Buddhism, *Śaivism* was typically ascetic in character. When Buddha achieved realisation in the second phase of his life, he preached: "Universal brotherhood, universal equality and universal compassion for all forms of animal life", which was remarkably similar to the beneficent *Viṣṇu*. In effect, these two Hindu sects offered the very ideas Buddhism was offering to the confused Hindu populace. According to Monier, this is how Hinduism yet again dissipated the formidable challenge confronting *Brahmanism*.[27]

At first glance, *devāpūjā*, which appears to be in conflict with the doctrine of an omnipresent, impersonal, formless and passionless spiritual essence pervading and animating the universe, was not repudiated by the *Brahmanical* sect. The concept of *nirguṇa* and *saguṇa Brahman* coexisted within the folds of *Brahmanism*. In the words of Monier, "The more closely the theistic phase of the Hindu religion is examined, the more plainly will it be found to rest on a substratum of *Brahmanism*." He goes on to add that "the one system is to a great extent a development of the other, and to draw a line of separation between the two, or to say where one ends, and the other begins, is impossible."[28] With the availability of this kind of flexibility within the system to accommodate a conflict in ideas, it is little wonder that "it has artfully appropriated Buddhism, and gradually superseded that competing system by drawing its adherents within the pale of its own communion." Monier marvels that "without doubt the most remarkable fact in the history of the interaction between *Brahmanism* and the mighty movement initiated by one of this earth's greatest teachers was the resolution of his teaching into *Śaivism* and *Vaisnavism*."[29]

Explaining how the sects came to be formed[30] (600-300 BC), Romila Thapar observes that this was the period of competing ideologies and philosophies when "rivalries and debates were rife," and "people gathered around the new philosophers in the *kutuhala-shālās*." According to Thaper, the ambience was different "from that of a Vedic thought where the teachings or disputations were not held in public. The presence of multiple, competing ideologies was a feature of urban living." It was in this milieu that "some of those expounding different ideas were identified as sects. This meant that they were a small group usually supporting a single doctrine of belief who had voluntarily come together." Out of the many sects that blossomed, not all survived, and only "some of these sects grew in number in the subsequent period through a following or incorporation and where they were successful in finding support and patronage they emerged as an order, being referred to as various *sanghas* or assemblies." Thaper believes that this is how Buddhism and Jainism came to stay as two sects.

It is highly likely that *Śaivism* and *Vaiśnavism* also evolved in a similar vein, due to which they retain very large followings even today.

This period, as you will recall, belonged to Axial age discussed in an earlier chapter.

There were, however, two key differences between the *Sanātana Dharma* sects (*Śaivism* and *Vaiśnavism*) and the newly born Buddhism and Jainism. While Buddhism encouraged monks to live a life of renunciation in monasteries, this was rare in the *Sanātana Dharma* sect. Buddhism insisted on abjuring differentiations based on *varṇa* and assimilation of customs, practices, cults and deities. It did not restrict the continuation of old practices - a late Bhushana monastery in the Mathura area received donations from those appreciating the fertility deity worshipped by the popular *nāgā* cult of the area, associated with snake worship, despite Buddhism curtailing deity-worship.[31] On the other hand, the *sanātana* sects could not ignore *varṇa*, and collective renunciation was rare, except in hermitages.

Between 200 BC and the beginning of the Christian era, a movement arose within Indian Buddhism that altered it radically. The earliest sources for this movement were the Mahāyāna sūtras, scriptures that were first compiled nearly four centuries after the Buddha's death[32]. The idea of *Bodhisattva* and reincarnation brought about the idolisation of Gautama Buddha. In the words of Romila Thapar, "the Buddha had opposed the deification, yet by the first century AD, his image was carved in stone, engraved on rock or painted, and worshipped."[33]

Mahāyāna, literally 'the great vehicle', as this movement was known, became the dominant sect in Buddhism. Apart from the *bodhisattva*, it also propagated the concept of merit transfer and idol worship, both of which were directly in conflict with the teachings of Buddha. Various cults, especially the fertility cult and goddesses like *yakṣa*, *yakṣani*, *nāgā*, et cetera, soon became a part of the mythology of all these major religions. It is difficult to say with any amount of certitude whether this was a result of competition or simple influence over each other that both Buddhism and *Sanātana Dharma* sects started following *mūrti pūjā*. What is certain is that by this time, *mūrti* had become an integral part of Buddhism, *Śaivism* as well as *Vaiśnavism* (it was perhaps already a part of *Śaivism* since earlier times). Many Vedic gods like *Mitrá*, *Varuṇa* and *Índra* were now losing popularity and newer gods were taking centre stage.

Mūrti pūjā obviated the role of the *purohita*. It was a private, even a personal, act of worship by an individual within the confines of the walls of his home, akin to the *panca mahā yajñas*. Nevertheless, in public *devālayas*, there was scope for the *purohita* to appropriate the role of a designated priest who had to perform numerous duties regularly. It was inconceivable that an idol of a god could be left unattended based on the assumption that a member of the public would tend to the *devālaya* and the *mūrti*. The *purohitas* were quick to seize such an opportunity. One must bear in mind that despite the flourishing Buddhism and Jainism, and the emergence of *Śaivism* and *Vaiśnavism*, *yajñas* did not disappear. As kingdoms expanded, their rulers needed larger displays of power, such as the coronation of the king and other ceremonies. This was done through various *yajñas* like *rajasūya*, *aśvamedha*, *putraishtaprapti*, et cetera; the *Shungas*, the *Sattvāhānas*, the *Ikshvakus* and other dynasties kept this tradition alive.

Chapter 31

The Worship - *Pūjā*

'The act of worship in Hinduism, which may take place in a temple or at home'[1] - is how most Hindus understand and describe *pūjā*. The worship often involves making offerings to the image of gods and goddesses, or to any one or more of innumerable animate or inanimate objects like animals, rivers, mountains, treated as divine by Hindus.

There are many theories on the etymology of the word *pūjā* : Jarl Charpentier, a Swedish Indologist and Sanskrit scholar whose research focused on etymology, believes '*pūjā*' has its origin in Tamil root '*puchu*' or Kannada '*pūsu*' meaning 'to smear'[2]; German Indologist and scholar of Vedic Sanskrit, Paul Thieme, on the other hand suggests '*pūjā*' is derived from the Sanskrit word '*pranca*' meaning 'to prepare the mixture (for someone)' which is used in context of *madhuparka* (a ceremony in which curd mixed with honey is offered to a guest) and conceives *pūjā* as the 'honouring of a guest'[3], and many others. So far, no unanimity has yet been reached on this topic.

An earlier chapter on *mūrti pūjā* tries to explain how the form-less Vedic gods assumed anthropomorphic forms and not only found a place in homes, but also in *devālayas* built for public worship of idols. There are also strong evidences that idol worship had become popular few centuries before the beginning of the Christian Era, as can be seen by the rules laid down by Manu (200 AD-100 BC) for public conduct in the vicinity of *devālayas*. Although the change is discussed in the preceding chapter on *mūrti pūjā*, we still need to understand why, and how, a society which for nearly 1500 years had *yajña* at the very core of its religious practices, chose to transform into a *pūjā*-centric society in which mantras came to occupy centre stage, and displaced *yajña* (*homa*) to a secondary place?

To understand this, we must first acquaint ourselves with *Vidhāna*. We should also have a look at the contribution of *āgama* and *tantra* before studying how *pūjā* is performed.

There are many reasons why *Vidhāna*-texts are important in the history of Vedic literature, but perhaps the most important reason is : 'They mark a new period of literature and a new outlook in the religious life of India, since they were written with a practical object in view, to wit: the simplification of the complicated and burdensome ceremonies treated in the *śrauta* and *gṛyha sūtras*, and this was done by adjusting the matters, with the help of magic, in such a way that observances became easier in practice.'[4]

The word *vidhāna*, meaning precepts, has two interpretations[5] - (i) *vidhi* or sacred precept; and (ii) sorcery practice, which is strictly *Atharvanic*."A whole class of writings, the *vidhāna*, the origin (of) which is besides very ancient, have no other object then to direct in the observance of a kind of cultus at a reduced rate, which should procure the same advantages as the great sacrifices."[6]

These magic practices are of two kinds- the 'white' and the 'black'. Where as 'white' magic refers to the *bheṣajani* or the auspicious practices, and 'black' refers to *abhicara* or *ghora*.[7]

For each Veda, there are separate *vidhāna* texts - Ṛg Vidhāna, for Ṛgveda, composed by Śaunaka; Samávidhāṇa Brahmaṇa (not a real Brahmaṇa) for Sāmaveda; ŚhuklaYajur Vidhāna Sūtras for white Yajura by Kātyāyana (a grand disciple of Śaunaka); and Kauśika Sūtras (though not a *vidhāna*, but regarded as a representation of Atharvaveda Vidhāna) composed by Kauśika, about whom we know very little. Śaunaka's composition is belived to be of around ~ 500 BC period.

Just as Brahmaṇas laid down procedures of *śrauta* rituals and application of mantras to *yajña* to achieve *kāmya*, *vidhāna* laid down procedure for achieving *kāmya* through magical power of mantras. An important feature of *vidhāna* is use of Vedaic mantra in truncated *pratika* (symbolic) form.

Pratika, meaning a symbol, are usually the first few words, or a part of the Vedic mantra, used in place of the whole mantra. In Ṛgvedic schools, if the first quarter verse (*pada*) of the mantra is recited, then the whole verse is indicated; if less than a *padā* is recited, then a whole sūkta hymn is indicated; and if more than a *padā* is cited, then a triplet is indicated. It will not be wrong to say that *vidhānas* are an abridged version of *śrauta* and *smṛta* rituals relying on the magical power of mantras to attain the objective or *phala*.

The period from 500-300 BC was one of turmoil for Āryans in India. A rapidly urbanizing society, suffocating in ritualism and disenchanted with Brahminism, was experiencing serious exodus to Buddhism and Jainism. Even the rich, who could afford expensive *śrauta* ceremonies, and the young, who had numerous new opportunities that the urbanization offered, were getting disillusioned with the ritualism of Vedic life and taking to the life of *śramaṇas* and acetic wonderers. Questions were being raised on the efficacy of Vedic mantras from within the Āryan fold. Through his famous six questions, Kautsa attacked the very roots of Veda by calling mantras meaningless and nothing more than a mere conglomerate of words[8]! The resilient Hinduism did not lie low, it fought back - fiercely and effectively. On one hand, reformists initiated debates on the 'superiority of knowledge over rituals' and the unity of *Ātman* with *Brahman*, on the other hand, *ācāryas* like Yaska effectively countered questions on the efficacy of Vedic mantras through the grand work of Nirukta. Sages like Jaiminy put forward formidable reasoning in the form of *Mimāmsa* to counter the anti-Vedic wave, at times going too far - insisting that every single word of the Vedas is meaningful. *Vidhāna* was one more such attempt by sages like Śaunaka and Kātyāyana to reassert the importance of Vedas and power of mantras.

Śaunaka was an orthodox *vedin* and Kātyāyana his grand disciple. Both believed that the mantras had magical powers and through its recitation - even a few words - almost anything could be achieved. In the *vidhāna* scheme of things, time consuming and tedious *śrauta* and *smṛta* rituals were replaced by short ceremonies using *pratikas* (part of mantras), *japa* and *homa*. An exhaustive list detailing suitable mantras for attainment of specific objectives was compiled in text form. In the modern-day language, *vidhāna* is a targeted delivery system wherein for specific end results, use of specific mantras and their method of application is prescribed. For these two staunch followers of Veda, composing the *vidhāna* texts was an extension of their valuable work of indexing (*anukramaṇīs*) the hymns, seers, metres and deities, in the order they occur in the various Vedic *Saṃhitās*. Out of the five *anukramaṇīs* ascribed to Śaunaka, the three extant ones are the Arshanukaramani, which gives the seers of the Ṛgveda; the Candonukramani, which enumerates the meters in which the Ṛgvedic hymns are composed; and the Anuvākakramani, which give the *pratikas* of each of the 85 *anuvākas* of the Ṛgveda and the number of hymns contained in them.

The Sarvānukramaṇīs of Kātyāyana composed in the *sūtras* style is a more systematic work. It combines the data contained in all the *anukramaṇīs* listed above and for every hymn in the Ṛgveda, even a single verse, it gives the *pratika*, the number of verses, as well as the ṛṣi, the deity, and the metres, respectively.

Although the *anukramaṇīs* and the *vidhānas* do not form part of the *vedānga* literature, they are inseparable from the auxiliary literature of the Vedas on account of their close relation with the *kalpa*.

Śaunaka, in his *vidhāna*, lists long life (*āyuṣ*), heaven (*svarga*), wealth (*dravinam*) and sons (*sunnavah*) as the four-fold objects of desire in this life. All of these, according to him, can be achieved through mantras - if employed using correct method, and in conformity to the precepts. Self-control, freedom from envy and enmity, truthfulness, endurance and tranquillity are the (important) means of achieving these four desires. To overcome miseries, the *vidhāna* asks the twice-born to engage in prayers (*japa*) and burnt offerings (*homa*).

The inclusion of objects of desires, such as countering poison (*viśaghnam*) and hostility (*vidveśam*), and removing disease (*roganāśam*) and propitiating (*samvananam*), in the eyes of many, made the *vidhānas*, an 'inferior way' and a 'way of magic and charms'. Whereas it is easy to defend use of religion in curing disease - in pre Christian era curing disease through religious rites was a common practice - use of religion to win charm of a woman next door, or making a man impotent, do make *vidhānas* appear 'an inferior way'.

Importance of *Vidhāna*

The importance of *vidhāna* lies in the way it changed the way the society practised religion. *Yajña*, which was always central to the religion of Āryans, along with the rituals, had become all important in the time of the Brahmaṇas. So much so that *yajñas*, initially considered a medium for carrying food (through the fumes) to the manes and propitiating gods, were now believed to have power to compel even the gods to deliver the desired results. Even though mantras were important because without their recitation *yajñas* could not be completed, they were second to *yajña* in importance. The *vidhāna* changed this scheme of things by making *yajña* secondary in importance, thus rendering the elaborate rituals of *śrauta* and *gṛhya* nearly obsolete. The mantra power, through *pratikas*, was brought centre stage in the *vidhāna* way of doing things, and *homa* was pushed away from the place it occupied on the high pedestal.

Vidhāna, undoubtedly, was a conscious effort to provide an easy and affordable means of fulfilling everyday common desires (*kāmya*) by using the power of Vedic mantras without having to go through tedious, time-consuming and expensive rituals. In this scheme, the belief in the efficacy of Vedic mantras remained intact, while the rituals which had taken *yajñas* out of reach of an ordinary man were marginalised. An important feature of the *vidhāna* practices is that it offers solutions for everyday problems ranging from want of a potential spouse, undivided attention of the husband (by eliminating the influence of a co-wife), protection from wild animals during long journeys, and prevention and cure from life-threatening diseases. These every day '*kāmya*' (desires) were fundamentally different from desire for afterlife in *svarga* or *go-loka* that *śrauta* and most *smṛta* rituals offered.

Nearly all everyday issues could be tackled with the help of a specific mantra or charm. It was no more left to the army of sixteen or seventeen priests to conduct an elaborate *putraprāpti* (begetting a son) *yajña*, which king Dasaratha performed in the Rāmāyaṇa. The same objective (*kāmya*) could be achieved by any ordinary man through a simple, inexpensive *vidhāna* procedure employing basic resources and services of a single priest.

This was no ordinary change. By making mantras a tool of 'daily use' for a common man who was less bothered about attaining moksha than improving the declining harvest yield, or earning more money in his business, *vidhāna* practices dealt a devastating blow to *śrauta* and *smṛta* rituals. Moreover, it broke the stranglehold of priests and the ritualism associated with *yajña*-centric Āryans' religious practices. The consequent collateral damage to *śrauta* and *smṛta* practices was immense. A society which had so far aimed at noble rewards, such as an afterlife in *svargaloka* or *brahmāloka*, suddenly started using knowledge of the Vedic mantras for mundane and often 'baser' objectives like destroying enemies and winning favours of a neighbour's wife.

This shift was important in another way too - once the people broke through the rigid shell of Vedic ritualism centred around sacrifices, they were open to any other form of worship. Thus, apart from the traditional Vedic gods, gods like *Viṣṇu*, *Śiva* and *Sarasvatī* started emerging in the *gṛhya sūtras*, and getting worshipped differently. Clothes, fragrances and seats were offered to them instead of mere oblations in fire. This new form of worship of gods in their anthropomorphic forms came to be known as *pūjā*. Probably it was also a consequence of emergence of personal gods.

∞

Āgama* and *Tantra - Another push towards *pūjā* came from the *āgama* and tantric practices. These are non-Vedic texts and many believe that the *āgamic* tradition belongs to the pre Mauryan period (322-298 AD). A few references to this tradition, which blossomed in the Puraṇic times with emergence of multiple mythologies and gods, are found in the Atharvaveda. *Āgamas* are a collection of Sanskrit and Tamil *grantha* scriptures, chiefly dealing with construction of temples, *mūrti* making, worshipping deities, meditative practices, and philosophical doctrines. Tantrism, linked with *āgama*, is a widely misunderstood term; people usually associate it with magic, sorcery and dark practices, which is untrue. Professor Ariel Glucklich, a PhD from Harvard, offers courses in Hinduism, Psychology of Religion and Anthropology of Religion. According to him, "Scholars generally define tantrism as the use of specialized ritual techniques to achieve both ritual liberation (*jivanmukti*) and worldly perfection (*siddhi*) without renouncing the world or denying its value. The origins of this religious outlook are shrouded in mystery, but it clearly owed more to Atharvaveda and Ayurveda than to the Veda and Upaniṣads."[9]

According to Kulluka, a commentator during 1150-1300 AD, on Manu 2.1, the Harita Dharma Sūtra opens with the words - "*Vaidiki tantrums caviar dvividha śrutih kirtita*", meaning,

"Now then we shall explain Dharma; Dharma based upon the revealed texts *Śruti*; revealed texts are of two kinds, the Vedik and the Tantrik."[10]

Here Tantrism is unambiguously called a revealed text, just as Vedism.

Pūjā occupies an important place in *āgama* or tantric literature of the *śaivas*, *vaiśnavas* and *śaktas*, as well as different smaller groups like *pāśupatas*, *nāthas*, worshippers of *dattātreya*, and *vīra-śaivas*. Tantrism of the *vāmācāra* or *vāmāpantha* (practices of leftists) associated with *aghoras* and *kāpālikas*, who often live and conduct *pūjā* and other tantrik practices in the *śmaśana* (cremation or burning grounds), such as drinking wine out of a human skull and eating raw meat (at times of a corpse), is undeniably a part of the *śakta* tantric practices, but a small part of *śaktism*. *Śakta* are those who worship *Śakti* in her many manifestations - and the *vāmāpanthic* practices occupy a very small, yet important, space in *śaktaism*. According to Woodroffe, "this ritual, whatever may in truth be said against it, was not understood; that it was completely ignored that the Tantras contained a remarkable philosophic presentment of religious teaching, profoundly applied in a ritual of psychological worth." The strong sentiment against tantrism (*vāmāpantha*) continues to make us ignore, indeed detest tantrism. In the words of Woodroffe, we overlook "that the *śastras* were also a repertory of the alchemy, medicine, law, religion, art and so forth of their time. It was sufficient to mention the word "tantra" and there was supposed to be the end of the matter."[11]

Be that as it may, *śakta* is a very popular form of worship of *Śakti* as *Mahādevi* or *Pārvatī*. She is considered the real power behind *Śiva*.

Śaivas and *Vaiśnavas*, as the name suggests are worshippers of *Śiva* and *Viṣṇu*, two major sects of *mūrti pūjā*.

These *pūjā* practices are identified as *āgama* or tantrik in contradistinction with the Vedic practices which are called *nigama* or never changing. Another distinguishing feature of the *āgama* is that they refer to non-Vedic texts which were accessible to all, unlike Vedas, which were accessible only to three *varṇa*s.

∞

Pūjā is a ritual of worship of a deity (in the form of an idol or a picture) or anything considered sacred, such as a man (guru), a mountain (*Kailāsa*), a river (Ganges), a tree (*vata vṛiksha*) or even an animal (snake or elephant). *Archana* and *pūjāna* are synonyms of *pūjā*.

Offerings are a common feature of all *pūjās* made with or without any ritualism, and more importantly, with or without the accompaniment of any mantras, Vedas or otherwise. Though offerings are a common feature in any *pūjā*, big or small, it's quality or quantity is of no importance. It can be almost anything - a few drops of water, a flower, few leaves of a plant, fragrance or sandalwood paste. Likewise, the *pūjā* itself can be an elaborate, structured affair of a sequence of offerings, *homa*, et cetera, or simple acts - of bowing the head and joining palms or murmuring a simple praise like 'Jai ho' while standing in front of an image. A properly organised *pūjā* consists of a sequence of offerings called *upacāras* which consist of five or sixteen offerings, i.e., *panca* or *ṣoḍaśa upacāras*. These two are the standard *upacāras* which continue to be performed even in our present time.

As one would have noticed, offerings are a common denominator in Vedic sacrifices as well as non-Vedic form of worship (*pūjā*), which many believe existed in the pre-Vedic period among non-Āryans.

Earliest records of the *pūjā* form of worship are found in Baudhāyana Gṛhya Śeṣa-sūtras (*Śeṣa* - appendix, or supplement - Oxford Hindi-English Dictionary). These *sūtras* describe *Viṣṇu pūjā* as a mixture of *pūjā* and Vedic rituals. Vaikhansa Śrauta Sūtras also deal with the worship of *Viṣṇu* in a similar manner.

While the Baudhāyana Gṛhyasūtras belong to the 500-300 BC period, its appendix, the Śeṣasūtras, are of an uncertain later day origin. However, in the Agniveṣa GS, which are texts of a much later origin, full blown *pūjā* accounts giving additional details of worship of *navagrahas* (nine planets), *Viṣṇu bali* and other gods, complete with offerings of *vastra* (garment), *gandha* (fragrance), *puṣpam* (flower), *dhūpa* (incense) and *anulepan* (unugeten) are provided.[12]

(अथ देवमावाहयामि इति केशवदीनामभिरवाहया अथ वस्त्रं प्रदाय युवं वस्त्राणि इति अथ गन्धं प्रदाय गन्धद्वाराम इति अथ पुष्पम प्रदाय यो अपाम पुष्पम वेद इति अथ धूपं प्रदाय धूरसि इति अथ दीपं प्रदाय इति तच्छेषेणानुलेपनं करोति ।)

Interestingly, all three *sūtra* compositions (Baudhāyana, Vaikhansa and Agniveṣa) above are from South India, indicating that by this period, South India had truly taken to *mūrti pūjā* without giving up its old Vedic traditions. But after reading *Parṣishta* of *Gṛhyasūtras* (*Śeṣasūtras*), by Aśvālanya - a sage from north India, it becomes evident that *pūjā* was not a south specific. These *sūtras* provide a long list of non-Vedic gods, such as *Sarasvati* 15.2, *Śiva* 11.22, *Vasudeva* 2.6.2, *Hare*, *Mahādeva*, *Śaṅkara*, *Īśāna* 4.8.9.

In Baudhāyana's Śeṣasūtra, there is a proper description of consecration of idol worship of *Viṣṇu* and *Rudra-Śiva*. The consecration description is followed by instructions (when, where and how) to perform *pūjās* (2.13 ff) of *Durgā*, *Sarasvati*, *Vināyaka*, *Ravi*, *Viṣṇu*, *Rudra*, *Śrī*, *Upaśruti* and *Jyēṣṭha* (3.3ff). A subsequent section of the *sūtra* goes on to describe *punḥpratisṭhā*, the procedure of re-consecration to be followed if the worship of an idol had been neglected for some time.

In *Viṣṇu's* consecration, according to Baudhāyana Śeṣasūtras, starting with a seat (*kurca*) *Viṣṇu* was offered ten items in following sequence -

i. A seat (*kurca*),
ii. Water for washing feet (*pādya*),
iii. Water for sipping (*ācamaniya*),
iv. *Arghya* (water),
v. Sandalwood paste (*gandha*),
vi. Garland (*māla*),
vii. Flowers (*puṣpa*)
viii. Incense (*dhūpa*)
ix. Lamp (*dīpa*)
x. Food (*pāyasa* - a sweet milk and rice preparation)

Each offering was made with a submission - a typical gift of flower (*puṣpam dadāti*) is prescribed (*praśna* 2.13.29) with the following pronouncement -

पुष्पं ददाति
इमे पुष्पाश्शुभा दिव्यांस्सर्वपुष्पैरलङ्कृताः।
पूता ब्रह्मापवित्रेण पुतास्सूर्यस्य रश्मिभिः २९

A similar procedure - with some variations - is required to be followed for other offerings as well. Remarkably, the same procedure is followed in *Viṣṇu pūjā* even today.

The consecration of *Rudra-Śiva* follows an almost identical course.

The worship of *Durgā*, *Vināyka*, *Viṣṇu*, et cetera is given separately in BGS (appendix 3.3 onwards). The section (3.13) called '*Durgā Kalpam*', sacred precepts or law for *Durgā* worship, starts on an auspicious time, the earlier part of *krattika nakṣatra*. The typical format includes preparation and cleaning of a place of an area equal in size to a cow hide, and offering a chair and sacred thread to *Durgā*, followed by various invocations and prayers for her blessings. This format was also used in worshipping other deities.

We know from the Aśv GS Parṣishta that in those days, the north-Indian style of *pūjā* was more or less same as in the south, with some minor differences, such as inclusion of half a dozen more offerings in Aśvalāyana's *pariṣishṭa* than Baudhāyana. The essence of *pūjā*, treating a god's idol as a living human being, and offering to an idol what one would offer a very special guest visiting home is common to both Gṛyha Śeṣasūtras. The sixteen offerings of Aśvālayana begin with an invocation and offering of seat, washing of feet, and *arghya* - a standard practice followed by the host welcoming the guru or an important guest. Thereafter, the worshipper bathed, wore new garments, and after a formal bath offered the sacred thread, followed by a series of other offerings, making the idol's reception treatment only slightly different from the one accorded to any human guest. The ceremonies concluded with offerings of food, mouth freshener, hymns of praises and the all important circumambulation before dispersal. The exact sequence of these *upacāras* remained sacrosanct. Following are Aśvā's sixteen *upacāras* -

1. Invocation (*āvāhana*)
2. Seat (*āsana*)
3. Water for washing the feet (*pādya*)
4. Water offered at the respectful reception of a guest (*arghya*)
5. Water for sipping (*acamanīya*)
6. Bath (*snāna*)
7. Garments (*vastra*)
8. Sacred thread (*upavita*)
9. Sandalwood paste (*gandha*)
10. Flowers (*puṣpa*)
11. Incense (*dhūpa*)
12. Lamp (*dīpa*)
13. Food (*naivedya*)
14. Mouth perfume (*mukha-vāsa*)
15. Hymn (*stotra*) and prostration (*praṣama*)
16. Circumambulation (*pradakṣinā*) and dismissal (*visarjana*)

Ṛg vidhāna, which deals with the worship of *Viṣṇu*, also lists sixteen services (*upacāras*) - beginning with *āvāhana* or invocation, and ending with *pradakṣinā* (circumambulation) and *dāna* (gift). These *upacāras*, and a few other *pūjā* rites, are accompanied by mantra's *pratīkas* from the Ṛgveda. Adoption of shortened form of Vedic mantras in Ṛg vidhāna practices indicating reduced importance of Vedic practices, is a classic example of how Hinduism never entirely rejects any of its old practices while moving on with the changes.

Thus, the arrival of *pūjā* also did not signal end of the Vedic form of worship centred around *yajñas* and mantras.

Among the earlier *smṛtis*, Manu's (200 BC-100 AD) does not described any *pūjā*, though it does talk of '*devatābhyarchana*' or worship (of image of god)[13]. Unlike Manu's text, Yājñavalkya's smṛti, a later text (100- 300 AD), does contain verses of *vināyaka pūjā* and *gṛhya śānti*. But, it is in *smṛtis* of 600 AD and thereafter that *navagraha pūjā* (worship of the nine planets) and *gṛhya śānti* (pacification), consecration of images, *vratas*, glorification of *tīrtha*, *saṃdhyā*, *homa*, et cetera became important topics. Purāṇas of this period (600 AD and later), like Śiva, Nārada, Agni, Padāma and Garuda are very rich in *pūjā* details.[14] By this time, *pūjā* had obviously blossomed fully and nearly replaced the Vedic *yajñas*, both from the private and the public life.

Medieval writers came to look upon *vaiśvadeva* as *devayajña*, while others held the view that *homa* to gods was different from *vaiśvedevā* (Hardatta, 1150-1300 on Āp.DS. I.4.13.1).

According to Smritymuktaphala by Vaidyanatha Dikshita - composed sometime about or after 1700 AD - which covers several branches of *Āhnika* (Āhnika p 383), quoting Māric and Harita, both authorities on *āhnika* - "*Devapūjā* is performed after morning *homa*, or after *Brahmāyajña* and *tarpaṇa* in the noon."[15]

So far, the most elaborate edited treatise on *pūjā* is Pūjā-Prakāśa by Mitramisra whose literary activity was between 1610 and 1640 AD. It forms the fourth part of the twenty-two sections of a monumental work called Vīramitrodaya. The PP is divided into several parts according to the five deities: *Viṣṇu*, *Śiva*, *Sūrya*, *Durgā* and god *Brahman*, which were probably the main deities worshipped in northern India at that time.

Readers may find it interesting to see (Table T-2) how over last 100 years, starting 1918, *pūjā* changed.

Chapter 32

Rules of deity worship - *Vidhi* of *Mūrti Pūjā*

Generally, when we talk of *pūjā*, it is understood in the sense of *mūrti pūjā* or idol worship. In fact, the word 'icon' itself is defined by the Oxford dictionary as 'a devotional painting of Christ or another holy figure, typically executed on wood…'. But, in context of Hindu worship, word icon is not restricted to a picture or painting; it is not even limited to an idol of a god. It relates to one of several objects which are worshipped. Beginning with the four elements - earth, water, air and fire - Hindus also practice *pūjā* of humans - *guru pūrṇimā* (worshipping the guru), *kumāri pūjā* (worshipping young pre-puberty girls during *navrātri* festival), *batuka-pūjā* (worshipping young boys after the *upanayana*), and plants and trees, for example - *tulsī pūjā*, especially on *tulsī vivāha* days, and *vata* or Banyan tree *pūjā*, especially during *vatasāvitri vrata*. Coconut and areca nuts are invariably used in the *Satyanārāyaṇa kathā* (*pūjā*) representing different deities. Then there is the famous example of Bharata, son of king Daśaratha, who worshipped the *caraṇ pāduka* (wooden sandals) of his eldest brother Rāma for fourteen long years while Rāma was in exile. Even implements and vessels used in conducting *pūjā* are entitled to *pūjā* - the water vessel *kumbha* or *kalaśa*, the small brass bell, the conch shell, et cetera. Even the ground on which *homa* is to be performed is washed and often given a coat of cow dung - *sthandila* - before it is worshipped. The list is endless.

A list of main items that are usually required for *pūjā*, and basic preparations is given below:

- *Kumbha* or *kalaśa* is integral to every *pūjā* - *Kumbha* is a narrow-necked copper (sometimes brass) vessel which is filled with water, and is a symbol of plenty and welfare. During the *pūjā*, the vessel is never ever kept empty. It is filled with water mixed with other auspicious objects to the chants of Vedic mantras. Typically, *durba* grass, twigs of mango tree, sandal paste, *akṣata* (unbroken rice) as a substitute for jewels, areca nuts and usually gold (a gold coin) are mixed with the water and the mouth of the vessel is covered with a shallow bowl filled with unbroken rice or other grains. The vessel is seated on a heap of grains for stability. It is then covered with mango leaves and a piece of red cloth tied around it. The auspicious sign of *svastika* is drawn on the vessel and an areca nut is placed in the small cover on top representing the main deity. Many times, a coconut - also representing the main deity - is kept on the mouth of the *kalaśa*.

The choice of icon materials are restricted to

i. Stone
ii. Wood
iii. Clay
iv. Sand
v. Metal
vi. Jewels
vii. Painted figure

Quoting Skāṇḍa Purāṇa, Pūjā Prakāśa[1] allows all the above, except sand. In a descending order, jewels are considered the best, and clay is the least preferred material.

- Clothes - Only unstitched, clean, freshly washed cotton, silk or woollen clothing is allowed for men during the *pūjā*. The lower garment is a *dhotī*, usually a six-yard long piece of cloth tied round the waist, while the upper garment is a sufficiently long piece of cloth called *pravaraṇa*. Women use *saubhāgya* marks (marks indicating blessed state of women, especially married women, e.g. vermilion in hair parting) and are appropriately dressed in a saree and blouse for the *pūjā*. Both men and women are required to keep their heads covered during the ceremony.
- Seat - The place of worship is swept clean, and washed and plastered with cow dung, if possible. The worshipper must be seated preferably facing east or north. He should not sit in direct contact with the ground and must use an *āsana* (mat). In a descending order, the preferred *āsana* materials include deer skin, wool, cotton or unsacrificial wood. *Āsanas* made of bamboo, sacrificial wood, brass, green leaves or stone are not to be used.

The deity and *navagrahas* are installed on a metal plate kept on a wooden *caukī* - a low stool, washed, cleaned and usually covered with a new unstitched red cloth. Sometimes the deity is directly kept on the red cloth itself.

- Flowers - There are detailed rules about flowers. Flowers of thorny plants are not to be used, unless they are white, sweetly fragrant, and red in colour; those springing in ponds or lakes may be employed. Flowers with overpowering smells or no smell at all are not to be used. In order of preference, *vanamalika* (wild *Jasminium grandiflorum*), *campaka* (*Michelia campaca*), *aśoka* (Jonesia asoka), *vāsanti* (a variety of Jasmine), *mālati* (a variety of Jasmine) and *kuṇḍa* (Jasmine) are considered suitable. Some flowers are specifically used for worshipping particular deities. For example, for *Śiva* worship, *arka, karavira*, blue lotus, *dhaturā* flower, and leaves of *apamārga, bilva, sami* and blue lotus are considered most suitable. For *Viṣṇu*, the *jati* flower is considered the best.

The flowers should be plucked after the morning bath, and are not to be washed because un-plucked flowers are considered pure. A mere sprinkling of water makes them suitable for use in *pūjā*. But once plucked, they should not be smelt or kept in an unclean place. Before offering fresh flowers to the deity, flowers offered the previous day are removed. These flowers, called '*nirmalya*', are treated with great reverence. According to Smṛti Candrikā (I point page 204), those who touch *nirmalya* to their head, never fall from their place in heaven[2].

Damaged or burnt flowers and flower buds are considered unsuitable for *pūjā*.

- Water - Another very important article used in *pūjā*, water should be freshly drawn the same day. Water collected and kept overnight should not be used for *devapūjā* or the rites.
- Conch shell, brass lamp, brass bell and other small implements employed in the *pūjā* are thoroughly cleaned, washed, dried and kept ready for use. Just like the idols, *pūjā* utensils, conch shell and the bell are never kept on the bare ground, but on the *caukī*. Many a times, a small heap of grain is used as a seat for *Gauri* and *Gaṇeśa* when areca nuts are used as a substitute for them. A general principle observed is that objects which have been in contact with the divine power are not kept directly on the ground.

∞

Prāṇa praṭhishṭhā - The icon by itself is nothing more than a toy in the shape of a deity. For it to become the deity, it is instilled with *prāṇa* (breath) or life. In Hinduism, the rite of infusing *prāṇa*, in an otherwise inanimate object, is crucial to idol worship. The rites and rituals associated with this process are called *prāṇa praṭishṭhā*. The moment an idol is damaged, it ceases to be fit for worship.

There are three types of *pūjā*:

i. Daily and regular (*nitya*) *pūjā*
ii. Occasional (*naimittika*) *pūjā*
iii. Optional (*kāmya*) *pūjā*

The daily or *nitya pūjā*, enjoined as a duty of the householder, must follow strict timings - morning before sunrise, midday or noon, and at the time of sunset. In a sense, *nitya pūjā* follows the Vedic *saṃdhyā* pattern, which is also performed thrice daily at the same times. If it is not possible to perform *pūjā* in its proper form three times in a day, then an elaborate *pūjā* is prescribed to be done in the morning (considered most suitable for worshipping gods), and in the afternoon and evening in a short form.

Usually, even *kāmya pūjās* are performed and concluded in the forenoon.

Preliminaries

- *Āchamana* - The act of sipping water at the root of the thumb (considered '*Brahman tīrtha*') in the right hand palm, curled in the shape of a cow's ear, is *āchamana*. This act is a means of achieving inner purification using the great purifier, water. *Āchamana* is prescribed at the beginning of all ritual acts.
- *Prāṇayāma* - It is breath control while reciting mantras. It consists of three stages - inhalation called *pūraka*, retention called *kumbhaka*, and exhilaration called *recaka* - done in a sequence in which the nostrils are closed using the thumb and a finger in the prescribed manner. The mantras employed are - the syllable *auṃ* (*prāṇava*), which is to be connected with each of the utterances (*vyāhṛtis*) of names of the seven worlds; the *gāyatri mantra*; and the *gāyatṛṣisha mantras*. There are different ways of employing mantras to the three stages of *prāṇayāma*. An example of the seven *vyāhṛtis* is - *oṁ bhuḥ oṁ bhuvaḥ oṁ svaḥ oṁ mahāḥ oṁ janaḥ oṁ tapaḥ oṁ satyaṁ*
- Salutation - Gods, parents and all *brahmaṇas* are invoked to make the conduct of the *pūjā* free of hurdles and obstacles. *Gaṇeśa*, the destroyer of all hurdles, tops this list. A typical salutation to the village deity is *grāma-devatābhyo namaḥ*. Roughly meaning - homage or obeisance to village deity; exactly the same homage is repeated for all those who are invoked.

Salutation are offered to the noble great leader of the troops (*Gaṇeśa*); *Lakṣmi* and *Nārāyaṇa* (*Viṣhnu*); *Umā* and *Maheśvara* (*Śiva*); *Śachi* and *Índra*; father and mother; favorite deities; the deities of the family; the deities of the village; the deities of the place; the deities of the house; the deities of the nine heavenly bodies (*navagraha*) beginning with the sun; all gods; all *brahmaṇas*; and the deities presiding over this rite.

- Prayer - Verses are addressed to *Gaṇapaṭi*, mother goddess, *Viṣṇu*, various other deities, *Gaṇapaṭi* again, *Brahman*, *Viṣṇu* and *Śiva* seeking their protection.
- Place, time and aim declaration - *saṃkalpa* (vow or resolution) are rites in which the devotee makes a commitment. While declaring his resolution and the purpose for which he is conducting this *pūjā*, *yajmāna* gives his own name, *gotra*, the exact coordinates of his location, and time in accordance with the almanac, for example -

Today, in the second grand half of *Brahman*, in the noble *śveta-vārāha-kalpa*, in the epoch of *vaivasvata manu*, in the twenty-eigth *yuga* out of the unit of four *yugas*, in the first quarter of *kaliyuga*, in the Jambu continent, in the country of

Bharata, in the north/south/east/west region, XXX city/ village, under the auspices of the Buddha incarnation, in the year named X, in the month X, in the X (bright/ dark) half of the month, on the lunar date X, on the day X; I, X *gotra*, X Sharma/ Varma/Gupta, shall perform *pūjā* in the morning/noon/evening for obtaining the fruit for myself, which is vouched for in the *śruti*, *smṛti* and the Purāṇas; for obtaining for us with family and dependents' increase of happiness, stability, life, health, wealth and all-out prosperity; for the satisfaction of the noble deity so and so; with the materials of service as they are available, I shall perform *pūjā* with five/sixteen services.

If the *pūjā* is for a specific purpose, it is clearly stated in the *saṃkalpa*.

From region to region, there are minor variations in the above *saṃkalpa* format, but these pronouncements must be made before the commencement of the *pūjā*. A small quantity of water is poured onto the palm of the worshipper which flows over the tip of his stretched middle finger called *devāya tīrtha* into a metal dish kept under the arm, while he pronounces, "I perform worship", thus making a commitment to perform the *pūjā*. Without the saṃkalpa performance, *pūjā* yields only a part of its benefits.

- Remembering *Gaṇapaṭi* (*Gaṇapaṭi smaraṇa*) - *Gaṇeśa* is recalled through prayers and mantras, but this time alone unlike in the prayer above (in point 4), where he, along with many other deities is remembered for making the *pūjā* free of interruptions or hindrances. As we know, many mantras employed in *pūjā* are from Vedas; mantra employed in *Gaṇapaṭi* worship - *ganānāṁ tvā gaṇapatiṁ havāmahe* - is a Ṛgvedic mantra, which though originally addressed to Brahmaṇaspati (RV 2.23.1) uses the word *Gaṇapaṭi*. It is employed in the *Gaṇeśa smaraṇa* because of this *viniyoga*.[3]
- Offering seat - Three rites are performed here: for the earth's support for a firm and stable seat; driving away evil spirits and inviting gods; and removing human odour (*manuṣyagandha*). For successful performance of the *pūjā*, a firm and stable support of earth is a must and a mantra is employed for invocating the same. The devotee is not supposed to move once he occupies a seat, until completion of the *pūjā*. While performing the mantra, the devotee keeps his left hand turned upwards on his right knee, and anything that is kept in the upturned palm is then covered with the right hand. While performing this ritual, the worshipper is seated on an *āsana* (mat of cloth, wool, grass or deer skin).

The worshipper then recites three mantras to drive away evil spirits, bows to *Bhairava*, hits the ground with the heel of his left foot thrice in a symbolic gesture of driving away evil spirits, and makes hand gestures (*nyāsa*) as if to drive away the spirits.

For removing human odour or *manuṣyagandha*, two mantras from the Ṛgveda (10.6 3.3 and 4.5 0.6) are recited. The chosen mantras have *viniyoga* connection with *manuṣyagandha*.

Nyāsa - This is a Sanskrit term, literally meaning 'placing, putting down or inserting'.[4] In *anga nyāsa*, the body is stabilised and readied before meditation by touching different parts of the body and reciting appropriate mantra. The sixteen verses of *Puruṣasūkta* are assigned to sixteen limbs of the worshipper's body - to each hand, foot, knees, hips (lower waist), arms, eyes, head, mouth, throat, heart and the navel. In the second instance, *nyāsa* is performed by touching the heart, head, the top knot and shoulders while employing the last five verses of *Puruṣasūkta*. Uttering 'for the weapon phat' (in Sanskrit), the worshipper strikes the palm of his left-hand with the index and middle finger of the right-hand, producing a slight sound.

- Worship of the *kalaśa* (jar of water in which twigs/leaves of sacred tree have been put) - This is done by invoking deities. The vessel is filled with water; it is believed that *Viṣṇu*, *Rudra*, *Brahman*, the mother goddesses, the sea, earth and the four Vedas reside in its various parts. An eight-petal lotus is drawn where the *kalaśa* must be installed. Various auspicious objects as described earlier are added to the water one by one accompanied by mantras. Various gods and goddesses, and the holy rivers, the *Gaṃgā*, *Yamunā*, *Godāvari*, *Sarasvatī*, *Narmadā*, *Sindhu* and *Kāveri* are invited in this water.

While some offer all *upacāras* to the *kalaśa*, others offer only *gandha*, *akṣata* and *puṣpa*.

- Conch shell, bell and lamp worship - Uttering the sacred syllable *oṁ*, the conch shell is filled with water from the vessel (*kalaśa*). Several verses are recited describing the residence of the deities - moon, *Varuṇa*, *Prajāpati* and the rivers *Gaṃgā* and *Sarasvatī* - in different parts of the conch. The conch is then worshipped by offering sandalwood paste and a flower. Unbroken rice (*akṣata*), is not offered to the conch. Finally, the conch (*śaṅkha*) *mudrā* is made imitating the shape of a conch. *Mudrās* are shapes that are made using fingers of one or both hands. In Yogic meditation too they have great significance - it is believed they stablise body and mind.

The bell is washed and rung by the worshipper imitating the shape - *mudra* - of a bell. The bell ringing announces arrival of the gods and is believed to drive demons away. Devotee worships it by offering sandalwood paste, unbroken rice (*akṣata*) and a flower. The bell is then kept on the left hand side in front of the devotee, while the conch is kept on the right side.

Oil lamp is worshipped reciting Ṛgvedic hymn where *Índra* 'smashed apart the nine and ninety walls of *Sambara*' (RV. VI.47.21), symbolizing the oil lamp drives away darkness the way *Índra* destroyed ninety nine forts of *dasyu Sambara*.

- Sprinkling with water (*prokṣaṇa*) - In Hindu religion water is considered a universal purifier and sprinkling with water is part of *śrauta* ritual. By sprinkling water from the vessel and the conch by a flower or *durva* grass, the worshipper by purifying himself prepares self and the utensils for *pūjā*.

Following mantra, a purificatory verse - used on many other similar occasions - is recited. It essentially means, he who having sprinkled with water from the jar and the conch remembers *puṇḍarikākṣaṁ*, i.e. lotus eyed *Viṣṇu*, is cleansed within (mentally) and without (bodily) of all impurities.

(*prokṣaṇa*)
apavitraḥ pavitro vā sarvāvasthāṁ gato 'pi vā |
yaḥ smaret puṇḍarikākṣaṁ sa bahyābhyantaraṁ suciḥ ||
ātmānaṁ prokṣya | pūjā dravyāṇi ca saṁprokṣayet |

Having thus purified himself, the devotee also sprinkles the *pūjā* utensils.

- Meditation - worshipper collects flowers or unbroken rice in the hollow of the joined hands and recites the meditation verses. The flowers, consecrated by the mantras, are then offered to the deity.

The laudatory verses - they differ from place to place- are recited praising the five deities (*Viṣṇu, Śiva, Gaṇeśa, Sūrya, Devī*). Since the verses are chosen keeping in mind description of special attributes of the deity, it helps the devotee think of the physical form of the deity (*viniyoga*) and meditate on it.

Though the devotee is expected not only to recite the verse, but also to meditate on the form of the deity, in reality, the meditation is reduced to simple recitation of verses.

Viṣṇu, Śiva, Gaṇeśa, Sūrya, Devī are arranged in such a way that one's favorite deity is placed in the center, surrounded by the other deities arranged in a particular order. The verse addressed to the favourite deity (here: *Viṣṇu*) is recited first.

Śiva		*Gaṇeśa*
	Viṣṇu	
Devi		*Sūrya*

Ṣoḍaśopacāra **and** ***pancopcāra*** **(daily** ***Pūjā*** **)**

First a word about *upacāra*. The *upacāras* or services are imitation of how a revered and important guest was invited and treated on his arrival. Gods are similarly invited (*āvāhana*) and offered a seat upon arrival. As per the tradition, feet of the guests were washed with water (*pādya*) mixed with auspicious objects offered to signify his honour. Just as the human guest acknowledged the honour by accepting water offered in the hollow of his palm and pouring it out, *arghya* or water for the hands is offered to the murti. This is followed by water offered for sipping (*ācamana*), an act of purification. Like any guest who arrived after a long journey, the idol of the deity is offered a bath (*snāna*), and because the guest in this case is no ordinary guest, the *snāna* consists of a series of baths with curd, milk, honey, *ghī* and sugar, and finally water mixed with sandalwood paste. Kings too, at the time of their coronation, were given bath with milk, juice, sugar et cetera. Each of the five baths is followed by a pure water bath, *ācamana* and sandalwood paste, unbroken rice and flower offering.

Upacāras

The sixteen *Upacāras*

As mentioned earlier, there is no unanimity in the texts as to which sixteen *upacāras* constitute part of *ṣoḍaśopacāra*. Moreover the number of *upacāras* invariably exceeds sixteen, necessitating clubbing two or more services as one in order to keep the final figure as sixteen. The reason why number sixteen is important is because for each of the *upacāras* the mantra that is applied is taken from the famous *Puruṣa sūkta* of the tenth *manḍala* of Ṛgveda (RV. X.90), and the total number of mantras in this hymn is only sixteen. The mantras of *Puruṣa sūkta* have not been chosen for any overt link or association with the actual service being performed, their connecting link is *viniyoga*. And since the number of services usually exceed sixteen, for the spillover services mantras from Brahmaṇas or Āranyaka have been chosen following a long tradition.

An important thing that is noticeable is, the variation in types of *upacāras* chosen to constitute sixteen *shodashopacāra* occurs only after *snāna*. Upto *snāna*, all lists have common *upacāras*.

Following seven steps are common to both, the long and the short version of *pūjā*.

1. *āvāhana* (invocation)
2. *āsana* (seat)
3. *pādya* (water for washing the feet)
4. *arghya* (water for the hands)
5. *ācamanīya* (water for sipping)
6. *snāniya* (material for bath)
7. *snānottarasvalpa pūjā* (short *pūjā* after the bath)

1. *Āvāhana* (invocation) - the *pūjā* begins with the invocation to gods to come. The first mantra of *Puruṣa sūkta* is recited - inviting gods to arrive. In another mantra - from Nityakarma Pūjā Prakaśa - *Viṣṇu*, the superior of all gods, is requested to come and stay where the *pūjā* is being performed.
2. *Āsana* (seat) - He is then begged to take the jewel embedded seat. The *Puruṣa sūkta* recited on the occasion seemingly has no connect with what is being offered.

Seat is offered with salutations and pronouncement - ‘For the seat I offer a *tulsī dala* (tulsī leaf)’.

3. *Pādya* (water for washing the feet) - there was tradition of offering water for washing feet. The gods being very special guests, their feet were washed with water with the third mantra of *Puruṣa sūkta*; along with the salutations, submission was made, 'I offer water for washing the feet.'

Nityakarma PP offers *pādya* with a mantra saying - O lord, I offer the best water from the Ganga and other holy places for welcoming you to my house.

4. *Arghya* (water for the hands) - Important guests were entitled to special honour, *arghya* was one such ceremony. In this the special guest was offered water mixed with certain ingredients like, sandalwood paste, flowers, unbroken rice etc which he accepted in the hollow of the joined palms and poured out, signifying acceptance of the honor accorded. The fourth mantra of *Puruṣa sūkta* was recited on this occasion.

With salutation to the deity, submission was made - I offer *arghya*.

5. *Ācamanīya* (water for sipping) - as per the tradition, after *arghya*, guest was offered - *ācamanīya* - flavoured water to sip. This was a purifactory action. Accordingly god was also offered water flavoured with camphor, to sip with the fifth mantra of *Puruṣa sūkta*.

In Nityakarma PP the accompanying mantra says - I offer flavoured tasty cold water for *ācamana*, O god please accept it.

6. *Snāna* (bath) - These are of six kinds - (i) *payaḥ snāna* (bath with milk); (ii) *dadhi snāna* (bath with curd); (iii) *ghṛta snāna* (bath with *ghī*); (iv) *madhu snāna* (bath with honey); (v) *śarkarā snāna* (bath with sugar); and (vi) *gandodhka snāna* (bath of water with sandalwood paste).

The deity is next offered bath - first with water of sacred rivers, followed by bath with the *pancāmritas* - the five nectors viz milk, curd, *ghī*, honey and sugar, followed by sandalwood paste mixed water - *gandhodaka-snana*. The bath/s are given with recitation of *Puruṣa sūkta* and some other Ṛgvedic mantras.

Finally the deity is bathed with plain water and wiped and dried with a fresh cloth while reciting *apo hi stha*...(RV. X.9.1-3).

With salutation, submission is made offering various baths.

This sets the stage for any of the two forms of *pūjā*, short or long.

Short *pūjā* or *pūjā* with *pancopācara*

After the bath, a short *pūjā* follows where the icon is offered sandalwood paste for be-smearing the body, besides unbroken rice (as a substitute for ornaments), flowers and leaves, incense, a lamp and food. The food (usually, left-overs of the substances used for the baths with the five nectars, i.e., *pancāmrita*) is offered in a specific manner.

After the meal, water for rinsing hands and mouth, sandalwood paste for rubbing on hands, betel and a gift are offered. The worshipper performs circumambulation and prostrates himself before the icon.

Each and every offering or service is accompanied by description and purpose of the offering and one or more appropriate mantra. Thus in case of betel offering, recitation is -

pūgīphalaṁ mahad divyaṁ nāgavallī-dalair yutam |
ailālavang-samāyuktaṁ tāmbūlaṁ pratigṛhyatām ||

Meaning - Accept this whole betel, the divine areca nut together with leaves of the betel plant together with cardamom and clove.

The accompanying mantra is -

Om Viṣṇupanchaytan devatābhyo namaḥ |

Meaning - slutations to *Viṣṇu panchaytan*, i.e. *Viṣṇu* and *Shiva*, *Gaṇeśa*, *Devi* and *Sūrya* (*panchāytan* - five deities arranged with *Viṣṇu* in centre).

Offering of *tāmbūla* concludes by saying -

tambūlaṁ samarpayāmi |

Meaning - I offer betel.

Long *pūjā* or *pūjā* with *Ṣoḍaśopacāra*

1. *abhiṣeka-snāna* (*abhiṣeka* bath)
2. *vastra* (garments)
3. *upavīta* (sacred thread)
4. *saubhāgya-dravya* (substances signifying wifehood)
5. *parimāla-dravya* (aromatic substances)
6. *candana* (sandalwood paste)
7. *akṣata* (unbroken rice)
8. *puṣpa* (flowers)
9. *dhūpa* (incense)
10. *dīpa* (lamp)
11. *naivedya* (food)
12. *tambūla* (betel)
13. *phala* (fruit)
14. *dakṣiṇa* (gift)
15. *mahā-nīrājana-dīpa* (principal lamp for waving)
16. *namaskāra* (prostration)
17. *pradakṣiṇa* (circumambulation)
18. mantra *puṣpañjali* (a handful of flowers consecrated by mantras)

1. *Abhiṣeka* - The proceedings start with the *abhiṣeka* bath - a special kind of bath in which water is substituted by different fluids and the number of baths vary depending on the deity - sixteen times for *Viṣṇu*, eleven times for *Śiva*, twenty-one times for *Gaṇapaṭi*, nine times for the *Devi*, and twelve times for *Sūrya*. Several different copper implements are specifically used for *abhiṣeka*. This practice was copied from the *abhiṣeka* practice of the kings wherein, on

the occasion of *rājyabhiṣeka* (coronation), the ruler ascending the throne was given a bath by one or more liquids like milk, curd, and sugarcane juice.

A continuous stream of liquid is poured on the deity to the accompaniment of mantra - once or continuously or for a fixed number of times - depending on the deity (*Viṣṇu sūkta*: sixteen times, *Śiva* or *mahimá stotra*: eleven times, *Gaṇapaṭi Arthavaśīrṣa*: twelve times, *Śrī sūkta* for the *Devi*: nine times, and *Saurasūkta* for the sun: twelve times). These mantras are drawn from the Vedas - *Viṣṇu sūkta* from Ṛg 1.2 2.16 - 21, *Śiva* from Taittirīya 4.5.1 - 11, and *Sūrya* from Ṛgveda 1.50. Since the *Devi* and *Gaṇapaṭi* are later-day gods, they do not find mention in the mantra texts of the Vedas. An original Vedic mantra is drawn for either of them, although the mantra for the *Devi* is drawn from the later texts of the Ṛgveda khilas (5.87). The *abhiṣeka* concludes with the recitation of texts from AB. 8.7.9.

The idol is then treated to *punarabhiṣeka* (meaning one more *abhiṣeka*) imitating the practice followed in case of consecration of the kings using the eight substances - curd, honey, *ghī*, rain water fallen during sunshine, fresh sprouts of grass, green barley, liquor and *durva* grass.

The icon is thoroughly bathed with pure water, wiped dry with a piece of cloth and offered *āchamana* - water for sipping. Then, it is reinstalled in its original place with the pronouncement - 'May the deity be well established'.

2. Garments - Unstitched pieces of clothes, both lower and upper garments, are then offered. *Akṣata* or unbroken rice is often used as a substitute for garments. After the garments have been offered, sipping of water follows.
3. Sacred thread - In imitation to the practice of the *dvijas*, the male deities are offered the sacred thread on the left shoulder under the right arm. The ceremony must follow after the garments have been offered, since *yajñopavita* cannot be worn unless a person is properly dressed.
4. '*Saubhāgya*' offerings - Female deities, just like their human counterparts, are offered substances worn by a married woman, signifying that her husband is alive. These items include *cuṛi* (bracelet), vermilion on the forehead and hair parting, *maṃgala sūtra* (a special necklace), collyrium, et cetera.
5. Perfumes - Various kinds of perfumes or scents are offered to the accompaniment of Ṛgveda (V. 6.7 5.14), which strangely is in context to a hymn on a war weapon. This could be because of some *viniyoga*, which is not quite clear.
6. Sandalwood paste - Sandalwood has a special place not only in religious ceremonies, but also in the everyday life of Indians. For centuries, the lore of snakes wrapping themselves around sandalwood trees have been told and retold in many stories and poems. Sandalwood's cooling effect and medicinal properties have made *candana*, as it is called in Sanskrit and Hindi, an item for keeps among all Hindu families. In its present application, a piece of *candana* wood is rubbed on a flat stone while pouring small quantities of water to

produce a thick paste, which is then transferred to a dish to apply to the deities and foreheads of the worshippers. It is applied with the ring finger of the right hand to the deities.

The paste is offered to the deities with the accompaniment of the following mantras -

'*Oṁ* "From that great general sacrifice *ṛcas* and saṁa-hymns were born: Therefrom were horses born."

This sandalwood paste is divine sandal, rich in scent [and] very pleasing. Best of the gods, accept the sandal for besmearing.

Salutation to the deities so and so. I offer sandalwood paste.

7. Unbroken rice - Unbroken and uncooked rice called *akṣata*, Sanskrit word meaning - 'un-damaged', is used in many religious ceremonies as a substitute for an unavailable object. Here, it is used as a substitute of ornaments offered to male deities with -

    Salutation to the deities so and so. [As a substitute] for ornaments I offer unbroken rice.

8. Flowers - Flowers and leaves, plucked in accordance with the rules discussed earlier, are offered using only the right hand with-

    Salutation to the deities so and so. I offer flowers.

Different deities favour different flowers and leaves. There are detailed rules about the preferences of deities as well as contra-indications, e.g. *tulsī* leaves are never used in a *Gaṇapaṭi pūjā*.

Worshipping the deity with *tulsī* leaves or other material is accompanied by the recitation of twenty-four names of *Viṣṇu*, beginning with *Keśava*, or 108 names, or 1000 names.

9. Incense - Incense sticks are waived in front of the icon while ringing a bell in the left hand. The incense is believed to purify the air, and more importantly, drive away evil spirits. The following mantra is recited -

    Accept this incense, the best scent rich in odour which has come from the secretion of the grown-up tree, fit to be smelt by all gods.

10. Lamp - A small lamp, also called *dīpa*, in which only *ghī* is used, is very important and auspicious in Indian religious ceremonies at homes and in temples. It was offered to an honoured guest by way of *ārtī*, a ceremony in which it is waived in a clockwise circular motion, the head and upper torso is kept covered. Traditionally, it is offered to someone visiting home after a long time or going away on an important mission. It is also offered to revered guests. In the *pūjā*, the same ceremony is followed with the prayer -

    With devotion I offer this lamp to the deity, the 'highest self.

    Save me from the terrible darkness [of ignorance]. Accept this lamp.

    Salutation to the deities so and so. I offer a lamp.

11. Food - The well bathed and attired deity is offered food served on a plate sprinkled with water, and one or more *tulsī* leaves, to make it pure. The plate is kept in a small quadrangular area drawn with water to protect the food from evil spirits. Once the food is offered, either the worshipper closes his eyes, or a screen is drawn in front of the idol and food. A bell is rung inviting the idol to partake the offerings. This act is consistent with the *brahmaṇa's* practice of eating food away from the gaze of any person. Like humans, gods are also believed to have favourite foods, such as *modaka* for Gaṇapaṭi, *laddūs* for *Hanumān*, et cetera.

The leftover food is of great significance and is distributed among the devotees to be consumed as *prasāda*. The deity, like any other human, is offered water for rinsing the mouth and washing hands with -

> Accept the food, candied sugar, eatables and curd, milk, *ghī*, and the food of all kinds.
>
> Salutation to the deities so and so. I offer food. You are the seat of nectar. *Śvāha.*
>
> I offer water for washing the hands. I offer water for washing the mouth.
>
> I offer sandalwood paste for rubbing on the hands.

12. Betel - Conforming to the Indian tradition, betel is offered as mouth freshener to the deity with -

> Accept this whole betel, the divine areca nut together with leaves of the betel plant together with clove and cardamom.
>
> Salutation to the deities so and so. I offer betel.

13. Fruit - The deity is then offered a fruit, normally sprinkled with water and marked with *kumkuma*, with the following recitation -

> With this fruit may I attain everything - with offering of fruit the three worlds with the movable and immovable is accomplished. Therefore may my wishes bear fruit by the giving of fruit.
>
> Salutation to the deities so and so. I offer a fruit.

14. Gift - A gift of money kept on washed betel leaves and sprinkled with water for purification is offered to the deity with accompaniment of a purāṇic mantra praising gold. After the *pūjā* ceremony, the worshipper - usually a *pujārī* - takes all the offerings along with the money. Gold was offered as gift in the olden days, as is evident from the accompanying prayer -

Gold is the seed of fire which is in the womb of *Brahman*. It gives endless merit as fruit. Therefore, give me peace.

> Salutation to the deities so and so. I offer the gift.

15. Main *ārtī* - This *ārtī* is similar to the one described earlier with minor differences. The lamp is usually kept in a plate with one or five wicks alongside camphor. The camphor and the wicks are lit and waved in a clockwise, circular motion.

Camphor has purificatory properties and is supposed to keep evil spirits away. *Ārtī* is done with the accompaniment of Vedic mantras - AB. 9.9 4.4, A.B. 3.7.11 - 13, 2.4 0.8. These mantras are connected with *nīrājana*, a means of obtaining prosperity and welfare, which also forms a part of *puṇya-vacana.*

The act of waving lit lamps called *ārtī* is also called *nīrājana*. In modern-day practices, it is the climax of the *pūjā* accompanied by ringing of the bell, clashing of the cymbols and singing bhajanas and prayers, which form part of, and are also called, *ārtī*.

Salutation to the deities so and so. I offer the great lamp for waving (*nīrājana*).

Highest Lord, accept the spotless lamp of camphor which I offer with devotion, which is able to remove the darkness of ignorance in heart.

Salutation to the deities so and so. I offer the lamp of camphor for waving (*artikya*).

16. Prostration - Salutation has many forms in India. The forms of salutation change depending on the relationship, just like in other societies. God, being the highest and most revered, is naturally paid the highest obeisance, either in *aṣṭāṅga* (eight limbs), one of the forms of the prostration in which the man lies flat on his stomach, eight parts of his body touching the ground; or a simple act of bowing with folded hands. These acts are believed to evoke blessings of the person being respected. Prostration is done with the formal pronouncement -

Salutation to the deities so and so. I offer prostrations.

17. Circumambulation - One of the highest ways of showing respect, it involves going around the object of worship in a clockwise direction. This is to imitate the daily movement of the sun and shake off evil. The devotee goes around the idol once or twice, except for *Śiva's mūrti*, in which case the worshipper travels half the circle and retraces his steps. The worshipper prays -

Whatever evil deeds one has committed in previous lives they vanish at every step of the circumambulation.

Salutation to the deities so and so. I offer circumambulation.

18. Flowers consecrated by mantras - The worshipper takes *akṣata* and a few flowers consecrated with Vedic mantras in the right hand, and offers them to the icon at the end of the worship with -

I offer a handful of flowers consecrated by mantras.

Conclusion

Concluding the *pūjā*, the worshipper seeks forgiveness of the gods for mistakes and deficiencies. A few rites are followed for atonement (*prāyaścitta*), since it is believed that a *pūjā* performed with deficiencies results in evil consequences, and causes harm to the worshipper and the object for which the *pūjā* was performed. Normally it consists of the following three rites-

1 *prārthana* (prayer)
2 *saṅkalpa pūrti* (completion of the declaration)
3 *tīrtha grahaṇa* (taking the holy water)

This begins with invocation of *Gaṇapaṭi*, followed by oblations made in fire, offerings of flowers, and ends with the invocation of *Viṣṇu*. Mantras from Ṛg are employed for this along with the purāṇic prayer, '*Tvameva māta ca pitā tvameva...*', ending with -

I immediately bow to *acyuta* by recalling whom and uttering whose name a deficiency in austerity, *pūjā* and ritual, et cetera is made up for. Thus, ends the prayer.

Next is completion of the declaration in which the *pūjā* along with the merits is dedicated to the *pujārī* with the pronouncement -

This is not mine, *omtat sat*. Made to be offered to *brahmaṇa*.

By this act of dedicating the worship to the *pujārī*, it is believed that the god blesses the worshipper with the actual fruit of the *pūjā* -

By this worship which I have performed according to (my) knowledge, with the materials of service as they are available may the noble deities so and so be pleased.

The worshipper then takes the *nirmalya* flowers (offered in the *pūjā*) along with water in the conch shell and drinks the water. Putting the flowers to his head, he waits his hands over the flame of the *ārtī* lamp and touches his eyes or forehead. Usually, this is done three times.

And the *devapūjā* concludes.

PART V

देवपितृकार्याभ्यां न प्रमदितव्यम् | मातृदेवो भव | पितृदेवो भव | अचार्यदेवो भव |
अतिथिदेवो भव | यान्यनवद्यानि कर्माणि | तानि सेवितव्यानि | नो इतराणि |
यान्यस्माकं सुचरितानि | तानि त्वयोपास्यानि | नो इतराणि ||

The Ācārya, who is well-versed in Scriptures, instructs his pupil-
Don't swerve away from the duties to devas and parents. To you, may your mother, father,
Ācārya and guest be devas. You must do only unobjectionable Karmas, not others.
You follow only the virtuous acts of ours, not vicious ones.

(Tait 1.11.2)

Chapter 33

Rites of passage - *Saṃskāras*

Meaning of *saṃskāras*

In the present context of Hinduism, *saṃskāra* broadly has two meanings. First, a set of rites and rituals that identify the practitioner with Hinduism, and, second, "the tendencies and qualities that accumulate around a person in succeeding lives and influences his fate."[1]

[Ref to chapter on *Dāna* for *iṣṭapurta*, a word first used in the Ṛgveda to imply 'the humility of a spiritual result or merit due to a man's performance of sacrifice and charitable acts'.]

One can see the two meanings of *saṃskāra* are interrelated and interdependent in the sense that a Hindu accumulates merit by performing the rites and rituals, and to be a Hindu (in the sense of following the Vedas teachings), one is required to perform these rites and rituals. Though some *saṃskāras* like *vivāha* do find mention in the oldest of the Vedic texts, the Ṛgveda (1700 BC or before), the word *saṃskāra* itself is not used anywhere in the Ṛgveda - the closest we come to is *saṃskrāta*, which is used in the sense of 'purified' in the context of '*gharma*' vessel - "*Aśvins* do not harm the *gharma* that has been purified." (RV. V.7 6.2.). Even in Śatapatha, this word is not used anywhere - though we do come across similar sounding *saṃskruru* and *saṃskrutam*, occuring in relation to preparing or purifying *havis* (oblations) for the gods (1.1.40). The first mention of the word *saṃskāra* is found in Jaimini's *sūtras* (around 500-200 BC), who first uses it categorically for *upanayana* ceremony in PMS (VI.1.35), and several other times in his subsequent *sūtras*, where it generally means purificatory act in a sacrifice. *Saṃskāra* is applied to the actions of shaving of the head, cleansing the teeth, and paring the nails of the sacrifice in *jyotiṣṭoma* (II I.8.3), and sprinkling of water (*prokkṣana*) in I X.3.25. Harita (pre Āpastamba, i.e. 500-300 BC) divides *saṃskāras* into two heads -

(i) *Brahman* - *Saṃskāras* described only in *smṛtis*; and

(ii) *Daiva* - *Saṃskāras* that allow a purified man to stay (in afterlife) in the world of forefathers.

But it is Śabara (200-500 AD), who while commenting on PMS (3.1.3) explains *saṃskāra* as that which makes a thing or person fit for a certain purpose. He goes on to explain that, "fitness is of two kinds; it arises by the removal of taints (sins) or by the generation of fresh qualities. *Saṃskāras* generate fresh qualities, while tapas brings about the removal of taints." Elucidating he adds that one has blemishes due to not doing his duties in the previous or this life, or doing what is forbidden. If not removed, these actions prevent the sacrificer from harvesting the reward of even a perfect and defect-less sacrifice!

∞

In the Indian school of *darśana* (philosophy), while the *Advaita Vedantists* debunk *saṃskāras* as a false attribution of physical action to the soul, the *Naiyāyikas* (students of *nyāya* branch who believe in realism, logic and analytic philosophy) consider it to mean a self-productive quality, and the *Vaiṣeśekas* (students of *vaiṣeśeka* branch - who believe in naturalism and atomism) recognise it as one of the 24 *guṇas* (qualities). Kumarila in Tantravartika (650-750 AD) regards *saṃskāras* as acts and rites that impart fitness.

In the early 15th century, *saṃskāras* came to be defined as "a peculiar excellence due to the performance of rites ordained (by the *śastra*) which resides either in the soul or the body" (Pandit Mitra Mishra in Vīramitrodayā, 1610-1640 AD). Here, it was explained that *saṃskāras* are of two kinds - those that make a person eligible for performing other actions, such as the *upanayana* which makes a person eligible for Vedas' study, and those that remove evil taints, like *jātakarma*, which removes the taint of seed and uterus.

Given this journey of meaning and understanding of *saṃskāras* through the ages, it is safe to say that *saṃskāras*, at their least, are a set of rites and rituals performed by Hindus making them fit or ready for certain purposes. The purpose may be a crossover from one stage of life to another, such as the *upanayana*, where leaving parental home one goes to the guru's house for education, or *vivāha*, where one moves from bachelorhood to a married householder, or *garbhādhāna* (conception) wherein a woman is made ready or fit for bearing a child. Apart from this, it appears that another important purpose of *saṃskāras* was simply to share the joy and happiness of an important family occasion, such as *karṇavedha* (ear piercing), *annaprâsana* (tasting solids first time), *niṣkrmana* (taking child out of home first time) or *námahkarana* (naming the child). Whereas *annaprâsana*, a ceremony in which a child is fed solid food for the first time, is technically a crossover or transition from one stage of life to another, primarily, it is an occasion of great joy for the immediate family of the new born in a social - as opposed to the religious - way signifying healthy growth of the baby. Likewise, *niṣkramaṇa*, a ceremony in which the child is taken out in the sun for the first time, is also an occasion for parents and members of the immediate family to enjoy and remember. This *saṃskāra* can hardly be called purificatory in nature, or an act which makes the child 'fit or ready for a certain purpose'. Similarly, *varṣavardhana*, monthly celebration of the birth of the child for a whole year, also falls in the category of a family celebration. However, *caula* or *cudakarma* (*mundan* or shaving of head) does appear to be a rite to remove 'taints of seed and uterus', as the child was believed to carry impurities from the womb in its hair.

All in all, it appears that the purpose of *saṃskāras* was manyfold. Some *saṃskāras*, like *annaprâsana*, *karṇavedhana* and *nāmahkarṇa*, were occasions for the family to express joy and happiness. Others, like *upanayana*, were important landmarks in the crossover from one stage of life to other. *Vivāha*, also a cross over from one to other stage of life, marked the entry of a man into a new *āśrama*, *gṛhastha* (one of the four *āśramas* in life), which changed the status of the individual from that of a *brahmācarin*, to a special social status of *gṛhastha* in the society.

Many scholars assert that *saṃskāras*, from *garbhādhāna* (conception) to *antyeṣṭi* (cremation), are mere symbolic milestones in the life of a Hindu, an assertion this author does not subscribe to. It does not matter what else a Hindu does or does not do, whether he is a believer or an atheist, whether he belongs to the mainstream *Sanātana Dharma* or is a practitioner of any of the several fringe forms, a Hindu does go through at least one of the sixteen, or forty, *saṃskāras* during his life time, or after death. The *saṃskāras* are thus much more than mere symbolic milestones - they are the single most important defining feature of a Hindu's life.

On one hand, *saṃskāras* identify its practitioner as a member of the unique religion of Hinduism, on the other they impart a unique characteristic by which Hinduism is identified as Hinduism. Just as anyone observing even one of the *saṃskāras* is identified as a Hindu, the definition and understanding of Hinduism - which otherwise is so difficult to define and explain - cannot be considered complete without the inclusion of *saṃskāras* as one of the attributes of this religion.

Having said this, one has to admit that the *saṃskāras* were not the defining attribute of Hinduism in the earliest times of the Vedic religion. Though the Ṛgveda describes *vivāha*, *garbhādhāna*, *antyeṣṭi*, and *upanayana* in its hymns, in all probability, only these few (of the sixteen or forty in the present-day) *saṃskāras* existed (as customs) and were practised in the Ṛgvedic society. Described as stand-alone customs, scattered in the texts, these were neither called nor grouped as *saṃskāras* at that time. With the passage of time, the Brahmaṇas came to be compiled as a directory of rites and rituals. And as the rituals became more complex and detailed, texts had to be created describing in minute detail how to perform these elaborate ceremonies. While the *dharma sūtras* (sixth to seventh century BC), born out of the necessity to codify Hindu law, describe customs and ethics as well as details of many *saṃskāras*, it is the *gṛyha sūtras* (400 BC to 400 AD) that are considered the natural repository of *saṃskāras*. In addition, the *gṛyhasūtras* also describe the daily sacrifices that a householder should perform. In the beginning, only important or perhaps even necessary practices were prescribed as *saṃskāras*, however, over a period of time even lesser practices like *annaprâsana* and *niṣkramaṇa* came to be consolidated as a group, and by the time of *gṛhya sūtras* were institutionalised as *saṃskāras*.

The oldest three: *Vivāha*, *Upanayana* and *Antyeṣṭi*

In the following few passages we will have a quick look at the original description - when they first occur in Ṛg - of the three of the most important *saṃskāras* - *vivāha*, *upanayana* and *antyeṣṭi*.

Vivāha is mentioned in the Ṛgveda only as a social event. It does not enjoin or recommend performance of this rite as Dharma of a Hindu. In Ṛgveda *Saṃhitā*, which is simply a collection of mantras, the *vivāha* (marriage) ceremony of *Sūryā*, *Savitaṛ's* daughter (RV. X.85) has been described in detail. The Ṛgvedic sages were simply describing prevalent *vivāha* customs when they described *Sūryā's* bridal friends leading her home in her bridal clothes and readying the steers of her bridal cart, singing holy Sāma hymns -

Raibhi was her dear bridal friend, and Narasamsi led her home.
Lovely was *Sūryā's* robe: she came to that which *Gatha* had adorned ...6
Thought was the pillow of her couch, the sight was the unguent for her eyes:
Her treasury was Earth and heaven, when *Sūryā* went unto her Lord ...7
Hymns were the crossbars of the pole, *Kuriera-metre* Decked the car:
The bride's men were the *Aśvin* pair *Agni* was leader of the train ...8
Soma was he who wooed the maid: the groomsmen were both *Aśvins*, when
the Sun God *Savitar* bestowed his willing *Sūryā* on her Lord ...9
Thy steers were steady, kept in place by holy verse and *Sama* hymns:
all car were thy two chariot wheels: thy path was tremulous in the sky, ...11
(RV. X.85 Griffith)

Vivāha finds two more references in the fifth *manḍala* - considered older than the tenth *manḍala* (cited above) - of the Ṛgveda; tenth is widely accepted to be latest additions to the Ṛg *Saṃhitā*. In these two earliest references to *vivāha* in the *Saṃhitā*, both hymns are dedicated to the *Agni* deity and the sage poets unambiguously speak of a husband, wife and a household -

"As a kind friend with the streams of milk they balm thee what kind thou makest a wife and lord one minded." (V.5.3, Griffith)

"Make easy to maintain our household Lordship, and overcome the might of those who hate us." (V.28.3, Griffith)

Interestingly, till this stage there is no indication of any insistence or emphasis on 'must do' in the Ṛgveda as far as *vivāha* is concerned. That comes later, as expected, in the Brahmaṇa, when Śatapatha prescribes that "the wife is indeed half of one's self; therefore, as long as a man does not secure a wife so long he does not get a son and so he's till then not complete; but when he secures the wife he gets progeny and then he becomes complete."[2] The formal union of a man and woman, from being a purely an optional social event became an obligation in the Brahmaṇa's time. And by the time of the *dharma sūtras* it took the form of a religious injunction. Āpastamba (500-300 BC), in his *dharma sūtras*, observes that there are two main purposes of marriage - it enables a man to perform religious rites (which will be incomplete if he is not accompanied by his wife), and the wife provides sons who perform the rites after the death of their father to save him from going to hell (I I.5.11 - 12). Manu too states that procreation of sons was dependant on the wife (i.e. marriage), and heaven for oneself and ancestors was dependant on performance of religious rites involving the wife (MS I X.28). Here, Manu and Āpastamba, both are referring to redemption of *pitŕiṇarina* through *śraddhā* - one of the three *riṇas* (indebtedness) with which every human is born - which is performed by the son. Thus, we can see how an optional formal union of a man and a woman got embedded in the *dharma sūtras*, *smṛtis*, and *gṛyhasūtras* not only as a religious ceremony, but 'a must-do', an injunction. A man who did not marry was considered committing a serious crime and failing to perform his duty towards his forefathers. He thus shut the door for himself for *pitŕiṇaloka* in the afterlife, and worse, ensured hell for himself. This is a typical example of how a social custom got transformed/ institutionalised into a *saṃskāra*.

Upanayana and *antyeṣṭi* both, likewise, appear to have had a similar journey. The two are also among the oldest recorded practices (apart from *garbhādhāna*) mentioned in ancient Vedic literature.

"Well robed, enveloped he is come, the youthful: springing to life his glory waxeth greater.

Contemplative in mind and god adoring, sages of high intelligence upraise him."[3]

The above quote fits the description of an *upanayana* initiated student. In Upaniṣad period, *upanayana* was performed in a simple way - young student approached teacher with no more than few sacrificial fuel sticks called '*samidhā*', indicating he was ready to serve the teacher; in return, the teacher assured to protect him (Br. U. VI.2.1; CU. V). Describing the initiation of a student by the teacher, *Śatapatha* says that the teacher touches the pupil with his right hand and becomes pregnant (with the pupil). In the third night, he is born as a Brahmaṇa with *Savitṛi*. The Brahmaṇa belongs to *Agni*. At once the Brahmaṇa with *Savitṛi* teaches the pupil.[4]

Upnayana developed into a full-blown ritual much later in the *gṛyhasūtras* (S. GS. I I.1; A. GS. I.19.3.5; P GS. I I.10; G GS. I I.10; H GS. I.1.2.18).

Anteyeṣṭi as a rite/custom finds mention in the tenth *manḍala*. However, the narration of the custom is sketchy, as can be seen in the following translations (Ralf T H Griffith) of *ṛcas* -

Come, *Agni*, come with countless ancient Fathers, dwellers in light, primeval, God-adorers,
Eaters and drinkers of oblations, truthful, who travel with Deities and *Índra*.............10
Fathers whom *Agni's* flames have tasted, come ye nigh: ye kindly leaders, take ye each your proper place.
Each Sacrificial food presented on the grass: grant to riches with a multitude of hero sons. 11
thou, *Jātavedas*, when entreated, didst bear the offerings which thou madest the fragrant,
and give them to the fathers who did eat them with *Svadha*. Eat, thou God, the gifts we bring thee. 12
and
Burn him not up, nor quite consume him, *Agni*: let not his body or his skin be scattered.
O JātaVedas, when thou hast matured him, then send him on his way unto the fathers. 10.16.1.
Again, *O Agni*, to the fathers send him who, offered in thee, goes with our oblations.
Wearing new life let him increase his offspring: let him rejoin a body, *JātaVedas*...[5]

And finally, in[5] RV (X.18.7-8) -

Let these unwidowed dames with noble husbands adorn themselves with fragrant balm and unguent.
Decked with fair jewels, tearless, free from sorrow, first let the dames go up to where he lieth. ...7
Rise, come unto the world of life, O woman: come he is lifeless by whose side thou liest. 8

As expected, the Brahmaṇas give a detailed description of these rites (SBXIII), and Aśva, Gobhila, Baudhāyana Gṛhya Sūtras go on to institutionalize it.

Meaning of *saṃskāras*

In last few pages, various aspects of *saṃskāras*, their first mention in the texts, evolution and growth, importance in Hinduism, and in a Hindu's life have been briefly discussed. However, one may still be left wondering what is the exact meaning of this Sanskrit word *saṃskāra*. Dalal[6] tells us that the term *saṃskāra* is used in two ways: "It indicates ceremonies and rituals practised in Hinduism, as well as the tendencies and qualities that accumulate around a person in succeeding lives and influences his fate"; in English, 'Sacrament', perhaps is the closest word to *saṃskāra*, which Oxford dictionary defines as '(in the Christian church) a ceremony regarded as imparting a spiritual grace'. The Roman Catholic and many Orthodox churches refer to the word sacrament as the seven rites of baptism - confirmation, the Eucharist, penance, anointing of the sick, ordination, and matrimony. According to the Oxford dictionary, it is a thing of mysterious and sacred significance, a religious symbol. Most of these definitions are close to *saṃskāras*, more particularly, 'a religious symbol', and 'a thing of mysterious and sacred significance'. In Hindu scriptures, apart from purification, *saṃskāras* have a deeper meaning, and serve a greater purpose.

Broadly speaking, we can classify *saṃskāras* under following categories based on the purpose -

1. In the ancient times, superstitions involving evil spirits and personification of destructive phenomenon of nature were central to a man's life. The householder was ever so anxious these evil powers, beyond his control, may interfere in his or his family's life causing pain and destruction. Plus, the fear and anxiety of things going wrong, such as birth of a deformed or a stillborn baby, haunted men in the Vedas period just as much as they do now in the twenty first century, when modern diagnostic medical help is easily available. In those days fear of mischievous spirits interfering with the peaceful conduct of a householder's life could only be countered by these religious ceremonies.
2. Material gain was another important purpose of *saṃskāras*. A man getting married, prayed and asked the gods e.g. during the *sapta-padi* rite of *vivāha saṃskāra* - for animals, children, corn, a good physique and sharp intellect
3. Self-expression was perhaps the chief purpose of *saṃskāras*. Beginning from *garbhādhāna* (conception), child birth, to the first time when the child is taken out of the house, fed his/her first solid food, given a name, sent to a guru's house for education, to *vivāha* - all must have been occasions of extreme joy then, just as they are now. These landmarks were occasions not only for the parents, but for all near and dear ones to get together, celebrate and watch the progression of the child into adulthood.
4. Many scholars think that, the cultural purpose, in a way, accorded a more serious colour to what were otherwise purely family social functions. Washing away

the impurities of birth was serious business in a society which rested heavily on the concept of *śauca* and *aśauca*, i.e. pure and impure. Bodily purity was a prerequisite to initiation of any religious or social ceremony, or even ordinary daily acts of cooking and eating. The physical aspect of procreation was considered a sin of seed and it was thought necessary to remove this impurity, as well as the impurity arising out of staying in the mother's womb. From Manu, Yājñavalkya, Kulluka to Harita, there is extensive discussion of these pre- and post-natal impurities which were removed through the *saṃskāras*. *Saṃskāras* like *upnayana* also imparted a special social status to members of the three superior castes, *brahmaṇa*, *kṣatriya* and *vaiśya*, by helping them attain the status of *dvija*, i.e. twice born. However, *śūdra* and non-Āryans were not entitled to the *saṃskāras*.

Saṃskāras also helped in attainment of heaven and even *moksha*. Speaking about this benefit in Vīramitrodayā Saṃskārasprakāśa, Harita says, "One who is consecrated with the *Brahman saṃskāras* attained the status of ṛṣis, becomes there equal, goes to their world and lives in their close vicinity. One who is consecrated with *Daiva Saṃskāras* attains the status of God et cetera."

But, was there a greater purpose, such as spiritual, of these rites and rituals called *saṃskāras*?

The answer is yes. *Saṃskāras* were never regarded as an end, they were considered preparation for attainment of higher goals in life viz. realisation of the self or the absolute truth. According to Hindu scriptures[10a], this self-realisation can be achieved through the development of eight *ātmā guṇas* or inner virtues, which are -

i. *Dayā* (compassion) - consideration and sensitivity for all
ii. *Kṣamā* or forbearance - the ability to face a procreative situation without getting agitated
iii. *Anasūya* - freedom from jealousy
iv. *Śauca* or purity - both internal as well as external
v. *Anayasam* or staying cool - freedom from burden
vi. *Akarpanya* - not being miserly
vii. *Aspṛha* - free of desire or attachment
viii. *Ānandam* - state of blissful peace

Once these eight *gunas* are cultivated, a man is considered ready to proceed on the path of self-realisation. It is the *saṃskāras* that are believed to make a man fit for this journey.

Saṃsakāra - 16 or 40?

It is unclear as to how and when social and religious customs like *caula*, *aanaprâsana*, *upanayana*, *vivāha* and *antyeṣti*, some perhaps from times even prior to Vedas period, came to be grouped together and given the name *saṃskāras*.

While some *saṃskāras* like *annaprāśana* and *niṣkramaṇa*, were 'private' affairs (celebratory occasions for the immediate family), others like *vivāha* necesserily involved participation of at least two different families, and their relatives. It is evident from various references in the concerned texts that to the key rites like *upanayana*, *vivāha* and *antyeṣṭi*, as the society evolved from pre-Vedic period to early and late Vedas period, i.e., Brahmaṇa and Upaniṣadic days, many more rites got added. However, these events were not yet clubbed together and labelled as *saṃskāras*. As mentioned earlier, the word *saṃskāra* came to be used repeatedly only around 400-200 BC - by Jaimini - though he too did not use it in the sense of a series of rites or rituals as a group, as it is used today. He used it in a typical *Mīmāṃsā* context - of purification of *yajña* materials for the sacrificial fire.

The *gṝha-sūtras*, where we expect to find enlightenment in this respect of the study of *saṃskāras*, again disappoint; here too the word is used in the sense of *Mīmāṃsākas*: *sūtras* 'speak of the *ancabhusaṃskāras* and *pāka-saṃskāras* by which they mean sweeping, sprinkling and purifying the sacrificial ground and boiling and preparing food for sacrifice'[7].They, unsurprisingly, include bodily *saṃskāras* in the list of *pākayajñas*; 'unsurprisingly' because *gṛhyasūtras* were composed under the heavy influence of sacrificial thinking, and it is natural - "they classify the entire domestic rituals under the names of different sacrifices."[8]

Accordingly in many *gṝha-sūtras*, *saṃskāras*, from *vivāha* to *sīmantonnayana*, have been classified under *huta* (type of *yajña*), where offerings are made to the fire directly; and *jātakarma* to the *caula saṃskāras* under *prahuta* sacrifice, where offerings are thrown in the fire and the *brahmaṇa* are given gifts! [As explained earlier, *pāka yajñas* were divided by different *sūtrakaras* in various ways - Pāraskara and Sanhkyayana divide these sacrifices under four heads *huta*, *ahuta*, *prahuta* and *praśita* - चत्वारः पाकयज्ञा हुतोऽहुतः प्रहुतः प्राशित इति ॥ (1.4.1)]

It appears that *saṃskāras* had not yet achieved a separate identity covering the series of rites from conception to death under one umbrella.

The credit for making this distinction, between the bodily *saṃskāras* and the sacrifices (performed to propitiate the gods), must go to Vaikhānasa, who for the first time mentions this difference in his *Smṛtasūtras* (available texts are of 200-500 AD antiquity). In nearly 2000 year long history (1700 BC or before to nearly 200 AD) of Hinduism, there hasn't been either clarity, or consensus, on what constituted *saṃskāras*. Different *Gṝha-sūtras*' authors made their own selection of family, social and religious events they deemed fit to be included in their list of *saṃskāras*. The number in different *gṛhya sūtras* and subsequent *smṛti* texts varies wildly from forty in Gautama, twenty one in Angiras, to sixteen in Vedavyāsa (I.14-15). Manu and Yaj Smṛtis, and Viṣṇu Dharma Sūtras do not specify a number, but agree that all events from *garbhādhāna* (*niśheka*) to *antyeṣṭi* are *saṃskāras*.[9]

The forty *saṃskāras* of Gautama DS are listed below[10b] -

Garbhādhāna, puṁsavana, sīmantonnayana, jātakarma, nāma karma, annaprâsana, caula, upanayana, the four *vratas* of Vedas, *snāna, vivāha*, the five daily *mahāyajñas*, the seven *pākayajñas*, the seven *haviryajñas*, and the seven *soma* sacrifices.

Obviously, Gautama uses *saṃskāra* word in its earlier wider sense, and includes *soma* and *havir* yajñas in its ambit. During his time, "there was no clear distinction between the *saṃskāras* proper and the sacrifices" and "the word '*saṃskāras*' is used in the sense of religious rites in general."[11] By the time of the *smṛtis*, when the practice of sacrifices was on wane, the number of *saṃskāras* - excluding the *yajñas* - was pared down to sixteen or twenty. Manu underlining the importance of *saṃskāras*, exhorts 'the transformative rituals for the bodies of the twice born, beginning with the rites of the infusion (of semen), which purified them here on earth and after death, should be performed with excellent Vedic rites'[12], and goes on to discuss several rites, without however giving exact number of rites. Rajbali Pandey claims[13] Manu has listed thirteen *samsakars* in his *smṛti* -

Garbhādhāna, puṁsavana, sīmantonnayana, jātakarma, nāma dheya, niṣkramaṇa, annaprâsana, cudakarma, upanayana, keśānta, samāvartana, vivāha and *śmaśāna*.

∞

Texts make all *dvijas* duty bound to perform *saṃskāras*, for women and *śūdras* there are a few special provisions. *Jātakarma* to *cudakarma* rites for a girl child - unlike in case of a male child - are prescribed to be performed without Vedic mantras (Manu I I.66, Yaj I.13; Aśva GS I.15.10, 16.6, 17.18). However texts permit Vedic mantras for girl's *vivāha-saṃskāra* (Manu I I.67, Yaja I.13) - provided girls belong to any of the three higher class. *Śūdras* were permitted restricted number of *saṃskāras*; only ten, from *garbhādāna* to *caula* according to Veda Vyāsa, and only eight according to Aprārka. Vedic mantras were not permitted in *saṃskāras* of *śūdra*.

While exhorting performance of *saṃskāras* with 'excellent Vedic rites' as a duty of Hindus, Manu does not enumerate *saṃskāras* that a Hindu should perform - though he must have been fully aware of the divergent opinions on this issue. It is evident that Manu, a man known for a detailed and prescriptive approach, skirted the issue deliberately - he did not want to give a fixed list of rites.

In more recent times, the Smṛti Candrika and Smṛti Mukta phala (~300-year old) observe that *saṃskāras*, from *garbhādhāna* to *upanayana*, were necessary in case of a twice born. Likewise, the Vīramitrodayā and Saṃskārasmayukha also deal with *Brahman Saṃskāras* from *garbhādhāna* to *vivāha*, although they quote the entire list of forty *saṃskāras* as provided by Gautama.

It appears people were left to choose from the list of forty *saṃskāras* what they preferred to perform, at a time of their choosing. What gave considerable flexibility to people was the provision of rectification in case a *saṃskāra* (except *upanayana*) was not performed at the prescribed time. For each *saṃskāra* not performed, the *padakrcchra* penance had to be performed. Various *prāyaścitta* (expiation) were prescribed for rectification depending on the circumstance due to which *saṃskāra* could not be performed at the prescribed time. All in all, *saṃskāras*, excepting a few key ones like *upanayana*, *vivāha* and *antyeṣṭi*, came to be performed as a matter of choice and convenience. Moreover, they were often performed in a perfunctory manner, more for ticking the box rather than performing the rite in its true spirit, and in the prescribed manner.

∞

Currently, sixteen *saṃskāras*, from *garbhādhāna* to *vivāha*, are widely accepted. Not only have the latest *Paddhatis* adopted this number, Swami Dayānand Saraswati in his Saṃskārasvidhi has also included only these sixteen *saṃskāras*, commonly called the *ṣoḍaśa saṃskāras*[14]. In actual practice however, only *upanayana*, *vivāha* and *antyeṣṭi* are performed in accordance with the *saṃskāra* texts. *Upanayana* is often clubbed with the *vivāha* ceremony. *Cudakarma* and *annaprâsana* are invariably performed without the help of a priest, and *karṇavedha*, restricted only to baby girls these days, is often performed at the family doctor's clinic! Interestingly, *garbharakśana/sīmantonnayana*, performed, without a priest, more as a celebration by women, also known as *godabharāī* (literally- filling the lap) has become popular among the modern crowd, particularly in towns, cities and metros, where it is celebrated as 'baby shower'. *Námahkarana* is a must for every child, but these days there is no ceremony attached to giving a name to the child. It is an act in which the immediate family and friends participate, but only by way of suggesting a suitable name for the new born.

The reason many of the *saṃskāras* gradually disappeared from our lives is because some became irrelevant, and many others, like pre-natal, a source of acute embarrassment to couples. It is embarrassing for a young couple to announce to the world at large that the husband is going to impregnate his wife in order to father a child, as *garbhādhāna* demands, or organise a ritual to beget a baby boy, thereby indicating his lack of preference for a daughter! Another important reason why in progression of modern society many of the *saṃskāras* fell by the wayside is paucity of time and resources. Urban life has its own pressures, and the working couple can hardly keep abstaining from work for one or another rite. In big cities, working couples go out to work. Living away from their parents, they do not have enough resources to organise these prenatal and postnatal *saṃskāras*. Fortunately, their task has been made easy by Hindu texts offering simple rectification measures.

One niska (about 38.88 gram) of silver or corn of the prescribed value is all that is required to be given in *dāna* for not performing some of these *saṃskāras*. It makes more sense for the people to pay this small penalty rather than go through a tedious and time-consuming process of performance of a *saṃskāra*.

Kane[15a] sums it up succinctly: "The whole life of a person was so very minutely worked out and overlaid with so much ritual in the *gṛyhasūtras* and the *smṛtis* that the tendency to neglect and change became insistent and inevitable. This tendency was helped by the accommodating spirit of the Brahmaṇa authors of later *smṛtis* and digests that were ready to prescribe easier and easier substitutes for non-observations of the elaborate sacraments, prenatal and postnatal."

As things stand today, only *upanayana*, *vivāha* and *antyeṣṭi* continue to be performed by all Hindus. Well, nearly all Hindus.

[Note - According to Kane, four *annas* (a fourth of rupee) for each of *saṃskāras* not performed up to *caula* and eight *annas* for *caula* was the going *prāyaścitta* rate in his time (~1930)[15b].]

Chapter 34

Types of *Saṃskāra* - Description

Since early times there has been no consensus on the number of *saṃskāras* to be performed by a Hindu. *Dharmasūtras*, *gṝhasūtras*, *smṛtis*, and various *nibandha* and *paddhati* texts prescribe different lists, making it difficult for practitioners and scholars to arrive at any conclusion. There is also confusion on whether the *saṃskāras* that figured in one GS, but were absent in list of another GS author, qualified as *saṃskāra* or not. And yet, the institution of *saṃskāra* continued uninterruptedly in every Hindu family as an important hallmark of their faith. This was made possible primarily because of the inherent flexibility that the Hindu Dharma offers to its followers in its practices. But more importantly, it was because initially these were only customs and practices, not yet formalised and codified as *saṃskāra* by sage scholars like Manu and Yājñavalkya.

For easy comprehensibility, an exhaustive list of forty *saṃskāras* of Gautama is provided here. The list includes both, the *Brahman Saṃskāras* (body *saṃskāras*) and *Daiva Saṃskāras* (sacrifices or *yajñas*) like *soma* and *haviryajñas*. Against this list of *saṃskāras*, names of various sages like Āpastamba and Vyāsa, and the *saṃskāras* that they chose to include in their texts, is also provided in a matrix form - Table T-3. A brief description of most *saṃskāras* is given below, but various *yajñas* have been left out since they have already been dealt with in the chapter on *yajñas*.

Later in the chapter, a detailed account of two of the three most widely practiced *saṃskāras* of our time - *vivāha* and *upanayana* - is given. Third important *saṃskāra* - *antyeṣṭi*, deals with the last rites of the dead. Keeping in view the sensitivity of readers who may find description of some of the funeral rites disagreeable and off-putting, your author has decided to exclude this important *saṃskāra* from this book.

i. *Garbhādhāna* - This is an old *saṃskāra*, which finds mention in Atharava (V.25.3) and Br A. U (VI.4.21). The act of copulation is driven by one of the most fundamental of human desires. Within the framework of matrimony, apart from fulfilling a bodily need, sexual intercourse serves the greater purpose of producing progeny. In Vedic contexts, this hinged around getting at least one male child. Only a son, by performing the last rites and *śrāddha*, could ensure the diseased father's soul's journey to *pitŕiṇaloka*. Sons were important in Vedic times because they were required by fathers to redeem themselves from the three debts (*ṛṇas*) inherited by birth. On a more practical level, son also helped in settling and discharging any fiscal debt of his father.

It is difficult to comprehend as to how this private act borne out of a natural human desire came to assume a ceremonial form. But, a healthy pregnancy ending in a healthy child and mother, must have been a matter of great concern in a householder's life, which in those days was full of fears and superstitions, just as they are even now. Today, we have highly advanced medical science with its diagnostic instruments available at our disposal to confirm a healthy pregnancy, but in the olden days, rites and rituals aided by prayers to god, were the only thing the family could rely upon. This, coupled with the religious necessity of having a son, almost certainly shaped *garbhādhāna* as an event of the greatest importance in the life of a householder.

Thenceforth, it was just a matter of time before these ceremonies got codified as *saṃskāra* in *sūtras*, complete with such minute details that even our sexually liberal modern generation may find it awkward and embarrassing to talk about publicly.

In the *saṃskāra* proper, at the end of the third day of menstruation, after the wife has bathed, the husband should make her pounded rice, which is boiled and eaten with various other things, based on the desires for a fair, brown or dark skinned son, or a learned son or daughter. Towards the morning, after performing the ceremony for preparing clarified butter, husband sacrifices from *sthalipāka*[1] and takes out the rest of the rice, eats it and gives some of it to his wife. After washing his hands, he sprinkles her thrice with water, embraces her and makes certain prescribed utterances[2] which cannot be literally translated for reasons of decency. He has intercourse with her and repeats certain *mantras*[3].

While the even nights (2, 4, 6, et cetera) were prescribed most suitable for conceiving a male child, copulation on the odd nights begot a female child (Manu I I I.48). Only nights were considered suitable for conception, daytime was prohibited, as it was believed that vital airs of a man cohabiting with his wife during the day leapt out. It also resulted in the birth of unlucky, weak and short lived children.[4]

The birth of a son was of utmost importance to every couple. Without a son, the last rites and *shrāddha* of the father could not be performed, which meant a certain journey to hell. If a man could not produce a son because of bad luck or physical shortcomings, a provision was made for the woman to invite her brother-in-law to impregnate her. The Ṛgveda too sanctifies a widow to take her brother-in-law to raise children for her husband (X.4 0.2). Subsequently, the *smṛtis* also made a provision for the wife of an impotent or invalid male, or a widow to bear children from the brother of her husband, a *sagotra*, or a *brahmaṇa*. (Yaj. S. I.68 and Manu MS I X.59)

There is a debate whether *garbhādhāna* is a *saṃskāra* of the child in the womb or of the woman - Gaut. V I I I.24. Manu I.16 and Yaj I.10 considered it a *saṃskāra* of the child in the womb which must be performed repeatedly i.e. for every childbirth. Later works like Smṛti Chandrika and saṃskāras-tattva, prescribe it to be performed only once and quote Harita in support.

'All *saṃskāras* other than *garbhādhāna* can be performed by any *agnate* (substitute or representative) in the absence of the husband' became a norm in the later period with the change in the idea of female chastity. In this context, Manu's condemnation of begetting a child from a male other than the husband as 'animal like' (*paśu* Dharma)[5] is confusing as it is in direct conflict with his earlier observation (MS. I X.59) endorsing this practice.

The significance of this *saṃskāra* lies in the creation of an institution of matrimony in the Vedic society wherein the relationship of a man and a woman was moved beyond one of pure sexual gratification. It aimed at a lifelong partnership for the greater purpose of building a home with the woman, and producing children to discharge one's moral duty of debt redemption to one's forefathers and liberation of the soul.

ii. *Puṁsavana* - Broadly speaking, it is a rite for begetting a male child[6]. According to Kane[7a] *puṁsavana* is so called because 'in virtue of it a male is born' whereas, according to Rajbali Pandey, "the word *puṁsavana* is rendered in English by 'a rite quickening a male child'."[7b]

Begetting a male child was critical in Vedic India for salvation of one's soul. It was one of the main, if not the sole purpose, of getting married. In the Atharvaveda, there are prayers by the husband to let 'a hero be born' (AV I I I.23). The *prājāpatya* ceremony recommends a medicinal herb for the pregnant woman to acquire a son (AV 23.6).

In the third month of pregnancy, the wife was supposed to fast, and under the constellation of *tishya* (PGS i.14.2; BGS i.1), she was given to eat two beans and one barley grain each with three portions of curd of a cow's milk - which has a calf of the same colour as the cow. On being asked what she drinks, the woman had to reply thrice - generation of a male (Aśva GS I.13.2-7). There are diverging views in the *gṛyhasūtras* about the timing and details of how the ritual is to be performed. Manu and Yājñavalkya recommend performing it before the foetus begins to move in the womb.

There is no clarity in the *smṛtis* whether the *saṃskāra* was to be performed in every pregnancy or just the first one.

The *saṃskāra* had only one purpose - the birth of a male child. Apart from the prayers, the then existing medicinal knowledge recommended herbs which were inserted in the right nostril of the woman.

Garbha rakśana or *anāvalobhana* - Apparently, this rite was a part of *puṁsavana* and is so called because its performance kept the foetus from falling out or getting destroyed. The husband inserted the sap of an herb called *durvarasa*, in the right nostril of the women, touching her heart and offered praise to the gods for safety of the foetus. This was performed in the fourth month of pregnancy.

iii. *Sīmantonnayana* - It literally means 'parting of the hair (of the pregnant woman) upward.'

The safety of the foetus was the driving force behind this *saṃskāra* performed in the fourth or fifth month of pregnancy. It was believed that demons came to the woman in her first pregnancy to devour the foetus and suck its blood[8a]. The husband invoked goddess *Śri* for protection. Another important reason was to bring prosperity and long life to the mother and the unborn child. Many scholars hold the view that the formation of the brain of a child begins in these months, therefore, care had to be taken by the woman to ensure that no damage was done to the unborn child through physical shock (Dr JD Parker of Lilavati Hospital, Mumbai, explained to this author that the brain formation begins in the twentieth week. All six layers of the brains are formed by two years of age). The mother, at all times, had to be kept in a cheerful mood for a healthy baby.

Also called *sīmānta* and *sīmāntakarṇa*, *homa* is performed in the fourth or fifth month of the pregnancy during the fortnight of the waxing moon when the moon is in conjunction with a *nakṣatra* with a masculine or male name. The deity *Raka* is invoked with the verse, 'Oh *Prājāpatya*, no one other than you' (Ṛgveda X.12 1.10), and the husband parts his wife's hair upwards three times beginning from the front, using a bunch of unripe *uḍumbara* fruits in even numbers, a porcupine quill with three white spots, three bunches of *kusha* grass, a stick of *viratara* wood and a full spindle, while saying, '*Bhūr bhuvaḥ svaḥ*'. Or, after partitioning the hair, with each of the three *mahāvyāhṛtis*, the *udumbara* branch was tied around the neck of the wife with a string of three twisted threads (PGS I.15.4) with the words, "Rich in sap is this tree; like the tree rich in sap, be thou fruitful." (PGS I.15.6) The wife was asked to look at the mess of rice, sesame and *ghī* and imagine prosperity and long life for her husband (G GS I I.7.10 -12).

To keep the pregnant woman happy, this rite was of a social and festive nature, lute was played accompanied with singing. It ended with feeding the *brahmaṇas*. Realising the importance of the well-being of the mother, and her state of mind and conduct influencing the unborn child, a set of duties were prescribed for the pregnant mother which included securing her from evil spirits. This was achieved by meticulously observing purity and writing sacred mantras. To avoid overexertion, she was advised not to mount an elephant or horse, climb mountains or many storeyed buildings. She also had to give up exercise, swift walking, journey in a bullock cart, sitting on an ordure, mace, pestle and mortar, an anthill, et cetera. To keep her in good spirits, she had to avoid quarrel in the family, engage in worship of her father and mother-in-law and avoid uttering inauspicious words[8b].

The husband was enjoined to fulfil the wishes of his pregnant wife and keep her in good humour because "by not meeting the wishes of a pregnant women, foetus becomes unhealthy; it is either deformed or it falls down. Therefore, one should do as desired by her" (Yaj S. I I I.79). Aśvalāyana, in his *smriti*, forbids the husband[8c] "coition, pilgrimage and performing *śrāddha*" after the sixth month of pregnancy.

According to Mānava Gṛyha Sūtras I.1 2.2, parting of the hair is also a part of the marriage rite. By the time of Manu, the *saṃskāra* had lost its importance, as is evident from its lack of mention by the great lawmaker, even though Yaj does mention it. In some parts of the country, in the eighth month of pregnancy, this rite continues to be performed, wherein the pregnant woman is made to wear a garland of *udumbara* fruit around her neck.

Clearly, this *saṃskāra* had one purpose - good physical and mental health of the pregnant woman. However, it gradually lost its importance. Today, devoid of any religious ceremony, this *saṃskāra* is performed in a different *avatāra* called *godhabharāī*. Urban couples have suddenly taken to this ceremony, also called 'baby shower', wherein friends and relatives of the pregnant woman assemble for a feast to celebrate the pregnancy. The celebration is accompanied by none of the rituals associated with *Sīmantonnayana* of the olden times.

iv. *Viṣṇu bali* - This ceremony is performed in the eighth month of pregnancy during the bright fortnight, on the second, seventh or twelfth *tithi*, when the moon is in an auspicious constellation. The aim is to eliminate any harm to the foetus and promote an easy delivery, and is performed during every pregnancy. A *homa* has to be performed by offering *ājyabhāga* to the fire after *nandī śrāddha* has been performed the previous day. During special occasions like marriage or birth of a boy, *vriddhi śrāddha*, also known as *nandī śrāddha* is performed to get blessings of the ancestors.This is followed by sixty four oblations of boiled rice to *Viṣṇu* with recitation of verses from Ṛgveda, namely I.20 2.15 - 21, 154.1 - 6, VI.60 9.1 - 8, VI I.10 4.11, X.9 0.1 - 16, and X.184.1 - 3.

v. *Soṣhyantikarma* - This means 'a rite for a woman who is about to be delivered of a child'. It is an ancient rite described in the Ṛgveda V.78.7 - 9 (J &B) "As the wind sways a lotus-pond in every direction, so let your unborn child stir. Let him in his tenth month come out. As the wind, as the forest, as the ocean stirs, so you in your tenth month - descend together with the after birth. Having lain for ten months within his mother, let the boy come out, alive and unharmed - a life from his living mother." The husband draws water from a river or spring in an unused earthen cup, places *turyanti* plant at the feet of his wife and touches her head with both hands while chanting mantras. He sprinkles her with water from the cup and recites three appropriate verses. If the baby does not come out, he sprinkles more water while reciting two additional verses.

Even though some scholars hold the view that this is not really a *saṃskāra*, according to some other, this is a rite which has 'a seen result' (even though *saṃskāras* are deemed to have an unseen result).

vi. *Jātakarma* - In ancient times, the occasion of childbirth was both a time of excitement, and also anxiety and fear for the parents and immediate family. Since they did not fully understand the medical process of conception and delivery, the phenomenon of childbirth left them wide-eyed with wonderment and suppressed excitement. But even during this joyful time, they were seized with the fear of safety of the mother and child- not so much due to natural health risks of a pregnancy, as due to the harm caused by evil spirits and demons,who were believed to be constantly on the lookout for flesh and blood of the new born. Thus, on one hand, the possibility of the birth of a son, who would redeem the father of all ancestral debts, made the occasion religiously significant, on the other, concerns about the safety of the mother and child made the family take help of magic and religion (ref Atharvavedic magico religious ceremonies recommended for this occasion), to ward off any undue attention from evil forces. Equal attention was paid to the health and hygiene of the expectant mother. All possible help, and company of women who had already mothered children to share their own personal experience and knowledge, was provided to her.

In the medieval treatises, we come across a detailed account of the preliminary preparations made before the delivery. A month before delivery, on an auspicious day and time, a room called *sūtika bhavan* (maternity home) was built by expert architects on a firm and even ground. An auspicious and strong structure, the *bhavan* faced east or north, and was built for use during the last ten days of the pregnancy. The expectant mother was moved here a day or two before the delivery. Before shifting to the maternity home, the mother ceremoniously worshipped the gods, *brahmaṇa*, and cows, with the accompaniment of auspicious verses and musical instruments. Women who had already produced children joined the nervous expectant mother. They played a crucial role at the time of delivery since they had their own past experiences and knowledge. They made the pregnant lady lie down while the *brahmaṇa* loosened all the knots in the house, symbolising loosening of the foetus in the womb for an easy delivery. Fire, water, staff, lamp, weapons, mace and mustard seeds were kept in the house[9] and *turyani* plant was kept next to the mother to ward off lurking evil spirits and demons (HGS2.1.2.8; Āp GS 6.14.14).

The *soṣhyanti karma* ceremony was performed to expedite the delivery and make labour easy for the mother. Many authors, as has been described earlier, consider it a separate *saṃskāra*. Immediately after childbirth, fire was lit inside the room for its purifying influence. For the next ten days, this fire was kept alive. It was extinguished only after the mother and child had undergone the purification rite. Grains of rice and seeds of mustard were constantly thrown in the fire accompanied by appropriate mantras to keep away the evil spirits.

The actual *jātakarma* ceremony was performed before severing the umbilical cord[10]. After gaining the news of childbirth, the husband went to his wife to see his child. If it was a son, the father was absolved from all ancestral debts and attained immortality.[11] The husband then bathed in full clothes and performed *nandī śrāddha* and other *jātakarma* ceremonies.[12]

[Note - Not all *śrāddhas* are inauspicious ceremonies. Some, like *nandī śraddhā*, are auspicious.]

Medha-jñāna was performed by the father for developing intelligence in the child. In this ceremony, while 'four other persons touch him', the father makes the child lick honey and clarified butter in a gold spoon with the verse, "I give unto thee the Veda (Wisdom or knowledge) of honey and *ghṛita*, (Veda) which is produced by the God *Savitaṛ* (who urges on) the bountiful; may you have long life and may you live in this world for 100 autumns being protected by the gods."[13] The father's whisper of *medhajñāna* verse in the child's ears was believed to develop intelligence. Rajabali Pandey quotes Suśruta explaining *ghī* was included because, "it is producer of beauty; it is greasy and sweet; it is remover of hysteria, headache, epilepsy, fever, indigestion, excess of bile", and "it is increaser of digestion, memory, intellect, talent, lustre, good sound, semen and life"[14]

Thereafter, the father patted the son's shoulders with the Ṛgvedic mantras I I.1.6, I I I.3 6.10 and gave him a name. Aśva and Samkhya both describe giving a secret name to the child on the day of birth and do not prescribe a separate *nāma karna* ceremony (Asv GS 1.15.3-8).

Next came a rite for long life (*āyuṣa*) of the child in which the father murmured either near the navel or the right ear of the new born various utterances, such as '*Agni* is long-lived', 'through the trees he is long-lived', '*soma* is long-lived', 'ṛṣis are long-lived', et cetera He also repeated the verse 'the threefold age' three times (Vaj. S. I I I.62 - PGS I.16.6 - 7, SBE volume 29). Then, five *brahmaṇas* or the father himself read to the child symbolising a long life. The father then thanked the soil (the earth) on which the child was born.

The rite for strength of the child was performed next, wherein the child was asked to be a stone, an axe, or imperishable gold. Wishing him a life of hundred years, the father praised the mother for bearing him a son, and called her the daughter of *Mitra* and *Varuṇa-Ida*.

The navel cord was then severed, the child bathed and given to the mother for breast feeding. A jar of water was kept near the mother's head to ward off evil spirits.

The ceremony ended with offering presents to the *brahmaṇas* and distributing alms.

The different components of this rite in different *gṛyhasūtras* are put together beolw -

1. *Homa*;
2. *Medha jñāna* (muttering in ear of the boy '*vāk*');
3. *Āyuṣa* (muttering over the navel or right ear of the child);
4. *Aṃśabhimarśaṇa* (touching child on shoulder);
5. *Mātrabhimantraṇa* (addressing the mother);
6. *Panca Brahmaṇasthapana* (breathing over the child by five *Brahmaṇas*);
7. *Stanpratidhana* (offering breast feed to child);
8. *Deśābhimantraṇa* (touching the ground where the child is born);
9. *Nāma karna* (giving name to the child);
10. Keeping evil spirits away[15]

vii. *Utthāna* - It is getting up from child- bed on tenth or twelfth day after birth. The father shaves, bathes, purifies the house, and performs a sacrifice to the earth through a person of a different gotra. He feeds the *brahmaṇas* after bringing the *aupāsna* fire back and offers oblations to *Dhatr*, *Varuṇa* and other gods.

viii. *Nāmakarṇa* - The reason for conducting a ceremony for naming the child or *nāma karṇa* needs no explanation. What is unclear is why the father gives the new born a secret name within a couple of hours of birth. The explanation, even for those who are superstitious, that it is to keep evil away is perplexing. *Nāma karṇa*, however, is not the same as giving the child a secret name right after birth. It is a ceremony in which the father and mother jointly give a name to the child on the tenth day (according to Āpastamba, Baudhāyana and Pāraskara) of his birth. While Yaj I.12 prescribes the eleventh day for the ceremony, Hiraṇyakeśin advocates the twelfth day, Vaikhānasa, Baudhāyana and Manu, tenth or twelfth day. To add to the confusion, Gobhilla and Khadira (GGS I I.8.8 and Kh. GS I I.3.6) provide the flexibility of any day after ten nights, a hundred nights or a year from birth. It appears that every *gṛhya sūtra* went its own way for prescribing a suitable time for the naming ceremony. This made Aprārka say that one may follow one's own *gṛyhasūtras*[16].

Four Names: Interestingly, a person could have up to four names in the Vedic period - a secret name given by the father right after birth, name given during the *nāma karṇa saṃskāra*, a *nakṣatra nāma* (name of the *nakṣatra* in which a person was born was attached to the child's name), and the name received for the performance of a sacrifice, *e.g. agnihotṛi*, et cetera. In yet another common practice, a person had three names - the ordinary name, a name derived from his father, and a name from his *gotra* or a famous ancestor. The most common Vedic way, however, is for a person to have two names - his own name followed by the name of his *gotra*, e.g. Cyavana Bhargava.

Rules for naming child : Different *gṛhya sūtras* prescribe different rules for naming the male child. These are summarised below -

- The name should have even number of syllables, such as 2, 4, et cetera
- The name should begin with the consonant and contain a semivowel in the middle
- The name should end in a long vowel
- The name should end in a *visarga* immediately after a long vowel
- Many also suggest that the name should be formed from a root by a *krit* affix and should not be formed from a noun by an affix

Interestingly, the Mānava Gṛyha Sūtras forbids giving the name of a deity, but allows giving a name derived from a deity's name or *nakṣatra* (I.18). In Vedic literature, one can observe the absence of any human named after a Vedic god's name. But, names like Viṣṇumitra, Bhanuka or Yajñadatta which are derived from the names of deities are common. According to Kane[17a] this practice probably began in the first century of the Christian era and became common by the fifth century, as evidenced by names like Viṣṇu Gupta.

While the child could not be given his father's name (Mānava GS I.180), it was a common practice to name him after his grandfather. This practice was particularly common among the rulers of ancient and mediaeval period.

In modern times, contemporary works like Saṃskāra Prakāśa, part of Mitra Mishra's twelve volume Vīramitrodaya (page 237), recommend that names may be given based on *devtā námah*, *masa nāmah*, *nakṣatra námah* and *vyāvahārika námah*.

Special rules were laid down for naming girls. Her name had to contain three syllables, ending in *a*, *da* or *ani*, and a long vowel. Vāraha Gṛhya Sūtras prescribe that while the name should have vowel 'a', it should neither be after a river, a *nakṣatra*, or name of the sun, moon or *pūṣan*, nor imply that a name was given by god, or having the word *rakshita*. Manu I I.33 prescribes the name should be easy to pronounce, have a long vowel, not suggest any harsh acts, should be auspicious and convey a blessing. In a subsequent *sūtras*, Manu lays down the rule that one should not marry a girl named after *nakṣatras*, trees or rivers. However, Āpastamba over rides this view of Manu (I I I.13).

It appears that the practice of having two names, one given and the other indicating *varṇa*, came into existence a couple of centuries before Christ, in Manu's time[17b]. Though Manu does not specifically suggest what this second name should be, Pāraskara is more specific, he suggests - Śarman for *brahmaṇa*, Varman for *kṣatriya*, and Gupta for *vaiśya*, Aprārka a commentator and a king (widely accepted to have ruled be somewhere between 1100-1200 AD) and Viṣnu Purāna - a pre Christian era text, also suggest *varṇa* specific second names[17c]: Śarmā or Deva for *brahmaṇa*, Verma or Trātā for *kṣatriya*, Bhūti or Datta for *vaiśya*, and Dāsa for *śūdra*.

Ceremony: Towards the end of the naming ceremony, the house was washed and purified to remove impurities caused by birth, and the child and the mother were given a bath. The child was covered with fresh pure raw silk cloth and his head sprinkled with water. He was handed over to father after which offerings were made to *prājāpatya*, date, constellation, the deities, *Agni* and *Soma*. Alternatively, *homa* was performed in the *aupāsna* fire with oblations to *Dhatr*, *Anumati*, *Rākā*, *Sinvali*, and according to some, to *Kuhu*.

Thereafter, the father touched the breath of the child and gave him a name. The following procedure was followed, though these details are not available in *gṛhya sūtras* -

The father whispers in the right ear of the child, "O child! Thou art the devotee of the family deity so thy name is such and such; thou art born in such and such month so thy name is such and such; thou art born under such and such constellation, so thy name is such and thy popular name is such and such." The *brahmaṇa* confirms by saying, "may thee name be established." Thereafter, the child is made to salute the *brahmaṇas*, who bless it with long life, and the ceremonies end with feeding the *brahmaṇas* (Ref. Saṃskāra vidhi, Swami Dayānand Saraswati; and Sodasha Saṃskāra vidhi, Pandit Bhima Sena Sarma).

ix. *Karṇavedha* - It is piercing of the ear lobes of the child, generally on the twelfth day after birth; some GS suggest the seventh or tenth month. In case of girls, the left ear is pierced first. Nirukta too talks of ear piercing, indicating the antiquity of this *saṃskāra*. In modern days this ceremony is hardly ever performed by the parents in case of boys in their child hood. Many of adults have started getting their ears pierced - not as observance of *saṃskāra* but to be in tune with modern fashion.

x. *Niṣkramaṇa* - This is a minor rite wherein the child is taken out of the house for the first time. According to most *gṛyha sūtras*, the child is taken out and shown the sun with the recitation of Vaj S. 4.36.24 verse in the fourth month or the twelfth day.

xi. *Annaprāśana* - This involves feeding child cooked food for the first time - usually in the sixth month from birth. In a brief procedure, the father prepares food from goat's flesh, flesh of partridge, fish and boiled rice, for nourishment, holy lustre, swiftness or splendour respectively, and mixes them with curd, honey and *ghī*. (This practice of feeding animal flesh is hardly ever practiced in modern times, and refers to *gṛyha sūtra* period). He feeds this to the child with recitation of the *mahāvyahrtis -'Bhūr bhuvaḥ svaḥ*'. The father then offers oblations to fire with the four verses of Ṛgveda IV.12.4 - 5, recites I X.6 6.19 over the child, and sits the child down northwards on *kusha* grass with the verse I.2 2.15. The mother eats remnants of the food.

This was an important ceremony as it signalled weaning the child away from breastfeeding to solid and semisolid *anna*. It was important for the health of the mother as well as child. It was an occasion for the family to rejoice seeing the child transit from being completely dependent on the mother's milk to sustaining on solid food, indicating a normal and healthy growth.

xii. *Varṣavardhana* - This ceremony involves making a sacrifice to *Agni* and *Índra*, heaven, earth and *Viśvedevās* every month on the birthday of the child for one year, and subsequently, every birthday every year throughout life. Having sacrificed to these deities, the father should sacrifice to the *tithi* and *nakṣatra* (Gobhila GS. I I.8.19 - 20). A few other *gṛyhasūtras* prescribe a *homa* every month for a year after *nāma karṇa*, with offerings of goat flesh and sheep to *Agni* and *Dhanavantri* (in the same way as *námakarma*) followed by offering food to the *brahmaṇa* (Kathka GS. 36.12 and 14).

xiii. *Caula* or *cudākarma* - The first haircut of child is mentioned in every *gṛhya sūtra*. *Cuda* means a lock or tuft (*śikha*) of hair left on the head while the rest is shaved.

Reasons for shaving head has two explanations -

i. Long hair and nails were recognised as health hazard. It was believed that shaving head resulted in a long life (Aśhv GS I.1 7.12). This view was supported by Suśruta, an ancient Indian physician and author of Suśruta Saṃhitā (600 BC), and by Carka, author of the famous Caraka Saṃhitā (600-200 BC). Both *Saṃhitās* are the two most valuable texts which can be called the foundation stone of Āyurveda (ancient Indian medicine system). Both are of the view[18a] that shaving and cutting the hair and nails gave strength, vigour, light, happiness and life. Rajbali, quoting Suśruta, says, "Inside the head near the top, is the joint of *śira* (artery) and *sandhi* (a critical juncture). There in the eddy of hairs is the vital spot called *adhipati* (overlord). Any injury to this part causes them to death."[18b]

ii. In a society obsessed with *śauca* and *aśauca* i.e. pure and impure, shaving hair on head had another compelling reason - impurities of the seed and womb had to be (physically) removed as soon as possible.

As soon as a razor could be used on the tender skin of a new born child, the head was shaved. Atharvaveda contains a prayer reflecting the awareness of the danger of exposing the tender skin of the child and the head, when the skull is not fully formed, to the sharp edge of a razor. This prayer praises and requests razor to be harmless - "Thou art friendly by name. Thy father is hard iron. I salute thee; do not injure the child" (Atharvaveda 68.1). Although there are references of hair cutting and shaving of the head in the Yajurveda, the Ṛgveda does not contain any direct reference to the existence of this practice in early Vedic times.

While in most *gṛhya sūtras*, *caula* is prescribed to be performed in the third year of birth, Baud I I.4, Pāraskara I I.1 and Manu I I.35 suggest performing it in the first year or the third year. As usual, there is no unanimity on the exact age - while Aśva prescribes the third year or in accordance with the family custom, Vīramitrodaya Samskāra quoting him adds "but it can be performed in the seventh year or with the *upanayana*."[33]

The ceremony was performed when the sun was in the *uttarāyaṇa*, during the daytime, and the mother was not impure due to menstruation. The ceremony was prohibited if the mother was five months or more pregnant. In the earlier times, it was performed at home because that is where the domestic fire was kept burning, and consequently, home was the theatre of all domestic sacrifices including the *saṃskāras*. With the decline of the practice of keeping domestic fire and rise of idol worship, many people started choosing temples or bank of a holy river for performing *caula* and *upanayana saṃskāras*.

The actual ceremony was performed on an auspicious day and consisted of the principal act of shaving the hair of the child, *homa*, feeding the *brahmaṇas*, receiving benedictions of the *brahmaṇa* and giving *dakṣiṇā*. Finally, the cut hair was disposed in a way that no one could find it.

The preliminary ceremonies of *saṃkalpa*, *Gaṇeśa* worship, *maṅgala śrāddhā*, et cetera were performed first. Then, food was distributed among the *brahmaṇas*. The child was bathed by the mother who then clothed him in unwashed new garments and held the child in her lap next to the sacrificial fire. The father made *ājya* oblations holding her hand, and then partook in the sacrificial food. He then mixed warm water into cold inviting *Vāyu* and *Aditi*, all the while looking at the barber. After mixing a bit of butter, *ghī* or curd with the water, the father moistened the hair near the right ear invoking *Savitaṛ*, "On the impulse of *Savitaṛ*! May the divine waters moisten the body in order that long life and splendour may be thine."

Using a porcupine quill with three white spots, the father dishevelled the hair of the child and put three *kusha* shoots in to it with the mantra, "Herb, protect this child. Do not inflict pain on it." He cut the *kusha* shoots alongwith the hair praying "Thy father is iron: salutation be to thee. Do not hurt the child" with the additional words, "I cut off the hair for a long life, properly digesting food, productivity, prosperity, good progeny, and valour. The razor with which *Savitaṛ*, the knowing one, has shaven the beard of the kings *Sóma* and *Varuṇa*, with that ye brahmán, shave the head, in order that he may be blessed with long life and may reach old age." The cut hair and the *kusha* grass are thrown on a lump of bull's dung kept north of the fire. The head is shaved three times from left to right with appropriate verses. Then, the razor is given to the barber to shave off the rest and give a shape to the remaining locks according to the family tradition, with the verse "when the shaver shaves its head with the razor, wounding the well-shaped, purify his head, but do not take away his life."[34]

The cut hair is placed in the dung of a bull and buried in a cow stable, or thrown in a pond or near the water (Bharadvaja GS I.28, Pāraskara GS I I.1), or buried in the root of an *udumbara* tree, in a bunch of *durba* grass or the forest. The reason for this is rooted in the fear that inimical elements can cast a magical spell or commit acts of sorcery using personal possessions, hair, nails, et cetera There are divergent views on the number of locks of hair to be left on the head. According to Baud DS (I I.41), one or three or five locks may be left according to family usage. He further adds that according to some sages, as many locks as the *pravaras* invoked by the father may be left, but never four.

The *shikha* or top knot remains to be one of the characteristic outward signs of all Hindus - without the *yajñopavīta* and *śikhā* 'performance of religious ceremonies is tantamount to non-performance'[35]. The twice born 'who out of infatuation, ignorance or hatred cut off the top-hair, bcome purified by undergoing the *taptakrecchra* penance'.[36]

Aśhva GS I.1 7.18 specifically says that *cudakarma* was to be performed for girls too, but without the Vedic mantras. Manu (I I.66) and Yaj (I.13) also say the same thing.

xiv. *Vidyāraṃbha* - Although the *gṛyhasūtras* and *dharma sūtras* are silent on this topic, Kauṭilya, in his Arthaśāstra, speaks of prince engaging in the study of alphabet and arithmetic after *caula*. Bana talks of the prince entering the temple of learning at the age of six. Aprārka and Smṛtichandrika, citing Mārkaṇḍeya Purāṇa, speak of the ceremony to be performed when the child begins learning. It should be conducted in the fifth year of the child on a day between twelve of bright half of *kārtika* to eleven of bright half of *āsādha*, but excluding first, sixth, eighth, fifteenth and rikta tithis. *Viṣṇu*, *Lakṣmī* and *Sarasvatī* are worshipped and oblations are offered in the fire to various deities, followed by honouring the *brahmaṇas* and giving *dakṣiṇā*. The teacher begins the first lesson after the boy has received benediction of the *brahmaṇa*, which should be stopped on the days of *anādhyaya* (days of break).

xv. *Upanayana* - Literally meaning 'leading or taking near', it appears that it originally meant taking the child to the *ācārya* for learning, or introducing the novice to the stage of student-hood.

The earliest reference to *upanayana* and *brahmācārya* is in the Ṛgveda (III.8.4.5 and X.109.5). The celibate student is much extolled in two hymns in the subsequent Vedic text, the Atharvaveda. We find details of *upanayana* here-in Atharvaveda - which were later institutionalised in *upanayana saṃskāras* ceremonies. The Atharvaveda also describes the initiation of the student by the teacher as, "The teacher, taking him in charge, makes the Vedas student an embryo within", which he bears "in his belly three nights; gods gather unto him to see him when born" (AV XI. 5.3). This is perhaps how *upanayana* came to be regarded as the second birth of the student. The Atharva goes on to describe that the student so-initiated wore a sacred girdle, put on a deer skin, practiced austerity and collected alms and fuel, observed strict celibacy while living in the guru's house. And above all, his stay with guru was for the sole purpose of *vidyā* or learning; not any learning, but learning the Vedas from his guru. This appears to have been a standard practice for anyone desirous of learning. In the time of Brahmaṇas, true to the character of Brahmaṇas, this assumed form of a ceremony with fixed procedures (SB. I.2.1-8). In the *gṛhyasūtras* period (PGS II.2.5), anyone desirous of studentship under an *ācārya* simply had to approach the guru with fuel sticks and a humble submission, "I have come for *brahmachārya*; let me be a *brahmachārī*." The teacher asked him about his family background and took him in his charge. He explained the dos and the dont's, and taught the *gāyatri mantra* to the student. For the next three days, the teacher observed continence (exercising restraint, especially sexual - Oxford dictionary). The teacher became even more important in the times of the Upaniṣads because in the age of reason or the ultimate knowledge, *Brahman vidyā* could only be learnt by sitting at the guru's feet. This is the period when *upanayan* shed its frills and retained only the 'learning' part of the earlier ritual. Anyone desirous of learning could go to a guru with fuel sticks and express his desire to be a disciple. The teacher decided (among other things, depending on *varṇa* considerations) whether to accept the applicant as his student or not. (Ref Aruni and Jabali etc for ignoring *varṇa* restriction)

By sin, a man becomes degenerate, by grace, he becomes regenerate, or is conducted (*nayana*) to nearness (*upa*) of spirit. This is the *dvijatva* or new birth. This concept is symbolised in the Atharvavedic teacher when he makes his 'Veda student an embryo within', which he bears 'in his belly three nights; gods gather unto him to see him when born' (AV. XI. 5.3). However, the *dvijata* could only belong to the *brahmaṇa*, *kṣatriya* and *vaiśya varṇa*; *śūdra* was strictly excluded and called *ekajāta* or once born. In the beginning - the Ṛgvedic times - the *varṇāśrama vyavasthā* (*varṇa* order/arrangement) was nothing more than a vague idea of classification of the society, according to the livelihood of different sections of society, But by the Atharva period, it had taken a firm shape, and the *smṛtis* cast this system in steel.

In the *upanayana* rite, the guru (preceptor) accepts a boy as his pupil for learning Vedas, but through a purificatory rite. This rite signified purity and spirituality of a second birth, open only to the three higher *varṇa* or *dvijats* of the Hindu society. In his *smṛti*, Manu explained that there are three births - first from the mother; second, when a girdle is tied on (i.e. when *upanayana* takes place); and third, when one is initiated in a Vedic sacrifice. The latter two births were permitted only to members of the three higher *varṇa*s.

The *upanayana* was important because it enabled a *dvijata* to learn the Vedas. The student could enter the *gṛhastha āśrama* only after completion of his Veda studies. Once married, he could produce a son and perform the various rites without which neither could he redeem life's debts nor avoid going to hell. Thus, the *upanayana* was not just any learning; it was the initiation of learning the Vedas and preparing to enter the *gṛhastha āśrama* for higher goals of life, a second birth. This is why *upanayana saṃskāra* is considered an initiation ceremony signifying purity and spirituality unrelated to other *saṃskāras*.

Thus, the ritual for initiating a student for study of the Vedas under an *ācārya*, the vows and restraints, the observances, and the vicinity of a god, was called *upa-nayana*. The *upanayana* ritual developed into a philosophy which covered the simplicity and discipline of the educational life, symbolized by wearing a girdle of *munja*-grass, and taking *Savitaṛ* as the mother and the teacher as the father. Yajñavalkya states that the learning of the Vedas was the main object of the *upanayana*. (Yaj.S. I.33-34)

Age and time: Different age were prescribed for the initiation ceremony of the three *varṇa* - eighth year for *brahmaṇa*, eleventh year for *kṣatriyas*, and twelfth year for *vaiśya* (Aśhva GS I.19, Baud I I.5, Āp XI, GGS I I.10, Manu I I.36, Yaj I.11). The reason for prescribing different age for different *varṇa* is unclear. A practical reason could be that since a *brahmaṇa* child did not have to leave his home for initiation (his father could perform the ceremony and usually did), he could be initiated at a young age. Both *kṣatriya* and *vaiśya* children had to leave their home and stay with a guru, so their departure from the care and comfort of the home was delayed by three or more years. There is also some merit in the argument that these age limits were fixed by the *brahmaṇas* out of conceit. They regarded a *brahmaṇa* child to be more intelligent than the other two, and fit to receive education at a younger age.

The un-initiated, regardless of the class of his birth, was likened in many *Dharmasūtras* to *śūdras* who were also excluded from Vedic rituals. So, we find statements like "they do not put any restrictions on the acts of (a child) before the initiation for he is on the level with a *śūdra* before his (second) birth through the Veda."[19]

Just like the different ages for initiation, for different *varṇa*s, different seasons are recommended for performance of the *upanayana* ceremony - 'Let him initiate a *Brahmaṇa* in spring, a *kṣatriya* in summer, a *vaiśya* in autmn' (Āp.GS 1.1.1.19). These seasons were symbolic of the temperament and occupation of the different *varṇa*s. The moderation of spring symbolized the moderate life expected of a *brahmaṇa*; the heat of summer represented the fervour associated with a *kṣatriya*; and autumn was when the commercial life of early India reopened after the rainy season suggesting wealth and prosperity of a *vaiśya*.[20]

Depending on the special benefit intended from the learning, the age of initiation was modified. "One desirous of only lustre should perform the *upanayana* in the eleventh year, of long life in the eight year, of glory in the ninth year, of food in the tenth, of cattle in the twelvth, of talent in the thirteenth, of strength in the fourteenth, of brothers in the fifteenth and of all on the sixteenth." (Baud GS I I.5.5) Manu has prescribed different ages for initiation to secure special merits - 'For a priest who desires the splendour of the Veda, it is to be done in the fifth year; for a king who seeks strength, in the sixth; and for a commoner who is ambitious, in the eighth' (MS II.37, Doniger). Interestingly, the ages that Manu prescribes are different from the one prescribed by Baudhāyana. The ambiguity of different ages for acquisition of special merits is left to speculation, as these sages have not explained the co-relation of age with the special merits.

The upper age limit for performance of the *saṃskāra* was sixteen for *brahmaṇa*, twenty-two for *kṣatriya* and twenty-four for *vaiśya* (P GS. I I.5.36 - 38). However, it had to be performed before the marriage of the twice born. This laxity in the age of *upanayana* is not unexpected; with the passage of time, the society changed in many ways, particularly after the eleventh century when Muslim rulers started governing different parts of the country.

Punishment for not undergoing initiation: Initially, anyone belonging to the three higher *varṇa*s had to undergo the initiation, failing which he was excommunicated from the community of Āryans - "After that (past the age of initiation), if these three (classes) have not undergone the transformative rituals at the proper time, they lose their chance of learning the words to the Sun God and become outlaws, despised by Āryans." (MS I I.39) Such people were clubbed with the non-Āryan tribe of *Vrātya*, and called *Vrātyas* - "A priest should never, even in extremity, forge a Vedic or sexual bonds with these people who have not been purified."[21] According to Rajbali Pandey[22], the *Vrātyas* were Āryans in race, but they were not Vedic in religion. This inference is supported by the fact that, "the door of Āryandom was always open for them if they sought admission, while it was closed against the *śūdras*." (Rajbali quotes PGS I I.5.44 in support of the latter statement).

***Upanayana* not compulsory in the beginning**: There is no evidence in the Vedic literature suggesting that the *upanayana* was compulsory. Rajbali argues that in the pre-*sūtras* times, *upanayana* was not compulsory but optional. His argument is based on the fact that the *upanayana* was regarded as the second birth (AV. X I.5.3) in the Atharvaveda, but this idea of second birth was not unique to the *upanayana*. All initiations preparatory to Vedic sacrifices were called second birth, as is evident in Śatapatha (I I.3.4). Therefore, it can be concluded that the second birth is referred in the religious context rather than social context. He has further quoted the example of Aruni advising his son Svetaketu that their family did not claim *brahmānism* by birth (Chāndogya Upaniṣad VI.1.1). Another argument put forth by him is that the *varnāśrama* was not yet firmly in place, and the word *Vrātya* did not denote a person who had not performed the *upanayana*, but was used in the sense of a person who did not offer sacrifice or keep the sacred fire.[23]

There is little doubt that *upanayana* had become compulsory for the *dvijas* in and around the Upaniṣadic period. This is understandable because the Upaniṣads represent a period of knowledge, a move away from rituals. In this period, there was a great emphasis on learning *vidyās* relating to *Ātmā* and *Brahman*, invariably done sitting at the feet of the guru. With increase in the popularity of education, it was natural for *upanayana* to assume great importance and become a 'compulsory' *saṃskāra*. However, with the passage of time, when the practice of sending children to the guru's house for several years at a stretch became out of sync with the changed reality of the society, though the *saṃskāra* continues to be performed, but as a farce; these days, a man, who has already finished his university education, pretends to go to a guru's home in the caricature of *upanayana saṃskāra* proper.

The ceremony proper: The *upanayana* had taken firm shape as a formal ceremony by the time of the *sūtras* and *smṛtis*. Even though the components of the initiation are common in all *sūtras* and *smṛtis*, each - as is the wont of Hindu texts - has its own variations, e.g. the age limit, the material and colour of the garments, and more importantly, the Vedic mantras, all differ in different texts.

An important feature of the various rites performed in the *upanayana* is the apparent conscious effort to bring to the fore *varṇa* based distinctions of the 'would be' *brahmācariṇ*. Thus, a different age for initiation was prescribed for *brahmaṇa*, *kṣatriya* and *vaiśya*. The length and material of the staff or *ḍaṇḍa* differed for different *varṇa* - *palāsa* wood for *brahmaṇa*, *udumbara* for *kṣatriya* and *vilva* wood for *vaiśya*. The staff of the *brahmaṇa* student had to be as high as his hair, up to the forehead for *kṣatriya* and up to the nose for *vaiśya*. On every step, we come across this *varṇa*-based distinction in conduct of the ceremony, indicating that by this time, the society had adopted a rigid *varṇa* based system.

The first step was choosing an auspicious time for the ceremony - spring for *brahmaṇa*, summer for *kṣatriya* and autumn for *vaiśya* is recommended. By this time, the caste system had also emerged, and there is specific mention of the rainy season as most suitable for *rathakaras*. Many scholars believe that the seasons symbolise the main characteristic of the different *varṇa*s.

A canopy was erected at a suitable place to perform the *saṃskāra* and on the day of the initiation, the boy was given something to eat. Usually, he shared this meal with his mother symbolizing his crossover to the next stage of life. After this meal, he was forbidden to share a meal with her or any other lady. His head was shaved and he was bathed.

After the bath, the boy was given *kaupīna*, a piece of cloth to cover his modesty, while the rest of his body remained naked. He then approached the *ācārya* and announced his intention to become a *brahmāchari*. Once accepted, he was offered new clothes accompanied with the verse, "In the way in which *Bṛhaspati* put the garment of immortality on *Índra*, thus I put this garment on thee, for the sake of long life, of old age, of strength, of splendour."[24] Apart from symbolising a new identity, it carried a strong message of protection that the *ācārya* offered his new disciple.

The teacher then gave a staff, referred as *ḍanda*, to the student, which he was advised to maintain all the time. As mentioned earlier, the length of the staff varied depending on whether the recipient was a *brahmaṇa*, *kṣatriya* or *vaiśya*. Apart from the wood used for the staff (*palāsa*, *udumbara* or *vilva*), scholars have also prescribed for it to be unbroken and unscratched. The bark (Gautam DS) should be straight, fine looking and unburnt by fire (Manu I I.47). *Ḍanḍa* signified the boy becoming a guardian of the Vedas - an analogy drawn from the *ḍanḍa* of a king that symbolised him as protector and upholder of Dharma, the law. More practical use of the staff were perhaps herding the guru's cattle, protection from animals in the forest during his forays to collect sacred fuel, and as a defensive weapon when he ventured out in the dark (Yājñavalkya S. I.29). The purpose of the *ācārya* presenting the initiate with the staff is encapsulated in the verse spoken by the student while accepting it - "My staff which fell down to the ground in the open air, that I take up again for the sake of long life, of holiness, of holy lustre" (PGS I I.2.12). The same *sūtraskara* goes on to add that according to some teachers, the student accepts the staff because "he enters upon a long *sattra* (sacrificial period)."[25]

A girdle was then tied around the waist of the student by the *ācārya* to ward off evil spirits (PGS II.2.8) and protect his purity. One practical reason of tying the girdle perhaps was to support the *kaupina*. Depending on the *varṇa* of the student, the girdle was made of *munja* grass for *brahmaṇa*, bow string for *kṣatriya* and wool for *vaiśya*.

Although cotton clothes were also prescribed (GDS I.17.18) as an option, many scholars prescribed hemp, silk and *kusha* grass, for "the *Brahmaṇa* reddish yellow one, the *kṣatriya* a light red one, the *vaiśya*, a yellow one" (Aśhva GS.I.19.11). Alternately, an antelope skin for *brahmána*, skin of a spotted deer for *kṣatriya* and a goat's skin for *vaiśya*, were also prescribed (Aśhva GS I.19.10).

This marked the end of an important part of the *upanayana* ceremony in which the student was prepared and equipped for life in the *gurukula*.

A series of symbolic acts followed leading to the *ācārya* taking over the charge of the student. The first act was purification in which - " (the teacher then) fills the two hollows of (his own and the student's) joined hands with water, and with the verse, 'That we choose of *Savitaṛi*'(Ṛg. V.8 2.1) he makes with the full (hollow of his own hands the water) flow down on the full (hollow of) his, (i.e. the student's hands). Having (thus) poured (the water over his hands) he should with his own hand seize his (i.e. the student's) hand together with the thumb, with (the formula) 'By the impulse of the God *Savitaṛi*, with the arms of the two *Aśvins*, with the *Pūṣan's* hands I seize thy hand, N. N.!' (Aśva GS. I.2 0.4). And then '*Savitaṛi* has seized thy hand, N.N.', and yet again '*Agni* is thy teacher, N.N.' the *Ācārya* causes the student to look at the Sun saying 'God *Savitaṛi*, this is thy *brahmācariṇ*; protect him; may he not die'.[26]

Pāraskara says it a little differently though. After making the student look at the sun, the teacher touches the heart of the student over his right shoulder and seizing the student's right-hand says, "What is thy name?" The student replies, "I am N.N, Sir!" The teacher then specifically asks him, "Whose pupil art thou?" The student replies, "Yours!" At this point, the teacher points out that the student is *Índra's* pupil, *Agni's* pupil and his own pupil[27]. Pāraskara's account is more explicit as far as the pupil asking to be taken in charge and the guru taking his charge is concerned. Both Aśhva and Pāraskara conclude that 'The student becomes belonging to *prājāpatya*' is understood in the *sruti*! (Aśhva I.2 0.11 and Pāraskara I I.2.2).

After taking the charge, the student and teacher go around the fire and make *ājya* oblations. After partaking in remains of the sacrificial food, the teacher gives the commandments, the first set of instructions to the student - "A student art thou. Take water. Do the service. Do not sleep in the daytime. Keep silence. Put fuel on (the fire). Take water" (PGS 2.3.2).

Thereafter, the student and *ācārya* look at each other while the *ācārya* recites *Savitaṛi* to him, "*Pada* by *pada*, (then) hemistich by hemistich, and the third time the whole (verse), reciting it together (with the student)" (PGS 2.3.5). Here again, based on the student's *varṇa*, the *Savitaṛi* verse is to be recited in *gāyatri* - metre to a *brahmaṇa*, *trishtubha* to *rājanya* and *jagati* to *vaiśya* student (2.3.7-10). In this critical part of the *upanayana* ceremony, the boy requests the teacher to accept him as a *brahmāchāri* (student). The teacher holds the boy's hand and addresses him, "You are the *Brahmāchari* of *Índra*: *Agni* is your teacher, I am a teacher, N.N. (addressing the boy by his name)"[28] and consigns the boy to the care of the elements. The student is then given his first set of instructions - drink water, work in the teacher's house, put fuel sticks on fire, do not sleep in the daytime and repeat the sacred *Savitaṛi mantra.*

Interestingly, in ancient times, the sacred *gāyatri* verse was imparted by the teacher to the students one year, six months, twenty five, twelve or three days after the *upanayana*. But in case of a *brahmaṇa* student, this was supposed to be done immediately. (SB.XI.5.4.6 - 12)

This teaching of the sacred mantra signalled the second birth of the child, as the teacher was regarded the father and *Savitaṛi* the mother of the child (MS I I.170).

The next rite was of sacred fire. The student went around the fire with folded hands uttering, "*Agni*, glorious one, make me glorious. As thou, glorious *Agni*, art glorious, thus, O glorious one, bring me glory. As thou, *Agni*, art the preserver of the treasure of sacrifice for the gods, thus may I become the preserver of the treasure of the Veda for men." After sprinkling water around the fire, he stood up and put a piece of wood in the fire saying, "To *Agni* I have brought a piece of wood, to the great *jātavedas*", and "may my teacher be the father of living sons; may I be full of insight, not forgetful (of what I have learned); may I become full of glory, of a splendour, lustre, and enjoyer of food. *Svāhā*!" After putting wood in the fire, he sprinkles water round the fire, warms his hands, wipes his mouth and utters the formula for *Agni* to give him life, vigour and restore fullness to his body. He concludes with the formula, "May the God *Savitaṛi* bestow insight on me, may the goddess *Saraswati*, may the two divine *Aśvins*, wreathed with Lotus, (bestow) insight (on me)." (PGS 2.4.3 - 8).

This was also the beginning of a life of collecting alms - the chief means of the student's maintenance - for the rest of his stay at the guru's place. The ceremonious beginning was made on the day of *upanayana* by collecting alms from his mother and other relatives who would not refuse. The form of address for begging was fixed and yet again, *varṇa* was prominently on display. In case of a *brahmaṇa*, the word lady was inserted at the beginning of the sentence while requesting for alms, in the middle of the sentence for a *kṣatriya*, and at the end for a *vaiśya.*

This custom of begging was to make the student understand that he was not contributing anything to the society while learning, and was dependent on their charity. It also deeply imbibed humility and humbleness in every student and brought the rich and poor at the same platform.

After the initiation ceremony, the student was required to observe three days of continence called *triratra vrata*. On the day of the *upanayana*, after finishing his round of begging, the student announced to the teacher what he had received and stored for the rest of the day. After sunset, he cooked boiled rice for the *anupravachaniya* sacrifice - a sacrifice performed after a part of the Veda has been studied - and announced it to the teacher. Four oblations were made by the teacher 'while the student takes hold of him' and food was offered to the *brahmaṇas*. The teacher then requested the *brahmaṇas* to pronounced the beginning of the Veda study. Thereafter, the student was forbidden to eat saline food; he observed chastity and slept on the ground for three or twelve nights, or one year. After he fulfilled these observances, the *medhajñāna* ritual was performed to evoke divine help in sharpening his intellect, memory and retaining power[29].

The qualification of an *ācārya* was important since, "he whom a teacher devoid of learning initiates enters from darkness into darkness and he also (i.e. an *ācārya*) who is himself unlearned (enters into darkness)."[37] The *ācārya* had to be a *brahmaṇa* who had studied at least one *śākhā* of a Veda. Though, in absence of a *brahmaṇa ācārya*, the guru could be a non-*brahmaṇa*, as is evident in multiple instances where *brahmaṇas* approached *kṣatriya* rulers for knowledge.

It normally took twelve years for a student to learn one Veda, which was the minimum period of student-ship. One desirous of learning all the four Vedas had to spend forty-eight years with the guru, i.e., his studentship lasted fifty-six years if he was a *brahmaṇa* - since for a *brahmaṇa* learning of Vedas commenced at the age of eight years.

According to Kane, a woman *Brahman vedini* (students of sacred lore) was allowed to go through *upanayana*, keep fire and study Vedas, but her begging was restricted to her parental home. Gobhila also speaks of the bride "who is wrapped in her robe, and wears the Sacrificial cord over her left shoulder, she should murmur (the verse), '*Sóma* gave her to the *Gandharva*'. But, this view is refuted by the translator/editor Oldenberg in his footnotes (17-19) - "*Yajñopavīta* or *śikhā nim* in *sūtras* 19 means, according to the commentary, that she wears her outer garment arranged like the Sacrificial cord, over her left shoulder; for women are not allowed to wear the Sacrificial cord itself."[30] On the other hand, this view is supported by Kh. GS. I.3.6 where the bride takes a bath and is "dressed in a garment that has not yet been washed with (the verse) 'they who spun' (MB I. I.7)." Kane has quoted Yama and Manu in support of his point. Manu speaks of *saṃskāras* from *jātakarma* to *upanayana* for both men and women in entirety (I I.66), but goes on to add that these were old practices that belonged to another *yuga*. Even when *saṃskāras* were performed for women, it was without *mantras*[31].

The student spent long years at the guru's house. During this period, he served the guru and his wife while the guru gave him shelter, food and knowledge. As a *brahmāchārī*, the student had to observe *brahmāchārī* dharma, some of which were for a short term, such as not eating saline food, observing chastity and sleeping on the ground (Aśhva GS I.20 2.19), besides avoiding milk (Kh GS I I.4.32), honey, flesh, bathing for pleasure, sitting on high seats, going to women, falsehood, and accepting water not given to him (PGS I I.5.12). Such observances lasted for three or twelve nights or one year after the *upanayana*. Other observances had to be continued for the entire period of his student hood, including worshipping the fire, begging for food, *saṃdhyopāsanā* (*saṃdhyā* involved *japa* of *gāyatri* and other sacred mantras apart from *āchamana*, *prāṇāyāma*, *mārjana*, offering water to the sun, et cetera), study of the Vedas, serving the guru, his family and other elders, and observing the *vrata* of a *brahmāchari̅*.

Any breach in begging for food and offering fuel sticks to the fire every day was a serious offense. If the student failed in this duty for seven days continuously (except when he was ill), he had to put on the skin of a donkey and beg for food from seven houses proclaiming his own act (Manu I I.124), the same penance is prescribed for sexual intercourse.

Life at the teacher's house: The student was required to be dependent on the teacher and under his complete control. He could stay with no one but the teacher, had to serve the teacher by tending the cattle, beg for food and inform the teacher, and look after the sacred fires (Chāndogya IV.4.5; 3.5). He could only attend his study of the Veda after completing the rest of the work for the guru (Chāndogya Upaniṣad a VI I I.1 5.10. He was required to help the teacher in his twilight, bathe and shampoo his body, and take food left by him (Baud DS. I.2.34 and 37). He was not to sit in the presence of his teacher, cross his legs, lean against a wall, nor stretch his feet, clear his throat loudly, laugh or crack his knuckles. He was required to respond to the teacher's call at once, always occupy a seat lower than his teacher, go to sleep after his teacher and wake up before him (Gautama I I.20 - 21, 30 - 32). Furthermore, the student was not to pronounce the name of his teacher without prefixing or affixing an honorific even in the absence of the teacher.[32]

Corporal punishment: Corporal punishment was allowed in ancient India. If it was not possible to control the pupil by words, then he could be struck with a split bamboo or slender rope. But, if the teacher hit the student any other way, he attracted punishment by the king (Gautama I I.48 - 50). Āpastamba recommends the teacher to use words of censor and if the nature of the offence demanded severe punishment, the student was refused food, drenched in cold water and not allowed to come in the presence of the teacher. Manu however suggests a soft tone and sweet persuasion in imparting instructions about the right path of conduct - "Living beings must be taught what is best for them without violence, and a man who wants to uphold the law should use sweet, smooth speech" (2.159).

One of the most important features of the education system in those days was the absence of commercial transaction. At the end of the studies, whatever the student offered according to his abilities was accepted by the teacher as *dakṣiṇā* (roughly translated as fees). According to Manu, after finishing his education, when the student received his guru's permission to leave, before his graduation bath (*snāna*), he had to bring a present for his guru to the best of his ability (2.245) be it a field, gold, cow, horse, an umbrella, shoes, grain, clothing or vegetables to please his guru (2.246). *Dakṣiṇā* was offered to the teacher before departing- not as a compensation for the knowledge imparted, but as a token of gratitude. Chāndogya (I I.11.6) declares *Brahmāvidyā* to be more valuable than the wealth of the entire earth put together.

With time, the study of Vedas gave way to the pursuit of real knowledge, i.e. Upaniṣadic teachings of *Ātmā* and *Paramātmā*. Although interested students still approached gurus for acquiring knowledge, the teaching process was unlike the olden days. Gradually, other forms of *vidyās* emerged and the tradition of oral learning also declined. The *upanayana* slowly ceased to be a ceremony centred around initiation of the student to Vedic study.

Chapter 35

Marriage - *Vivāha*

In Mahābhārata Ādiparva (chapter 122), Pandu makes an indirect reference to promiscuous and unregulated relationship between men and women of former ages in the country of Uttara Kuru. Svetaketu, son of Uddālka, is credited for the first time to have tried and stopped this licentious lifestyle; he laid down the rule that if a woman was unfaithful to her husband or *vice versa*, a grave sin would be incurred. It is quite likely that such a practice existed in certain parts of India which Pandu was aware of. Even today, strange practices, such as polyandry, are followed in isolated small pockets of India amongst tribes of the hilly regions. Polyandry is only one of the many such examples. One should keep in mind that Mahābhārata is a much later text as compared to the Ṛgveda, and by its time the Āryan culture had spread far beyond the Ṛgvedic land 'in which black antelopes wandered', and where it encountered practices unknown, and often abhorrent, to the Āryan customs. But there is no evidence in any ancient Vedic text of men and women living together, or procreating, without a formal relationship within the Vedic society. In fact, this formal relationship, the institution of marriage, is amongst the oldest rites described in the Ṛgveda tenth *manḍala*, and later institutionalised as the most important *saṃskāra* which is practiced even today.

Purpose: Performing sacrifice to gods was the core feature of the Vedic religion for which being a *gārhapatya* or householder was necessary. A son was essential for performing the last rites and *śrāddha* of the father and forefathers, and ensuring they went to *pitṛloka* instead of hell. These twin objectives could only be achieved if a man got married, secured a wife, acquired the status of *gārhapatya* and produced a male child. Marriage, a Vedic religious necessity, thus firmly dovetailed in the Vedic social custom. This comes out clearly in the early Ṛg texts where blessings and protection of *Agni* is sought for the well-being of the *gārhapatya* (V. 28.3). The Brahmaṇas went further and changed its status from one of necessity to essentiality, and proclaimed anyone who did not enter married life as '*ayagyo*' (Taittirīya Brahmaṇa I I.2.2.6) or 'one without sacrifice.'[1] They further added that he is himself a half man, the second half is wife. This point was made more emphatically and unambiguously in the Śatapatha. While emphasising the importance of marriage and producing a son, it went a step further and called a man 'incomplete' until he secured a wife: "The wife is indeed half of one's self; therefore as long as a man does not secure a wife so long he does not get a son he is not complete; but when he secures the wife he gets progeny and then he becomes complete."[2] Aitareya Āraṇyaka also regards securing a wife an act which makes the man complete, implying that without a wife he is incomplete: "Therefore a man after securing a wife regards himself as more complete." (I.2.4) Unsurprisingly, with time, marriage became a religious compulsion without which, not only a man was not complete, but failed in discharging his most fundamental duty of redeeming the three debts (*riṇas*) and incurred great sin. The *sūtrakaras* made it clear that "heaven, for oneself and one's ancestors depends on a wife (who begets him a son)."[3]

Neatly summing up the main purpose of marriage, Āpastamba says (DS. I I. 5. 11. 12) that by becoming a householder it enables a man to -

i. perform sacrifices to the gods; and
ii. procreate sons

With the establishment of *āśrama* theory in Upaniṣadic times, life was divided into four parts - *brahmacārya*, *gṛhastha*, *vānaprastha* and *saṃnyāsa*. In this arrangement, after spending the initial quarter of life in learning, every Hindu was enjoined (Manu 4.1) to get married and lead the life of a *gṛhyastha* for the next quarter (twenty-five years). Married life was considered essential - divenely ordained and a sacred duty. The order of the first three *āśrama* could not be changed; it was considered sinful to do so (Dakṣa Sūtra I.12).

But, securing a wife was not only meant for solemn acts such as sacrifice and worship of gods, it was also for 'the ultimate sexual pleasure' which depended upon a wife (Manu 9.28). The four aims, or *puruṣārtha*, of a Hindu's life are *dharma*, *artha*, *kāma* and *mokṣa*. The Vedas enjoin every Hindu to pursue these four in the given order. Thus, pursuit of sensual pleasure or *kāma* is an integral part of a Hindu's aim in life, his duty. But this was not to be mistaken as a licence to indulge in free sex or unbridled indulgence with one and all just for pleasure. Indulgence in sex was permitted, but in a regulated manner, and within the institution of marriage, i.e. *gṛhastha āśrama*. The *smṛtis* clearly lay down *Dharmasampatti* (Dharma), *prajā* (procreation) and *rati* (sexual and other pleasures) as the principal purposes of marriage.

Meaning: *Vivāha*, or marriage, literally means taking the girl away in a special way or for a special purpose. Other commonly used words for *vivāha* are *parṇasya*, going around fire; *udvaha*, taking the girl out of her parental home; *pāṇi-grahaṇ*, accepting or holding the girl's hand, et cetera, all of which indicate one or the other component in the rite of marriage.

Essentially, *vivāha* is a composite rite which has several components performed in a given sequence culminating in a man accepting the woman as his wife, and taking her away from her parent's home to his own home.

The process starts with choosing the bridegroom.

How to choose a bridegroom: The *sūtras* and *smṛtis* have commented extensively on the selection criteria. Sifting through the maze of these recommendations and prescriptions, the author has found that scholars considered the bridegroom suitable if he had -

i. good learning and mental calibre
ii. good family
iii. good character

While Aśvalāyana[4] solely focused on intelligence of the bridegroom: "Let him give the girl to a (young man) endowed with intelligence," Āpastamba's bridegroom was supposed to have five accomplishments including "a good family, a good character, auspicious characteristics, learning, and good health" (Āp GS I.3.19), which were stretched to seven by *Yama*, "Good family, good character, bodily appearance, fame, learning, and wealth and support (of relatives and friends)"[5]. For a *brahmaṇa*, it appears, tougher guidelines were prescribed: ten generations of learning, austerity and meritorious work for those who participated in certain types of *yajñas*. (Aśva Śrauta Sūtra. I X.3)

A good family or *kula* seems to have been of great importance and was placed in the forefront for both the bride and the groom (Asv.I.54). It seems that scholars/ thinkers had also become conscious of eugenic considerations i.e. 'improving population by controlled breeding to increase the occurrence of desirable heritable characteristics through the science' empirically, as is evident from Yaj's emphasis on the importance of a good family, famed for ten generations and freedom from hereditarily transmitted diseases (I.54 - 55). Manu prescribed to forgo families even though they were richly endowed with cattle, wealth, et cetera, but didn't perform *saṃskāras*, or did not have a male progeny, or were devoid of Veda (study), had hairy members, suffered from piles, consumption, indigestion, epilepsy, or white/ black leprosy (III.6-7). Harita's observation that the offspring is in accordance with the qualities of the family and parents, further confirms that those formulating guidelines and laws had a hereditarian view in mind.

In those times, it was believed that women were created for bearing children. While she was called *kṣetra* (field), the man was termed *bīja* (seed). The *kṣetra* should be given to one who has *bīja*. Thus, an impotent man, who lacked or had a defective *bīja* was considered unfit to be a bridegroom. A mad man, a 'fallen' man, one who had leprosy, a eunuch, one bearing the same *gotra*, blind, deaf or epileptic[6], all were considered unfit for marriage. Yet, some impotent men got married and managed to have offspring using services in conformity with the law of other males. The children so produced were called *kṣetraja*; they had the right to inheritance, e.g. Dhṛtarāṣṭra and Pandu in Mahābhārata. (MS 9.203)

Choosing bride: Bharadvāja gives - wealth, beauty, intelligence and family - in that order, as four inducing reasons for marrying a girl (GS I.11). He explains that their importance is in the reverse order, i.e. if it comes to forgoing, then wealth should be dropped first, beauty next, intelligence after that, making a family the most important criteria in selection of a girl for marriage. Although, there is talk in the texts of broad hips and slender waists making woman attractive[7], surprisingly, none of such bodily attributes are mentioned while according beauty a priority. The *sūtras*' approach will please any modern-day Indian or western feminist - the Kāmasūtra, the world famous book on the art of love making, speaks of a girl "born of a highly respectable family, possessed of wealth, well-connected, and with many relations and friends" as most suitable for marrying, before broaching on her looks in a perfunctory manner: "She should also be beautiful, of a good disposition, wear lucky marks on her body and with good hair, nails, ears, eyes and breasts, neither more nor less than they ought to be, and no one of them entirely wanting."[8] The reader will notice that in the selection of a life companion, Vātsyāyana, the great guru of the art of love making, puts beauty fifth in order of priority - after respectable family, wealth, good connection and a large number of relations and friends. Aśvalāyana is not much different. He also pushes beauty to second place, after intelligence: "A girl that shows the characteristics of intelligence, beauty, and moral conduct, and who is free from disease." (GS I.5.3)

Āpastamba's advice to a young suitor is that "a girl on whom his mind and eyes are riveted will bring him happiness (or prosperity), he should pay no heed to other things; this is the view of some"(GS. I I I. 21). Vātsyāyana's (III.1.3) advice to the would-be-bridegroom in Kāmasūtra is that "he should proceed to marry a girl, and in taking her home as his wife, he would regard himself as blessed and would not be blamed by his friends (or persons in a similar station in life)", reflecting the sensible approach that prevailed over every other recommendation or suggestion. Āpastamba and Vātsyāyana's views indicate that in the end, it was pretty much the personal choice of the bridegroom that mattered.

Disqualifications: These, strangely, make a longer list than qualifying characteristics for a girl, and mainly include physical attributes, like tawny hair, an excessive limb, a deficient limb, too much hair or hair-less, or one who is talkative and has yellowish eyes (Manu I I I.8 and 10). Marked hair growth on chin or lips, hoarse voice or a crow-like voice, dwarfish or very tall were added disqualifications (Viṣṇu Purāṇa I I.10.18 - 22). Vātsyāyana's list (Kāmasūtra) includes a girl with a depressed nose, upturned nostrils, bent posture, a male-like structure, crooked thighs (how will one know?), projected forehead, affected with *gulma* (glandular growth) and a *vrśākhāri*, one who perspires excessively in the palms and sole of feet.

Most of these are considered negative points against a girl even in present-day in the society, particularly in case of 'settled marriage'(a term popularly used to describe an arrangement wherein parents of the boy and girl take the initiative of getting their children married.)

The case of dimples is an intriguing one. Dimples on cheeks, which have been a sign of beauty for the past two centuries for both men and women, were a sign of disqualification in times of Viṣṇu Purāṇa I I I.10.18 - 22. Equally perplexing is the disqualification due to perspiring palms.

Lakṣaṇa: One should marry a healthy girl endowed with intelligence, beauty, a good character and auspicious characteristics (Asv. GR. I. 5. 3).

Note the importance of 'auspicious characteristics' as an attribute in the above statement. In a rough translation, it means auspicious indications or *lakṣaṇas* - they play an important part in the Hindu society even today. These *lakṣaṇas* are of two kinds - physical/bodily or visible characteristics; and invisible or nonphysical characteristics. These are called *bahya* and *abhyantara* respectively in Hindi language, meaning external and internal.

Nārad in *Stripunsayoga*[36] considers - "when they suffer from long-standing or disgusting diseases, when they are devoid of a limb or have already had connection with another man, when they are wicked or have their minds fixed on another" - as disqualifying attributes. Āpastamba goes on to add few more to these: that one should not choose a girl who is asleep, weeps or leaves the house when prospective families come to see whether she can be chosen. (Āp. GS. I I I. 11 - 12)

Name of the bride: Another reason, more perplexing than her perspiring palms, for rejecting a bridal candidate is on account of her name. There are various names that make the prospective bride ineligible for marriage. She should not bear name of the lunar mansion, such as *Revathi* and *Ardra*, or trees and rivers. She must not bear a *mleccha* name or that of a mountain, bird, snake, a slave, or a name that is terrific (a great amount, size, et cetera) (Manu I I I. 9 and Āp. GR. I I I. 13). While it is understandable why a girl should not be named after one of the several varieties of snakes (many people do not like these reptiles) or a slave, shunning names of trees, rivers, mountains or stars is baffling. More baffling is the prescription that a girl whose name ends with the letters R or L, such as Kamal, should not be chosen (Kāmasūtra I I I. 1. 13 Richard Burton).

A possible explanation is that in those times, great importance was attached to the name of a person. You may recall that the first time the father saw his new born child, immediately after birth and even before the umbilical cord was severed, he gave the child a secret name. And when the *nāmakaraṇa* ceremony was performed, the child was given another name, a formal name, beginning with any of the letters considered appropriate and auspicious based on astrological considerations - determined by the time and place of birth. Apart from these two, a third name was used to indicate his *gotra* or *pravara*, and a fourth name was one what he strived for. If found worthy, he acquired it based on his qualification to perform one of the *yajñas*. Those Āryans were very superstitious about names. Certain names like those of constellations, mountains, rivers and trees were considered inauspicious and harbingers of bad luck.

Brother-less girl

"She seeketh men, as she who hath no brother, mounting her car, as it were to gather riches.

Dawn, like a loving matron for her husband, smiling and well attired, unmasks her beauty."

In this beautiful piece of Ṛgveda hymn dedicated to dawn, the poet draws similarity between a brother-less maiden seeking her man, rising to mount a chariot, and the dawn rising late in the night. But, the simile of a brother-less matron leaves one puzzled. The answer to the puzzle lies in an ancient term *putrikā* which was used for a brother-less girl. In Vedic India, a man got married so he could perform *yajñas*, and beget a son. It was the son who performed the last rites and the *pinḍadāna* to save him from going to hell. If a man could not have a son, he had a choice - to declare his daughter as his *putrikā*. In this case, the daughter's son after marriage could act as a substitute and perform the rites essential for his journey to heaven. However, there was a catch in the system - his daughter's son became ineligible to perform the last rites of his own (biological) father and paternal forefathers, thus leaving them in the same position as his mother's father (own maternal grandfather).

In this arrangement, a man without a son, at the outset stipulated with the man marrying his daughter that her (his daughter's) son would be treated as his own son, and would offer *pinḍas* as a son to him i.e. to mother's father. He proclaimed his daughter to be a *putrikā*. Obviously, while this was an ideal arrangement for the father of the girl, for the daughter's husband it was a disaster because it deprived him of a son. He had nobody left to perform his own last rites and *pinḍadāna* if he failed to beget a second son. It defeated the very purpose of his getting married! What made matters worse was that some teachers (according to some sages - Gautama. 28.17) went so far as to say that a daughter became a *putrikā* by the mere mental resolve of the father i.e. without an agreement with the bridegroom, or a formal declaration. No wonder this practice of a brother-less daughter being declared a *putrikā* by her father had a serious social repercussion and men stopped marrying maidens who had no brothers, but were otherwise eminently suitable.

The ill-consequences of the *putrikā* system became evident in the time of early Ṛgveda itself: "As she who in her parent's house is growing old, I pray to thee as *bhaga* from the seat of all" (I I.17.7 Griffith). A brother-less maiden was not chosen as a bride, and *gṛhya-sūtras* and *smṛtis* started prescribing that a man should not marry a brother-less girl for the fear of her being declared a *putrikā* - "A wise man will not marry a woman who has no brother or whose father is unknown, for fear that she may be an appointed daughter (*putrikā*) or that he may act wrongly." (Manu I I I.12)

In the medieval times, gradually this practice got diluted and faded away. There are no traces of this system left in modern India.

Age, caste and virginity

Age - Men

In the Vedic period, a man married only after he had completed his study of Vedas. The minimum period of *brahmacārya* (time to learn one Veda) lasted twelve years. Given that the *upanayana saṃskāra* of a *brahmaṇa* boy ordinarily was when he was at least eight years old (in case of *kṣatriya* and *vaiśya* boys, *upanayana* took place at eleven and twelve years of age respectively), it meant that a *brahmaṇa* male would usually be twenty years old at the time of marriage, and twenty-three and twenty-four years old respectively, if he was a *kṣatriya* and *vaiśya*. Since the period of Vedas study could last twelve, twenty-four, thirty-six or forty-eight years, depending on whether one chose to learn one, two, three or all four Vedas, men got married at thirty-two years of age or more. This flexibility accorded to men is supported by many instances quoted in the scriptures and is clearly reflected in Manu's (I X. 94) remarks that a man of thirty may marry a girl of twelve years of age, or a man of twenty-four may marry a girl of eight years, only if in a hurry to become a householder.

There is no upper age restriction for men anywhere in the texts, and a male could also choose to remain celibate throughout his life.

Women

Age, dowry and inter-caste alliances are the three most controversial aspects of a Hindu marriage. *Sati*, the evil practice of burning brides was legally banned during the British rule thanks to the efforts of the great reformer Rāja Rām Mohan Roy, and has been discontinued (except few stray incidents) for over a century now. But the other three continue to play a crucial part in Hindu marriages to a varying degree, depending on how traditional or modern is the family. One may think that those blessed with modern education and living in urban centres would have stopped considering caste, dowry and age of the spouse (particularly in case of girls), but the fact remains that modern education and urban living has failed to penetrate the rigid-shell of ancient traditions, and a large number of Hindus still hold these beliefs dear, as a part of their religion, and surprisingly, even non-Hindu families at times tread this path.

In ancient times, determining the right age for the girl to participate in a physical union with a man must have been a simple task. It may have been guided primarily by considerations of her puberty and visible physical maturity: body devalopment as a sign of her ability and fitness to participate in sexual intercourse and to procreate. Very little information is available to us on the marriageable age for girls in the pre-Vedic period society. But there is adequate, though not age-specific information from the earliest Vedic times that a girl was considered suitable for marriage only when she became physically and mentally mature. The Ṛgveda, the oldest of the Vedic texts, talks of a man and woman's union in marriage for the purpose of being lovers and parents (I.66.3; X.30.5-6). It is a clear indication that the girl in the union was not a child, was capable of adult love as well as physically mature to produce a child and undertake the job of parenting - functions which are not expected from a girl child. The later Ṛgvedic texts (X.8 5.21, 22) emphatically show that the girl must be physically developed in her father's house before her marriage - 'Seek some other girl sitting in (the house of her) father, adorned (for marriage) / smeared with menstrual blood. That is your share by nature. Know this.' The tenth *maṇḍala* is widely accepted to have been a much later addition to the *Saṃhitās* and one of least vintage in the Ṛgveda. This practice of marrying girls only when they were past their childhood and had attained maturity continued in the Atharvaveda times. The Vedic texts, several hundred years younger than the Ṛgveda, reflect that after marriage the girl may run her household as *samragyi* (empress), while the brothers, sisters, father and mother of her husband comply with her wishes and commands (AV. X IV.1.44). Rajbali notes,[10] the maidens grew up in their father's home mixing with the youth of the village, something that was possible only if they had come out of their childhood. Numerous verses of the Atharvaveda deal with charms for lovers and lost love (AV 5.28, RV or AV 3.31.7; 33.10, X.96.20) which reveal prevalence of a normal healthy interaction between the opposite sexes prior to marriage; it wouldn't have taken place if girls were married in their early childhood (eight years or so).

Based on these and many more evidence available to us in the Vedic texts, it is safe to assume that girls were married when they had grown up and child marriage was not practised in the times of Vedas. Girls were given away in marriage after they had developed physically in their father's home, where they led a normal healthy life, interacting with male counterparts. From all accounts, the Vedic society appears to have been liberal in this respect, and in a way, even more advanced than some sections of the present-day modern Hindu society. Nearly 4000 years back, it gave the girl freedom to choose her own husband: "Bride is fine looking and well adorned she by herself seeks her friend from among men."

(Ṛgveda X. 27. 12). Yet, people still murder their daughters in the name of honour - 'honour killings' - for committing the crime of 'love marriage' in many parts of north India. The above Ṛgvedic quote also indicates that girls were allowed to grow up before they selected their husbands.

It is uncertain as to when and why the age of marriage for girls was lowered, and lowered to absurd levels of three years, and at one point, even before she started wearing clothes (*naganika*). Extant literature doesn't throw any light on these issues. Nor do we have any texts from foreign sources belonging to that period which throw any light on this subject. However, we do have copious material dealing with the suitable age for marrying girls in the *gṛhya* and *dharma sūtras* as well as *smṛtis*. While we know that the antiquity of these texts generally follow the order of *gṛhya sūtras* being the oldest and the *smṛtis* youngest, the problem is that all *gṛhya sūtras* were not necessarily composed before the dharmasūtras. For example, Kane places *gṛhya sūtras* of Aśvalāyana and Āpastamba between 800-400 BC and dharmasūtra of Āpastamba, Baudhāyana, Gautama along with Pāraskara Gṛhya Sūtras in the 500-300 BC period - one can see the overlap of more than a century. At least we are fortunate in this respect with the *smṛtis*, which came later and have a definite cut-off point e.g. Manu is accepted by all scholars to belong to a period after 200 BC and probably before 100 AD.

Why is the precise period of composition of the various *gṛhya* and *dharma sūtras* important to us?

First, the answer to the above question will enable us to chart out how the marriageable age of girls, a crucial element of the oldest and most important Hindu *saṃskāra*, changed from the period of Vedas to the times of *smṛtis*, i.e. 1700 BC to 200 AD. Second, once we have drawn these timelines, this information will help us co-relate the dips and spikes in the age chart to important socio-political changes that took place in the region at that time. This may provide a possible answer as to why the age was lowered, and the factors that triggered a liberal Vedic society to change its thinking and resort to child marriage.

The *gṛhya sūtras* offer us a mixed bag on their stand on marriageable age of girls. While some *sūtras* tell us in a definitive and unambiguous way that girls should be married post puberty, others say just the opposite.

For example, Aśvalāyana's *gṛhya-sūtras*, in the first *adhyāya*, enjoin newlyweds who (after marriage) have made their journey and arrived at their new home, following course of action after they have finished offering the necessary sacrifice -

"From that time, they should eat no saline food, they should be chaste, wear ornaments, sleep on the ground three nights or twelve nights", and "when he has fulfilled (this) observances (and has had intercourse with his wife), he should give the bride's gift to (the Brahmaṇa) who knows the *sūrya* hymn." (8 and 12)

Śankhayana speaks on the same lines: "Through a period of three nights let them refrain from conjugal intercourse" (I.17.5), and "the mouth of the *gandharva viśvasu* art thou" - with these words let him touch, when he is about to cohabit with her (I. 19.2).

Khadira, I.4.9, Āp 8.8 - 9, Gobhila I I.5.7 and others, all say that the newlywed should cohabit after three nights of marriage and practice continence during this interval.

From all these *gṛhyasūtra* directions, it becomes clear that the bride was expected to be physically mature enough to cohabit three days after the wedding. Gobhila (II.5.8) and Baudhāyana have even provisioned[11] for menses at the time of marriage further indicating that the brides had attained puberty.

The problem arises when we come across several other *gṛhya sūtras* directing the girl should be a '*naganika*', a Sanskrit word which has two meanings 'naked,' and 'a girl before mensuration' (Sanskrit English Dictionary, Monier). Talking about the suitable age for girls to become a bride, Gobhila commands, "The best, however, is a naked girl"[12], and Hiraṇyakeśhin directs that "with their permission he should take a wife belonging to the same caste and country, 'a naked girl', a virgin who should belong to a different *gotra* (from our husband's)[13]. In both these instances, SBE, like most other translators, has preferred 'naked' over the other meaning. If we stay with this meaning, there are two different ways of interpreting the *sūtras*' instructions-

(i) a naked girl should be chosen for marriage, an absurdity that does not deserve a second look; and

(ii) a girl who is too young to be bothered about being covered (clothed) fully should be favoured, though again an absurd interpretation in the present context, but with a micron thin edge over the earlier one.

It may appear unthinkable, but a sizeable section of the society went with this mind-boggling interpretation! It is unthinkable, and mind-boggling, because an alternative and a far more contextually appropriate interpretation of *naganika* as 'a girl before mensuration', i.e. a pre-puberty girl, was known and available from the Mahābhārata days (Sanskrit English dictionary, Monier, and his reference to use of *naganika* in this sense in Mahābhārata). In fact, Gobhila, who commands that a *naganika* be chosen as a bride in the first *prapāṭhaka* of his *gṛhya sūtra*, in the very next *prapāṭhaka*, enjoins that "after three nights (after marriage) have passed, they should cohabit, according to some (teachers)[14]" (I I.5.7), an impossibility if the bride was a child wandering about naked at her father's home few days before her marriage, but possible if *naganika* meant 'a girl before mensuration'. The immediate next *sūtra* further confirms that Gobhila had 'a girl before mensuration' in mind while using *naganika* in his *sūtra* - "When she has had her monthly illness and the blood has ceased to flow, that is the time for cohabiting"(I I.5.8). Baud

Gṛhya Sūtra IV.1.10, specifically prescribes a purificatory ceremony if the bride has mensuration during the progress of the marriage ceremonies[15] - yet another confirmation that girls were married near, or after attaining the age of puberty.

From all these examples, it can be concluded that during the *sūtra* period, girls were married generally past their puberty or close to puberty.

Things changed during and after the dharmasūtra period, and by the time of the *smṛtis*, not marrying a girl by the time she was ten years old came to be regarded as a grave sin. According to Parāśara, a girl is a virgin when ten years old, thereafter she becomes *rajaswala*, similar to a female who has monthly menses (VII. 4). Kane[16] has quotes Vasiṣṭha DS 17.70 - 71 and Baudhāyana Dharmasūtra, that if the girl was not married before she attained puberty, "the father or guardian incurs the sin of destroying an embryo at each appearance of menses as long as the girl is unmarried." Gautama also says, "The girl should be given in marriage before she attains the age of puberty. He who neglects it commits sin." (18.20 - 23). The dharma sūtra period is generally accepted to be around 500 BC and later, so it will be safe to assume that in this period, there was insistence that girls be married before they reached the age of puberty and failure to do so started being labelled a sin, though interestingly, no *prāyaścitta* (propitiation) was prescribed for this sin.

While in the *dharmasūtra* period there was insistence on marrying girls before they reached puberty and suggestion that failure to do so was sinful, in the *smṛti* period, things became stricter and non obseravane of age criterian attracted horrible consequences. Parāśara takes a position that if a person's daughter reaches her twelfth year without marriage, "her forefathers drink, without interruption, during each succeeding month, whatever blood is passed in her courses," a terrible and abhorrent prospect. But the punishment does not end there. The Parāśara Smṛti (VII.5-6) suggests that "the mother, and the father, and likewise the eldest brother, all these three relatives will go to hell, if before mensuration they neglect to marry the girl."[17] Kane quotes[18] Samavarta's verse 67 where marriage of an eight year old is highly commended, and Māric (quoted in Parāśara Madhviya I.2. p.177) says that choosing a girl of five years of age is best.

After approximately 200 AD, the *smṛtis* consistently lowered the age of marriage for girls, and since there was insistence on pre-puberty as the cut off age for marriage, debates ensued among *smṛtis* and other texts about a more exact interpretation of pre-puberty, a term which could theoretically cover the entire period from birth to the time the girl had her first menses.

Naganika, gauri, rohni, kanyā and *rajaswala* - All girls

Naganika, gauri, rohni, kanyā and *rajaswala* are labels used by various *smṛtikaras* and scholars of 200-500 AD period for describing the age group of girls between eight and twelve years. Perhaps, in no other society in the world such a detailed classification of pre-adolescent girls has ever been made. Our forefathers were truly men of details!

As we have seen, by 200 AD, i.e. by the time the Yājñavalkya Smṛti was composed, the society had veered to prepuberty marriages of girls. And with time, this tendency became a rigid rule. One must keep in mind that many of the conditions and restrictions that we are going to discuss below were applicable strictly to *brahmaṇa* brides; girls of all other castes were exempt.

"A Brahmaṇa should marry a Brahmaṇa girl who is *naganika* or *gauri*," says Vaikhānasa in his Smṛta sūtras (V I. 12) and explains *naganika* as a girl who is eight years old but less than ten, and a *gauri* as one who is between ten and twelve and has not started menstruation. But, Parāśara calls an eight-year-old a *gauri*, and a ten-year-old a *kanyā*. He fine tunes the age grouping by classifying a nine-year-old as *rohini*, and one who is more than ten years as *rajaswala* (VI I.6 - 9). Kane has quoted[19] - Kaśyapa classifying *gauri* as a seven-year-old girl, a *kanyā* as ten and *kumāri* as twelve, and Aprārka saying - '*naganika* is one who is ten years old'.

As we can see, there was no consensus among texts assigning the specific age to various classes of preadolescent girls. *Gauri* is a prepuberty girl between the age of ten and twelve for Vaikhānasa, but eight years for Parāśara. *Naganika*, likewise, is a girl of eight for Vaikhānasa, but a ten-year-old in Bhaviṣya Purāṇa. However, there was complete unity and consensus in all these texts on one point - the girl had to be married before she reached puberty, failing which the guardians faced serious consequences, including an ensured spell in hell.

It is remarkable that from the Vedas period to that of the *smṛtis*, a span of nearly 2000 years, while the society became increasingly conservative and regressive, and the marriageable age of girls kept reducing, the girl was allowed to be married only if her father found "a distinguished, handsome suitor who is like her" (MS 9.88), otherwise it was considered better "even after she has reached puberty, to stay in the house until she dies then for him to give her to a man who has no good qualities." (MS 9.89). Not only was the great insistence on finding a suitable boy an important condition which superseded the rigid criterion of marriage before the age of puberty, if the guardians failed to find a suitable boy, the girl had the freedom to choose a husband of her liking - "When a girl has reached puberty she should wait for three years, but after that period she should find a husband like her." (MS 9.91). According to the great lawmaker Manu, "If she herself approaches a (would be) husband when she has not been given one, she commits no error, nor does the man whom she approaches."[20] Gautama in his Dharmasūtra also permits a girl in this situation to find for herself a blameless man on her own will. (18.20 - 23)

From these statements, it appears that starting from the times of the early Vedas down to nearly 600 AD, although the society did become more conservative and regressive, it was so only with respect to the marriageable age of its daughters. It continued to entertain liberal views by insisting on suitability of a husband who had to be distinguished, handsome, and had good qualities; three conditions which were non-negotiable. Meeting the deadline of the constantly decreasing age limit prescribed for the marriage came with one important caveat - it was subject to finding a husband of good qualities, failing which the same conservative society had a liberal approach of providing the girl the freedom to continue to stay with her father, and/or find a suitable husband for herself. How do we explain this dichotomous approach of the society?

It appears that the attitude of the society didn't harden towards its women in general, the apparent rigidity and constant lowering of marriageable age was a function of socio-political changes that took place during this period (600 BC to 500 AD), i.e. from the *gṛhya sūtras* to *dharma sūtras* and the *smṛtis*.

We know that the earliest foreign invasions go back to nearly 560 BC when the Persians first entered north-western India and Cyrus probably subjugated a number of tribes living to the south of Hindu-Kush mountains[21]. Later, Daius's (522-486 BC) rule extended to the Sindh. Greeks first entered India under the rule of Alexander in 327 BC and reached Sindh and Punjab via Taxila, eventually retreating from the banks of river Beas in Punjab. Thereafter, the Parthian king Mithradates I carried his arms up to the Sindhu in the middle of the second century BC, and Maues, a chief, managed to establish a principality in western Punjab. The Śakas followed next and three of their *satraps* ruled with their capitals in Mathura and Taxila in the north, and Malwa in western India.[22] During the fifth century, two new religions, Buddhism and Jainism were born in north India in the adjoining present-day Nepal, and states of UP and Bihar. Mahāvīra died in 468 BC at the age of seventy-two, and Buddha in 486 BC at 80 years of age. Buddhism spread quickly across India since it had a special appeal among youth who were disillusioned by the *Brahmanical* ritualism.

It was probably the encounter of Hinduism, a highly developed, Dharma-abiding society, with these foreign invaders, who, in the words of Rajbali, "were physically stronger, but less civilised than the Indians", and who regarded women "as an article of enjoyment."[23] This triggered fear for women's safety among Indians, and at the same time, they started to copy the invader's social customs 'for fashion'. Other socio-religious factors that had an impact on lowering of the marriage age for girls were -

i. Buddhism had spread widely in India during this period and the institution of monks and nuns became increasingly popular in the society. With such rapid popularity, a growth in the number of nuns indicates that many accepted this difficult way of life - many perhaps because it had become a fad. An early marriage may have been seen as a solution to prevent such conversion.
ii. From the time of Ṛgveda X. 85. 40 - 41., there was a mystical belief that *Soma*, *Gandharva* and *Agni* were the divine guardians of girls. It was believed that

Soma enjoys a girl first, then *Gandharva* enjoys her when her breasts develop, and finally the *Agni* or fire enjoys her when she menstruates.[24] It appears that as time passed, many started taking god's threat of getting physical with the young girls rather seriously and decided to marry them even before puberty.[25]

iii. Another possible reason was that marriage was looked upon as the *upanayana* in the case of girls/women. Hence, the age for *upanayana*, i.e. eight year came to be looked upon as proper age for marriage. (Samskarkaustubha p 699; year 1650 - 80)

Rajbali Pandey in his Hindu Saṃskāras[26] has quoted Mahābhārata (Anuśāsana Parva 33) and Brahman-Purāṇa (chapter I.5) where a daughter is described as suitable for husband at birth, and a daughter who is a child and plays with dust is considered fit for being given away in marriage, respectively. Both these examples, if genuinely part of the original Mahābhārata and Purāṇa, which in all probability are later day interpolation as suggested by Rajbali himself, cannot be justified by any of the reasons given above.

While Hinduism fought back against the growing conversions to Buddhism and was gloriously revived during the Gupta period (320 AD), the age of marriage for girls again went up, and stayed up, until the beginning of the thirteenth century and the advent of Muslim rule in India. With the spread of Muslim rule, the age of marriage dipped again, primarily to safeguard the honour of girls, and also in imitation of Muslim culture of marrying girls very young. After decline of the Muslim rule, when the reigns of power came in hands of the British, they followed a policy of 'normally do not interfere with religion, and customs of natives'. Consequently, this abhorrent practice of child marriage continued unabated in the subcontinent. A strong opposition was however building, not only among Indians exposed to western education and culture, but also among the British public in England, who were shocked beyond belief at the exposures brought to them through newspapers and books like 'Mother India' by Mayo. All these efforts finally culminated in the enactment of law against this blot on Hindu civilisation.

Interestingly, Child marriages were common in all European countries in earlier times. According to Chamberlain 'From Dio Cassius we learn that in Rome, at the beginning of the Empire, marriage of children under ten years occasionally took place.'[27] He refers to the work of FJ Furnivall -"no fewer than twnty-seven cases of the actual marriage in church of the little boys and girls of middle-class folk"[28] - on child marriages, divorces, et cetera between 1560-66 AD in England when children of nine or ten and rarely even two or three years were married (in England) only 300 years ago. Describing Dr Furnivall's research findings Chamberlain says, 'Perhaps the youngest couple described are John Somerford, aged about three years, and Jane Brerton, aged about two years, who were married in the parish church of Brerton about 1553. Both were carried in arms to the church, and had the words of the marriage service said for them by those who carried them.'[29]

In India, until 1929, this limit was fourteen and twelve years for boys and girls respectively as per English law. After 1929, it was revised at sixteen years for both.

The Child Marriage Restraint Act of 1929, also called the Sarda Act, was a law to restrict the practice of child marriage. The punishment for a male between eighteen and twenty-one years marrying a child became imprisonment of up to fifteen days, a fine of 1,000 rupees, or both. The British colonial law set the minimum age for men and women to get married at eighteen and fifteen years respectively. Through subsequent amendments, the law now permits twenty-one years for a male and eighteen years for females to marry.

We now have again come back to an age where not only are boys and girls marrying closer to their thirties, but increasingly choosing a partner of their liking. Amen.

Chapter 36

Types of *Vivāha*

Although the institution of marriage finds its first references in the early parts of the Ṛgveda, the first exhaustive classification of types of marriages was done more than 1000 years later by Aśvalāyana in his *Gṛhya Sūtra*. According to him, there are eight forms of marriages - *brahman*, *daiva*, *prājāpatya*, *ārṣa*, *gandharva*, *asura*, *paiśāca* and *rākṣasa* (GS 1.6.1 - 8). Authors of *dharma sūtras* (Gautama and Baudhāyana) and subsequent *smṛtikaras* - Manu included - also acknowledge these eight forms of marriage. However, Āpastamba has notably omitted *prajāpātya* and *paiśāca* forms, pruning Aśvalāyana's list down to six. Vasiṣṭha, also has the same six as Āpastamba, but calls the *rākṣasa* form by the name of *kṣatra*, and *asura* by the name of *manuṣya* (I.29 - 36).

All texts call *Brahman* the best form of marriage and *rākṣas* the worst in a descending order. The reason of this gradation will become clear after going through the below given description of each form -

i. *Brahman* - In this form, the father gives his daughter, dressed in good clothes and decked up in ornaments that he can afford, to a man of character and learning, invited by him to his house. In return, he does not take anything. (MS I I I.27)

ii. *Daiva* - The girl is given as *dakṣinā*, i.e. sacrificial fee to the *brahmaṇa* for conducting a sacrifice. The rich, the powerful, and the kings of ancient time gave their daughters to ṛṣis in this manner. (MS I I I.28)

iii. *Ārṣa* - The girl is given away by the *brahmaṇa* father and the chosen man in return gives a pair (or more) of cattle for use, as prescribed by law. (MS I I I.29)

iv. *Prājāpatya* - The father gives away his daughter to a man against the bond that the couple will perform their social and religious duties together. (Yaj S I.60)

v. *Asura* - Here, the husband pays money to the girl's relation and the bride, and accepts her out of free will. (MS I I I.31)

vi. *Gandharva* - Manu (III.32) describes it as: "When the girl and her lover join with one another in sexual union because they want to, out of desire."

vii. *Rākṣasa* - A weeping girl is captured by force against her will, often using violence, resulting in injury and death to the relatives. (MS 3.33)

viii. *Paiśāca* - According to the *śāstras*, it is the worst form of marriage which involves carrying away or ravishing the woman when she is alone, asleep, senseless or intoxicated (MS I I I.34). This form of marriage is prohibited.

It is not as if a few wise men sat together and created these eight forms of marriage. These different forms of marriages were being practiced as the local social customs for more than 1000 years before the *sūtrakaras* observed and studied these divergent practices and grouped them under eight (or six) heads. More importantly, even a cursory study of these eight forms of marriages reveals that either the Vedic Dharma, beginning from the period of the Vedas up to the *sūtra* period, did not have a 'standard form' of marriage, or if such a template existed, it is not extant. The very fact that the *sūtrakaras* and the *smṛtikaras* came up with this classification is indicative of the fact that the society had a very broad outlook, and different sections of the society freely followed different customs and practices. The institution accommodated a couple driven by desire to copulate, just as it did the union of an abducted girl by the high and mighty. But, it didn't do so in an unreserved manner. The four marriages - *brahman*, *daiva*, *arśa* and *prājāpatya* - were called *praśasta* (literally - praised, commended) and were favoured by the society and approved by the sages. On the other hand, *apraśasta* were the 'unapproved' forms of marriage, these included *asura*, *gandharva*, *paiśāca* and *rākṣasa*. Inevitably, once *varṇa* and caste system got institutionalised, the great lawmaker Manu associated each of the eight types with the appropriate *varṇa*. According to his verdict *brahman*, *daiva*, *arśa*, *prājāpatya*, *asura* and *gandharva* forms were right for a priest; *asura*, *gandharva*, *rākṣasa* and *paiśāca* for rulers; and *asura*, *rākṣasa* and *paiśāca* for *vaiśya* and *śūdra*. He further observed that *paiśāca* and *rākṣasas* "are traditionally regarded as wrong and are never to be performed." (III. 25)

When it comes to gradation, the first four are considered superior to each succeeding one, and overall, *brahman* is considered the best and *paiśāca* the worst. (Āp DS I I.5.12.4, Baud DS I.11.11) But, Kāmasūtra, as expected, has different preferences. It calls *brahman* the best but next to it is *gandharva*! (I I I.5.29 - 30)

∞

The ruler class, *kṣatriya*, often faced war and conflict situations where it was traditional to acquire women at the military camp as booty. These relationships had the society's approval and formed a passing custom which was later sanctified as *rākṣasa* marriage. Arjuna's marriage with Subhadrā in Mahābhārata is a well-known instance of this form of marriage, which interestingly didn't receive approval of Balram, *Krişņa's* elder brother. But it is almost universally accepted by the present-day society! The *asura* form of marriage, in which a man acquires his wife by making a payment to the father of the girl attracted censure, just as it does now, for obvious and justifiable reasons. It reduced the marriage to the despicable level of a commercial transaction - not very different from sale and purchase of a commodity, which the girl was not. The then society most certainly did not look at girls as commodities. According to scholars like Dr Rajbali Pandey, this form of marriage, also called *manuṣya* marriage, "was a great improvement, in early times, on the *paiśāca* and the *rākṣasa* form of marriages where fraud and force were applied." Explaining it as a consequence of the patriarchal system where children were regarded as family property and "the girls could be given away in marriage for money," he quotes instances of the Vedic period (Ṛgveda I.10 7.2) when "sometimes bargains were struck, and the bride was practically sold for a heavy price."[1] Pandey, quoting RV (X.2 7.2), adds that "sometimes girls themselves selected wealthy though otherwise unfit, husband for money." Soon this practice degraded into a greed-driven money transaction and started attracting stern warning and censure from heavyweights of that time; terms like pimp and prostitution were used to castigate the practice - "No learned father should take a bride price for his daughter, no matter how small, for a man who, out of greed, exacts a bride price would be selling this child like a pimp." (MS 3.51). Manu came down heavily on those who tried to justify giving cow and bull as price for the bride. To block this loophole to the evil practice, he announced, "Some say that the cow and bull (given) during the (wedding) of the sages is a bride price, but it is not so. No matter how great or small (the price), the sale amounts to prostitution." (3.53) He further clarified "that (gift) is merely honorific and the mercy to maidens," (5.54) making it amply clear that the practice of giving cows is not a payment for the girl, it is a gift to the bride.

These different forms of marriages had Vedic roots. The *kanyādāna* of *brahman* form is described in Ṛgveda X.85; payment for acquiring a wife, i.e. *asura* form, is illustrated in Ṛgveda (I.10 9.2) and Nirukta VI.9; the *gandharva* form was practised in *svayaṃvaras*, as depicted in the Ṛgveda I.11 9.5; and the *daiva* form of marriage occurs in the RV. V.61, when Rathaviti's hand is asked for Syavasa. Priests often received from princely patrons, noble maidens or slave girls called '*vadhus*'- a term in current use - for services at sacrifice.

Chapter 37

Rules of marriage - *Vivāha Vidhi*

Marriage is the most important relationship that we enter into in our life. Making someone a partner for life and producing progeny - the core of institution of marriage - is more than a social need and personal necessity in Hinduism, it is Dharma, the root of which can be traced down to the Ṛgveda.

The mission of every Hindu's life is the four *puruṣārthas* - *dharma*, *artha*, *kāma* and *mokṣa*. These are possible only if one goes through each of the four phases (*āśramas*) of life sequentially - *brahmacārya*, *gṛhyastha*, *vānaprasthas* and *saṃnyāsa*. The *Dharmaśāstras* proclaim *gṛhyasthasrāma* as the most important of the four *āśramas*. Little wonder then that *vivāha* occupies central place amongst all *saṃskāras*.

It is also one of the few *saṃskāras* described in detail in the oldest of Hindu text, the Ṛgveda, not as a *saṃskāra*, because the word *saṃskāra* did not exist at that time, but as a socio-religious event of *Sūryā's* (daughter of the sun) wedding with *Soma* in the tenth *manḍala* (X.85).

Soma was the bridegroom; the *Aśvins* are both wooers,
When *Savitar* gave *Sūrya* to her husband, as she pronounced (her vow)
with her (whole mind). 9
Mind was her wagon, and heaven was her canopy,
The two glowing ones [=sun and moon] were the draft oxen, when
Sūrya drove to her (new) home. 10

Unfortunately, the Ṛgveda poet neither follows the discipline of proper sequential narration of events, nor does he pay much attention to details in these hymns. But he does put across the outlines of the *vivāha* ceremony as practiced in the society in his time. Fortunately, both of these shortcomings were duly amended a few centuries later by poets of the Atharvaveda - we find a sequential and fairly detailed account of the *vivāha* ceremony of that period in this Veda (AV. 14.1 &14.2).

Later, sages in the *sūtra* period did what they were very good at: collecting, collating and arranging the floating mass of rituals and customs. Using their wisdom and judgement, they compiled and edited account of the *vivāha* ceremony practiced in their times by different sections of the society and produced a final product in their respective *sūtra* texts. While this excercise did provide a standard work on *vivāha* for the followers of different sages, e.g. Aśvalāyana or Baudhāyana, it did not provide a uniform and standard product across the *gṛhyasūtras*, since different sages followed different practices (*śākhās*), and customs peculiar to their regions, which had their own local variations. But it is not something unique only to *vivāha* ceremonies; it applies to almost all rites and rituals in a Hindu's life. No two *gṛhyasūtras* prescribe exactly the same way of performing any rite or ritual.

The procedures prescribed by these *sūtras* however have a large common denominator - a core, which has remained unchanged over last 2500 years. It is this core of the *vivāha* ceremony that is solemnised even today in Hindu marrages. This core comprises rites and rituals described in great detail in the Atharvaveda, and in the Ṛgveda before that. A remarkably great number of verses of the Ṛgveda are used in this ceremony. According to Kane[1], the Āpastamba Mantrapatha - used in marriages today - employs twenty-nine of the forty-seven verses of Ṛgveda (X.85)!

But outside this core, there is great divergence. There was no uniformity in the rites of marriage even in olden times. The rites changed from people to people, and place to place, according to local customs - a fact which was duly recognised by the sages in their *sūtras* -

"Now the various indeed are the customs of the (different) countries and the customs of the (different) villages: those one should observe at the wedding."[2]

"And one should learn from women what ceremonies (are required by custom)."[3]

Veda sources

In the tenth *manḍala* of the Ṛgveda, an entire hymn, *Sūrya sūkta* (X.85), in which the wedding ceremony of *Sūryā* (daughter of the sun) with *Soma* (the moon) is described; and the fourteenth *kāṇḍa* of the Atharvaveda, entirely devoted to entry in the *gṛhyastha āśrama*, and duties of a husband and wife - a total of sixty-four and seventy-five verses in two *anuvākyas* - are the two Veda sources which tell us how marriages were performed in the Veda's period.

Starting with a vivid and colourful description of *Soma*, the bridegroom (RV 85.1 - 5; AV 14.1.1 - 5), the next mantra of Ṛgveda is about the trousseau (RV.85.6, 8, 10 - 13; AV 14.1.6 - 10). *Pāṇigrahaṇa* (85.36; AV 14.1.48-52), *keśhamochan* (RV.85.24; AV 14. 1.55-56), *udvaha* (*vidāi*) or the bride's departure to the bridegroom's house (RV.26 - 32, 33; AV 14.1.60-64), arrival and entry in the father-in-law's house (RV.85.27, 41 - 46; AV 14.2.13) and *kanyādāna* (RV.85.39 - 41) are the other events covered in the *Sūryā sūkta*. As one can see, the events are not in the chronological order in which the ceremonies are performed these days. This could be either because the poet did not pay sufficient attention to the chronology of the events, or when the tenth *manḍala* was compiled, this disorderliness crept in due to lack of attention by the compilers. There is yet another, though remote, possibility that in times of the Ṛgveda, things were actually done in the manner that the poet has described. In any case, all these rites continue to be performed in today's marriages.

The Atharvaveda contains more detailed account of *Sūryā's* marriage with *Soma* than the Ṛgveda. The entire fourteenth *kāṇḍa* of the Atharvaveda is devoted to *vivāha* and related topics. Additionally, there are a few hymns in the second *kāṇḍa* (36) and third *kāṇḍa* (28) as well. Apart from all the ceremonies given in the Ṛgveda, Atharvaveda also has *aṣmārohaṇa*, wherein the bride steps on stone (14.1.47), gifted bridal clothes (14.1.45), given a bridal bath and a pre-nuptial bath (14.1.39). A peculiar ceremony of yoke is performed in which water is poured on the bride through the hole of one of the yokes (14.1.40). Thereafter, the bridal procession departs, and the bride mounts the chariot (14.1.61). The next phase includes the bride's arrival at the groom's house (14.2.13), *Agni pūjā*, homage to *Sarasvatī* and father (14.2.20) followed by seating the bride on a red-bull hide strewn with grass (14.2.22), and a baby boy is put in her lap (14.2.23). Thereafter, the family and friends of the bridegroom come to see the bride for the first time (14.2.28). After this starts the final phase leading to consummation - the bride mounts the bed (14.2.31) and the couple unites (14.2.32-37 and 40). The clothes are then given to a *brahmaṇa* (14.2.4 2) followed by homage to gods (14.2.46). The used garments are tied to a pillar (14.2.62) and shrivelled rice is scattered to drive away the evil (14.2.63), and finally, the bridegroom pronounces to the bride: "I am this, that you are. I am *Sama*, you are the *Rik* and I am heaven, you are the Earth. Let us both unite here. Let us generate progeny." (14.2.71). Clearly, by the time of the Atharvaveda, the simple marriage ceremony of Ṛgveda, in which *pāṇigrahaṇa* was the central piece, had become a long drawn affair incorporating several new rites, undoubtedly because these had become common practices.

Gṛhya Sūtras

As seen earlier, the simple ceremony of Ṛgveda, which centred around the father handing over his daughter to a suitable boy by *pāṇigrahaṇa* and *kanyādāna* rites, transformed into a series of rites and rituals by the time of the *sūtra* period. These rituals varied every few miles within India. The *sūtrakaras* specialised in grasping the heart of the matter and reducing the procedures and discourses to extremely short *sūtras* - they standardised these practices of *vivāha* and included it in their respective *gṛhya sūtras*. But this failed to bring 'across-the-board' uniformity in procedures, because the rites, rituals and customs among the followers of different *śākhā* of the Vedas differed. But by and large, the works of the *sūtrakaras* had a large common denominator, embellished by local customs and practices of the area and community. These *gṛhya sūtras* included the rites as well as mantras employed while performing the rites.

To study how the *vivāha* rituals changed from the Atharvavedic to *sūtra* period, study of Kauśika Sūtra is ideal since it is attached to the Atharvaveda. Although nothing much is known about Kauśika himself, there is near unanimity that these *sūtras* belong to a period prior to Pāṇini, making it one of the earliest *gṛhya sūtras*.[4]

Samples of Aśvalāyana and Parāśara *gṛhya sūtra* below will help study the change from the Atharva Vedas period (as detailed in Kauśika), especially since Aśvalāyana has the distinction of being perhaps the oldest *gṛhya sūtra*, while Parāśara's is among the more popular *gṛhya sūtras* for *vivāha*.

∞

The guests at the marriage arrive in a procession and are greeted and offered seats, *arghya* (water) and *madhuparka* (1.3.4 - 5). *Madhuparka* is a mixture of honey with butter or curd in which some *gṛhyasūtras* mix barley, while others offer goat meat to bestow special honour to a guest. The father of the bride offers the bridegroom a cow as *dāna* - a part of the *madhuparka* rite on all occasions. Thereafter, the groom offers garments (*vastradāna*) to the bride accompanied with Atharva mantra 14.1.45, wherein a long-life of a hundred years full of sons and wealth is prayed for. The groom is prescribed to clothe the bride in the *sūtra* period, but nowadays the bride does it herself. Pāraskara has described *kanyādāna* in passing: "(The bridegroom), having accepted her who is given away by her father, takes her and goes away (from that place)." (1.4.15) (RV X.85.39-41). Next, the bride and groom come face-to-face and look at each other in *parasparsamikshana* to the accompaniment of Ṛg mantras in which the groom repeats the verse: "With no evil eye, not bringing back to thy husband, brings luck to the cattle, be full of joy and vigour. Give birth to heroes; the godly and friendly. Bring us luck, to men and animals." (RV X. 85.37,40,41,44). In *agnisthāpana* and *homa*, an important rite of *vivāha*, the bridegroom leads her round the fire, with the fire on his right side (clock-wise), and sits down to make oblations while the bride touches him. Pāraskara prescribes the normal oblations - the two *aghara*, two *ājjya*, the *mahāvyahrtis*, the general expiation, the *prājāpatya* oblation, and the *svishtakrit* - followed by twelve oblations of *rashtrabhrata*, thirteen oblations of *japa homa* and eighteen of *abhyatana homa*. After the *homa* comes *pāṇigrahaṇa*, a critically important *vivāha* rite in which the bride and groom hold each other's hand and take a vow to stay together. In Aśvalāyana's account (I.7.3-5), "having placed to the west of the fire a millstone, to the north-east (of the fire) a water pot, he should sacrifice, while she takes hold of him." Thereafter, "standing, with his face turned to the West, while sitting and turns her face to the east, he should seize the thumb if he desires only sons, her other fingers for daughter, and the hand on the hair-side together with the thumb for male and female children both with the mantra 'I seize thy hand for the sake of happiness'." He leads her three times around the fire and the water pot in a way that their right sides are turned towards the fire. The groom murmurs the Taittirīya Brahmaṇa mantra (3.7.11): "This am I, that art thou; that art thou, this am I; the heaven I, the Earth thou; the Saman I, the Rik thou. Come! Let us here marry. Let us beget offspring. Loving, bright, with genial mind may we live a 100 autumns." (AGS 1.7.3 - 6). In the ritual, the brother of the bride follows the couple around the fire holding a jar of water.

After each round around the fire, the groom makes the bride tread on the stone with the words: "Tread on this stone; like a stone be firm. Overcome the enemies; tread the foes down." (AGS 1.7. 7) The rite of *aṣmārohaṇa* is followed by the ceremony of *laja-homa*, wherein the bride's brother or someone on his behalf pours fried grain twice over the wife's joined hands with the mantra: "To God *Āryaman* the girls have made sacrifice, to *Agni*; may he, God *Āryaman*, loosen her from this, and not from that place, *Svāhā*!" The groom sacrifices the fried grain without opening her joined hands, and "without leading around (the fire, she sacrifices grain) with the neb of a basket towards herself silently a fourth time." (I.7.14) Thereafter, the bridegroom loosens two locks of her hair with the mantra: "I release thee from the fetter of *Varuṇa*," (RV.X.8 5.24) (AGS I.7.17) in what is known as *keśhamocana*.

Next is the all-important rite of *saptapadī* in which the groom makes the bride take seven steps forward in north-east direction with the words: "For the sap with one step, for juices with two steps, for thriving of wealth with three steps, for comfort with four steps, for offspring with five steps, for the seasons with six steps. Be friend with the seven steps. So be thou devoted to me. Let us acquire many sons who may reach old age!" (AGS 1.7.19)

After completion of the seven steps, the priest sprinkles water from the water jar on the joined heads of the bride and bridegroom in *murdhabhiṣeka*. The couple should then spend that night in the house of an older *brahmaṇa* woman whose husband and children are alive. When the bride has seen the polar star, the star *Arundhatī* and the seven Ṛṣis (*Ursa Major*), she breaks her silence with the words: "May my husband live, and I get offspring." (AGS I.7. 21-22)

If the newly married couple have to make a journey to their new home, i.e. *vidāi*, the bride is made to mount the chariot with the (verse): "May *Pūṣans* lead thee from here holding thy hand." (RV. X.8 5.26). On arrival at the bridegroom's father's place, she enters the house with the verse: "Here let your heart'sdesire be realized through children." (RV. X.85.27 J&B). She is then made to sit on a bull's hide with its neck to the east and hair facing upwards, and hold the groom, who makes oblations in the nuptial fire (just brought in) with the verse: "May *Prajāpati* create offspring to us" (RV. X.8 5.43 seq) and four verses. Thereafter, with the verse: "May all the gods unite" (RV. X.8 5.47), the groom should eat curd and give the rest to the bride or smear the remnant *ājya* (*ghī*) on the bride and his heart, signifying complete union of the two. (AGS I.8)

The couple are enjoined to abstain from eating saline food, stay chaste, wear ornaments, sleep on the ground for three (*Triratra Vrata*) or twelve nights or one year before having sexual intercourse (ASG 1.8.10).

Kauśika Sūtra is yet another *sūtra* in the *gṛhya sūtra* class, but it is of special interest to us because it forms part of the Atharvaveda tradition, and therefore follows this Veda closely. The study of Kauśika Sūtras - believed to have been created before Pāṇini's time (600-300 BC) by Kauśika- provides us valuable insight on how marriage rites of the Atharvaveda period gathered new customs and rituals.

Broadly, the *saṃskāra* of marriage has three components -

1. Preliminary rites
2. Core rites of the *saṃskāra*, e.g. *pāṇigrahaṇa*, *homa*, *saptapadī*, et cetera
3. Rites performed after the core rites

1. Preliminary rite - An auspicious time for performing the wedding ritual is prescribed starting the full moon day of *kartika* to full moon day of *vaiśākhā*. It seems to be based on AV(14.1.13); however, complete flexibility was given to solemnise the marriage on any day chosen by the parents.

The wedding rituals begin with oblations accompanied by sixteen verses of the first wedding hymn of AV, AV 14.1.23 - 24 and 2.36. A wooer, a friend and the *brahmaṇa* go to the bride and bring grass from the bride's house at night, which is kindled (perhaps) to remove evil elements. Then, the bridegroom scatters shrivelled grains and sends a person to guard the bride.

Three persons including a *brahmaṇa* fetch water from a stream. The same water is used whenever required in the wedding ritual. The *brahmaṇa* breaks a lump of clay from the stream and fetches water from a different place along the flow of the stream. The water jar is tied to a branch of *palaska* tree to the north of the fire outside the *vedi*.

The bridegroom enters the wedding place, loosens the bride's hair, and offers the clarified butter. This is followed by the bridal bath - originating from the Atharvaveda - where the priest mixes remnants of the sacrificial butter in hot water. The bride is bathed in this water while she faces the north-east corner. She is then sprinkled with cold water, and after drying her limbs the cloth is taken away on *tumber ḍanda* (stick) and tied to a tree in a forest.[5]

Then bride wears new garments, her hair is combed once with a comb of 100 teeth, she is girded and an amulate made of *mandugha* (licorice) is tied with a red thread to her ring finger with the amulet inside and the knot facing outside.

A piece of gold is tied with grass blade to the hole of the yoke based on a branch and the gold is made to touch the bride's forehead. Water is sprinkled into the yoke hole and collected in a pot below. The bride is led away from the northern side of the fire.

These constitute the preliminary rites.

2. The Core rites - The main marriage rites include *aṣmārohaṇa*, *laja-homa*, *agniparinayana* and the *saptapadī*, performed in this sequence.

A stone without edges is placed on a lump of bull dung and the bride is made to step on it. She offers shrivelled grains in the fire three times in continuation and makes four offerings to the deity *Kāma* (*laja-homa*). Then, the bridegroom leads her around the fire three times (*Agni parinayana*). *Saptapadī* was unknown in the Atharvaveda times; it was introduced in the Kauśika Sūtra period. In *saptapadī*, seven lines are drawn extending towards the east to the northern side of the fire, and the bride walks on these lines taking one step after another.[6]

3. Post Core rites - In the post marriage rites, the bride sits on the bed and a *dāsi* (maid) washes her feet (unique to Kauśika Sūtra) accompanied by a mantra provided by Kauśika.[7] The girdle tied to her waist is loosened by the servants who mock fight to appropriate it. Fragrant powder is then scattered on her head and she stands on the bed. She is then led to her husband's house.

She ascends the vehicle with the *brahmaṇa* leading the procession. The *svastyayana* rite is performed leading the direction on the road. The *brahmaṇa* stands on the tip of the bridal garment from the right side placing it on the crossroad and lets the procession pass through. On reaching the bridegroom's house, he recites AV (14.2.12) and sprinkles water on the vehicle, setting it free.

After the *udvaha* ritual, the rites to be performed at the bridegroom's house begin. On entering her new house, she sprinkles it with water (AV 14.2.19). A second *aṣmārohaṇa* is repeated in which a leaf is kept on the stone which is kept on bull dung and *durba* grass is spread on it. The bride steps on the stone and is then led into the house by a friend holding a jar of water. The bridegroom leads her around the fire three times and she worships the household fire and other deities.

She then sits on a red bull hide spread with grass and a *brahmaṇa* boy is placed in her lap. Offerings are made into the fire and remnants of the sacrificial butter are added to the couple's heads and to a water jar. The *brahmaṇa* pours water from the jar on their folded hands.

The *brahmaṇa* makes them have curd, honey and water, and cooked food.

The bridegroom offers a handful of barley and clarified butter into the fire.

The *cathurthikarman* or consummation is performed on the fourth day, after the couple have practised chastity for three days. On the morning of the fourth day, the bridegroom offers rice, barley or sesame seeds into the fire. The couple smear each other's eyes and the bridegroom makes the bride touch the bed and sit on it. They lie down together on the bed and the *brahmaṇa* covers them with a garment. He makes them come together three times, throws the amulet tied to bride in a mixture called *auksa*, and the couple unite. The bridegroom knots her hair, makes her get up and covers her with a garment. He sprinkles clarified butter with a grass blade on her parted hair and places rice and barley on it. He loosens her hair knot with a bunch of grass and she ties her hair with the piece of hemp which she wears for three nights.

The *sulka* or the bride price is divided between the bride and bridegroom. The bridal white garment is given to the priest who then wraps it around the tree, takes a bath, wears another garment and returns. This is followed by a concluding offering with the AV (14.1.46 and 14.2.59).

The consummation is a symbolic rite that takes place in presence of the *brahmaṇa*.

It is important to remember that all these rituals were accompanied with appropriate Ṛg/Atharva Vedic mantras.

This is end of the wedding ritual which Kauśika calls *Saurya Vivāha*.

As mentioned earlier, apart from these two *gṛhya sūtras*, there are many *gṛhya sūtras* which describe *vivāha*. For convenience, a chart C-4 is attached listing out the rites prescribed in some of more important texts. A few important rites which were not included in the works of the above two sages are -

i. *Vara Preṣaṇa* - Here, the groom's father sends a representative to look for a suitable bride. The *Aśvani* brothers had acted as the wooers of *Soma* in the Ṛgveda (X.8 5.9). Interestingly, a friend of the groom was usually chosen as the representative and he was called *vara*! As we know, *vara* is now used exclusively for the bridegroom. Subsequently, Baud GS (I.1.14 - 15), Āp GS (2.16.4.1 - 2, 7) and a few others included this in their texts. This practice continued in times of Kālidāsa (Kumara Sambhava 6.28 - 29); how and why this practice changed into the present practice wherein the girl's parents send their representatives to the groom's house is not known.

ii. *Vaga Dāna* is a practice mentioned only in Shankya Gṛhya Sūtra (1.6.5 - 6). The consent of the bride's father to the marriage proposal brought by the messenger is called *Vaga Dāna*. This is in practice even today.

iii. *Vivāha muhūrta* - Just like in any other important religious ceremony, the auspicious time for *vivāha* was of great importance. The Ṛgveda (10.8 5.13) mentions the month of *phalguna* as auspicious for marriage. Aśvalāyana went a step further in defining the auspicious period, but Baud, Āpastamba et cetera went in great detail prescribing the month, date and time of the year ideally suited for a marriage ceremony. The Rāmāyaṇa and the Mahābhārata, both give details of how the time of the wedding was chosen depending on the position of constellations and other astrological conditions. This continues to be a very important factor in today's weddings, and the exact *muhūrtam* is strictly adhered to for the well-being and happiness of the couple.

iv. *Maṇḍapa* erection - Erection of a temporary structure 'in the open' finds mention for the first time in Paraskara Gṛhya Sūtra (1.4). Over time, the *maṇḍapa* - temporary structure where the main marriage ceremony is performed - became extremely important. Several customs and practices have emerged in different parts of the country associated with erection and dismantling of the *maṇḍapa.*

Nandī śrāddha and a few other associated *pūjās* find their beginnings in the times of Baudhāyana Gṛhya Sūtra (I.1.24), which continue even today.

A huge mass of Sanskrit text was composed to enable perform the steps in a ritual in the correct order and form, and to list the mantras that accompany the actions. These ritual handbooks normally called *paddhati* (compendium), *vidhi* (rules/norms), *prayoga* (manual), *prakaraṇa* (dissertation), *vidhāna* (prescriptions/manuals) (see Patton 2005, 27-31), or in case of metric texts, *karika*, which means texts that are manuals for the practice as well as liturgy, are available to us.

We can gather valuable information on changes in the performance of *vivāha* post the *sūtra* period, from *prayogas* and *paddhatis* of the Atharvaveda tradition and literary works of the medieval period.

Keśhava's Kauśika Paddhati is one such important undated composition. Instead of explaining Kauśika's *sūtras* one by one, Keśhava has tried to explain the rituals in detail. The reader quickly realises that there is hardly any change in the main rites, either by modification or introduction of a new rite. However, there are numerous modifications and additions to the peripheral acts accompanying the main rites. He adds the practice of feeding a dish made of sesame with remnants of sacrificial butter to the bride. There is also a rite for bringing the water to be used in the wedding ritual. Furthermore, the bride's clothes are collected on a stick and disposed in a cattle hurdle instead of the forest; the bride's garments are tied with a sacred thread and the *madhuparka* ritual is performed after tying the *madugha* amulet. After *laja homa*, Keśhava includes the ritual of *kanyādāna*, and after the *pāṇigrahaṇa*, recitations of AVS (2.36, 14.1, 20.126 and 3.30). A bath is recommended for everyone at the end of the wedding ceremony.

In the Saṃhitā Vidhivivarana (1618 AD), which seems to be a text of Ātharvaṇa Paddhati, we find many small variations in the peripheral activities associated with important rites like fetching water. Furthermore, according to this text, the wooer should be well-dressed and must put on ornaments; the *brahmaṇa* goes to the bride to narrate qualities of the groom. Here it is prescribed that if the water originally fetched from the river for the bride's bath gets exhausted, then any other water can be used for sprinkling. There are a few mantra additions too, like incorporation of one more mantra after *aṣmārohaṇa* and *laja-homa*. More important is introduction of tying *kankaṇa* and singing of songs by young and old women after the *lokcāhara* (custom) practice of presenting barley, garland and mirror to the bride. The tying of *kankana* and singing of women are an integral part of modern-day wedding ceremonies as well.

From the Atharvaveda Prayoga Bhanu, another *prayoga* text of the Atharvaveda tradition of the late eighteenth century, we find that *vaga dāna* or betrothal, *simanta karma* and *svastípuṇyavacana* were introduced in this period, and so was the important ceremony of *maṃgala sūtra*. All these additions also form part of today's wedding ceremonies.

Accepting the importance of the custom and its incorporation in the marriage ceremony, Sudarsanācārya notes that certain rites like worship of planets, *ankuraropana*, tying of the *pratisara* (the marriage string) around the wrist are performed with Vedic mantras, while others like *naga bali*, *yaksah bali* and the worship of *Índrani* are performed without Vedic mantras.

∞

According to Kane, the main outline of the marriage *saṃskāras* show a remarkable continuity of several thousand years from the time of the Ṛgveda to our modern times; though the essential or core rites are mentioned by all *sūtrakaras*, but there is great divergence in the details of rites preceding and succeeding these core rites, i.e. components 1 and 2 above.

Even the core or essential rites have different sequence according to different *sūtrakaras* -

- Asv GS I.7.7 - Going around the fire first followed by *saptapadī*
- Āp GS IV.16 - The *saptapadī* precedes going around the fire
- Gobhila GS I I.2.16, Khadira GS I.3.31, Baud GS I.4.10 - Performing *pāṇigrahaṇa* after *saptapadī*; many other *sūtrakaras* place it before *saptapadī*

Some ceremonies/acts are omitted by some *sūtrakaras*, for example -

- *Madhuparka* - It is not mentioned in Asv. GS, although Āp GS I I I.8 and Baud GS I.2.1, Mānava GS I.9 mention it.
- *Madhuparka*, *homa*, going around the fire, *pāṇigrahaṇa*, *laja-homa* and *ardrakashata ropan* are described as principal ceremonies in Kāli Dāsa's Raghuvamsha VII.

Kane prepared an exhaustive list based on "as many *sūtras* as I could read," and "of the different matters described in the *saṃskāra* of marriage."[8] These are given below -

1. *Vara vadhu guṇa parikśa* - In this rite, the suitability of a girl or bridegroom is

examined.

2. *Varapreshna* - This rite includes sending to the girl's father representatives to negotiate for the hand of the girl (Ṛgveda X.85.8 –9). Same practice is given in BGS (I.1.14 - 15), Āp GS (I I.16 and IV.1 - 2 and 7). In the medieval times, the bridegroom was the first to seek the hand of the girl, particularly among *kṣatriyas*. For instance, in Harishcharitra, Prince Grahavarma sent messengers asking for the hand of Princess Rājyaśrī.

Today this custom has completely changed. The girl's father has to select the bridegroom. In the early twentieth century, according to Kane, *śūdras* and several other castes still followed the old practice.

3. *Vaga dāna* or *vān niśeya* - This refers to settling the marriage described in San. GS (I6.5-6). Medieval works like SRM (p 529-33) deal with it at great length.
4. *Maṇḍapa karṇa* - It comprises erecting a *pandala* (shed) where ceremonies are to be performed. Par GS I.4 says marriage (and some other *saṃskāras*) should be performed outside the house in a *pandala* (Vide Sam.Prakasha. p 817-18).
5. *Nandī śrāddha* and *puṇyahavacana* - This is referred by BGS (I.1.24). Most *sūtras* are silent about these (For details please see page 317 *nandī śrāddha*).
6. The bridegroom goes to the bride's house (San GS I.12.10).
7. *Madhuparka* - It refers to the reception of the bridegroom at the bride's house. In *madhuparka*, honey is offered to honour the distinguished guest (Āp GS I I I.8, BGS I.2.1, Mānava GS I.9 and Kathaka GS 24.1 –30).

Two *madhuparka*s, one before, and one after the marriage, where the bridegroom returns to his own house, have been referred by San GS I.12.10.

8. *Snapana, paridhapana* and *samnahana* - These include making the bride bathe, put on new clothes and girding her with a string or rope of *darbha*. (Āp GS IV.8 and Kathaka GS 25.4)

Par GS I.4 refers to putting on two garments.

Gobhila GS I I.1.17 - 18 refers to bathing and putting on garment and also speaks of sprinkling the girl with the best of *sura* wine I I.1.10.

Mānava GS I.11.4 - 6 refers to *paridhapna* and *samnahana.*

9. *Samanjana* - This includes anointing the bride and bridegroom. San GS I.12.5, Gobhila GS I I.2.15, Par GS I.4 - all three cite Ṛgveda X.80 5.47 as the mantra for this rite.
10. *Pratisarabandha* - It refers to tying an amulet string on the bride's hand. (San GS I.12.6 - 8, Kauśika Sūtra 76.8)
11. *Vadhu vara nishkramana* - This rite refers to the bride and groom coming into the *pandala* from the inner part of the house. (Par GS I.40)
12. *Parasapara samikśana* - It requires the bride and groom to look at each other (Par. GS I.4, Āp GS IV.4, BGS I.1.24 - 25). Parāśara asks the bridegroom

to cite Ṛgveda (X.80 5.44.40, 41 and 37) while Āpastamba and Baudhāyana *sūtras* suggest that he recites Ṛgveda (X.80 5.44).

Asv GS Parṣishta I.23 says that first, a piece of cloth is held between the bridegroom and bride, and at the proper astrological moment, it is removed and then the two see each other. Laghu Aśvalāyana Smṛti 15.20 also says the same.

This practice is prevalent even now, especially among communities in Andhra Pradesh.

13. *Kanyādāna* - This refers to the gift of the bride (vide Par GS I.4, Mānava GS I.8.6 –9, Varaha GS.13).

Half a dozen different methods of uttering the formula in *kanyādāna* are given by Sam. Kaustubha of Anantadeva. Page 779. The Aśvalāyana GS Parṣishta sets out the procedure of *kanyādāna*, practiced even today. In this rite, the father of the girl says that the bridegroom should not prove false to the bride in the *dharma*, *artha* and *kāma*, and the groom responds with the words: "I shall not do so." This too is practiced today.

14. *Agnisthāpna* and *homa* - In these rites, the fire is established and offered *ājjya* oblations. There is great divergence of views about the number of *āhutis* and the mantras to be recited. Vide Asv GS I.7.3 and I.4.3 - 7, Āp GS V.1 prescribe sixteen *āhutis* and mantras each.
15. *Pāṇigrahaṇa* - This refers to holding the bride's hand.
16. *Laja-homa* - It includes offering fried grains into the fire by the bride.

The first three offerings of fried grain are repeated by the bridegroom while chanting the mantras, and the fourth is made of remaining *lajas* by the bride silently (Asv GS I.7.7 - 13, Par GS I.6, Āp GS V.3 - 5, San GS I 13.15 - 17, Gobhila GS I I.2.5, Mānava GS I.11.11, Baud GS I.4.25, et cetera). A few other GSs talk of only three offerings by the bride.

17. *Agniparinayaṇa* - This rite requires the bridegroom to walk in front of the bride around the fire with a water jar. While doing so, he utters the word '*amohasmi*' (vide San GS I.13.4, Hir GS I.20.2).
18. *Aṣmārohaṇa* - It consists of making the bride tread on a millstone.

These last three rites, i.e. *lajahoma*, *agniparinayaṇa* and *aṣmārohaṇa* are repeated thrice, one after another.

19. *Saptapadī* - This rite involves taking seven steps together to the north of the fire. The bridegroom makes the bride step upon each of the seven small heaps of rice made with her right foot beginning from the west.
20. *Murdhabhiṣeka* - It consists of sprinkling holy water on the bride and bridegroom's head according to some, and only on the bride's head according to others. (Asv GS I.7.20, Par GS I.8, Gobhila GS I I.2.15 - 16)
21. *Suryodikṣana* - It requires the bride to look towards the sun. (Par GS I.8)
22. *Hṛdaya sparśa* - Here, the groom touches the bride's heart with a mantra. (Par

GS I.8, Bhar GS I.17, BGS I.4.1)

23. *Prekśākhānumantrana* - In this rite, the spectators are addressed with reference to the newly married bride. (Mānava GR I.12.1, which employs Ṛgveda X.85.33)
24. *Dakṣinādāna* - This act consists of giving gifts to the *ācārya*. Par GS I.8, and San GS I.14.13 - 17 both prescribe a cow as the fee in the case of *brahmaṇas*, a village in case of marriages of kings and nobles, and a horse in marriages of *vaiśyas*. Gobhila GS I I.3.23, and Baud GS I.4.38 only speak of a cow.
25. *Gṛyha pravesha* - Here, the bride enters the groom's house.
26. *Gṛyha praveshaniya homa* - This includes performance of a sacrifice on entering the groom's house. (San GS I.16.1 - 2, Gobhila GS I I.3.8 - 12, Āp GS VI.6 - 10)
27. *Dhruva Arundhatī darśana* - In this rite, on the day of marriage, the polar star and *arundhatī* is pointed to the bride at night. Both bride and groom remain silent through the day until night, when *dhruva*, et cetera are shown to them. (San GS I 17.2, Hir GS I.22.10) However, according to Asv. GR, only the bride remains silent.

There are many other views on which other heavenly bodies - apart from *dhruva* - are shown in the night.

28. *Agneya sthālipāka* - This is a mess of cooked food offered to *Agni*. (Āp GS VI I.1 - 5, Gobhila I I.3.19 - 21, Bhar GS I.18, Hir GS I.20 3.1 - 6)
29. *Triratri vrata* - This rite includes keeping certain observances, such as *vrata*, for three nights after marriage. Furthermore, according to Aśvalāyana and almost all other *sūtrakaras*, the couple should not eat *kshara* and *lavaṇa*, should observe celibacy, wear ornaments and sleep on the ground for three nights or twelve nights or even a year according to some.
30. *Caturthi karma* - This is the rite on the fourth night after marriage when the married couple have intercourse.

A few ceremonies, mentioned in medieval digests, which are observed even today are listed below -

1. *Simantapūjāṇa* - This includes honouring the bridegroom and his party on their arrival at the bride's village.[9] This is done before *vaga dāna* in the modern times.
2. *Gauri hara pūjā* - Worship of *Śiva* and *Gauri*[10]

Images of *Gauri* and *Hara* made of gold or silver, or their pictures drawn on a wall or a piece of cloth or a stone, is worshipped by the intending bride after *puṇyahavacana* and before *kanyādāna* (vide Laghu - Aśvalāyana 15.35).

3. *Índrani pūjā* - This requires worship of *Índrani*, the consort of god *Índra*.[11]
   Kāli Dāsa in Raghuvamsha V I I.3 refers to this ancient practice.
4. *Taila hardidraropana* - This consists of applying turmeric powder to the

bridegroom's body from what is left after the bride's body has been been applied with it[12].

5. *Ardraksataropana* - Here, the bride and groom together shower wet unbroken rice grains.[13]
6. *Maṃgala sūtra bandhana* - This involves tying a string with golden and other beads around the bride's neck; the *sūtras* are entirely silent about it.

Among the earliest references, Śaunaka Smṛti and Laghu Aśvalāyanas Smṛti 15.33 prescribe it along with the appropriate mantra.

Gadadhara (exponent of *Navya-nyāya* branch of *Nyāya* school of philosophy from Bengal, around 1450 AD) in his *bhashya* on Par. GS (I.8), says that *maṃgala sūtra* should be worn and garlands must be placed around necks of the bride and bridegroom. The *sūtra* of Paraskara is silent on the point. The Baud GS. Śeṣasūtra (V.5), in describing '*arkavivāha*', speaks of *maṃgala sūtra* to be tied to a plant. It is unclear whether it means the same as the one women wear around their necks today.

Nose ring or nose ornaments, to which all women whose husbands are alive attach great importance to in modern times, find no mention in the *sūtras*, *smṛtis* or even the early digests. According to Dr Altekar, "nose ring was unknown throughout the whole of India during the entire Hindu period[14]," i.e., until nearly 1000 AD. This is evident from sculptures found across India belonging to that period.

7. *Uttariyapranta bandhana* - This involves tying turmeric pieces and a betel nut onto the end of the upper garment of both the bride and groom, and knotting their garments together.[15]
8. *Airinidāna* - It includes presenting several gifts and a large wickerwork basket with lit lamps to the groom's mother, and requesting her and the relatives of the bridegroom to treat the bride affectionately. This is done when the bride is about to leave the father's place to go to the bridegroom's house after marriage.[16]
9. *Devakotthapna and mandapodvasna* - This involves taking leave of the deities invoked before the ceremonies began and taking down the *pandala*.[17]

Chapter 38

Caste Factor

The caste factor in marriage

Before we proceed to discuss the important role that the caste factor plays in Hindu marriages, we need to understand - what may appear as totally unrelated topic - Why the *smṛtis* were composed at different times and in different parts of the country? The main, if not the sole, purpose was to provide guidelines to the people to carry out their duties and responsibilities in a righteous way, i.e., according to their Dharma, in changed environment. So the *smṛtis* were composed to fulfil a popular want and reflect the prevailing state of the society.

Consequently, the direction and instructions that the *smṛtis* contained kept changing - from time to time, and from place to place. As the society evolved over time - differently in different parts of the country - new *smṛtis* were composed to incorporate these factors. They constaly modulated their stance with time.

∞

It will be worthwhile to briefly recapitulate the *varṇa* and caste system and its evolution, particularly with reference to marriage in the Hindu society. As we know, the early Ṛgvedic period talks only about *varṇa* and not caste. It is nearly universally accepted that the caste system evolved subsequently and is the outcome of the union of men and women of different *varṇa*s. This union was of two kinds, *anuloma* and *pratiloma*.

Anuloma and *pratiloma* literally mean 'along' and 'against' the '*loma*', a Sanskrit word meaning hair. In the English language, the expression 'going against the grain' best describes *pratiloma*, and *anuloma* is the opposite of it.

In the present context, when a man of a higher *varṇa* married a woman of a lower *varṇa*, the marriage was called *anuloma*, and the offspring was an *anuloma*.

And when a woman of a higher caste married a man of a lower caste, it was a *pratiloma* marriage, and their offspring was called *pratiloma*. Thus, there were six primary *anulomas* and *pratilomas* each (Manu X.10- 12; Yaj.91-94) resulting in twelve castes.

	Pratiloma		***Anuloma***	
S.No.	**Female**	**Male**	**Male**	**Female**
1.	*Brahmaṇa*	*Kṣatriya*	*Brahmaṇa*	*Kṣatriya*
2.	*Brahmaṇa*	*Vaiśya*	*Brahmaṇa*	*Vaiśya*
3.	*Brahmaṇa*	*Śūdra*	*Brahmaṇa*	*Śūdra*
4.	*Kṣatriya*	*Vaiśya*	*Kṣatriya*	*Vaiśya*
5.	*Kṣatriya*	*Śūdra*	*Kṣatriya*	*Śūdra*
6.	*Vaiśya*	*Śūdra*	*Vaiśya*	*Śūdra*

Further sub-castes were produced from -

(i) Union of twelve *anuloma* and *pratiloma* castes with the four *varṇa*s;

(ii) Union of six *anuloma* with six *pratiloma* castes;

(iii) Union among six *anuloma* castes; and,

(iv) Union among six *pratiloma* castes

The resultant sub-castes further multiplied as their progeny married spouses from other sub-castes, thereby producing more new sub castes. So, when we come across a mind-boggling number of castes - running into hundreds - enumerated in the *smṛtis* and *dharmaśāstras*, they may have actually existed at the time. Kane collated 169 castes from these texts compiled between 500 BC to 1000 AD[1]. In fact, Kane's numbers do not take into account cates based on sub divisions - *brahmaṇas* alone number more than a hundred. However, the reasoning given in the *smṛtis* - the permutations and combinations of the inter-*varṇa* cum *pratiloma* cum *anuloma*, and intra-*anuloma* and intra-*pratiloma* marriages resulting in birth of specific castes - appears to be farfetched, and a bit of guesswork.

Although, as described above, many scholars agree that new castes resulted from inter-*varṇa* marriages, it is not right to conclude, as many other scholars do, that this was the only way castes came into existence. All castes did not originate from inter-*varṇa-pratiloma-anuloma* marriages. There were at least two other social fields where the caste system germinated and grew.

First, as the society evolved and urbanised, a whole new and different class of people performing specialised tasks/duties emerged. This new class of artisans and professionals passed on their skills to their descendants/progeny and over few generations these family occupations became hereditary. It is not difficult to imagine - a carpenter or a weaver father, attracting the fancy of the growing child of the house, who as he grew up, started sharing the burden of his father. He eventually inherited the business and skills from his father, and adopted that profession for himself. Perhaps, over generations these skills became part of the DNA, giving him an edge over a new entrant to that profession. It is not uncommon to see even today, a carpenter's or a barber's son following in the footsteps of his father. These family occupations over time came to be identified as caste.

And secondly, some castes were also born with emergence and formation of guilds. With growth in urbanization emerged new class of people engaged in specialised commerce leading to formation of guilds, which in due course of time became an important and powerful factor in urban centres. These guilds started wielding considerable influence in the cities, and over time, their activities got identified as their separate caste.

Coming back to our subject of castes and marriage, there is no disagreement among scholars that -

(a) Four *varṇa*s - *brahmaṇa*, *kṣatriya*, *vaiśya* and *śūdra* - had a recognized social status in the given descending order since ancient times, they started crystallizing from later part of Ṛg.

(b) Marriages were permissible between a male of a higher *varṇa* with a woman of a lower *varṇa*. The marriage of a woman of higher *varṇa* with a man of lower *varṇa* was reprehensible, but common.

(c) By medieval ages, caste was determined only by birth provided birth was lawful, i.e. in lawful wedlock of parents belonging to the same *jāti* or *varṇa*.

The four *varṇa*s were a fact of life in times of the *Saṃhitās* (the tenth *manḍala* of the Ṛgveda unambiguously talks of the four *varṇa*s), and the issue of superiority and inferiority had started firming up. But the rigidity of not partaking food outside of one's *varṇa*, and not marrying outside the *varṇa* was still in a faraway future. Following are two of many such examples of *inter-varṇa* union from Ṛg -

In the early part of the Ṛgveda i.e. (*manḍala* 5.61), there is a story of *Archananas*, a *hotṛ* (*brahmaṇa*) asking for the hand of a *kṣatriya* king's daughter Rathaviti for his son Syavasa, and their subsequent marriage (*Sūkta* V.(LXI) fourth *aṣṭaka*, third *adhyāya*, Wilson). In later texts of Brahmaṇa, there is an account of *kṣatriya rāja* Saryata marrying his daughter Sukanyā to ṛṣi: "*Chyavana* the *Bhārgava*, or *Chyavana* the *Angirasa*."[2]

The practice of inter-*varṇa* marriage began to be looked at differently in the GS and DS period. Unfortunately, what is right and in accordance with *śāstras*, is not always easy to interpret, since these texts often give contradictory signals. For example, the recommendation in Gauta DS that "*Gṛhastha* should marry in (same) *jāti* and *kula*, one who is not previously married (unmarried) and younger girl"[3] is clearly prescriptive and not directive in nature. Āpastamba also prescribes more or less the same in his DS: "Sons begotten by a man who has sex in the proper season with a woman of equal caste, who has not been married to another man, and who has been married legally, have a right to (follow) the occupations (of their castes)."[4] But while Gautama, in the following *sūtra* - (DS.4.13-17) - goes on to describe *anuloma* and *pratiloma* marriages and the status of their offspring without any adverse observations, implying these were common practices, Āpastamba, in the subsequent *sūtras* - (Āp DS.3 and 4) - calls inter-*varṇa* marriage a transgression or offence and declares that the son born out of such a union is blameworthy!

As we progress from the Vedas to *dharmasūtra* and *smṛti* period, it appears that there was a growing tendency to move from inter-*varṇa* marriages to intra-*varṇa* marriages (evident from the different *dharmasūtras* and *smṛtis*). Although marrying a woman of the same *varṇa* was considered more favourable in the beginning of the Christian Era, inter-caste marriages continued and were allowed by lawmakers: "A woman of the same class is recommended to twice born man for the first marriage; but for men who are driven by desire, these are the women, in progressively descending order." (MS 3.12)

The *anuloma* and *pratiloma* marriages, permitting union even with a *śūdra* girl, thus continued to flourish through the Christian Era with some restrictions. However, some sages held the view that a *dvija* should not marry a *śūdra* girl. (Yaj I.57)

Now we shall see sample of what different *dharma* and *gṛhya sūtras* say about the same *varṇa* and *inter-varṇa* marriage -

i. One should marry a girl of the same *varṇa* and marriage should be solemnised in accordance with the *śāstra* - contravention of this rule results in sin being incurred. (Āp.DS. I I.6.13.1 and 3).
ii. Mānava GS (I. 7.8) and Gautama (IV.1) require that one should marry a girl of the same *varṇa*, but are silent about marriage with a bride of another *varṇa*.
iii. Manu (I I I. 12) and others (Saṅkha and Nārada etc.) observe that marriage to a girl of one's own caste is the best course or *pūrva kalpa*, i.e., the foremost or the best procedure.
iv. A less advisable course, i.e., *anukalpa* is that a *brahmaṇa* may take a wife of any caste; a *kṣatriya* may marry a woman of his own caste or *vaiśya* or a *śūdra* woman; a *vaiśya* may marry a *vaiśya* woman or a *śūdra* woman; and a *śūdra* may marry only a *śūdra* woman.(Baud.DS.I 8.2; Manu I I I. 13, Viṣṇu DS. 24.1- 4.)
v. Some teachers allowed *dvijas* to marry a *śūdra* woman, but without Vedic mantras. (Parāśara GS I. 4; and Vas DS. I. 25)

Interestingly Vasiṣṭha himself condemns such mixed marriages severely: "One should not do so, i.e. marry a *śūdra* girl, for by doing so the declination of the family is certain and loss of heaven after death." It appears that he's in company with Viṣṇu Dharmaśāstra and Manusmṛti which state that the *dvijati* may marry a *śūdra* girl but go on to condemn it - the union (of *dvijāti*) with a *śūdra* woman can never produce religious merit Viṣṇu DS (26. 5-6).It appears that the contradiction is due to the fact that such a practice had become prevalent in the society, so at one place they were stating the state of affairs (as it existed) and at the other place, they were prescribing the rule. Yaj I.57 while allowing a *brahmaṇa* to marry a girl of his own *varṇa* or of the *varṇa*s next in order, critically opines that a *dvijāti* should not marry a *śūdra* girl.

Such marriages were not only common, but even children borne of a *śūdra* wife from a *brahmaṇa* had the legal sanctity and right to inheritance. This is evident from the fact that if a *brahmaṇa* had sons from his *brahmaṇa*, *kṣatriya*, *vaiśya* and *śūdra* wives, they were entitled to four-tenth, three-tenth, two-tenth and one-tenth share of the father's property respectively. (Manu IX.152-153 and Yaj 11.125)

Interestingly, contradicting himself in I. 91 - 92, Yaj recognises the marriage of a *brahmaṇa* with a *śūdra*, calling the son of such a union as *parasava*. Mentioning the marriage of *śūdra* girl with one of higher caste/class and accepting the sanctity of *pratiloma*, Manu also says that she holds the hem of the garment of a bridegroom of a higher class. (I I I. 44)

So, it appears that while *smṛtis* recognised without reservation marriages between a *brahmaṇa* and *kṣatriya* or a *vaiśya* girl, the opinion was divided about the marriage of a *brahmaṇa* with a *śūdra* woman. Such marriages, though did take place, were looked down upon.

While the *anuloma* offspring is entitled to the *saṃskāras* (e.g. *upanayana*, which are performed for the *dvijas*), according to Manu X. 41, *pratiloma* castes are like *śūdras* and not entitled to any of the *saṃskāras* that *dvijas* are (even when the offspring is from *dvija* parents, but a result of *pratiloma* marriage, e.g. a *brahmaṇa* woman with a *kṣatriya* man).

∞

According to Kane[5], *anuloma* marriages were frequent until ninth or tenth century AD, but later became rare, and for last several hundred years they have hardly occurred, or perhaps they were not recognised as valid by the communities concerned.

With passage of time, around first half of ninth century AD, intercaste marriages between *dvijāti*s came to be prohibited by the *smṛtis* and writers of digests. Aaccording to Visvarupa on Yaj I I I. 283, a *brahmaṇa* could marry a *kṣatriya* girl, but around 980 AD, according to Medhatithi on Manu (I I I. 14), a *brahmaṇa* rarely married *kṣatriya* and *vaiśya* girls. And by 1100 AD, though *anuloma* marriages among *dvijāti* were allowed by Manu and Yaj, they had entirely ceased to be regarded as valid. Al Beruni, an Arab scholar who spent nearly thirteen years in India (1017-1030 AD) wrote a valuable account of the prevailing religion, philosophy, literature, astronomy, customs and laws, among other things.

He noted that the caste system in his time had become so rigid that "each of the four castes, when eating together, must form a group for themselves, one group not being allowed to comprise men of different castes."[6] Inter-dining and inter-marriage are two important characteristics of the caste system (people outside the caste are excluded from both), and by 1030 AD, inter-caste marriages had ceased.

The position remained unchanged in the thirteenth century - Hemādri (1260-1270 AD) and Smṛti Candrika (1200-1225 AD) qoute Āditya Purāṇa and Brahman Purāṇa to say that intercaste marriages are included in the list of matters forbidden in the *kāli* age, i.e. *kālivarjya.*

Nearly 500 years later, during the British rule, by the Special Marriage Act I I I of 1872 as amended by Act XXX of 1923, both *anuloma* and *pratiloma* marriages were validated if they were registered and solemnised according to the procedure prescribed by the act. But if the marriage was not so solemnised under that act, but under the general rule of Hindu law, then all *pratiloma* marriages were invalid throughout British India.

Anuloma marriages were recognised as valid by some High Courts in India; the Allahabad High Court however regarded all *anuloma* marriages as invalid until India's independence.[7]

∞

Historical evidences demonstrate the practice of *anuloma* and *pratiloma* marriages in the society - the Kadamba family, founded by Mayursarman (a *brahmaṇa*), got their daughters married to the Gupta and other kings who were not *brahmaṇas*; Lokanātha's ancestors belonged to the Bharadvāja *gotra*, and the maternal grandfather of Lokanātha was Keśhava (a *parasava*)[8]; Virupadevi, daughter of Vijaynagar king Bukka I was married to a *brahmaṇa* named *Brahman*, who was the governor of the Araga province between 1268-1298 AD.[9]

There are instances of intercaste marriages in the Sanskrit literature of Kālidāsa as well.

Chapter 39

Gotra, *Piṇḍa* and *Pravara*

The rule about choosing a girl for marriage of the same caste was essentially based on endogamy i.e. a rule requiring marriage within a certain large community. But within this large community, there were certain groups which were excluded from marrying a person belonging to another group in the same community.

This exogamy i.e. rule of marrying outside one's own group, which had to be practised within endogamy, was determined by three defining factors - *gotra*, *pravara* and *piṇḍa*.

Marriage in the same *gotra* or *pravara* or *piṇḍa* was totally prohibited. Marriage between two members could not take place even if one of the three was common to both. It is not quite clear as to why such marriages were prohibited, but the reason this rule had to be adhered to was in view of the canon of the *Pūrva Mīmāṃsā* : If there is a seen or easily perceptible reason for the rule stated in the sacred texts, it is only recommendatory and a breach of such a rule does not nullify the principal act. But if there is an unseen reason for the rule, i.e. a reason which is not perceptible and there is a breach of such a rule, then the principal act itself becomes invalid.[1]

While interpreting -

i. One of the maxims of interpretation is that where there is conflict between *smṛti* texts, the preferable rule is to follow the opinion of the majority[2].Notably Gautama, Manu, Yaj, Marici and many other *smṛtikaras* are opposed to this dictum.

ii. The second rule is that Manu has the highest authority among *smṛtis*, and a *smṛti* which is opposed to the dicta of Manu is not commended.[3]

Sapiṇḍa

The prohibition on account of being *sapiṇḍa* in marriage is absolute - it applies to all *varṇa*s including *śūdra*[4]. *Sapiṇḍa* relationship, apart from marriage, has an important bearing on inheritance, and impurity on birth and death, i.e. *aśauca*.

Meaning of *sapiṇḍa*

Many of us who are familiar with Hindu rituals have heard of *piṇḍas*, especially in context of *śrāddha* ceremonies where it is used for a 'ball of rice'. But in the Ṛgveda, where the word occurs nearly a dozen times, nowhere is it used in the sense of a 'ball of rice' e.g. RV (I.16; 2.19), here it is used in the sense of a part of the sacrificial animal offered in the fire. In subsequent Brahmaṇa and Taittirīya, it is used in the present day sense of 'ball of rice' offered to the manes. Nirukta very specifically talks of '*pinddanya*' - *dāna* or gift of *piṇḍa* or ball of rice - in the same sense as we do now, 2000 years later, in our *śrāddha* ceremonies. The word came to be used very frequently in the *sūtra* and other literature.

There are two schools of thought about the meaning of *sapiṇḍa* - i. Mitākṣarā, and ii. Jimutvahana - author of the Dayabhaga. Both agree that *sapiṇḍa* marriage cannot take place.

Sapiṇḍa means one who has the same *piṇḍa* i.e. body (or particle of the body), and a *sapiṇḍa* relationship arises from being connected by having particles of the same body. Thus, a son has a *sapiṇḍa* relationship with his father because particles of the father's body continue in him. Similarly, there is *sapiṇḍa* relationship with the paternal grandfather and the like because through his father, particles of the grandfather's body continue in the grandson. On the mother's side too, the son has particles of his mother, who in turn has particles from her own mother and father, thus establishing a *sapiṇḍa* relationship with maternal grandparents similar to the paternal side.

All brothers and sisters on the father's side i.e. paternal uncle and aunt, and maternal uncle and aunt also become *sapiṇḍa* by this definition. Apart from the husband and wife becoming *sapiṇḍa* after marriage - the wife has particles of her husband in her - the brothers and sisters in the family also fall under this catogary.

Given this understanding and definition, an individual may eventually be found to have a *sapiṇḍa* relationship with the whole *saṃsāra* (world), thereby making restrictions on *sapiṇḍa* marriages impractical and meaningless. Recognising the problem of making *sapiṇḍa* relationship open-ended, sages like Yājñavalkya came up with the solution of imposing reasonable restrictions on the number of generations for which the restriction of *sapiṇḍa vivāha* remained valid; after seventh on the father's side and fifth on the mother's side, the *sapiṇḍa* relationship was declared to be inconsequential. The counting of seven began from the father, going up to the father's father and so on.

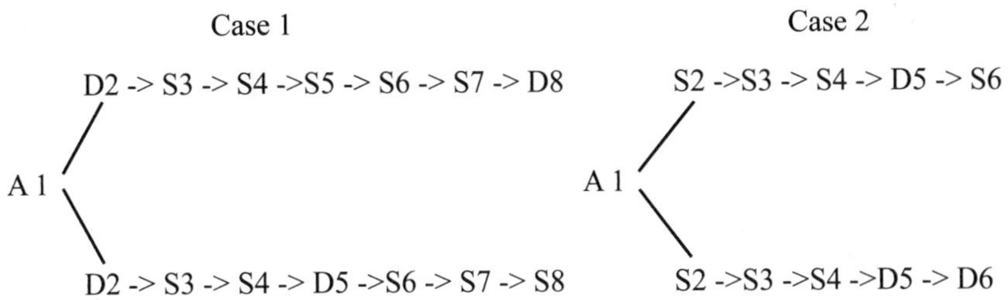

(A is ancestor, D - daughter & S - son)

In case 1, marriage between D8 and S8 is traced through their respective fathers, therefore rule of both sides' ancestors removed by more than seven generations is applicable. Marriage between S8 and D8 is permitted.

In case 2, marriage relationship of both S6 and D6 is through their mothers, hence rule of both ancestors removed by five generations is applicable. Marriage between D6 and S6 is permitted.

Although separation of seven and five generations in case of father and mother respectively was accepted, and by and large continues to be observed, there has been a dispute about the numbers right from beginning - some believed that after five generations from the father's side and three from the mother's side, *sapiṇḍa* ceases to be of any consequence.

Given this prohibition on marriage in a *sapiṇḍa* relationship, the first question that comes to mind is: How marriage with one's maternal uncle's daughter, and paternal aunt's daughter, is prevalent amongst many South Indian communities?

The prohibition of marriage on the ground of *sapiṇḍa* relationship, where a person is connected through females, has not been observed in numerous instances over wide areas since very ancient times. Whether a man can marry his maternal uncle's or paternal aunt's daughter has remained a topic of hot debate in this context. On this point, sharply divided opinions hav existed from ancient times.

Āpastamba, while listing out actions causing loss of caste (a grave sin), terms this relationship as incestuous -

'Now (follows the enumeration of) the actions which cause loss of caste (*Patnīya*).'

'[These are] (a) stealing (gold), (b) crimes whereby one becomes an *Abhiśasta*, (c) homicide, (d) neglect of the Vedas, (e) causing abortion, (f) incestuous connection with maternal or paternal uncles or aunts, (g) and with the offspring of such persons (cousin), (h) alcoholism, and (i) socializing with persons the interaction with whom is forbidden.' (Āp.DS 1.7.21.7-8)

In support of this practice of marriage with the maternal uncle's daughter[5], Parāśara Mādhviya and Smṛty Candrikā cite two Veda passages, one from Śatapatha (I. 8. 3. 6), and a verse from a Khila sūkta. But there are disagreements on the meaning of the two passages. Separating the two spoons for making offerings to *Índra* and *Agni*, Śatapatha says: "Thus the separation (of the eater and the eaten) is effected in one and the same act; and hence from one and the same manner spring both to the enjoyer (the husband) and the one to be enjoyed (the wife): for now kinfolk (*jātyah*) live sporting and rejoicing together." He further adds: "In the fourth (or) third man (i.e. generation) reunite," and "this is so in accordance with that (separation of the spoons)."[6] This can hardly be interpreted to mean anything other then what it specifically says i.e. the restriction of marrying a *sapiṇḍa* applied only up to fourth-generation in the Vedic times. The Khila Sūkta, admittedly, unambiguously says: "Come, O *Índra*, by commanded paths to this sacrifice and partake of your portion. They (the priests) have offered the fat seasoned with *ghī* that is thy portion, as the maternal uncle's daughter or the paternal aunt's daughter (is one's lot in marriage)."[7] *Khila* is the designation 'of certain hymns appended to the received text of the Ṛgveda' that occur only in the *sūtra* period[8], and is widely used to mean a supplement. Those in support of this view believe that *Khila* (being a part of *śruti*) supersedes what is said to the contrary in the *dharma śāstras* and the *smṛtis* like Gautama DS, Baudhāyana DS and MS.

This controversy was very much alive in the period of *dharma sūtras* and *smṛtis*, and yet the practice continued in the whole of south, Mahārāshtra, and parts of Odishā, and was accepted by *sūtrakaras* as a custom or *shishta* peculiar to south. Baudhāyana, while observing that south had five peculiarities, says: "There is a dispute regarding five (practices) both in the south and in the north." Explaining those peculiar to the south, Baudhāyana says: "They are, to eat in the company of an uninitiated person, to eat in the company of one's wife, to eat stale food, to marry the daughter of a maternal uncle or of paternal aunt,"[9a] and adds that the north also had its share of peculiarities - to deal in wool, to drink rum, to sell animals that have teeth in the upper and lower jaws, to follow the trade of arms, and to go to sea.[9b] What Baudhāyana states next is very significant because it shows how these peculiarities were accepted and accommodated as part of Dharma: "If a man follows the practices of the former in the latter, and those of the latter in the former, he becomes defiled." "Each practice is based solely on the authority of the customs of that region."[9c]

Very interestingly, Baudhāyana also notes that Gautama declares 'that that is false' and 'one should not take heed of either (set of practices) because they are opposed to the tradition of *shishtas*'.[9d]

With the two opposing sides firmly holding their ground, the practice continues in south India to this day, except among *nambūdiri* Brahmaṇas in Kerala, who traditionally did not adopt cross-cousin or maternal uncle marriage customs. *Nambūdiris* followed their other rule - that only the eldest son marries a *nambūdiri* girl. The younger sons enter spousal relationships with women of other castes that were matrilineal and matriarchal in their practice.

Kane quotes[10] *Dharma Sindhu* (1790 AD) of Kāśī Nath, who is categorical in stating that only in calamities, when one is unable to secure a girl, one may enter into a *sapiṇḍa* marriage, but that those who can secure another girl must not go for a *sapiṇḍa* marriage as the sin of incest would be incurred. He adds that the approach of Saṃskārakaustubha and Dharma Sindhu is most sensible and practical, and that even in the *kāli* age, only those whose families or countries where the limits of *sapiṇḍa* relationship are narrowed down, and marriage with the maternal uncle's daughter has been in vogue for ages, may do so.[11]

Truly a gem!

Gotra

To us, *gotra* denotes all persons who can trace their descent in an unbroken line from a common male ancestor. So when someone says that he's of Vasiṣṭha *gotra*, he's understood to be claiming his descent from the ancient sage Vasiṣṭha. In our oldest Vedas text - Ṛg, where we do come across this word several times, nowhere has this word been used in this sense; everywhere it is used to mean cows, cow pens, or cow's shelter. Monier's Sanskrit English dictionary first lists the meaning of *gotra* as: 'Protection or shelter for cows, cow pen, cow shed, hurdle, enclosure - Ṛg VIII.50.10'. Obviously, the concept of *gotra* as we understand it now had not crystallized in the Ṛgveda time. However, we do know that *kula* (family) was a frequently used term from the early Vedic times. The first time that we come across its use in the present sense is when Gautama asks Satyakāma his *gotra* in Chāndogya (IV.4.1-5) - an Upaniṣad attached to Sāmaveda, a much later creation. Subsequently, we come across *Viśvagotrah* - belonging to all families - in the Atharvaveda (V. 21. 3), and a mantra in Kauśika Sūtra (I V. 2 in which *gotra* means 'a group of persons'.

By Pāṇini's time (~600-300 BC), '*gotra*' had become sufficiently popular for the grammarian to include its definition in his treatise - "The word *gotra* denotes (in my work on grammar) the progeny (of a sage) beginning with son's son".

The eight *gotras* and how they formed: The fate of 80,000 sages, that Āpastamba DS. II.9.23. 3-5 referring to two verses of Purāṇa tells us about, who desiring no offspring passed on to the south by *Āryaman's* road and practiced celibacy, is not known to us. But the other 80,000 sages who desired offspring and passed by *Āryama's* road to north did have among them eight ṛṣis from who the original eight *gotras* started and whose progeney proliferates Indian subcontinent today. Patañjali in his *Bhāshya* confirms: "There were 80,000 sages who observed celibacy. ..... The spread of progeney was due to the *sapta ṛṣis*' plus Agastya's lines. The offspring of these eight are *gotra* and other then these are called *gotravayava.*[12]

So, since the ancient times, it is accepted that there were eight primary *gotras* - the progeny of the eight sages, namely Viśvamitra, Jamadāgni, Bharadvāja,

Gautama, Atri, Vasiṣṭha and Kasyapa. These seven '*sapta ṛṣis*', and the eighth, Agastya, together constitute the eight gotras.

Importance of *gotra* - Over time, along with *varṇa* and caste system, family lineage (a subset of caste system) became a determining factor in marriage, inheritance and part of one's identity - one had to pronounce one's *gotra* in *saṃkalpa*, *saṃdhyā* and *śrāddha* ceremonies. *Sagotra* marriages were strictly forbidden - meaning that the bride to be chosen must not belong to the same *gotra* as the bridegroom (Gobhila GS. I I I. 4. 4, Āpastamba DH.S. I I. 5. 11. 15, Hir. GS. I. 19. 2).

Although the period in which *sagotra* marraiges got prohibited is not known, one can gather from the *śrauta* literature that even in that time - since 'long before' marriages in the same *gotra* were forbidden. According to Kane, "It must be supposed that prohibitions on sameness of *gotra* in marriage had its origin long before the period of the *sūtras* in the times of the Brahmaṇa works (if not earlier)."[13] Even now, *sagotra* marriages continue to be a big 'no', especially in the north, where non-observance of this prohibition results in village *pancāyats* annulling such marriages.

Importance of *gotra*: In five important events of a Hindu's life, listed below, *gotra* is of great importance-

(i) Marriage - spouse should not be of same *gotra*

(ii) Matters of inheritance - the wealth of the one dying (without an issue) went to his near *sagotras*

(iii) *Śrāddha* - the Brahmaṇas to be invited should not be (as far as possible) *sagotra*

(iv) While offering water to *preta* of the deceased, his name and *gotra* were to be repeated, and

(v) At the time of daily *saṃdhyā* prayer, one has to repeat one's *gotra*.

Dvigotras - There are certain families that are *dvigotra*, i.e. they have two *gotra*. These three families are *Saunga saisiri*, *Samkritis*, and *Laugaksis*.

Pravara

Although the literal meaning of *pravara* is *prārthana*[14] i.e. choosing or invoking, *pravara* came to denote one or more illustrious ṛṣis who belonged to that particular *gotra* to which a person belongs. Some others define *pravara* as "the group of sages that distinguishes the founder, i.e. the starter of one *gotra* from another."[15]

The word *pravara* does not occur in the Ṛgveda, but the word '*arseya*' does (IX. 97. 51) which means 'descendants of sages of those who are related to sages'(Atharvaveda XI. 1. 16, XI. 1. 25, 26, 32, 33, 35. X I I 4. 2 and 12, XVI 8. 12 - 30). Subsequently, as in Yaj I. 52, *arseya* or *arsa* became synonym of *pravara*.

Baudhāyana Pravaradhyāya gives 500 names of *gotras* and *pravara* sages, while Pravarāmanjari quotes the verse: "There are three crores of them and so the *gotra* system is difficult to comprehend," and mentions about 5000 *gotras*. Therefore, the *nibhandhas* endeavour to place the innumerable *gotras* under groups and distribute them among forty-nine *pravaras*.[16]

The *pravara* identifies the association of a person with three or five, sometimes seven, and interestingly, sometimes even nine (as seen in some places) ṛṣis. For example, those who have only one sage are Mitrayus, Vasiṣṭha, Śaunakas and Agastya,[17] while Kaśyapa Gothram has three ṛṣis associated with it, viz. Kaśyapa, Daivala and Āvatsāra.

In Vedic rituals, the importance of *pravara* appears to be in its use by the ritualist for extolling his ancestry and proclaiming that one is fit to do the act that he is performing as a descendant, in a manner worthy of the ancestors. The sacred thread called *upavita* or *yajñopavita* has close connection with the concept of *pravaras* related to the *brahmaṇa gotra* system. While tying the knots of the sacred thread, an oath is taken in the name of each of these three, five, seven or nine of the ṛṣis belonging to one's *gotra*.

Marriage between *sagotra* or *sapravara* parties is considered invalid. Since the boy and the girl each may have more than one ṛṣis in *pravara*, the rule of prohibition applies even if one ṛṣi is common to the two.

The consequences of such a union, in olden days, were extremely serious. If a man had intercourse with a *sagotra* girl, he had to undergo the penance of *candrayana*, after which he was supposed to not abandon the woman, but only maintain her as if she were a mother or sister. If a child is born, it does not incur sin and is given the *gotra* of Kaśyapa.[18]

Aparārka quotes Sumntu and prescribes *candrayana* penance if a man marries the girl unknowingly, which is the same as Baudhāyana quoted above. However, if the marriage takes place knowingly, then penance was the same as that for incest, and if he has intercourse with her or begets a child, he loses his caste and the child will be a *candala*.[19]

PART VI

न चक्षुषा गृह्यते नापि वाचा नान्यैर्देवैस्तपसा कर्मण वा ।
ज्ञानप्रसादेन विशुद्धसत्त्वस्ततस्तु तं पश्यते निष्कलं ध्यायमानः ॥

Brahman is not grasped by the eye, nor by speech, nor by the other senses, nor by penance or good works. A man becomes pure through serenity of intellect; thereupon, in meditation, he beholds Him who is without parts.

(Mundaka Upanishad 3.1.8)

Chapter 40

Do Rituals Have Meaning?

Rituals, difficult to define, are necessarily physical acts that always involve some 'doing '.

The drawback with such description and understanding is that a very wide, disparate range of practices - everyday ‘interaction rituals’ (Goffman 1967), governmental and non-governmental bureaucratic procedures, everyday habits like the brushing of teeth or showering, magical or religious practices, even compulsive and neurotic behaviour that require medical treatment - qualify as rituals. We are then presented with the very formidable task of culling out attributes that are common to these diverse activities, and working out a satisfactory definition of the thing we call ritual. Most attempts to find traits that are common to such a wide range of practices yield such diffused results that they are rendered meaningless.

Alternately, we can follow Crossley’s advice. Nick Crossley is a Professor of Sociology at the University of Manchester and author of several books on social theory, embodiment, and the sociology of social movements. Here we are more interested in his paper ‘Ritual, Body technique, and (inter) Subjectivity'. According to Crossley, “We would be ill-advised...to attempt to define ritual in a neat or conclusive fashion." He recommends a different approach: "we must work with its 'fuzziness."[1] Crossley takes on a bigger question - Are there any attributes sufficiently exclusive to these very diverse activities? He suggests these are like Wittgenstein's (1953) 'games' that “enjoy a family resemblance rather than a fixed and clear essence."

[Fuzzy logic is a form of many-valued logic in which the truth values of variables may be any real number between 0 and 1. It is employed to handle the concept of partial truth, where the truth value may range between completely true (i.e. 1) and completely false (i.e. 0), for example - asking persons participating in an experiment on the colour of a disc, which may be described differently by participants. By contrast, in Boolean logic, the truth values of variables may only be the integer values 0 or 1.]

Since rituals do not share a common given likeness or function, Crossely reasons that, "the meaning, function, and characteristics of rituals will be different in different cases. Indeed, even the same ritual may change in these respects over time, as rituals necessarily belong to the flow of historical time."[2]

If we choose Crossley's view as the path to understand religious rituals, we must examine the fundamentals of rituals in general, and compare ritual practices from different religions across eras. But before that, let's look at how the Oxford dictionary defines rituals -

'A religious or solemn ceremony consisting of a series of actions performed according to a prescribed order'.

Though this chapter is essentially about rituals in context of Hinduism, any such study of Hindu rituals will necessarily be a subset of the study of rituals per se.

Any analysis of religious rituals will remain incomplete unless one has fully understood the basic characteristics of the rituals. One will then be better equipped to draw inferences from the ritual acts in other religions. Such inferences are better served if we bear in mind that each religion has its own system of beliefs, and rituals are deeply rooted in the culture and religious beliefs of societies, and are also affected by their geographical locations.

Though most societies have a fair share of adherents who practice (religious) rituals, they, usually, also have an appreciable number of critics, who consider rituals meaningless. The criticism of rituals comes mainly from two quarters - those who belong to the religion in which these rituals are practiced, and those who belong to the scholarly class. The thrust of the argument from both quarters is largely the same - rituals are meaningless acts with no purpose (other than just being there, like fillers in a TV program, totally unrelated to the main program for which the viewer tuned into the particular programme). It is interesting that the two groups reach similar conclusions by employing entirely different set of arguments.

Let us first examine the arguments of the scholarly quarter - heavyweights like Frits Staal, Macaulay, and many others fall firmly in this class. While Staal finds rituals almost unintelligible - not a human language of communication and fit to be studied in the same way as bird songs[3], Macaulay views rituals as transparently irrational acts bereft of any meaning.

∞

Frits Staal, an eminent Indologist and logician of repute, deems rituals meaningless. He believes, the assumption that 'ritual expresses or conveys meaning as if it were a kind of language', is mistaken.[4]

In his essay '*Theories and facts on ritual simultaneities*' (*Thinking Through Rituals*, Ed.K. Schilbrack), Staal argues that any language has a speaker and a hearer, who follow certain rules of communication. One basic rule on which such communication hinges is of speakers taking turns successively. Any instances of simultaneous speech or response can be logically reduced to a succession.[5] He adds - communications, which are simply conversations or dialogues between two or more people, are also characterized by gaps and follow certain other rules.

Staal visited India in 1975 and witnessed *agnicayana*, a twelve-day long *Soma* ritual performed by seventeen *Nambūdri brahmanṇs* of Kerala at Panjal in Thrissur district.

In *apyāyana*, a part of *agnicayana*, (dry) *Soma* stalks are sprinkled with water and made to swell before the juice is extracted. This follows a complex, protracted ritual that has been described in the chapter on *Soma* rituals in this book. In this ceremony, sixteen priests and the *yajamāna* simultaneously recite different mantras while performing different tasks. Citing this, Staal surmised that *Soma* rituals follow the rule of simultaneity, in direct conflict with the rule of succession that is followed in languages.

Another feature which caught Staal's eye was *saṁtataṁ*, meaning 'linked' or 'continuous'. This term expresses that gaps are avoided in time, not unlike the avoiding of any gaps in spaces in the *horror vacui* seen in some ancient and medieval European art. *Horror vacui* is a Latin term meaning a fear or dislike of leaving empty spaces, especially in artistic composition. Staal explains: "*saṁtataṁ* means that in long recitations from the Ṛgveda like the *śāstra* recitations, verses are recited without interruption, taking care that the flow of sound is as continuous as possible."[6] This is an important part of Vedas recitation - the *śrauta sūtras* contain detailed rules explaining how continuity is affected, and prescribing when, and how, to breathe mid verse.

Staal finds "the most important, general and characteristic simultaneity of Vedic ritual "between mantra and act, and in support quotes *ekāmantrani karmani*, "each act is accompanied by one mantra"[7] in the *śrauta sūtras*, e.g. Āpastamba śrauta sūtras 24.1.38. This, according to Staal is a characteristic which is implicit throughout the ritual.

∞

For Staal, the purpose of any language is 'communication of knowledge'. And communication necessarily presupposes the presence of at least two subjects - a speaker and a hearer. The absence of any one subject will disqualify the act as a form of communication.

One (essential) purpose of language is to convey meaning, emotion, a thought, or an idea of the speaker to the hearer. Language employs words, sentences and syntax to achieve this objective. Additionally, languages follow a discipline - there is an entire field of linguistics that covers the study of languages.

Staal argues that in rituals, the priests are the speakers, but there are no hearers. He says the gods are not hearers and, hence, rituals fail to qualify as a form of communication[7a].

Raising issue of simultaneity, Staal says - communication, the main purpose of languages, is done sequentially rather than simultaneously. In any civilised conversation or dialogue, the hearer and the speaker both do not speak simultaneously. The dialogue is carried out in a sequence, i.e., the speaker speaks first and the hearer hears him, and when the hearer speaks, the earlier speaker becomes the hearer. In such communications, following the rules of language, the same word or sentence is not repeated. Giving the example of *Soma* rituals that he attended, Staal argues that the priests participating in the ritual talk simultaneously e.g. they simultaneously recite mantras taking great care to not leave any gaps in the recitation; a stringent requirement of the ritual. For Staal, such a performance is not dialogical, does not conform to the principles or laws of communication and makes the act meaningless. The incessant repetitiousness, ensuring that there are no gaps between sentences, and simultaneous speaking, are attributes which disqualify "the symbolic acts and utterances associated with the rituals" as a (human) language or communication of any knowledge.

To illustrate an important point, let's pause the Staal-related discussion and indulge in a sports analogy with the help of India's favourite sport: How the two forms of game of cricket - five day Test match and its current short form of T20 - differ? Cricket matches are massively popular in India and have an enormous following. When the Indian team reaches the final of, say, the T20 World Cup, the media claims that one billion hearts throb in excitement. The attire of the players and umpires, the size of the cricket field, the duration of the game (usually three hours), the time of day when the game is played (evening/night), and the restrictions on field placements et cetera are all governed by a detailed set of rules which are significantly different from the rules of the more traditional Test match cricket which is played over five days.

The important thing to note here is, a five-day Test match as well as a 180-minute-long T20, both are games of cricket, though played quite differently. If we apply the rules of five-day Test match to a T20 game, the shorter form would barely qualify as a proper game of cricket! A cricket fan frozen in time in the 1960s, when T20 did not exist (the first T20 match was played in February 2005), if woken up in the present day, would be fairly disoriented watching a T20 game. No doubt, he will instantly recognize that the sport being played is cricket. But an unfamiliar and very strange version of cricket. He would not understand any of the several new 'signals' made by the umpires - like rotating the arm over the head indicating a free hit award for a 'no-ball', or signal indicating commencement of 'power-play'. Nor the 'new' rules governing the leg-bye or the bouncer. The confusion in the mind of this spectator, whom the sport passed by for 50 years, would arise due to the following reasons -

- he would be applying the rules of Test cricket - the only format of the game he knows - to a modern T20 format, and (erroneously) conclude T20 does not qualify as 'cricket proper'
- the signals, rules, players' jersey, the settings et cetera will leave him confused, especially the attitudes, and the behaviour of players and the umpires on the field, and the scantily-clad cheerleaders off the field, breaking into a bottom wriggling dance beside the boundary line to high-decibel music every time the batsmen score a four or a six - are important features of T20 cricket. He would be finding these aspects of the game at great vriance from the aspects he associates with 'cricket proper'

Now, if this 'traveller in time' spectator was asked (from a purist's point of view) whether what he watched (the T20 event) was a legitimate cricket match, the gentleman's answer would most likely be a firm no. On the touchstone of the core values of cricket, namely -

(a) the rules governing the game, particularly the limitation of the number of overs that a bowler could deliver, and the number of overs that each side could bat

(b) the general outlay of the field, the distance of the boundary from the batting pitch, the dress code of players and umpires, the behaviour of spectators, and the general atmosphere in the stadium

this game would hardly pass muster (under the conventions of the sixties) as a proper game of cricket.

From this analogy, it is easy to see that the problem arises because of the attempt to overlay the rules of one format of the game on another format which follows markedly different rules; even though the equipment used - such as the cricket ball, the wickets et cetera - and the two umpires and the scoreboard remain common features of the two formats.

The same thing happens when we try answereing - what is a ritual? - by applying defining features of one form, to an entirely different form of events that function in different environments!

Staal too applies a modern definition of 'language', formulated barely a couple of centuries ago, to judge the 'language' and style of recitation of mantras in ritual practices, created nearly 4000 years ago. He judges mantras and rituals independent of their own rules which had evolved over two millennia before the modern 'language' rules came in to existence. He uses this modern definition of 'language', time and again, as the touchstone to test whether a particular form of word, syntax or order of sentence - predating Staal's definition by over 2000 years - qualifies as 'language'. The point I am trying to make is that Sanskrit, in its spoken as well as written forms, had been in use until about 1000 years ago, and had acquired - what is now regarded - amongst the most sophisticated of generative grammars of any human language, codified by Pāṇini. Most ritual practices and mantras are in use and practise for more than three millennia without a break. Linguistics, and the modern definition of language came into existence no more than a few hundred years back. While framing these modern rules of linguistics, scholars failed to recognise, or ignored, the unique features and equally unique applications of Sanskrit, an ancient and demonstrably sophisticated language, in various situations, including religious rituals, and chose a narrow definition of 'language'. Now a more serious error is being committed : judging Sanskrit (which pre-existed these imperfect rules) by applying to it modern rules of 'language'. The fact is Sanskrit, as a language (including the mantras), need not adapt change/s in order to fit the modern definition of language. It is the definition of language that needs to be modified. It should accommodate some of the unique features of this ancient language, including mantras and the form in which they are practised, to arrive at a more holistic and comprehensive definition of language.

The topic of 'mantras not qualifying as a language' using more recent advancements in linguistics that accept additional classes of types of languages (descriptive, instructive, et cetera), has been dealt with in detail in the following chapter.

∞

McCauley and some other scholars find rituals transparently irrational acts, but their reasons are different from Staal's. Most Hindus, especially the younger generation of the twenty first century, also consider rituals meaningless and irrational acts, but not for the same reason as Staal or McCauley. Their reasons are largely rooted in ignorance of the Sanskrit language and religious rituals. They view ancient rituals as residues of past irrational practices which haven't died away because, in their opinion, the light of reason and scientific thought (temper) did not illuminate this part of the world i.e. India, as it did the western world in the nineteenth and twentieth century. Colonised Indians who, in their opinion, were deprived of education thus continued practicing these rituals.

This class of modern Indian differs from scholars in one imoprtant respect. Whereas the scholars' rejection of rituals comes after a deep study of religious texts and Vedic scriptures - often the original texts in Sanskrit (Staal, Doniger, Patton, Olivelle all possess deep knowledge of Sanskrit and an understanding of ancient Sanskrit texts) - contemporary Indian youth has near zero knowledge of Sanskrit and its literature. Their rejection is based on other factors.

Nearly all of the urban and semi urban population in India, particularly north of Mahārāshtra, has no knowledge of Sanskrit as a language which they can really use. In fact, Sanskrit ceased to be a language of communication more than 1000 years ago. The only time it is now used, apart from religious ceremonies, is by news readers in government-owned TV channels on Door Darśan, and in a quaint little village Mattur (or Mathur) in Shimoga district near the city of Shivamogga in Karnātaka state. In Mattur, Sanskrit is still used for day-to-day communication by the entire village, although the common language of the state is Kannada.

Given this absence of familiarity with Sanskrit, it is not surprising that most educated Indians readily concur with the view that mantras (and rituals conducted in Sanskrit) are meaningless. It is not that they think it to be meaningless after having understood the meaning of the words, the syntax and the message being communicated. For them, mantras are indeed meaningless because they do not understand the language. They have had little to no exposure to any authentic ancient text dealing with such practices either. Simply put, they find rituals unworthy of their time. In India, many of the urban educated tend to blame 'time constraints', and show little patience for these rituals where a priest utters words in a near-alien language (Sanskrit) and conducts rituals too complex to understand or even correlate to the strange utterances. Participation in religious rituals is viewed as a necessary evil that cannot be avoided. Their compromise with this strange thing called a 'religious ritual' is to clench ones teeth and 'rush' through it. Cosequently there is a great insistence by the main 'actor' (*yajmāna*), and an even greater demand by the 'audience' (attendees), to pare down the duration of the rituals and expedite conclusion of religious part of ceremony.

On the other hand, the rural Indian population (nearly 70%) - having much lower literacy rate than urban - seems to demonstrate an implicit faith in the efficacy of mantras and rituals. This attitude, ironically, is born of blind faith rather than knowledge. Similar to the urban populace, rural folk also do not comprehend, either the rituals, or the language used, but they have all the time and the patience to go through the rituals.

∞

A comparable situation had prevailed in England (and some parts of Europe) when that society was rapidly transforming in the wake of the Industrial Revolution. It is widely believed that in a more industrialised society, people have less 'disposable time' for rituals and religious congregations. Apart from organisational and logistic constraints, the participation (in rituals) does not have much to show by way of immediate results for the invested time.The returns (if any) are not always visible or tangible - at least not obviously. Participation in rituals is thus viewed as a case of poor returns on invested time, and avoided by industrial urban societies. This has naturally led people, and scholars, to conclude that industrialisation of society has taken people farther away from rituals.

The behaviour of modern Indians is also transformed in much the same ways. They have not rejected rituals outright. They continue to participate, albeit grudgingly, in deference to the feelings of the aging generation of their elders, and to project an image of a modern *saṃskāri* (one who observes *saṃskāras*) Hindu. This reluctant participation is, however, not without a trade-off. The religious rituals are getting truncated; they consume less time. And the accompanying celebrations, which the current generation understands and accepts as the 'main' ritual and is happy to invest time in, have correspondingly expanded to occupy centre stage. For instance, marriage celebrations these days extend over three to four days, or more, attracting large numbers for 'main course' events like *mehandī*, and cocktails which begin in the evening and extend into the wee hours of the morning. The core religious rituals are reduced to perfunctory necessities, shrunk to an hour or two, in a *mandapa* measuring 100-200 square feet tucked in a corner of the sprawling 100,000 square feet lawn usually reserved for the reception, dancing, dinner and photo ops. The wedding ceremony proper, during which the priest is urged to conclude the ritual proceedings quickly, is not attended by more than a handful of close relatives and friends.

Be that as it may, question is - Is the inverse relationship between the rise of industrialization and number of people participating in rituals as straightforward as it appears? Is the society really becoming less ritualistic because of this industrialization? Some scholars believe that is not the case. They claim industrialisation does not cause people to get less ritualised, it causes people to get 'ritualised differently' (L McWhorter using Focoult's perspective). A study of this very interesting distinction based on keen observations and forceful arguments from both sides is dealt with elsewhere in this book.

Returning to the views and conclusions of Staal, Macaulay, et al - let's examine whether these are irrefutable. Can ritual practices be examined differently by applying other philosophical tools that are available to us, thereby leading to alternative interpretations?

We can employ two broad approaches for this purpose -

i. Interpret rituals using modern philosophical tools like pragmatics, existentialism, et cetera, and see whether they (rituals) have meaning
ii. Use 'organic reasoning and logic' i.e. rely on the 'definitions' and 'rules' of Vedic literature and the *dharma-śāstras* - the alternative interpretation - and try to study the thought and rationale of rituals, if any

In the following pages, we shall first examine rituals by applying more suitable modern philosophical tools that are available to us. Then we will see how rituals can be understood and interpreted by applying reasoning drawn from the Vedas and the *dharma śāstras* themselves i.e. the organic logic of approach (ii). The chapter will be concluded with the listing of different purposes that rituals serve. To put it another way, we will examine what the society and the individuals gain by practising rituals.

∞

Kevin Schilbrack is a Professor and Department Chair of Philosophy & Religion at Appalachian State University in Boone, North Carolina who writes on philosophical and methodological questions involved in the cross-cultural study of religions. According to his biography, he is presently interested in the relevance of embodied cognition and social ontology for understanding what religion is and how it works. He is of special interest to us for his own contributions[8] and as Contributing Editor of 'Thinking through Rituals: Philosophical perspectives'.

∞

Pragmatist philosophers believe that apart from reason (for rationalists) and senses (for empiricists) as the two sources of knowledge, action is the third source of reliable knowledge.

All rituals are actions, gestures and utterances in play. For pragmatists, actions and thoughts are closely linked. In fact, actions are embodied thoughts.

It is worthwhile at this stage to examine the meanings of thought and belief - two terms that are used frequently in the following passages. The Oxford dictionary defines 'thought' as 'an idea or opinion produced by thinking or occurring suddenly in the mind', and 'belief' as a 'religious conviction' or 'an acceptance that something exists or is true, especially without proof'.

So if we believe that the car keys are lying on the dining table, we will move in a premeditated manner in the direction of the dining room (rejecting other locations like bedrooms or the kitchen) to look for the keys. In this sense, the belief became a guiding rule, making us proceed in a particular direction to a specific location. Thus, the belief became a rule for the action. This is why Charles Pierce's pragmatism concludes that belief is a program, a rule for action.

Over time, deeply held beliefs affect the conduct of a person. Repeated actions or conduct result from this deep-set belief system which triggers actions, making these repeated actions habitual over time.

One must pause to look at the consequences of deeply entrenched beliefs and habitual actions. In Pierce's pragmatism, beliefs are habits, and habits become entrenched over time. What that means is, over time actions become habit-driven and are carried out without the application of thought, leading to the conclusion that rituals are thoughtless actions!

Raposa thinks that "a number of historically prominent theories would fit this type, perhaps the most extreme examples being those psychoanalytic accounts that portray religious ritual as a form of neurotically compulsive behavior."[9a]

Admitting that "This is not to deny that there might be a kind of activity for which such theories supply an adequate description,' he adds, 'But not all or even most of religious ritual can be reduced to activity of that kind. A richer, more complex account is required. Ritual is less appropriately conceived as thoughtless action than as a thinking through and with the body."[9b]

The gestures, movements, utterances and other actions that comprise religious rituals represent a form of deliberate behavior - habit formation being one of its purposes. To regard a ritual as such is to conceive it as a form of spiritual exercise. Moreover, these exercises are governed by a logic that Peirce's pragmatism can help understand.

Therefore, just as deeply-held beliefs are embodied in the habits of their conduct, the repeated acts (rituals) mould their beliefs. From this perspective, Raposa considers rituals to be "thinking through and with the body."

Can the rituals then be just random, meaningless and casual actions as Staal says, similar to the casual movement of our hands when we are standing or sitting, doing nothing in particular? Religious rituals are not random actions, gestures and utterances, they are very precise in nature - every action and utterance must be in perfect conformity with the prescribed methods and rules, following a specified sequence. A religious ritual is a complex performance which doesn't permit personal choices in its praxis; it demands exactitude and inculcates in ritualists a respect for discipline. Every action performed, as well as how and when every word is uttered in a ritual, is prescribed in great detail. Since pragmatists view conduct as embodied thought, shaping the conduct (by demanding complete adherence to what is prescribed) results in affecting and shaping the belief. And since entrenched beliefs are habits, over time the person starts behaving in conformity with his belief. Constantly repeated rituals thus get firmly entrenched as beliefs and shape our conduct. For Pierce, beliefs result in shaping conduct/behaviour, which when entrenched over time, become a habit and help transform the believer.

For example, if a person is not inherently racist, but chooses to deliberately behave in a racist fashion, then he is at a risk of transforming into a racist. This way, by shaping our beliefs, rituals shape our conduct.

For Raposa, religious rituals, in a way, try to capture attention by consciously removing other unwanted thoughts. They are an effort towards bringing consciousness 'under discipline' i.e. exercising self-control.

This act of self-control necessarily involves deliberately choosing objects of attention, and the degree and intensity of attention applied in the present moment, which results, gradually, in transforming belief and inclination by the process of habit formation.

Attention is a process in which the unwanted thoughts and ideas, excluding the subject under consideration, are squeezed out. Essentially, it means - from the multiple thoughts and ideas crowding the mind, only that which is 'under consideration' is allowed to take centre stage. All other thoughts and ideas are consciously subdued or driven out. In a manner of speaking, this is a selection process - choosing and focusing only on a given subject out of the many choices. [The induction process of logic/reasoning entails looking for and identifying similarities (of properties). For instance, there are a hundred swans in a lake, all the swans in the lake are white, so all swans are white.]

The precise nature of religious rituals calls for carefully looking at various possible actions, gestures, objects, utterances, and making the right choices after paying close attention. Thus rituals train ritualists in achieving a higher degree of attention in their application.

Religious rituals, being repetitive in nature, unfold in a way that leads to a build-up of expectation among the participants. Over time, these believers develop a habit of expectation.

As observed earlier, the habit of expectation is also a type of belief (like the car keys on the dining table from the earlier example). Apart from being a program for action, it also develops in us certain habits or powers of perception.

How?

Scientific research is carried out in the laboratory for validation of hypotheses as true or false. By observing the results, a belief system (of secured beliefs) gets established, which operates as a habit of thought. This acts as a template that guides the individual through future enquiries and investigations. In other words, the experiences of observation and analysis bring us to certain conclusions after rejecting many other possibilities/options. We then follow the maxim of 'not reinventing the wheel', and in the next instance, this new belief becomes our starting point. Hence, a belief system develops and operates as a habit of thought, 'a given', a starting point for further investigation. Such a habit, rooted in a belief that is a consequence of verification and validation, represents cognitive skill - a skill that facilitates scientific insight and discovery.

For pragmatists, the primary model for understanding human inquiry is evolution rather than revolution. A belief system which operates as a habit of thought triggers a discipline of self-transformation, and in this way, a ritual is a discipline of self transformation.

∞

Let us try and understand why scholars, and a large section of educated and not so educated 'religious' people (with little knowledge of Sanskrit or scriptures dealing with ancient ritual texts) who do not understand the mantras chanted during rituals, consider Vedic rituals to be nothing more than random or meaningless and irrational acts. Besides a lack of understanding and sound knowledge of rituals, another important reason is the widely prevalent belief that the body is not capable of thinking. So body's movements, outside of activities like yoga, athletics, dancing and so on, do not deserve any attention except in a physiological sense. This is Cartesian philosophy.

In Cartesian thought, the body is just an object, like any other object - chair, table, building et cetera - in this world, and it is only the mind that really matters. Because it can think. This philosophy is based on the conclusion that the great French philosopher-mathematician Rene Descartes reached in his Discourse on Method (1637), denying the existence of everything except his self (mind) -

Cogito, ergo sum, i.e. "I think, therefore I am."

The body is mere matter, an object in this scheme, physical acts are purely mechanical actions performed by various parts or limbs of the body, and our mind feels the presence of our own body like it does of any other object around us.

Maurice Jean Jacques Merleau-Ponty (1908–61), French philosopher and public intellectual, was the leading academic proponent of existentialism and phenomenology in post-war France. He is best known for his pioneering work on embodiment, perception and ontology. Ponty disagrees with the Cartesian notion.

He argues that we do not experience our own body as an object (as we do other objects in the world). Rather, we experience the world lying beyond or outside our own corporeal body '*by our body*' (emphasis mine). Thus, our body is not another external object in our experience. Our sensuous experiences are directed outwards (of our body) - "The (our) body is the very texture of this experience."

In his phenomenology, it is not the mind alone that experiences the world with the body acting as an inert medium to transmit the experience to the mind. The body also experiences the world. For Ponty: "*I'm not front of my body, I am in it, or rather, I am it...*" (Merleau-Ponty 1962:150; emphasis mine)

Going a step further, the body experiences the world and also itself - it is always embodied experience.

∞

Body techniques' is a term that is applied to the things we do with our body.

All rituals, including religious rituals, involve physical movements of the body. Therefore, any study of rituals must necessarily include a thorough examination of bodily movements or techniques of the corporeal body.

The term 'body technique' was first used by Marcel Mauss (1872-1950) who argued that from society to society, men make culturally-specific use of their bodies. A French sociologist and anthropologist who conducted a renowned comparative study of the relation between forms of exchange and social structure, Mauss was a soldier during WWI and, subsequently, a patient in a hospital where he observed soldiers and nurses in what he called 'miscellaneous actions' - walking, sitting, standing, sleeping, et cetera. He noticed differences in these simple activities among people belonging to different genders, ages, countries and so on. He noted the different ways in which men and women clinched their fists (thumb 'out' in the case of men, and the opposite for women); the difference in the strides of soldiers belonging to different nationalities; the ability of Asian men to sit in a squatting position and the inability of Europeans to do so - all these were confirmations to Mauss that such skills are acquired socially. He used the Latin term '*habitus*' to describe these variations between different societies, educations and fashions, differentiating it from habits which vary from individual to individual (as against society to society).

Studying actions like walking, running and sitting activities/techniques from the stand point of a purely single discipline - mechanical, physiological, psychological or sociological - is not adequate. According to Mauss, it cannot be done unless one introduced a triple consideration instead of a single consideration, be it physical (like an anatomical and physiological theory of walking) or psychological or sociological.

This triple viewpoint consists of biological, psychological and sociological influences, and is the 'total man' of Mauss.

To understand it more clearly, let's look at an example given by the man himself.

All human children are born with the ability to walk on two feet, and this 'bipedal' capability is innate. Thus, to be able to walk, they must have biological and psychological capabilities in the right measure. Most babies (with the exception of the few unfortunate ones) are able to walk on their feet because of this innate capability, but it is also true that this is possible because of the availability of physically suitable limbs. It is the presence of both legs which makes walking possible. Mauss goes on to propose a few questions - Since all children in the world are born with this innate program and also have two legs, why, then, do they not walk alike? Why do their walking styles differ from society to society, and yet bear similarity to those belonging to their own community/group?

In body techniques, walking style is an outcome of not just our physical and psychological abilities, but also a third social factor - the mind. We acquire the skills of walking, talking, et cetera by being immersed in the social environment around us. Thus, walking is not simply a biological and psychological combination, it is a product of a bio-socio-psychological mix - the triple consideration.

When a child imitates an elder, respected and known for exemplary action, say talking or swimming, the imitation which follows has physical/biological as well as psychological elements. However, these are conditioned by a third element, the social element of prestige, or respect towards the person being emulated.

Tim Ingold, an anthropologist (previously a Professor at Manchester City and subsequently, Chair of Anthropology at University of Aberdeen), questioned the body techniques of Mauss, where "the whole ensemble is conditioned by the three elements indissolubly mixed together."[10]

Interestingly, Ingold does not question the inclusion of 'mind' as one of the three elements in Mauss's idea of body techniques, he accepts the vital role that the mind plays (in what Mauss calls 'acquired skills'). He disagrees with Mauss on the 'reason of variations' from society to society, in the way we walk or talk et cetera. According to Ingold, the variations are not a result of culturally acquired skills, which are different from society to society owing to differences in culture, but a consequence of the natural process of development as properties of human organisms, and are, thus, fully biological.

Hence, differences in the style of walking/talking are neither due to genetic coding nor culture - they are purely biological. To support this, Ingold gives the example of the skeleton, which grows in the body that is actively doing things, and its precise form is liable to bear the mark of these activities. ['Developmentally enhanced achievements of the organism-person, at once body and mind positioned within an environment'.[11]]

Ingold recommends a new approach to evolution to fully understand this concept.

Lets go back to Mauss's 'body techniques'. Body techniques are social and habitual in nature and belong to the realm of Practical Reason. In philosophy, practical reason (as against theoretical) is the use of reason to decide how to act. With this argument of linking body techniques with reason, Mauss distanced himself from Cartesianism.

Humans function in this world through their knowledge, understanding and intention (in phenomenology), and knowledge is constituted of practical know-how.

The Oxford dictionary defines the word 'knowing' as 'to be aware of through observation, enquiry or information' - an act of doing something, e.g. observing, just like 'understanding'. And 'doing something' always involves using the body - all knowledge and understanding are essentially bodily acts. Now that we have linked thinking and understanding to bodily acts, let us examine a few everyday bodily acts and analyse how much thinking is involved in carrying them out.

With repeated use, we can type on a word processor without having to look at the board, and with time, we become adept at it. This is muscle memory - the body acquiring the understanding and expertise of moving fingers precisely on the word processor keyboard. But, this bodily act is not conscious. If one was to do it consciously, the chances are that one would do so haltingly, and make more mistakes than usual. This act cannot be called an act of habit in the sense of a stimulus (a response situation), it is a case of pre-reflective response, where the body responds as a result of an acquired skill, a practical know-how.

This practical know-how, acquired skill or cultural competence of the human body is the embodied knowledge of rituals. While activities like cycling or swimming have an explicit purpose of use, a similar purpose or function for rituals has to be identified. The following pages will attempt to throw light on this topic.

∞

So we have seen that rituals, including religious ones, are not bereft of meaning. They are an outcome of complex interactions between ideas, thoughts, and disciplined body techniques deeply influenced by the cultural sphere. Now, let us try to analyse their practicality for individuals and societies.

Before that however, we must recall Crossley's observation on fuzziness of rituals and body techniques -

"The meaning, function, and characteristics of rituals will be different in different cases. Indeed, even the same ritual may change in these respects over time, as rituals necessarily belong to the flow of historical time."[12]

And also remember -

(Moreover), as the word 'habit' suggests, we generally use body techniques without recourse to thought or reflection and, at least in some cases, the know-how they embody remains unintelligible and inaccessible to our reflective, discursive consciousness.[13]

In the first instance, it is fairly evident that the performance of ritual requires a basic, embodied know-how.

Know-how - Semiotics is the study of signs and symbols, of their use or interpretation. All rituals are semiotic acts and, to that extent, the agents must learn the gestures, postures and movements of body parts in a given order e.g. in Yajur recitations, movements of hands are considered so important, students are separately trained to coordinate these movements with the recitation. At times, these acts may require a high level of precision, and at other times, less so. However, there will always be a common denominator - a ritual will always include some sort of doing, involving not only the agent's understanding of how to perform these activities, but also how to read others' activities and respond appropriately(an example is oblations are poured in fire just as the priest utters *svāha*). Therefore, it will always entail an awareness of the appropriate social situation, and to respond thusly the agent must recognise and understand the act of 'doing', as well as the action of other agents. A part or all of this may be pre-reflective, but never without historical knowledge of how social groups conduct themselves.

Deference - Similarly, the rituals of deference are also acceptance of authority, submission and a continued demonstration of a familial or tribal hierarchy, or simply conveying acceptance of the other person's position in the social pecking order. Even in the more westernised urban societies of India, the participants in a religious ritual - particularly the *yajamāna* couple - reverently touch the feet of the *paṇḍita* at the end of a *Satyanārāyaṇa Pūjā*, regardless of the *paṇḍita's* age! This is a typical example of acknowledgement of the status of the *paṇḍita* in a *pūjā*. In a rural setting, the same event may involve a greater show of submission to the *paṇḍita* - all participants will touch the *paṇḍita's* feet and invariably show greater deference. This example illustrates the recognition by the *yajamāna* and other participants of the *paṇḍita*, and the historical background of the *pūjā*, when *paṇḍitas* (always *brahmaṇa*) were treated with reverence for hundreds of years, not just because they conducted the *pūjā*, but because as *brahmaṇas*, they had been at the top of Hindu society's social ladder since antiquity. Even in a bureaucratic setup, such as workplaces (particularly government offices in northern India), visible deference through bodily acts stand out starkly.

Hand-shake - The western ritual of shaking hands, which has many meanings apart from welcoming or greeting, is now widely accepted as a symbol of agreement between two parties. When two individuals shake hands over a deal, it signifies an agreement. Here, a body technique conveys the understanding of a social situation and the conclusion of a social transaction, such as a negotiation culminating in an agreement. Here, a ritual, the body technique of shaking hands, encapsulates the understanding and acceptance of the meaning and the obligations of that negotiation. The logic may again appear a bit ambiguous to be spelt out clearly.

As we saw in above examples, rituals as practical knowledge of social relationships are important.

In this way, rituals are undoubtedly vital in perpetuating awareness, thereby keeping the social order alive.

Ritual as a technique of transformation - In the Hindu way of life, there are sixteen *saṃskāras* which are important milestones indicating crossovers from one stage of life to another. The *upanayana* or sacred thread ceremony - when a young boy enters studentship - is perhaps one of the most important such crossover. Accepting a sacred thread, he is recognised by society as *dvija* or twice-born. Rituals can thus transform the relationship of an individual with the society around, and the ritual technique is key in achieving this transformation.

Ritual as a 'call to order' - During wars, India has stood united, putting aside differences, quarrels and disputes over languages, rivers, reservations, and employment. How does this happen? How are all the raging controversies and disputes suddenly forgotten?

This happens because we, as a society, feel collectively under threat. But this is also a result of the 'call of duty', a duty to contribute towards defending the country. Rituals, in a similar vein, are also 'call to order'.

The initiation of a ritual is a call to all adherents to participate jointly - the 'call to order'. These believers are members who have consciously accepted to be a part of society, and have developed deep rooted cultural commitments over time. They act as a closely-knit group and respond in an expected way, due to social compulsions. The response to the national anthem is an apt example of social compulsion - anyone who does not immediately respond to this 'call to order' by standing up, not only suffers acute embarrassment and guilt (even if it is due to a physical disability), but may also have to face unpleasant, even aggressive, response from those that do stand up.

For the time being, let's stay with the responses of 'call to order' and compulsions in the context of the national anthem. The listener's strong urge to stand up is not driven by an external force or authority, nor is it a 'conscious consent'. It is something in between absolute mechanism and absolute voluntarism. These ritual activities are not standard examples of 'reflexes' that our behaviourists tell us, nor are they appropriate examples of reflective thought. They are pre-reflective in nature.

These ritual activities are meaningful, purposive and mindful (in contrast to mechanical response or reflex) calls-to-order.

Bourdieu has identified them with socially structured dispositions which operate below the level of conscious volition.

Collective effervescence - All of us have experienced the change that the festive season and its accompanying ceremonial rituals bring not only in our emotions, but practical life as well. Individuals, along with the society, start behaving differently in an obvious manner. The preparation for ceremonial rituals becomes a priority, not only over routine work, but also important professional and personal commitments. These happy occasions or celebratory rituals bring out a collective change or transformation in individuals as well as in society. This palpable change takes place across the social order, even when there is a geographical disconnect between the parent society and the individuals - Diwali celebrations among the Indian diaspora in far-flung lands is one of many such examples.

The rituals, thus, have a purpose of binding the individuals in a group, and the society, together

Order, discipline, and submission - Rituals bring order, discipline and submission to authority. The example of the national anthem clarified that the individual and societal response is neither guided by an external force, nor is it well considered. It is called pre-reflective response - a 'call to order'. Likewise, the rituals of deference, quotidian as well as ceremonial in nature, remind the agent of his status with respect to the subject being revered. Rituals are a constant reminder to juniors of their position vis-a-vis the boss, or nephews and nieces vis-a-vis elders in the family, and citizens in relation to state authority. Interestingly, those in positions of authority also use ceremonial rituals to constantly reaffirm their superiority over their subjects. The national anthem is one more such example where the state reaffirms its authority over the citizens.

These are only few of the many effects of rituals on individuals and societies. They serve many more purposes but these examples should suffice to show their purpose and usefulness.

∞

It is true that rituals are difficult to define precisely. It is also true that what applies to a given set of rituals may not apply to another set of rituals, making it equally difficult to generalise our observations. But once we recognise and accept this ambiguity associated with rituals, enormously interesting avenues emerge, expanding our understanding of rituals and the role they play in our lives, both at the individual as well as societal level.

Then why is it that most of us, including those who willingly participate regularly, have stated and unstated reservations about rituals? Why is it that many people - the pious who have unquestionable faith in the existence of god, visit temples and participate in *pūjā* with great reverence - are unable to invoke the same passion for rituals? Why do they not comply rigorously, meticulously, passionately with the prescribed procedures for performing rituals? Most people exude a '*chaltā hai*' (loosely translated as *anything goes*) or a dismissive attitude when asked to face east direction while getting a *rākhi* tied to the wrist or getting their head shaved after the passing of an uncle or a grandfather. Another example is the attitude of Hindus towards solar and lunar eclipses. Apart from key transitional *saṃskāras* - like *upanayana*, marriage, et cetera - rituals associated with these celestial occurrences were considered serious matters and occupied an important position in the hierarchy of rituals. In the ancient Hindu belief system, as per the mythology, it is a time when the demons Rahu and Ketu try to swallow the sun or the moon, both of which are considered *devas*. A long list of do's and dont's are prescribed in the scriptures, which includes the rituals of fasting, bathing in holy rivers, giving *dāna* and, more importantly, abstaining from daily commercial activities. All this is done to save the two *devas* from the demons duo. Most of us simply continue with our everyday lives during solar or lunar eclipses and do not bother to pray or perform the rituals that are said to save the sun and moon gods. Why?

The answer is simple - the scientific progress we have made has changed our view of cosmology, it has changed our view of several natural and biological processes in our surrounding world, which we did not understand in the past and were in awe of. The moon is no more a *deva* in danger of being swallowed by demons, or even a novelty - not only has man walked on the moon, we have brought back rocks from the surface of the moon for everyone on earth to see. We know exactly how these eclipses occur and, apart from predicting the exact time of their occurrence through accurate mathematical calculations, we also have television networks telecasting how these celestial events occur into every home in real-time.

It is easy, therefore, for us to understand why even temple-going, fast-observing individuals do not consider these celestial events as impending disasters requiring - to save the day - personal and collective intervention through rituals. One would think that the scientific knowledge gained by humanity has eliminated this area of darkness and the space for rituals has shrunk.

But this reasoning is only partly true.

Childbirth (except in cases of complicated delivery) is an event that families await with great expectation and anxiety. The excitement of the arrival of a new-born is always preceded by anxiety over the health of the foetus, safe delivery of a healthy, fully-formed child, and the good health of the mother. Ultrasound was first used for clinical purposes in 1956 in Glasgow and, by the 1970s, it was used regularly in American hospitals. In the past fifty years, progressive developments in ultrasound and other scientific techniques have made it possible for us to not only see the foetus in the womb, but also identify its sex, listen to its heart beat, and even capture its smile! Those who started their families prior to the seventies obviously did not enjoy the benefit of ultrasound technology. They experienced fear and anxiety - not the joy of watching the foetus grow and smile - wondering if the baby in the womb had 'all limbs intact', whether it was a boy or a girl, whether the foetus was growing properly et cetera. But they did have qualified medical practitioners and other (less sophesticated) medical equipment to give them reasonably well-informed alerts and inputs about the health of the foetus and the mother.

In ancient times, when scientific medical care was lacking, delivery of an ill-formed child or loss of life during pregnancy came as a complete shock. It was attributed to the conjunction of celestial bodies, a malevolent spirit or an evil eye. The only insurance against such tragedies were the gods and the rituals that placated them.

People fervently prayed to the gods and performed the prescribed religious rituals to ward off the evil eyes, evil spirits and the ill effects of an eclipse, or an unfavourable congregation of the *nakṣatras*, or other such celestial events occurring millions of miles away. Even today, many families routinely perform rituals for the safe delivery of a healthy child. However, the expecting couples increasingly rely more on modern medical facilities. They participate in these rituals more to indulge the wishes of family elders than out of fear, anxiety, or the belief that the ritual will provide protection to the yet-to-be-born child.

Let us take an example of a young mother to be, Lakṣmī - a modern, educated, urban woman expecting a child. She encounters two eclipses - one before, and another a few weeks after, she has conceived i.e. during her pregnancy. In the first instance of an eclipse, she will hardly put her heart into the rituals meant to save *Candra Deva* from being ingested by the demons because she believes she knows the science behind the eclipse, and is therefore aware that such rituals can be safely ignored. But in the second case - when she is pregnant - she will be more compliant with rituals during the second eclipse, not wanting to risk the well-being of the child in her womb! Therefore, the same person may use 'reason' and 'logic' differently in different situations. How do we explain these dichotomous responses?

Is it simply fear psychosis - non-observance of rituals may result in paying a heavy price (vis-a-vis the health of the unborn child)? Or is it a question of selective rationality?

There are no clear-cut answers to such complex human behaviour.

If we step away from the conflicting responses of an individual (such as Lakṣmī's) to collective responses in different parts of the society within our country, we find that as we move farther from urban centres, there is greater adherence to rituals. More people abstain from work during solar or lunar eclipses in the rural and tribal areas, than in cities and bigger towns.

These contrasting attitudes may be more directly attributed to rational thought, which is a dominant reason the younger generation questions the very basis of rituals. Because modernisation and scientific developments are superseding ancient cosmology and old world knowledge of natural and biological phenomena, two things are happening -

1. Modern minds naturally reject the tenets of religious cosmology, such as *Pṛthvī* (earth) resting on the head of the great snake *Sheshnāga*, or solar and lunar eclipses being the result of the demons Rāhu and Ketu attempting to swallow the moon and the sun etc. By applying inductive logic, they tend to reject all other rituals as equally nonsensical.
2. They judge rituals using tools they are familiar with, and have been trained to judge events of the natural world with. In so doing, they often reach conclusions which make no sense and are truly baffling (since they were originally inappropriately deduced).

∞

Objectively, the degree of success or failure of an effort can only be measured in terms of how much the performer achieved vis-a-vis the stated goal that he set for himself, or was set by others to judge his performance. If one attends an Indian classical music performance as a 'linguistics expert' and not as a critic of classical music, s/he would rate the performance 0/10 because in the entire duration of sixty minutes or so of the *rāga* rendition, the vocalist may have enunciated barely a dozen intelligible words. The singer would have certainly repeated few words incessantly, and replaced several words with meaningless sounds. In short, the score of 0/10 is a consequence of judging the performance using an entirely inappropriate yardstick. On the other hand, if another person attends the same classical music performance as a music critic, s/he might grant a score of 9/10 for superlative *tāna*, *alāpa*, *gamaka* and purity of *sur* - all important components of a successful vocal performance. In the latter case, application of tools (entirely different from linguistic tools of word, syntax, semantics and grammar, repetitiousness, et cetera) that are appropriate in comprehending the quality of the 'musical' performance and the overall purpose of the performance, resulted in a high score of 9/10.

The Organic Approach

At the beginning of this chapter, the author had proposed to examine the purpose, if any, of rituals, using two methods -

i. By using modern interpretive tools of pragmatics, existentialism, phenomenology, genealogy, et cetera
ii. Taking the organic route, using interpretive tools and methods available within the local texts and scriptures of Hinduism i.e. Vedas and *dharmaśāstra* texts

Since the first method (point i) has been sufficiently examined, let us now examine the organic method (point ii).

Indians are an argumentative people.

This trait, which became a popular notion following Noble laureate Amratya Sen's book *The Argumentative Indian*, has been a part of our culture since time immemorial. Even those Indians who do not agree that we have earned this dubious distinction, will concede that arguing is in our blood, it is genetic. It is no surprise, therefore, that our ancient texts, couched delicately in deferential language, are full of arguments in a question-answer form (dialogical form). From the Vedas to the Purāṇas and the *Itihāsa*, everything is in the form of questions and answers. In this author's view, the dialogical method of narration was the most preferred in ancient times. Not because the scriptures' authors were unimaginative or could not conceive of any other form, but because of what they saw around them in society. A classic example of literature being a mirror of society!

What it also reflects is that nothing was accepted without close examination and inquiry. In the Gītā, the great warrior Arjuna keeps questioning the teachings of Kṛṣṇa till he is fully satisfied with the replies. This is an example of remarkable spirit on the part of the disciple friend Arjuna, who, on a battlefield, tests the patience of Kṛṣṇa, a self-admitted incarnation of god! Gītā therein contains a larger message - the primacy of reason. Nothing is to be accepted blindly from anyone under any circumstances, even god himself, until one is fully satisfied. In the case of Arjuna and Mahābhārata - not even when the first arrow is waiting to be unleashed on the battlefield.

The lesson imparted in the Bhagavad Gītā is : put to rest all doubts through reason before action. Only then can one succeed in one's endeavour against all odds.

This is the cornerstone of Hindu Dharma. The quest for knowledge of *dharma* and *adharma* involves ascertaining what is right and what is wrong, which can only be done by applying reason. Only by asking questions does one come upon the right answers. No wonder then that the *dharma śāstra* is based on rules in a dialogical form, reflecting the many questions and doubts that kept emerging in the minds of readers, and providing answers aided by illustrative examples in the form of stories, real or imaginary, illuminating the Righteous course forward. In a way, many of these narratives can be called modern day FAQs (Frequently Asked Questions). This is how Dharma evolved - first in the oral tradition and subsequently in the written texts.

The origin of Hindu Dharma are the Vedas.

It is interesting that the Vedas hardly mention practices, or dos and don'ts. Most of Hinduism's codes-of-conduct came from the works of great sages like Manu, Yājñavalkya, Kapila, Vasiṣṭha, et cetera over many centuries, originating in different locations across Bhāratvarṣa (as it was then called). These literary works were influenced, naturally, by local customs and practices followed by diverse sets of people. Hence, it is not surprising to find conflicting practices recommended by different sages in different scriptures. To resolve such conflicts, a simple rule was laid down which is followed uniformly by all practitioners of Hinduism. A strict order of precedence is to be followed by all - teachings of Vedas are considered supreme, followed by the Upaniṣads, the *sūtras*, the Purāṇas and, finally, the *Itihāsa* citations. In addition to these scriptures, customs and practices followed by the wise men of society were to be treated as the Righteous path to follow.

Mīmāṃsākas (600-400 BC) were a class of people who believed every word of Veda to be true and meaningful - Vedas were to be followed literally. This created a serious problem - How to interpret some of the inane passages? Or explain what appeared inconvenient and at odds with the general flow of things? Besides being intellectuals of high calibre, the *Mīmāṃsākas* were extremely hard working, diligent and men of detail. By their time, rituals had become very elaborate and complex affairs, forming an integral part of Hindu thoughts and practices. *Mīmāṃsākas* established the rules of the game by defining all-important terms. They developed several allied branches of philosophy for interpreting the scriptures. These definitions and principles have been used extensively in interpreting, explaining, even justifying the 'why' and 'how' of several aspects of Hinduism.

Let us have a quick look at the ground rules, and their reasoning, which are to be used to interpret these scriptures -

The root of the religion is the Ṛgveda, and (then) the tradition and customs of those who know (the Veda), and the conduct of virtuous people, and what is satisfactory to oneself.[14]

This set the ball rolling, clearly defining the place of Veda as the very root of religion. And then -

The Veda should be known as the revealed Canon, and the teachings of religion and the tradition. These two are indisputable in all matters, for religion arose out of the two of them.[15]

That these laws are sacrosanct was made indubitably clear by Manu -

Any twice born man (*dvija*) who disregards these two roots (of religion) because he relies on the teachings of logic should be excommunicated by virtuous people as an atheist and the reviler of the Veda.[16]

This last quote is critical - the position of the (first) two rules has been put beyond any question or reasoning; any twice born who disregards this runs the risk of excommunication. In today's Khāpa panchayat's language, he becomes an outcast - an existence considered worse than death.

The *Mīmāṃsākas* went on to develop sophisticated theories of reason, identifying and defining situations that could arise and create uncertainty, and ways to deal with such situations.

It is these set of rules that have to be applied to rituals.

Jonardon Ganeri is a Professor of Philosophy at New York University and a Fellow of the British Academy who has taken great interest in the organic approach of interpreting rituals. According to him[17], rituals are incorrectly seen as a mechanical repetition of invariant tradition. In performing rituals, decisions have to be made regarding not only what to do and what not to do, but also deciding the sequence and when to do that which is required to be done. Such decisions involve hermeneutics (the branch of knowledge that deals with interpretation, especially religious texts). Thus, there is reason within rituals.

According to Ganeri, the problem arises due to the training received by scientists. Their training familiarises them with only one kind of ritual - science. As a consequence of this, they try using the same reason they use in science with all other rituals. Therefore, it is a question of using an appropriate tool.

But what was the purpose of all this i.e. performing rituals?

The purpose was to know what is to be done; the Right thing to do, the Right way to do that, and how to choose the Right course of action in conflicting situations by applying reason.

In this manner, ritual laws become a training ground for reason. With the help of the teachings and techniques of *Mīmāṃsā*, one can apply these reasons in other contexts, both ritual and non-ritual, with the ultimate aim of becoming an ethical, Righteous being.

Chapter 41

Do Mantras Have Meaning/Power?

From the time of the Ṛgveda, mantras formed the core, the very nucleus around which Vedic society revolved. Borrowing from the Vedic simile - *Nāda* is *Brahman* - one could say that mantras are the Vedas. Vedic texts developed sequentially: mantras came first, then came the Brahmaṇas, followed by the Upaniṣads, the *śrauta*, and the *gṛhya sūtras*. The *vidhāna* texts came last.

Before we delve into the subject matter of this chapter - the claim that mantras are meaningless - we must first understand what mantras are.

∞

The first use of the word mantra was in the context of *ṛcā* of the Ṛgveda. Sage Śaunaka provides *lakṣaṇa* (distinguishing features) of Veda verses *ṛcā* in Ṛgveda (RgVeda - Prātiśākhya V 1); Viṣṇumitra, who wrote a *vṛtti* (commentary) on Śaunaka's Prātiśākhya, explains that *ṛcā* are Veda's utterances or mantras having definite numbers of syllables (*akṣara*), quarter (*pada*) or half (*ardharca*) verses[1]. But this exegesis doesn't really venture beyond informing us that Veda's utterances or *ṛcā's* are mantras.

One is left wondering whether all *ṛcā's* are mantras? And what of *sāman* and *yajus* in the Sāma and the Yajurveda - are they mantras too?

These answers are found in *Mīmāṃsā* and *śrauta sūtra* texts. *Mīmāṃsā* - roughly translated - means reflection or investigation. For this purpose *mīmāṃsākas* (*Mīmāṃsā* commentators/scholars) divided the Vedas into five parts - *Vidhi* (injunction or hortation); *Artha-Vada* (commendation); *Nāmadheya* (proper names of sacrifices); and *Pratiśedha* (prohibitions). Jaimini, though not the founder of the doctrine of *Mīmāṃsā* philosophy, occupies highest place as *mīmāṃsāka* (commentator). According to him, mantra is that which simply asserts (and is not hortatory) -

'Those are mantras that are so called on account of their asserting something' - (PMS II.1.31-32).

This, unfortunately, fails to explain adequately what are mantras.

Śabara, who is known for his commentary (*bhāṣya*) on Jaimini's PMS (Pūrva Mīmāṃsā Sūtra), commenting on PMS I.4.1, clarifies Jaimini but not sufficiently. He describes mantra as one that, at the time the procedure of sacrifice is being followed, makes clear to the performer the matter that is prescribed. Again not wholly satisfactory descriptiption, because there are mantras not directly related to procedures of sacrifice. Admittedly, these injunctive mantras e.g. 'the stronger man should give to one in need' (RV. X.11 7.5, J & B) - are rare and barring a few exceptions, they are expressive or assertive, calling to mind things connected with the acts enjoined by the *vidhi vākyas* (injunctive passages).

Mantras are classified under three heads - *Ṛk, Sāman* and *Yajus*. *Ṛk* is applied to mantras that are divided into metrical *padás*, (often) based on the meaning; *Sāman* denotes those mantras that are sung (the mantra texts are not called *Sāman*, but only the music). And *Yajus* are Vedic mantras that are neither *Ṛk* nor *Sāman*.

Kumarila Bhatta (~700 AD), another distinguished *mīmāṃsāka*, in Tantravartika (Exposition on the Sacred Sciences, his commentary on the Śabara-bhasya) observes that the Ṛgveda alone contains over 10,000 mantras. Of these, only one third are employed in all the Vedic rites; the rest are employed in *japa* (repetition of mantra). Besides, other Vedas also contain thousands of mantras. Therefore, no formal definition of mantra is attempted, and all that is stated is - mantras are those that have been recognised as such by the learned.[2]

Āpastamba (~600 BC), a formidable figure whose works on *śrauta*, *gṛha* and *dharma sūtras* are considered invaluable, was also an accomplished mathematician. But here we are concerned with his Yajña Paribhasa Sūtras, which, as the title suggests, explains the definitions (*Paribhaṣa*) of Vedic terms. Unfortunately, Āpstamba too disappoints - though he elucidates what the Brahmaṇas are (precepts for the sacrifice), he defines/explains mantras using the principle of exclusion - 'all the rest are mantras'! The great scholar of mathematics and religion says[2a]-

The rules for the sacrifice are the mantras and Brahmaṇas (Sūtras XXX).

The name Veda belongs both to the Mantras and to Brahmaṇas (Sūtras XXX I).

The Brahmaṇas are the precepts for the sacrifice (Sūtras XXX I I).

The rest of the Brahmaṇa - that which does not contain precepts - consists of explanations, i.e. reproof, praise, stories, and traditions (Sūtras XXX I I).

The next two *sūtras* are critically important -

All the rest are Mantras (Sūtras XXXIV).

But the passages which are not handed down, are not to be classed as Mantras, as for instance the pravara, the words used in choosing priests, divine or human; uha, substitution of one word for another; and namadheya-grahana, the mentioning of the names of particular sacrificers (Sūtras XXXV).

It appears Kane is right when he claims,"It is difficult to define what a Vedic mantra is and it is generally understood, as said by Sabra, that passages or verses are Mantras that are recognised as such by the learned."[3]

∞

In this respect, your author found Monier's Sanskrit-English dictionary more rewarding. Describing *mantras*[4] comprehensively, Monier says mantras are -

'instrument of thought', speech, sacred text or speech, a prayer or song of praise - RV; AV; TS; a Veda hymn or sacrificial formula, that portion of the Veda which contains the texts called Rik or *Yajus* or Saman as opposed to the Brahmaṇa or Upaniṣad portion - BR; GSS et cetera; a sacred formula addressed to any individual deity (e.g. *Om Sivaya námah*), a mystical verse or magical formula (sometimes personified), incantation, charm, spell (especially in modern times, employed by the *Śaktas* to acquire superhuman powers; the primary mantras believed to be 70 million in number, and the secondary innumerable).

Dealing with mantras in the context of tantric practices, elsewhere, Monier says[5] - 'A mantra, as most persons know, is properly divinely inspired Veda text, but with the *Śhakta's*, and indeed with the great mass of the Hindus in the present day, it loses this character and becomes a mere spell or charm.' He clarifies,'Even though the text be taken from the Ṛg, Yajur or Atharva Veda, and be generally employed as a prayer or invocation with a definite meaning and application attached to the words, it becomes with the *Śaktas* a mere collection of magical letters and sounds, which, if properly uttered and repeated according to prescribed formularies, possesses in itself a mystical power capable of causing every conceivable good to oneself or evil to one's enemy.'

Yaska (800-500 BC), the etymologist and 'linguist' who has authored texts explaining meanings of words in Veda, says - the sages possessed an intuitive perception of Dharma, and they transmitted mantras by way of oral instruction to those that came after them and that or those who had no intuitive perception of Dharma (Nirukta I.20).

Mantras, even in Ṛgvedic times, were believed to have power - they induced the gods to attend the sacrifice and bestow on the reciters cattle, crop, and sons et cetera. (RV. I.102.1 - 5, I I.24.15 - 16, 25.2, I I I.3 1.14, I X.2 0.7, I X.7 2.9, X.7 8.8, X.10 5.1)

During the age of the *Pūrva Mīmāṃsā*, the *vidhi* (*yajña*) gained ascendancy but mantras retained their stature - it was definitely understood, says the Tantravartika, that religious acts performed with mantras, led to prosperity or to *svarga*. Later, in *Vidhāna*, and subsequently in Pauranic literature, this position again shifted - mantras once again came to occupy centre stage.

Today, to most Hindus, mantras mean sacred Sanskrit words or verses that praise gods and goddesses. It is widely believed that mantras, when repeated with single-minded concentration, are so potent as to coax a deity into bestowing on the practitioner special powers and favours. Consequently, they are widely used for attaining desired results (*phala*) through their special application in *pūjā* (*kāmya*), or (even) independently, in the form of *japa* - fervent repetitions, silent or spoken. Traditionally, repetitions are 108, 1008, or, in cases where the desired result is of extraordinary value, one lac and eight times. For greater effect, mantras are often used in conjunction with *havana* (*yajña*), typically conducted by a priest, in which participating members of the family or public throw *āhuti* (oblations) in the holy fire.

But what Monier wrote a century and a quarter ago (1883, Religious Thought and Life in India) about *Ṣaktas*, continues to hold true for most Hindus even today: they view mantras as something beyond mere 'prayer or invocation'; they see them as a 'collection of magical letters and sounds, which, if properly uttered and repeated according to prescribed formularies, possesses in itself a mystical power capable of causing every conceivable good to oneself or evil to one's enemy.'

∞

Before continuing further, it is necessary to draw a distinction between the religious world (religious frame work) as it exists now and as it existed in pre-*gṛhya sūtras* times.

Today a ritual, absent the mantra, is not unusual. A householder visiting a *Śiva* temple may pour water on the *linga* of *Śiva* without uttering *Oṃ Namaḥ Śivāya* or any other *Śiva mantra*. But in the Ṛgvedic times this was unthinkable. Conducting an *aśvamedha yajña* without the accompaniment of the appropriate mantra would have meant reducing that solemn ceremony to a caricature, a social occasion of horse slaughter for a feast. Similarly, in the case of *pravagya*, an important *iṣṭi* rite, merely boiling *ghī* and pouring goat or cow milk over it, minus the mantra, would be an act reduced to creating a pillar of fire to display pyrotechnics purely for entertainment!

It is the mantra that elevates an otherwise mundane and routine ceremony into a religious rite. The simple act of adding *ghī* to a fire suddenly assumes special significance - it becomes an *āhuti* when accompanied by a mantra. Only through mantra is this simple physical act transformed into a religious one. No song or poem, no matter how popular, meaningful, appropriate, or pleasing to the ear, can replace the mantras. For mantras are not created by man; they are part of *śruti*, and were passed on to us.

In Vedic time, clearly, mantras were applied to different ritual situations chiefly to secure the '*kāmya*,' (desired object). Another important reason was that mantras infused life in the rituals. Without mantras, any ritual was akin to a body bereft of a soul. Later, in *Mīmāṃsa* days, the *yajña* became all important - in *mīmāṃsakaras* world, it was *yajña* that compelled the gods to attend the ceremony, and deliver the '*kāmya*'. But even in this situation mantras played very important role; admittedly they were relegated to second place, after sacrifice (*yajña*) in order of importance.

There are several questions about mantras that need satisfactory answer - What is the importance of mantras? Do they have any meaning? What is the purpose of application of mantras to rituals? What outcome/s do they achieve? Is there any rationale, method, or a set of rules that act as guiding principles, in determining which mantra is to be recited with which rite? And do these religious rites and rituals, themselves, really have any meaning, or are they meaningless?

An attempt is made in the following pages to answer questions: Are the mantras meaningless? Do they have any power?

The claim 'mantras have almost no meaning, and even if they do it is secondary' has been championed by Frits Staal. He has a unique way of looking at mantras : through the prism of linguistics. Here is a summary of his theories on mantras (the author's comments are within brackets) -

i. Mantras are, at best, sounds (mantras are just human sounds, without any meaning)
ii. This sound is temporal i.e. worldly or belonging to this world (has a biological structure)
iii. The ritual behaviour too shares this basic biological structure that mantra, as sound, possesses
iv. The meaning of the mantra lies in the syntax it creates with the ritual and its ability to create repetitious patterns
v. The semantic (meaning), referential, poetic or aesthetic properties (capacity) of a mantra and ritual are secondary, if at all relevant to this biological i.e. the sound' universe (world)

Several scholars have countered the above arguments at various times - notably Hans Penner, Glucklich (recent), Lawson and, more recently, McCauley.

i. Penner and a few others have demonstrated the capacity of mantras and rituals through a huge number of referential cases
ii. Glucklich and other scholars have assessed the observation of Staal as partially (but not universally) true

McCauley and Lawson insist that even though the ritualized behaviour has biological roots, it does not confirm that it has no meaning. They give the example of language, which is biological in structure/origin yet contains consistent theories of meaning and semantics developed by linguists.

To justify his theory that 'mantras are meaningless', Staal relies heavily on the original 'seven arguments' of the famous Kautsa controversy that dates back 2500 years. This controversy is detailed in Yaska's Niruktam.

Niruktam are texts that attempt to explain the meaning of Ṛgvedic words. They form a part of the six '*Vedāngas*' (limbs of Vedas) without which the study of Vedas is considered incomplete. According to the Muṇḍaka Upaniṣad[6]

"Those who know Brahmaṇa (part of Veda) say that there are two sciences which should be known - the spiritual (*parā*) and the empirical (*aparā*). The empirical sciences are (the mastering of) the Ṛgveda, the Yajurveda, the Sāmaveda, the Atharvaveda, and the ancillary disciplines *vedānga*: *śikṣā* (phonetics), *kalpa* (ritual sciences), *vyākaraṇa* (grammar), *nirukta* (etymology), *candasa* (prosody) and *jyotiṣa* (astrology)."

Although there are references of several Niruktams by other authors in the texts, only *ācārya* Yaska's Niruktam (800-500 BC) is extant. It is invaluable in understanding the proper meaning of archaic Sanskrit words used in the Vedas. The *ācārya* himself has underlined its importance saying, "Without this science (Nirukta) there can be no understanding of the Vedic mantras."

It is said there were seventeen commentators who explained meaning of Ṛgvedic words in Yaska's time, and Kautsa was one of them. Kautsa declared the Ṛgveda meaningless - and put forth series of powerful arguments to support his pronouncement. Kautsa claimed the science of etymology as a tool for comprehending the meaning of scriptural texts, was worthless because the Vedas had no meaning at all! In Kautsa's opinion, the scriptural texts were reduced to non-linguistic sounds.

Kautsa's (from the Sanskrit '*kutsa,*' meaning revile) arguments were repudiated by *ācārya* Yaska in his first Niruktam - *prathama adhyāya padā* 5.

Like most Vedic texts, this narrative too is in 'question and answer' form. In the beginning of *padā* 5, Kautsa remarks that it is pointless to study Nirukta because mantras are meaningless. He employs his famous seven arguments[7] in support of his theory, first two arguments are -

1. Vedas language is fixed and frozen in both word and syntax; if the meaning of the Vedas were so important, the form would not have such huge emphasis.
2. Mantras are meaningless and do not have the power to do anything by themselves. Otherwise, why would they require the detailed supplementary texts of Brahmaṇas for their efficacious application, or interpreting their meaning (lengthy and farfetched associations) using *Viniyoga*?

Kautsa's other five arguments are: there nonsensical features - like talking to a plant, such as "save him, O plant!" (TS1.2.1.1); mantras contradict each other - one says there is one *Rudra* (TS1.8.6.1), while VS (1.6.54) says they are countless; priests (*adhvaryu*) make a show of telling other priests (*hotṛ*) specifically what to say and do at different times during a ritual, knowing full well the other priest is fully trained, and already knows what he has to say and do, making whole act meaningless. Therefore one will be right in concluding that mantras, similarly, must also be meaningless; some mantras address things that are different (and seen as different) as one. For example, *aditih sarvama* in Ṛgveda 1.6.16.5.; some mantra verses have obscure meanings - such as the word '*amyak*' which occurs only once in Ṛgveda 1.16 9.3. (these words are known as *hapax legomena* - words occurring only once in the text).

Yaska demolishes each of the arguments made by Kautsa in his Niruktam. Using examples, many from the Vedic texts themselves, he successfully demonstrates that mantras are indeed meaningful, and their meaning can be understood through the study of Nirukta. However, Staal remains unconvinced of the *ācārya's* arguments; countering them with good reasoning.

It will be interesting to see how these two scholars, Staal and Kautsa, separated by over two millennia, using similar arguments but different routes, arrive at the same conclusions, as is evident from the examples they give to support their respective contentions.

Kautsa's opening argument is -

"Mantras are meaningless because, in it, a given word cannot be replaced by its synonym and the order cannot be changed."

For example, in '*agni āyahi*' (SV 1.1.1.1), the synonym '*vibhasa*' cannot replace '*agni*', and '*ayāhyagne*' cannot be used in place of '*agni āyahi*'.

Simply put, it means - whereas in an ordinary sentence we can

- interchange positions of words
- freely replace a word with any of its synonyms, e.g. *agni* with its synonyms *anal* or *pavak*, the same freedom is not permitted in the case of mantras.

Yaska's (who, according to Staal, was a linguist and grammarian) rejoinder in Niruktam is simplicity itself: It is illogical to reject the validity of the mantras and regard them as meaningless (on this ground) because, even in the 'non-mantra world', there are numerous examples in every day speech where this fixity is observed without anyone ever calling such expressions meaningless, for example, '*pitāputrāu*' or '*Índrāgni*'.

One doesn't have to be a linguist, or a grammarian, to appreciate Yaska's argument.

Those who are familiar with the Hindi language will be able to appreciate the sound logic of the above example better. A Hindi speaker will never say '*putra pitā*' while referring to a father-son duo; it is always '*pitā putra*'. Similarly, even in uneducated circles, while referring to parents, the phrase '*mā-bāpa*' is not interchanged with '*bāpa-mā*'. Therefore, if fixity does not render words meaningless in the 'non-mantra world', then why should its insistence make them meaningless in the 'mantra world' of the Vedas?

Interestingly, Staal uses much the same argument as Kautsa[8], he only replaces 'word' with 'sound': "The sound of mantras may not be changed unlike in language where sounds may change provided meaning remains the same."

Staal appears to argue that when a word is replaced with its synonym, its sound (neccesserily) changes; whereas language allows this change of sound - since it does not change the meaning - mantras simply do not permit any change of sound (irrespective of change of meaning or not). And therefore mantras are not language.

I will put forward two arguments here.

i. While as Staal says, change of a word, by its equivalent or synonym - without changing meaning - may 'generally' be acceptable as a defining feature of language, this is not applicable to all situations. In situations where an exactness, a precise meaning is imporatant, eqivalents or synonyms are strictly not permitted.

In Constituitions of the nations, just as in legal agreements, every word is 'sancrosanct'- any substitution of a word by its equivalent in these documents is simply not permitted. Oath taking ceremonies are yet another example where the person taking oath has to repeat exactly the same words, in the same order - any change in order, or use of synonym, or equivalent word, renders the oath void. This is because any change will change the meaning - howsoever subtely - and destroy the sanctity of these documents and the oath.

ii. As we have seen in previous chapters, Ṛg mantras are in Sanskrit language, and part of *Śruti* - what was heard- by the *ṛsis*. *Ṛsis*, the original recipients of the mantras passed it to other sages, and *dvijas* who they considered worthy of this knowledge. This transmission was done strictly orally. The correct pronunciation of each Veda syllable and letter, with appropriate accents, is absolutely essential in recitation of Vedas. In order to retain absolute purity of mantras, 100% fidelity in transmission was a must. With this end in mind a unique system of memorising Vedas was devised in which every single *ṛca* was recited in eleven different ways. These recitations, called *pathas-ghana, dhvaja* etc., involved memorisation of the same text in eleven different ways. In addition, a very exhaustive discipline called *Vedanga* was created with specific purpose of teaching phonetics and grammar. This ensured that any recitation of Vedas was totally error free. A student spent a minimum of 12 years to learn a single Veda. Prodigous energy was expended by ancient Indian culture in ensuring that these texts were transmitted from generation to generation with inordinate fidelity for over 1500 years. It is a classical example of Zero-D quality control.

This system succeded because absolutely no change was permitted to be made in the texts. If the system had allowed changes to be made, the Vedas as we know them today would have been totally transformed version of the original.

If at every stage of reprint, even 5% replacement of original words with their synonyms and equivalents is permitted, after a mere ten reprints the original text will appear very different, and after twenty five reprints, unrecognisable. Imagine reading 250th edition of Rāma Carita Mānasa by Tulsī (Gita Press Gorakhpur) with 5% change in word order and replacement of words by its synonyms/equivalents!

The only change that was permitted to be made in Ṛgvedic mantras was when they were adapted for chanting in the Sāmaveda; by insertion of *stobhas* - meaningless words like *bhh*, *bhū*, et cetera.

According to Staal[9], in *stobha*, "Syllables are replaced by others that keep the same vowel, but replace the initial consonant by *bh*." Explaining the word '*stobha*', Staal says[10] (elsewhere): "When words do not fit, they are changed or transformed, and embellishments called *stobha* inserted. They are meaningless, like the sounds of lullaby."

Consider. In the Sāmaveda, all but seventy-five of the 1800 odd *Ṛks* are from the Ṛg. These are modified for chanting, attracting comments that they are "the Ṛgveda set to music."[11] While the Ṛgveda has vertical and horizontal accents, the Sāmaveda uses numbers 1, 2 and 3 to mark the accents; indicative of the importance of phonetics in both texts. A mantra from the Ṛgveda is chosen and its words are marked in this manner, this is called *ādhār* (base, foundation) or *yoni* (source). The Sāmaveda text consists of these *yonis* which are then modified by changing, transforming or embellishing the words, and, where necessary, inserting meaningless sounds or words called *stobha*. These *stobha* - words like *huva*, *hova*, *Bhū* - are crucial in fitting an existing string of words into a melody.

Insertion of modified words or inclusion of meaningless words in a text is a regular, indeed essential, feature of melody composition - an integral part of music all over the world. Using *stobhas Ṛk* verses were modified to fit Sāman melodies. It is difficult to understand how this change robs *Ṛk mantras* of all meaning and leaves them as meaningless as 'sounds of lullaby'.

Staal further argues, "Meaninglessness belongs to the nature of mantra. It is a feature of mantras as such. Kautsa's arguments showed this clearly and the core of the argument is that mantras are not language."[12]

Calling Kautsa a linguist (which he probably was), Staal analysed the mantras using modern linguistic parameters and reached the conclusion that "mantras incorporate recursive structures. They may be long and there are many of them. But mantras are not learnt in the way language is picked up." According to him (Staal), the incessant repetition of mantras is an additional reason in support of his argument that mantras are meaningless.

Giving example of a man who asks another person sharing the dining table - 'please give me salt', Staal attempts to establish that repetitiousness is not a quality of languages. For example, the phrase 'please give me' will remain meaningful even if changed to 'please, please give me'. It would hardly be acceptable if the phrase is further changed to 'please, please, please, please give me'. Staal observes: "It would definitely be looked upon as eccentric", and rightly so. He adds: "Mantras, on the other hand, are happily repeated," and gives examples of two mantras - '*Oṃ*' and the '*gāyatrī mantra*' - which are repeated many times for long periods without intermission.

∞

[Staal has used the term 'language' keeping languages such as English or Sanskrit, modern or classical, world or tribal languages, in mind.]

The author would like to raise a few questions here.

While requesting for salt on a dining table, although repeating the word 'please' four times, definitely looks eccentric, as Staal suggests. But will it sound even slightly out of place if somebody about to be shot by a captor begs, "Please, please, please, please let me go!"? Or, when caught with drugs on him, a teenager pleads with the Headmaster in school, "Please, please, please don't tell my mother!"? There are innumerable situations in everyday life where repeated use of a word, or a sentence, lends an added force: an adolescent lover seeking sexual favours from his partner; a young child pleading with her mother to let her play with friends; a physically abused wife begging her husband to let her go. This is particularly true in situations where something is being sought from a superior (authority).

In fact, to emphasise a point in situations of extreme emotional stress, we automatically become repetitive; even those of us who are otherwise proficient in the language and possesses perfect knowledge of vocabulary, semantics and syntax lapse in to this mode of speech.

Does the repetitiveness render the sentence meaningless?

In your author's opinion no. It actually adds force, and lends power to what is being conveyed in these situations. In other words, repetitiveness, many-a-time, is used to emphasise the intent of the speech. It becomes a sort of force multiplier or, more accurately (mathematically speaking), a force adder. When someone repeats a word, it's almost like he is following mathematical logic, as if he is making a mathematical statement - just as the number 2 repeated four times becomes (2+2+2+2)=8, four times bigger than the original 2.

Why does this happen?

The author would like to present another aspect of repetitiveness. As remarked earlier, the state of repetitiveness is usually associated with a heightened emotional state of mind of the individual. While psychologists are best equipped to study this tendency among humans, what we can safely discuss and analyse here is another aspect of such human behaviour - Prayers. Nearly all prayers - irrespective of their language - are repetitive. In most cases, a prayer is (offered) to receive something favourable from the almighty. For the purpose of the present discussion, let us call these prayers *kāmya* - A student asking for good grades, an athlete praying for the gold medal, or a mother praying for the recovery of her child - are typical examples of prayers for a very specific short term objective. In all three examples, the student, the athlete, and the mother, may start praying for desired results once they reach a 'critical' emotional level, which will vary depending on their personality, mental make-up, and stress threshold. As their anxiety increases, the frequency and repetitiveness of the prayer will also increase. For example, initially, the athlete may simply pray, "Oh God, please get me the gold!", only a few times a week prior to his race. He may start repeating the sentence every five minutes on the day of event, and even chant it non-stop when he is on the track waiting for the signal to start running. This is a typical example of a prayer 'sentence' (or, language of a prayer) repeated over and over again, where the seeker uses frequency of repetition as the force multiplier (or force adder) for a favourable result.

Repetitive use of a word, such as '*Oṃ*', is a subset of repetitive prayer sentence. A situation which makes the seeker repeat a word, rather than the whole sentence, over and over again, is born of the seeker's belief that such usage is a force multiplier. When a child learns a language from everyday experience with adults, s/he learns the increased effectiveness, and enhanced power, of words and sentences when they are repeated. This repetition does not make the sentence (and their intentions) any less meaningful. We apply the same knowledge and experience of repeating things in appropriate situations, expecting that it would make what we are saying more forceful and meaningful.

Use of 'many, many, many thanks', for expressing excessive gratitude; 'no, no, no and no again!' to make one's strong resolve known, are but two such examples.

We are now only a step away from understanding 'meaning' of repetitiousness in mantras.

In the preceding paragraph, the author has dealt with situations where the prayer is said for attaining a specific *kāmya* - a short-term objective. Many people find that offering the same set of prayers daily, or multiple times a day, gives 'a sense of calm' to the mind. Many others do it because it gives them confidence to face trying situations in life, and many also believe that in a prayer, the same set of sentences, said in a fixed order, will ward off unknown unpleasant situations, such as an accident involving oneself or near and dear ones. For the present discussion, let us call such prayers, which are repeated regularly without any specific short-term objective in mind, 'general prayers'. These two types of prayers are not unlike the accident/theft and burglary insurance policy vs general or all risks cover insurance policy.

These 'general prayer's - a fixed order of words - are present in many languages. They are repetitive in nature without becoming meaningless. The frequency of repetition may vary from individual to individual, or situation to situation, but the content (i.e. the exact words and their order) normally remains fixed in each case. A mother, whose sons have been in an unfortunate accident in a car racing event in which one son lost his life, may pray for the safety of the surviving son. Every time the surviving sibling participates in the circuit, the mother may offer the same set of prayers with folded hands in front of a deity, or mentally repeat the prayer while carrying out her daily chores, or mouth the words while watching a program on television. One can say with near certainty that every time she offers the same prayer, the order of every single word and sentence would remain unchanged. Why?

The answer is rather simple - to the seeker who is offering the prayer, the repetitiousness makes the prayer more meaningful, powerful and efficacious (Oxford Dictionary - 'of something abstract - successful in producing the desired or intended result').

More importantly, the fixity of the order, in which the words and sentences are arranged in an individual's prayer, is of critical importance. This order does not get changed; even though by altering the order and changing the syntax, the content remains unchanged. This purity of 'fixity of the order' is what Kautsa questioned in the case of mantras. Two and half millennia later, Staal questions in a similar vein - Why should mantras be treated as a language when they lack flexibility? Both insist that flexibility is the very life and soul, the absolutely necessary condition for an assembly of words to qualify as a language. Yet there are abundant examples in many languages where the repetition of a word, a sentence, or even an entire stanza, constituting a prayer, has been used by humans for centuries to make repetition more powerful, more efficacious and more meaningful. Judging by the yardstick of Kautsa and Staal - Do they all stand rejected as 'language' and 'meaning less'?

The author would like to add two more instances of repetitiveness of words. Although the two are employed in entirely different situations, they share the 'force multiplier' effect. First is an example of a powerful 'speech act', unfavoured by Staal and his followers; and the second, what Staal may have called a case of extreme madness rather than simple 'eccentricity'[13] (ref his earlier example of using the word 'please' four times in a sentence instead of just once, ref Discovering the Vedas, page 204). In this second example, in a very solemn social intercourse, the same word is repeated 108 or even 1008 times!

The two examples are from two different languages, and two different cultures, geographical locations and religions.

First is the common Sanskrit and Hindi word '*Śrī*' (meaning splendour, radiance, etc) an honorific, and the other is '*Ṭalāq*', an Arabic term meaning 'divorce'.

It is common practice in India to attach '*Śrī*' before a person's name, much like 'Mr' in English language. A successful 1955 Bollywood film, produced and directed by Raj Kapoor, was caustically titled 'Shree 420' (Shree and Sri are same). While *Śrī* is normally used only once before a person's name, in many cases e.g. while addressing kings or highly esteemed members of society, the title of *Śrī* 108 (i.e. '*Śrī*' repeated 108 times) is used before their name to show extreme respect.

Similarly, *Śrī* 1008 (i.e. '*Śrī*' repeated 1008 times) is used as sign of extreme reverence/respect to extraordinary and revered personalities, such as a saint, a benefactor, divinity, an emperor, or an exceptionally learned man. Does this repetitiveness of the word '*Śrī*', disqualify the address as 'not part of the language' and meaningless?

The answer is no.

The second, example of '*Ṭalāq*', is even more interesting. It attracts Staal's 'disqualification' (meaninglessness) on two counts - its repetitiveness, and on account of being the 'speech act'. But first let's understand what a 'speech act' is. There are certain utterances that are considered as an action. For example, a Priest in Church pronouncing a man and a woman, husband and wife (married). The pronouncement changes status of their relationship.

According to Islamic law, when a husband repeats the word '*ṭalāq*' to his wife three times in succession, it nullifies his *nikāḥ* (marriage). This 1300-year-old Islamic practice is prevalent across continents and uniformally followed by adherents of Islam, both literate and illiterate.

The repetitive use of the word '*ṭalāq*', a powerful speech act with serious consequences, can hardly be dismissed as meaningless by the 1.2+ billion followers of Islam across the globe.

As discussed earlier, repetitiousness is a powerful tool, and the practitioner, or seeker, uses it both in religious and nonreligious situations. Not only does repetitiousness not make mantras or any statement meaningless merely because such words or sentences are not part of a language (repetitive words, phrases or sentences do not fit in a modern linguist's definition of language proper), these are the very characteristics (the fixity of order of words and sentences, and repetitiveness) which make mantras powerful 'speech acts'.

We are yet to fully understand how this repetitiveness has become an all-important factor in elevating an 'ordinary' prayer to the status of a powerful tool in languages across the world, a tool that is believed to deliver the desired result. And why the 'meaningless' mantras become powerful when repeated over and over again? True, it is not entirely attributable to the 'force multiplier' effect, and involves an associational angle with *kāmya* (the desired result), plus a certain degree of imagery. This associational aspect is beautifully described by the great contemporary scholar of Vedic texts Laurie Patton in her detailed studies of *viniyoga*, and in a limited way by Jan Gonda in his concept of *bandhu*.

∞

Many scholars claim that mantras are not a language, but meaningless sounds. And because sound is a biological activity, mantras too are biological activity, just like rituals.

Let's examine this. But before that let's have a brief understanding of language and linguistics.

Language is a mass noun that the Oxford dictionary defines as - 'the method of human communication, either spoken or written, consisting of the use of words in a structured and conventional way'.

The scientific study of language and its structure, including the study of grammar, syntax and phonetics is linguistics.

Specific branches of linguistics include socio linguistics, dialectology, psycholinguistics, computational linguistics, comparative linguistics and structural linguistics. (Oxford Dictionary)

Any human language enables its speakers to communicate with each other and express ideas, emotions, desires and all other things that need expressing. It is a function of knowledge and ability, and linguistics is the study of these knowledge systems. The branches of linguistics dealing with the structure of language can be categorized as follows[15] -

- Phonetics - The study of speech sounds in their physical aspects
- Phonology - The study of speech sounds in their cognitive aspects
- Morphology - The study of formation of words
- Syntax - The study of formation of sentences
- Semantics - The study of meaning
- Pragmatics - The study of language use

If we accept that mantras are not a language or language proper and, hence, cannot be studied using the tools applied for studying language, such as linguistics, we are faced with a question - What are the suitable tools then to study and analyse mantras?

The answer is Pragmatics, possibly.

Like semantics is the study of meaning of a language, and syntax, the study of formation of sentences, Pragmatics is -

The branch of linguistics dealing with language in use and the contexts in which it is used, including such matters as deixis, the taking of turns in conversation, text organisation, presupposition and implicature.

One should not confuse it with the more commonly used word 'pragmatic', which has an entirely different meaning and is not a term of Linguistic studies. The word 'pragmatic'is defined as dealing with things sensibly and realistically in a way that is based on practical rather than theoretical considerations.

A closer examination of the various components of Linguistics suggests that Pragmatics is a more suitable tool to understand and study mantras. The standard/ conventional tools had earlier declared that mantras are not a language because it failed the crucial tests of recursiveness, substitution of a word by its synonyms and its repetitiveness.

By definition, Pragmatics deals with -

i. 'language in use and the contexts in which it is used' - which is what we require for our discussion

ii. 'in matters such as deixis' - deixis is a function or use of words whose meaning is dependent on that context in which it is used, such as you, me, here, next Tuesday, et cetera. Deixis, also known as indexical, are of special interest because their meaning is different to different people at the same time. For example, in the phrase 'come here', the meaning of the word 'here' is different to the person saying it and (different) to the person it is said to, thereby making it highly contextual and situation-dependent. In the case of the mantras, this, prima facie, is of great interest

iii. 'Implicature' - the action of implying a meaning beyond the literal sense of what is explicitly stated. For instance, one may use the phrase 'the frame is nice', implying that the person does not like the picture in it. This too seems to be extremely important and relevant in the case of mantras. Within Pragmatics, 'speech acts' are a subcategory of Indexicals, which are defined as 'an utterance considered as an action, particularly with regard to its intention, purpose, or effect' (Oxford Dictionary)

Therefore, Pragmatics seems to be a better suited tool, maybe even ideal to study and analyse mantras.

Searle and a few other scholars have also used such an approach in the past.

Introduced in 1962, by Austin, a philosopher linguist at Oxford University, the 'speech act' theory was further developed seven years later by John Rogers Searle, Professor of Philosophy at Berkeley, University of California. 'Speech acts' are language utterances by which an act is performed. Searle classified them, according to function, into the following -

1. Assertives - which commit their speaker to the truth of a proposition
2. Directives - which get the hearer to do something
3. Commissives - which make the speaker commit to a future course of action
4. Expressiveness - which express the psychological attitude toward the proposition
5. Declarations - which bring about the state of affairs, as indicated in the proposition, merely by being said

Many scholars argue that mantras are 'speech acts'.

According to Patton, these are speech/ utterances that change the state of affairs, for example, a priest's words of declaring a couple husband and wife. If anyone else makes those utterances, the relationship between a man and woman will not be affected and their status will remain unchanged.

Just as many Indologists are convinced that mantras are powerful 'speech acts', others outright reject it: "Calling an utterance an act is such a misleading suggestion. For we would still have to distinguish between acts that merely speak and acts that are really act... conclude that mantras are neither language nor speech acts."[16] Staal recommends and explores other areas for a possible solution. He suggests "we should widen our net and study them in the context of the animal kingdom", and observes, "mantras are in some respect close to birdsong than to language."

Interestingly, Staal questions neither the power of mantras, nor their meaning. His contention is that mantras are a powerful entity, like an elephant. We cannot explain what an elephant is just by language, and resort to using other means - like genetics, DNA or biological evolution. Similarly, we cannot explain the mantra using language. Hence, the 'word meaning' of mantra is not the 'meaning' of mantra.

What are *mantras* then, if not language?

If mantras are not language (because the word order cannot be changed, words cannot be replaced by their synonyms, and they are incessantly repetitive), then what are they?

The house of Indologists stands divided on this question.

According to one group, mantras are simply sounds, biological acts. And according to another group, they are powerful speech acts.

Interestingly, those who consider the mantras sounds, a purely biological act, see religious rituals also as purely biological acts. For them, the spoken mantras and the accompanying rituals, say a ritual performed to get a son, are adaptive behaviour with biological roots. Hence, they are devoid of meaning. In other words, these are purely physical acts in the domain of biological actions.[17]

Macaulay and Lawson have argued that language is also biologically rooted, and yet, linguists develop theories of meaning and semantics.

They put forward compelling arguments opposing the biological root conjecture. They counter that even though language has biological roots, this reasoning alone cannot be used to reject it as meaningless, since linguists have themselves developed theories of meaning and semantics of this 'biological action' based language!

[Similarly, ritualised behaviour, which has biological roots, cannot be said to have no meaning. Macaulay and Lawson make a clear distinction between religious acts and religious ritual. While religious action involves agents doing something, religious ritual involves agents doing something to a patient. In the latter, the agent acts on the patient, thus changing the status of a religious act. More importantly, in case of religious rituals, it is prerequisite to conduct a series of events of a prescribed quality before proceeding with the ritual itself. The history, quality and exact specifications are as demanding of men as they are regarding materials employed in the rituals. In a *yajña*, the water to be used must only come from specified sources, the wood of the spatula can only come from specified trees, and the priest conducting the ritual must at least be someone who has undergone the *upanayana* ceremony.]

They have attempted to make a distinction between a simple biological action, like a religious action, and other biological actions, like ritual action.

- **Religious action** is when an actor does anything in the domain of religion
- **Religious ritual** is when an actor does something to the patient, and the efficacy of the action lies in a precondition being met, e.g. actions of a Roman Catholic priest become a ritual because he is already ordained, as opposed to a religious act, where a non-priest performs the same act, such as baptism.

Thus, the efficacy of a ritual act is contingent on a sequence of requisite events.

For this section of people/scholars, mantras and rituals hold great meaning, and the power and efficaciousness of the mantras come from their fixity and repetitiveness. These speech acts, as described by linguists like Searle, are harnessed and used in various forms in and non-Vedic rituals.

As seen earlier, speech acts do alter the status. All religious rituals are performed with the object of changing the status of the doer. Ṛgvedic mantras were uttered to beget a son, or a better crop, which essentially meant that prayers changed the status of a man to that of a father, of a farmer to a wealthy man, et cetera. But these mantras, these prayers, didn't become speech acts, they remained just prayers.

In a religious ritual, an agent does something to a patient. For that, certain conditions must be met. Some of these conditions may require prerequisite events to have taken place in the past. For instance, a man who desires to get married can only do so after completing the *upanayana saṃskāra*. The efficacy of a religious ritual depends on some of these critical conditions being satisfied, including quality of the materials being used (for example, un-boiled milk of a cow, source of the water to be used, shape and size of the *yajña vedi*, et cetera).

In their study, Macaulay and Lawson arrived at the conclusion that the state of mind of the ritual participant may be immaterial to the efficacy of ritual, but -

The actor's emotional engagement and conceptual control of the ritual's special agents (the gods, in case of Vedic rituals), along with its associational history, are quite important.

Appendix 1

Agniṣṭoma: *Soma Yajña* (Deatil Description)

Day 1 - The main events of the day are -

1. Selection of the priests - *ṛtvija-varṇa*
2. Construction of the *prācīnaavamsha vedi - shālā nirmāṇa*
3. Consecration - taking of the *dīkṣā* by *yajamāna* - the *dīkṣāniya iṣṭi*

The ceremony starts with *yajamāna* taking *saṃkalpa* for the *yajña*, a resolve to perform the sacrifice. The priests are ceremonially welcomed and honoured, and the sacrificer carries out a ritualistic selection of the officiating priests with the accompaniment of *varṇamantra*. Next, is *devayāchnā* rite in which the sacrificer approaches king for a piece of land suitable for *deva yajña* (sacrificial arena) with the words '*Dev yajñam me dehi*'. The ground must be free from salinity and holes, inclined towards the north-east, east or north, and "which lies highest, and above which no other part of the ground rises" (SB. 3.1.1). On this ground, a hall or a shed is built with the top beams running from west to east, enclosed on every side 'lest it should rain upon', and because the one who is consecrated "truly draws nigh (near) to the gods and becomes one of the deities. Now the gods are secreted from men and secret also is what is enclosed on every side: this is why they enclose it on every side" (SB. 3.1.8). Only a *rājan* or *vaiśya*, other than a *brahmaṇa*, are allowed to enter the hall. During this period the *yajamāna* is prohibited from speaking to a *śūdra*.

On this day, the *pragvanshālā* (a shed admeasuring 30 feet long and 22 feet wide is erected using east-oriented upper beams, also called *prācīnavamsha*, where *vedi* shaped like a woman is located and the three fires are kept), the *patnī-shālā* (a hut for the wife within *prācīnavamsha*), and the *vratasṛapangār* (place where milk is warmed) are erected (ref diagram D-1).

At his home, the *yajamāna* warms on the *gārhapatya* fire the two pieces of wood (*araṇīs*) for producing the *āhavanīya* fires by friction. After extinguishing the fires, the *yajamāna* and his wife go back to the sacrificial arena, *devayājan*, and enter the *pragvanshālā* through the eastern door. Various articles of the *yajña* are also taken to the sacrificial arena where the fire is then produced through the *araṇīs* by the *adhvaru* to ceremonially light the *gārhapatya* and *āhavanīya* fires.

The rite of consecration (*dīkṣā*) - In the afternoon, *dīkṣā* is performed. Śatapatha Brahmaṇa gives a detailed account of the *dīkṣā* ceremony. The *yajamāna* eats what he likes and then to the north of the hall in an inner enclosed place a barber shaves his hair and beard, and cuts his nails. Thereafter the *yajamāna* bathes with accompaniment of Ṛgveda mantras - "may the waters, the mothers, cleanse us!" (X.1 7.10), wears a new piece of garment that has been beaten by *pratiprasthatṛ* priest so that "whatsoever part of it an unclean woman has spun or woven will become clean" (3.1.19).

The wife, guided by the *pratiprasthatṛ* priest, also goes through these rites except cutting of the hair.

Next, everyone is seated in the *pragvanshālā* to perform *dīkṣāniyeshti*, the ceremony of imparting *dīkṣā*. *Agnaviṣṇu* is the deity of the ceremony; and cakes (shaped like tortoise and as large as a horse's hoof), made of pounded rice or barley flour based on eleven potsherds of *gārhapatya*, are offered as *havis*. The *yajmaná* is then anointed with butter (*navnīta*) in a purificatory ceremony. After purifying the *yajamāna* with the *pavitrīs*, the *adhvaryu* makes him perform *audgrahana homa* - a name of the six elevatory *ājya* (*ghī*) oblations, also called *dīkṣāhuti*, in which twelve ladling oblations take place

The *adhvaryu* spreads two black deer skin (*kriṣṇamṛga-charma*) in north of *āhavanīya* with the neck parts of the skin facing east and *yajamāna* and his wife sit on these and pronounce beginning of the benediction[4] from the white Yajurveda, "We approach you, O Gods, for a desirable good, at the opening of sacrifice; we call on you, O Gods, for holy blessings". In a significant symbolic gesture, the sacrificer bends his fingers inwards clinching his fists, pretending to hold the ether, sky and the earth as a representation of the sacrifice. After a series of sacrificial rites, the *pratiprasthatṛ*, or another priest, announces completion of consecration by calling out "consecrated is this *Brahmaṇa*, consecrated is this *Brahmaṇa*."

It is believed that through the consecration (*dīkṣā*) of the *agniṣṭoma*, the sacrificer simulates an embryo (*garbha*) to be reborn as one of the gods. This is based on the assumption that prior to the *dīkṣā*, he meets with ceremonial 'death'. The clenching of the fist is in imitation of the embryo.

Thereafter the priests, as per rules, cook prescribed food for them on *gārhapatya* fires. *Yajamāna* is served in an iron pot and his wife in a copper pot. After the meal the *yajamāna* and his wife remain silent until the first star shines. The *yajamāna* fasts during the day and drinks only milk in the night before going to sleep.[5]

This ends the first day of *agniṣṭoma.*

Day 2 - The main events of the second day are - *prāyṇīyā iṣṭi*, *somakrayaṇa*, *atithyeṣṭi* and *pravargya*, and *upasad* which are performed twice, morning and evening, daily.

Opening sacrifice or *prāyṇīyāeṣṭi* - After the *dīkṣā* day, this is first introductory (opening) rite of *soma* sacrifice in which one goes forth (*prāyan*) to buy *soma* stalks.The sacrifice consists of offering of *caru* cooked in milk to *Aditi* and four libations of *ājya* for *Parthya svasti*, *Agni*, *Soma* and *Savitṛ*. The *sviṣṭakṛita* oblation is offered to *Agni* - *Sviṣṭakṛit*. The mantras of the call of invitation to the deity (*anuvākyā*) are recited in praise of *yājya mantras* and vice versa in this *iṣṭi*. The initiated person begins the *soma* sacrifice with this rite.

Hiraṇyavati āhuti - This involves purchase of *soma* and an offering of gold (*hiraṇya*) and homage to *soma* cow, purchased by the sacrificer earlier, to be given to the *soma* seller in exchange of *soma* stalks. In this interesting ritual -

The seller of *soma* removes weeds from *soma latā* (creeper) - priests and *yajamāna* do not participate or look at weeding - and places it on red ox hide. The seller sits on the northen part of the hide, a jar of water is kept in front of *soma* and the doors of sacrificial hall are shut. *Adhvaryu* makes offerings of *ājya* with *juhu* spoon, to which a piece of gold is tied with *durbha* grass. This offering is called *hiraṇyavati āhuti*. The doors of hall are opened. Out side a tawny or red colour heifer, not older then three years, which has yellowish brown eyes but not red, and which has no deificiency, is kept ready. The cow is not to be tied by rope or held by ears or horns. It is held by its neck. It is then made to walk seven steps; in the seventh hoof print, a piece of gold is put. Oblations with mantra are offered and gold piece tied to *yajamāna*'s little finger. Servant of *yajamāna* fetches three pieces of cloth - one for tying *soma*, second for covering *soma* from all sides, and the third is used as turban of the *soma* bundle. They then tie and cover the *soma* stalks, tie the turban on it and hand it over to the seller who then enters into a mock haggling drama with *adhvaryu* for the price of *soma*. The deal is concluded in which in exchange for *soma* seven cows, gold piece, clothes and a she goat are offered. Procured *soma* is kept on black antelope skin spread in the box of the bullock cart.

Procession and entrance of king *soma* - After the purchase, *soma* kept in a *sakata* (bullock cart) is brought in a procession to the entrance of the eastern door of *pragvanshālā*, where the *atithyeṣṭi* (guest offering) ceremony of *soma* is performed. On a throne made of *uḍumbara* wood, carried by four men, king *soma* makes an entry with the sacrificer, accompanied with chants "whatsoever hours of thine they worship with offering, may they all encompass the sacrifice! Go forth to our dwellings, O *soma*, prospering our homes, ever helpful, bestowing abundance of men, not slaying of man!" (RV. I.90 1.19; Vaj. S. IV.37) and is placed to the south of *āhavanīya*.

Like any special guest, king *soma* is greeted with *atithyeṣṭi*. In this *iṣṭi navakapāla - puroḍāśa* (rice/barley cakes made on 9 potsherd) is offered to *Viṣṇu*. The *ājya* is placed in *tānūnaptra-pātra* - a pot, so called after deity '*Tānūnaptra*'.

Tānūnaptra - The ceremony of the covenant of *tanunapat*, or the 'self-generated one', is called *tānūnaptra*. Once during a guest offering, unwilling to yield to each other's excellence, the gods had a serious discord and formed rival groups. However, they managed to make amends and took oaths (*tānūnaptra*) to work together.

As a sign of commitment for mutual cooperation, *yajamāna* and the sixteen priests touch *ājya* placed in *tānūnaptra-pātra*. Each priest is requested by the sacrificer to participate, and form a ritual alliance to shun any discord for the successful completion of the sacrifice.

Avāntaradīkṣā or Intermediary consecration - Imitating the gods who had fallen in discord and repaired their relationship through *tānūnaptras* (oaths), in this intermediary consecration or *avāntaradīkṣā*, the *yajamāna* tightens his girdle and clinches his fist more tightly. The priests envelope (until expiatory bath) the *yajamāna* with a skin by means of fire[6] - "Fire being fervour, and the consecration being fervour, he thereby undergoes an intermediate consecration" (SB. I I I.4.3.3). He puts on the kindling stick repeating, "O *Agni*, protector of vows, on thee, O protector of vows - what bodily form there is of thine, (may that be) here on me; and that bodily form there is of mine, (may that be) on thee! May my vows be bound up with thine, O Lord of vows!"[7] (Vaj S. V.6).

Then follow *pravargya* and *upasads* rites, in that or in reverse order. *Pravargya* and *upasad* are two different ceremonies which form an important part of *soma yajña*. Both are done morning and afternoon for three days (second, third and fourth day) if *soma* is to be pressed on fifth day; if *soma* pressing is on seventh day or later then *upasad* and *pravagya* are performed till one day before the pressing day. These are very important rites - according to SB - the *upasads* or homages are the neck of the sacrifice, and *pravargya* is the head.[8]

Pravargya and *Upasads* - *Pravargya* is an independent *iṣṭi* incorporated in the *soma* sacrifices. Although *Apastambā* does not consider it as an essential part of *agniṣṭoma*, he considers it important enough to deal with it separately in detail in *śrauta sūtras* (Āp. SS. XV.5 - 12). In the first part of *pravargya*, earthen vessels for the sacrifice are made. To prepare clay for the vessels, earth drawn from east of *āhavanīya*, soil dug by a wild boar, dust from an ant-hill are mixed with *putika plant*[9], hair of goat and black antelope; goat's milk is drawn on mix directly from its udder and hot water from *madanti* is added next.

One principal and two supplementary vessels called *mahāvīra*, two milking bowls, and two plates for baking (*puroḍāśa*) cakes are made using this clay. *Mahāvīra* is ten to twenty inches in diameter, round, flat bottom vessel, with a collar and a hole or snout to pour out liquid. The vessels are dried in sun, polished with a new bride's garments and *gavidhuka*[10], fumed with horse dung and finally baked in a pit. Baked vassels are cooled by pouring goat's milk over them.

Next day, i.e. on the day of *pravargya* performance, there are recitations of the *ardhvayu*, the *brahmaṇa* and the *hotṛ*. The main vassel - *mahāvīra* - is held over the *āhavanīya* fire and anointed with *ghī* and transferred to a raised platform (*āsandī*). A series of actions are performed now: a silver plate inserted in the *āsandī*, sheaths of reeds kindled in the *gārhapatya* placed on top of the mound, and *vikantaka* wood sticks put around *mahāvīra*. *Mahāvīra* is then covered by a gold disk and a blaze produced using fan made of black antelope skin. Once the blaze is produced, gold plate is removed and *mahāvīra* heated till it becomes red hot. *Ghī* is poured in the vessel and to the boiling *ghī* is added freshly drawn milk of a cow and a goat (which has a male young). This instantly produces a column of fire. The hot mix of the milk and *ghī* is called *gharma*.

The vessel is then taken to the *āhavanīya* fire and milk poured in *mahāvīra* till it overflows from all direction. Offerings are made to *Aśvin*, *Vāyu*, *Índra*, *Savitṛ*, *Bṛahspati* and *Yama*. The sacrificer drinks the remainder *gharma* by *upayamanī*, the priests only smell it. *Mahāvīra* - addressed as *samrāt* (emperor) - is kept back on its throne (*āsandī*) which is made higher than the throne of king *soma* - symbolizing its pre-eminence. At every stage the *mahāvīra* is to be lifted using wooden tongs.

Other two secondary *mahāvīra* vassels are not used at any stage; through out the ceremony, wrapped in cloth, they are kept on an *āsandī* on one side of the throne.

After the last *pravagya* performance, the implements are buried at *uttaravedi* or disposed in water. 'One must not perform the *pravargya* at one's first *soma* sacrifice, since that would be sinful, and lest *Índra* should cut off his head;'[11] is the dictum of Śhatpatha. It was not to be performed 'for any and every one' - but 'for him who is known', or 'who has studied sacred writ (Vedas).'[12]

The *upasads* are *homa* ceremonies involving oblations of *ghī* offered to *Agni*, *Soma* and *Viṣṇu* in *āhavanīya* with a *juhu* ladle, and are performed twice a day, at sunrise and sunset, along with the *pravargya*.

Upasads are performed after *prvargya*, and *somāpyāyana* (wetting *soma* stalks with water so that they swell and yeid juice) and *nihanva* (an act of begging pardon by the priests) are performed after the *upasad*. Thereafter *Índra* is invoked by the priests under the leadership of *Subramanya* to come and partake of the *soma*.

Day 3 - The main events of the day three are - *pravargya*, *gharma* and *upasad iṣṭis* - performed twice daily; and construction of covered *mahā* and *uttara-vedi*.

Pravargya, *gharma* and *upasad iṣṭis* are performed as described in earlier paragraphs.

The *soma* stalks bundles are untied by the *brahmaṇa* and touching these stalks, the priests recite mantras praising *soma*.

The *adhvaryu* goes to the south of the *āhavanīya* after taking *juhu* and *upabhṛta* oblation spoons filled with *ājya*, and offers its oblations to *Agni*, in the east; to *Soma* in the centre; and to *Viṣṇu* in the west from central point of *āhavanīya*. Thereafter commence *vedi* preparations.

1. *Soma* and high altar preparation - *Mahāvedi* - also called *saumika* - is the high altar, and is prepared by *adhvaryu*. It is a trapezium measuring appox 67 feet (36 *prakramas* or 72 *padas* or steps) east to west and 56 feet (30 *prakramas* or 60 *padas*) north to south facing *shālā*, and 45 feet (24 *prakramas* or 48 *padas*) north to south on the east (ref diagram D-1). A rope marks the boundary of the *mahāvedi* within which the *sadas* (tent/shed), *havirdhānamandapa* and *uttaravedi*, are constructed in a way that its visibility is not obstructed.
2. *Uttara vedi* or high altar is erected in the east and is situated within sacrificial arena but outside the *shālā*;

Day 4 - The main events of the day are - *Pravargya* and *upasads*, the digging of *uparavas* and the *agniṣomiya-paśu yaga*.

Pravargya and *upasad* are performed as already described.

The following rites are then performed in sequence.

1. Leading forward the fire to the high altar or *agniprṇayana*: In this ceremony, the fire is transferred from *āhavanīya* to the *nābhi* (navel) of *uttaravedi* located in *mahāvedi* (ref diagram). Once the fire is set ablaze with five ladles of *ghī*, the *adhvaryu* instructs *hotṛ* to recite (eight) verses while the fire is carried eastwards and laid down on the high altar in the navel. Simultaneously, the priest pours *ghī* praying for abundant offspring and wealth, and for gods to be brought to the sacrifice.
2. Construction of sheds and preparation of pressing place and *dhiṣṇiya* -
   i. Cart shed or *havirdhāna* - *Havirdhāna* is the name of two carts on which the *havis* - the *soma* plant - is placed. Cart shed has two doors and is constructed using twelve posts and four beams, covered with triple *chadis* (covering for the *havirdhāna* carts) and enclosed by a mat cover. It is located in the *mahāvedi* for parking these carts.
   ii. Sound holes or *uparava* - These are holes of resonance (*rava*). Four holes, in two rows of two holes each, are dug by *adhvaryu* below the fore part of the southern cart. Each hole is one span (appox 8.5 inches) in diameter and one span from each other. Holes are one arm (appox 18 inches) deep and interconnected. In an interesting ceremony *adharvayu* and sacrificer insert their right-hand in the south-east and north-west holes. When the two hands touch, *adharvayu* asks, "Sacrificer! What is there?" The sacrificer replies 'welfare (or happiness)' and the *adharvayu* in a low voice says 'may that belong to us both'. This is done twice.[13] Holes are first covered with *kusha* grass blades and then by two wooden

boards (*adhisavana phalaka*) kept on them. Skin of a red bull, cut up to fit the boards, is spread over the boards. To extract *soma* juice, when *soma* stalks are pounded on these boards by four stones, the pounding/crushing produces sound which reverberates (*rava*) through the holes. (Compare it with 4 holes in head.)

iii. Sheds/tents or *sadas* - According to the black Yajur, erection of the *sadas* precedes the digging of *uparavas*. These are oblong sheds or tents facing east measuring 27 *aratnis* (40 feet) in length and 20 feet in breadth (or half of the length). The *uḍumbara* post stands exactly in the centre of the shed. The middle shed is supposed to be as high as the sacrificer's height with the slanting ends reaching the sacrificer's navel. The shed is covered with nine mat roofs.

iv. *Dhiṣṇiya* - These are eight small seats raised for the *soma* priests. Of these, six are situated within the *sadas*, separated by 14 inches (18 *angulas*) - either square or in diameter - made of soil taken from the *cātvāla* (a pit dug outside measuring 2.25 feet or one *samya* square) from where loose earth is drawn for constructing *dhiṣṇiyas*, *uttara vedi* et cetera, or made of sand. Fire is installed on them and oblations can be offered in it.

3. *Vaisarjana* offerings, and leading *Agni* and *Soma* or *Agniṣṭomapraṇayana* - In *agniṣṭomapraṇayana*, there is a ceremonial procession in which wife and relatives of the sacrificer are called out from *patnīśālā*, the sacrificer touches the *adhvaru*, the wife touches the sacrificer, and sons and brothers of the sacrificer touch the wife of the sacrificer. *Adhvrayu* covers them with a fresh piece of cloth and offers *ājya* libations called *vaisarjina*.[14] This is done with the objective of setting them all free.[15]

Next, firewood is put on *ahávaniya* (now serving as *gārhapatya*) and transferred to the *uttara vedi*. Then they deposit the pressing stones, *soma* trough and cups, and other implements for use in animal sacrifice at appropriate place. A black deer skin is spread on the enclosed part of the southern *soma* cart and king *soma* (stalks) deposited thereon saying, "O divine *Savitṛi*, this is thy *soma*: shield him; may they not injure thee!" (Vaja S. V.39). This way, king *soma* is left in god *Savitṛi's* protection.

The *yajmāna* now gives up his vow of silence and fast, and hands over the staff (to *maitravarunā*). He unclenches his fist which he had kept clenched from the time of *dīkṣā*.

4. Animal sacrifice to *Agni* and *Soma* -

i. Setting up of sacrificial stake - The sacrificial stake called *yūpa* is cut from the forest and is chosen based on - "Thee have I found on the nearer side of the farther, and on the farther side of the nearer" (SB I I I.6.4.6) - and cut into 5 to 15 *aratnis* (1 *aratni* = 1.5 feet) in length. The stake is eight cornered or octagonal, tapering on the top, as high as the sacrificer standing with or without raised hands or on the chariot, with one fifth of the chiselled end, called *havirdhāna*, planted inside the pit. The stake is then planted on the ground and anointed with *ghī* while Ṛgvedic verses praising *Viṣṇu* are chanted.

ii. Slaying victim - The animal is bound to the stake and fire is churned around to make the animal know "that this truly is the manner of sacrificial food, this its resort; that it is truly in fire that Sacrificial food is offered: and accordingly they will resign themselves and will be favourably disposed to the slaughtering."[16] A noose is made and thrown around the victim - "with the noose of sacred order I bind thee, O oblation to the gods!"[17] - binding it to the stake while pronouncing "at the impulse of the divine *Savitṛi*, I bind thee with the arms of the *Aśvins*, with the hands of *Pūṣan*, the agreeable to *Agni* and *Soma*!" (Vaj S. VI.9) The victim is sprinkled with water and the permission of its mother and father is prayed for. The animal is given a drink of water to purify it internally and anointed with *ghī* from *juhu*.

iii. Oblations - The *hotṛ* urges *adhvaru* to proceed with oblations -

(a) Offerings with *āprī* verses (there are total 11 fore offerings) - after the tenth offering, the butcher's knife is called for and anointed to touch forehead of the victim, while exclaiming, "anointed with the *ghī*, protect ye the animal!" (Vaj. S. V I.11) The slaughtering knife is handed over to the butcher with, "be this thine approved edge!" The *agnīdh* (the priest who kindles fire) carries the fire around the victim which is led to the slaughtering place while *pratiprasthṛtṛṛi* holds it from behind by means of two spits. The *adhvaryu* holds the *pratiprasthṛtṛṛi* and the sacrificer holds the *adhvaryu*.[18] They then return to the altar and sit down turning away and facing *āhavanīya* "lest they should be eyewitnesses to its being quieted (strangled)."[19] "They do not slay it on the frontal bone, for that is human manner; nor behind the ear, for that is after the manner of the fathers. They either choke it by merely keeping its mouth closed, or they make a noose. Therefore, he says not, 'slay! kill!' for that is human manner, but 'quiet it! It has passed away!' for that is after the manner of the gods. For when he says, 'it has passed away,' then this one (the sacrificer) passes away to the gods: therefore, they say, 'it has passed away." When they hold the victim down before strangling, the butcher offers "Hail, to the gods!" and after slaying, "quieted is the victim" he offers "to the gods, hail!" Thus, some gods are preceded and some succeeded by hail!

(b) Offering of omentum or *vapa* - Once the slaughterer announces that the animal has been quieted, the wife of the sacrificer carries water to wipe the mouth, nostrils, eyes, ears, sexual organs and legs of the victim, and washes the remaining half of the body with the wound. They cut the animal and pull out the omentum from all sides of its belly. The *agnīdh* then heats the omentum and propitiates it while pouring *ghī* over it. With each drop that reaches the fire, "may *Agni* graciously accept the *ghī*, *svāhā* (hail)!" (I I I.8.2.21) is chanted. After the omentum is roasted, they cleanse themselves over the pit with Ṛg mantra.[20]

Next follow - (c) cake offerings or *paśu puroḍāśa* (d) cutting and offering of flesh portions (e) offering of gravy or vasa (f) offering to *vanaspati* (g) after-offerings (h) purificatory bath.

5. *Vasativari* water - It is the name for water used to extract *soma* juice. Before the sun sets on the day before *sutyā*, this water is fetched by dipping a pitcher against the current from a stream originating in a hill. The water is carried around the fire and altar by the *adhvaryu* and later mixed with the *ekadhanā* water (water brought earlier on the very day of pressing, mixed with *soma* juice and stored in a clay trough with large opening, *pūtabhṛt*), thereby transforming it into *nigrābhya*.[21]
6. The *agnīṣomiya* rite ends with *patnīsāmaveda yaja* (SB VI I.8). Literally meaning offerings made to the wives of gods, these are four offerings of *ājya* made to *Soma*, *Tvṣṭṛ*, the wives and *Agni gṛhapati*.
7. *Subrahmaṇya* brings in the jar water flowing from river which starts from mountain, filling it against the stream with appropriate utterances - this water is called *vasativari* water which is placed in *āgnīdhra* shed. Sacrificer keeps awake that night in *agnīdhra* shed and guards *soma* while wife keeps awake in *prāgvaṃśa* - the sacrificial hall.

Day 5 - The main events of the day are - The three *soma-savanas* (pressing of *soma*) and the principal-sacrifice, *dakṣiṇā*, *samiṣṭayajus-homa avbhṛta* and *udayanīyā iṣṭi*.

Savana constitutes the *soma* rite proper. It is the rite of pressing of *soma* stalks on *sutyā* day. The word '*savana*' designates time divisions of the *sutyā* day on which, besides the actual pressing, various other rites - such as *prātah savana* (morning pressing and service), *mdāhyānandī śrāddhana savana* (midday) and *tritīya savana* (the third pressing) - are performed. The climax is reached at the mid-day service.

The day starts very early - priests wake up soon after midnight in order to finish all actions up to *upāṃśu* before sunrise. *Adhvaryu* makes thirty three offerings of *ājya* - yajñatanu - in *agnīdhra* fire with mantras, various *pātras* are placed on the mounds, *upāṃśu* and *antarbṛhaspati* and *yamapātra* are kept between two gravan stones. Sitting between the yokes of the two *havirdhāna* carts, *hotṛ* recites *prātaranuvākya* (morning invocation) in three parts - called *kratu*. First is for *Agni*, second for *Uṣa* and third for *Aśvins*. In all about 2000 verses or nearly one fifth of Ṛgveda is recited in low or base (*mandrá*) scale, repeated if necessary, till sunrise. While morning invocation is going on, five offerings of cake on eleven potsherds for *Índra*, *dhana* (fried barley) for *Índra's* two bay horses - Haris, *karambha* (barley flour mixed with curd) for *Puṣān*, curd for *Sarasvati*, and payas for *Mitra* and *Varuna* are made.

Next, *adharvayu* goes to a pond and makes offering of *ājya* with the cup of *Maitra Varuṇa* to *Maitravaruna*, fills it with water - called *vasativari*. *Vasativari* water is poured in the *hotṛa's* cup to prepare *nigrabhya* water. Thereafter an offering of curds from cup called *dadhigraha* is made.

Savana - The 'little pressing' and 'the great one': *Upāṃśu* and *Mahābhishvana*

The 'little pressing' - *Upāṃśu*

Upāṃśugraha, sometimes simply referred as *upāṃśu*, is the name of first drawing of *soma* before sunrise in the 'morning pressing' which takes place without the recitation, except a few formulas muttered in silence without breathing or thinking. *Soma* stalks sufficient for one cup are taken out of the heap and placed over the *upara* stone (one of the lower crushing stones on which *soma* stalks are laid out for pressing). These are sprinkled with *nigrabhya* water (consecrated *vasativari* water) taken from *hotṛ's chamaṣa* and the stalks are pressed with the *upāṃśu savana* stones in three turns of eight, eleven and twelve beatings respectively. The extracted juice is poured into the *upāṃśu* cup without straining. This pressing is called small pressing (*kṣhullakābhiṣāva*) to distinguish it from 'the great pressing' (*mahābhiṣava*). A portion of it is offered in southern part of fire and a portion is kept in a vassel for keeping the drawing - called *āgrayanasthali*.

Mahābhiṣhava - This is the 'great' pressing of *soma* stalks for extraction of juice, which is then transferred in various cups (*graha*) for libation. The actual pressing is done by *adhvaru* and his assistants, *pratiprasthṛtṛṛ*, *neshtṛ* and *unnetṛ* in three rounds of three turns, with unlimited strokes of pressing stone (unlike the preliminary pressing where strokes are limited). This exercise is done three times on the final day of *soma* sacrifice: the morning pressing is called *pratahsavana*, the mid-day and afternoon pressings are called *madhyadina* and *tritīya savana* respectively. The ritual involves several acts which have been described in detail in texts like Āpastamba Śrauta Sūtras.

Extraction of *soma* juice

The *adhvaru* places the *upara* stone on a piece of red bull rawhide (*adhisavanacharma*), cut round and folded over four times (*puta*) for holding the pressing stones. *Soma* stalks are measured on the side and placed over the planks covered with red hide for pressing and extracting the juice.

Then comes the great principal pressing : *mahābhisava.*

Adhavaniya trough is filled with water by *adharvayu*. A large portion of *soma* stalks are brought and kept on *upara* stone on the hide, *nigrabhya* water poured on it and the stalks are beaten by the priests with other stone held in their right hand. This is called first round - *pāryaya*. Scattered stalks are collected into a vessel called *samabharaṇi* and transferred to *adhavaniya* trough which already contains water. The contents are thoroughly stirred, stalks are washed, pressed and taken out and placed on *adhysavana* hide for collecting the sediment or dregs (*ṛjsa*). The stalks are again kept on *upara* stone and sprinkled with water and pounded. This way the stalks are pounded three times (including *pāryaya*). The *droṇa kalaśa* is carried from its place and kept over four pressing stones by *udgātṛ* priests who spread over it a woollen strainer held on wooden frame or stool. *Unnetṛa* priest takes in a vessel *soma* liquid from *āhavanīya* trough, pours it into the *hotṛa camasa* containing *nigrabhya* water held by sacrificer, who pours a continuous stream onto the woollen strainer.

The filtered *soma* liquid is called *śukra* (pure). From the stream of *soma* juice flowing down from the (wool) strainer, several wooden cups are filled - the first being *antarbṛhaspati* and *yama* cup. Other cups - *a Índravaiva*, *maitra varuṇa*, *śukra*, *manthin*, *agrahayana*, *ukhtya*, *dhruva* - filled with *soma* are placed on various spots of mound. The *soma* that falls in *droṇa kalaśa* is called *śukra.*

The *upāṃśu* cup is offered before sunrise, while *adharvayu* offers *āntarbṛhaspati* and *yama* when the sun rises.

Viprudd homa is performed so that the *soma* drops spilt during the pressing of *soma* stalks reach the gods. These are four expiatory oblations of clarified butter performed by priests.

Bahishpavamāna stotra - *Stotra* chant during which *soma* is 'purified' is called *pavamāna stotra*. This is the first of the *stotras* chanted in *trivṛit* ('three fold') style (*ṣṭoma*) in the *soma* sacrifice and consists of nine verses of the Ṛgveda, i.e. X.1 1.1 - 3; 64.28 - 30; 66.10 - 12. This is called 'outside *pavamāna*' (*bahiṣ*) because the *stotra* in which *soma* is praised is chanted outside the *sadas* or *vedi.*

Next follow offering of *savanīya paśu*, in which an offering of goat is made to *Agni* (other details are similar to animal sacrifice given above), offerings of *puroḍāśa* cake, followed by *soma* libations to the seasons or *ritu graha*, *Índragana graha*, *vaiśvedevā graha* accompanied with *ājya śāstra*.

The *yajamāna* offers *samiṣṭa* (literally a *yajus* indicating end of a sacrifice) *homa* oblations - oblation to wind god. This ends the morning oblations.

Mid-day pressing or *Madhyānandina savanas*

Abhisavana (pressing of *soma*) rites of the morning are followed in mid day pressing too. *Yajamāna* and priests chant *pavamāna strota*. There are three pressings but there are no cups for joint deities and no cups for seasons.

Gravastut priest (an assistant priest who uses crushing stones) praises stones used in *soma* crushing, enters *havirdhāna* pavilion and takes cloth in his joined hands, folds it round his head and face from left to the right three times. When stalks of *soma* are placed before being crushed he recites *madhyānandī śrāddhana pavamana* (certain verses) during which *yajamāna* mutters several texts. Next comes *dadhigharma* ritual in which *pratiprasthatṛ* brings curd in *uḍumbara* wood ladel - curd is heated on *agnīdhriya* fire to the accompaniment of Ṛg mantra and offered in *āhavanīya* two times and the remnant eaten by those who had participated in *pravargya* rite. Then *paśu puroḍāśa* (cakes of the animal killed in the morning), and the other offerings, such as *puroḍāśa* on eleven potsherds are made and remnant eaten. Next ten cups are filled and offering of *soma* from the *śukra* and *manthin* cups are made by the priests and remainder *soma* partaken by priests and *yajamāna*. Thereafter the *yajamāna* gives the *dakṣiṇā* to the priests.

Dakṣiṇā - Three libations of *ājya* in the *shālāmukhiya* fire, accompanied with the solemn ceremony of giving sacrificial fees is called *dakṣiṇā homa*. If no fees is paid the sacrifice is considered singed and the sarificer is believed to become short-lived.

Numerous rules are given about the *dakṣiṇā*: SB (IV.3.4) states no priest should take less than 100 cows; it may consist of 7, 21, 60, 100, 112, or 1000 cattle or an unlimited number or a man may give all his wealth except the share of eldest son; when he gives thousand cattle or all his wealth, he is to give one mule in addition (Āp. S S. X I I I.5). A man may give his own daughter in marriage as fee.

On making gifts sacrificer does obeisance to the priests and utters an invocation as to animals donated with the words 'who gave to him.'

When the gifts are taken away by priests, the sacrificer casts away with two mantras, the antelope horn which he carries right through the entire *soma* sacrifice, in the *cātvāla*. *Adharvayu* offers five offerings of *ājya* called *vaishvvāmana* in fire with five mantras from Taittiriya. *Adharvayu* and *pratiprasthātṛ* take two cups for *Índra* (*Marutvat*) and offer them. Priests partake of the remnants and *strotas* and *śāstras* are recited.

Middle pressing comes to an end.

***Tritīya savana* or evening pressing - a series of rites in which various libations are offered** - These consist of *āditya graha prachar*, *abhishava*, *gragrahana*, *prasarpana*, *arbhvapavamanastotra*, *savaniya havi prachar*, *hotṛak achamsha prachar*, *savitṛ graha prachar*, *vaiśvadeva graha grahana*, *vaiśvedevā śāstras*, *vaiśvadeva graha prachar*, *sowmya caru* and *patnī vatagraha prachar* rituals. Drawing of *soma* (or any liquid) for libation is called *graha*; it also relates to cup. *Prachar* in Sanskrit is to proceed, in present context, to proceed to perform rite. *Śastra* is a verse which is recited, whereas *stotra* is a verse which is chanted.

Concluding ceremonies - The main events are *samiṣṭayajus*. These are *yajus* formula indicating completion of sacrifice. This is an *iṣṭi* connected with *Varuṇa* wherein the sacrificer, his wife and priests bathe either in a river or reservoir, and dispose various sacrificial implements/utensils smeared with *soma* into the water. This rite is called *avabhritheshti* and takes place in water, not fire. *Udaynīya iṣṭi* is the concluding *soma* rite at the end of *yajnapuchha*, i.e. tail of sacrifice. It is based on *prāyṇīyā* (described in the beginning) and is opposite of it.

Adharvayu takes *soma* from *āditya* cup, offers it in fire with two AV mantras, thereafter he consecrates *āśira*, a mixture of curd or milk mixed with *soma* prepared by the wife of sacrificer with AV mantras. Next *prastotṛ* chants *pavamāna strotra*, *agneyapaśu avadāna homa* is consecrated with mantra related to *Agni*, and thereafter *paśuekadaśni homa* is performed in which eleven animals of different colour and kind are offered to *Agni*, *Soma*, *Viṣṇu*, *Sarasvatī*, *Pūṣan*, *Bṛhaspati*, *Viśvedevā*, *Índra*, *Índragni*, *Savitar* and *Varuṇa*. *Brahmaṇa* consecrates these offerings with mantras. Next *savaniya puroḍāśas* of principal offerings are offered according to first two *savanas*, and *prasthita homa* in which *soma* libations are offered with AV mantras.

In *havirdhāna mandapa* priests and *yajamāna* place *puroḍāśa*, for their manes, in groups of three small portion each. These are consecrated by AV mantras. After partaking remnant offerings, *āgnīdhra* offers series of *homa* - *savitṛagraha homa*, *vaiśvadeva yājya* and *dhishnya dhiṣṇiya homa* respectively.

Thereafter *patnī vātahoma* is performed in which AV mantras are whispered (*upāṃśu*); in *vātahoma*, offerings of air are made by joining hands.

Next comes an action that has created a controversy. *Āgnīdhṛ* consumes remnants of *patnīvata* cup - sitting in the lap of *nestṛ* or near the *dhiṣṇiya* fire. While Kane, giving view of Āpastamba Śrauta Sūtras, says idea of sitting in lap is not appreciated[22], according to Āpastamba Śrauta 13.15.1 it results in impotence, and according to Gopatha Brahmaṇa (2.4.5) - partaking it in lap makes *yajamāna prajāvāna*[23].

After chanting *agniṣṭoma soma strota*, *dhruva*, *agnimaruta yājya homa*, *hari homa* are consecrated by *brahmaṇa* and *prāyaścitta* (expiation) rite is performed in *agnīdhṛa* fire.

Patnisamiṣṭayāja homa is performed next, in which oblations are offered to the spouses of the deity.

There after *dakṣiṇā*, according to previous pressings, is distributed.

With offerings of *samiṣṭayajus* and *samiṣṭa homa* in *āhavanīya* fire, third pressing comes to end. *Samiṣṭayajus* is a *yajus* formula indicating completion of a sacrifice.

Final purificatory bath

Yajamāna, wife, and all priests go to river or any other place of water for purificatory bath (*avabhṛtha*) after collecting articles placed near *cātvāla*. *Yajamāna* offers *homa* oblations with AV mantra in water, and *samsthita homa* oblations related to *pātras* of extractions of *soma*. After some oblations, *adhvaryu* throws utensils of pressing, and vessels, smeared with *soma* in water. At that time *yajamāna* offers oblations with mantras where *soma pātras* are thrown, puts *krişṇa mṛga charma* (black antelope skin) on earth, sprinkles it with water reciting mantras.

After sprinkling water on each other with hymns related to water - *apah* - and *pradakṣiṇā* (circumambulation) of water they return home reciting mantras.

After reaching *vedi* they pray to *āhavanīya* fire and offer *samidhas* in fire.

At the end of *iṣṭi* they touch their mouth with their hands reciting mantras.

Concluding rite or *Udaynīyeṣṭi*

This *soma* rite is at the end of *yajanpuchha*, i.e. tail of sacrifice. *Udaynīyeṣṭi* is performed on *prācīna vedi* - the rite is same as in in rite of initiation (the *prayāṇiyeṣṭi*).

All offerings are made in the same order with few exceptions.

Next is rite of *anubandhya* in which a sterile cow is immolated and offered to *Mitra* and *Varuṇa*[24], it follows the pattern of *nirūḍh paśu baṃdha*.[25]

Once the performance is complete, the *sadas* (cart shed), *āgnīdhṛa* (firehouse) and other temporary structures are set on fire, and the sacrificer and priests go home.

T-1 : Puranas

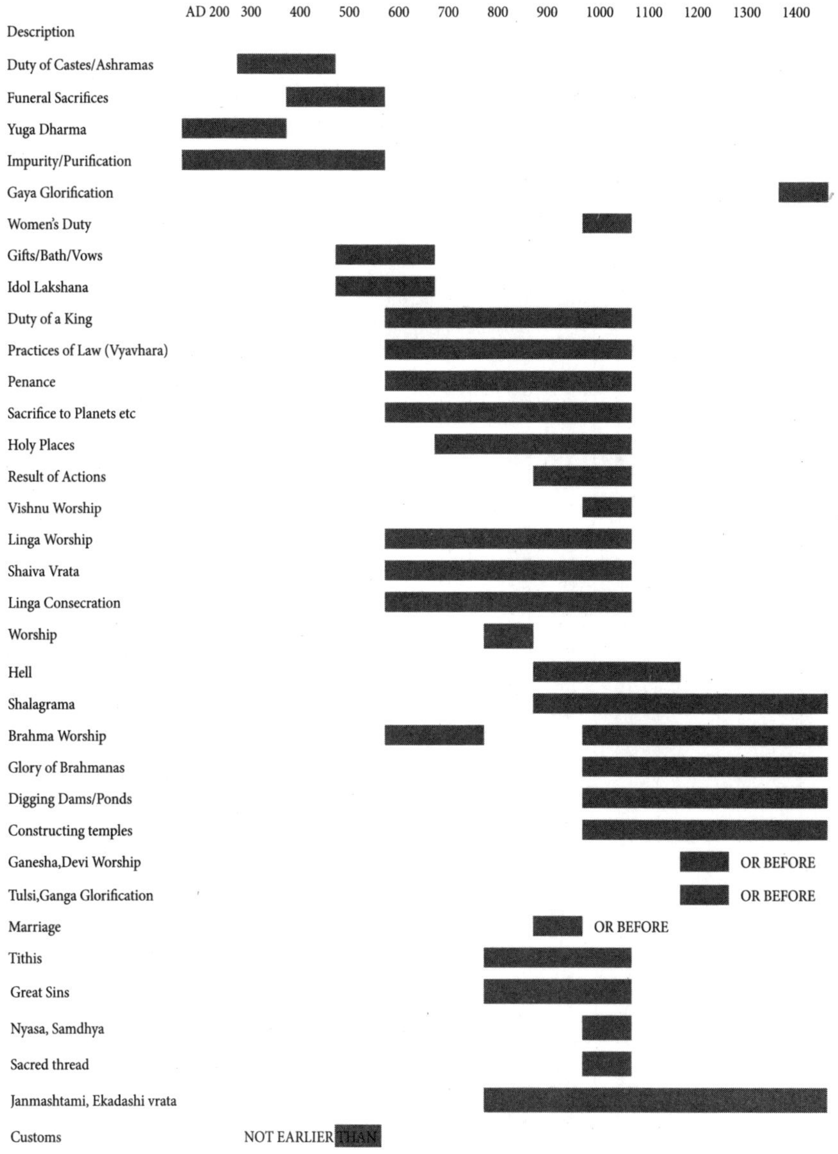

Chart showing Time period in which Hindu practices/ customs evolved (Found first mention in different Puranas).

X-axis is year in AD; Y-axis gives description of practice/ custom.

T-2 : Saṃskāra

	Gauta-ma	Vaikh	Angiras	Apstam-ba	Ashva-layan	Baud-hayan	Gobhila	Hiren.	Katyaya-na	Khadira	Manu	Yaj	Veda Vyasa	Parasar	Sank	Present Day
Descripton of Samskara														13		16
Ritu-samagama		***														
Garbhadhana /Chaturhikarma/Niseka/ Homa	***	***		***	***	***					***	***		***	***	***
Pumsvana	***	MOST														***
Garbharakshana					***										***	
Simantonayana	***	ALL														***
Vishnubali		***	***			***										
Sosyanti-karma or homa				***			***	***		***						
Jatakarma	***	ALL														***
Utthana		***													***	
Namakarana	***	ALL														***
Nishkramana/ Adityadarshan/Nir-nayana											***	***		***	***	***
Karnavedha									***				***			***
Annaprasana	***	MOST														***
Varshavardhana/Abdapurti						***	***							***	***	
Chaula/Chudakarma/Chudakarna	***	ALL														***
Vidyarambha		NOT IN ANY SMRITY BUT IN MARKENDEYAPURANA QUOTED BY APARARKA AND SMRI-TY CHANDRIKA														***
Upanayana	***	ALL														***
Vratas(4)/ Vedarambha		MOST														***
Keshanta/Godana		ALL														***
Samavartana/ Snana	***			***	***	***	***	***			***	***		***	***	***
Vivaha		ALL			***											***
Mahayajnas(5)		MOST				Angiras,	Gautama	& OTH-ERS								
Utsarga		***	***													
Upakarma		***	***													***
Antyshti					***	***					***	***		***		

A chart displaying list of Saṃskāra, and Smrity texts (by various sages) in which Saṃskāra finds a place.

***- Indicates presence in the Smrity
ALL – Indicates presence in all Smritys
MOST – Indicates presence in most of the Smritys

T-3 : Pūjā

Year 1918	Year 1930	Year 1985	Year 2014
Acmana	Achmana	Achmana	Achmana
Snana	Pranayama	Pranayama	Dhyana
Offering Tulsi	Ganapati & other deity Adorataion	Devatavandana	Asana shuddhi
Samanya Arghya	"Hymns of praise to Ganesha, Gauri, Vishnu"	Prarthana	Manasa puja
Asana Shuddhi	Co-ordinates etc	Deshkaloccharana - Samkalpa	Ganaesha Smarana
Pushpa shuddhi	Samkalpa	Ganapati Smarana	Samkalpa
Driving away elements	Coordinates etc	Asanavidhi	Ghanta Pujan
Bhuta shuddhi	Contemplation on Ganapati	Nyasa	Shankha Pujan
Pranayama	Asanavidhi	Kalasha Puja	Kalasha Puja
Panch Deva Puja	Nyasa	Shankha Puja	Panch Deva Smaran
All Deva Puja	"Invocation of Rivers to jar & Chandana, flower etc offerings"	Ghanta Puja	**Upacharas**
Nyasa	Invocation Conch shell, Bell etc	Dipa Puja	Arati
Gurupranama	Sprinkling of self & material	Prokshana	Shankha bhramana
Dhyana-Narayana	Dhyana of Panch Devas	Dhyana	Pradakshina
Second Dhyana	**Upacharas**	**Upacharas**	Mantra Pushpanjali
Special Arghya	Final benedictiction	Prarthana	Namaskar
Upacharas		Samkalpapurti	Charnamrat paan
Japa		Tirthagrahana	Atonement
Nivedana			Prasad grahana
Pranama			

Upacharas	1918	1930	1985	2018
Avahana		X	**	
Asana		X	**	
Padya	scv	X	**	*
Arghya	scv	X	**	*
Achmana	scv	X	**	*
Panchamrata snana		X	**	*
Gandhdaka snana			**	*
Shudhodaka snana			**	*
Achmana				
Vastra- Upavasrea		X	**	*
Abhushana or yajnopavita		X	**	*
Achmana				
Chandana	scv	X	**	*
Pushpamala	scv	X	**	*
Tulsidala Manjari				
Dhoop		X	**	*
Deep	scv	X	**	*
Naivaidya	scv	X	**	*
Achmana	scv	X		*
Tarpana	scv	X		*
Karpoor Arati-Stavapatha		X		*
Rituphala				
Tambula	scv	X		*
Namaskara/Dakshina		X	**	*
Pradkkshina		X	**	
Visarjana/ mantra-push-panjali			**	

Chart showing how Actions in Puja changed in last 100 years - from year 1918 thru 2014. Upachara column indicates how upacharas changed in corresponding years.

Year 1918 -Vasu Srisa C(2008). The Daily Practice of Hindus. New Delhi. Cosmo Publications. p128ff.

1930 - Kane PV(1997). *History of Dharmshastra*, Vol II, partII. Pune, Bhandarkar Oriental Research Institute, p.739

1985 - Buhnemann Gudrun (1988), Puja- A study in Smṛta Ritual, Viennna, Publication of The Nobilei Research Library, p.63ff

2014 -Mishra PP (Samvat 20171). Nityakarm Puja Prakasha. Gorakhpur. Gita Press. p 129ff

Upachars : scv indicates upacharas in 1918, x indicates upacharas in 1930, ** indicates upacharas in 1985, and * indicates upacharas in 2014.

References and Notes

Prologue

Are we Āryans?

The Beginning: From Mehrgarh to Surkotada Horse

1. This is reported in an International journal of science by research scholars of IIT - Kharagpur. Their work shows declining monsoon in the areas inhabited by the pre-Harappan to mature Harappan civilization resulted in decline of the Indus valley Harappan civilization. According to the paper - 'Isotope and archaeological data suggest that the pre-Harappans started inhabiting this area along the mighty Ghaggar-Hakra rivers fed by intensified monsoon from 9 to 7kaBP.' Here 'ka' denotes kilo year i.e. 1000 years, and BP stands for 'Before Present'. Sarkar A, Deshpande Mukherji A, Bera MK, Das B, Juyal N, Morthekai P, Deshpande RD, Shinde VS & Rao LS (2016). *Oxygen isotope in archaeological biopatites from India: Implications to climate change and decline of Bronze Age Harappan civilization.* Scientific Reports volume 6, Article number: 26555 (2016). p.1 Published in nature, an international journal of science. Available from: https://www.nature.com/articles/srep26555
2. Sindhav HD Dr (2016). *The Indus Valley Civilization (Harappan Civilization).* In: International Journal of Social Impact (Vol. 1, Issue 2, DIP:18.02.015/20160102) April-June, 2016 Makvana SM Ed.Lunawad. Red Shine Publication. p.101 cit Davreau, Robert (1976). "Indus Valley". In Reader's Digest. World's Last Mystries. For more details readers may read - Davreau Robert, World's Last Mysteries. Reader's Digest, 1976; ISBN 089577044X, 9780895770448. Available from: https://www.cse.iitk.ac.in/users/amit/books/davreau-1976-worlds-last-mysteries.html
3. Dalal R (2014). *The Vedas*. New Delhi, Penguin Group, p. 174
4. Dalal R (2014). *The Vedas*. New Delhi, Penguin Group, pp. 174-76
5. Kalibangan-1 or KLB-1 - is period from 3500-2800 BC to 2500-1750 BC
6. Dalal R (2014). *The Vedas*. New Delhi, Penguin Group, p.175
7. Majumdar RC (2003). *Ancient India*. Delhi, Motilal Banarsi Dass
8. Dalal R (2014). *The Vedas*. New Delhi, Penguin Group, p.184
9. Ratnagar S (2008). *The End of the Harappan Civilisation*. In: Trautmann TR Ed. The Aryan Debate, New Delhi, Oxford University Press, p.131
10. Staal Frits(2014). *Discovering the Vedas*. Gurgaon, Penguin Group
11. Trautmann TR (2008). In: *Trautmann TR Ed. The Aryan Debate*. New Delhi, Oxford University Press, p.xl.

12. Lal BB. *It is Time to Rethink.* In: Trautmann TR Ed.The Aryan Debate, New Delhi, Oxford University Press, p.153

13a,b. Gupta SP (2008). *Indus Sarasvatī Civilisation.* In: Trautmann TR Ed. The Aryan Debate, New Delhi, Oxford University Press, p. 183 & 189

14. Parpola A(2008). *The Horse and the Language of the Indus Civilisation.* In: Trautmann TR Ed.The Aryan Debate, New Delhi, Oxford University Press, p. 235

15. Parpola A(2008). *The Horse and the Language of the Indus Civilisation.* In: Trautmann TR Ed. The Aryan Debate, New Delhi, Oxford University Press, p.236

Chapter 1

Arrival of Āryans and Vedas

1. Macdonell AA (1897). *Vedic mythology.* Strassburg. Verlag Von Karl J. Trubner. p.1. Available from: https://archive.org/details/vedicmythology00macduoft/page/n9
2. Monier W (1974). *Religious Thought and Life in India.* New Delhi, Oriental Books Reprint Corporation. p.7
3. Monier W (1974). Religious Thought and Life in India. New Delhi, Oriental Books Reprint Corporation.p.7

Chapter 2

Hinduism – Dharma, not A Religion

1. Anthony David W (2007). The Horse The Wheel And Language. Princeton. Princeton University Press. p.462
2. White David G (2003). Kiss of the yogini: "Tantric Sex" In Its South Asian Contexts. Chicago. The Chicago University Press. p.28 cit Bernard Sergent. According to White, the J. F. Rowny Professor of Comparative Religions at the University of California, Santa Barbara-many scholars-like Asko Parpola, Frits Staal and Bernard Sergent, have 'emphatically demonstrated' that 'the religion of the Vedas was already a composite of the Indo-Aryan and Harappan cultures and civilization'.
3. The New Encylopaedia Britannica (1990).Vol. 20, p. 519
4. Eraly Abraham (2002). Gem in the Lotus. New Delhi. Penguin Books, p.215 quote, "And sometimes they-even Buddha and Mahavira- hurled dire invectives against each other."

Chapter 3

Dharma – What is it if not 'religion'?

1. Manu (I I.4) (2009). In: tr. Buhler G, Max Muller F Ed. The Sacred Books Of The East (Vol.25).Delhi. Motilal Banarsidass
2. The Kama Sutra of Vatsyayana (1883) tr. By Richard Burton (1883) Ch. II, pp.1-20 retrieved from http://www.sacred-texts.com/sex/kama/kama102.htm
3. Bhandarkar DR (1989). Some Aspects of Ancient Indian Culture. New Delhi, Asian educational Services, p.67

Chapter 4

Hindu Dharma and its Sources

1. Ādi Parva,MB, chapter 74.162.
2. The Chandogya Upanishad (2009). In: Max Muller F Ed. The Sacred Books Of The East (Vol.1).Delhi. Motilal Banarsidass
3. The Taittriyaka Upanishad (1.11.1) (2009). In: Max Muller F Ed. The Sacred Books Of The East (Vol.15). Delhi. Motilal Banarsidass
4. Pandey UC (1966). The Gautama Dharma Sutra.Varanasi. Chowkhamba Sanskrit Series Office, p.18 citing Mckenzie,Hindu ethics p. 38
5. Monier W (2003). Indian Wisdom. New Delhi, Rupa & Co. p. 1706.
6. Kane PV (1997). History of Dharmshastra, Vol I. Pune, Bhandarkar Oriental Research Institute, p.10 7.
7. Pandey UC (1966). The Gautama Dharma Sutra.Varanasi. Chowkhamba Sanskrit Series Office, p.9

Chapter 5

Sanatana Dharma

1. Santana Dharma. Encylopaedia Britannica. Available from https://www.britannica.com/topic/sanatana-dharma
2. Besant Annie & Bhagwan Das (2002). Sanatana Dharma.Chennai, The Theosophical Publishing House, p.3
3. Bharathi KS (1998). Encyclopaedia of Eminent Thinkers, Shri Aurobindo, Volume 6. New Delhi. Cocept Publishing Company, p.84 The Uttarapara Speeches, op. cit. p 20
4. Mall RA (2000), Intercultural Philosophy, Lanbam, Rowman & Littlefield Publishers, Inc., p.29

5a,b. Bhandarkar DR (1989). Some Aspects of Ancient Indian Culture. New Delhi, Asian educational Services, p.67, pp.67-68

6. Bose ML (1998). Social and Cultural History of India. New Delhi. Concept Publishing House, pp.40-41, f.n.70

Chapter 6

Earliest Body of Indian Scripture: Veda

1. Monier W (1974). *Religious Thought and Life in India.* New Delhi, Oriental Books Reprint Corporation, p.7
2. Kothari Rita (1999). *Indian Literature in English Translation: The Social Context* (Thesis for Degree of Doctor of Philosophy), p.22 superscription 27 citing PJ Marshall,ed The British Discovery of Hinduism in the Eighteenth Century (London: Cambridge UP, 1970) 189. Available from http://shodhganga.inflibnet.ac.in/bitstream/10603/46404/9/09_chapter%202.pdf.
3. Kothari Rita (1999). Indian Literature in English Translation: The Social Context (Thesis for Degree of Doctor of Philosophy), p.25 superscription 32 citing Majeed J, Ungoverned Imaginings: James Mill's The History of British India and Orientalism (Oxford: Calrendon Press,1992) p.20. Available from http://shodhganga.inflibnet.ac.in/bitstream/10603/46404/9/09_chapter%202.pdf
4. Kothari Rita (1999).Indian Literature in English Translation: The Social Context (Thesis for Degree of Doctor of Philosophy), p.26 citing Said E, Orientalism (New York) : Vintage Books,1979), p.78. Available from: http://shodhganga.inflibnet.ac.in/bitstream/10603/46404/9/09_chapter%202.pdf
5. *The Upanishad* (2009). In: tr. Max Muller F Ed. The Sacred Books Of The East (Vol. 15). Delhi. Motilal Banarsidass, p.Ixi.
6. Molendijk AL (2016). *Friedrich Max Muller and the Sacred Books of the East.* Oxford. Oxford University Press, p.15
7. Molendijk AL (2016). *Friedrich Max Muller and the Sacred Books of the East.* Oxford. Oxford University Press, p.15.

8a. Molendijk AL (2016). *Friedrich Max Muller and the Sacred Books of the East.* Oxford. Oxford University Press, p.15.

8b. Molendijk AL (2016). Friedrich Max Muller and the Sacred Books of the East. Oxford. Oxford University Press, p.16

9. Molendijk AL (2016). *Friedrich Max Muller and the Sacred Books of the East. Oxford.* Oxford University Press, p.20.
10. P.J. Marshall Ed. (1970). *The British Discovery of Hinduism in the Eighteenth Century.* London. Cambridge University Press, p. 189 fn 27 Max Muller.

11. Gaurinath Sastri (1998). *A Concise History of Sanskrit Literature*. Delhi. Motilal Banarsidass, p.15.
12. Abhyakar Tryambak B(2010), Svaramanjari, 7. Available from http://sanskritdocuments.org Accessed on Dt. 271018.
13. Gaurinath Sastri (1998). *A Concise History of Sanskrit Literature*. Delhi. Motilal Banarsidass, p.16.
14. Monier-Williams Sir Monier(2010). A Sanskrit English Dictionary. New Delhi. Bhartiya Grantha Niketan, p.x- p.s. to Prefacw by Monier's son, dated - May 1899, Preface.
15. Monier W(2003). Indian Wisdom. New Delhi, Rupa & Co.p.182

Chapter 7

Constituents of Vedas

1. Encyclopaedia Britannica, Pyramid Texts: Ancient Chinese Text. Available at https://www.britannica.com/topic/Pyramid-Texts
2. Mark Joshua J(2018). *Enuma Elish - The Babylonian Epic Of Creation*. Ancient History Encyclopaedia. Available at https://www.ancient.eu/article/225/enuma-elish---the-babylonian-epic-of- creation---fu/
3. Encyclopaedia Britannica, Yijing: Ancient Chinese Text. Available at https://www.britannica.com/topic/Yijing [Accessed on 251016]
4. Dalal R (2014). *The Vedas*. New Delhi, Penguin Group, p.294.
5. Wilson HH. *Rigveda* Sanhita, N Trubner & Co.p.ix.
6. Wilson HH (1866). *Rigveda* Sanhita, N Trubner & Co.p.I.
7. Wilson HH (1866). *Rigveda* Sanhita,London, N Trubner & Co.pp.1-9.
8. Monier W (2003). *Indian Wisdom*. New Delhi, Rupa & Co.p.9.
9. Monier W (2003). *Indian Wisdom*. New Delhi, Rupa & C,p.xxxix.
10. Wilson HH (1866). *Rigveda Sanhita*. London, N Trubner & Co. p.viii.
11 Wilson HH (1866). Rigveda Sanhita, London, N Trubner & Co. p.viii.
12. Monier W (2003). *Indian Wisdom*. New Delhi, Rupa & Co.p.27
13. Dalal R (2014). *The Vedas*. New Delhi, Penguin Group,p.288.
14. http://www.censusindia.gov.in/Census_Data_2001/Census_Data_Online/Language/Statement1.aspx Dt. 03072018

Chapter 8

Ṛg - The Collection Mantras

1. Saxena Dr Pravesh (2003) *Vedoṃ meṃ kyā hai?,* Delhi, Pustaka Mahal, p.29
2. RV(VI 27. 7-8).
3. *Śatapatha Brāhmaṇa* (11.5.1) (2009). In: Max Muller F Ed. The Sacred

Books Of The East vol. 40). Delhi. Motilal Banarsidass Urvaṣi narrative

4. RV(X. 10)
5. RV(X. 108)
6. Monier W (2003). Indian Wisdom. New Delhi, Rupa & Co.p.27. Hymn to Night - RV(X.127)
7. RV (VIII.29.1-4),
8. Monier W(2003). Indian Wisdom. New Delhi, Rupa & Co.p.25. *Puruṣasūkta* RV(X.90) - not translated literally.
9. *Monier W(2003). Indian Wisdom. New Delhi, Rupa & Co.* p. 23. *Nasadiyasūkta* or the Sūkta of CreationRV(X.129)

Chapter 9

Yajur - The Veda of Rituals

1. Dalal R (2014).*The Vedas*. New Delhi, Penguin Group, p.10
2. Dalal R (2010). *Hinduism An Alphabetical Guide.* New Delhi, Penguin
3. Dalal R (2010). *Hinduism An Alphabetical Guide.* New Delhi, Penguin
4. Mehta BS (1990). *Critical and Comparative Study of Vaitana Srauta Sutra : With special reference to the Srauta Sacrifices* - Thesis for Doctor of Philosophy.p216.Avaible from: http://shodhganga.inflibnet.ac.in/handle/10603/116852
5. Saxena Dr Pravesh (2003) *Vedoṃ meṃ kyā hai?,* Delhi, Pustaka Mahal, p.94
6. *Shukla,* sixteenth *adhyāya* and *Kṛṣṇa, adhyāya* (4-5).

Chapter 10

***Sāma* – The Veda of Songs**

1. Staal Frits (2014). *Discovering the Vedas*. Gurgaon, Penguin Group, p.4
2. Witzel Michael (n.d.). *The Development of Vedic Canon and its School : The Social and Political Milieu*, p.269 fn 49. Available at http://www.people.fas.harvard.edu/~witzel/canon.pdf
3. Staal Frits (2014). Discovering the Vedas. Gurgaon, Penguin Group, p.107
4. Staal Frits (2014). *Discovering the Vedas*. Gurgaon, Penguin Group, pp. 107-08
5. Staal Frits (2014). *Discovering the Vedas*. Gurgaon, Penguin Group, p.115
6. Dalal R (2014). *The Vedas*. New Delhi, Penguin Group, p.19
7. Monier W (2003). *Indian Wisdom*. New Delhi, Rupa & Co. p.174
8. Saxena Dr Pravesh (2003) *Vedoṃ meṃ kyā hai?*. Delhi, Pustaka Mahal, p.107

Chapter 11

Atharva – Veda?

1. Dalal R (2010), *Hinduism An Alphabetical Guide.* New Delhi, Penguin Group
2. *Hymns of the Atharvaveda* (2009). In:Max Muller F Ed. The Sacred Books Of The East (Vol.42). Delhi. Motilal Banarsidass, p. xvii.
3. *Hymns of the Atharvaveda* (2009). In:Max Muller F Ed. The Sacred Books Of The East (Vol.42). Delhi. Motilal Banarsidass, p.lxxiii.
4. Witzel Michael (n.d.). The Development of Vedic Canon and its School : The Social and Political Milieu, p.281. Available from: http://www.people.fas.harvard.edu/~witzel/canon.pdf
5. Brockington J (2005). *The Origins Of Indian Philosophy.* In Brian Carr, Indira Mahalingam, Companion Encyclopedia of Asian Philosophy (part II Indian Philosophy) Taylor & Francis e-Library, p.91.
6. *The Laws Of Manu* (1991) translated by Doniger W & Smith BK, New Delhi, Penguin Books India (P) Ltd, p.xviii.
7. *Hymns of the Atharvaveda* (2009). In:Max Muller F Ed. The Sacred Books Of The East (Vol.42). Delhi. Motilal Banarsidass, p.xxxi.
8. *Hymns of the Atharvaveda* (2009). In: tr. Bloomfield M, Max Muller F Ed. The Sacred Books Of The East (Vol.42). Delhi. Motilal Banarsidass,p.xxxi.
9. *Hymns of the Atharvaveda* (2009). In: tr. Bloomfield M, Max Muller F Ed. The Sacred Books Of The East (Vol.42). Delhi. Motilal Banarsidass, p.xxxii.
10. *of the Atharvaveda* (2009). In: tr. Bloomfield M, Max Muller F Ed. The Sacred Books Of The East (Vol.42). Delhi. Motilal Banarsidass, p.xxxiv
11. *Hymns of the Atharvaveda* (2009). In: tr. Bloomfield M, Max Muller F Ed. The Sacred Books Of The East (Vol.42). Delhi. Motilal Banarsidass, p.xxxv.
12. *Hymns of the Atharvaveda* (2009). In: tr. Bloomfield M, Max Muller F Ed. The Sacred Books Of The East (Vol.42). Delhi. Motilal Banarsidass,p.xliv
13. *Hymns of the Atharvaveda* (2009). In: tr. Bloomfield M, Max Muller F Ed. The Sacred Books Of The East (Vol.42). Delhi. Motilal Banarsidass,p.xlv
14. *Hymns of the Atharvaveda* (2009). In: tr. Bloomfield M, Max Muller F Ed. The Sacred Books Of The East (Vol.42). Delhi. Motilal Banarsidass,p.lxix
15. *Hymns of the Atharvaveda* (2009). In: tr. Bloomfield M, Max Muller F Ed. The Sacred Books Of The East (Vol.42). Delhi. Motilal Banarsidass, pp.lxx-lxxi
16. *Hymns of the Atharvaveda* (2009). In: tr. Bloomfield M, Max Muller F Ed. The Sacred Books Of The East (Vol.42). Delhi. Motilal Banarsidass,p.lxxi

Chapter 12

The Ritual Sacrifice - *Yajña*

1. Monier W (1974). *Religious Thought and Life in India*. New Delhi, Oriental Books Reprint Corporation, pp.11-13

1a. Apastamba Yajña Paribāhaṣa Sūtras (Sūtra1) (2009). In:Max Muller F Ed. The Sacred Books Of The East (Vol.30,part 2). Delhi. Motilal Banarsidass. p.315

2. *Manu II.4* (2009). In:Max Muller F Ed. The Sacred Books Of The East (Vol.25). Delhi. Motilal Banarsidass

3. T*he Kama Sutra of Vatsyayana* (1883) tr. By Richard Burton, Ch.II, pp.1-20. Available from: http://www.sacred-texts.com/sex/kama/kama102.htm

4. *Apastamba Yajña Paribāhaṣa Sūtras (sutra I)* (2009). In: Max Muller F Ed. The Sacred Books Of The East (Vol.30,part 2). Delhi. Motilal Banarsidass

5. Śatapatha Brāhmaṇa (I.9.3.1)(2009). In: Max Muller F Ed. The Sacred Books Of The East (Vol.12). Delhi. Motilal Banarsidass

6. Śatapatha Brāhmaṇa (2.2.3.28) (2009). In: Max Muller F Ed. The Sacred Books Of The East (Vol.12). Delhi. Motilal Banarsidass

7. *Ashvalayana Grihya Sutras* (I.9.1-2) (2009). In: tr. Oldenberg H & Max Muller F Ed. The Sacred Books Of The East (Vol.30). Delhi. Motilal Banarsidass, p.172

8. Many texts have explained why Mahayajnas are called great. *Taittirīya Āraṇyaka* II. 10 and Apstamba Dharma Sutra (1.4.12.14) are just two of many such examples.

9. *Manusmṛti* 3.68, The Laws Of Manu (1991) translated by Doniger W & Smith BK, New Delhi, Penguin Books India(P) Ltd.

10. *Grihya Sutras* (2009). In: tr. Oldenberg H & Max Muller F Ed. The Sacred Books Of The East (Vol.30). Delhi. Motilal Banarsidass, p.xxi.

11. *Grihya Sutras* (2009). In: tr. Oldenberg H & Max Muller F Ed. The Sacred Books Of The East (Vol.30). Delhi. Motilal Banarsidass, p.xxii

12. *Grihya Sutras* (2009). In: tr. Oldenberg H & Max Muller F Ed. The Sacred Books Of The East (Vol.30). Delhi. Motilal Banarsidass, p.xvii f.n.

13. Śatapatha Brāhmaṇa (I .5.1) (2009). In: Max Muller F Ed. The Sacred Books Of The East (Vol.29). Delhi. Motilal Banarsidass

14. Charles Malamoud (1998). *Cooking the World: Aspects of Hindu Castes and Ritual*. Delhi.Oxford University Press, p.36 page 28.

15. Buhler G (2009). *Sacred Laws of the Aryas*. In: Max Muller F Ed. The Sacred Books Of The East(Vol.14).Delhi. Motilal Banarsidass, p.xxxi, fn. 1- citing Baudhāyana

16. Sen C (2001). A *Dictionary of the Vedic Rituals*. Delhi.Concept Publishing Company, p.73
17. Sen C (2001). A Dictionary of the Vedic Rituals. Delhi. Concept Publishing Company, p.114
18. Sen C (2001). A *Dictionary of the Vedic Rituals*. Delhi,Concept Publishing Company, p.113, 115
19. Sen C (2001). A *Dictionary of the Vedic Rituals*. Delhi, Concept Publishing Company, p.93
20. Sen C (2001). A *Dictionary of the Vedic Rituals*. Delhi, Concept Publishing Company, p.70
21. Sen C (2001). A *Dictionary of the Vedic Rituals*. Delhi, Concept Publishing Company, p.43
22. Dalal R (2014). *The Vedas*. New Delhi, Penguin Group, p 264.
23. Tripathi V. *Agnicayana* (1990). Varanasi. HCM Tripathi, Sampurnanand Sanskrit University
24. *Śatapatha Brāhmaṇa* (2009). tr. Eggling In: Max Muller F Ed. The Sacred Books Of The East (Vol. 41). Delhi. Motilal Banarsidass, page xxxviii.
25. *Śatapatha Brāhmaṇa* (2009). tr. Eggling In: Max Muller F Ed. The Sacred Books Of The East (Vol. 41). Delhi. Motilal Banarsidass. In SB. VI.2.1 the names of the five victims- including head of a human - is clearly indicated. Subsequently, in SB. VI I. 5.2, once again detailed reasoning, why the four animals and a human head are chosen, is given. Apart from what Eggling says about this refers to a practice which was long shunned, there are texts which say the head of a man who had died due to reasons other than natural death, was sought for the sacrifice.

Chapter 13

Soma Yajna

1. *Mahānarayananopnishad* (section 79/9)(1968). tr. Swami Vimlananda. Madras. The President, Sri Ramkrishna Math, Mylapore. p.335

Chapter 14

Soma Yajña Ritualss

1. Alvar RS(2010). *An Introduction to Somayagnas and Vedic Yagnas in General*, eds. Laksmithathachar MA, Alwar MA. Mysore, Samskriti Foundation, p.27. Available at https://archive.org/details/an_introduction_to_somayagnyas_and_vedic_yagnyas_in_general [Accessed 18th June 2015]

2. RV. VI I I.4 8.6. (J&B)
3. Śatapatha Brāhmaṇa (3.1.1.9) (2009). In: Max Muller F Ed. The Sacred Books Of The East (Vol.26). Delhi. Motilal Banarsidass

Chapter 15

From Action to Knowledge – Veda to Vedānta

1. *RV (IV. 57) verse 5,7 and 8 (2017).* In: tr. Jamison SW, Brereton JP. New Delhi. Oxford University Press
2. Eraly Abraham (2011). *The First Spring*: *The Golden Age of India*. New Delhi. Penguin Books, p.194
3. *The Munduka Upanishad (III.1.5)*(2009). In: tr. Max Muller F Ed. The Sacred Books Of The East (Vol. 15). Delhi. Motilal Banarsidass
4. *The Kaushitaki Upanishad (I.2)*(2009). In: tr. Max Muller F Ed. The Sacred Books Of The East (Vol. 1).Delhi. Motilal Banarsidass
5. Ford James L (2016). *The Divine Quest : East and West*. Albany. State University of New York Press, p.142
6. Aslan Reza (2013). *Zealot*. Noida. Harper Collins. p.37

Chapter 16

Questioning Minds and Unanswered Questions

1. *Maha-bharata(Book 12, Vol. 3)(2017).* tr Wyenne Alexander.New York. New York University Press. p.xviii.cit TW Rhys Davids (1908:47). Wynne calls 'Ancient India, in the last few centuries BCE' as a land of great fervor. It was a time when its 'religious culture had exploded into life with a movement of world - renunciation'. According to Wyenne this was on an unprecedented scale, and 'peripatetic sages meditated under trees, devout ascetics practiced austerities in forest groves, and wandering sophists conducted debates in the towns and cities. There has been nothing comparable before and since'.p.xviii.
2. *The Munduka Upanishad (III.1.5) (2009).* In: tr.Max Muller F Ed. The Sacred Books Of The East (Vol. 15). Delhi. Motilal Banarsidass
3. Ref. Pali Language in Encyclopaedia Britannica. Available from: https://www.britannica.com/topic/Pali-language
4. *Buddhist Suttas* (2009). In: tr. Rhys David TW, Max Muller F Ed. The Sacred Books Of The East (Vol. 11). Delhi. Motilal Banarsidass, pp.298 - 300
5. Kane PV(1997). History of Dharmshastra, Vol I, partI. Pune, Bhandarkar Oriental Research Institute, p.943

6. *The Saundarananda Of Ashvaghosha* (XVI. 28 – 29)(1928). Johnnston EH Ed.London. Oxford University Press.
7. Kane PV (1997). *History of Dharmshastra*, Vol I, partI. Pune, Bhandarkar Oriental Research Institute, p.10
8. Kane PV (1997). History of Dharmshastra, Vol I, part I. Pune, Bhandarkar Oriental Research Institute, p.944

Chapter 17

The Reforms: Upaniṣads

1. Black B (2007). *The Character of the Self in Ancient India*. Albany. State university of New York press, p.4
2. Max Muller (2009). *The Upanishads*. In:Max Muller F Ed. The Sacred Books Of The East(Vol.1). Delhi. Motilal Banarsidass, p.xxxiii
3. Arthur Schopenhauer was a German philosopher (1788-1866) often called 'philosopher of pessimism' and is known as exponent of metaphysical doctrine of the will (Britannica). The above quote is his famous reaction after he was exposed to Upanishads. Ref. Max Muller (2009). *The Upanishads.* In:Max Muller F Ed. The Sacred Books Of The East (Vol.1). Delhi. Motilal Banarsidass, p.Ixi
4. Max Muller (2009). *The Upanishads*. In: Max Muller F Ed. The Sacred Books Of The East (Vol.1). Delhi. Motilal Banarsidass, p.lxviii
5. Deussen: *A.G.Ph., I.2.S.22f.* Deussen adds that he published a chronological theory of the same import in *Transactions of the Third International Congress for the History of Religions*, II,Oxford, 1908, pp.19-24. Deussen(1908). Transactions of the Third International Congress for the History of Religions, II. In: Nakamura Hajime (1983), *A History of Early Vedānta Philosophy*, Part One, tr. Leffett T, Mayeda S, Unno T & others, Ed. Lancaster LR & Shastri JL, Delhi. Motilal Banarsidass, p.10. Available at https://archive.org/details/AHistoryOfEarlyVedantaPhilosophyHajimeNakamura

Chapter 18

The Upanishadic Reforms

1. *The Chandogya Upanishad* (IV.1.4-5) (2009). In: Max Muller F Ed. The Sacred Books Of The East (Vol.1). Delhi. Motilal Banarsidass
2. *The Chandogya Upanishad* (IV.1.3-5) (2009). In: Max Muller F Ed. The Sacred Books Of The East (Vol.1). Delhi. Motilal Banarsidass
3. The legend of Mathava, according to Prof Weber distinguishes three successive stages of the eastward migration of Brahminical Hindus. In

the first stage- in the times of Rigveda hymns - they were already settled in Punjab region as far as Sarasvati, then they pushed east, as far as river Sadanira, led by Mathava the king and his priest of this legend. This formed the eastern boundary of Videha. *Śatapatha Brāhmaṇa (I .4 .1 .10; 14-17) (2009). In: Max Muller F Ed. The Sacred Books Of The East (Vol.12). Delhi. Motilal Banarsidass*

4. Olivelle Patrick (1996). *Upanishads*. Oxford. Oxford University Press. p.xxxv
5. *The Aitreya Aranyaka*. Tr. & Ed. AB Keith. (1909). Oxford. Clarendon Press. p.15. According to Keith, the secret explanation tended to grow independent of ritual until Araṇyaka passed onto the Upaniṣad. For him, this knowledge therefore does not replace rituals.
6. *The Chandogya Upanishad* (I.I.X)(2009). In: Max Muller F Ed. The Sacred Books Of The East (Vol.1). Delhi. Motilal Banarsidass
7. *The Chandogya Upanishad* (V.24.1-3) (2009). In: Max Muller F Ed. The Sacred Books Of The East (Vol.1). Delhi. Motilal Banarsidass

Chapter 19

Age of Reason: Ritual Gurus as Teachers of Knowledge

1. *Śhatpatha Brāhmaṇa* (X I I .9 .1 .1 and X I .6 .1)
2. Mookerji Radha K (1947). *Ancient Indian Education: Brāhmaṇical and Buddhist*. London. Macmillan, p. 29
3. *The Chandogya Upanishad* (V.24.1-2)(2009). In: Max Muller F Ed. The Sacred Books Of The East (Vol.1). Delhi. Motilal Banarsidass
4. *The Chandogya Upanishad* (VII.1.3)(2009). In: Max Muller F Ed. The Sacred Books Of The East (Vol.1). Delhi. Motilal Banarsidass
5. Staal Frits (2014). *Discovering the Vedas*. Gurgaon, Penguin Group. p.159

Chapter 20

Cosmos, the Creator and the Self: Matters of Life, Death, and Eternal Bliss

1. Olivelle Patrick (1996). *Upanishad*. Oxford. Oxford University Press. p.lvi
2. *The Chandogya Upanishad* (1.1.10) (2009). In: Max Muller F Ed. The Sacred Books Of The East (Vol.1). Delhi. Motilal Banarsidass
3. *The Chandogya Upanishad* (1.1.10) (2009). In: Max Muller F Ed. The Sacred Books Of The East (Vol.1). Delhi. Motilal Banarsidass, p.3, fn.2
4. *The Chandogya Upanishad* (1.10.10) (2009). In: Max Muller F Ed. The Sacred Books Of The East (Vol.1). Delhi. Motilal Banarsidass

Chapter 21

Meeting of Saguṇa Brahman and Vedānta

1. Encyclopaedia Britannica. Mohanty JN (n.d.) *History of Indian philosophy*. Available from https://www.britannica.com/topic/Indian-philosophy
2. *Encyclopaedia Britannica*. Mohanty JN (n.d.) History of Indian philosophy. Available from https://www.britannica.com/topic/Indian-philosophy - see 'Roles of sacred texts,mythology, and theism'
3. Kane PV (1997). *History of Dharmshastra*, Vol V, part II. Pune, Bhandarkar Oriental Research Institute, pp. 1624-25

Chapter 22

Īśvara, the Personal God: Para and Aparabrahman

1. RV (I.125.4-7)
2. Śatapatha Brāhmaṇa (12.9.1.1; also 11.6.1) (2009). In: Max Muller F Ed. The Sacred Books Of The East (Vol.44).Delhi. Motilal Banarsidass
3. *RV (1.125.4-7)*
4. *RV (IX.113.7)*
5. *The Brihadāranakya Upanishad (III.7) (2009). In: Max Muller F Ed. The Sacred Books Of The East (Vol.15).Delhi. Motilal Banarsidass*
6. *The Kaushitaki Upanishad* (III.8) (2009). In: Max Muller F Ed. The Sacred Books Of The East (Vol.1). Delhi. Motilal Banarsidass
7. *The Brihadāranakya Upanishad* (1.4.10) (2009). In: Max Muller F Ed. The Sacred Books Of The East (Vol.15). Delhi. Motilal Banarsidass

Chapter 23

Pūrva and Uttara Mīmāṁsā

1. PV(1997). *History of Dharmshastra*, Vol V, partII. Pune, Bhandarkar Oriental Research Institute, p.1208
2. Kane PV(1997). *History of Dharmshastra*, Vol V, partII. Pune, Bhandarkar Oriental Research Institute, p.1209
3. Kane PV(1997). *History of Dharmshastra*, Vol V, partII. Pune, Bhandarkar Oriental Research Institute, pp.1207-10
4. Kane PV(1997). *History of Dharmshastra*, Vol V,partII. Pune, Bhandarkar Oriental Research Institute,p.1214, f.n.1969, cit. Dupattikka on PMSVI.2.4
5. Kane PV(1997). *History of Dharmshastra*, Vol V,partII. Pune, Bhandarkar Oriental Research Institute, p.1209

6. Kane PV(1997). *History of Dharmshastra,* Vol V, part II. Pune, Bhandarkar Oriental Research Institute, p.1216-17
7. http://svbf.org/newsletters/year-2014/purva-mimamsa-philosophy/ Ref *Mīmāṁsā* notes M. R. Dwarakanath, *Purva Mīmāṁsā* Philosophy

Chapter 24

Vedānta

1 Nakamura Hajime(1983). *A History of Early Vedānta Philosophy*, part one. Delhi. Motilal Banarsidass, p.6-7

Chapter 25

Ancient Sacred Mythology and Legends - Purāṇas

1a,1b. Bhatt MS(1998), *Vedic Tantrism*. Delhi. Motilal Banarsidass, p.3
2. Dalal R (2010), *Hinduism An Alphabetical Guide*. New Delhi, Penguin Group
3. Dalal R (2010), *Hinduism An Alphabetical Guide*. New Delhi, Penguin Group
4. Dalal R (2010), *Hinduism An Alphabetical Guide*. New Delhi, Penguin Group
5. Dalal R (2010), *Hinduism An Alphabetical Guide*. New Delhi, Penguin Group
6. Hazra RC (1940). Studies in the Puranic Records on Hindu Rites and Customs. Dacca. University of Dacca, p.4
7. Kane PV (1997). *History of Dharmshastra,* Vol V, part I. Pune, Bhandarkar Oriental Research Institute, p.841
8. Hazra RC (1940). *Studies in the Puranic Records on Hindu Rites and Customs.*Dacca. University of Dacca, p.188, f.n. 1
9. Hazra RC (1940).*Studies in the Puranic Records on Hindu Rites and Customs*. Dacca. University of Dacca, p.189
10. Hazra RC(1940).*Studies in the Puranic Records on Hindu Rites and Customs.*Dacca. University of Dacca, p.189
11. Hazra RC (1940).*Studies in the Puranic Records on Hindu Rites and Customs.*Dacca. University of Dacca, p.193
12. Thompson RS (2007), *The Cosmology of the Bhagavata Purana*, Delhi, Motilal Banarsidass, p.33
13. Thompson RS (2007), *The Cosmology of the Bhagavata Purana*, Delhi, Motilal Banarsidass, pp.25-26
14. Speaking at the Third Annual Patanjali Lecture Series at University of Mass

Dartmouth in May 2004, Cornell mathematician Dr Richard Thompson presented a 'technical lecture' on 'An Accurate Map of the Solar System in an Ancient Sanskrit Text.He described a system of cosmic geography based on the *Bhagvata Purana,* using ring-shaped features labelled as oceans and islands. Available from: https://www.umassd.edu/media/umassdartmouth/center-for-indic-studies/newsletter_fall04.pdf

15. *Brihad Āraṇyaka-Upaniṣad* (3.9.2)(2009). In:Max Muller F Ed. The Sacred Books Of The East(Vol.15).Delhi. Motilal Banarsidass
16. Doniger W(1993). *Purana Perennis*, New York, State University Of New York Press,p.24-25
17. Hazra RC(1940). *Studies in the Puranic Records on Hindu Rites and Customs*. Dacca. University of Dacca, p.218
18. Hazra RC(1940). *Studies in the Puranic Records on Hindu Rites and Customs*.Dacca. University of Dacca, p.188

Chapter 26

Devotion -*Bhakti*

1. Dalal R (2010), *Hinduism An Alphabetical Guide*. New Delhi, Penguin Group
2. Prentiss KP (1999).*The Embodiment of Bhakti*, Oxford, Oxford University Press, p.5
3. Prentiss KP (1999).*The Embodiment of Bhakti*, Oxford, Oxford University Press, p.4
4 Prentiss KP(1999).*The Embodiment of Bhakti*, Oxford, Oxford University Press, 18
5. Dalal R(2010), Hinduism An Alphabetical Guide. New Delhi, Penguin
6. Mallik BK (1992). *Social Protest and Popular Movement in Medieval Orissa (circa 1450-1600AD)* Thesis for Doctor of Philosophy. pp.1-2. Available from: http://shodhganga.inflibnet.ac.in:8080/jspui/handle/10603/14987
7. Mallik BK (1992). *Social Protest and Popular Movement in Medieval Orissa (circa 1450-1600AD)*Thesis for Doctor of Philosophy. p.2. Available from: http://shodhganga.inflibnet.ac.in:8080/jspui/handle/10603/14987

Chapter 27

The Gift-*Dāna*

1. Kane PV (1997). *History of Dharmshastra*, Vol I. Pune, Bhandarkar Oriental Research Institute, p.33
2. RV (I .125), (I .126 .1 – 5), (VI .47 .22-25)

3. RV (I .126 .3), (VI .2 7.8), (VI I .1 8.22), (V I I I .1 9.36)
4. *Śatapatha Brāhmaṇa* (II.2.2.6) (2009). In: Max Muller F Ed. The Sacred Books Of The East (Vol.12).Delhi. Motilal Banarsidass
5. (Kane PV(1997). History of Dharmshastra, Vol II, part II. Pune, Bhandarkar Oriental Research Institute, p.843
6. Kane PV(1997). *History of Dharmshastra*, Vol I. Pune, Bhandarkar Oriental Research Institute, p.843
7. *Manu Smriti* (4.235) *The Laws Of Manu*(1991) tr. by Doniger W & Smith BK, New Delhi, Penguin Books India (P)Ltd
7. *Matsya Purana* (83.3)
8. *Matsya Purana* (205.1-9)

Chapter 28

Pilgrimage-*Tīrtha*

1. Kane PV(1997). *History of Dharmshastra*, Vol IV. Pune, Bhandarkar Oriental Research Institute, p.555
2. Knut JA(2018). *Pilgrimage*. In: Olivelle Patrick & Davis DR Eds., *The Oxford History of Hinduism-Hindu Law*, Oxford, Oxford University Press, p.337
3. MB, book 3, chapters 78 -148
4. MB, book 9, chapters 35 - 54
5. MB, book 13, chapter 25 - 26
6. Kane PV(1997). *History of Dharmshastra*, Vol IV. Pune, Bhandarkar Oriental Research Institute, p.562 cite Vanaparva 82.9-12 and Anushashna 108.3-4

http://www.bbc.com/news/world-asia-india-20778818 Dt.02052018

Chapter 29

Pious Observances - Vrata

1. Kane PV(1997). *History of Dharmshastra*, Vol V, partI. Pune, Bhandarkar Oriental Research Institute, pp.25-26
2. Kane PV(1997). *History of Dharmshastra*, Vol V, partI. Pune, Bhandarkar Oriental Research Institute,p.28
3. Davis DR(2018). *Vows and Observances: vratas*. In The Oxford History of Hinduism: Hindu Law. Patrick Olivelle, Donal R Davis Jr. Eds. Oxford. Oxford University Press, p. 334
4. Kane PV(1997). *History of Dharmshastra*, Vol V,partI. Pune, Bhandarkar Oriental Research Institute, p.54 citing Shantiparva 65.13 – 25, *Brahmā*

Parva 16.61 – 62

5. Davis DR Jr.(2018) *Vows and Observances: vrata*. In The Oxford History of Hinduism: Hindu Law. Patrick Olivelle, Donal R Davis Jr. Eds. Oxford. Oxford University Press, pp.326-27
6. Davis DR Jr.(2018) *Vows and Observances: vrata*. In The Oxford History of Hinduism: Hindu Law. Patrick Olivelle, Donal R Davis Jr. Eds. Oxford. Oxford University Press, p.334
7. Davis DR Jr. (2018) *Vows and Observances: vrata*. In The Oxford History of Hinduism: Hindu Law. Patrick Olivelle, Donal R Davis Jr. Eds. Oxford. Oxford University Press, p.334 citing McGee 1987:86, footnote 27
8. Kane PV(1997). *History of Dharmshastra*, Vol V, partI. Pune, Bhandarkar Oriental Research Institute,p.51
9. *The Agni Purāṇa (275.4-9),* (1998)tr. Shastri JL,Bhatt GP & Gangadharan N. Delhi. Motilal Banarsidass
10. *The Agni Purāṇa* (175.4-9), (1998)tr. Shastri JL, Bhatt GP & Gangadharan N. Delhi. Motilal Banarsidass
11. Kane PV(1997). *History of Dharmshastra*, Vol V, partI. Pune, Bhandarkar Oriental Research Institute, p.31
12. *The Agni Purāṇa* (175.59-62), (1998) tr. Shastri JL,Bhatt GP & Gangadharan N. Delhi. Motilal Banarsidass
13. *The Agni Purāṇa (*175.59-52), (1998) tr. Shastri JL, Bhatt GP & Gangadharan N. Delhi. Motilal Banarsidass
14. Kane PV (1997). *History of Dharmshastra*, Vol V,partI. Pune, Bhandarkar Oriental Research Institute, p.41
15. Kane PV(1997). *History of Dharmshastra*, Vol IV. Pune, Bhandarkar Oriental Research Institute, p.149, note 343
16. Kane PV(1997). *History of Dharmshastra*, Vol V, partI. Pune, Bhandarkar Oriental Research Institute,p.42
17. *MB, Udyogapárva* 39.71-72; *The Agni Purāṇa (*175.43), (1998) tr. Shastri JL,Bhatt GP & Gangadharan N.Delhi. Motilal Banarsidass
18. Kane PV (1997). *History of Dharmshastra*, Vol V,partI. Pune, Bhandarkar Oriental Research Institute,p.49 citing Hemadri
19. Kane PV(1997). *History of Dharmshastra*, Vol V,partI. Pune, Bhandarkar Oriental Research Institute, p.54
20. Kane PV(1997). *History of Dharmshastra*, Vol V,partI. Pune, Bhandarkar Oriental Research Institute, p.55
21. Kane PV(1997). History of Dharmshastra, Vol V,partI. Pune, Bhandarkar Oriental Research Institute, p.57
22. Kane PV(1997). *History of Dharmshastra*, Vol V, part I. Pune, Bhandarkar Oriental Research Institute, p.47

Chapter 30

Arrival of Mūrti and Many Gods

1. Kane PV (1997). History of Dharmshastra, Vol II, partII. Pune, Bhandarkar Oriental Research Institute, p.707
2. Kane PV (1997). History of Dharmshastra, Vol II, partII. Pune, Bhandarkar Oriental Research Institute,p.708
3. Dalal R (2010), Hinduism An Alphabetical Guide. New Delhi, Penguin Group.
4. Kane PV(1997). History of Dharmshastra, Vol II, part II. Pune, Bhandarkar Oriental Research Institute, p. 707-8
5. Kane PV(1997). History of Dharmshastra, Vol II,partII. Pune, Bhandarkar Oriental Research Institute, p. 708
6. Kane PV(1997). History of Dharmshastra, Vol II, partII. Pune, Bhandarkar Oriental Research Institute,p. 708-9 cit Haradtta, Ref SBE volume 30 part 2 page 290.
7. Āpastamba Gṛhya Sūtra (I.11.31–22) (2009).In: tr. Max Muller F Ed. The Sacred Books Of The East (Vol. 30, part1). Delhi. Motilal Banarsidass
8. Dalal R(2010), Hinduism An Alphabetical Guide. New Delhi, Penguin Group
9. Āpastamba Yajña Paribhāshā Sūtra (Vol.30, partII) In: tr. Oldenberg H,Max Muller F Ed. The Sacred Books Of The East (Vol.30,part 2). Delhi. Motilal Banarsidass .p.315
10. Monier W(1974). Religious Thought and Life in India. New Delhi, Oriental Books Reprint Corporation, pp.11-13
11. (Manu II.28) The Laws Of Manu (1991). tr. by Doniger W & Smith BK, New Delhi, Penguin Books India (P) Ltd
12. Kane PV (1997). History of Dharmshastra, Vol II, partI. Pune, Bhandarkar Oriental Research Institute, p.33, p.703
13. Kane PV (1997). History of Dharmshastra, Vol II, partII. Pune, Bhandarkar Oriental Research Institute,p.705
14. Kane PV (1997). History of Dharmshastra, Vol II, partII. Pune, Bhandarkar Oriental Research Institute, p.706
15. Max Muller (2009). The Upanishads. In:Max Muller F Ed. The Sacred Books Of The East (Vol.1). Delhi. Motilal Banarsidass, p.xxiii.
16. Kane PV (1997). History of Dharmshastra, Vol II, part II. Pune, Bhandarkar Oriental Research Institute,p.712
17. Patton LL (2005). Bringing the Gods to Mind. Berkley. University of California Press. p.64.
    Amplifying 'This and other related phrases' Patton says - 'Related phrases

and concepts, such as knowledge and ignorance of the deities, and the necessity of knowledge of the deities for the efficacy of sacrifice, are also found in these and many other related texts; see BD1. 22ff; Sarvanukramani 1; Nirukta 7.13, 10.42; Sayana in his introduction to Rg Veda, and so on'. p.64

18. Jaiminiya Brahmana (I, l-65) tr. Bodewitz. H. p.23, point 13. Available from https://archive.org/details/jaiminiyabrahmana [Accessed 011115]
19. Śatapatha Brāhmaṇa (XI.2.6.13)(2009). In: Max Muller F Ed. The Sacred Books Of The East (Vol.44). Delhi. Motilal Banarsidass
20. Śhatapatha Brāhmaṇa (11.2.6) (2009). In: tr.Various Authors,Max Muller F Ed. The Sacred Books Of The East (Vol. 44). Delhi. Motilal Banarsidass
21. Śhatapatha Brāhmaṇa (XI.2.6.1-3)(2009). In: tr.Various Authors, Max Muller F Ed. The Sacred Books Of The East (Vol. 44). Delhi. Motilal Banarsidass, p.35.fn 1
22. Śhatapatha Brāhmaṇa (XI.2.6.11)(2009). In: tr.Various Authors,Max Muller F Ed. The Sacred Books Of The East (Vol. 44). Delhi. Motilal Banarsidass
23. Patton LL (2005).Bringing the Gods to Mind.Berkley. University of California Press. p.64
24. According to Patton, 'viniyoga shows a bringing of the gods and many other things to mind.' And 'the guides for this usage or application are based on laws of association. In Vedic ritual texts there is the law of association of yathalingam. It is a term used in a number of Sanskrit commentaries and Ritual Sutras to describe the characteristics of a deity.' Patton LL (2005). Bringing the Gods to Mind. Berkley. University of California Press. p.64. The belief that 'what sounds alike must be alike' was founded on the theory that the essence of a thing was expressed in its name and its visible appearance – *nāma-rūpa*. The importance given to speech sounds is evident in the discussions of special sounds like *bhū, bhuvaḥ, svaḥ* (sounds that correspond to three worlds), as well as the most basic and powerful sound of all - '*Oṃ*'. These speech sounds are both powerful in themselves and provide access to the basic reality of the world, *Brāhmaṇa.*
25. Monier W(1974). Religious Thought and Life in India. New Delhi, Oriental Books Reprint Corporation, p.36
26. Monier W(1974). Religious Thought and Life in India. New Delhi, Oriental Books Reprint Corporation, pp.43-44
27. Monier W(1974). Religious Thought and Life in India. New Delhi, Oriental Books Reprint Corporation, p.58-59
28. Monier W(1974). Religious Thought and Life in India. New Delhi, Oriental Books Reprint Corporation, p.57
29. Monier W(1974). Religious Thought and Life in India. New Delhi, Oriental

Books Reprint Corporation, p.58
30. Thapar Romila (2001). Early India. London. Penguin Group,pp.164-67
31. Thapar Romila (2001). Early India. London. Penguin Group,pp.270-274
32. Encyclopaedia Britannica. Available from https://www.britannica.com/topic/mahayana)
33. Thapar Romila (2001).Early India. London. Penguin Group, p.271

Chapter 31

The Worship - *Pūjā*

1. Dalal R(2010), Hinduism: An Alphabetical Guide. New Delhi, Penguin Group
2. Encylopaedia of Oriental Philosophy and Religion: Hinduism:J-R(Vol.2). Ed. Singh NK, Mishra AP.(2005). New Delhi. Global Vision Publishing House.p.629, cit Jarl Charpentier, "Uber den Begriff und die Etymologie von puja",Beitrage zur Literatur Wissenschaft und Geistesgeschichte Indiens: Festgabe Herman Javcobi, ed. By Willibald Kirfel, Bonn,1926,pp.276-297
3. Encyclopaedia of Oriental Philosophy and Religion: Hinduism: J-R(Vol.2). Ed. Singh NK, Mishra AP.(2005). New Delhi. Global Vision Publishing House.p.629 cit Thieme Paul, Puja, Journal of Oriental Research 27,1957-58, pp.1-16
4. Bhatt MS(1998), Vedic Tantrism, Delhi, Motilal Banarsidass, p.3
5. Bhatt MS(1998), Vedic Tantrism, Delhi, Motilal Banarsidass,p.15
6. Bhatt MS(1998), Vedic Tantrism, Delhi, Motilal Banarsidass, p.16
7. According to Bloomfield, the 'fifth Kalpa of AV, usually known as *Angirasa-kalpa*, bears also the names *Abhicara-kalpa* and *Vidhana-kalpa*, 'textbook of sorecery;' Bloom Field(2009).Hymns Of The Atharva Veda. In:Max Muller F Ed. The Sacred Books Of The East (Vol.15).Delhi. Motilal Banarsidass. pp.xvii-xix
8. Staal Frits(2014). Discovering the Vedas. Gurgaon, Penguin Group, pp.141-45
9. Glucklich A(2008), The Strides of Viṣṇu : Hindu Culture in Historical Perspective. Ocford. Oxford University Press, p.143
10. Kane PV(1997). History of Dharmshastra, Vol I. Pune, Bhandarkar Oriental Research Institute,p. 129 fn 120
11. Woodroffe Sir John (1918). Śakti and Śakta.London.Luzac & Co.,Ch.4. Available from http://www.sacred-texts.com/tantra/sas/sas04.htm [Dt.221016]
12. Āgniveshya Gṛyha Sūtram(Praśna2, Adhyaya 4.9).p.40 at http://vedicreserve.mum.edu/kalpa/grihya/agniveshya_grihya_sutram.pdf

13. The Laws Of Manu(2.176)(1991)tr. by Doniger W & Smith BK, New Delhi, Penguin Books India(P)Ltd
14. Buhnemann Gudrun (1988), Puja- A study in Smṛta Ritual, Viennna, Publication of The Nobilei Research Library, p.13
15. Kane PV(1997). *History of Dharmshastra*, Vol II, partII. Pune, Bhandarkar Oriental Research Institute,p.705

Chapter 32

Rules of Deity Worship - Vidhi of Mūrti Pūjā

1. *Viramitrodaya:Pūjā Prakāśa* (Vol. 4) (Vikram 2044 Samvat Varanasi. Chaukhamba Sanskrit Series Office, p. 11. Available from: https://archive.org/detailsViramitrodayaVol04PujaPrakasaVishnuPrasadSharmaChowkambhaReprint [Accessed on 031216]
2. Kane PV(1997). *History of Dharmshastra*, Vol II,partII. Pune, Bhandarkar Oriental Research Institute,p.732 cit. Smṛti Candrikā (I point page 204)
3. Buhnemann Gudrun (1988), *Puja- A study in Smṛta Ritual*, Viennna, Publication of The Nobilei Research Library,p.34
4. Dalal R(2010), *Hinduism An Alphabetical Guide*. New Delhi, Penguin Group

Chapter 33

Rites of Passage - Saṃskāras

1. Dalal R(2010), *Hinduism An Alphabetical Guide*. New Delhi, Penguin Group
2. Śhatapatha Brāhmaṇa (V .2 .1 .10)(2009). In: tr.Various Authors,Max Muller F Ed. The Sacred Books Of The East (Vol. 41) .Delhi. Motilal Banarsidass
3. RV (I I I .8 .3)
4. *Śhatapatha Brāhmaṇa* (XI.5.4.12)(2009). In: tr.Various Authors,Max Muller F Ed. The Sacred Books Of The East (Vol. 43) .Delhi. Motilal Banarsidass. Ref. teacher becoming pregnant : Some authorities describe the *upanayana* as the teachings of *Savitṛ*i. The *ācārya* teaches the *Savitṛi* mantra to the pupil and the latter learns it wholeheartedly. It was a union between the teacher and the pupil. (Yaj.S. I.14)
5. *The Hymns Of Rigveda(1896)*.tr. Griffith RTH, ed. Shashtri JL, are available in PDF file and can be accessed at: http://www.sanskritweb.net/rigveda/griffith.pdf
6. Dalal R(2010), *Hinduism An Alphabetical Guide*. New Delhi, Penguin Group

7. Pandey R (2006). *Hindu Saṃsakāras*. Delhi, Motilal Banarsidass, p.17
8. Pandey R (2006). *Hindu Saṃsakāras*. Delhi, Motilal Banarsidass, p.17
9. Kane PV(1997). *History of Dharmshastra*, Vol II, part1. Pune, Bhandarkar Oriental Research Institute,p.194

10a. *The Gautama Dharma Sutra*(VIII.24-26)(1966). Tr. Pandey UC. Varanasi. Chowkhamba Sanskrit Series Office

10b. *The Gautama Dharma Sutra* (VIII.14-24)(1966). Tr. Pandey UC. Varanasi. Chowkhamba Sanskrit Series Office

11. Pandey R (2006). Hindu Saṃsakāras. Delhi, Motilal Banarsidass, p.20
12. *he Laws Of Manu*(2.26)(1991)tr. by Doniger W & Smith BK, New Delhi, Penguin Books India(P)Ltd
13. Pandey R (2006). Hindu Saṃsakāras. Delhi, Motilal Banarsidass, p.21
14. Pandey R (2006). Hindu Saṃsakāras. Delhi, Motilal Banarsidass, p.23

15a. Kane PV(1997). History of Dharmshastra, Vol II, part1. Pune, Bhandarkar Oriental Research Institute,p.200

15b. Kane PV(1997). History of Dharmshastra, Vol II, part1. Pune, Bhandarkar Oriental Research Institute,p.200

Chapter 34

Types of Saṃskāra- Description

1. *sthalipāka* is described as a dish of rice or barley boiled in milk- Macdonell AA and Keith AB(2007).Vedic Index of Names and Subjects (vol. II).Delhi. Motilal Banarsidass, p.487
2. Br. Up.VI .4 .21 – 22 – which cannot be literally translated for reasons of decency.
3. Kane PV(1997).*History of Dharmshastra*, Vol II,Part I. Pune, Bhandarkar Oriental Research Institute,p.202
4. Pandey R (2006). *Hindu Saṃsakāras*. Delhi, Motilal Banarsidass, p.52 cit. Vīramitrodaya Saṃskāras volume 1
5. 'animal like' (paśu dharma) - *The Laws Of Manu(*IX. 66)(1991)tr. by Doniger W & Smith BK, New Delhi, Penguin Books India(P)Ltd
6. Pandey R (2006). Hindu Saṃsakāras. Delhi, Motilal Banarsidass, p.60 cit. Śaunaka quoted in Vīramitrodayā volume 1 page 166.

7a. Kane PV(1997).History of Dharmshastra, Vol II,Part I. Pune, Bhandarkar Oriental Research Institute,p.21cit Sudarsana on Ap GS 14.9

7b. Pandey R (2006). Hindu Saṃsakāras. Delhi, Motilal Banarsidass, p. 60

8a. Pandey R (2006). *Hindu Saṃsakāras*. Delhi, Motilal Banarsidass, p.60 (*Aśvalāyan* quoted in VMS volume 1 page 172).

8b. Pandey R (2006). *Hindu Saṃsakāras*. Delhi, Motilal Banarsidass, pp.67-68 cit various Puranas

8c. Pandey R (2006). *Hindu Saṃsakāras*. Delhi, Motilal Banarsidass, p.69 cit Asv quoted by Harihara PGS (i.15)

9. Pandey R (2006). *Hindu Saṃsakāras*. Delhi, Motilal Banarsidass, p.72

10. Pandey R (2006). Hindu Saṃsakāras. Delhi, Motilal Banarsidass, p.73 cit. Samvyarta quoted in VMS volume 1 page 187.

11. Pandey R (2006). *Hindu Saṃsakāras*. Delhi, Motilal Banarsidass, p.73,fn17

12. Pandey R (2006). *Hindu Saṃsakāras*. Delhi, Motilal Banarsidass, p.74,fn 18

13. *Aśvalayana Gṛyha Sūtra* (I.1 5.1 – 4)(2009). In: tr. Oldenberg H,Max Muller F Ed. The Sacred Books Of The East (Vol. 44). Delhi. Motilal Banarsidass

14. Pandey R (2006). *Hindu Saṃsakāras*. Delhi, Motilal Banarsidass, p.74

15. Kane PV(1997). History of Dharmshastra, Vol II,partI. Pune, Bhandarkar Oriental Research Institute, pp. 232-235

16. Kane PV(1997). *History of Dharmshastra*, Vol II,partI. Pune, Bhandarkar Oriental Research Institute, p.240

17a. Kane PV(1997). *History of Dharmshastra*,Vol II,partI. Pune, Bhandarkar Oriental Research Institute, p.245

17b. *The Laws Of Manu(II.31-32)*(1991)tr. by Doniger W & Smith BK, New Delhi, Penguin Books India(P)Ltd. Manu says that the name of a priest should have a word for auspiciousness, of a ruler strength, of a commoner property, and of a servant –one that breeds contempt. Pāraskara goes on to suggest the second name for the three *vārnas* GS(I.17). *The Prāskara Gṝyha-Sūtras*(2009). In: tr. Oldenberg H,Max Muller F Ed. The Sacred Books Of The East(Vol.29).Delhi. Motilal Banarsidass

17c. Kane PV(1997). *History of Dharmshastra*, Vol II, partI. Pune, Bhandarkar Oriental Research Institute, p.251 cit Aprārka p.27 and Viṣnu Purāna (III.10).

18a. Pandey R (2006). *Hindu Saṃsakāras*. Delhi, Motilal Banarsidass, pp.94-95.

18b. Pandey R (2006). *Hindu Saṃsakāras*. Delhi, Motilal Banarsidass,p.101 cit *Sharirasthana* chapter 6.83.

19. Bhushan S(2009).*Samsakaras in the Sutras and the Ramayana: A comparative study* (Thesis for Doctor of Philosophy), Ch. 3. Available from http://shodhganga.inflibnet.ac.in/bitstream/10603/17667/9/09_chapter%203.pdf)

20. Bhushan S(2009). *Samsakaras in the Sutras and the Ramayana:* A comparative study (Thesis for Doctor of Philosophy), p.94. Available from http://shodhganga.inflibnet.ac.in/bitstream/10603/17667/9/09_chapter%203.pdf)

21. *The Laws Of Manu(*II.40)(1991)tr. by Doniger W & Smith BK, New Delhi, Penguin Books India(P)Ltd

22. Pandey R (2006). *Hindu Saṃsakāras*. Delhi, Motilal Banarsidass,p. 121
23. Pandey R (2006). *Hindu Saṃsakāras*. Delhi, Motilal Banarsidass,p.122
24. *Paraskara Gṛyha Sūtra* (I.1 5.1 – 4)(2009). In: tr. Oldenberg H,Max Muller F Ed. The Sacred Books Of The East (Vol. 29). Delhi. Motilal Banarsidass
25. *ParaskaraGṛyha Sūtra* (II.2.12-13)(2009). In: tr. Oldenberg H,Max Muller F Ed. The Sacred Books Of The East (Vol. 29). Delhi. Motilal Banarsidass
26. *Asvalayana Gṛyha Sūtra* (I.20.4-6)(2009). In: tr. Oldenberg H,Max Muller F Ed. The Sacred Books Of The East (Vol. 29). Delhi. Motilal Banarsidass
27. *Paraskara Gṛyha Sūtra* (II.2.16-20)(2009). In: tr. Oldenberg H,Max Muller F Ed. The Sacred Books Of The East (Vol. 29). Delhi. Motilal Banarsidass
28. *Paraskara Gṛyha Sūtra* (II.2.16-20)(2009). In: tr. Oldenberg H,Max Muller F Ed. The Sacred Books Of The East (Vol. 29). Delhi. Motilal Banarsidass
29. Ref. *Asvalayana Gṛyha Sūtra* (I.2.2.1-19)(2009). In: tr. Oldenberg H, Max Muller F Ed. The Sacred Books Of The East (Vol. 29). Delhi. Motilal Banarsidass
30. Kane PV(1997). *History of Dharmshastra*, Vol II,partI. Pune, Bhandarkar Oriental Research Institute, p.294 (RV.X.85.41)
31. Kane PV(1997). *History of Dharmshastra*, Vol II,partI. Pune, Bhandarkar Oriental Research Institute, p.295
32. Kane PV(1997). History of Dharmshastra, Vol II,partI. Pune, Bhandarkar Oriental Research Institute, p.333
33. Pandey R (2006). *Hindu Saṃsakāras*. Delhi, Motilal Banarsidass,p. 97 cit *Vīramitrodaya Samskāra* vol 1, p.296 quoting Aśva.
34. *Paraskara Gṛyha Sūtra* (II.1)(2009). In: tr. Oldenberg H,Max Muller F Ed. The Sacred Books Of The East (Vol. 29). Delhi. Motilal Banarsidass
35. Pandey R (2006). *Hindu Saṃsakāras*. Delhi, Motilal Banarsidass,p. 99 cit *Vīramitrodaya Samskāra* vol 1, p.315 quoting Devala
36. Pandey R (2006). *Hindu Saṃsakāras*. Delhi, Motilal Banarsidass,p. 99 cit Laghu-Hārita
37. Kane PV(1997). History of Dharmshastra, Vol II,partI. Pune, Bhandarkar Oriental Research Institute, p.324 cit Ap.DS. I.1.1.11 referring to Brāhmaṇa texts

Chapter 35

Marriage - Vivāha

1. *The Tatteriya Brāhmana*(II.2.2.6)(1862).Tr. Rajendralala Mitra. Calcutta. The Baptist Mission Press, Vol II
2. Śatapatha Brāhmaṇa (V.2.1.10)(2009). In: Max Muller F Ed. The Sacred Books Of The East (Vol.5).Delhi. Motilal Banarsidass
3. *The Laws Of Manu*(9.28)(1991)tr. by Doniger W & Smith BK, New Delhi,

Penguin Books India(P)Ltd

4. *Aśvalāyana Gryha Sūtra*(I.5.2).In: Max Muller F Ed. The Sacred Books Of The East (Vol.29).Delhi. Motilal Banarsidass
5. Kane PV(1997). *History of Dharmshastra*, Vol II,partI. Pune, Bhandarkar Oriental Research Institute,p.430 cit *Smṛti Candrikā* I., p. 78
6. Kātyāyana - Smṛtimuktaphala, p.159
7. Śatapatha Brāhmaṇa (I.2.5.16)(2009). In: Max Muller F Ed. The Sacred Books Of The East (Vol.12).Delhi. Motilal Banarsidass
8. *The Kama Sutra of Vatsyayana*(I I I.1.1 – 2) (1883)tr. By Richard Burton at http://www.sacred-texts.com/sex/kama/kama102.htm
9. *The Kama Sutra of Vatsyayana*(I I I.1.13) (1883)tr. By Richard Burton at http://www.sacred-texts.com/sex/kama/kama102.htm
10. Pandey R (2006). *Hindu Saṃsakāras*. Delhi, Motilal Banarsidass,p.183 cit. Macdonell AA & Keth AB. Keith(2007). Vedic Index (vol. II),Delhi. Motilal Banarsidass. p 485. Keith and Macdonnell actually say,'the maiden may be assumed to have grown up in her fathers house, enjoying free intercourse with the youth of the village, and sharing in the work of house.'
11. Pandey R (2006). Hindu Saṃsakāras. Delhi, Motilal Banarsidass,p.184 cit. (Baudhayana GS IV.1.16)
12. *Gobhila Gryha Sutra*(III.4.6).In: Max Muller F Ed. The Sacred Books Of The East (Vol.30).Delhi. Motilal Banarsidass
13. *Hiraṇyakeśhin Gryha Sutra*(I.19.2).In: Max Muller F Ed. The Sacred Books Of The East (Vol.29).Delhi. Motilal Banarsidass
14. *Gobhila Gryha Sutra*(II.5.7).In: Max Muller F Ed. The Sacred Books Of The East (Vol.30).Delhi. Motilal Banarsidass
15. Kane PV(1997). *History of Dharmshastra*, Vol II,partI. Pune, Bhandarkar Oriental Research Institute,p. 442
16. Kane PV(1997). *History of Dharmshastra*, Vol II,partI. Pune, Bhandarkar Oriental Research Institute,p.442
17. *Parāśara Smṛti* (VII.5-6). Available from http://www.indiadivine.org/content/files/file/17-Śrī-parashara-smṛti-with-english-translation-pdf/ [Accessed 16April2016]
18. Kane PV(1997). *History of Dharmshastra*, Vol II,partI. Pune, Bhandarkar Oriental Research Institute,p. 445
19. Kane PV(1997). *History of Dharmshastra*, Vol II,partI. Pune, Bhandarkar Oriental Research Institute,p.444-45 cit Kaśyapa in *Gṛhyastha ratnākara* (page 4), and Aprarka page 85 quoting *Bhaviṣya Purāṇa*
20. *The Laws Of Manu*(9.91)(1991)tr. by Doniger W & Smith BK, New Delhi, Penguin Books India(P)Ltd
21. Majumdar RC (2003). *Ancient India.* Delhi, Motilal Banarsi Dass, p.97

22. Majumdar RC (2003). *Ancient India.* Delhi, Motilal Banarsi Dass,p.120-121
23. Pandey R (2006). *Hindu* Saṃsakāras. Delhi, Motilal Banarsidass, p.186
24. Kane PV(1997). *History of Dharmshastra*, Vol II, part I. Pune, Bhandarkar Oriental Research Institute,p.443 cit *Gṛhyasamagraha* as quoted in the commentary on Gobhila GS III. 4. 6.
25. Kane PV(1997). *History of Dharmshastra,* Vol II,partI. Pune, Bhandarkar Oriental Research Institute,p.443 cit. Verses 64 and 67 quoted by SM. C. I. Page 79 and GR. R. Page 46
26. Pandey R (2006). *Hindu Saṃsakāras*. Delhi, Motilal Banarsidass,p.188 -89
27. Chamberlain AF(2018), *The Child and Childhood in Folk-Thought.* Frankfurt am Main, Outlook Verlag GmbH,p.202
28. Chamberlain AF(2018), *The Child and Childhood in Folk-Thought.* Frankfurt am Main, Outlook Verlag GmbH,p.202
29. Chamberlain AF(2018), *The Child and Childhood in Folk-Thought.* Frankfurt am Main, Outlook Verlag GmbH,p. 203

Chapter 36

Types of Vivāha

1. Pandey R (2006). *Hindu Saṃsakāras*. Delhi. Motilal Banarsidass,p.164

Chapter 37

Rules of Marriage - Vivāha Vidhi

1. Pandey R (2006). Hindu Saṃsakāras. Delhi, Motilal Banarsidass,p.164
2. (Asv GS I.7.1 – 2, SBE volume 29)
3. (Ap.GS I.2.15, SBE vol 30)
4. Śilpa Prakāsh Sumant quotes Rām Gopāl (1959.82) having taken this view considering Bloomfield, Keith and Gastra – ref Vivāha: The Development of the Ritual from Saṃhitā to Prayoga in the Atharvaveda Tradition, p.188.
5. Atharvavediya Kaushik Gṛha sūtrasm(10th adhyaya, 75-76th kandika,sutra 23-26;1-3) (Samvat 1999), translated by Thakur Udainarayan Singh. Madhurapur. ShastraprakashBhavan.pp.182-83. Available at https://archive.org/details/Atharvavediya_Kausika_Grihya_Sutra_With_Samkshipta_Tika_And_Hindi_Translation_Uday_Narayan_Singh_1942
6. Atharvavediya Kaushik Gṛha sūtram(10th adhyaya, 76th kandika, sūtras 19-25) (Samvat 1999), translated by Thakur Udainarayan Singh. Madhurapur. ShastraprakashBhavan.pp.183-84. Available at https://archive.org/details/Atharvavediya_Kausika_Grihya_Sutra_With_Samkshipta_Tika_And_Hindi_Translation_Uday_Narayan_Singh_1942

7. Atharvavediya Kaushik Gṛha sūtrasm(10th adhyaya, 76th kandika, sūtras 26-27) (Samvat 1999), translated by Thakur Udainarayan Singh. Madhurapur. ShastraprakashBhavan.pp.184-85. Available at https://archive.org/details/Atharvavediya_Kausika_Grihya_Sutra_With_Samkshipta_Tika_And_Hindi_Translation_Uday_Narayan_Singh_1942.
8. Kane PV(1997). History of Dharmshastra, Vol.III,part I Pune, Bhandarkar Oriental Research Institute, p.531
9 &10. Kashinath Upadyaya(1986). *The Dharmasindhu*. Dehi. Sri Satguru Publications, p.213
11. Bhatt Gopinath Dikshit (1899)Samsakara Ratna Mala. Agashe KS,Phadke B. Eds. Anandashram Mudralaya. pp.545 Avalable from https://archive.org/details/SAMSKARARATNAMALA1
12. Bhatt Gopinath Dikshit (1899)Samsakara Ratna Mala. Agashe KS,Phadke B. Eds. Anandashram Mudralaya. pp.538 Avalable from https://archive.org/details/SAMSKARARATNAMALA1
13. Bhatt Gopinath Dikshit (1899)*Samsakara Ratna Mala*. Agashe KS,Phadke B. Eds. Anandashram Mudralaya. pp.545-48 Avalable from https://archive.org/details/SAMSKARARATNAMALA1
14. Altekar AS(1938). *Coalition of Hindu Women in Hindu Civilisation.* Benares.The Culture Publication House, pp.362-64
15,16,17. Kane PV(1997). *History ofDharmshastra*, Vol II,partI. Pune, Bhandarkar Oriental Research Institute, p.536-38 cit. Samsakara Kaustubha p. 799,811 & 532

Chapter 38

Caste Factor

1. Kane PV(1997). *History of Dharmshastra*, Vol II,partI. Pune, Bhandarkar Oriental Research Institute,p.69ff
2. Śatapatha Brāhmaṇa (IV.1.5.1 & 7)(2009). In: Max Muller F Ed. The Sacred Books Of The East (Vol.26).Delhi. Motilal Banarsidass
3. *The Gautama Dharma Sutra(4.1)(1966)*. Tr. Pandey UC. Varanasi. Chowkhamba Sanskrit Series Office
4. *Apstamba Dharma Sutra*(Praśna2. Patala6.Khanda13.1) (2009). In: Max Muller F Ed. The Sacred Books Of The East (Vol.2).Delhi. Motilal Banarsidass
5. Kane PV(1997). History of Dharmshastra, Vol II,partI. Pune, Bhandarkar Oriental Research Institute,p. 49
6. Sachau EC(2002). *Alberuni's India*.New Delhi.Rupa & Co.p.86
7. Kane PV(1997). *History of Dharmshastra*, Vol II,partI. Pune, Bhandarkar

Oriental Research Institute,p.451

8,9. Kane PV(1997). History of Dharmshastra, Vol II,partI. Pune, Bhandarkar Oriental Research Institute, p.450 cit. E I volume 15 p 301 FF approximate 650 AD.

Chapter 39

Gotra, Piṇḍa and Pravara

1. Kane PV(1997). *History of Dharmshastra*, Vol II,partI. Pune, Bhandarkar Oriental Research Institute,p. 437
2. Kane PV(1997). *History of Dharmshastra*, Vol II,partI. Pune, Bhandarkar Oriental Research Institute,p.464,fn1093
3. Kane PV(1997). History of Dharmshastra, Vol II,partI. Pune, Bhandarkar Oriental Research Institute,pp.464-65 fn 1093c cit. Bṛhaspati quoted by Aparарka on Yaj I I. 21 and Kulluka on Manu I. 1
4. Nārada in Stree Pumsah section 7 page 108, Mitākṣarā on Yaj I 53, Nirnaya Sindhu I I I. Pūrvardh p to 84).
5. Kane PV(1997). *History of Dharmshastra*, Vol II,partI. Pune, Bhandarkar Oriental Research Institute,p.460
6. (SBE volume 12)
7. Kane PV(1997). *History of Dharmshastra*, Vol II,partI. Pune, Bhandarkar Oriental Research Institute,p. 461
8. Macdonell AA and Keith AB(2007).Vedic Index of Names and Subjects. Delhi. Motilal Banarsidass, Vol.I
9. *Baudhayana Dharma Sutra*(I.1.2. 1 and 3) (2009). In: Max Muller F Ed. The Sacred Books Of The East (Vol.2).Delhi. Motilal Banarsidass
10. Kane PV(1997). *History of Dharmshastra*, Vol II,partI. Pune, Bhandarkar Oriental Research Institute,p.466 cit. Dharma Sindhu I I I. Pūrvardh p 29 – 1790 AD of Kasi Nath
11. Kane PV(1997). *History of Dharmshastra*, Vol II,partI. Pune, Bhandarkar Oriental Research Institute,p.468.
12. Mahābhāshya volume I I.p to 233 on the Sūtra-gotravaivata) (Patañjali I V. 1. 78
13. Kane PV(1997). *History of Dharmshastra*, Vol II,partI. Pune, Bhandarkar Oriental Research Institute,p.481
14. Kane PV(1997). History of Dharmshastra, Vol II,partI. Pune, Bhandarkar Oriental Research Institute,p.482 fn 1124 cit. Samskarpraksh p 598
15. Kane PV(1997). History of Dharmshastra, Vol II,partI. Pune, Bhandarkar Oriental Research Institute,p.486 cit. Udhavatattva page 111 ref Parāśarāmadhviya I part 2 page 70
16. Kane PV(1997). History of Dharmshastra, Vol II,partI. Pune, Bhandarkar Oriental Research Institute,p.489 cit. Smṛtiarthasara,p.15

17. Kane PV(1997). *History of Dharmshastra,* Vol II,partI. Pune, Bhandarkar Oriental Research Institute,p.491

17. Kane PV(1997). *History of Dharmshastra,* Vol II,partI. Pune, Bhandarkar Oriental Research Institute,p.497

18. Kane PV(1997). *History of Dharmshastra*, Vol II, partI. Pune, Bhandarkar Oriental Research Institute, p, 497, fn 1164

Chapter 40

Do Rituals Have Meaning?

1. Nick Crossley Nick(2004).*Thinking Ritual, body technique, and (inter) subjectivity.* In: Schillbrack K Ed. Thinking Through Rituals. Newyork. Routledge. p. 32

2. Nick Crossley Nick(2004).*Thinking Ritual, body technique, and (inter) subjectivity*. In: Schillbrack K Ed. Thinking Through Rituals. Newyork. Routledge. p. 32

3. Staal Frits(2014). *Discovering the Vedas*. Gurgaon, Penguin Group, p.208

4a. Staal Frits(2004).*Theories and facts on ritual simultaneities*. In: Schillbrack K Ed. Thinking Through Rituals. New York. Routledge. p. 175

5. Staal Frits(2004).Theories and facts on ritual simultaneities. In: Schillbrack K Ed. Thinking Through Rituals. New York. Routledge. p. 176,"No doubt, it is not infrequent that people talk at the same time, interrupt each other or simply shoot back without waiting for a speaker to finish, but such cases are probably best analysed by reducing them to cases of succession."

6. Staal Frits(2004).*Theories and facts on ritual simultaneities*. In: Schillbrack K Ed. Thinking Through Rituals. New York. Routledge, p.179

7. Staal Frits(2004).*Theories and facts on ritual simultaneities*. In: Schillbrack K Ed. Thinking Through Rituals. New York. Routledge. p. 185

7a. Staal Frits(2004).*Theories and facts on ritual simultaneities*. In: Schillbrack K Ed. Thinking Through Rituals. New York. Routledge. p. 175. In countering argument that Gods are hearer in rituals, Staal relies heavily on Mimamsa philosophy where it is the yajña, and not mantras, that are of any consequence in delivering *phala*. Conceding 'it was not true (Gods are not hearers) when Vedic verses were first composed', he bases his argument on frangible logic- 'Vedic rituals, and the later ritual philosophy of the Mimamsa are concerned with rules observed by priests, not rules observed by Gods'- to assume that Gods are not hearers.

8. Schillbrack K(2004).*Ritual metaphysics*. In: Schillbrack K Ed. Thinking Through Rituals. New York. Routledge.

9 a,b. Raposa ML(2004). *Ritual inquiry: the pragmatic logic of religious practice*. Ritual metaphysics. In: Schillbrack K Ed. Thinking Through Rituals.

Newyork. Routledge. P.114

10. Mauss Marcel(1934).*Techniques of the Body*.p.5. Available from http://monoskop.org/images/c/c4/Mauss_Marcel_1935_1973_Techniques_of_the_Body.pdf. This lecture was given at a meeting of the Societe de Psychologie, May 17th, 1934 and published in the Journal de psychologie normal et patholigique,Paris, Annee XXXII, 1935, pp. 271-93.
11. Ingold Tim(revised text 1999). *Three in one: on dissolving the distinctions between body, mind and culture*. Conclusions. Available from: http://lchc.ucsd.edu/mca/Paper/ingold/ingold2.htm[Accessed 15th July 2015]
12. Crossley Nick(2004).*Ritual, body technique, and (inter) subjectivity*. In: Schillbrack K Ed. Thinking Through Rituals. Newyork. Routledge. p. 32
13. Crossley Nick(2004).*Ritual, body technique, and (inter) subjectivity*. In: Schillbrack K Ed. Thinking Through Rituals. Newyork. Routledge. p. 36
14. *The Laws Of Manu(2.6)*(1991)tr. by Doniger W & Smith BK, New Delhi, Penguin Books India(P)Ltd
15. *The Laws Of Manu(2.20)* (1991)tr. by Doniger W & Smith BK, New Delhi, Penguin Books India(P)Ltd
16. *The Laws Of Manu(2.11)* (1991)tr. by Doniger W & Smith BK, New Delhi, Penguin Books India(P)Ltd
17. Ganeri J(2004).*The ritual roots of moral reason*. In: Schillbrack K Ed. Thinking Through Rituals. Newyork. Routledge. p.207

Chapter 41

Do Mantras Have Meaning/ Power?

1. Mishra Anand(2010). *On the descriptive techniques of the Prātiśākhya and the Aṣṭādhyāyī*. In. Houben JanEM, Rotaru Julieta(eds.). Romania.The International Symposium, The Book. Romania. Europa. 20–24 September 2010,p.ff247,2.1 http://www.bibmet.ro/Uploads/Simpozionul%20International_Cartea_Romania_Europa_III_V3_mic.pdf accessed Dt.221215
2. Kane PV(1997). History of Dharmshastra, Vol V, partII. Pune, Bhandarkar Oriental Research Institute, p.1098 cit Sābra on Tantra Vartika on PMS I I.1.34

2a. *Apastamba Yajña Paribāhaṣa Sūtras* (2009). In:Max Muller F Ed. The Sacred Books Of The East(Vol.30,part 2).Delhi. Motilal Banarsidass

3. Kane PV(1997). History of Dharmshastra, Vol V, partII. Pune, Bhandarkar Oriental Research Institute, p.1098
4. Monier W(2010). *The Sanskrit English Dictionary*. New Delhi. Bhartiya Grantha Niketan.

5. Monier W(1974). Religious Thought and Life in India. New Delhi, Oriental Books Reprint Corporation, p. 197
6. *Muṇḍaka Upaniṣad (61.4-5)* (2009). In: tr. Buhler G, Max Muller F Ed. The Sacred Books Of The East(Vol.15).Delhi. Motilal Banarsidass
7. Patton LL(1996). *Myth as Argument: Brahaddevtā as Canonical commentary*. Berlin. de Gruyter. p.21. I have relied on Pt Sitaram Shastri(2014) edited Hindi commentary titled Nirukta of Yaska Muni Vol 1 prathama adhyāya padā 5, Delhi. Parimal Publication. p 72.
8. Staal Frits(2014). Discovering the Vedas. Gurgaon, Penguin Group, p.203
9. Staal Frits(2014). Discovering the Vedas. Gurgaon, Penguin Group, p.109
10. Staal Frits(2014). Discovering the Vedas. Gurgaon, Penguin Group, p.107
11. Staal Frits(2014). Discovering the Vedas. Gurgaon, Penguin Group, p.4
12. Staal Frits(2014). Discovering the Vedas. Gurgaon, Penguin Group, p.194
13. Staal Frits(2014). Discovering the Vedas. Gurgaon, Penguin Group, p.203
14. Staal Frits(2014). Discovering the Vedas. Gurgaon, Penguin Group, p.204
15. (Ref University of California, Santa Cruz, http://linguistics.ucsc.edu/about/what-is-linguistics.html)
16. Staal Frits(2014). *Discovering the Vedas*. Gurgaon, Penguin Group, p.208
17. Patton Laurie L (2001).*Bringing the Gods to Mind*. Berkley. University of California Press.p.39

Appendix 1

***Agniṣṭoma*: *Soma Yajña* (Deatil Description)**

4. *Vajasanein Samhita* (IV.5).
5. Śatapatha Brāhmaṇa (3.2.2.1-10)(2009). In: Max Muller F Ed. The Sacred Books Of The East (Vol.26).Delhi. Motilal Banarsidass
6. Śatapatha Brāhmaṇa (3.4.3.3)(2009). In: Max Muller F Ed. The Sacred Books Of The East (Vol.26).Delhi. Motilal Banarsidass
7. Vajasaneyin Samhita (IV.6).
8. Śatapatha Brāhmaṇa (3.4.4.1)(2009). In: Max Muller F Ed. The Sacred Books Of The East (Vol.26).Delhi. Motilal Banarsidass
9. *putika* plant is usually identified with *Guilandina Bonduc*- Macdonell and Keith (2007), *Vedic Index of Names and Subjects vol II*. Delhi. Motilal Banarsidass.
10. *gavidhuka* a species of grass- *Coix barbata* – Macdonell and Keith (2007), *Vedic Index of Names and Subjects vol I*. Delhi. Motilal Banarsidass.
11. Śatapatha Brāhmaṇa (14.2.2.44)(2009). In: Max Muller F Ed. The Sacred Books Of The East (Vol.44).Delhi. Motilal Banarsidass
12. Śatapatha Brāhmaṇa (14.2.2.46)(2009). In: Max Muller F Ed. The Sacred Books Of The East (Vol.44).Delhi. Motilal Banarsidass

13. Kane PV(1997).*History of Dharmshastra,* Vol II,partII. Pune, Bhandarkar Oriental Research Institute, p.1195
14. Sen C(2001).A Dictionary of the Vedic Rituals. Delhi, Concept Publishing Company, p.108 cit Apstamba Shrauta Sutra (XI.16.15)
15. Śatapatha Brāhmaṇa (3.6.3.2)(2009). In: Max Muller F Ed. The Sacred Books Of The East (Vol.26).Delhi. Motilal Banarsidass
16. Śatapatha Brāhmaṇa (2.7.3.4)(2009). In: Max Muller F Ed. The Sacred Books Of The East (Vol.12).Delhi. Motilal Banarsidass
17. Vajasaneyin Samhita. (V I.8)
18. Śatapatha Brāhmaṇa (3.8.1.9)(2009). In: Max Muller F Ed. The Sacred Books Of The East (Vol.26).Delhi. Motilal Banarsidass
19. Śatapatha Brāhmaṇa (3.8.1.15)(2009). In: Max Muller F Ed. The Sacred Books Of The East (Vol.26).Delhi. Motilal Banarsidass
20. Ṛgveda mantras that are recited while concerned persons cleanse themselves are (I.20 3.22; X.9.8) hymns; the cleansing over the pit, according to Śatapatha Brāhmaṇa (3.8.2.30)(2009). In: Max Muller F Ed. The Sacred Books Of The East (Vol.26).Delhi. Motilal Banarsidass, was undertaken because the animal was wounded and water was a means of soothing it.
21. Sen C(2001).A Dictionary of the Vedic Rituals. Delhi, Concept Publishing Company, p.104
22. Kane PV(1997). *History of Dharmshastra,* Vol II,partII. Pune, Bhandarkar Oriental Research Institute, p.1995
23. Mehra BS(1990).*A Critical and Comparative Study of theVaitana Srauta Sutra with Special Reference to the Srauta Sacrifices*, A Thesis for the Degree of Doctor of Philosophy, p.212. Available from: http://shodhganga.inflibnet.ac.in/handle/10603/44465
24. Kane PV(1997). *History of Dharmshastra,* Vol III,partII. Pune, Bhandarkar Oriental Research Institute, p.1200
25. Sen C (2001). *A Dictionary of the Vedic Rituals*. Delhi, Concept Publishing Company,p.37

Bibliography

Some of the important Books, Journals, and Doctoral Thesis are listed below.

1. *Aitreya* and *Kausitaki Brahmanas* - Various translations

2. Altekar AS (1938). *Coalition of Hindu Women in Hindu Civilisation*. Benares. The Culture Publication House

3. Alvar RS (2010). *An Introduction to Somayagnas and Vedic Yagnas in General*, eds. Laksmithathachar MA, Alwar MA. Mysore, Samskriti Foundation. Available at https://archive.org/details/an_introduction_to_somayagnyas_and_vedic_yagnyas_in_general

4. *Apastamba Yajña Paribāhaṣa Sūtras* (2009). In: Tr Oldenberg H, Max Muller F Ed. The Sacred Books Of The East (Vol.30, part 2). Delhi. Motilal Banarsidass

5. *Apastamba Dharma & Griyha Sutras*. Tr various scholars Ed Sri Rama Ramanuja Achari. Available from: www.srimatham.com

6. *Atharvavediya Kaushik Gṛha Sūtrasm* (Samvat 1999), tr. Thakur Udainarayan Singh. Madhurapur. Shastraprakash Bhavan.

7. Author(s): Jan E. M. Houben. *The Ritual Pragmatics of a Vedic Hymn: The "Riddle Hymn" and the Pravargya Ritual*. Journal of the American Oriental Society, Vol. 120, No. 4 (Oct. - Dec., 2000), pp. 499-536. Available from : http://www.jstor.org/stable/606614

8. *Authority, Anxiety, and Canon : Essays in Vedic Interpretation* (1994), Patton Laurie L, Albany. Sate University of New York Press

9. *Baudhayana Srauta Sutram* (2003). New Delhi and Delhi. Indra Gandhi National Centre For The Arts and Motilal Banarsidass Publishers P Ltd.

10. Besant Annie & Bhagwan Das(2002). *Sanatana Dharma*. Chennai, The Theosophical Publishing House

11. Bhandarkar DR (1989). *Some Aspects of Ancient Indian Culture*. New Delhi, Asian educational Services

12. Bharathi KS (1998). *Encyclopaedia of Eminent Thinkers, Shri Aurobindo*, Vol 6. New Delhi. Cocept Publishing Company, The Uttarapara Speeches

13. Bhatt MS(1998), *Vedic Tantrism*, Delhi, Motilal Banarsidass

14. Bhushan S (2009). *Samsakaras in the Sutras and the Ramayana: A comparative study* (Thesis for Doctor of Philosophy). Available from http://shodhganga.inflibnet.ac.in/bitstream/10603/17667/9/09_chapter%203.pdf

15. Black B (2007). *The Character of the Self in Ancient India.* Albany. State university of New York press

16. Buhnemann Gudrun (1988), *Puja - A study in Smṛta Ritual*, Viennna, Publication of The Nobilei Research Library

17. Chomsky, Noam. 1988. *Language and Problems of Knowledge*. The Managua Lectures. Cambridge, Massachusetts: The MIT Press.

18. Crossley Nick (2004). *Thinking Ritual, body technique, and (inter) subjectivity*. In: Schillbrack K Ed. Thinking Through Rituals. New York. Routledge.

19. Dalal R (2010), *Hinduism: An Alphabetical Guide*. New Delhi, Penguin Group

20. Dalal R (2014). *The Vedas*. New Delhi, Penguin Group

21. Doniger W(1993). *Purana Perennis*, New York, State University Of New York Press

22. Dr Yagnasubramanian. *Vaidika Sansakaras*. Available from : http://svbf.org/vaidika-samskaras

23. *Encyclopaedia Britannica*. Available from: https://www.britannica.com/topic/Pali-language

24. *Encyclopaedia Britannica*: Available from https://www.britannica.com/topic/mahayana

25. Eraly Abraham (2002).*Gem in the Lotus*. New Delhi. Penguin Books

26. *Fire Yajna and Upanayana Procedure*. Compiled by Swami Bhakti Kanan Giri. Available from : www.scsmath.com/n_corner/trove/yajna_info.pdf [Accessed on 120115]

27. Ganeri J (2004). *The ritual roots of moral reason*. In: Schillbrack K Ed. Thinking Through Rituals. New York. Routledge.

28. Hazra RC (1940). *Studies in the Puranic Records on Hindu Rites and Customs*. Dacca. University of Dacca

29. *History of Science*. ELECTRONIC JOURNAL OF VEDIC STUDIES (EJVS)

30. Houben Jan EM (2012). *Vedic ritual as medium in ancient and pre-colonial South Asia : its expansion and survival between orality and writing*. Available from: https://halshs.archives-ouvertes.fr/halshs-00673190

31. http://www.indiadivine.org/content/files/file/17 - *Śrī-parashara-smṛti-with-english-translation-pdf/*

32. https://archive.org/details/Atharvavediya_Kausika_Grihya_Sutra_With_Samkshipta_Tika_And_Hindi_Translation_Uday_Narayan_Singh_1942

33 https://archive.org/details/hymnsrigveda02grifgoog/page/

34. Ref for quotes of RV hymns free download site - http//:www.holybooks.com/Rg-Veda/

35. Ingold Tim (revised text 1999). *Three in one: on dissolving the distinctions between body, mind and culture*. Conclusions. Available from: http://lchc.ucsd.edu/mca/Paper/ingold/ingold2.htm

36. *Jaimini Sutras* (1984) - transliteration Bangalor Suryanarain Rao and revised. published by Sri G. K. Ananthram fc IBH Prakashana. Bangalore

37. *Jaiminiya Brahmana*. tr. Bodewitz. H. Available from https://archive.org/details/jaiminiyabrahmana [Last Accessed 011115]

38. Kane PV (1997). *History of Dharmshastra*. Pune, Bhandarkar Oriental Research Institute

39. *Katyayana's Sarvanukramani of the Rigveda* Edited by AA Macdonell, Oxford University Press, Oxford 1886

40. Knut JA (2018). *Pilgrimage*. In: Olivelle Patrick & Davis DR Eds., *The Oxford History of Hinduism-Hindu Law*, Oxford, Oxford University Press

41. Kothari Rita(1999). *Indian Literature in English Translation: The Social Context* (Thesis for Degree of Doctor of Philosophy), p.22 superscription 27 citing PJ Marshall, ed The British Discovery of Hinduism in the Eighteenth Century, London: Cambridge UP,1970) 189. Available from http://shodhganga.inflibnet.ac.in/bitstream/10603/46404/9/09_chapter%202.pdf .

42. *Language and Reality*, Bronkhorst Johannes (2011), tr Allen Michael S, Raghunathan Rajam, Leiden, Brepols Publishers

43. Macdonell AA and Keith AB (2007). *Vedic Index of Names and Subjects*. Delhi. Motilal Banarsidass, Vol. I and II.

44. Macdonell AA (1917). *Vedic Reader*. London. Oxford University Press.

45. *Maha-Bharata* (Book 12, Vol. 3) (2017). tr Wyenne Alexander. New York. New York University Press.

46. Majumdar RC (2003). *Ancient India.* Delhi, Motilal Banarsi Dass

47. Mall RA (2000), *Intercultural Philosophy*, Lanbam, Rowman & Littlefield Publishers, Inc.

48. Mallik BK (1992). *Social Protest and Popular Movement in Medieval Orissa* (circa 1450-1600AD) Thesis for Doctor of Philosophy. Available from: from:http://shodhganga.inflibnet.ac.in:8080/jspui/handle/10603/14987

49. *Manu (*2009). In: tr. Buhler G, Max Muller F Ed. The Sacred Books Of The East (Vol. 25). Delhi. Motilal Banarsidass

50. *Manu-Smrti*: with the 'Manubhashya' of Medhatithi Edited with the help of several *Manuscripts* By GN Jha Publisher Royal Asiatic Society Bengal, 1939, Calcutta

51. Mauss Marcel (1934). *Techniques of the Body*. Available from http://monoskop.org/images/c/c4/Mauss_Marcel_1935_1973_Techniques_of_the_Body.pdf. This lecture was given at a meeting of the Societe de Psychologie, May 17th, 1934 and published in the Journal de psychologie normal et patholigique,Paris, Annee XXXII, 1935, pp. 271-93.

52. Mehra BS (1990). *A Critical and Comparative Study of the Vaitana Srauta Sutra with Special Reference to the Srauta Sacrifices*, A Thesis for the Degree of Doctor of Philosophy. Available from: http://shodhganga.inflibnet.ac.in/handle/10603/44465

53. Mishra Anand (2010). *On the descriptive techniques of the Prātiśākhya and the Aṣṭādhyāyī.* In. Houben JanEM, Rotaru Julieta(eds.). Romania. The International Symposium, The Book. Romania. Europa. 20–24 September 2010.

54. Molendijk AL (2016). *Friedrich Max Muller and the Sacred Books of the East.* Oxford. Oxford University Press

55. Monier W (1974). *Religious Thought and Life in India.* New Delhi, Oriental Books Reprint Corporation

56. Monier W (2003). *Indian Wisdom.* New Delhi, Rupa & Co.

57. Monier W (2010). *The Sanskrit English Dictionary.* New Delhi. Bhartiya Grantha Niketan.

58. Nirukta-Pt Sitaram Shastri edited Hindi commentary titled *Nirukta of Yaska Muni* Vol 1 and 2

59. Olivelle Patrick (1996). *Upanishads*. Oxford. Oxford University Press.

60. *Panca Mahayajna Vidhi* (1874 & 1877). Maharshi Dayanand. First published in 1875 from Bombay (not available) and then published again from Lazerus Press, Benaras in 1878. Available from : co

61. Pandey R (2006*). Hindu Saṃsakāras.* Delhi, Motilal Banarsidass

62. Parāśara Smṛti. Available from *http://www.indiadivine.org/content/files/file/17-Śrī-parashara-smṛti-with-english-translation-pdf/*

63. Patton Laurie L (1996). *Myth as Argument: Brahaddevtā as Canonical commentary*. Berlin. de Gruyter.

64. Patton Laurie L (2001). *Bringing the Gods to Mind.* Berkley. University of California Press.

65. *Philosophy of Pancaratra (Agama Shastra)* by S Rangachar, Sridevi Prakashna, Mandya, 1991

66. *Poetry: The Missing Link?* J.H. de Roder, University of Maastricht Available from http://uahost.uantwerpen.be/apil/apil101/deroder.pdf [220116]

67. Purkayastha D (2009). *A Study of the Asvalayana Srauta Sutra* with Reference to the Principal Sacrifices - Their Structural and Sequential Affinity. Thesis for Doctor of Philosophy. Silchar. Assam University.

68. *Ramayana Valmiki, Mahabharata, Bhagvad, Puranas*, Gita Press, Gorakhpur

69. Raposa ML (2004). *Ritual inquiry: the pragmatic logic of religious practice. Ritual metaphysics*. In: Schillbrack K Ed. Thinking Through Rituals. New York. Routledge.

70. *Rigveda* - Sanskrit

71. *Rigveda Brahmanas: The Aitreya And Kausitaki Brahmana* (1920). tr Keith Arthur B. Cambridge, Mass. Harvard University Press. Avalable from: https://archive.org/details/rigvedabrahmana00keitgoog/

72. *Rigveda Samhita* (1977). tr. Sarasvati Satya Prakash, Satykam Vidyalankar. New Delhi. Veda Pratishthan

73. *Rig-Veda Sanhita* (1987). Wilson HH. Delhi. Cosmos Publications.

74. Sachau EC (2002). *Alberuni's India*. New Delhi. Rupa & Co.

75. *Samsakara Chandrika arthat Maharshi Dayananda praneet Samsakara Vidhi Ki Tika*, Bhimsen Sharma, Atmaram Radhakrishna, Vikram Samvat 1970, Dehradun

76. Sastri Gaurinath (1998). *A Concise History of Sanskrit Literature*. Delhi. Motilal Banarsidass, p.15

77. *Śatapatha Brāhmaṇa* (2009). In: Max Muller F Ed. The Sacred Books Of The East (Vol. 12). Delhi. Motilal Banarsidass

78. Saxena Dr Pravesh (2003).*Vedoṃ meṃ kyā hai?,* Delhi, Pustaka Mahal

79. Sen C (2001). A *Dictionary of the Vedic Rituals*. Delhi, Concept Publishing Company

80. *Smruti Chandrika The*, Devana Bhat, tr T Krishnasawmy Iyer, J Higginbotham, Madras, 1867

81. Staal Frits (2001). *There Is No Proof But*... Addendum to EJVS 7-3 on Vedic Geometry & the Staal Frits (2014). *Discovering the Vedas*. Gurgaon, Penguin Group

82. Staal Frits. *The Meaninglessness of Ritual*. Numen, Vol XXVI, Fasc. I. Available from: https://religion.ua.edu/wp-content/uploads/2018/06/The-Meaningless-of-Ritual.pdf

83. T. P. Mahadevan & Frits Staal (2003) *The Turning Point in a Living Tradition. Somayāgam* (2203). Available from: https://www.namboothiri.com/articles/FRITS%20STAAL-MAHADEVAN.PDF

84. Thapar Romila (2001). *Early India*. London. Penguin Group,

85. *The Chandogya Upanishad (*2009). In: Max Muller F Ed. The Sacred Books Of The East (Vol. 1). Delhi. Motilal Banarsidass

86. *The Gautama Dharma Sutra* (1966). Tr. Pandey UC. Varanasi. Chowkhamba Sanskrit Series Office

87. *The Hymns of Rigveda*. Tr Griffith Ralph TH (1896).

88. *THE INTERNATIONAL SYMPOSIUM THE BOOK*. ROMANIA. EUROPA. 20–24 September 2010. Available from: http://www.bibmet.ro/Uploads/Simpozionul%20International_Cartea_Romania_Europa_III_V3_mic.pdf

89. *The Kama Sutra of Vatsyayana* (1883) tr. By Richard Burton at http://www.sacred-texts.com/sex/kama/kama102.htm

90. *The Laws Of Manu* (1991) tr. by Doniger W & Smith BK, New Delhi, Penguin Books India (P) Ltd

91. *The Munduka Upanishad* (2009). In: tr. Max Muller F Ed. The Sacred Books Of The East (Vol. 15). Delhi. Motilal Banarsidass

92. *The Sacred Books Of The East* (Different years of publication). Delhi. Motilal Banarsidass

93. *The Saundarananda Of Ashvaghosha* (1928). Johnnston EH Ed. London. Oxford University Press.

94. *The Taittriyaka Upanishad (*2009). In: Max Muller F Ed. The Sacred Books Of The East (Vol.15). Delhi. Motilal Banarsidass

95. Thompson RS (2007), *The Cosmology of the Bhagavata Purana*, Delhi, Motilal Banarsidass

96. Trautmann TR Ed. *The Aryan Debate*. New Delhi, Oxford University Press

97. *Vedanta Sutras*. tr Thibaut George. Available from : www.yoga-breathing.com

98. *Viramitrodaya: Pūjā Prakāśa* (Vol. 4) (Vikram Samvat 2044). Varanasi. Chaukhamba Sanskrit Series Office, Available from: https://archive.org/details/ViramitrodayaVol04PujaPrakasaVishnuPrasadSharmaChowkambhaReprint [Accessed last on 031216]

99. Witzel Michael (n.d.). *The Development of Vedic Canon and its School : The Social and Political Milieu*. Available at http://www.people.fas.harvard.edu/~witzel/canon.pdf

100. Woodroffe Sir John (1918). *Śakti* and *Śakta*. London. Luzac & Co.,Ch.4 at http://www.sacred-texts.com/tantra/sas/sas04.htm

101. *Yajnavalakya Smrity with commentary of Vijnanesvara* (Mitakshara) (1918). Book 1 Acahara Adhyaya, tr Srish Chandra Vidyarnava, Panini Office, Bhuvneshvari Asrama, Allahabad

Index